BOOK TWO

RESEARCH OF FAMILY NAMES

Joyce Sutton

Order this book online at www.trafford.com
or email orders@trafford.com

Most Trafford titles are also available at major online book retailers.

Printed in the United States of America.

ISBN: 978-1-4669-0323-4 (sc)
ISBN: 978-1-4669-0324-1 (e)

Library of Congress Control Number: 2011919842

Trafford rev. 11/03/2011

Trafford PUBLISHING® **www.trafford.com**

North America & international
toll-free: 1 888 232 4444 (USA & Canada)
phone: 250 383 6864 • fax: 812 355 4082

1700'S HOFFMAN/HOVATTER 1600'S

1600'S SUMMERS/SHAHAN 1700'S

1800'S SHUMATE/SMITH/JONES 1800'S

1800'S MANCUSO TO SUTTON

Descendants of Hannes John Hoffman

1 Hannes John Hoffman
.. +Barbara
..... 2 John Hoffman 1741 - 1790
.... +Margaret J.
.... 3 Barbara Hoffman
.... 3 Catherine Hoffman
.... 3 Christian Hoffman
.... 3 Elizabeth Hoffman
.... 3 John Hoffman 1775 - 1856
.... +Sarah Ann Godwin 1773 - 1861
.... 4 Daniel Hoffman
.... 4 Squire Hoffman - 1850
.... +Mary Debolt 1809 - 1833
.... 5 Mary Ellen Hoffman 1830 - 1866
.... +Cary Armistead Doggett 1827 - 1887
.... 6 Martha Luella Doggett 1856 - 1939
.... +Max A. Hostetler 1857 - 1927
.... 5 Eva Albina Huffman Hoffman 1832 - 1854
.... 4 Phillip Hoffman 1797 - 1879
.... +Aletha Summers 1799 - 1849
.... 5 Mary Ann Hoffman 1821 - 1886
.... +David William Shahan 1825 - 1910
.... 6 Thomas Shahan 1844 -
.... 6 Philip Nelson Shahan 1848 - 1913
.... +Barbara Bowman 1864 - 1946
.... 7 Charles L. Shahan 1884 - 1885
.... 7 Ernest Uriah Shahan 1885 - 1969
.... +Lula Jane Robinson
.... 7 Datis Alvin Shahan 1887 - 1955
.... +Martha M. Davis
.... 7 Elizabeth Ina Shahan 1890 - 1969
.... +Alexander Nestor 1871 - 1944
.... 8 Woodrow Charles Nestor 1922 - 1969
.... +Norma Owens 1935 -
.... 8 Ellis Nestor
.... 8 N.C. Riley Nestor
.... 8 Ira Nestor
.... 8 Ruth Nestor
.... +Mr. Digman
.... 8 Ruby Nestor
.... +Mr. Thompson
.... 8 Elsie Nestor
.... +Mr. Shrout
.... 8 Bertha Nestor
.... 8 Ace Nestor
.... 7 Florence Lulu Shahan 1893 - 1983
.... +Orville Burr
.... 7 Alta Wilson Shahan 1896 - 1918
.... 7 Gay Tona Shahan 1899 -
.... +Minerva M. White
.... 7 Male Shahan 1903 - 1903
.... 7 Waitman Philip Shahan 1904 - 1953
.... *2nd Wife of Philip Nelson Shahan:
.... +Mary Edna Lipscomb 1847 - 1881
.... 7 Rebecca Alice Shahan 1875 - 1957
.... +Loman Sanford Stalmaker
.... 7 Charles Tilden Shahan 1877 - 1962
.... +Lee Verna Keller
.... 7 Cyrus Walter Shahan 1879 - 1961
.... +Oleta C. Poling
.... 7 Ira D. Shahan 1880 - 1958
.... +Jennie Knotts
.... *3rd Wife of Philip Nelson Shahan:
.... +Mary E. Lipscomb 1847 -
.... 6 Rebecca E. Shahan 1851 -
.... 6 David William Shahan 1853 - 1931
.... +Caroline A. Bolyard 1857 - 1949
.... 7 Lula V. Shahan 1875 -
.... +James A. Knotts
.... *2nd Husband of Lula V. Shahan:
.... +M. D. Wolfe
.... 7 Florence E. Shahan 1877 - 1959
.... +Eli Nose
.... *2nd Husband of Florence E. Shahan:
.... +Harrison Serman Hornbeck

7 Ulysses S. Grant Shahan 1879 - 1880
7 Noah Shahan 1881 - 1934
+Dona Bolyard
7 Waitman C. Shahan 1888 - 1894
7 Anna Shahan 1889 - 1894
7 Flora Shahan 1893 - 1894
7 Flora E. Shahan 1895 -
+Ernest Lee
6 Christina E. Shahan 1855 - 1921
+William Sein Rosier
6 Columbia Jane Shahan 1857 - 1860
6 John Washington Shahan 1858 - 1930
+Sarah A. Mitchell 1864 - 1939
7 Clarence Shahan 1881 - 1885
7 Della May Shahan 1886 - 1962
+Charles Alva Phillips
7 Daisy Ellen Shahan 1889 - 1923
+Bolyard
*2nd Husband of Daisy Ellen Shahan:
+Uriah C. Phillips
7 David Roy Shahan 1890 - 1926
+Ivey Pearl Nestor
7 Ida Belle Shahan 1893 - 1893
7 Albert Troy Shahan 1894 - 1958
+Virginia Pearl Harsh
7 Dona Victoria Shahan 1901 - 1952
+Silals Runner
*2nd Husband of Dona Victoria Shahan:
+Wilburt L. White
6 Charlotte L. Shahan 1860 - 1943
+Lemuel Knotts
5 John Alexander Hoffman 1822 - 1893
+Amy Elizabeth Brunner 1828 - 1862
6 Aletha Ann Hoffman 1846 -
6 Susannah Hoffman 1849 -
6 Ursuley Ann Hoffman 1852 -
6 Mary Jane Hoffman 1852 -
6 Amy Elizabeth Hoffman 1858 -
6 William Francis Hoffman 1861 -
*2nd Wife of John Alexander Hoffman:
+Lucinda Barnes 1841 - 1895
6 Nathan Squire Hoffman 1868 -
6 Cenith E. Hoffman 1870 -
6 Marion P. Hoffman 1874 -
6 David Milton Hoffman 1875 -
6 George Irvin Hoffman 1879 -
5 Elijah S. Hoffman 1824 - 1894
+Martha Ann King 1823 - 1899
6 David Hennon Hoffman 1849 -
6 Abbalona Clamenc Hoffman 1850 -
6 Rosalie Maranda Hoffman 1852 -
6 Henry Milton Hoffman 1853 -
6 Ruall Nanzilla Hoffman 1855 -
6 Enoch Madison Hoffman 1857 -
6 Elijah McGee Hoffman 1859 -
6 John Nelson Hoffman 1861 -
5 Nimrod Nelson Hoffman 1827 - 1890
+Nancy Ann Elizabeth Saer 1844 - 1917
6 Willie U.S. Hoffman 1865 - 1938
6 Anna Aminia Hoffman 1866 - 1935
6 Ada Gregg Hoffman 1868 - 1868
6 Cora Lee Hoffman 1871 - 1925
6 Nellie Grant Hoffman 1873 -
6 John Thompson Hoffman 1875 - 1947
6 Harry Hagans Hoffman 1878 - 1879
5 George Washington Hoffman 1831 - 1865
+Elizabeth Eliza Knotts 1831 - 1905
6 Mary Elizabeth Hoffman 1849 - 1930
+Robert Corneloius Wagner 1847 - 1919
6 Martha Jane Hoffman 1850 -
6 Aletha Hoffman 1860 -
5 Francis Marion Hoffman 1836 - 1904
+Christena Shahan 1839 - 1871
6 John Martin Hoffman 1858 - 1942
+Martha Anne Burgoyne 1863 - 1935
7 Russell Reed Hoffman 1890 - 1956
+Sara Louise Porter 1898 - 1998

8 Russel Reed Jr. Hoffman 1921 - 1972
+Adela Gloria Teixeira 1916 -
9 Dianne Marie Hoffman 1947 -
+Wayne Charles Wunderlich 1947 -
10 Robert Christopher Wunderlich 1966 -
*2nd Husband of Dianne Marie Hoffman:
+Daniel Balduck 1949 - 1997
10 Bret Alan Balduck 1970 - 1975
*3rd Husband of Dianne Marie Hoffman:
+Carl Albert Reinert, Jr. 1928 -
6 Charity Elizabeth Hoffman 1860 - 1923
6 Ursula Jane Hoffman 1864 - 1939
6 Sarah Ann Hoffman 1864 - 1934
6 Charles Nelson Hoffman 1866 - 1926
6 Rebecca Hoffman 1868 - 1957
+Arthur Ellsworth Alexander
7 Clarence Harold Alexander 1894 -
7 Oscar Granville Alexander 1896 - 1918
7 Lottie Alice Alexander 1898 - 1919
7 Nellie Gay Alexander 1900 - 1978
7 Gladys Murl Alexander 1902 -
7 Audra Dot Alexander 1903 -
7 John Thomas Alexander 1907 - 1981
+Mary Ann Wells
7 Manti Lee Alexander 1909 -
7 Agnes Blanche Alexander 1911 -
*2nd Wife of Francis Marion Hoffman:
+Mary Amelia Martin 1842 - 1922
6 Oriona Alice Hoffman 1873 - 1948
+James R. Phelps
7 Leita Phelps 1910 -
+?? Lunk
6 Emma Florence Hoffman 1875 - 1936
+William N. Goff
7 Eulalia Luella Goff 1899 - 1980
*2nd Husband of Emma Florence Hoffman:
+Joseph L. Shrout
6 Rutherfold B. Hayes Hoffman 1876 - 1953
+Effie
7 Jean Hoffman
*2nd Wife of Rutherfold B. Hayes Hoffman:
+Gladys
7 ?? Hoffman
6 Lelia Eugenia Hoffman 1877 - 1925
+W. Irvin Watts
7 Mary Sue Watts 1908 - 1933
+W. R. Schooley
6 Jenivee Hoffman 1879 - 1974
+Franklin Blakeney Pierce
7 Lola Hazel Pierce 1902 -
7 George Francis Pierce 1905 -
7 Harold Blakeney Pierce 1917 - 1975
6 Lola Velle Hoffman 1881 - 1966
+Robert Munsen
6 James Gillispi Blaine Hoffman 1884 - 1956
+Nora A. Burgoyne
7 James Blaine Hoffman 1917 - 1974
7 Charles Francis Hoffman 1919 - 1919
7 Virginia Lee Hoffman 1919 - 1919
*2nd Wife of James Gillispi Blaine Hoffman:
+Clarissa M. Todd
7 David Roger Hoffman 1937 -
*3rd Wife of James Gillispi Blaine Hoffman:
+Edith P. Fox
5 Louisa Marion Hoffman 1836 - 1885
+George Washington Shahan 1830 - 1891
6 Alethea Elizabeth Shahan 1851 - 1860
6 William Francis Shahan 1852 - 1942
+Michelle / Melvina L. Nestor
7 Amelia Shahan 1880 -
7 Louisa C. Shahan 1881 -
+J. Patrick Loughry
7 Sarah E. J. Shahan 1885 - 1974
7 George A. F. Shahan 1885 - 1962
7 James Peter Shahan 1888 - 1966
+Nellie Agnes Plum
7 John M. Shahan 1890 -

7 Chloe F. Shahan 1892 -
7 Bertha M. Shahan 1897 -
+Everett Wallace
7 Marry Jessie Shahan 1901 - 1986
6 John Wesley Shahan 1854 - 1855
6 Sarah Minerva Shahan 1856 -
+Thomas Dewalt Poling 1856 -
6 Christina L. Shahan 1858 - 1933
+David T. Hovatter 1853 - 1929
7 Charles E. Hovatter 1878 -
+Ella Agnice Burns 1883 -
8 Claudene Elwood Hovatter
+Arietta Shockley
8 Elston Gerald Hovatter
+Myra E. Howard
8 Charles Woodrow Wilson Hovatter
+Madeline Kausch
8 Wanda Lorraine Hovatter
+Albert H. Hearn
8 Earl Gay Hovatter 1912 - 1934
8 Thomas David Hovatter 1908 -
+Elsie Ambrosio
9 Timothy Hovatter
8 Elmer Dallas Hovatter 1902 - 1970
+Jessie B. Noce 1898 - 1919
8 Etta Ives Hovatter
+Earl C. Cathel
8 Delbert Ray Hovatter 1904 - 1974
+Barbara Chandler
9 Barbara Lindsay Hovatter 1944 - 1968
9 Sandra Lee Hovatter 1946 -
+James Moore
9 Martha Jean Hovatter 1953 -
+Kenneth Speer - 1988
10 Barbara Anne Speer 1974 -
10 Donald Ray Speer 1977 -
*2nd Husband of Martha Jean Hovatter:
+Charles Reno
8 Leoda Pearl Hovatter
8 Ora Marie Hovatter 1914 - 1937
+Herbert Fues, Sr
8 Elford Harold Hovatter 1924 - 1924
7 Lellie C. Hovatter 1880 -
+John Patrick Burns 1877 - 1950
7 Wilbert F. Hovatter 1882 - 1969
+Hattie Lee Jones 1885 - 1969
8 Eula Hovatter 1903 - 1937
+Samuel Linton
9 Voncile Linton
*2nd Husband of Eula Hovatter:
+Hope Watson
9 Junior Lee Watson
9 Francis Watson
9 Joyce Watson
8 Odie Hovatter 1905 - 1905
8 Wilbertie Valentine Hovatter 1908 - 1987
+Hazel Dell Clevenger 1907 - 1988
9 Marjorie Hovatter 1927 -
9 Dolores Hovatter 1929 -
9 Berta Jayne Hovatter 1938 - 1988
+Harold Snyder
10 Pam Snyder 1959 -
11 Brian Snyder 1976 -
*2nd Husband of Berta Jayne Hovatter:
+Thomas Moser 1930 -
10 Thomas Moser 1969 -
*Partner of Wilbertie Valentine Hovatter:
+Ruby Barnett 1915 -
9 Rosalie J. Hovatter 1932 -
+Charley Jenkins
*2nd Husband of Rosalie J. Hovatter:
+David Faulknier
8 Boyd Hovatter 1910 - 1975
8 Floyd Hovatter 1913 - 1913
8 Lois Hovatter 1914 - 1983
+Thomas Mancuso 1912 - 1985
9 Joyce F.. Mancuso 1934 -

.... +Robert Thomas Sutton 1932 -
.... 10 Dolores Lea Sutton 1958 -
.... 10 Susan Joyce Sutton 1964 -
.... +Christopher Keating
.... 11 Christopher Keating Jr.
.... 11 Benjamin Keating
.... 10 Bobbi Lynn Sutton 1968 -
.... +Karl Frank Chase
.... 11 Shawn Joseph Chase 1995 -
.... 11 Samantha Joyce Chase 1997 -
.... *Partner of Bobbi Lynn Sutton:
.... +Mr. McHenry
.... 11 Dani-Lynn McHenry 2006 -
.... 9 Patrina Mancuso 1937 - 1937
.... 8 Hattie Almalee Hovatter 1917 -
.... 8 Aubrey Hovatter 1920 -
.... 8 Dessie Hovatter 1921 - 2001
.... +Edgar Thom 1922 - 1982
.... 9 Dennis Thom 1949 - 1971
.... *2nd Husband of Dessie Hovatter:
.... +William F. Putnam 1932 - 2002
.... 9 Robin Putnam 1963 -
.... +Edison Richard Walker
.... 10 Stephen Randall Walker 1987 -
.... 10 Jaren Dawn Walker 1993 -
.... 9 William F. Putnam 2 1966 -
.... +Bernetta Graham 1970 -
.... 10 William F. Putnam 3 1990 -
.... 10 Olivia Lucille Putnam 1997 -
.... 8 Vernon Hovatter 1924 - 1996
.... 8 Kenneth Gene Hovatter 1927 - 1983
.... 7 Ira J. Hovatter 1885 - 1968
.... +Dessie Thomas
.... 8 Nina Hovatter
.... 7 Mary L. Hovatter 1887 -
.... +Andrew Jackson Brown 1877 - 1932
.... 8 Andrew C. Brown 1904 - 1975
.... +Mildred Fortney
.... 9 Donald Brown
.... 9 Keith Brown
.... 9 Larraine Brown
.... 9 Swanee Brown
.... 9 Frank Brown
.... 9 Paul Brown
.... 8 Albert Leroy Brown 1908 - 1994
.... +Marie Mizell
.... 8 Ruby Brown 1908 -
.... +Bryan Hovatter - 1996
.... 9 William Hovatter
.... 9 Prudence Hovatter
.... 8 Wilber Jackson Brown 1912 - 1912
.... 8 Homer Jennings Brown 1914 - 1972
.... +Mary Myrtle Deese or Dees 1918 - 1989
.... 9 Cecile Leota Brown 1934 - 1937
.... 9 Andrew Jennings Brown 1937 - 1994
.... +Jackine Lou Tallet
.... 9 Homer Ray Brown 1938 -
.... +Anna Cecelia Stevens
.... 10 Tracy Lee Brown 1966 -
.... 8 Delbert Jennings Brown 1917 - 1998
.... 8 William Henry Brown 1920 -
.... 8 Nellie Mae Brown Brown 1923 -
.... 8 David Elmer Brown 1926 - 1929
.... 7 George E. Hovatter 1889 -
.... +Cecil May Burns
.... 8 Ernest Ray Hovatter 1916 -
.... +Mildred Kinter
.... 9 Gary Ray Hovatter 1949 -
.... +Linda Hunnicut
.... 10 Health Hovatter
.... 10 Heather Hovatter
.... +Anthony Galvez
.... 11 Daniel Galvez
.... 11 Rebecca Galvez
.... 11 Allisa Galvez
.... 9 Vickie Lynn Hovatter 1954 -
.... +William Claypool 1949 -

.... 10 Daniel Claypool 1978 -
.... 10 Kevin Claypool 1981 -
.... *2nd Wife of Ernest Ray Hovatter:
.... +Evelyn ?
.... 9 Patti Ann Hovatter
.... +? Smith
.... *3rd Wife of Ernest Ray Hovatter:
.... +Francis Boyer
.... 9 Francis Lee Hovatter
.... 8 Violet Mildred Hovatter 1915 -
.... +Fred Baiocchi - 1987
.... 9 Yvonne Baiocchi
.... 8 Velma Arizonia Hovatter 1917 -
.... 8 Beryl Hovatter
.... +Page Evans
.... 9 Male Child Evans
.... 8 Mary Elizabeth Hovatter 1923 -
.... +Mr. Pert
.... 9 Jean Pert
.... 9 Larry Pert
.... 9 unknown Pert
.... *2nd Husband of Mary Elizabeth Hovatter:
.... +Leonard Blackmon
.... 8 Darrell Hovatter
.... +Shirlee
.... 9 Donna Hovatter
.... 9 Kathy Hovatter
.... 7 Lloyd A. Hovatter 1891 -
.... +Lulu Sterringer
.... 7 Maudie P. Hovatter 1893 -
.... +Samuel Dumire
.... 7 Arlie David Hovatter 1895 - 1977
.... +Laura Poling
.... 8 Lester Hovatter
.... 7 Boyd E. Hovatter 1897 - 1980
.... +Hilda Davis
.... 6 Mary Catherine Shahan 1860 - 1941
.... +Martin M. Poling 1860 -
.... 7 Rhoda Poling
.... 7 Jonas Poling
.... 7 Ira Poling
.... 6 Cyrena Margaret Shahan 1862 - 1943
.... +Isaac M. Poling 1860 -
.... 6 George Emery Shahan 1864 - 1966
.... +Cora Jane Hovatter 1876 - 1948
.... 7 Walter Brown Shahan
.... 7 Agnes Shahan 1892 - 1986
.... 7 Minnie Pearl Shahan 1894 - 1959
.... 7 Donna Jane Shahan 1896 - 1972
.... 7 Mary Elizabeth Shahan 1897 - 1918
.... 7 Daisy Virginia Shahan 1899 - 1978
.... 7 Flora Shahan 1904 - 1904
.... 7 Dora Shahan 1904 -
.... 7 Charles Lee Shahan 1907 - 1971
.... 7 Cora Louise Shahan 1908 - 1987
.... +Floyd Edward Sayre
.... 7 Ruby Bessie Shahan 1910 -
.... 7 Georgia Oletha Shahan 1912 - 1975
.... 7 Lillian Ann Shahan 1916 -
.... 7 Victoria Arabelle Shahan 1919 -
.... 6 Richard Jefferson Shahan 1867 - 1954
.... 6 Louisa Olive J. Shahan 1868 - 1900
.... 6 Elizah Squire Shahan 1873 - 1874
.... 6 Caroline Josephine Shahan 1874 - 1951
.... +Mr. Hebt
.... 6 Stillborn Twin One Shahan 1874 -
.... 6 Stillborn Twin Two Shahan 1874 -
.... 6 David Charles Shahan 1880 - 1947
.... 6 Virginia Catherine Shahan 1882 -
.... +Mr. Spare
.... 5 Abalona Rebekah Hoffman 1839 -
.... 5 Nancy Jane Hoffman 1840 -
.... 5 Sarah A. E. Huffman 1841 - 1901
.... +Robert Johnson
.... 6 Robert Leland Johnson 1864 -
.... +Sarah J. Phillips 1858 - 1918
.... 6 James Thomas Johnson 1867 -

.... 6 John Pendelton Johnson 1869 -
.... 6 Charles William Johnson 1874 -
.... 6 Rosetta Johnson 1879 -
.... *2nd Wife of Phillip Hoffman:
.... +Phoebe Ann Goff 1823 - 1904
.... 5 Harrison Dortman Hoffman 1855 -
.... 5 Phoebe Luella Hoffman 1857 -
.... 4 Elizabeth Hoffman 1808 -
.... 4 Nancy Ann Hoffman 1810 - 1881
.... +William Henry Phillips
.... *2nd Husband of Nancy Ann Hoffman:
.... +Capel Howell 1805 - 1881
.... 5 Sarah Howell 1828 -
.... 5 Mary Howell 1830 -
.... 5 Elizabeth Howell 1832 -
.... 5 Susan Howell 1838 -
.... 5 John H. Howell 1840 -
.... 5 Cleon C. Howell 1840 -
.... 5 Christian Howell 1843 -
.... 5 Isaac Scott Howell 1848 -
.... 5 Harriet Howell 1850 -
.... 5 Mary Alice Howell 1855 -
.... 4 Sarah Hoffman 1815 - 1899
.... +Unknown Hoffman
.... 5 George Hoffman 1837 -
.... *2nd Husband of Sarah Hoffman:
.... +John Meredity
.... 4 John Hoffman 1815 - 1850
.... +Rebecca Ann Bunner 1818 - 1875
.... 5 Squire Washington Hoffman 1836 -
.... 5 Amos Huffman Hoffman 1836 -
.... 5 John Hoffman 1839 -
.... 5 Margaret Hoffman 1839 -

Descendants of John Hoffman

Generation No. 1

1. JOHN[2] HOFFMAN *(HANNES JOHN[1])* was born October 23, 1741 in Tulpehocken Twnsp, Berks Co. PA, and died Aft. 1790 in Fayette County PA. He married MARGARET J. April 22, 1772 in 1790 Uniontown, Pa.

Notes for JOHN HOFFMAN:
Ancestor's Service
Pennsylvania Archives, Volume 23, Third Series. Also Series Five 1777-1778. He received depreciationary pay for his services as a Ranger. (Westmoreland County formed from Bedford County 1773, and Fayette from Westmoreland, 1783) In the home of Mrs. Edith McCay Bloom, 487 North High Street, Morgantown, WV. (living, February 1955) has been handed down, the hand painted baptismal certificate of this ancestor, born John Hoffman, on October 23, 1741. see National No. 122366 and National No. 196768. the said John Hoffman served in the capacity of Ranger on the Frontier from Bedford County, PA. Pennsylvania Archives Series 3, Volume 23, page 236.[]

More About JOHN HOFFMAN:
Fact 10: Capt. in the Revolutionary War11,12
Berks County History
Created Oct. 14, 1751 from parts of Philadelphia, Chester, and Lancaster counties; organized 1752. From it came part of Northumberland Co. in 1772 and part of Schuylkill Co. in 1811.

Tulpehocken; settled about 1707; incorporated 1729 while part of Lancaster Co.
The Tulpehocken bi-centennial commemorated in a four-day celebration at Womelsdorff, Pa. : June 28th, 29th, 30th and July 1st, 1923, being a series of historical sketches covering two hundred years, 1723-1923.

Ancestor's Service
Pennsylvania Archives, Volume 23, Third Series. Also Series Five 1777-1778. He received depreciationary pay for his services as a Ranger. (Westmoreland County formed from Bedford County 1773, and Fayette from Westmoreland, 1783) In the home of Mrs. Edith McCay Bloom, 487 North High Street, Morgantown, WV. (living, February 1955) has been handed down, the hand painted baptismal certificate of this ancestor, born John Hoffman, on October 23, 1741. see National No. 122366 and National No. 196768. the said John Hoffman served in the capacity of Ranger on the Frontier from Bedford County, PA. Pennsylvania Archives Series 3, Volume 23, page 236.

(the following received from Ken Huffman 6-19-1998)
Private 4th Class, Lancaster Co. Militia under Capt. Martin Weaver. Mustered 4-23-1781?
served in the capacity of Ranger on the Frontier from Bedford Co. Pa., for which he received depreciation pay.
Reference: 5th Ser. Pa. Archives, Vol 6, pages 201 and 606.
3rd Ser. Pa. Archives, Vol 23, years 1777 - 1778.
A Mrs. Cora Mckay, one of John's descendants had in her possession a hand painted birth certificate of John Hoffman. It shows him to have been born Oct. 23,1741.
In a book called "Monongalhela of Old", by Judge Veech, is a statement that John Hoffman lived in Springhill Township, Fayette County, Pa. as early as 1772. All the southwestern part of Pa. was called Bedford County until 1773.
A court record in Uniontown, Pa. shows a transaction in the sale of land in 1790, by John Hoffman. Nothing is shown at a later date. This would indicate that he died after 1790. His wife Margaret signed her name to one or two records at Uniontown, Pa.
The first census of Pa. taken in 1790 show John Hoffman to have had three white males and four females in his family.

John & Margaret Huffman's Deed dated 25th July 1789

This indenture made the twenty fifth day of July in the year of our Lord one thousand seven hundred and Eighty nine, between John Huffman of German Township, Fayette County and common wealth of Pennsylvania yeoman and Margaret his wife of the one part and James Wilson of Pennsylvania the same place yeoman of the other part witnessed that whereas the commonwealth of Pennsylvania by their patent or confirmation bearing date the eighth day of June in the year of our Lord one thousand seven hundred and eighty six did grant unto George Huffman one hundred and thirty acres of Land called 'Germany.' _located on the Waters of Browns Run, a branch of Monongahela River in German Township, Fayette County, adjoining the land of the said John Huffman. Barney Gilbert Edward Green and Jacob Hester by the said patent and enrollment in the Rolls office of said state in patent book No. 6 page 323 dated the 28th June AD 1786 will appear.And whereas the said George Huffman by Deed duly executed bearing Date the Sixth day of February in the year of our Lord one thousand seven hundred and eighty eight did convey the same unto the said John Huffman as by the said Deed Recorded in the office for Recording Deeds in said County in Book 45 the 11th July Anno Domini 1789. And whereas the commonwealth aforesaid by their Patent or confirmation dated the fifth day of March in the year of our Lord one thousand seven hundred and eighty nine did grant unto the said John Huffman and a certain tract of land called 'Partnership' situated on the Waters of Browns Run in German Township, Fayette County adjoining Lands of Hugh Gilmore, George Huffman aforesaid John Harris Hieronimus Ramley ? as by the said patent or confirmation enrolled in the Rolls Office for the State of Pennsylvania willfully appears. Now know ye that the said John Huffman and Margaret his wife for and in consideration of the sum of two hundred Pounds, Two Shillings lawful Money of the Commonwealth of Pennsylvania aforesaid to him the said John Huffman in hand well and truly paid or served to be pain by the said James Wilson at and before the sealing and delivery hereof The Receipt or Security whereof is acknowledged by the signature of the said John Huffman. Have granted bargained _____ ______ released and confirmed and by these payments Do grant bargain ______ ______ release and confirm unto the said James Wilson his heirs and assigns. All the Estate, Right, Title, Interest ____ ________property, claim and Demand Whatsoever of them, the John Huffman and Margaret his wife ________and unto the following described part of the above described Tracts of Land called, Germany and Partnership the same being bounded? as followeth. Beginning at a Black Oak Tree a corner of Edward Green's Land thence by the same North sixty six degrees and three quarters West one hundred and four ? perches and five tenths to a pile of stones thence by Jacob Hoover's Land South Sixty eight degrees West one hundred and fifteen? Perches and five tenths to a pile stones on a Sugar tree stump, North eighty six degrees and three quarters West eleven perches and eight tenths? To a white Oak and South sixty four degrees and a quarter West Sixty three ? perches and five tenths? To a white walnut tree near the forks of a small Run Thence by Hugh Gilmore's land south two degrees and a quarter East one hundred and twelve perches to a post near same marked Trees thence by the other Lands of the said John Huffman being the residue? of both the Tracts above mentioned north seventy two degrees and a quarter East Three hundred and twenty five perches to a post on the line of Alexander Wilson's Land _______ Barney Gilbert's Thence by the same North twenty five degrees ______/ sixty five perches __ six tenths to a post in the line of Edwards Green's Land aforesaid thence by the same South thirty seven degrees and on the ____West twenty three perches to the place of Beginning containing one hundred and eighty five acres and half a quarter of an acre___ the one half part of both the above surveys now resurveyed and made to contain three hundred and seventy acres and one quarter be the same more or less. Together____ with all and Singular the Rights member's ? and ______hereunto belonging or in any wise of Right appertaining To have and to hold the said described part of the above described Tracts of Land _________and ___________with the ___________ and every part thereof unto the said James Wilson his heirs and assigns. To the only ______ _________ _________and Behalf of the said James Wilson his heirs and Executors, Administrators and assigns forever And the said John Huffman and Margaret his wife the aforesaid __________ gained__________and every past thing against them their heirs and against all and every other person or persons anything having a lawfully claiming in the same or any part thereof by from or under them or their heirs or by from or under any other person or persons whatsoever. The fifth part of all gold or silver are to be delivered at the _______ ______ clear of all charges. Reserved? For the use of the commonwealth aforesaid only accepted unto the said James Wilson his heirs and assigns shall and will warrant and forever by these ______? ______ Whereof the parties of these ________have set their hands and interchangeably affixed their seals the sixth day and year first above written.

Sealed and delivered in the presence of the words his heirs and assigns ________?
before signing
John _________ and Alexander _____________

Received the day of the above indenture of within named James Wilson the sum of Two hundred pounds ten shillings lawful money in full of the consideration herein mentioned.

John Huffman

Mark

Margaret Huffman

Testis} Alexander ________ John Huffman
Mark

Fayette County: The fourteenth day of July anno domini 1789 Before me the______ one of the Justice of the Peace and the Commonplace in and for the said county personally _________John Huffman and Margaret his wife and acknowledges the above instrument to be their deed and defined the same night be recorded as such. The said Margaret on examination previous hereto to having acknowledged when apart from her husband that she was fully acquainted with the contents and voluntarily became a party thereto.

Recorded and compared 25th July 1789

Note:
A perch is 16.5 feet

Notes for MARGARET J.:

Children of JOHN HOFFMAN and MARGARET J. are:

i. BARBARA^3 HOFFMAN.
ii. CATHERINE HOFFMAN.
iii. CHRISTIAN HOFFMAN.
iv. ELIZABETH HOFFMAN.
2. v. JOHN HOFFMAN, b. January 21, 1775, Bedford Co. PA.; d. March 19, 1856, Mongalia Co. VA.

Generation No. 2

2. JOHN^3 HOFFMAN *(JOHN^2, HANNES JOHN^1)* was born January 21, 1775 in Bedford Co. PA., and died March 19, 1856 in Mongalia Co. VA. He married SARAH ANN GODWIN Bef. 1797. She was born September 02, 1773 in Kent Co. DE, and died June 10, 1861 in Mongalia Co. VA.

Notes for JOHN HOFFMAN:
Written about in a book by Ella Mae Doggett Hostetler.
John & Sarah Hoffman are also known as John & Sarah Huffman. It seems that through different people's writing the name went from Hoffman to Huffman, Hoffman is the correct German spelling, but some adopted Huffman as the new American version of their name, whatever! Some say they adopted the name Huffman, but later descendants found baptismal certificates and misc. papers showing the real name of Hoffman and some descendants changed their names from Huffman back to the original Hoffman, so you can choose from here on out which is actually these people's names!
John and Sarah were very hard working industrious people. Sarah carded her own wool. They say that Sarah was a small wiry woman. According to Sarah's great grand daughter,(Ella Mae Doggett - Hostetler), a coverlet that Sarah made herself is on display at the Smithsonian Institution.

John and Sarah lived in Masontown, Pa. Till 1797(another source says 1830) then moved to Smithtown, WV. Monongalia County, just south of Morgantown

John and his wife were among the first member of the Goshen Baptist Church, about ten miles south of Morgantown, WV. Goshen was organized August 2, 1837, by the Reverends J.W.B. Tisdale and John Curry.

#282

In the name of God Amen, I John Huffman of Monongalia County in the State of Virginia, Do make this my last will and Testament in manner and form following that is to say First I give and bequeath to my wife Sarah Huffman the house where I at present reside and the whole of the house
hold furniture therein during her natural life time. I also give and bequeath to her the sum of one hundred dollars in money to be paid to her by my Executor or Executors herein after named in one year after my decease. Secondly I give and bequeath to my three grandchildren sons of my late son John Huffman namely Squire Huffman, Amos Huffman, and John Huffman one dollar each to be paid to them by my Executors herein after named. Thirdly I give and bequeath to my son Phillip Huffman and my son Daniel Huffman and my daughter Elizabeth Harris and to my daughter
Nancy Howell and to my daughter Sarah Meredith and to my grandson George I. Huffman son of daughter Sarah Huffman, now Sarah Meredith and my wife Sarah Huffman an equal share of the balance of my property both real and personal not heretofore devised or what may be devised in this will hereafter to them and their Heirs forever except the share of my daughter Sarah Meredith which I bequeath unto her son George I. Huffman at her decease. Fourthly I bequeath to my two grand children Mary Ellen and Abalina Elizabeth daughters of my son Squire Huffman and to my daughter in law Rebeckah Ann one dollar each to be paid to them by my Executors herein after named. Fifthly I do hereby constitute and appoint my wife Sarah Huffman and my friend Thomas Meredith Executrix and Executor of this my last will and Testament revoking all other and former willes by me hereto fore made.
17th January 1852.
R.C. Corrothers) his
Haymond Griggs) witnesses John X Huffman
James Stanley) mark
At a County Court held in and for Monongalia County March Term 1856 A paper writing purporting to be the last will & testament of John Huffman deceased was this day produced to the court fully proven by the oaths and examination of Robert C. Carrother and Haymond Griggs subscribing
witnesses thereto and ordered to be admitted to record as for the last will and testament of the said John Huffman.

A copy Teste: Marshall M. Dent clerk
At a County Court held in and for Monongalia County March Term 1856 A paer writing puporting to be the last will and testament of John Huffman deceased was this day produced to the court fully by the oaths and examination of Robert C. Corrothers and Haymond Criggs subscribing witnesses thereto and ordered to be admitted to record as and for the last will and testament of the said John Huffman dec'd.

A Copy Teste: Marshall M. Dent Clerk.
At a County Court held in and for Monongalia County in the March term of 1856 On motion of Henry Watson and for reasons appearing to the court (Sarah Huffman the widow & executrix named in the will having in having in writing decline to act as such and desired that said Watson should
administer) a certificate is granted him to obtain letters of Administration with the will annexed on the estate of John Huffman dec'd.
Whereupon the said Watson took the oath prescribed by law and entered into bond in the penalty of sixteen hundred dollars conditioned as the law directs with John Meredith and Haymond Griggs (who justified on oath as to their sufficiency) secureties therein.

Notes for SARAH ANN GODWIN:

Sarah's name has been found spelled both ways Goodwin and Godwin

More About SARAH ANN GODWIN:
Fact 9: October 17, 1773, christened in Hartford,Co.???27,28

Notes for JOHN HOFFMAN:
[For Jo Ann.FTW]

[AAA NewOne.FTW]

Written about in a book by Ella Mae Doggett Hostetler.
John & Sarah Hoffman are also known as John & Sarah Huffman. It seems that through different people's writing the name went from Hoffman to Huffman, Hoffman is the correct German spelling, but some adopted Huffman as the new American version of their name, whatever! Some say they adopted the name Huffman, but later descendants found baptismal certificates and misc. papers showing the real name of Hoffman and some descendants changed their names from Huffman back to the original Hoffman, so you can choose from here on out which is actually these people's names!
John and Sarah were very hard working industrious people. Sarah carded her own wool. They say that Sarah was a small wiry woman. According to Sarah's great grand daughter,(Ella Mae Doggett - Hostetler), a coverlet that Sarah made herself is on display at the Smithsonian Institution.

John and Sarah lived in Masontown, Pa. Till 1797(another source says 1830) then moved to Smithtown, WV. Monongalia County, just south of Morgantown

John and his wife were among the first member of the Goshen Baptist Church, about ten miles south of Morgantown, WV. Goshen was organized August 2, 1837, by the Reverends J.W.B. Tisdale and John Curry.

Children of JOHN HOFFMAN and SARAH GODWIN are:

i. DANIEL[4] HOFFMAN.
ii. SQUIRE HOFFMAN, d. 1850, Port Hudson LA; m. MARY DEBOLT, March 19, 1829; b. February 24, 1809; d. February 16, 1833, Masontown, PA.
iii. PHILLIP HOFFMAN, b. February 18, 1797, Monongalia Co. VA; d. January 09, 1879, Barbour Co. WVA; m. (1) ALETHA SUMMERS, August 26, 1820, Monongalia Co. VA; b. February 01, 1799, Prince George Co, MD; d. April 17, 1849, Preston, WVA; m. (2) PHOEBE ANN GOFF, January 19, 1854, Preston Co. WVA; b. Abt. 1823; d. January 17, 1904, Benwood, Marshall Co. WVA.

Notes for PHILLIP HOFFMAN:
[Brøderbund Family Archive #290, Ed. 1, Census Index: VA, WV, Preston County, 1870 West Virginia Census, Date of Import: Feb 17, 2001, Internal Ref. #1.290.1.16537.1]

Individual: Hoffman, Phillip
Race: W
Age: 73
Birth place: VA
Township: Portland Twp
Microfilm: Roll 1697, Page 155

Obituary Morgantown Post:

Philip Hoffman, father of one of the editors of the Post, died at his residence in Barbour County, WV at 6 o'clock on Thursday evening, January 09, age 82 years, 1 month, 9 days. He was for many years a resident of Monogalia County, and lived in what is the now Clinton District, the place of his nativity, he was the oldest son of John and Sarah Hoffman, who emigrated from Berks County, PA about the year 1795 or 1976, & settled on 'The Old Hoffman Farm' near Smithtown.

Newspaper Clipping: Phillip Hoffman, Father of one of the editors of the Post, died at his residence in Barbour County, West Virginia at 6 o'clock on Thursday evening, January 9th age 82 years, 1 month and 9 days. He was for many years a resident of Monongalia County and lived in what is now Clinton District, the place of his nativity. He was the oldest son of John and Sarah Hoffman, who emigrated from Berks County, Pa. about the year 1795 or 1796, and settled on the "Old Hoffman Farm" near Smithtown. In 1845 or 46 he moved to Preston County where he lived until about 5 years since, when he went to Barbour County. He was married in 1820 to Aletha Summers, daughter of Rev. Alexander Summers, of this county and raised to their majority 10 children, 8 of whom are still living. He leaves 8 children, 56 grandchildren, about 86 great-grandchildren, 3 sisters, and many friends to mourn his loss, but our loss is his gain, and we hope his troubles are over. "

From book "Hoffman Huffman 1741 - 1995" by Patsy Ann Brown

More About ALETHA SUMMERS:
Burial: Mathews Cemetery, Marquess, Preston, VA

More About PHOEBE ANN GOFF:
Burial: Barbour Co. WVA

iv. ELIZABETH HOFFMAN, b. April 06, 1808.
v. NANCY ANN HOFFMAN, b. March 10, 1810; d. February 10, 1881; m. (1) WILLIAM HENRY PHILLIPS, Monongalia Co. VA; m. (2) CAPEL HOWELL; b. August 03, 1805, VA; d. May 14, 1881.
vi. SARAH HOFFMAN, b. April 19, 1815; d. February 02, 1899; m. (1) UNKNOWN HOFFMAN; m. (2) JOHN MEREDITY, August 31, 1849.
vii. JOHN HOFFMAN, b. December 25, 1815, VA; d. Abt. 1850; m. REBECCA ANN BUNNER, March 05, 1835; b. October 29, 1818, VA; d. May 20, 1875.

Notes for JOHN HOFFMAN:
Buried At the Mt. Nebe Chruch of Christ.

Notes for REBECCA ANN BUNNER:
Buried at the Mt. Nebe Chruch of Christ
(Buried in Knotts Cemetery and moved to Clermont Cemetery in Fairmont, WV when highway went in.)
(Believe this information is wrong but left it in so as not to lose it.)

More About REBECCA ANN BUNNER:
Burial: Mt. Nebo Cemetary, Marion Co.

John's Baptism Certificate

HAND PAINTED BAPTISM CETIFICATE.
THIS WAS DAMAGED BY WATER.

Pennsylvania Archives

Third Series.

Printed under direction of

DAVID MARTIN,

Secretary of the Commonwealth.

Edited by

WILLIAM HENRY EGLE, M.D.

VOL. XXIII.

HARRISBURG:

Wm. Stanley Ray, State Printer.

1897.

Jacob Mallott.
John Lane.
Jacob Seaman.
James Applegate.
Nade Harden.
John Smith.
Evan Shelby.
Christian Sipes.
Christ'n Enslow.
Thomas Arnott.
Daniel Priale.
Jacob Shingletake.
Jacob Shoak.
Philip Longstreet.
Henry Sype.
Jn'o Cox, Colonel, New Jersey.
Charles Sipe.
George Shingletaker.
Henry Rush, Capt.
James John, Lieut.
George Isapice.
Thomas Herod, Ensign.
Wm. Hay.
Peter Rush.
Benjamin Davis.
John Peek.
George Walker.
Samuel Paxton.
Peter Mariles.
Benjamin Cox.
Joshua Pitman.
John Slaughter.
Moses Beamen.
Amos Beaker.
Mich'l Stall.
Emanuel Smith.
Lawrence Bishop.
John Hoffman.
Jacob Mellott.
James Applegate.
Henry Smith.
Thomas McFarren.
Robert Hill.
Powell George.

Jn'o Smith.
Timothy Covalt.
Richard Pittman.
James Collins.
Peter Rouff.
John Smith.
Jacob Rush.
Wm. Turner.
George Bailey.
John Neely, Serg't.
George Bishop.
Adis Lin.
Edw. Brethod.
Jacob Rush.
Benj. Williams.
James Ballou.
Joseph Thraulds.
Philip Truix.
Samuel Truix.
Henry Rush.
Adis Lin.
Hugh Alexander.
Benj. Stevens.
Philip Davis.
Henry Rush, Capt.
Peter Rush.
Benj. Milot.
John Milot.
James Longstretch.
Charles Leper.
Thomas Morton.
John Graham.
James Grimes.
Thomas Herrod.
Samuel John.
Benj. Cherry.
John Crossins.
Abraham Covalt.
Lott French.
John Livington.
Timothy Covelt.
Jeremiah French.
Adam Miller.
Bethual Covelt.
Benj. French.

John Moorhead.
Rich'd Kimbers.
Abraham Covelt, Jr.
Jacob Miers.
Ralph French.
Martin Myers.
John Miller.
Matheas Myers.
Abraham Covelt.
Lott French.
John Livingston.
Timothy Covelt.
Adam Miller.
Benj. French.
John Murhead.
Rich'd Kimbers.
Jacob Miers.
Martin Miers.
John Miller.
Mathew Myers.
Abraham Covelt, Jr.
Bethual Covert.
John Brealy.
John Thorleton, Capt.
James Eags.
Daniel Murphy.
Josiah Minor.
James McGinnis.
David Caldwell.
Jonathan Edenton.
Wm. Wright.
Mich'l McMullin.
Peter McMullin.

Peter Bailey.
John Gorman.
John McGuire.
Wm. Beatty.
John Tussey.
Charles Bradley.
Joseph Moore.
Joseph Sharp.
Woolrich Huffstater.
James Huffstater.
Samuel Montgomery.
Samuel Gibson.
Samuel Rhea.
John Williams.
Balser Rowler.
John Rowler.
Michael Rowler.
Hezekiah Rickets.
Nathaniel Rickets.
Edw. Rickets.
Edw. Cheney.
Thomas Rickets.
Robert Rickets.
John Hess.
Rob't Spencer.
Jacob Smith.
Charles Lamox.
James Wilson.
Wm. Templeton.
Joseph Neavorn.
George Hutchison.
John Branciff.
Wm. Barker, New Levies.

BEDFORD COUNTY.

John McClellan.
John Coyle.
John McKindly.
Rich'd Stephens.
James Alexander.
Wm. Sloan.

John Rankin.
James Gallaway.
Lewis Davis.
Wm. Scott.
Wm. Enyart, 2d Lieut.
John Enyart, Ensign.

MONONGALIA COUNTY, WEST VIRGINIA

[V. 1]

Births and Wills

Part 2

Will Books A, 1, 2, 3, 4, 5, and 6

Copied from Morgantown Court House Records

by

Works Progress Administration of West Virginia

Historic Marker Project

Ross B. Johnston, Director

1936

Retyped & Indexed by

Ann Harner Stocker
Ann Simpson Davis Chapter
Columbus, Ohio

1995

for the Bookworm Project, NSDAR Library

WILLS

TESTATOR	DATE OF INSTRUMENT PROBATE	DEVISEES	WITNESSES	BOOK NO. PAGE NO.
HUFFMAN, (X) John	1/17/1852 3/-/1856	Sarah Huffman, wife Squire, Amos and John Huffman, g.sons, sons of John Huffman, dec.son. Philip and Daniel, sons Geo.I.Huffman, g.son, son of Sarah, dau. Elizabeth Harris, dau Nancy Howell, dau. Sarah Meredith, dau. Mary Ellen and Abalina Eliz. Huffman, daus.of Squire Huffman, dec. son.	Robt.D. Corrothers Haymond Griggs James Stanley Exrs. Sarah Huffman Thomas Meredith	1-282
HUNT, Jonas	7/6/1826 12/-/1839	Jane Hunt, wife James Hunt, son Billy and Joshua, sons Matilda, Sally, Betty and Mary Hunt, daus.	James Seaton Jr. Thomas P.Seaton Exrs. Jane Hunt James Seaton Jr.	1-121
HURLEY, (X) Caleb	10/4/1833 4/-/1834	Sally Hurley, wife Eliza Cole, dau.& heirs	Caleb Tanzey Leven Fleming	A-8
HURRY, James	12/10/1830 1/-/1831	Margaret Hurry, present wife Rachel Hurry, dau. Other children	John Shisler N.B. Madera Michael Shisler Exrs. Thos. P. Ray Edgar C. Wilson	1-54
HURST, William	6/18/1802 7/-/1802	Elizabeth Hurst & heirs	Christian Whitchore Two other names in Dutch Extrx. Elizabeth Hurst	1-307
ICE, Thomas	4/13/1840 9/-/1840	Andrew Ice, son Drewsilla, Ice, wife Mary, Sarah and Phebe Ann Ice, daus. Isaac W. Ice, son Aaron Chriss, nephew	J.H. Martin Isaac Talkington Alex. Talkington	1-130

FAMILIES HOFFMAN BROWN

Brown, Patsy Saily

Hoffman - Huffman family tree

NSDAR

--- Presented by ---

James Tull Chapter in honor of Mrs. Virginia Stragall.

Date 5-7-1996 No. 126941

GGGG 8th G
G.F.

1. John Huffman 2A. John Huffman 1776
b. 23 October 1741 Berks County, Pennsylvania
md. Margaret ****John was in the Revolutionary War.****
DAR PATRIOT INDEX:FromPage335.Hoffman,includes(Huffman)John,b.,October 23,1741,dp 1790,m-Margaret PS-Patriotic Services, Pa. Pennsylvania.

th G
GGGG
G.F.

2A. John Huffman

b.1776,Bedford County,Pennsylvaina
d.1856 Monongalia County,Virginia
80 years old.md. Sarah Goodwin
b.ca.1776,Kent County,Delaware
d. Monongalia County, Virginia

3A. Philip Huffman 1797
3B. Squire Huffman P.767
3C. Female Huffman P.767
3D. Female Huffman
3E. Female Huffman

John and Sarah came from Berks County, Pennsylvania in 1795 or 1796 and settled in the vicinity of Smithtown, Monongalia, Virginia where they lived the remainder of their lives and raised their family of boys and girls. They are buried in an old abandoned cemetery (no markers) on side road between the Pisquah Church and the river on route 73 in Clinton district of Monongalia County.

1850 Cenus for Eastern District of Monongalia County,West Virginia.
Family 59:John Huffman,age 74,Born:Pennsylvania.
Sarah Huffman,age 74,Born:Delaware
George Huffman,age 13,Born:Virginia
Mary Huffman,age 16,Born:Virginia.

This census record is from William Knotts.

6th G
G-G-G
grand F.

They are enumerated in the1830Census ofMonongalia Co.From Roy Lockhart

3A.Philip Hoffman
b.18 February 1797
Monongalia County,Virginia
d.9January 1879,81 years old.
Barbour County,West Virginia
Bur.BarbourCounty,WestVirginia
md#1. 26 August 1820(Bond)
Monongalia County,Virginia
Aletha Summers(Letha)
b.1 February 1799
Prince Georges County,Maryland
d.17 April 1849, 50 years old.
Marquess,Preston,Virginia
bur.Marquess,Preston,Virginia,
Mathews Cemetery.Father:Rev.Alexander Summers-Mother Mary Ann Vinegar
md.#2.19 January 1854,Preston County,Virginia
Phoebe Ann Goff b.March ca.1823. * Picture Page 11.
d.17 January 1904,80 years old,Benwood,Marshall,West Virginia
bur.Wheeling,Ohio,West Virginia,Greenwood Cemetery
Father:Salathiel Goff - Mother:Malinda Garner
Name appears as Hoffman on Phoebe tombstone.

P.12.4A.Mary Ann Huffman1821(Shahan)
P.58.4B.John Alexander Hoffman 1822
P.577.4C.Elijah S.Huffman 1824
P.601.4D.Nimrod Nelson Huffman 1827
P.608.4E.George Washington Huffman 1831
P616.4F.Francis Marion Huffman(Twin1836)
P.648.4G.Louisa Marian Huffman (Twin1836)
P.708.4H.Abalona Rebekah Huffman 1839Hall
4I.Nancy Jane Huffman md.Hovey
P.750.4J.Sarah Huffman 1841 Johnson
Mother of above is Aletha
P.8.4K.Harrison Dortman Huffman 1855
P.2.4L.Phoebe Luella Huffman(Ella)1857
Mother of above is Phoebe
^P.768^

Marriage Bond Records, Monangalia County, West Virginia 1796-1850.
Page-51: Date and Groom: August 26, 1820-Phillip Huffman,Bride: Aletha Summers, Daughter of Alexander Summers, Bondsman, Alexander Summers

"Philip & Phoebe are enumerated in the 1860 & 1870 censuses of Preston Co. She is enumerated in the 1880 census of Barbour Co& 1990 census of Marshall Co.(Benwood). Phoebe was a resident of Benwood at the time of her death." above is from Roy Lockhart.

NEWSPAPER CLIPPING:PHILIP HOFFMAN. Philip Hoffman,Father of one of the editors of thePost,died at his residence inBarbour County,WestVirginia at6o'clock onThursday evening,January 9th,age 82years,1month& 9days.He was for many years a resident of Monongalia County,& lived in what is nowClinton District,the place of his nativity.He was the oldest son of

5 in G
Great-Great
G.M.

4G.Louisa Marian Huffman(Twin)P.1.
b.25January1836 Pic.*P.859.
Monongalia County,Virginia now
West Virginia
d.30 April 1885,49 years old
Tucker County,West Virginia
Died of cancer
md.1851,Preston Co.Virginia
George Washington Shahan(Bull)
b.29February1830^Pic.*P.859.
Preston County,Virginia
now West Virginia
d.20 June 1891,61 years old
Tucker County,West Virginia
Father:George Elias Shahan(Shehan)
Mother:Catherine Rosier
George md#2.22 February 1886
Mary Martha Mathew
b.1836,Preston County,Virginia
now West Virginia

5A.Alethe Elizabeth Shahan
b.3 August 1851
Virginia,Died ca.1860
P.649.5B.William Francis Shahan 1852
5C.John Wesley Shahan
b.27 July 1854
d.1 February 1855
Died of Whooping Cough
5D.Minerva Sarah Shahan 1856 P.651
P.651.5E.Christina LeVerna Shahan1858Tena
P.651.5F.Mary Catherine Shahan 1860-1861
P.652.5G.Cyrena Margaret Shahan 1862 Rena
P.652 5H.Rev.George Emery Shahan 1864
P.672.5I.Richard Jefferson Shahan1867Jeff
5J.Louisa Olive Shahan 1869 P.686
5K.Elizah Squire Shahan
b.27 July 1873
d.1 November 1874,15 months old
5L.Caroline Josephine Shahan1874Jo
5M.Stillborn Twin ^P.686^
5N.Stillborn Twin
5O.Stillborn Twin
5P.Stillborn Twin
P.687.5Q.David Charles Shahan 1880
P.706.5R.Virgina Catherine Shahan 1883

From Beulah & Jeanette Shahan: George Elias Shahan & his 2 brothers, John & David came from Downs County, Ireland & settled in a Colony in Delaware. Then George went to a colony in Virginia. George was a stone mason & a carpenter. The first 5 children of George & Louisa Huffman Shahan were born in the Colony of Virginia. Then it was made the State of West Virginia 20 June 1863. George & Louisa lived in Tucker County, West Virginia on Licking Creek by a schoolhouse, near Blackwater River & Tucker County that goes up into Arundel County. George served in the Confederate Army during the Civil War. Book: History of Tucker County, West Virginia by Hu Maxwell 1884,Kingwood,West Virginia,PrestonPublishing Company.Page 495:George W.Shahan,of Irish descent,born in Preston, 1830, son of George Shahan.In 1851 he married Louisa Hoffman, owns 111 acres of land on Licking,&has 20 acres improved,8 miles from St.George He was in the Confederate Army under Garnett.Children:WilliamF.Minerva Christina, Mary C. George E. Richard J, Olive J.& Carolina.George died after a lingering illness, probably what is known in modern medical terms as diverticulosis.****Look in section forRev.George Emery Shahan for more history for George &Louisa Shahan.George Washinton Shahan and David W.Shahan were brothers & Louisa Marian Huffman& Mary Ann Huffman were sisters. These 2 brothers married these 2 sisters so all of their children are double cousins.From Elizabeth Shahan Book:Cenus of Population;Monongalia County Nation Archives Microfilm Publication roll1364; pg.50.53. Eighth Census of the United States;NA.George (VI)& Louisa M. (Huffman) Shahan reside in Tucker County with a son & two daughters: William,age eight;Sarah M.age three.and Christina,age two.Their second son,John W.died of whooping cough 1February1855.*****From Roy Lockart: Louisa Marian Huffman born Monongalia Co.Jan 25,1834 & died Tucker Co. Apr 28,1885,aged 49yrs.3mos.3ds.married in Preston Co in1851 to George Washington Shahan born Preston Co.Feb29,1830 & died Tucker Co.June 20, 1891,son of George &Catherine(Rosier)Shahan.They are enumerated in the 1860census of Tucker Co,1870 census of PrestonCo&1880 census of Tucker Co.Lived near St.George,Tucker Co.having previously lived near Rowlesburg,Preston Co. George served in the Confederate Army during the Civil

*Luella Tankersley lives in Seymour,Indiana.
*Virginia and Francis lives in Danville,New York

6G.Chloe F.Shahan P.649
b.6 July 1892
md.Clifford Boyen or Boylan

7A.Male Boyen
7B.Male Boyen
7C.Male Boyen

All three of Chloe's son's are Ministers.One Minster is on T.V.& Dora Shahan watches him.******

6H.Bertha M.Shahan P.649,b.28 October 1897
md.Everett Wallace

5D.Minerva Sarah Shahan P.648, Pic.*P.858. b.20 October 1856,Virginia. Now. West Virginia md. 1 November 1877 Thomas Dewalt Poling.

(4th G Great G-M)

5E.Christina LeVerna Shahan(Tena)
b.16 May 1858^P.648.Pic.*P.862.^
St.George,Tucker,Virginia
now West Virginia
d.2 February 1933,74 years old
md.23 December 1877
Hannahsville,Tucker,West Virginia
David T.Hovatter Pic.*P.862.
b.15 June 1853
St.George,Tucker,Virginia
now West Virginia
d.31 October 1929,76 years old
Father:David Hovatter

6A.Charles E.Hovatter
b.11 October 1878
St.George,Tucker,West Virginia
6B.Lellie C.Hovatter
b.18 April 1880
St.George,Tucker,West Virginia
6C.Wilbert F.Hovatter (3rd G my grandfather)
b.1 April 1882(April Fools Baby)
St.George,Tucker,West Virginia
6D.Ira J.Hovatter
b.17 April 1885
St.George,Tucker,West Virginia
6E.Mary L.Hovatter
b.7 March 1887
St.George,Tucker,West Virginia

6F.George E.Hovatter,b.15 February 1889,St.George,Tucker,West Virginia
6G.Lloyd A.Hovatter,b.29 June 1891,St.George,Tucker,West Virginia
6H.Maudie P.Hovatter,b.21 July 1893,St.George,Tucker,West Virginia
Pic.*P.862.6I.Arlie David Hovatter 1895
6J.Boyd E.Hovatter, b.24 September 1897,St.George,Tucker,West Virginia Pic.*P.862.This information is taken from the Old Family Bible record, which I have. And about my Grandmother Huffman, I do not any records.I have often heard mother talk of her grandparents who were Huffmans. Arlie D. Hovatter,Grafton,West Virginia.****From Jeanette Shahan:Book: History of Tucker County, West Virginia by Hu Maxwell 1884, Kingwood, West Virginia.Preston Publishing Company.Page 413: David Hovatter,from Barbour County,is the son of David Hovatter,& was born in 1853;in 1877 he married Tena L. daughter of George Shahan; is a farmer, owning 72 acres, 10 of which are improved; lives 5 miles from St.George, on Bull Run.Children:Charles,Lillie C.& Wilbert.*******

6I.Arlie David Hovatter
b.15 August 1895,St.George,Tucker,West Virginia
md.Laura M.Poling

7A.Lester Hovatter

*Lester lives in Fort Myers,Florida.

5F.Mary Catherine Shahan P.648
b.22 June 1860or1861 Pic.*P.861.
Virginia,now West Virginia
d.15 December 1941,80 years old
bur.Knottsville Cemetery,Taylor County,West Virginia
md.11 July 1882
Martin M.Poling.bur.Knottsville Cemetery,Taylor County,West Virginia

6A.Rhoda Poling P.652
6B.Jonas Poling P.652
6C.Ira Poling P.652

This Census was transcribed by Kary Wild <Karywild@aol.com>
for the USGenWeb Census Project http://www.rootsweb.com/~usgenweb/census/.
NOT YET PROOFREAD

1790 Census Reference Chart:
1) Free White Male age 16 and upwards (including Head of Household)
2) Free White Males under age 16
3) Free White Females (including Head of Household)
4) All other free persons, except Indians, not taxed
5) Slaves
****

Census_Year	1790
Microfilm #	M637-8
State	PENNSYLVANIA
County	Berks

---------------------Begin Actual Transcription----------------------------------

Start of Exeter

CENSUS YEAR: 1790 STATE: PA COUNTY: Berks DISTRICT: Exeter ENUMERATOR: M

PG#	LN#	HEAD OF HOUSEHOLD LAST NAME	FIRST NAME	FREE WHITE Males 16 up	FREE WHITE Males to 16	Females	ALL OTHER FREE Persons	Slaves	R
35	1	Cinly	John	3	1	4	.	.	
35	2	Hoffmaster	Henry	1	2	2	.	.	
35	3	Noll	Peter Jr.	1	1	3	.	.	
35	4	Rapp	Michael	1	2	3	.	.	
35	5	Morris	Thomas	1	1	2	.	.	
35	6	Wicks	Christian	2	.	1	.	.	
35	7	Wicks	George Adam	1	1	2	.	.	
35	8	Mourer	Philip	1	3	5	.	.	
35	9	Feger	Conrad	4	3	4	.	.	
35	10	Coppelberger	Christian	1	.	1	.	.	
35	11	Schlier	George	1	1	2	.	.	
35	12	Letloff	Henry	1	.	5	.	.	
35	13	Miller	Jacob	1	2	4	.	.	
35	14	Ganzer	Andrew	1	3	1	.	.	
35	15	Ganzer	John	1	1	1	.	.	
35	16	Koch	Jacob	1	1	2	.	.	
35	17	Thom	Henry	2	1	3	.	.	
35	18	Moyer	John	2	3	3	.	.	
35	19	Hoffman	Christian	1	1	3	.	.	
35	20	Hartman	Valentine	2	2	5	.	.	

37	4	Spohn	John	2	2	6	.	.
37	5	Huert	Henry	2	3	4	.	.
37	6	Huert	Jacob	2	.	3	.	.
37	7	Huert	John	1	.	3	.	.
37	8	Christ	Michael	3	3	2	.	.
37	9	Ullrich	Balzer	1	2	2	.	.
37	10	Fucks	Henry	1	.	4	.	.
37	11	Dougherty	Edward	1	2	5	.	6
37	12	Bower	John	1	2	3	.	.
37	13	Beard	Adam	2	3	4	.	.
37	14	Hoffman	John	2	5	2	.	.
37	15	Horner	Daniel	1	.	1	.	.
37	16	Boone	Jonathan	1	.	6	.	.
37	17	Swartz	Philip	4	2	3	.	.
37	18	Patrick	Widow	.	.	2	.	.
37	19	Henzel	Conrad	1	2	2	.	.
37	20	Noll	Peter Sr.	2	.	3	.	.
37	21	Lees	Henry Jr.	1	.	3	.	.
37	22	Lees	Henry Sr.	3	.	4	.	.
37	23	Boyer	Henry	3	1	6	.	.
37	24	Bechtel	John	3	3	4	.	.
37	25	Bailer	John	3	1	6	.	.
37	26	Rodermel	Peter	2	4	2	.	.
37	27	Horner	Mary	.	1	2	.	.
37	28	Dieder	Conrad	1	4	3	.	.
37	29	Klose	Henry	3	2	7	.	.
37	30	Boyer	Daniel	1	2	1	.	.
		Carried Up		143	125	275	1	6

2 males over
5 males under
2 females

CENSUS YEAR: 1790 STATE: PA COUNTY: Berks DISTRICT: Exeter ENUMERATOR: M

PG#	LN#	HEAD OF HOUSEHOLD LAST NAME	FIRST NAME	FREE WHITE Males 16 up	to 16	Females	ALL OTHER FREE Persons	Slaves	R
38	1	Hahn	Valentine	1	.	4	.	.	
38	2	Herner	Nicholas	2	2	3	.	.	
38	3	Miller	Philip	1	2	1	.	.	
38	4	Hoffman	Valentine	1	.	1	.	.	
38	5	Dotinger	John	1	.	2	.	.	
38	6	DeTurk	John	2	2	4	.	.	
38	7	DeTurk	Samuel	2	3	3	.	.	
38	8	Arman	Henry	1	2	2	.	.	
38	9	Bitem	George	2	.	4	.	.	
38	10	Boone	Isaac	1	1	2	.	.	
38	11	Kern	Michael	1	2	2	.	.	
38	12	Lee	Jno. Senr.	1	.	3	.	.	
38	13	Lee	Mordacai	2	2	3	.	.	
38	14	Hughes	Samuel, Sr.	2	.	2	.	.	
38	15	Hughes	Thomas, Sr.	2	1	3	.	.	
38	16	Hughes	Samuel, Jr.	2	.	1	.	.	
38	17	Charrington	Thomas	1	5	4	.	.	
38	18	Lee	Samuel	2	.	2	.	.	
38	19	Lee	Ester	.	.	1	.	.	
38	20	Lee	Elias	2	1	4	.	.	
38	21	Houter	John	2	.	1	.	.	
38	22	Krouss	Henry	2	3	3	.	.	
38	23	VanRead	Jacob	1	.	2	.	.	
38	24	Colter	Andrew	1	2	2	.	.	

John Hoffman

Notes

Written about in a book by Ella Mae Doggett Hostetler.

John & Sarah Hoffman are also known as John & Sarah Huffman. It seems that through different people's writing the name went from Hoffman to Huffman, Hoffman is the correct German spelling, but some adopted Huffman as the new American version of their name, whatever! Some they adopted the name Huffman, but later descendants found baptismal certificates and misc. papers showing the real name of Hoffman and some descendants changed their names from Huffman back to the original Hoffman, so you can choose from here on out which is actually these people's names!

John and Sarah were very hard working industrious people. Sarah carded her own wool. They say that Sarah was a small wiry woman. According to Sarah's great grand daughter,(Ella Mae Doggett - Hostetler), a coverlet that Sarah made herself is on display at the Smithsonian Institution.

John and Sarah lived in Masontown, Pa. Till 1797(another source says 1830) then moved to Smithtown, WV. Monongalia County, just south of Morgantown

John and his wife were among the first member of the Goshen Baptist Church, about ten miles south of Morgantown, WV. Goshen was organized August 2, 1837, by the Reverends J.W.B. Tisdale and John Curry.

#282

In the name of God Amen, I John Huffman of Monongalia County in the State of Virginia, Do make this my last will and Testament in manner and form following that is to say First I give and bequeath to my wife Sarah Huffman the house where I at present reside and the whole of the house

hold furniture therein during her natural life time. I also give and bequeath to her the sum of one hundred dollars in money to be paid to her by my Executor or Executors herein after named in one year after my decease. Secondly I give and bequeath to my three grandchildren sons of my late son John Huffman namely Squire Huffman, Amos Huffman, and John Huffman one dollar each to be paid to them by my Executors herein after named. Thirdly I give and bequeath to my son Phillip Huffman and my son Daniel Huffman and my daughter Elizabeth Harris and to my daughter

Nancy Howell and to my daughter Sarah Meredith and to my grandson George I. Huffman son of daughter Sarah Huffman, now Sarah Meredith and my wife Sarah Huffman an equal share of the balance of my property both real and personal not heretofore devised or what may be devised in this will hereafter to them and their Heirs forever except the share of my daughter Sarah Meredith which I bequeath unto her son George I. Huffman at her decease. Fourthly I bequeath to my two grand children Mary Ellen and Abalina Elizabeth daughters of my son Squire Huffman and to my daughter in law Rebeckah Ann one dollar each to be paid to them by my Executors herein after named. Fifthly I do hereby constitute and appoint my wife Sarah Huffman and my friend Thomas Meredith Executrix and Executor of this my last will and Testament revoking all other and former willes by me hereto fore made.

17th January 1852.

R.C. Corrothers) his
Haymond Griggs) witnesses John X Huffman
James Stanley) mark

At a County Court held in and for Monongalia County March Term 1856 A paper writing purporting to be the last will & testament of John Huffman deceased was this day produced to the court fully proven by the oaths and examination of Robert C. Carrother and Haymond Griggs subscribing

witnesses thereto and ordered to be admitted to record as for the last will and testament of the said John Huffman.

A copy Teste: Marshall M. Dent clerk

At a County Court held in and for Monongalia County March Term 1856 A paer writing puporting to be the last will and testament of John Huffman deceased was this day produced to the court fully by the oaths and examination of Robert C. Corrothers and Haymond Criggs subscribing witnesses thereto and ordered to be admitted to record as and for the last will and testament of the said John Huffman dec'd.

A Copy Teste: Marshall M. Dent Clerk.

At a County Court held in and for Monongalia County in the March term of 1856 On motion of Henry Watson and for reasons appearing to the court (Sarah Huffman the widow & executrix named in the will having in having in writing decline to act as such and desired that said Watson should

administer) a certificate is granted him to obtain letters of Administration with the will annexed on the estate of John Huffman dec'd. Whereupon the said Watson took the oath prescribed by law and entered into bond in the penalty of sixteen hundred dollars conditioned as the law directs with John Meredith and Haymond Griggs (who justified on oath as to their sufficiency) secureties therein.

John Hoffman

Notes

Ancestor's Service

Pennsylvania Archives, Volume 23, Third Series. Also Series Five 1777-1778. He received depreciationary pay for his services as a Ranger. (Westmoreland County formed from Bedford County 1773, and Fayette from Westmoreland, 1783) In the home of Mrs. Edith McCay Bloom, 487 North High Street, Morgantown, WV. (living, February 1955) has been handed down, the hand painted baptismal certificate of this ancestor, born John Hoffman, on October 23, 1741. see National No. 122366 and National No. 196768. the said John Hoffman served in the capacity of Ranger on the Frontier from Bedford County, PA. Pennsylvania Archives Series 3, Volume 23, page 236.[]

More About JOHN HOFFMAN:

Fact 10: Capt. in the Revolutionary War11,12

Berks County History

Created Oct. 14, 1751 from parts of Philadelphia, Chester, and Lancaster counties; organized 1752. From it came part of Northumberland Co. in 1772 and part of Schuylkill Co. in 1811.

Tulpehocken; settled about 1707; incorporated 1729 while part of Lancaster Co.

The Tulpehocken bi-centennial commemorated in a four-day celebration at Womelsdorff, Pa. : June 28th, 29th, 30th and July 1st, 1923, being a series of historical sketches covering two hundred years, 1723-1923.

Ancestor's Service

Pennsylvania Archives, Volume 23, Third Series. Also Series Five 1777-1778. He received depreciationary pay for his services as a Ranger. (Westmoreland County formed from Bedford County 1773, and Fayette from Westmoreland, 1783) In the home of Mrs. Edith McCay Bloom, 487 North High Street, Morgantown, WV. (living, February 1955) has been handed down, the hand painted baptismal certificate of this ancestor, born John Hoffman, on October 23, 1741. see National No. 122366 and National No. 196768. the said John Hoffman served in the capacity of Ranger on the Frontier from Bedford County, PA. Pennsylvania Archives Series 3, Volume 23, page 236.

(the following received from Ken Huffman 6-19-1998)

Private 4th Class, Lancaster Co. Militia under Capt. Martin Weaver. Mustered 4-23-1781?

served in the capacity of Ranger on the Frontier from Bedford Co. Pa., for which he received depreciation pay.

Reference: 5th Ser. Pa. Archives, Vol 6, pages 201 and 606.

3rd Ser. Pa. Archives, Vol 23, years 1777 - 1778.

A Mrs. Cora Mckay, one of John's descendants had in her possession a hand painted birth certificate of John Hoffman. It shows him to have been born Oct. 23,1741.

[illegible] book called "Monongalhela of Old", by Judge Veech, is a statement that John Hoffman lived in Springhill Township, Fayette County, Pa. as early as 1772. All the southwestern part of Pa. was called Bedford County until 1773.

A court record in Uniontown, Pa. shows a transaction in the sale of land in 1790, by John Hoffman. Nothing is shown at a later date. This would indicate that he died after 1790. His wife Margaret signed her name to one or two records at Uniontown, Pa.

The first census of Pa. taken in 1790 show John Hoffman to have had three white males and four females in his family.

Descendants of Phillip Hoffman

Generation No. 1

1. PHILLIP[4] HOFFMAN *(JOHN[3], JOHN[2], HANNES JOHN[1])* was born February 18, 1797 in Monongalia Co. VA, and died January 09, 1879 in Barbour Co. WVA. He married (1) ALETHA SUMMERS August 26, 1820 in Monongalia Co. VA, daughter of REV. SUMMERS and MARY VINEGAR. She was born February 01, 1799 in Prince George Co, MD, and died April 17, 1849 in Preston, WVA. He married (2) PHOEBE ANN GOFF January 19, 1854 in Preston Co. WVA. She was born Abt. 1823, and died January 17, 1904 in Benwood, Marshall Co. WVA.

Notes for PHILLIP HOFFMAN:
[Brøderbund Family Archive #290, Ed. 1, Census Index: VA, WV, Preston County, 1870 West Virginia Census, Date of Import: Feb 17, 2001, Internal Ref. #1.290.1.16537.1]

Individual: Hoffman, Phillip
Race: W
Age: 73
Birth place: VA
Township: Portland Twp
Microfilm: Roll 1697, Page 155

Obituary Morgantown Post:

Philip Hoffman, father of one of the editors of the Post, died at his residence in Barbour County, WV at 6 o'clock on Thursday evening, January 09, age 82 years, 1 month, 9 days. He was for many years a resident of Monogalia County, and lived in what is the now Clinton District, the place of his nativity, he was the oldest son of John and Sarah Hoffman, who emigrated from Berks County, PA about the year 1795 or 1976, & settled on 'The Old Hoffman Farm' near Smithtown.

Newspaper Clipping: Phillip Hoffman, Father of one of the editors of the Post, died at his residence in Barbour County, West Virginia at 6 o'clock on Thursday evening, January 9th age 82 years, 1 month and 9 days. He was for many years a resident of Monongalia County and lived in what is now Clinton District, the place of his nativity. He was the oldest son of John and Sarah Hoffman, who emigrated from Berks County, Pa. about the year 1795 or 1796, and settled on the "Old Hoffman Farm" near Smithtown. In 1845 or 46 he moved to Preston County where he lived until about 5 years since, when he went to Barbour County. He was married in 1820 to Aletha Summers, daughter of Rev. Alexander Summers, of this county and raised to their majority 10 children, 8 of whom are still living. He leaves 8 children, 56 grandchildren, about 86 great-grandchildren, 3 sisters, and many friends to mourn his loss, but our loss is his gain, and we hope his troubles are over. "

From book "Hoffman Huffman 1741 - 1995" by Patsy Ann Brown

More About ALETHA SUMMERS:
Burial: Mathews Cemetery, Marquess, Preston, VA

More About PHOEBE ANN GOFF:
Burial: Barbour Co. WVA

Children of PHILLIP HOFFMAN and ALETHA SUMMERS are:

2. i. MARY ANN[5] HOFFMAN, b. June 15, 1821, Mongalia Co. WVA; d. December 23, 1886, Preston Co. WVA.
3. ii. JOHN ALEXANDER HOFFMAN, b. November 01, 1822, Mongalia Co. WVA; d. August 14, 1893, Kansas City, Jackson Co. Missouri.
4. iii. ELIJAH S. HOFFMAN, b. July 01, 1824; d. April 06, 1894, Preston Co. WVA.

Phillip Hoffman

Notes
[Brøderbund Family Archive #290, Ed. 1, Census Index: VA, WV, Preston County, 1870 West Virginia Census, Date of Import: Feb 17, 2001, Internal Ref. #1.290.1.16537.1]

vidual: Hoffman, Phillip
Race: W
Age: 73
Birth place: VA
Township: Portland Twp
Microfilm: Roll 1697, Page 155

Obituary Morgantown Post:

Philip Hoffman, father of one of the editors of the Post, died at his residence in Barbour County, WV at 6 o'clock on Thursday evening, January 09, age 82 years, 1 month, 9 days. He was for many years a resident of Monogalia County, and lived in what is the now Clinton District, the place of his nativity, he was the oldest son of John and Sarah Hoffman, who emigrated from Berks County, PA about the year 1795 or 1976, & settled on 'The Old Hoffman Farm' near Smithtown.

Newspaper Clipping: Phillip Hoffman, Father of one of the editors of the Post, died at his residence in Barbour County, West Virginia at 6 o'clock on Thursday evening, January 9th age 82 years, 1 month and 9 days. He was for many years a resident of Monongalia County and lived in what is now Clinton District, the place of his nativity. He was the oldest son of John and Sarah Hoffman, who emigrated from Berks County, Pa. about the year 1795 or 1796, and settled on the "Old Hoffman Farm" near Smithtown. In 1845 or 46 he moved to Preston County where he lived until about 5 years since, when he went to Barbour County. He was married in 1820 to Aletha Summers, daughter of Rev. Alexander Summers, of this county and raised to their majority 10 children, 8 of whom are still living. He leaves 8 children, 56 grandchildren, about 86 great-grandchildren, 3 sisters, and many friends to mourn his loss, but our loss is his gain, and we hope his troubles are over. "

From book "Hoffman Huffman 1741 - 1995" by Patsy Ann Brown

Know all men by these presnts, That we Philip Huffman

Alexander Summers are held and firmly bound unto

Esq governor or chief magistrate of the commonwealth of Virginia, for the time being and his successors. to the use of the said commonwealth, in the sum of one hundred and fifty dollars to which payment well and truly to be made we bind ourselves. our and each of our heirs, executors and administrators, jointly and severally firmly by these presents, sealed with our seals and dated this 26 day of August 1820

WHEREAS. a marriage is suddenly intended to be had and solemnised between the above bound Philip —— and Aletha Summers daughter of the above named Alexander both of this county.

Now the condition of the above obligation is such, That if there be no lawful cause or just impediment to obstruct the said marriage, then the above obligation to be void else to remain in full force and virtue.

Signed sealed and delivered in the presence of

Philip Huffman (SEAL)

Alexander Summers (SEAL)

5. iv. NIMROD NELSON HOFFMAN, b. May 21, 1827; d. November 04, 1890, Mongalia Co. WVA.
6. v. GEORGE WASHINGTON HOFFMAN, b. Abt. 1831, Monogalia Co. VA; d. January 22, 1865.
7. vi. FRANCIS MARION HOFFMAN, b. January 25, 1836, Mongalia Co. WVA; d. January 23, 1904, Preston Co. WVA.
8. vii. LOUISA MARION HOFFMAN, b. January 25, 1836, Monogalia Co. VA; d. April 30, 1885, Tucker Co. WVA.
viii. ABALONA REBEKAH HOFFMAN, b. May 12, 1839.

Notes for ABALONA REBEKAH HOFFMAN:
Sister mentioned in Louisa M. Shahan's Obit Mrs. Rebecca Hall of Wetzel County is believed to be Abalona Rebekah Hoffman Married to Mr. Hall

ix. NANCY JANE HOFFMAN, b. Abt. 1840.
9. x. SARAH A. E. HUFFMAN, b. August 09, 1841; d. 1901.

Children of PHILLIP HOFFMAN and PHOEBE GOFF are:
xi. HARRISON DORTMAN[5] HOFFMAN, b. Abt. 1855.
xii. PHOEBE LUELLA HOFFMAN, b. December 02, 1857.

Generation No. 2

2. MARY ANN[5] HOFFMAN *(PHILLIP[4], JOHN[3], JOHN[2], HANNES JOHN[1])* was born June 15, 1821 in Mongalia Co. WVA, and died December 23, 1886 in Preston Co. WVA. She married DAVID WILLIAM SHAHAN December 25, 1846. He was born October 30, 1825 in Preston Co. WVA, and died Aft. May 1910.

Notes for MARY ANN HOFFMAN:
Picture on page 35 in the Book "Generations of Hoffman to Hovatter

More About MARY ANN HOFFMAN:
Burial: George & Isabella Shahan Cemetery, Preston Co. WVA

Children of MARY HOFFMAN and DAVID SHAHAN are:
i. THOMAS[6] SHAHAN, b. 1844, va.
ii. PHILIP NELSON SHAHAN, b. September 09, 1848; d. January 22, 1913, St. George Tucker VA; m. (1) BARBARA BOWMAN; b. 1864; d. 1946; m. (2) MARY EDNA LIPSCOMB, February 16, 1865, Tucker Co. WVA; b. 1847; d. 1881; m. (3) MARY E. LIPSCOMB, February 16, 1865, Tucker Co. WVA; b. Abt. 1847.
iii. REBECCA E. SHAHAN, b. Abt. 1851.
iv. DAVID WILLIAM SHAHAN, b. February 08, 1853, Preston Co. WVA; d. January 13, 1931; m. CAROLINE A. BOLYARD; b. 1857; d. 1949.
v. CHRISTINA E. SHAHAN, b. March 09, 1855; d. March 09, 1921; m. WILLIAM SEIN ROSIER.
vi. COLUMBIA JANE SHAHAN, b. June 22, 1857; d. 1860.
vii. JOHN WASHINGTON SHAHAN, b. March 06, 1858, St. George Tucker VA; d. February 04, 1930, St. George Tucker VA; m. SARAH A. MITCHELL, March 09, 1880, Tucker Co. WVA; b. 1864; d. 1939.
viii. CHARLOTTE L. SHAHAN, b. May 30, 1860; d. 1943; m. LEMUEL KNOTTS.

3. JOHN ALEXANDER[5] HOFFMAN *(PHILLIP[4], JOHN[3], JOHN[2], HANNES JOHN[1])* was born November 01, 1822 in Mongalia Co. WVA, and died August 14, 1893 in Kansas City, Jackson Co. Missouri. He married (1) AMY ELIZABETH BRUNNER December 19, 1843 in Monongalia Co. VA. She was born April 18, 1828 in England, and died March 17, 1862 in Union, Bourbon KS. He married (2) LUCINDA BARNES May 07, 1865 in Bourbon Co. KS. She was born October 30, 1841 in Carthage, Jasper Co. MO, and died Abt. 1895 in OR.

Children of JOHN HOFFMAN and AMY BRUNNER are:
i. ALETHA ANN[6] HOFFMAN, b. March 28, 1846.
ii. SUSANNAH HOFFMAN, b. January 09, 1849.
iii. URSULEY ANN HOFFMAN, b. June 05, 1852.
iv. MARY JANE HOFFMAN, b. June 09, 1852.
v. AMY ELIZABETH HOFFMAN, b. Abt. 1858.
vi. WILLIAM FRANCIS HOFFMAN, b. Abt. 1861.

Children of JOHN HOFFMAN and LUCINDA BARNES are:

vii. NATHAN SQUIRE[6] HOFFMAN, b. September 02, 1868.
viii. CENITH E. HOFFMAN, b. Abt. 1870.
ix. MARION P. HOFFMAN, b. Abt. 1874.
x. DAVID MILTON HOFFMAN, b. May 01, 1875.
xi. GEORGE IRVIN HOFFMAN, b. December 27, 1879.

4. ELIJAH S.[5] HOFFMAN *(PHILLIP[4], JOHN[3], JOHN[2], HANNES JOHN[1])* was born July 01, 1824, and died April 06, 1894 in Preston Co. WVA. He married MARTHA ANN KING September 10, 1848 in Frederick Co., Maryland. She was born October 03, 1823 in Frederick Co. Maryland, and died January 16, 1899 in Preston Co. WVA.

More About ELIJAH S. HOFFMAN:
Burial: Mt. Zion Cemetery, Preston,Co. WVA.

More About MARTHA ANN KING:
Burial: Mt. Zion Cemetery, Preston,Co. WVA.

Children of ELIJAH HOFFMAN and MARTHA KING are:

i. DAVID HENNON[6] HOFFMAN, b. January 09, 1849.
ii. ABBALONA CLAMENC HOFFMAN, b. August 11, 1850.
iii. ROSALIE MARANDA HOFFMAN, b. May 30, 1852.
iv. HENRY MILTON HOFFMAN, b. September 06, 1853.
v. RUALL NANZILLA HOFFMAN, b. February 05, 1855.
vi. ENOCH MADISON HOFFMAN, b. January 19, 1857.
vii. ELIJAH MCGEE HOFFMAN, b. 1859.
viii. JOHN NELSON HOFFMAN, b. 1861.

5. NIMROD NELSON[5] HOFFMAN *(PHILLIP[4], JOHN[3], JOHN[2], HANNES JOHN[1])* was born May 21, 1827, and died November 04, 1890 in Mongalia Co. WVA. He married NANCY ANN ELIZABETH SAER April 21, 1864 in Morgantown, WVA. She was born February 27, 1844 in Morgantown, WVA, and died November 04, 1917 in Morgantown, WVA, Monongalia Co..

Notes for NIMROD NELSON HOFFMAN:
Editor Morgantown Post

More About NIMROD NELSON HOFFMAN:
Burial: Unknown, Oak Grove Cemetery - Morgantown, Monongalia Co., West Virginia328,329,330,331
Fact 3: Editor of the Morgantown Post (Newspaper)332,333,334
Fact 5: November 24, 1861, US Army, at Romney. Pvt. Co. A 1st W.Va. Calvary335,336,337
Fact 6: January 02, 1865, at Buckhannon, W.Va.338,339,340
Fact 7: April 03, 1862, 2nd Lt341,342,343
Fact 8: October 01, 1862, 1st Lt344,345,346
Fact 9: January 15, 1874, Mexican & Civil Wars, and was a W.Va. Delegate of the same347,348,349

Picture on page 34 of book The Generations of Hoffman to Hovatter.

More About NIMROD NELSON HOFFMAN:
Burial: Oak Grove Cemetery, Morgantown, Monongalia Co. WVA

More About NANCY ANN ELIZABETH SAER:
Burial: Oak Grove Cemetery, Morgantown, Monongalia Co. WVA

Children of NIMROD HOFFMAN and NANCY SAER are:

i. WILLIE U.S.[6] HOFFMAN, b. February 21, 1865, Mongalia Co. WVA; d. October 05, 1938, Elkins, Randolph, WVA.
ii. ANNA AMINIA HOFFMAN, b. September 26, 1866, WVA; d. January 26, 1935, Morgantown, WVA.

iii. ADA GREGG HOFFMAN, b. February 27, 1868, WVA; d. September 15, 1868, WVa.
iv. CORA LEE HOFFMAN, b. October 10, 1871, Mongalia Co. WVA; d. October 03, 1925, Morgantown, WVA.
v. NELLIE GRANT HOFFMAN, b. July 15, 1873.
vi. JOHN THOMPSON HOFFMAN, b. December 26, 1875, Monongalia Co. WVA; d. November 16, 1947, Parkersburg, Wood, WVA.
vii. HARRY HAGANS HOFFMAN, b. October 24, 1878; d. April 03, 1879.

6. GEORGE WASHINGTON[5] HOFFMAN *(PHILLIP[4], JOHN[3], JOHN[2], HANNES JOHN[1])* was born Abt. 1831 in Monogalia Co. VA, and died January 22, 1865. He married ELIZABETH ELIZA KNOTTS October 05, 1848 in Preston Co. VA, daughter of ABSALOM KNOTTS and ELIZABETH KELLER. She was born Abt. July 1831 in Preston Co. WVA, and died February 24, 1905.

Notes for GEORGE WASHINGTON HOFFMAN:
Note: George Washington Hoffman, spelling of name changed, Colonel in Civil War. ***From Roy Lockhart: He served in the Union Army during the Civil War as a Private of Company E, 15th Regiment, West Virginia Infantry. He was enrolled at Independence, Preston Co., Virginia, August 22, 1862; mustered into service at Wheeling, Virginia September 10, 1862 & served until his death in the service. He died of pneumonia at the Point of Rocks Hospital in Virginia.

More About GEORGE WASHINGTON HOFFMAN:
Burial: Unknown, National Cemetery - Grafton, Taylor Co., VA (now WV)426,427,428,429
Cause of Death: Pneumonia430,431

More About GEORGE WASHINGTON HOFFMAN:
Burial: National Cemetery, Grafton, Taylor Co. VA (now WVA)

Children of GEORGE HOFFMAN and ELIZABETH KNOTTS are:
i. MARY ELIZABETH[6] HOFFMAN, b. October 27, 1849; d. May 1930; m. ROBERT CORNELOIUS WAGNER, August 09, 1868, Near Fellowsville WV; b. June 15, 1847; d. June 1919.

More About MARY ELIZABETH HOFFMAN:
Burial: Howesville Methodist Cem. Howesville, wv

ii. MARTHA JANE HOFFMAN, b. Bet. 1850 - 1855.
iii. ALETHA HOFFMAN, b. February 29, 1860.

7. FRANCIS MARION[5] HOFFMAN *(PHILLIP[4], JOHN[3], JOHN[2], HANNES JOHN[1])* was born January 25, 1836 in Mongalia Co. WVA, and died January 23, 1904 in Preston Co. WVA. He married (1) CHRISTENA SHAHAN January 21, 1858 in Preston Co. VA, daughter of URSULA KNOTT. She was born October 22, 1839, and died April 26, 1871. He married (2) MARY AMELIA MARTIN September 05, 1872 in Grandsville, Monogalia Co. WVA, daughter of TURNER MARTIN and AMELIA CUMMINGS. She was born December 31, 1842 in Cassaville, Monongalia Co. WVA, and died August 05, 1922 in Cassaville, Monongalia Co. WVA.

Notes for FRANCIS MARION HOFFMAN:

For Days on the Field
By Francis Marion Huffman
National Tribune
6-4-1896

One West Virginian's Experience at the Battle of Manassas

Editor National Tribune: I have read with pleasure the recent account of the Second Bull Run. I was with Sigel's Corps, Milroy's Brigade. We cut McDowell out of a serious place on the evening of August 28. The Eleventh Corps fought in the cen6ter the next day, McDowell on the left and Fitz John Porter lay back on the right.

At about 2 o'clock p. m., while charging on the railroad embankment, I received a gunshot wound in the left knee, entirely disabling the limb. I was carried back by the Johnnies to the pike, 100 yard distant. The next morning when the battle opened I was in range of our guns. I crawled to a small oak tree for protection, and by so doing no doubt my life was saved. I was again removed September 2, a short distance in the direction of the gap, and in speaking distance of 40 or 50 wounded comrades, principally McDowell's men. We lay there with the earth for a bed and heavens for a shelter until the evening of the 5th, when the ambulance train was announced. If there are joys greater than ours when that ambulance train came I have never experienced them.

We were moved about one mile toward Alexandria and camped over night; started out again on the morning of the 6th, arriving at Georgetown College at 4 o'clock a.m. on the 7th. I had to have my leg amputated after that.
F. M. Huffman Corporal, Co. D, #rd W. Va. Marquess, W. Va.

More About FRANCIS MARION HUFFMAN:
Burial: Unknown, Mt Zion Church, Marquess, WV641,642

We were moved about one mile toward Alexandria and camped over night; started out again on the morning of the 6th, arriving at Georgetown College at 4 o'clock a.m. on the 7th. I had to have my leg amputated after that.
F. M. Huffman Corporal, Co. D, #rd W. Va. Marquess, W. Va.

[Brøderbund Family Archive #290, Ed. 1, Census Index: VA, WV, Preston County, 1870 West Virginia Census, Date of Import: Feb 17, 2001, Internal Ref. #1.290.1.16537.0]

Individual: Hoffman, Frank
Race: W
Age: 34
Birth place: VA
Township: Reno Twp
Microfilm: Roll 1697, Page 193

1880 Census Place: Reno, Preston, West Virginia

Source: FHL Film 1255412 National Archives Film T9-1412 Page 425A

Relation Sex Marr Race Age Birthplace Occupation

F. M. HUFFMAN Self M M W 44 WV
Farmer Fa: WV Mo: WV
Mary A. HUFFMAN Wife F M W 38 WV
Keeping house Fa: WV Mo: WV
John M. HUFFMAN Son M S W 21 WV Shoemaker Fa: WV Mo: WV
Sarah Ann HUFFMAN Dau F S W 16 WV Fa: WV Mo: WV
Ursula Jane HUFFMAN Dau F S W 16 WV Fa: WV Mo: WV
Charles N. HUFFMAN Son M S W 14 WV
Works On Farm Fa: WV Mo: WV
Rebecca HUFFMAN Dau F S W 11 WV Fa: WV Mo: WV
Onora A. HUFFMAN Dau F S W 6 WV Fa: WV Mo: WV
Emma F. HUFFMAN Dau F S W 5 WV Fa: WV Mo: WV
Hayes HUFFMAN Son M S W 4 WV Fa: WV Mo: WV
Lelia E. HUFFMAN Dau F S W 2 WV Fa: WV Mo: WV
Jenivee HUFFMAN Dau F S W 11M WV Fa: WV Mo: WV

Picture on page 36 in book "Generation of Hoffman to Hovatter"

More About FRANCIS MARION HOFFMAN:
Burial: Mt. Zion Cemetery, Preston,Co. WVA. Marquess

More About MARY AMELIA MARTIN:
Burial: Mt. Zion Cemetery, Preston,Co. WVA.

Children of FRANCIS HOFFMAN and CHRISTENA SHAHAN are:

i. JOHN MARTIN[6] HOFFMAN, b. November 07, 1858, Preston Co. WVA; d. May 07, 1942; m. MARTHA ANNE BURGOYNE; b. November 18, 1863; d. July 03, 1935.

Notes for JOHN MARTIN HOFFMAN:
Picture on page 37 in book "Generations of Hoffman to Hovatter"

Notes for MARTHA ANNE BURGOYNE:
Picture on page 37 in book "Generations of Hoffman to Hovatter.

ii. CHARITY ELIZABETH HOFFMAN, b. May 27, 1860, Preston Co. WVA; d. May 10, 1923, Kingwood, Preston Wva.

iii. URSULA JANE HOFFMAN, b. August 20, 1864, Marquess Preston, Wva; d. February 07, 1939, Rowlesburg, Preston WVA.

iv. SARAH ANN HOFFMAN, b. August 20, 1864, Marquess Preston, Wva; d. August 04, 1934, Davis, Tucker, WVA.

v. CHARLES NELSON HOFFMAN, b. June 10, 1866, Fellowsville, Preston, WVA; d. June 03, 1926, Marquess Preston, Wva.

vi. REBECCA HOFFMAN, b. October 24, 1868, Preston Co. WVA; d. December 01, 1957, Barbour Co. WVA; m. ARTHUR ELLSWORTH ALEXANDER, April 19, 1893.

Children of FRANCIS HOFFMAN and MARY MARTIN are:

vii. ORIONA ALICE[6] HOFFMAN, b. October 20, 1873, Fellowsville, Preston, WVA; d. February 22, 1948, Fairmont, Marion, WVA; m. JAMES R. PHELPS.

viii. EMMA FLORENCE HOFFMAN, b. January 19, 1875, Marquess Preston, Wva; d. August 09, 1936, Newburg, Preston, WVA; m. (1) WILLIAM N. GOFF; m. (2) JOSEPH L. SHROUT.

ix. RUTHERFOLD B. HAYES HOFFMAN, b. June 20, 1876; d. October 11, 1953; m. (1) EFFIE; m. (2) GLADYS.

x. LELIA EUGENIA HOFFMAN, b. September 10, 1877, Marquess Preston, Wva; d. June 12, 1925, Thornton, Preston, WVA; m. W. IRVIN WATTS.

xi. JENIVEE HOFFMAN, b. July 17, 1879, Marquess Preston, Wva; d. February 24, 1974, Kingwood, Preston, WVA; m. FRANKLIN BLAKENEY PIERCE, October 23, 1901, Marquess, Preston Co WV.

xii. LOLA VELLE HOFFMAN, b. June 02, 1881; d. August 29, 1966; m. ROBERT MUNSEN.

xiii. JAMES GILLISPI BLAINE HOFFMAN, b. October 27, 1884, Marquess Preston, Wva; d. July 07, 1956, Morgantown, Monongalia, WVA; m. (1) NORA A. BURGOYNE; m. (2) CLARISSA M. TODD; m. (3) EDITH P. FOX, June 08, 1942.

8. LOUISA MARION[5] HOFFMAN *(PHILLIP[4], JOHN[3], JOHN[2], HANNES JOHN[1])* was born January 25, 1836 in Monogalia Co. VA, and died April 30, 1885 in Tucker Co. WVA. She married GEORGE WASHINGTON SHAHAN 1851 in Preston Co. VA, son of GEORGE SHAHAN and CATHERINE ROSIER. He was born February 28, 1830 in Preston Co. VA, and died June 29, 1891 in Tucker Co. VA.

Notes for LOUISA MARION HOFFMAN:
ID: I25945
Name: Louisa Marian HUFFMAN HOFFMAN 1 2
Sex: F
Birth: 25 JAN 1836 in Monongalia Co., VA 3
Death: 28 APR 1885 in Tucker Co., WV
Reference Number: 25945
Note:
I had these obituaries in my files and wanted to share them with the List.
Roy Lockhart

The Preston County Journal - Kingwood, West Virginia - Thursday, May 14, 1885.
Vol. XVIII - - No. 37
Whole No. 978.
Page 3, Column 2

Deaths.

Announcements of deaths not exceeding 70 words, inserted free; but 1 cent per word for each word in excess of that number will be charged. In all cases, the money to be sent with the notice.

SHAHAN.--At her home in Tucker County, W. Va., April 28th, 1885, of cancer, Mrs. Louisa M. Shahan, aged 49 years, 3 months and 3 days. She was born in Clinton District, Monongalia County; was a consistent member of the M. E. Church for 37 years, and died with a glorious prospect of a home in Heaven. She leaves four brothers--John A. Hoffman, of Kansas, E. S. and F. M. Hoffman, of this county, and N. N. Hoffman, of Morgantown; and three sisters--Mrs. Mary A. Shahan, of this county, Mrs. Rebecca Hall of Wetzel County, and Mrs. Sarah Johnson, of Marion County.

Picture originally from Patsy Browns book, "Hoffman/Huffman

Notes for GEORGE WASHINGTON SHAHAN:
Originally from Patsy Browns book, Hoffman/Huffman

Children of LOUISA HOFFMAN and GEORGE SHAHAN are:

i. ALETHEA ELIZABETH[6] SHAHAN, b. August 03, 1851, va; d. Abt. 1860.

ii. WILLIAM FRANCIS SHAHAN, b. December 22, 1852, va; d. September 1942; m. MICHELLE / MELVINA L. NESTOR, April 22, 1879, Tucker County, WV.

iii. JOHN WESLEY SHAHAN, b. July 27, 1854; d. February 01, 1855.

iv. SARAH MINERVA SHAHAN, b. October 20, 1856, va; m. THOMAS DEWALT POLING, November 01, 1877, Tucker Co. WVA; b. Abt. 1856.

v. CHRISTINA L. SHAHAN[1], b. May 16, 1858, Sinclair, WV; d. February 02, 1933, Tucker Co.,WV; m. DAVID T. HOVATTER[1], December 23, 1877, Hannahsville, Tucker Co. WVA[1]; b. June 15, 1853, Kesson, WV[1]; d. October 31, 1929, Tucker Co.,VA now WV.

Notes for DAVID T. HOVATTER:
1880 Census Place: Licking, Tucker, West Virginia
Source: FHL Film 1255414 National Archives Film T9-1414 Page 378A
Relation Sex Marr Race Age Birthplace
D. C. HOVATTER Self MMW25 VA
Occ: LaborerFa: VA Mo: VA
Chrystena L. HOVATTER Wife FMW22 VA
Occ: Keeping House Fa: VA Mo: VA
Charles HOVATTERSonMSW1 WV
Fa: VA Mo: VA
Lilley C. HOVATTER Other FSW1M WV
Fa: VA Mo: VA

Barbour County Cities, Towns and Settlements
Kasson

According to an account found in Barbour County West Virginiapublished by the Barbour County Historical Society in 1979 Kasson, in Cove District, was first named Danville after the first settler Dan Highly. The hill he lived on, overlooking Kasson is still known as Highly Hill. Mr. Highly raised mulberry trees to feed his silkworms and produced silk thread was put on spools and shipped to Baltimore.

Danville was given the name Kasson because there was another WV Post Office called Danville. The first letter was mailed to a man named Kasson. The first Post Office was establised in 1862. Carr Bishop was the first postmaster. After him, Marion Newman, 1884; Lewis Coffman, 1904; George Coffman served from 1908 till his death in 1930. Hattie Coffman, his wife and two sons, Hayse & George Sherwood took it over until 1937 when Rachel Wilson Ball served till her death.

In the early days of Kasson the community included:
Stores:
Jack Bishop in 1870, John and Ed Compton, 1875; Marion Newman, 1880; Daniel J. Nester, 1890 and Lewis Coffman.

Blacksmith Shops:
David Hovatter, 1860; Ben Ekis in 1864; Albert Loar in 1891; and Lewis Coffman who learned the trade from his uncles Mike and Lige Coffman who had shops in Valley Furnace, Belington and Elkins. His first shop was near West Point

Churches:
The Kasson United Methodist Church, built in 1898. Daniel Nestor and Daniel Lohr were overseers.
The Church of the Brethren, David Hovatter had the Communion and Love Feast in his house, this was the beginning of the Shiloh Church of the Brethren which was organized in 1845 about 1 ½ miles from Kasson.

More About DAVID T. HOVATTER:
Burial: Preston Co. WV

vi. MARY CATHERINE SHAHAN, b. June 21, 1860, va; d. December 15, 1941, WVa; m. MARTIN M. POLING, July 11, 1882, Tucker Co. WVA; b. Abt. 1860.

vii. CYRENA MARGARET SHAHAN, b. September 08, 1862; d. August 15, 1943; m. ISAAC M. POLING, April 10, 1883, Tucker Co. WVA; b. Abt. 1860.

viii. REV. GEORGE EMERY SHAHAN, b. October 09, 1864, Rowlesburg, Preston WVA; d. December 18, 1966, Clarksburg, Harrison, WVA; m. CORA JANE HOVATTER, April 30, 1891, Tucker Co. WVA; b. October 05, 1876, Tucker Wv; d. March 28, 1948, Clarksburg, Harrison, WV.

Notes for REV. GEORGE EMERY SHAHAN:
Notes for REV. GEORGE EMERY SHAHAN:
[For Jo Ann.FTW]

[AAA NewOne.FTW]

[WFT3719_Vol10.FTW]

There is a picture of Elder G. Emory Shahan at age 100 on page 621 of "Alleghany Passage: Churches and Families" by Emmert F. Bittinger, and the following biography:

"The family lived near Rowlesburg for some years before moving near St. George in Tucker County. There the family lived within the boundary of the Union Chapel (Bull Run) branch of the Shiloh Congregation.

"The eighth child, George Emory Shahan, manifested special talents and an early interest in religion. He bagan a vigorous study [of] the Bible while still in his teens, soon mastering large portions by memory. His obiturary states that he began preaching at age fifteen, which would have been around 1879. The year after his marriage in 1891 to Cora Jane Hovatter, he was ordained to the ministry. He was advanced as an Elder in 1904 and thereupon given charge of the Shiloh Congregation, a position he held until 1907.

"He continued his labor for the Church at Union Chapel, serving as one of the ministers of that branch until his transfer to the Grafton Brethren Church which later became the Grace Brethren Church. He was called as pastor of the Grafton Church, a service which he fufilled for many years. He gave up this work in 1940 and moved to Clarksburg where he has retired.

"Most of his life he served in the free ministry, supporting his family by farming and carpentering. Before moving to Tucker County, he had accumulated a large tract of land, some of which was purchased for as little as $1.65 per acre. Most of the land was sold during an economic depression, and little gain was realized.

"Bro. Shahan was a man of high character and devotion. Much respected and loved by his fourteen children, ost of whom are now deceased, he left a strong impact on his family and those with whom he worked.

"A member of the National Fellowship of Brethren Ministers, he was the oldest member of that organization at the time of his death at the age of 102 in 1966. He still occasionally preached in the last decade of his life. Many will remember the occasion when he preached at the Grafton and Shiloh Churches after he had passed the age of 100. His ministerial work was greatly appreciated and respected."

More About REV. GEORGE EMERY SHAHAN:
Burial: Unknown, Clarksburg, WV2416,2417

- ix. RICHARD JEFFERSON SHAHAN, b. February 18, 1867, Rowlesburg, Preston WVA; d. May 13, 1954, Greenville, Darke, Ohio.
- x. LOUISA OLIVE J. SHAHAN, b. March 27, 1868, Preston Co. WVA; d. June 08, 1900, Rowlesburg, Preston WVA.
- xi. ELIZAH SQUIRE SHAHAN, b. July 27, 1873; d. November 01, 1874.
- xii. CAROLINE JOSEPHINE SHAHAN, b. June 10, 1874, St. George Tucker VA; d. August 22, 1951, Bethesda, Maryland; m. MR. HEBT.
- xiii. STILLBORN TWIN ONE SHAHAN, b. Bet. 1874 - 1880.
- xiv. STILLBORN TWIN TWO SHAHAN, b. Bet. 1874 - 1880.
- xv. DAVID CHARLES SHAHAN, b. May 05, 1880, Tucker Co. WVA; d. December 14, 1947, Union City, Randolph, Indiana.
- xvi. VIRGINIA CATHERINE SHAHAN, b. July 04, 1882; m. MR. SPARE.

9. SARAH A. E.[5] HUFFMAN *(PHILLIP[4] HOFFMAN, JOHN[3], JOHN[2], HANNES JOHN[1])* was born August 09, 1841, and died 1901. She married ROBERT JOHNSON.

Notes for SARAH A. E. HUFFMAN:
Lived in Marion County WV

Notes for ROBERT JOHNSON:

Notes for ROBERT JOHNSON:
[For Jo Ann.FTW]

[AAA NewOne.FTW]

[WFT3719_Vol10.FTW]

[Brøderbund WFT Vol. 10, Ed. 1, Tree #3719, Date of Import: Aug 6, 1998]

Robert served in the Union Army during the Civil War as a private of Company E. 7th Regiment, West Virginia Infantry; being drafted at Wheeling, West Virginia, April 9, 1865 and discharged at Munsons Hill, Virginia July 1, 1865.

Children of SARAH HUFFMAN and ROBERT JOHNSON are:

- i. ROBERT LELAND[6] JOHNSON, b. 1864; m. SARAH J. PHILLIPS; b. 1858; d. 1918.

ii. JAMES THOMAS JOHNSON, b. 1867.
iii. JOHN PENDELTON JOHNSON, b. 1869.
iv. CHARLES WILLIAM JOHNSON, b. 1874.
v. ROSETTA JOHNSON, b. 1879.

Endnotes

1. Mancuso.FTW, Date of Import: Sep 6, 2000.

The following 5 pages is about the Descendants of Harrison Dorton Hoffman.
This information was sent to me by Joyce Heigel, one of his descendants

Subj: **material**
Date: 11/14/2006 9:28:46 AM Eastern Standard Time
From: jheigel@sweetwaterhsa.com
To: JSutton639@aol.com

Yes, you may use what I sent you for your book. That must be an exciting endeavor.

Did I send you the article about William Goff Taylor ... It was in the Preston County Journal. Are you including photos in your book
would you want any?

I have not heard from Joanne.

Descendants of Harrison Dorton Hoffman

Generation No. 1

1. HARRISON DORTON[4] HOFFMAN *(PHILLIP[3], JOHN[2], JOHN[1])* was born 1855, and died November 22, 1892 in Preston Co. West Virgina. He married SUSAN VIRGINIA HILLIARD March 06, 1875, daughter of JAMES HILLARD and ELIZABETH (MEAZELLE). She was born October 1852 in Barbour CO., WV, and died October 05, 1910 in Preston Co. West Virgina.

More About HARRISON DORTON HOFFMAN:
Burial: Shay's Chapel United Methodist Church, Newberg, Preston CO., WV

More About SUSAN VIRGINIA HILLIARD:
Burial: Shay's Chapel United Methodist Church, Newberg, Preston CO., WV

Children of HARRISON HOFFMAN and SUSAN HILLIARD are:

i. GEORGE WASHINGTON[5] HUFFMAN, b. April 22, 1879; d. Abt. 1898.

Notes for GEORGE WASHINGTON HUFFMAN:
George died of typhoid fever.

ii. COLUMBUS "DOW" HUFFMAN, b. 1880; d. 1937.

Notes for COLUMBUS "DOW" HUFFMAN:
Dow served in the Spanish American War.

2. iii. WALTER GUY HOFFMAN SR, b. March 31, 1884, Preston Co. West Virgina; d. April 14, 1962, Morgantown, West Virginia.
3. iv. PHOEBE ELLEN "ELLA" HUFFMAN, b. 1886.
4. v. CARRIE AGNES HUFFMAN, b. February 18, 1890; d. Abt. 1983.

Generation No. 2

2. WALTER GUY HOFFMAN[5] SR *(HARRISON DORTON[4] HOFFMAN, PHILLIP[3], JOHN[2], JOHN[1])* was born March 31, 1884 in Preston Co. West Virgina, and died April 14, 1962 in Morgantown, West Virginia. He married MARY ANN WEAVER September 11, 1904, daughter of JAMES WEAVER and MARY RILEY. She was born August 07, 1889 in Preston Co. West Virgina, and died February 11, 1971 in Morgantown, West Virginia.

Notes for WALTER GUY HOFFMAN SR:
Grandpa and Grandma Hoffman were each born in Preston Co., WV.

They moved to Morgantowm in 1912.

More About WALTER GUY HOFFMAN SR:
Burial: Beverly Hills Memorial Gardens

More About MARY ANN WEAVER:
Burial: Beverly Hills Memorial Gardens

Children of WALTER SR and MARY WEAVER are:

5. i. GEORGIA VIRGINIA[6] HOFFMAN, b. January 11, 1906, Howesville, West Virginia; d. May 27, 1961, University Hospital, Morgantown, West Virginia.
6. ii. BEAUTY LOVE HOFFMAN, b. August 02, 1921, Home on McClain Ave./ Morgantown, WV.

iii. BETTY JANE CHARLENE HOFFMAN, b. February 13, 1925; d. March 17, 1934, Monongaila General Hospital, Morgantown, WV.

More About BETTY JANE CHARLENE HOFFMAN:

Burial: Beverly Hills Memeorial Gardens, Morgantown, WV

7. iv. WALTER GUY HOFFMAN JR, b. March 03, 1923, Home on McClain Ave./ Morgantown, WV; d. September 06, 2003, Ruby Memeorial Hospital (formerly U Hosp), Morgantown, WV.
8. v. DORIS JEAN "JEANNIE" HOFFMAN, b. August 30, 1927, Home on McClain Ave., Morgantown, WV.

3. PHOEBE ELLEN "ELLA"[5] HUFFMAN *(HARRISON DORTON[4] HOFFMAN, PHILLIP[3], JOHN[2], JOHN[1])* was born 1886. She married ELAM ROBINSON.

Children of PHOEBE HUFFMAN and ELAM ROBINSON are:

i. GOLDIE MAY[6] ROBINSON.
ii. CHARLES W. ROBINSON.
iii. HARRY R. ROBINSON.
iv. DAVID O. ROBINSON.
v. ROBERT W. ROBINSON.
vi. MARGARET ROBINSON.
vii. MABEL ROBINSON.

4. CARRIE AGNES[5] HUFFMAN *(HARRISON DORTON[4] HOFFMAN, PHILLIP[3], JOHN[2], JOHN[1])* was born February 18, 1890, and died Abt. 1983. She married BENJAMIN FRANKLIN TAYLOR.

Children of CARRIE HUFFMAN and BENJAMIN TAYLOR are:

i. PAUL[6] TAYLOR.
ii. IRA TAYLOR.
9. iii. BEATRICE TAYLOR, b. May 24, 1916, Tunnelton, WV; d. October 18, 2002.
iv. LEONARD TAYLOR.

Generation No. 3

5. GEORGIA VIRGINIA[6] HOFFMAN *(WALTER GUY HOFFMAN[5] SR, HARRISON DORTON[4] HOFFMAN, PHILLIP[3], JOHN[2], JOHN[1])[1]* was born January 11, 1906 in Howesville, West Virginia[1], and died May 27, 1961 in University Hospital, Morgantown, West Virginia[1]. She married JOSEPH LYONS JR[1] June 01, 1927 in Hoffman Home, McClain Ave, Morgantown West Virginia, son of JOSEPH LYONS and SADIE SAPP. He was born April 24, 1906 in Gladesville, West Virginia[1], and died September 22, 1988 in Tyrone Rd. Monongalia County, West Virginia[1].

More About GEORGIA VIRGINIA HOFFMAN:
Burial: Beverly Hills Memorial Gardens. Westover, West Virginia[1]

More About JOSEPH LYONS JR:
Burial: Beverly Hills Memorial Gardens. Westover, West Virginia[1]

Children of GEORGIA HOFFMAN and JOSEPH JR are:

10. i. JOYCE HOFFMAN[7] LYONS, b. March 16, 1944, Vincent Palotti Hospital. Morgantown, WV.
11. ii. JOENE VIRGINIA LYONS, b. February 09, 1947, Morgantown, WV.

6. BEAUTY LOVE[6] HOFFMAN *(WALTER GUY HOFFMAN[5] SR, HARRISON DORTON[4] HOFFMAN, PHILLIP[3], JOHN[2], JOHN[1])* was born August 02, 1921 in Home on McClain Ave./ Morgantown, WV. She married CHARLIE HAROLD STANSBERRY March 09, 1945 in Christian & Missionary Alliance Parsonage, son of FRANCIS STANSBERRY and BERTHA HAWKINS. He was born September 04, 1911 in Reedsville, WV, and died November 18, 1992 in Morgantown, WV.

Notes for CHARLIE HAROLD STANSBERRY:
Charlie died in his own bedroom at his home on Dorsey Ave., Morgantown, WV.

More About CHARLIE HAROLD STANSBERRY:
Burial: Beverly Hills Memeorial Gardens

Child of Beauty Hoffman and Charlie Stansberry is:

12. i. Alice Ann^{7} Stansberry, b. August 04, 1949.

7. Walter Guy Hoffman^{6} JR *(Walter Guy Hoffman^{5} SR, Harrison Dorton^{4} Hoffman, Phillip^{3}, John^{2}, John^{1})* was born March 03, 1923 in Home on McClain Ave./ Morgantown, WV, and died September 06, 2003 in Ruby Memeorial Hospital (formerly U Hosp), Morgantown, WV. He married Mary Rose Farkas, daughter of Zigmond Farkas and Barbala. She was born November 24, 1922 in Sabaraton, WV.

More About Walter Guy Hoffman JR:
Burial: Beverly Hills Memeorial Gardens, Morgantown, WV

Child of Walter JR and Mary Farkas is:

i. Bettie Lou^{7} Hoffman, b. September 19, 1943; m. Duane A. Haught, October 19, 1973; b. December 26, 1927; d. October 24, 1992.

8. Doris Jean "Jeannie"^{6} Hoffman *(Walter Guy Hoffman^{5} SR, Harrison Dorton^{4} Hoffman, Phillip^{3}, John^{2}, John^{1})* was born August 30, 1927 in Home on McClain Ave., Morgantown, WV. She married Everett Bowie July 28, 1950 in Christian & Missionary Alliance church, Morgantown, WV. He was born June 17, 1928 in Belmont, NC, and died August 17, 2002 in Zion, IL.

Children of Doris Hoffman and Everett Bowie are:

13. i. Ruth Ann^{7} Bowie, b. December 02, 1956, Morgantown, West Virginia.
14. ii. Martha Jean Bowie, b. May 10, 1954, Morgantown, West Virginia.

9. Beatrice^{6} Taylor *(Carrie Agnes^{5} Huffman, Harrison Dorton^{4} Hoffman, Phillip^{3}, John^{2}, John^{1})* was born May 24, 1916 in Tunnelton, WV, and died October 18, 2002. She married Harley McGuinnis. He died 1985.

Children of Beatrice Taylor and Harley McGuinnis are:

i. Shirley^{7} McGuinnis, m. William Immke.
ii. Linda McGuinnis, m. James Menear.
iii. Virginia McGuinnis, m. Michael Johnson.
iv. James F. McGuinnis, d. Bef. 2002; m. Dinah.
v. Elaine Ruth McGuinnis, d. Bef. 2002.

Generation No. 4

10. Joyce Hoffman^{7} Lyons *(Georgia Virginia^{6} Hoffman, Walter Guy Hoffman^{5} SR, Harrison Dorton^{4} Hoffman, Phillip^{3}, John^{2}, John^{1})*[1] was born March 16, 1944 in Vincent Palotti Hospital. Morgantown, WV[1]. She married (1) Donald Ray Burnside[1] April 13, 1963 in Christain Missionary Alliance Church. Morgantown, WV, son of Wallace Burnside and Ressie Harshman. He was born October 01, 1938 in Morgantown, West Virginia[1]. She married (2) LeRoy Heigel[1] June 10, 1995 in Hilltop Baptist Church. Green River, WY, son of John Heigel and Marie Gantz. He was born October 31, 1939 in Scottsbluff, NE[1].

Children of Joyce Lyons and Donald Burnside are:

i. Michael Eric^{8} Burnside[1], b. June 05, 1964, Morgantown, WV[1].
15. ii. Stephen Sean Burnside, b. July 16, 1968, Morgantown, WV.
16. iii. Thomas Llyn Burnside, b. May 07, 1970, Morgantown, WV.
17. iv. Cheryl Marie Burnside, b. April 16, 1973, at home in South Charleston, West Virginia.

11. Joene Virginia^{7} Lyons *(Georgia Virginia^{6} Hoffman, Walter Guy Hoffman^{5} SR, Harrison Dorton^{4} Hoffman, Phillip^{3}, John^{2}, John^{1})*[1] was born February 09, 1947 in Morgantown, WV. She married (1) Clifford Cutlip[1] August 13, 1966[1]. He was born March 02, 1946. She married (2) Howard Hildreth[1] February 1988[1]. He was born April 02, 1944, and died Abt. 1992. She married (3) Terry Ward November 25, 1995. He was born January 02, 1948.

Children of Joene Lyons and Clifford Cutlip are:

18. i. CLIFFORD ALLEN[8] CUTLIP, b. March 05, 1967, Fairmont, West Virginia.

19. ii. GREGORY BRIAN CUTLIP, b. March 29, 1971, University Hospital, Morgantown, West Virginia.

20. iii. JULIE ALANE CUTLIP, b. February 11, 1973, University Hospital, Morgantown, West Virginia.

12. Alice Ann[7] Stansberry *(Beauty Love[6] Hoffman, Walter Guy Hoffman[5] Sr, Harrison Dorton[4] Hoffman, Phillip[3], John[2], John[1])* was born August 04, 1949. She married (1) Ray Dixon Abt. 1965. She married (3) Gary Belmont Abt. 1988. He was born September 29, 1944, and died May 20, 2001.

More About Gary Belmont:
Burial: Beverly Hills Memorial Gardens, near Morgantown, WV

Child of Alice Ann Stansberry is:

i. LEAH JOYELLE[8] STANSBERRY, b. June 18, 1975, Morgantown, WV; m. BRIAN I. RICHEY; b. March 25, 1971, Kailua, Hawaii.

13. Ruth Ann[7] Bowie *(Doris Jean "Jeannie"[6] Hoffman, Walter Guy Hoffman[5] Sr, Harrison Dorton[4] Hoffman, Phillip[3], John[2], John[1])* was born December 02, 1956 in Morgantown, West Virginia. She married Matt Smiley. He was born June 24, 1961.

Children of Ruth Bowie and Matt Smiley are:

i. DAVID EVERETT[8] SMILEY, b. March 15, 1986.

ii. JOHNATHON "JOHN" LOREN SMILEY, b. August 29, 1991.

14. Martha Jean[7] Bowie *(Doris Jean "Jeannie"[6] Hoffman, Walter Guy Hoffman[5] Sr, Harrison Dorton[4] Hoffman, Phillip[3], John[2], John[1])* was born May 10, 1954 in Morgantown, West Virginia. She married Robert "Bob" Tackett. He was born August 29, 1953.

Children of Martha Bowie and Robert Tackett are:

i. ANDREA JOY "ANNIE"[8] TACKETT, b. January 25, 1978.

ii. ROCHELLE "SHELLY" TACKETT, b. October 23, 1979.

iii. JANELLE "JENNY" RUTH TACKETT, b. January 31, 1984.

Generation No. 5

15. Stephen Sean[8] Burnside *(Joyce Hoffman[7] Lyons, Georgia Virginia[6] Hoffman, Walter Guy Hoffman[5] Sr, Harrison Dorton[4] Hoffman, Phillip[3], John[2], John[1])*[1] was born July 16, 1968 in Morgantown, WV[1]. He married Pamela Marie Rambler[1] January 09, 1990 in Reno, Nevada. She was born February 26, 1968 in Arizona[1].

Children of Stephen Burnside and Pamela Rambler are:

i. DEANNA NIKOLLE[9] BURNSIDE[1], b. April 16, 1991, Fort Stewart, GA[1].

ii. JOSEPH RAY BURNSIDE[1], b. October 04, 1993, Belgium[1].

iii. JACOB ISSAC BURNSIDE[1], b. February 21, 1996, Phoenix, AZ[1].

16. Thomas Llyn[8] Burnside *(Joyce Hoffman[7] Lyons, Georgia Virginia[6] Hoffman, Walter Guy Hoffman[5] Sr, Harrison Dorton[4] Hoffman, Phillip[3], John[2], John[1])*[1] was born May 07, 1970 in Morgantown, WV[1]. He married Kristen Howery[1].

Child of Thomas Burnside and Kristen Howery is:

i. DRYDAN NYE[9] HOWREY[1], b. February 15, 1999, New Mexico[1].

17. Cheryl Marie[8] Burnside *(Joyce Hoffman[7] Lyons, Georgia Virginia[6] Hoffman, Walter Guy Hoffman[5] Sr, Harrison Dorton[4] Hoffman, Phillip[3], John[2], John[1])*[1] was born April 16, 1973 in at home in South Charleston, West Virginia[1]. She married Kevin Green[1] April 25, 1995 in Sheep's Creek on border of WY and UT[1], son of Lloyd Green and Ruth. He was born July 22, 1963 in Cheyenne, WY[1].

Children of Cheryl Burnside and Kevin Green are:

i. Nathaniel Lloyd[9] Green[1], b. November 21, 1995, Miner's Memorial Hospital. Rock Springs, WY[1].
ii. Nicholas Ray Green[1], b. December 16, 1997, Miner's Memorial Hospital. Rock Springs, WY[1].

18. Clifford Allen[8] Cutlip *(Joene Virginia[7] Lyons, Georgia Virginia[6] Hoffman, Walter Guy Hoffman[5] SR, Harrison Dorton[4] Hoffman, Phillip[3], John[2], John[1])*[1] was born March 05, 1967 in Fairmont, West Virginia[1]. He married Mellissa Ann[1] July 06, 1991[1]. She was born October 09, 1968[1].

Children of Clifford Cutlip and Mellissa Ann are:

i. Macie Ashton[9] Cutlip[1], b. July 03, 1994, Georgia[1].
ii. Korey Austin Cutlip[1], b. October 04, 1997, Georgia[1].

19. Gregory Brian[8] Cutlip *(Joene Virginia[7] Lyons, Georgia Virginia[6] Hoffman, Walter Guy Hoffman[5] SR, Harrison Dorton[4] Hoffman, Phillip[3], John[2], John[1])*[1] was born March 29, 1971 in University Hospital, Morgantown, West Virginia.

Child of Gregory Brian Cutlip is:

i. Travis[9], b. Abt. 1993.

20. Julie Alane[8] Cutlip *(Joene Virginia[7] Lyons, Georgia Virginia[6] Hoffman, Walter Guy Hoffman[5] SR, Harrison Dorton[4] Hoffman, Phillip[3], John[2], John[1])*[1] was born February 11, 1973 in University Hospital, Morgantown, West Virginia. She married Paul Bragg[1] September 25, 1995[1].

Child of Julie Cutlip and Paul Bragg is:

i. Hunter[9] Bragg, b. September 11, 2006.

Endnotes

1. Source_Working.FTW, Date of Import: Sep 14, 2004.

Harrison O. Hoffman

Mary Ann Weaver/Hoffman

Walter Guy Hoffman, 78, of Sabraton, died Saturday afternoon, April 14, 1962, in the Monongalia General Hospital. He was born in Preston County March 31, 1884, a son of the late Harrison and Susan Hilliard Hoffman. He was an employe of the West Virginia University maintenance department, and had been a resident of Monongalia County for the past 50 years.

In addition to his widow, Mrs. Mary Weaver Hoffman, he is survived by one son, Walter Guy Hoffman Jr. of Pittsburgh, Pa.; two daughters, Mrs. Charles Stansberry of Morgantown and Mrs. Everett Bowie of Illinois; one sister, Mrs. Carrie Taylor of

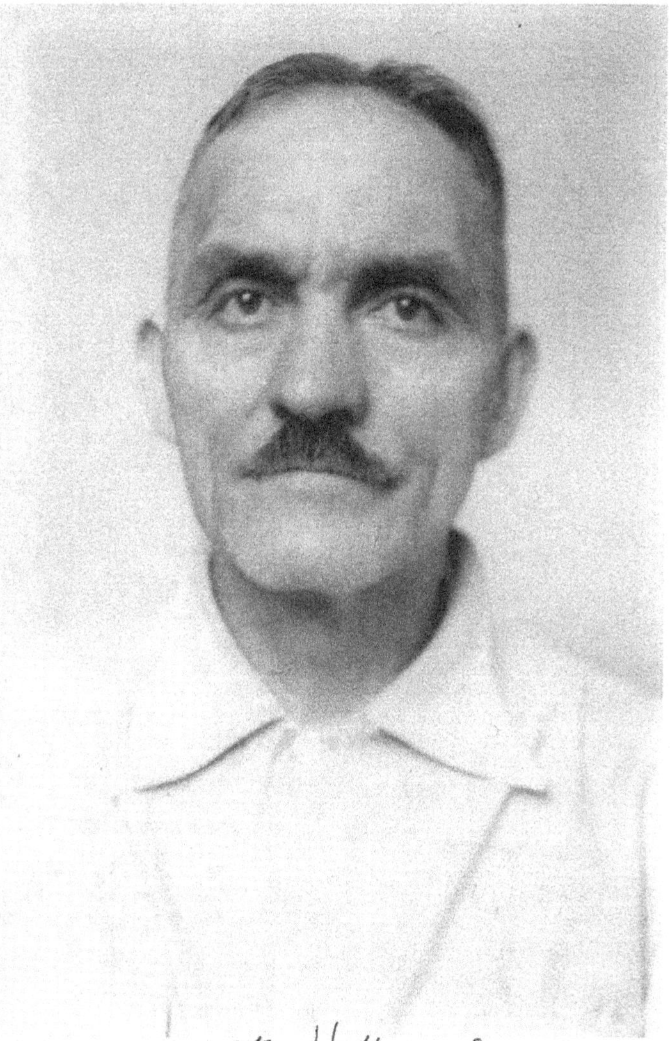

Walter Hoffman Sr.

Descendants of George Shahan

1 George Shahan 1795 - 1843
.. +Catherine Rosier 1795 - 1880
.... 2 George Washington Shahan 1830 - 1891
.... +Louisa Marion Hoffman 1836 - 1885
.... 3 Alethea Elizabeth Shahan 1851 - 1860
.... 3 William Francis Shahan 1852 - 1942
.... +Michelle / Melvina L. Nestor
.... 4 Amelia Shahan 1880 -
.... 4 Louisa C. Shahan 1881 -
.... +J. Patrick Loughry
.... 4 Sarah E. J. Shahan 1885 - 1974
.... 4 George A. F. Shahan 1885 - 1962
.... 4 James Peter Shahan 1888 - 1966
.... +Nellie Agnes Plum
.... 4 John M. Shahan 1890 -
.... 4 Chloe F. Shahan 1892 -
.... 4 Bertha M. Shahan 1897 -
.... +Everett Wallace
.... 4 Marry Jessie Shahan 1901 - 1986
.... 3 John Wesley Shahan 1854 - 1855
.... 3 Sarah Minerva Shahan 1856 -
.... +Thomas Dewalt Poling 1856 -
.... 3 Christina L. Shahan 1858 - 1933
.... +David T. Hovatter 1853 - 1929
.... 4 Charles E. Hovatter 1878 -
.... +Ella Agnice Burns 1883 -
.... 5 Claudene Elwood Hovatter
.... +Arietta Shockley
.... 5 Elston Gerald Hovatter
.... +Myra E. Howard
.... 5 Charles Woodrow Wilson Hovatter
.... +Madeline Kausch
.... 5 Wanda Lorraine Hovatter
.... +Albert H. Hearn
.... 5 Earl Gay Hovatter 1912 - 1934
.... 5 Thomas David Hovatter 1908 -
.... +Elsie Ambrosio
.... 6 Timothy Hovatter
.... 5 Elmer Dallas Hovatter 1902 - 1970
.... +Jessie B. Noce 1898 - 1919
.... 5 Etta Ives Hovatter
.... +Earl C. Cathel
.... 5 Delbert Ray Hovatter 1904 - 1974
.... +Barbara Chandler
.... 6 Barbara Lindsay Hovatter 1944 - 1968
.... 6 Sandra Lee Hovatter 1946 -
.... +James Moore
.... 6 Martha Jean Hovatter 1953 -
.... +Kenneth Speer - 1988
.... 7 Barbara Anne Speer 1974 -
.... 7 Donald Ray Speer 1977 -
.... *2nd Husband of Martha Jean Hovatter:
.... +Charles Reno
.... 5 Leoda Pearl Hovatter
.... 5 Ora Marie Hovatter 1914 - 1937
.... +Herbert Fues, Sr
.... 5 Elford Harold Hovatter 1924 - 1924
.... 4 Lellie C. Hovatter 1880 -
.... +John Patrick Burns 1877 - 1950
.... 4 Wilbert F. Hovatter 1882 - 1969
.... +Hattie Lee Jones 1885 - 1969
.... 5 Eula Hovatter 1903 - 1937
.... +Samuel Linton
.... 6 Voncile Linton
.... *2nd Husband of Eula Hovatter:
.... +Hope Watson
.... 6 Junior Lee Watson
.... 6 Francis Watson
.... 6 Joyce Watson
.... 5 Odie Hovatter 1905 - 1905
.... 5 Wilbertie Valentine Hovatter 1908 - 1987
.... +Hazel Dell Clevenger 1907 - 1988
.... 6 Marjorie Hovatter 1927 -
.... 6 Dolores Hovatter 1929 -
.... 6 Berta Jayne Hovatter 1938 - 1988

.... +Harold Snyder
.... 7 Pam Snyder 1959 -
.... 8 Brian Snyder 1976 -
.... *2nd Husband of Berta Jayne Hovatter:
.... +Thomas Moser 1930 -
.... 7 Thomas Moser 1969 -
.... *Partner of Wilbertie Valentine Hovatter:
.... +Ruby Barnett 1915 -
.... 6 Rosalie J. Hovatter 1932 -
.... +Charley Jenkins
.... *2nd Husband of Rosalie J. Hovatter:
.... +David Faulknier
.... 5 Boyd Hovatter 1910 - 1975
.... 5 Floyd Hovatter 1913 - 1913
.... 5 Lois Hovatter 1914 - 1983
.... +Thomas Mancuso 1912 - 1985
.... 6 Joyce F.. Mancuso 1934 -
.... +Robert Thomas Sutton 1932 -
.... 7 Dolores Lea Sutton 1958 -
.... 7 Susan Joyce Sutton 1964 -
.... +Christopher Keating
.... 8 Christopher Keating Jr.
.... 8 Benjamin Keating
.... 7 Bobbi Lynn Sutton 1968 -
.... +Karl Frank Chase
.... 8 Shawn Joseph Chase 1995 -
.... 8 Samantha Joyce Chase 1997 -
.... *Partner of Bobbi Lynn Sutton:
.... +Mr. McHenry
.... 8 Dani-Lynn McHenry 2006 -
.... 6 Patrina Mancuso 1937 - 1937
.... 5 Hattie Almalee Hovatter 1917 -
.... 5 Aubrey Hovatter 1920 -
.... 5 Dessie Hovatter 1921 - 2001
.... +Edgar Thom 1922 - 1982
.... 6 Dennis Thom 1949 - 1971
.... *2nd Husband of Dessie Hovatter:
.... +William F. Putnam 1932 - 2002
.... 6 Robin Putnam 1963 -
.... +Edison Richard Walker
.... 7 Stephen Randall Walker 1987 -
.... 7 Jaren Dawn Walker 1993 -
.... 6 William F. Putnam 2 1966 -
.... +Bernetta Graham 1970 -
.... 7 William F. Putnam 3 1990 -
.... 7 Olivia Lucille Putnam 1997 -
.... 5 Vernon Hovatter 1924 - 1996
.... 5 Kenneth Gene Hovatter 1927 - 1983
.... 4 Ira J. Hovatter 1885 - 1968
.... +Dessie Thomas
.... 5 Nina Hovatter
.... 4 Mary L. Hovatter 1887 -
.... +Andrew Jackson Brown 1877 - 1932
.... 5 Andrew C. Brown 1904 - 1975
.... +Mildred Fortney
.... 6 Donald Brown
.... 6 Keith Brown
.... 6 Larraine Brown
.... 6 Swanee Brown
.... 6 Frank Brown
.... 6 Paul Brown
.... 5 Albert Leroy Brown 1908 - 1994
.... +Marie Mizell
.... 5 Ruby Brown 1908 -
.... +Bryan Hovatter - 1996
.... 6 William Hovatter
.... 6 Prudence Hovatter
.... 5 Wilber Jackson Brown 1912 - 1912
.... 5 Homer Jennings Brown 1914 - 1972
.... +Mary Myrtle Deese or Dees 1918 - 1989
.... 6 Cecile Leota Brown 1934 - 1937
.... 6 Andrew Jennings Brown 1937 - 1994
.... +Jackine Lou Tallet
.... 6 Homer Ray Brown 1938 -
.... +Anna Cecelia Stevens
.... 7 Tracy Lee Brown 1966 -
.... 5 Delbert Jennings Brown 1917 - 1998

.... 5 William Henry Brown 1920 -
.... 5 Nellie Mae Brown Brown 1923 -
.... 5 David Elmer Brown 1926 - 1929
.... 4 George E. Hovatter 1889 -
.... +Cecil May Burns
.... 5 Ernest Ray Hovatter 1916 -
.... +Mildred Kinter
.... 6 Gary Ray Hovatter 1949 -
.... +Linda Hunnicut
.... 7 Health Hovatter
.... 7 Heather Hovatter
.... +Anthony Galvez
.... 8 Daniel Galvez
.... 8 Rebecca Galvez
.... 8 Allisa Galvez
.... 6 Vickie Lynn Hovatter 1954 -
.... +William Claypool 1949 -
.... 7 Daniel Claypool 1978 -
.... 7 Kevin Claypool 1981 -
.... *2nd Wife of Ernest Ray Hovatter:
.... +Evelyn ?
.... 6 Patti Ann Hovatter
.... +? Smith
.... *3rd Wife of Ernest Ray Hovatter:
.... +Francis Boyer
.... 6 Francis Lee Hovatter
.... 5 Violet Mildred Hovatter 1915 -
.... +Fred Baiocchi - 1987
.... 6 Yvonne Baiocchi
.... 5 Velma Arizonia Hovatter 1917 -
.... 5 Beryl Hovatter
.... +Page Evans
.... 6 Male Child Evans
.... 5 Mary Elizabeth Hovatter 1923 -
.... +Mr. Pert
.... 6 Jean Pert
.... 6 Larry Pert
.... 6 unknown Pert
.... *2nd Husband of Mary Elizabeth Hovatter:
.... +Leonard Blackmon
.... 5 Darrell Hovatter
.... +Shirlee
.... 6 Donna Hovatter
.... 6 Kathy Hovatter
.... 4 Lloyd A. Hovatter 1891 -
.... +Lulu Sterringer
.... 4 Maudie P. Hovatter 1893 -
.... +Samuel Dumire
.... 4 Arlie David Hovatter 1895 - 1977
.... +Laura Poling
.... 5 Lester Hovatter
.... 4 Boyd E. Hovatter 1897 - 1980
.... +Hilda Davis
.... 3 Mary Catherine Shahan 1860 - 1941
.... +Martin M. Poling 1860 -
.... 4 Rhoda Poling
.... 4 Jonas Poling
.... 4 Ira Poling
.... 3 Cyrena Margaret Shahan 1862 - 1943
.... +Isaac M. Poling 1860 -
.... 3 George Emery Shahan 1864 - 1966
.... +Cora Jane Hovatter 1876 - 1948
.... 4 Walter Brown Shahan
.... 4 Agnes Shahan 1892 - 1986
.... 4 Minnie Pearl Shahan 1894 - 1959
.... 4 Donna Jane Shahan 1896 - 1972
.... 4 Mary Elizabeth Shahan 1897 - 1918
.... 4 Daisy Virginia Shahan 1899 - 1978
.... 4 Flora Shahan 1904 - 1904
.... 4 Dora Shahan 1904 -
.... 4 Charles Lee Shahan 1907 - 1971
.... 4 Cora Louise Shahan 1908 - 1987
.... +Floyd Edward Sayre
.... 4 Ruby Bessie Shahan 1910 -
.... 4 Georgia Oletha Shahan 1912 - 1975
.... 4 Lillian Ann Shahan 1916 -
.... 4 Victoria Arabelle Shahan 1919 -

.... 3 Richard Jefferson Shahan 1867 - 1954
.... 3 Louisa Olive J. Shahan 1868 - 1900
.... 3 Elizah Squire Shahan 1873 - 1874
.... 3 Caroline Josephine Shahan 1874 - 1951
.... +Mr. Hebt
.... 3 Stillborn Twin One Shahan 1874 -
.... 3 Stillborn Twin Two Shahan 1874 -
.... 3 David Charles Shahan 1880 - 1947
.... 3 Virginia Catherine Shahan 1882 -
.... +Mr. Spare

Descendants of George Shahan

Generation No. 1

1. GEORGE[1] SHAHAN was born 1795, and died 1843. He married CATHERINE ROSIER. She was born 1795, and died 1880.

Child of GEORGE SHAHAN and CATHERINE ROSIER is:
2. i. GEORGE WASHINGTON[2] SHAHAN, b. February 28, 1830, Preston Co. VA; d. June 29, 1891, Tucker Co. VA.

Generation No. 2

2. GEORGE WASHINGTON[2] SHAHAN *(GEORGE[1])* was born February 28, 1830 in Preston Co. VA, and died June 29, 1891 in Tucker Co. VA. He married LOUISA MARION HOFFMAN 1851 in Preston Co. VA, daughter of PHILLIP HOFFMAN and ALETHA SUMMERS. She was born January 25, 1836 in Monogalia Co. VA, and died April 30, 1885 in Tucker Co. WVA.

Notes for GEORGE WASHINGTON SHAHAN:
Originally from Patsy Browns book, Hoffman/Huffman

Notes for LOUISA MARION HOFFMAN:
ID: I25945
Name: Louisa Marian HUFFMAN HOFFMAN 1 2
Sex: F
Birth: 25 JAN 1836 in Monongalia Co., VA 3
Death: 28 APR 1885 in Tucker Co., WV
Reference Number: 25945
Note:
I had these obituaries in my files and wanted to share them with the List.
Roy Lockhart

The Preston County Journal - Kingwood, West Virginia - Thursday, May 14, 1885.
Vol. XVIII - - No. 37
Whole No. 978.
Page 3, Column 2

Deaths.

Announcements of deaths not exceeding 70 words, inserted free; but 1 cent per word for each word in excess of that number will be charged. In all cases, the money to be sent with the notice.

SHAHAN.--At her home in Tucker County, W. Va., April 28th, 1885, of cancer, Mrs. Louisa M. Shahan, aged 49 years, 3 months and 3 days. She was born in Clinton District, Monongalia County; was a consistent member of the M. E. Church for 37 years, and died with a glorious prospect of a home in Heaven. She leaves four brothers--John A. Hoffman, of Kansas, E. S. and F. M. Hoffman, of this county, and N. N. Hoffman, of Morgantown; and three sisters--Mrs. Mary A. Shahan, of this county, Mrs. Rebecca Hall of Wetzel County, and Mrs. Sarah Johnson, of Marion County.

Picture originally from Patsy Browns book, "Hoffman/Huffman

Children of GEORGE SHAHAN and LOUISA HOFFMAN are:

- i. ALETHEA ELIZABETH[3] SHAHAN, b. August 03, 1851, va; d. Abt. 1860.
- 3. ii. WILLIAM FRANCIS SHAHAN, b. December 22, 1852, va; d. September 1942.
- iii. JOHN WESLEY SHAHAN, b. July 27, 1854; d. February 01, 1855.
- iv. SARAH MINERVA SHAHAN, b. October 20, 1856, va; m. THOMAS DEWALT POLING, November 01, 1877, Tucker Co. WVA; b. Abt. 1856.
- 4. v. CHRISTINA L. SHAHAN, b. May 16, 1858, Sinclair, WV; d. February 02, 1933, Tucker Co.,WV.
- 5. vi. MARY CATHERINE SHAHAN, b. June 21, 1860, va; d. December 15, 1941, WVa.
- vii. CYRENA MARGARET SHAHAN, b. September 08, 1862; d. August 15, 1943; m. ISAAC M. POLING, April 10, 1883, Tucker Co. WVA; b. Abt. 1860.
- 6. viii. REV. GEORGE EMERY SHAHAN, b. October 09, 1864, Rowlesburg, Preston WVA; d. December 18, 1966, Clarksburg, Harrison, WVA.
- ix. RICHARD JEFFERSON SHAHAN, b. February 18, 1867, Rowlesburg, Preston WVA; d. May 13, 1954, Greenville, Darke, Ohio.
- x. LOUISA OLIVE J. SHAHAN, b. March 27, 1868, Preston Co. WVA; d. June 08, 1900, Rowlesburg, Preston WVA.
- xi. ELIZAH SQUIRE SHAHAN, b. July 27, 1873; d. November 01, 1874.
- xii. CAROLINE JOSEPHINE SHAHAN, b. June 10, 1874, St. George Tucker VA; d. August 22, 1951, Bethesda, Maryland; m. MR. HEBT.
- xiii. STILLBORN TWIN ONE SHAHAN, b. Bet. 1874 - 1880.
- xiv. STILLBORN TWIN TWO SHAHAN, b. Bet. 1874 - 1880.
- xv. DAVID CHARLES SHAHAN, b. May 05, 1880, Tucker Co. WVA; d. December 14, 1947, Union City, Randolph, Indiana.
- xvi. VIRGINIA CATHERINE SHAHAN, b. July 04, 1882; m. MR. SPARE.

Generation No. 3

3. WILLIAM FRANCIS[3] SHAHAN *(GEORGE WASHINGTON[2], GEORGE[1])* was born December 22, 1852 in va, and died September 1942. He married MICHELLE / MELVINA L. NESTOR April 22, 1879 in Tucker County, WV, daughter of SAMUEL NESTOR and PERMILIA HOLT.

Children of WILLIAM SHAHAN and MICHELLE NESTOR are:

- i. AMELIA[4] SHAHAN, b. February 1880.
- ii. LOUISA C. SHAHAN, b. October 1881; m. J. PATRICK LOUGHRY, March 01, 1904.
- iii. SARAH E. J. SHAHAN, b. February 02, 1885, Tucker Wv; d. March 03, 1974, Greenville, Darke, Ohio.
- iv. GEORGE A. F. SHAHAN, b. December 04, 1885; d. 1962.
- v. JAMES PETER SHAHAN, b. September 13, 1888; d. July 28, 1966; m. NELLIE AGNES PLUM, March 21, 1920.
- vi. JOHN M. SHAHAN, b. April 01, 1890.
- vii. CHLOE F. SHAHAN, b. July 06, 1892.
- viii. BERTHA M. SHAHAN, b. October 28, 1897; m. EVERETT WALLACE.
- ix. MARRY JESSIE SHAHAN, b. December 19, 1901; d. May 04, 1986.

4. CHRISTINA L.[3] SHAHAN *(GEORGE WASHINGTON[2], GEORGE[1])*[1] was born May 16, 1858 in Sinclair, WV, and died

February 02, 1933 in Tucker Co.,WV. She married DAVID T. HOVATTER[1] December 23, 1877 in Hannahsville, Tucker Co. WVA[1], son of DAVID HOVATTER and SARAH THOMPSON. He was born June 15, 1853 in Kesson, WV[1], and died October 31, 1929 in Tucker Co.,VA now WV.

Notes for DAVID T. HOVATTER:

1880 Census Place: Licking, Tucker, West Virginia

Source:FHL Film 1255414 National Archives Film T9-1414 Page 378A

Relation Sex Marr RaceAge Birthplace

D. C. HOVATTER SelfM M W 25 VA

Occ:Laborer Fa: VA Mo: VA

Chrystena L. HOVATTER WifeFM W 22 VA

Occ:Keeping House Fa: VA Mo: VA

Charles HOVATTER Son M SW 1 WV

Fa: VA Mo: VA

Lilley C. HOVATTEROtherFSW 1MWV

Fa: VA Mo: VA

Barbour County Cities, Towns and Settlements
Kasson

According to an account found in Barbour County West Virginiapublished by the Barbour County Historical Society in 1979 Kasson, in Cove District, was first named Danville after the first settler Dan Highly. The hill he lived on, overlooking Kasson is still known as Highly Hill. Mr. Highly raised mulberry trees to feed his silkworms and produced silk thread was put on spools and shipped to Baltimore.

Danville was given the name Kasson because there was another WV Post Office called Danville. The first letter was mailed to a man named Kasson. The first Post Office was establised in 1862. Carr Bishop was the first postmaster. After him, Marion Newman, 1884; Lewis Coffman, 1904; George Coffman served from 1908 till his death in 1930. Hattie Coffman, his wife and two sons, Hayse & George Sherwood took it over until 1937 when Rachel Wilson Ball served till her death.

In the early days of Kasson the community included:
Stores:
Jack Bishop in 1870, John and Ed Compton, 1875; Marion Newman, 1880; Daniel J. Nester, 1890 and Lewis Coffman.

Blacksmith Shops:
David Hovatter, 1860; Ben Ekis in 1864; Albert Loar in 1891; and Lewis Coffman who learned the trade from his uncles Mike and Lige Coffman who had shops in Valley Furnace, Belington and Elkins. His first shop was near West Point

Churches:
The Kasson United Methodist Church, built in 1898. Daniel Nestor and Daniel Lohr were overseers.
The Church of the Brethren, David Hovatter had the Communion and Love Feast in his house, this was the beginning of the Shiloh Church of the Brethren which was organized in 1845 about 1 ½ miles from Kasson.

More About DAVID T. HOVATTER:
Burial: Preston Co. WV

Children of CHRISTINA SHAHAN and DAVID HOVATTER are:

i. CHARLES E.[4] HOVATTER[1], b. October 11, 1878[1]; m. ELLA AGNICE BURNS; b. March 07, 1883.

ii. LELLIE C. HOVATTER[1], b. April 18, 1880[1]; m. JOHN PATRICK BURNS; b. July 20, 1877; d. 1950.
iii. WILBERT F. HOVATTER[1], b. April 01, 1882, Preston Co. WV[1]; d. August 19, 1969, Greene Co. Miss.[1]; m. HATTIE LEE JONES[1], February 18, 1903, Greene Co. Miss.[1]; b. October 06, 1885, Greene Co, Miss.[1]; d. October 09, 1969, Greene Co, Miss.[1].

Notes for WILBERT F. HOVATTER:
87 years old 4 months and 18 days at time of death

More About WILBERT F. HOVATTER:
Burial: Stateline, MS
Social Security Number: Pennslyvania[1]

Notes for HATTIE LEE JONES:
84 years old and 3 days at time of death
Pictures on pages 106, 107 108 in book "Generations of Hoffman to Hovatter"

More About HATTIE LEE JONES:
Burial: Stateline, MS
Fact 5: Social Security #: 177-14-7342[2]
Fact 6: Issued in: Pennsylvania[2]
Fact 7: Residence code: Mississippi[2]
Fact 8: Last residence ZIP: 39451[2]

iv. IRA J. HOVATTER[3], b. April 17, 1885[3,4]; d. July 1968[4]; m. DESSIE THOMAS.

More About IRA J. HOVATTER:
Social Security Number: 232-22-9008

v. MARY L. HOVATTER[5], b. March 07, 1887[5]; m. ANDREW JACKSON BROWN, February 18, 1903, Greene Co MS; b. February 04, 1877; d. February 04, 1932.

Notes for MARY L. HOVATTER:

The information I received from Tracy had Fruitville listed in it but from Marriages in MS it seems that there was a double wedding, hers and her brother Wilbert. Both were married same day, same county and State. Greene Co. MS in Leakesville.

vi. GEORGE E. HOVATTER[5], b. February 15, 1889[5]; m. CECIL MAY BURNS.

Notes for CECIL MAY BURNS:
There is a possibility that the spelling of her name was different. May have been Cecilia or another variation.

vii. LLOYD A. HOVATTER[5], b. June 29, 1891[5]; m. LULU STERRINGER.
viii. MAUDIE P. HOVATTER[5], b. July 21, 1893[5]; m. SAMUEL DUMIRE.
ix. ARLIE DAVID HOVATTER[5], b. August 15, 1895, WVA[5]; d. December 1977[6,7]; m. LAURA POLING.

Notes for ARLIE DAVID HOVATTER:
[Broderbund Family Archive #110, Vol. 1 A-K, Ed. 7, Social Security Death Index: U.S., Date of Import: Jul 3, 2001, Internal Ref. #1.111.7.127438.120]

Individual: Hovatter, Arlie
Social Security #: 705-10-2282
Issued in: Railroad Board

Birth date: Aug 15, 1895
Death date: Dec 1977

Residence code: West Virginia

ZIP Code of last known residence: 26354
Primary location associated with this ZIP Code:

Grafton, West Virginia

More About ARLIE DAVID HOVATTER:
Fact 1: Issued in: Railroad Board[7]
Fact 2: Residence code: West Virginia[7]
Fact 3: Last residence ZIP: 26354[7]
Fact 6: Issued in: Railroad Board[8]
Fact 7: Residence code: West Virginia[8]
Fact 8: Last residence ZIP: 26354[8]
Social Security Number: Social Security #: 705-10-2282[8,9]

x. BOYD E. HOVATTER[10], b. September 24, 1897[10,11]; d. August 1980[11]; m. HILDA DAVIS.

More About BOYD E. HOVATTER:
Fact 5: Social Security #: 234-03-1597[11]
Fact 6: Issued in: West Virginia[11]
Fact 7: Residence code: Alabama[11]
Fact 8: Last residence ZIP: 36584[11]

5. MARY CATHERINE[3] SHAHAN *(GEORGE WASHINGTON[2], GEORGE[1])* was born June 21, 1860 in va, and died December 15, 1941 in WVa. She married MARTIN M. POLING July 11, 1882 in Tucker Co. WVA, son of REASON POLING. He was born Abt. 1860.

Children of MARY SHAHAN and MARTIN POLING are:
i. RHODA[4] POLING.
ii. JONAS POLING.
iii. IRA POLING.

6. REV. GEORGE EMERY[3] SHAHAN *(GEORGE WASHINGTON[2], GEORGE[1])* was born October 09, 1864 in Rowlesburg, Preston WVA, and died December 18, 1966 in Clarksburg, Harrison, WVA. He married CORA JANE HOVATTER April 30, 1891 in Tucker Co. WVA, daughter of DAVID HOVATTER and SARAH THOMPSON. She was born October 05, 1876 in Tucker Wv, and died March 28, 1948 in Clarksburg, Harrison, WV.

Notes for REV. GEORGE EMERY SHAHAN:
Notes for REV. GEORGE EMERY SHAHAN:
[For Jo Ann.FTW]

[AAA NewOne.FTW]

[WFT3719_Vol10.FTW]

There is a picture of Elder G. Emory Shahan at age 100 on page 621 of "Alleghany Passage: Churches and Families" by Emmert F. Bittinger, and the following biography:

"The family lived near Rowlesburg for some years before moving near St. George in Tucker County. There the family lived within the boundary of the Union Chapel (Bull Run) branch of the Shiloh Congregation.

"The eighth child, George Emory Shahan, manifested special talents and an early interest in religion. He bagan a vigorous study [of] the Bible while still in his teens, soon mastering large portions by memory. His obiturary states that he began preaching at age fifteen, which would have been around 1879. The year after his marriage in 1891 to Cora Jane Hovatter, he was ordained to the ministry. He was advanced as an Elder in 1904 and thereupon given charge of the Shiloh Congregation, a position he held until 1907.

"He continued his labor for the Church at Union Chapel, serving as one of the ministers of that branch until his transfer to the Grafton Brethren Church which later became the Grace Brethren Church. He was called as pastor of the Grafton Church, a service which he fufilled for many years. He gave up this work in 1940 and moved to Clarksburg where he has retired.

"Most of his life he served in the free ministry, supporting his family by farming and carpentering. Before moving to Tucker County, he had accumulated a large tract of land, some of which was purchased for as little as $1.65 per acre. Most of the land was sold during an economic depression, and little gain was realized.

"Bro. Shahan was a man of high character and devotion. Much respected and loved by his fourteen children, ost of whom are now deceased, he left a strong impact on his family and those with whom he worked.

"A member of the National Fellowship of Brethren Ministers, he was the oldest member of that organization at the time of his death at the age of 102 in 1966. He still occasionally preached in the last decade of his life. Many will remember the occasion when he preached at the Grafton and Shiloh Churches after he had passed the age of 100. His ministerial work was greatly appreciated and respected."

More About REV. GEORGE EMERY SHAHAN:
Burial: Unknown, Clarksburg, WV2416,2417

Children of GEORGE SHAHAN and CORA HOVATTER are:

i. WALTER BROWN[4] SHAHAN.
ii. AGNES SHAHAN, b. October 29, 1892, St. George, Tucker, W; d. September 03, 1986, Clarksburg, Harrison,WVA.
iii. MINNIE PEARL SHAHAN, b. June 04, 1894, St. George, Tucker, W; d. November 19, 1959.
iv. DONNA JANE SHAHAN, b. January 29, 1896, St. George, Tucker, WVA; d. January 24, 1972, Kingswood, Preston, WVA.
v. MARY ELIZABETH SHAHAN, b. September 23, 1897, Hannasville, Tucker, WV; d. November 01, 1918, Hannasville, Tucker, WV.
vi. DAISY VIRGINIA SHAHAN, b. June 25, 1899, St. George, Tucker, W; d. December 07, 1978, Clarksburg, Harrison, WV.
vii. FLORA SHAHAN, b. February 07, 1904, Hannasville, Tucker, WV; d. February 07, 1904, Hannasville, Tucker, WV.
viii. DORA SHAHAN, b. February 07, 1904.
ix. CHARLES LEE SHAHAN, b. February 1907, Hovatter, Preston, WV; d. May 21, 1971, Clarksburg, Harrison, WV.
x. CORA LOUISE SHAHAN, b. December 12, 1908, St. George, Tucker, W; d. June 22, 1987, St. Petersburg, FL; m. FLOYD EDWARD SAYRE, January 31, 1931, Clarksburg, Harrison, WV.
xi. RUBY BESSIE SHAHAN, b. September 14, 1910, St. George, Tucker, W.
xii. GEORGIA OLETHA SHAHAN, b. December 24, 1912, St. George, Tucker, W; d. July 12, 1975, Clarksburg, Harrison, WV.
xiii. LILLIAN ANN SHAHAN, b. March 31, 1916, St. George, Tucker, W.
xiv. VICTORIA ARABELLE SHAHAN, b. February 04, 1919, St. George, Tucker, W.

Endnotes

1. Mancuso.FTW, Date of Import: Sep 6, 2000.
2. Genealogy.com, Family Archive #110, Social Security Death Index: U.S. Ed. 9, Social Security Death Index, Release date: April 10, 2000, Internal Ref. #1.111.9.122873.123.
3. Mancuso.FTW, Date of Import: Sep 6, 2000.
4. Genealogy.com, Family Archive #110, Social Security Death Index: U.S. Ed. 9, Social Security Death Index, Release date: April 10, 2000, Internal Ref. #1.111.9.122873.131.
5. Mancuso.FTW, Date of Import: Sep 6, 2000.
6. Genealogy.com, Family Archive #110, Social Security Death Index: U.S. Ed. 9, Social Security Death Index, Release date: April 10, 2000, Internal Ref. #1.111.9.122873.61.
7. Broderbund Family Archive #110, Vol. 1, Ed. 7, Social Security Death Index: U.S., Date of Import: Jul 3, 2001, Internal Ref. #1.111.7.127438.120
8. Genealogy.com, Family Archive #110, Social Security Death Index: U.S. Ed. 9, Social Security Death Index, Release date: April 10, 2000, Internal Ref. #1.111.9.122873.61.
9. Broderbund Family Archive #110, Vol. 1, Ed. 7, Social Security Death Index: U.S., Date of Import: Jul 3, 2001, Internal Ref. #1.111.7.127438.120
10. Mancuso.FTW, Date of Import: Sep 6, 2000.
11. Genealogy.com, Family Archive #110, Social Security Death Index: U.S. Ed. 9, Social Security Death Index, Release

MY FAMILY BOOK TWO

4/G.GEORGE WASHINGTON SHAHAN(BULL)1830-1891.P.648.
4G.LOUISA MARIAN(HUFFMAN)SHAHAN1836-1885.P.1.648.

PICTURE WAS IN THE BOOK BY PATSY BROWN. TITLE HOFFMAN/HUFFMAN 1741

Descendants of Louisa Marion Hoffman

Generation No. 1

1. LOUISA MARION[5] HOFFMAN *(PHILLIP[4], JOHN[3], JOHN[2], HANNES JOHN[1])* was born January 25, 1836 in Monogalia Co. VA, and died April 30, 1885 in Tucker Co. WVA. She married GEORGE WASHINGTON SHAHAN 1851 in Preston Co. VA, son of GEORGE SHAHAN and CATHERINE ROSIER. He was born February 28, 1830 in Preston Co. VA, and died June 29, 1891 in Tucker Co. VA.

Notes for LOUISA MARION HOFFMAN:
ID: I25945
Name: Louisa Marian HUFFMAN HOFFMAN 1 2
Sex: F
Birth: 25 JAN 1836 in Monongalia Co., VA 3
Death: 28 APR 1885 in Tucker Co., WV
Reference Number: 25945
Note:
I had these obituaries in my files and wanted to share them with the List.
Roy Lockhart

The Preston County Journal - Kingwood, West Virginia - Thursday, May 14, 1885.
Vol. XVIII - - No. 37
Whole No. 978.
Page 3, Column 2

Deaths.

Announcements of deaths not exceeding 70 words, inserted free; but 1 cent per word for each word in excess of that number will be charged. In all cases, the money to be sent with the notice.

SHAHAN.--At her home in Tucker County, W. Va., April 28th, 1885, of cancer, Mrs. Louisa M. Shahan, aged 49 years, 3 months and 3 days. She was born in Clinton District, Monongalia County; was a consistent member of the M. E. Church for 37 years, and died with a glorious prospect of a home in Heaven. She leaves four brothers--John A. Hoffman, of Kansas, E. S. and F. M. Hoffman, of this county, and N. N. Hoffman, of Morgantown; and three sisters--Mrs. Mary A. Shahan, of this county, Mrs. Rebecca Hall of Wetzel County, and Mrs. Sarah Johnson, of Marion County.

Picture originally from Patsy Browns book, "Hoffman/Huffman

Notes for GEORGE WASHINGTON SHAHAN:
Originally from Patsy Browns book, Hoffman/Huffman

Children of LOUISA HOFFMAN and GEORGE SHAHAN are:

i. ALETHEA ELIZABETH[6] SHAHAN, b. August 03, 1851, va; d. Abt. 1860.
2. ii. WILLIAM FRANCIS SHAHAN, b. December 22, 1852, va; d. September 1942.
iii. JOHN WESLEY SHAHAN, b. July 27, 1854; d. February 01, 1855.
iv. SARAH MINERVA SHAHAN, b. October 20, 1856, va; m. THOMAS DEWALT POLING, November 01, 1877, Tucker Co. WVA; b. Abt. 1856.
3. v. CHRISTINA L. SHAHAN, b. May 16, 1858, Sinclair, WV; d. February 02, 1933, Tucker Co.,WV.
4. vi. MARY CATHERINE SHAHAN, b. June 21, 1860, va; d. December 15, 1941, WVa.
vii. CYRENA MARGARET SHAHAN, b. September 08, 1862; d. August 15, 1943; m. ISAAC M. POLING, April 10, 1883, Tucker Co. WVA; b. Abt. 1860.
5. viii. REV. GEORGE EMERY SHAHAN, b. October 09, 1864, Rowlesburg, Preston WVA; d. December 18, 1966, Clarksburg, Harrison, WVA.
ix. RICHARD JEFFERSON SHAHAN, b. February 18, 1867, Rowlesburg, Preston WVA; d. May 13, 1954, Greenville, Darke, Ohio.
x. LOUISA OLIVE J. SHAHAN, b. March 27, 1868, Preston Co. WVA; d. June 08, 1900, Rowlesburg, Preston WVA.
xi. ELIZAH SQUIRE SHAHAN, b. July 27, 1873; d. November 01, 1874.
xii. CAROLINE JOSEPHINE SHAHAN, b. June 10, 1874, St. George Tucker VA; d. August 22, 1951, Bethesda, Maryland; m. MR. HEBT.
xiii. STILLBORN TWIN ONE SHAHAN, b. Bet. 1874 - 1880.
xiv. STILLBORN TWIN TWO SHAHAN, b. Bet. 1874 - 1880.
xv. DAVID CHARLES SHAHAN, b. May 05, 1880, Tucker Co. WVA; d. December 14, 1947, Union City, Randolph, Indiana.
xvi. VIRGINIA CATHERINE SHAHAN, b. July 04, 1882; m. MR. SPARE.

Generation No. 2

2. WILLIAM FRANCIS[6] SHAHAN *(LOUISA MARION[5] HOFFMAN, PHILLIP[4], JOHN[3], JOHN[2], HANNES JOHN[1])* was born December 22, 1852 in va, and died September 1942. He married MICHELLE / MELVINA L. NESTOR April 22, 1879 in Tucker County, WV, daughter of SAMUEL NESTOR and PERMILIA HOLT.

Children of WILLIAM SHAHAN and MICHELLE NESTOR are:

i. AMELIA[7] SHAHAN, b. February 1880.
ii. LOUISA C. SHAHAN, b. October 1881; m. J. PATRICK LOUGHRY, March 01, 1904.
iii. SARAH E. J. SHAHAN, b. February 02, 1885, Tucker Wv; d. March 03, 1974, Greenville, Darke, Ohio.
iv. GEORGE A. F. SHAHAN, b. December 04, 1885; d. 1962.
v. JAMES PETER SHAHAN, b. September 13, 1888; d. July 28, 1966; m. NELLIE AGNES PLUM, March 21, 1920.
vi. JOHN M. SHAHAN, b. April 01, 1890.
vii. CHLOE F. SHAHAN, b. July 06, 1892.
viii. BERTHA M. SHAHAN, b. October 28, 1897; m. EVERETT WALLACE.
ix. MARRY JESSIE SHAHAN, b. December 19, 1901; d. May 04, 1986.

3. CHRISTINA L.[6] SHAHAN *(LOUISA MARION[5] HOFFMAN, PHILLIP[4], JOHN[3], JOHN[2], HANNES JOHN[1])*[1] was born May 16, 1858 in Sinclair, WV, and died February 02, 1933 in Tucker Co.,WV. She married DAVID T. HOVATTER[1] December 23, 1877 in Hannahsville, Tucker Co. WVA[1], son of DAVID HOVATTER and SARAH THOMPSON. He was born June 15, 1853 in Kesson, WV[1], and died October 31, 1929 in Tucker Co.,VA now WV.

Notes for DAVID T. HOVATTER:
1880 Census Place: Licking, Tucker, West Virginia
Source:FHL Film 1255414 National Archives Film T9-1414 Page 378A
Relation Sex Marr RaceAgeBirthplace
D. C. HOVATTER SelfM M W 25 VA

Occ:Laborer Fa: VA Mo: VA
Chrystena L. HOVATTER WifeFM W 22 VA
Occ:Keeping House Fa: VA Mo: VA
Charles HOVATTER Son M SW 1 WV
Fa: VA Mo: VA
Lilley C. HOVATTEROtherFSW 1MWV
Fa: VA Mo: VA

Barbour County Cities, Towns and Settlements
Kasson

According to an account found in Barbour County West Virginiapublished by the Barbour County Historical Society in 1979 Kasson, in Cove District, was first named Danville after the first settler Dan Highly. The hill he lived on, overlooking Kasson is still known as Highly Hill. Mr. Highly raised mulberry trees to feed his silkworms and produced silk thread was put on spools and shipped to Baltimore.

Danville was given the name Kasson because there was another WV Post Office called Danville. The first letter was mailed to a man named Kasson. The first Post Office was establised in 1862. Carr Bishop was the first postmaster. After him, Marion Newman, 1884; Lewis Coffman, 1904; George Coffman served from 1908 till his death in 1930. Hattie Coffman, his wife and two sons, Hayse & George Sherwood took it over until 1937 when Rachel Wilson Ball served till her death.

In the early days of Kasson the community included:
Stores:
Jack Bishop in 1870, John and Ed Compton, 1875; Marion Newman, 1880; Daniel J. Nester, 1890 and Lewis Coffman.

Blacksmith Shops:
David Hovatter, 1860; Ben Ekis in 1864; Albert Loar in 1891; and Lewis Coffman who learned the trade from his uncles Mike and Lige Coffman who had shops in Valley Furnace, Belington and Elkins. His first shop was near West Point

Churches:
The Kasson United Methodist Church, built in 1898. Daniel Nestor and Daniel Lohr were overseers.
The Church of the Brethren, David Hovatter had the Communion and Love Feast in his house, this was the beginning of the Shiloh Church of the Brethren which was organized in 1845 about 1 ½ miles from Kasson.

More About DAVID T. HOVATTER:
Burial: Preston Co. WV

Children of CHRISTINA SHAHAN and DAVID HOVATTER are:

i. CHARLES E.[7] HOVATTER[/], b. October 11, 1878[/]; m. ELLA AGNICE BURNS; b. March 07, 1883.
ii. LELLIE C. HOVATTER[/], b. April 18, 1880[/]; m. JOHN PATRICK BURNS; b. July 20, 1877; d. 1950.
iii. WILBERT F. HOVATTER[/], b. April 01, 1882, Preston Co. WV[/]; d. August 19, 1969, Greene Co. Miss.[/]; m. HATTIE LEE JONES[/], February 18, 1903, Greene Co. Miss.[/]; b. October 06, 1885, Greene Co, Miss.[/]; d. October 09, 1969, Greene Co, Miss.[/].

Notes for WILBERT F. HOVATTER:
87 years old 4 months and 18 days at time of death

More About WILBERT F. HOVATTER:

Burial: Stateline, MS
Social Security Number: Pennslyvania[1]

Notes for HATTIE LEE JONES:
84 years old and 3 days at time of death
Pictures on pages 106, 107 108 in book "Generations of Hoffman to Hovatter"

More About HATTIE LEE JONES:
Burial: Stateline, MS
Fact 5: Social Security #: 177-14-7342[2]
Fact 6: Issued in: Pennsylvania[2]
Fact 7: Residence code: Mississippi[2]
Fact 8: Last residence ZIP: 39451[2]

iv. IRA J. HOVATTER[5], b. April 17, 1885[3,4]; d. July 1968[4]; m. DESSIE THOMAS.

More About IRA J. HOVATTER:
Social Security Number: 232-22-9008

v. MARY L. HOVATTER[5], b. March 07, 1887[5]; m. ANDREW JACKSON BROWN, February 18, 1903, Greene Co MS; b. February 04, 1877; d. February 04, 1932.

Notes for MARY L. HOVATTER:

The information I received from Tracy had Fruitville listed in it but from Marriages in MS it seems that there was a double wedding, hers and her brother Wilbert. Both were married same day, same county and State. Greene Co. MS in Leakesville.

vi. GEORGE E. HOVATTER[5], b. February 15, 1889[5]; m. CECIL MAY BURNS.

Notes for CECIL MAY BURNS:
There is a possibility that the spelling of her name was different. May have been Cecilia or another variation.

vii. LLOYD A. HOVATTER[5], b. June 29, 1891[5]; m. LULU STERRINGER.
viii. MAUDIE P. HOVATTER[5], b. July 21, 1893[5]; m. SAMUEL DUMIRE.
ix. ARLIE DAVID HOVATTER[5], b. August 15, 1895, WVA[5]; d. December 1977[6,7]; m. LAURA POLING.

Notes for ARLIE DAVID HOVATTER:
[Broderbund Family Archive #110, Vol. 1 A-K, Ed. 7, Social Security Death Index: U.S., Date of Import: Jul 3, 2001, Internal Ref. #1.111.7.127438.120]

Individual: Hovatter, Arlie
Social Security #: 705-10-2282
Issued in: Railroad Board

Birth date: Aug 15, 1895
Death date: Dec 1977

Residence code: West Virginia

ZIP Code of last known residence: 26354
Primary location associated with this ZIP Code:

Grafton, West Virginia

More About ARLIE DAVID HOVATTER:
Fact 1: Issued in: Railroad Board[7]
Fact 2: Residence code: West Virginia[7]
Fact 3: Last residence ZIP: 26354[7]
Fact 6: Issued in: Railroad Board[8]

Fact 7: Residence code: West Virginia[8]
Fact 8: Last residence ZIP: 26354[8]
Social Security Number: Social Security #: 705-10-2282[8,9]

x. BOYD E. HOVATTER[10], b. September 24, 1897[10,11]; d. August 1980[11]; m. HILDA DAVIS.

More About BOYD E. HOVATTER:
Fact 5: Social Security #: 234-03-1597[11]
Fact 6: Issued in: West Virginia[11]
Fact 7: Residence code: Alabama[11]
Fact 8: Last residence ZIP: 36584[11]

4. MARY CATHERINE[6] SHAHAN *(LOUISA MARION[5] HOFFMAN, PHILLIP[4], JOHN[3], JOHN[2], HANNES JOHN[1])* was born June 21, 1860 in va, and died December 15, 1941 in WVa. She married MARTIN M. POLING July 11, 1882 in Tucker Co. WVA, son of REASON POLING. He was born Abt. 1860.

Children of MARY SHAHAN and MARTIN POLING are:

i. RHODA[7] POLING.
ii. JONAS POLING.
iii. IRA POLING.

5. REV. GEORGE EMERY[6] SHAHAN *(LOUISA MARION[5] HOFFMAN, PHILLIP[4], JOHN[3], JOHN[2], HANNES JOHN[1])* was born October 09, 1864 in Rowlesburg, Preston WVA, and died December 18, 1966 in Clarksburg, Harrison, WVA. He married CORA JANE HOVATTER April 30, 1891 in Tucker Co. WVA, daughter of DAVID HOVATTER and SARAH THOMPSON. She was born October 05, 1876 in Tucker Wv, and died March 28, 1948 in Clarksburg, Harrison, WV.

Notes for REV. GEORGE EMERY SHAHAN:
Notes for REV. GEORGE EMERY SHAHAN:
[For Jo Ann.FTW]

[AAA NewOne.FTW]

[WFT3719_Vol10.FTW]

There is a picture of Elder G. Emory Shahan at age 100 on page 621 of "Alleghany Passage: Churches and Families" by Emmert F. Bittinger, and the following biography:

"The family lived near Rowlesburg for some years before moving near St. George in Tucker County. There the family lived within the boundary of the Union Chapel (Bull Run) branch of the Shiloh Congregation.

"The eighth child, George Emory Shahan, manifested special talents and an early interest in religion. He bagan a vigorous study [of] the Bible while still in his teens, soon mastering large portions by memory. His obiturary states that he began preaching at age fifteen, which would have been around 1879. The year after his marriage in 1891 to Cora Jane Hovatter, he was ordained to the ministry. He was advanced as an Elder in 1904 and thereupon given charge of the Shiloh Congregation, a position he held until 1907.

"He continued his labor for the Church at Union Chapel, serving as one of the ministers of that branch until his transfer to the Grafton Brethren Church which later became the Grace Brethren Church. He was called as pastor of the Grafton Church, a service which he fufilled for many years. He gave up this work in 1940 and moved to Clarksburg where he has retired.

"Most of his life he served in the free ministry, supporting his family by farming and carpentering. Before moving to Tucker County, he had accumulated a large tract of land, some of which was purchased for as little as $1.65 per acre. Most of the land was sold during an economic depression, and little gain was realized.

"Bro. Shahan was a man of high character and devotion. Much respected and loved by his fourteen children, ost of whom are now deceased, he left a strong impact on his family and those with whom he worked.

"A member of the National Fellowship of Brethren Ministers, he was the oldest member of that organization at the time of his death at the age of 102 in 1966. He still occasionally preached in the last decade of his life. Many will remember the occasion when he preached at the Grafton and Shiloh Churches after he had passed the age of 100. His ministerial work was greatly appreciated and respected."

More About REV. GEORGE EMERY SHAHAN:
Burial: Unknown, Clarksburg, WV2416,2417

Children of GEORGE SHAHAN and CORA HOVATTER are:

i. WALTER BROWN[7] SHAHAN.
ii. AGNES SHAHAN, b. October 29, 1892, St. George, Tucker, W; d. September 03, 1986, Clarksburg, Harrison,WVA.
iii. MINNIE PEARL SHAHAN, b. June 04, 1894, St. George, Tucker, W; d. November 19, 1959.
iv. DONNA JANE SHAHAN, b. January 29, 1896, St. George, Tucker, WVA; d. January 24, 1972, Kingswood, Preston, WVA.
v. MARY ELIZABETH SHAHAN, b. September 23, 1897, Hannasville, Tucker, WV; d. November 01, 1918, Hannasville, Tucker, WV.
vi. DAISY VIRGINIA SHAHAN, b. June 25, 1899, St. George, Tucker, W; d. December 07, 1978, Clarksburg, Harrison, WV.
vii. FLORA SHAHAN, b. February 07, 1904, Hannasville, Tucker, WV; d. February 07, 1904, Hannasville, Tucker, WV.
viii. DORA SHAHAN, b. February 07, 1904.
ix. CHARLES LEE SHAHAN, b. February 1907, Hovatter, Preston, WV; d. May 21, 1971, Clarksburg, Harrison, WV.
x. CORA LOUISE SHAHAN, b. December 12, 1908, St. George, Tucker, W; d. June 22, 1987, St. Petersburg, FL; m. FLOYD EDWARD SAYRE, January 31, 1931, Clarksburg, Harrison, WV.
xi. RUBY BESSIE SHAHAN, b. September 14, 1910, St. George, Tucker, W.
xii. GEORGIA OLETHA SHAHAN, b. December 24, 1912, St. George, Tucker, W; d. July 12, 1975, Clarksburg, Harrison, WV.
xiii. LILLIAN ANN SHAHAN, b. March 31, 1916, St. George, Tucker, W.
xiv. VICTORIA ARABELLE SHAHAN, b. February 04, 1919, St. George, Tucker, W.

Endnotes

1. Mancuso.FTW, Date of Import: Sep 6, 2000.
2. Genealogy.com, Family Archive #110, Social Security Death Index: U.S. Ed. 9, Social Security Death Index, Release date: April 10, 2000, Internal Ref. #1.111.9.122873.123.
3. Mancuso.FTW, Date of Import: Sep 6, 2000.
4. Genealogy.com, Family Archive #110, Social Security Death Index: U.S. Ed. 9, Social Security Death Index, Release date: April 10, 2000, Internal Ref. #1.111.9.122873.131.
5. Mancuso.FTW, Date of Import: Sep 6, 2000.
6. Genealogy.com, Family Archive #110, Social Security Death Index: U.S. Ed. 9, Social Security Death Index, Release date: April 10, 2000, Internal Ref. #1.111.9.122873.61.
7. Broderbund Family Archive #110, Vol. 1, Ed. 7, Social Security Death Index: U.S., Date of Import: Jul 3, 2001, Internal Ref. #1.111.7.127438.120
8. Genealogy.com, Family Archive #110, Social Security Death Index: U.S. Ed. 9, Social Security Death Index, Release date: April 10, 2000, Internal Ref. #1.111.9.122873.61.
9. Broderbund Family Archive #110, Vol. 1, Ed. 7, Social Security Death Index: U.S., Date of Import: Jul 3, 2001, Internal Ref. #1.111.7.127438.120
10. Mancuso.FTW, Date of Import: Sep 6, 2000.
11. Genealogy.com, Family Archive #110, Social Security Death Index: U.S. Ed. 9, Social Security Death Index, Release date: April 10, 2000, Internal Ref. #1.111.9.122873.66.

Descendants of William Summers

1 William Summers 1645 -
.... 2 John Summers, 1st 1650 - 1705
.... +Rebecca Dent - 1711
.... 3 William Summers
.... 3 Sarah Summers
.... 3 Lucy Summers
.... 3 John Summers, 2nd 1685 - 1769
.... +Mary Moore 1696 - 1769
.... 4 John Summers, the 3rd
.... 4 George Summers
.... 4 William Summers
.... 4 Thomas Summers
.... 4 Benjamin Summers
.... 4 James Summers - 1761
.... 4 Joseph Summers
.... 4 Mary Summers
.... +Mr. Wheat
.... 4 Rebeckah Summers
.... +Mr. King
.... 4 Rachel Summers
.... +Mr. Johnson
.... 4 Ruth Summers
.... +Mr. Riggs
.... 4 Jemina Summers
.... +Mr. Caton
.... 4 Dent Summers 1727 - 1809
.... +Mary Ann Claggett - 1802
.... 5 Mary Ann Summers
.... +Mr. Hardy
.... 5 Sarah Summers
.... +White
.... 5 Paul Summers
.... 5 James Dent Summers
.... 5 Zadock Summers
.... 5 John Summers
.... +chloe (Cloy)
.... 5 Margaret Summers
.... +Hoskins
.... 5 William Dent Summers
.... 5 Hezekiah Summers 1750 - 1836
.... +Rebecker Glaz 1743 - 1800
.... 6 William Dent Summers
.... +Rebecca Jacobs
.... 6 Benjamin Summers
.... 6 John S. Summers
.... 6 Phillip Summers
.... 6 Thomas Summers
.... 6 Margaret Summers
.... 6 Nathan Summers
.... 6 Rev. Alexander Summers 1778 - 1847
.... +Sarah Stansberry
.... *2nd Wife of Rev. Alexander Summers:
.... +Mary Vinegar 1776 - 1832
.... 7 David Summers (twin)
.... 7 Jonathan Summers(twin)
.... 7 James Summers
.... 7 Chrystianna Summers
.... 7 Elijah Summers
.... 7 Rebecca Summers
.... +Baker
.... 7 Elias S. Summers
.... 7 Sarah Summers
.... 7 Mary Ann Summers
.... +Swisher
.... 7 Elizabeth Summers
.... +Snider
.... 7 Elisha Summers
.... 7 Aletha Summers 1799 - 1849
.... +Phillip Hoffman 1797 - 1879
.... 8 Mary Ann Hoffman 1821 - 1886
.... +David William Shahan 1825 - 1910
.... 9 Thomas Shahan 1844 -
.... 9 Philip Nelson Shahan 1848 - 1913
.... +Barbara Bowman 1864 - 1946
.... 10 Charles L. Shahan 1884 - 1885

10 Ernest Uriah Shahan 1885 - 1969
+Lula Jane Robinson
10 Datis Alvin Shahan 1887 - 1955
+Martha M. Davis
10 Elizabeth Ina Shahan 1890 - 1969
+Alexander Nestor 1871 - 1944
11 Woodrow Charles Nestor 1922 - 1969
+Norma Owens 1935 -
11 Ellis Nestor
11 N.C. Riley Nestor
11 Ira Nestor
11 Ruth Nestor
+Mr. Digman
11 Ruby Nestor
+Mr. Thompson
11 Elsie Nestor
+Mr. Shrout
11 Bertha Nestor
11 Ace Nestor
10 Florence Lulu Shahan 1893 - 1983
+Orville Burr
10 Alta Wilson Shahan 1896 - 1918
10 Gay Tona Shahan 1899 -
+Minerva M. White
10 Male Shahan 1903 - 1903
10 Waitman Philip Shahan 1904 - 1953
*2nd Wife of Philip Nelson Shahan:
+Mary E. Lipscomb 1847 - 1881
10 Rebecca Alice Shahan 1875 - 1957
+Loman Sanford Stalmaker
10 Charles Tilden Shahan 1877 - 1962
+Lee Verna Keller
10 Cyrus Walter Shahan 1879 - 1961
+Oleta C. Poling
10 Ira D. Shahan 1880 - 1958
+Jennie Knotts
9 Rebecca E. Shahan 1851 -
9 David William Shahan 1853 - 1931
+Caroline A. Bolyard 1857 - 1949
10 Lula V. Shahan 1875 -
+James A. Knotts
*2nd Husband of Lula V. Shahan:
+M. D. Wolfe
10 Florence E. Shahan 1877 - 1959
+Eli Nose
*2nd Husband of Florence E. Shahan:
+Harrison Serman Hornbeck
10 Ulysses S. Grant Shahan 1879 - 1880
10 Noah Shahan 1881 - 1934
+Dona Bolyard
10 Waitman C. Shahan 1888 - 1894
10 Anna Shahan 1889 - 1894
10 Flora Shahan 1893 - 1894
10 Flora E. Shahan 1895 -
+Ernest Lee
9 Christina E. Shahan 1855 - 1921
+William Sein Rosier
9 Columbia Jane Shahan 1857 - 1860
9 John Washington Shahan 1858 - 1930
+Sarah A. Mitchell 1864 - 1939
10 Clarence Shahan 1881 - 1885
10 Della May Shahan 1886 - 1962
+Charles Alva Phillips
10 Daisy Ellen Shahan 1889 - 1923
+Bolyard
*2nd Husband of Daisy Ellen Shahan:
+Uriah C. Phillips
10 David Roy Shahan 1890 - 1926
+Ivey Pearl Nestor
10 Ida Belle Shahan 1893 - 1893
10 Albert Troy Shahan 1894 - 1958
+Virginia Pearl Harsh
10 Dona Victoria Shahan 1901 - 1952
+Silals Runner
*2nd Husband of Dona Victoria Shahan:
+Wilburt L. White
9 Charlotte L. Shahan 1860 - 1943

+Lemuel Knotts
8 John Alexander Hoffman 1822 - 1893
+Amy Elizabeth Brunner 1828 - 1862
9 Aletha Ann Hoffman 1846 -
9 Susannah Hoffman 1849 -
9 Ursuley Ann Hoffman 1852 -
9 Mary Jane Hoffman 1852 -
9 Amy Elizabeth Hoffman 1858 -
9 William Francis Hoffman 1861 -
*2nd Wife of John Alexander Hoffman:
+Lucinda Barnes 1841 - 1895
9 Nathan Squire Hoffman 1868 -
9 Cenith E. Hoffman 1870 -
9 Marion P. Hoffman 1874 -
9 David Milton Hoffman 1875 -
9 George Irvin Hoffman 1879 -
8 Elijah S. Hoffman 1824 - 1894
+Martha Ann King 1823 - 1899
9 David Hennon Hoffman 1849 -
9 Abbalona Clamenc Hoffman 1850 -
9 Rosalie Maranda Hoffman 1852 -
9 Henry Milton Hoffman 1853 -
9 Ruall Nanzilla Hoffman 1855 -
9 Enoch Madison Hoffman 1857 -
9 Elijah McGee Hoffman 1859 -
9 John Nelson Hoffman 1861 -
8 Nimrod Nelson Hoffman 1827 - 1890
+Nancy Ann Elizabeth Saer 1844 - 1917
9 Willie U.S. Hoffman 1865 - 1938
9 Anna Aminta Hoffman 1866 - 1935
9 Ada Gregg Hoffman 1868 - 1868
9 Cora Lee Hoffman 1871 - 1925
9 Nellie Grant Hoffman 1873 -
9 John Thompson Hoffman 1875 - 1947
9 Harry Hagans Hoffman 1878 - 1879
8 George Washington Hoffman 1831 - 1865
+Elizabeth Eliza Knotts 1831 - 1905
9 Mary Elizabeth Hoffman 1849 - 1930
+Robert Corneloius Wagner 1847 - 1919
9 Martha Jane Hoffman 1850 -
9 Aletha Hoffman 1860 -
8 Francis Marion Hoffman 1836 - 1904
+Christena Shahan 1839 - 1871
9 John Martin Hoffman 1858 - 1942
+Martha Anne Burgoyne 1863 - 1935
10 Russell Reed Hoffman 1890 - 1956
+Sara Louise Porter 1898 - 1998
11 Russel Reed Jr. Hoffman 1921 - 1972
+Adela Gloria Teixeira 1916 -
12 Dianne Marie Hoffman 1947 -
+Wayne Charles Wunderlich 1947 -
13 Robert Christopher Wunderlich 1966 -
*2nd Husband of Dianne Marie Hoffman:
+Daniel Balduck 1949 - 1997
13 Bret Alan Balduck 1970 - 1975
*3rd Husband of Dianne Marie Hoffman:
+Carl Albert Reinert, Jr. 1928 -
9 Charity Elizabeth Hoffman 1860 - 1923
9 Ursula Jane Hoffman 1864 - 1939
9 Sarah Ann Hoffman 1864 - 1934
9 Charles Nelson Hoffman 1866 - 1926
9 Rebecca Hoffman 1868 - 1957
+Arthur Ellsworth Alexander
10 Clarence Harold Alexander 1894 -
10 Oscar Granville Alexander 1896 - 1918
10 Lottie Alice Alexander 1898 - 1919
10 Nellie Gay Alexander 1900 - 1978
10 Gladys Murl Alexander 1902 -
10 Audra Dot Alexander 1903 -
10 John Thomas Alexander 1907 - 1981
+Mary Ann Wells
10 Manti Lee Alexander 1909 -
10 Agnes Blanche Alexander 1911 -
*2nd Wife of Francis Marion Hoffman:
+Mary Amelia Martin 1842 - 1922
9 Oriona Alice Hoffman 1873 - 1948
+James R. Phelps

10 Leita Phelps 1910 -
+?? Lunk
9 Emma Florence Hoffman 1875 - 1936
+William N. Goff
10 Eulalia Luella Goff 1899 - 1980
*2nd Husband of Emma Florence Hoffman:
+Joseph L. Shrout
9 Rutherfold B. Hayes Hoffman 1876 - 1953
+Effie
10 Jean Hoffman
*2nd Wife of Rutherfold B. Hayes Hoffman:
+Gladys
10 ?? Hoffman
9 Lelia Eugenia Hoffman 1877 - 1925
+W. Irvin Watts
10 Mary Sue Watts 1908 - 1933
+W. R. Schooley
9 Jenivee Hoffman 1879 - 1974
+Franklin Blakeney Pierce
10 Lola Hazel Pierce 1902 -
10 George Francis Pierce 1905 -
10 Harold Blakeney Pierce 1917 - 1975
9 Lola Velle Hoffman 1881 - 1966
+Robert Munsen
9 James Gillispi Blaine Hoffman 1884 - 1956
+Nora A. Burgoyne
10 James Blaine Hoffman 1917 - 1974
10 Charles Francis Hoffman 1919 - 1919
10 Virginia Lee Hoffman 1919 - 1919
*2nd Wife of James Gillispi Blaine Hoffman:
+Clarissa M. Todd
10 David Roger Hoffman 1937 -
*3rd Wife of James Gillispi Blaine Hoffman:
+Edith P. Fox
8 Louisa Marion Hoffman 1836 - 1885
+George Washington Shahan 1830 - 1891
9 Alethea Elizabeth Shahan 1851 - 1860
9 William Francis Shahan 1852 - 1942
+Michelle / Melvina L. Nestor
10 Amelia Shahan 1880 -
10 Louisa C. Shahan 1881 -
+J. Patrick Loughry
10 Sarah E. J. Shahan 1885 - 1974
10 George A. F. Shahan 1885 - 1962
10 James Peter Shahan 1888 - 1966
+Nellie Agnes Plum
10 John M. Shahan 1890 -
10 Chloe F. Shahan 1892 -
10 Bertha M. Shahan 1897 -
+Everett Wallace
10 Marry Jessie Shahan 1901 - 1986
9 John Wesley Shahan 1854 - 1855
9 Sarah Minerva Shahan 1856 -
+Thomas Dewalt Poling 1856 -
9 Christina L. Shahan 1858 - 1933
+David T. Hovatter 1853 - 1929
10 Charles E. Hovatter 1878 -
+Ella Agnice Burns 1883 -
11 Claudene Elwood Hovatter
+Arietta Shockley
11 Elston Gerald Hovatter
+Myra E. Howard
11 Charles Woodrow Wilson Hovatter
+Madeline Kausch
11 Wanda Lorraine Hovatter
+Albert H. Hearn
11 Earl Gay Hovatter 1912 - 1934
11 Thomas David Hovatter 1908 -
+Elsie Ambrosio
12 Timothy Hovatter
11 Elmer Dallas Hovatter 1902 - 1970
+Jessie B. Noce 1898 - 1919
11 Etta Ives Hovatter
+Earl C. Cathel
11 Delbert Ray Hovatter 1904 - 1974
+Barbara Chandler
12 Barbara Lindsay Hovatter 1944 - 1968

12 Sandra Lee Hovatter 1946 -
+James Moore
12 Martha Jean Hovatter 1953 -
+Kenneth Speer - 1988
13 Barbara Anne Speer 1974 -
13 Donald Ray Speer 1977 -
*2nd Husband of Martha Jean Hovatter:
+Charles Reno
11 Leoda Pearl Hovatter
11 Ora Marie Hovatter 1914 - 1937
+Herbert Fues, Sr
11 Elford Harold Hovatter 1924 - 1924
10 Lellie C. Hovatter 1880 -
+John Patrick Burns 1877 - 1950
10 Wilbert F. Hovatter 1882 - 1969
+Hattie Lee Jones 1885 - 1969
11 Eula Hovatter 1903 - 1937
+Samuel Linton
12 Voncile Linton
*2nd Husband of Eula Hovatter:
+Hope Watson
12 Junior Lee Watson
12 Francis Watson
12 Joyce Watson
11 Odie Hovatter 1905 - 1905
11 Wilbertie Valentine Hovatter 1908 - 1987
+Hazel Dell Clevenger 1907 - 1988
12 Marjorie Hovatter 1927 -
12 Dolores Hovatter 1929 -
12 Berta Jayne Hovatter 1938 - 1988
+Harold Snyder
13 Pam Snyder 1959 -
14 Brian Snyder 1976 -
*2nd Husband of Berta Jayne Hovatter:
+Thomas Moser 1930 -
13 Thomas Moser 1969 -
*Partner of Wilbertie Valentine Hovatter:
+Ruby Barnett 1915 -
12 Rosalie J. Hovatter 1932 -
+Charley Jenkins
*2nd Husband of Rosalie J. Hovatter:
+David Faulknier
11 Boyd Hovatter 1910 - 1975
11 Floyd Hovatter 1913 - 1913
11 Lois Hovatter 1914 - 1983
+Thomas Mancuso 1912 - 1985
12 Joyce F. Mancuso 1934 -
+Robert Thomas Sutton 1932 -
13 Dolores Lea Sutton 1958 -
13 Susan Joyce Sutton 1964 -
+Christopher Keating
14 Christopher Keating Jr.
14 Benjamin Keating
13 Bobbi Lynn Sutton 1968 -
+Karl Frank Chase
14 Shawn Joseph Chase 1995 -
14 Samantha Joyce Chase 1997 -
*Partner of Bobbi Lynn Sutton:
+Mr. McHenry
14 Dani-Lynn McHenry 2006 -
12 Patrina Mancuso 1937 - 1937
11 Hattie Almalee Hovatter 1917 -
11 Aubrey Hovatter 1920 -
11 Dessie Hovatter 1921 - 2001
+Edgar Thom 1922 - 1982
12 Dennis Thom 1949 - 1971
*2nd Husband of Dessie Hovatter:
+William F. Putnam 1932 - 2002
12 Robin Putnam 1963 -
+Edison Richard Walker
13 Stephen Randall Walker 1987 -
13 Jaren Dawn Walker 1993 -
12 William F. Putnam 2 1966 -
+Bernetta Graham 1970 -
13 William F. Putnam 3 1990 -
13 Olivia Lucille Putnam 1997 -
11 Vernon Hovatter 1924 - 1996

.... 11 Kenneth Gene Hovatter 1927 - 1983
.... 10 Ira J. Hovatter 1885 - 1968
.... +Dessie Thomas
.... 11 Nina Hovatter
.... 10 Mary L. Hovatter 1887 -
.... +Andrew Jackson Brown 1877 - 1932
.... 11 Andrew C. Brown 1904 - 1975
.... +Mildred Fortney
.... 12 Donald Brown
.... 12 Keith Brown
.... 12 Larraine Brown
.... 12 Swance Brown
.... 12 Frank Brown
.... 12 Paul Brown
.... 11 Albert Leroy Brown 1908 - 1994
.... +Marie Mizell
.... 11 Ruby Brown 1908 -
.... +Bryan Hovatter - 1996
.... 12 William Hovatter
.... 12 Prudence Hovatter
.... 11 Wilber Jackson Brown 1912 - 1912
.... 11 Homer Jennings Brown 1914 - 1972
.... +Mary Myrtle Deese or Dees 1918 - 1989
.... 12 Cecile Leota Brown 1934 - 1937
.... 12 Andrew Jennings Brown 1937 - 1994
.... +Jackine Lou Tallet
.... 12 Homer Ray Brown 1938 -
.... +Anna Cecelia Stevens
.... 13 Tracy Lee Brown 1966 -
.... 11 Delbert Jennings Brown 1917 - 1998
.... 11 William Henry Brown 1920 -
.... 11 Nellie Mae Brown Brown 1923 -
.... 11 David Elmer Brown 1926 - 1929
.... 10 George E. Hovatter 1889 -
.... +Cecil May Burns
.... 11 Ernest Ray Hovatter 1916 -
.... +Mildred Kinter
.... 12 Gary Ray Hovatter 1949 -
.... +Linda Hunnicut
.... 13 Health Hovatter
.... 13 Heather Hovatter
.... +Anthony Galvez
.... 14 Daniel Galvez
.... 14 Rebecca Galvez
.... 14 Allisa Galvez
.... 12 Vickie Lynn Hovatter 1954 -
.... +William Claypool 1949 -
.... 13 Daniel Claypool 1978 -
.... 13 Kevin Claypool 1981 -
.... *2nd Wife of Ernest Ray Hovatter:
.... +Evelyn ?
.... 12 Patti Ann Hovatter
.... +? Smith
.... *3rd Wife of Ernest Ray Hovatter:
.... +Francis Boyer
.... 12 Francis Lee Hovatter
.... 11 Violet Mildred Hovatter 1915 -
.... +Fred Baiocchi - 1987
.... 12 Yvonne Baiocchi
.... 11 Velma Arizonia Hovatter 1917 -
.... 11 Beryl Hovatter
.... +Page Evans
.... 12 Male Child Evans
.... 11 Mary Elizabeth Hovatter 1923 -
.... +Mr. Pert
.... 12 Jean Pert
.... 12 Larry Pert
.... 12 unknown Pert
.... *2nd Husband of Mary Elizabeth Hovatter:
.... +Leonard Blackmon
.... 11 Darrell Hovatter
.... +Shirlee
.... 12 Donna Hovatter
.... 12 Kathy Hovatter
.... 10 Lloyd A. Hovatter 1891 -
.... +Lulu Sterringer
.... 10 Maudie P. Hovatter 1893 -

+Samuel Dumire
10 Arlie David Hovatter 1895 - 1977
+Laura Poling
11 Lester Hovatter
10 Boyd E. Hovatter 1897 - 1980
+Hilda Davis
9 Mary Catherine Shahan 1860 - 1941
+Martin M. Poling 1860 -
10 Rhoda Poling
10 Jonas Poling
10 Ira Poling
9 Cyrena Margaret Shahan 1862 - 1943
+Isaac M. Poling 1860 -
9 George Emery Shahan 1864 - 1966
+Cora Jane Hovatter 1876 - 1948
10 Walter Brown Shahan
10 Agnes Shahan 1892 - 1986
10 Minnie Pearl Shahan 1894 - 1959
10 Donna Jane Shahan 1896 - 1972
10 Mary Elizabeth Shahan 1897 - 1918
10 Daisy Virginia Shahan 1899 - 1978
10 Flora Shahan 1904 - 1904
10 Dora Shahan 1904 -
10 Charles Lee Shahan 1907 - 1971
10 Cora Louise Shahan 1908 - 1987
+Floyd Edward Sayre
10 Ruby Bessie Shahan 1910 -
10 Georgia Oletha Shahan 1912 - 1975
10 Lillian Ann Shahan 1916 -
10 Victoria Arabelle Shahan 1919 -
9 Richard Jefferson Shahan 1867 - 1954
9 Louisa Olive J. Shahan 1868 - 1900
9 Elizah Squire Shahan 1873 - 1874
9 Caroline Josephine Shahan 1874 - 1951
+Mr. Hebt
9 Stillborn Twin One Shahan 1874 -
9 Stillborn Twin Two Shahan 1874 -
9 David Charles Shahan 1880 - 1947
9 Virginia Catherine Shahan 1882 -
+Mr. Spare
8 Abalona Rebekah Hoffman 1839 -
8 Nancy Jane Hoffman 1840 -
8 Sarah A. E. Huffman 1841 - 1901
+Robert Johnson
9 Robert Leland Johnson 1864 -
+Sarah J. Phillips 1858 - 1918
9 James Thomas Johnson 1867 -
9 John Pendelton Johnson 1869 -
9 Charles William Johnson 1874 -
9 Rosetta Johnson 1879 -
7 Joseph Summers 1816 - 1887
+Julia Ann Tarleton 1812 - 1879
8 Alcinda Summers
+May
8 Thomas Marshall Summers
8 Elijah Summers
8 Alaxander Summers
8 William Caleb Summers
8 Sarah Elizabeth Summers
+Wofle/Bomer
8 James Summers 1850 - 1887
+Elmira (Almira) Francis Knapp - 1947
9 Ira Henson Summers
9 Charles Robert Summers
9 John Wesley Summers
9 Infant Summers
9 Joseph Willis Summers 1879 - 1956
+Iva Rebecca Burke
10 Leroma Blanche Summers
10 William Clair Summers
10 Christina Irene Summers
*2nd Wife of Hezekiah Summers:
+Ruth Dawson - 1866
2 Benjamin Summers
2 William Summers

Descendants of William Summers

Generation No. 1

1. WILLIAM[1] SUMMERS was born Abt. 1645 in ENGLAND.

Children of WILLIAM SUMMERS are:

2. i. JOHN[2] SUMMERS, 1ST, b. Abt. 1650; d. Abt. 1705.
ii. BENJAMIN SUMMERS.
iii. WILLIAM SUMMERS.

Generation No. 2

2. JOHN[2] SUMMERS, 1ST *(WILLIAM[1])* was born Abt. 1650, and died Abt. 1705. He married REBECCA DENT. She died Abt. 1711 in MD.

Notes for JOHN SUMMERS, 1ST:
The first reported Summers in your line was a John Summers. On 18 December 1671, a Captain John Boddy ...Having transported 12 persons to Maryland to inhabit, amongst whom was John Summers, proved his right to 600 acres of land.

John Summers was believed to be between 16 and 25 years of age (born about 1650), this being the age of most transported indentured servants. He would have faced a doubtful crossing of the Atlantic. A most dangerous thing at those times, where sickness, on board fires and ship wreaks were only some of the fears. The crossing if it went well would have taken 2 months.
Most of the time was spent below decks in cramped quarters with little light, sanitation or ventilation. Many died of disease on these journeys and John would had to have the true Pioneer spirit to make this trip.

John showed himself to be a rugged individualist, by 1682 he was already paying ground rent (tax) on 120 acres of land called Pitchcraft. It was on the Westside of the Patuxent River in the freshes, in Calvert County, Later called Prince Georges' County. As most people of the time, he was a Planter (Farmer) by trade. He also was active in the community. He testified for a Edward Gold (a Negro) and his freedon in June 1692. He served on Jury duty twice in 1698, and was appointed overseer of the Mount Calvert Hundred (a piece of property). He was married to a Rebecca Dent and had 4 chiuldren. He died about 1705 and left his estate to his wife Rebecca. When she remarried (to a Henry Mackbee in 170p8) the estate went to his two sons. Rebecca died about 1711.

Children of JOHN SUMMERS and REBECCA DENT are:

i. WILLIAM[3] SUMMERS.
ii. SARAH SUMMERS.
iii. LUCY SUMMERS.

3. iv. JOHN SUMMERS, 2ND, b. Abt. 1685, Prince Georges Co. MD; d. 1769.

Generation No. 3

3. JOHN[3] SUMMERS, 2ND *(JOHN[2], WILLIAM[1])* was born Abt. 1685 in Prince Georges Co. MD, and died 1769. He married MARY MOORE Abt. 1713, daughter of JAMES MOORE, SR.. She was born Abt. 1696, and died June 11, 1769 in Prince Georges Co. MD.

Notes for JOHN SUMMERS, 2ND:
John Summers, 2nd was born in Prince Georges County Maryland about 1685 and like his father he was a Planter. But John Summers the 2nd was a visionary and had a desire to grow with this new land. By 1709 he indentured (brought) his brother Williams' half of Pitchcraft for 1,500 pounds of Tobacco. It seems Wi8lliam Summers had some money problems and in 1708 the Sheriff was after him for an owed dept back in 1707 for the sum of 550

pounds of tobacco. It seems he was not at home when the sheriff called. By 1713 John Summers, 2nd married a Mary Moore, daughter of James Moore, Sr. and brought the land adjoining his father-in-laws called Moores Adition from a Thomas Clagatt. Moores Adition is 231Acres on the west side of the Patuxent River in the woods and in a fork of Piscataway Branch. John the 2nd and his fatherk-in-law must of got along well because on July 1723 James Moore indentured (sold) a tract of land (35 Acres) called Child's Portion to John the 2nd. John the 2nd then deeded the land back to him (James Moore) for "natural affection and loving duty". Besides working a growing farm, he and Mary Moore Summers had 13 children. All of them out lived him, excedpt James Summers who died in 1761 , John and Mary Summers died in 1769/

Children of JOHN SUMMERS and MARY MOORE are:

i. JOHN[4] SUMMERS, THE 3RD.
ii. GEORGE SUMMERS.
iii. WILLIAM SUMMERS.
iv. THOMAS SUMMERS.
v. BENJAMIN SUMMERS.
vi. JAMES SUMMERS, d. 1761.
vii. JOSEPH SUMMERS.
viii. MARY SUMMERS, m. MR. WHEAT.
ix. REBECKAH SUMMERS, m. MR. KING.
x. RACHEL SUMMERS, m. MR. JOHNSON.
xi. RUTH SUMMERS, m. MR. RIGGS.
xii. JEMINA SUMMERS, m. MR. CATON.
4. xiii. DENT SUMMERS, b. 1727, Prince Georges Co. MD; d. October 19, 1809, Montgomery co MD.

Generation No. 4

4. DENT[4] SUMMERS *(JOHN[3], JOHN[2], WILLIAM[1])* was born 1727 in Prince Georges Co. MD, and died October 19, 1809 in Montgomery co MD. He married MARY ANN CLAGGETT Abt. 1749. She died November 18, 1802 in Montgomery co MD.

Notes for DENT SUMMERS:
The fourth son of John Summers the 2nd, born in Prince George County, Maryland in 1727. He grew up on the farm with large extended family of brothers and sisters and aunts and uncles. He married about age 22 (about 1749) to Mary ann Claggett. On 18 April 1763 he obtained 100 acres of land called Joseph's Park. It was located on the east side of the Rock Creek Brance. When his parents died in 1769, he was willed 50 acres of the Adition, a portion laid off at the lower end next to theWood Yard. He needed this land because he and Mary Ann went on to have 9 children.
Dent Summers was a private, suspicious and bit of a obnoxious man. In 1776 when the new America commissioned a census of all its people, Dent Summers told the census taker there were 9 in the family but refused to give their ages. When they came back again to do another census in 1790, he was more co-operative and listed his kids along with 5 slaves. In 1802 his wife Mary Ann died he followed shortly in 1809.

Children of DENT SUMMERS and MARY CLAGGETT are:

i. MARY ANN[5] SUMMERS, m. MR. HARDY.
ii. SARAH SUMMERS, m. WHITE.
iii. PAUL SUMMERS.
iv. JAMES DENT SUMMERS.
v. ZADOCK SUMMERS.
vi. JOHN SUMMERS, m. CHLOE (CLOY).
vii. MARGARET SUMMERS, m. HOSKINS.
viii. WILLIAM DENT SUMMERS.
5. ix. HEZEKIAH SUMMERS, b. September 23, 1750, Prince Georges Co. MD; d. June 07, 1836, Mongalia Co. VA.

Generation No. 5

5. HEZEKIAH[5] SUMMERS *(DENT[4], JOHN[3], JOHN[2], WILLIAM[1])* was born September 23, 1750 in Prince Georges Co. MD, and died June 07, 1836 in Mongalia Co. VA. He married (1) REBECKER GLAZ Abt. 1772, daughter of JOHN GLAZ. She was born 1743, and died Abt. 1800. He married (2) RUTH DAWSON April 13, 1831 in Monongalia

Co. VA. She died Abt. 1866.

Notes for HEZEKIAH SUMMERS:
Life Appeared to be normal but these were not normal times. A nation was being born and Hezekiah soon found himself drafted on 71 August 1776 to fight in the Revolutionary War. He served 4 times in 6 years for a total of two and half years service. He stated he personally knew General Washinton and was a true Minuteman (enclosed is one of the letters for his pension request). He returned home after the war and was prosperous property owner, planter. He was living in Northwest Hundred, Federick County, by 1790 (Census) he had 10 slaves. It is believed that Rebecker Glaz Summers died about 1800 and the family was beginning to venture out to f8ind their own lives. Hezekiah Summers children went in many Different directions but most went to the western wilderness of Virginia (now West Virginia). Hezekiah moved to Monongalia County Virginia about 1810. It is believed that Hezekiah went west to be near his children and grandchildren. On 13 April 1831 he married Ruth Dawson in Monongalia County, Virgina, 30 plus years his younger. Both he and her petitioned the government for his war pension and land grants with no success. He died in 1836 in Monongalia County, Virgina. Ruth Dawson Summers lived on to about 1866.

Census Year: 1800 State: Maryland County: Montgomery Stamped no: 165A
Reel no: M32-11 Division: First Enumerated by: George Magruder

Transcribed by Janice Miles Parker and Proofread by James H. Parker for USGenWeb. Copyright: 2000

			Free White Persons					
			Male	Female	Not			
			0 10 16 16 26 45	0 10 16 26 45				
LN	Firstname	Lastname	10 16 18 26 45 +	10 16 26 45 +	Oth	Slv	SNDX	Remarks
1	Jeremiah	Lewis	0 0 2 0 1	0 1 1 0 1	1	0	L200	handwritten #44
2	Thomas	Lewis	1 0 0 1 0	1 0 0 1 0	0	0	L2 0	abd #224
3	Levy	Lewis	0 0 0 1 0	0 0 0 1 0	0	0	L200	
4	James	Lawson	2 0 1 0 0	1 0 1 0 0	0	6	L250	
5	George	Walker	1 1 1 1 0	1 1 1 1 0	0	0	W426	
6	Zadock	Summers	2 0 0 1 0	3 0 0 1 0	0	2	S562	
7	Joshua	Purdum	3 0 0 1 0	1 0 0 1 0	0	0	P635	
8	John	Ellis	1 2 0 0 1	0 0 2 0 0	0	0	E200	
9	Hezekiah	Summers	0 0 1 1 1	0 1 2 1 1	1	20	S562	
10	William	Lee	1 0 0 1 0	0 0 0 1 1	0	0	L 00	
11	Garrett T.	Lee	1 1 0 1 0	2 0 0 1 0	0	0	L000	
12	John	Boyd	0 0 2 0 1	2 3 1 0 1	0	0	B300	
13	Edward	King	2 0 0 1 1	1 0 0 1 0	0	0	K52	
14	Charles	Harvey	1 0 0 1 0	1 0 1 0 0	0	0	H610	
15	Charles	Miles	3 1 0 1 0	3 1 1 1 0	1	1	M420	
16	John	King	0 0 1 0 0	0 0 1 0 0	0	0	K52	
17	Joseph	Waters	0 0 0 2 1	0 1 0 0 0	0	8	W362	
18	Francis	McCater	2 1 0 1 0	2 0 0 1 0	0	3	M236	
19	Edward	Jones	0 0 3 0 1	2 4 1 0 1	0	0	J520	
20	Benjamin	Burdet	2 1 3 0 1	1 1 2 0 1	0	0	B633	
21	Levin	Mobly	2 1 0 1 0	3 2 0 1 0	0	0	M140	
22	Alexander	Summers	3 0 1 0 0	1 0 1 0 0	0	0	S562	

Children of HEZEKIAH SUMMERS and REBECKER GLAZ are:

i. WILLIAM DENT[6] SUMMERS, m. REBECCA JACOBS.

ii. BENJAMIN SUMMERS.

iii. JOHN S. SUMMERS.
iv. PHILLIP SUMMERS.
v. THOMAS SUMMERS.
vi. MARGARET SUMMERS.
vii. NATHAN SUMMERS.
6. viii. REV. ALEXANDER SUMMERS, b. March 09, 1778, Prince Georges Co. MD; d. April 12, 1847, Monogalia Co. VA.

Generation No. 6

6. REV. ALEXANDER[6] SUMMERS *(HEZEKIAH[5], DENT[4], JOHN[3], JOHN[2], WILLIAM[1])* was born March 09, 1778 in Prince Georges Co. MD, and died April 12, 1847 in Monogalia Co. VA. He married (1) SARAH STANSBERRY. He married (2) MARY VINEGAR March 25, 1797 in Frederick Co., Maryland. She was born April 15, 1776 in Ireland, and died February 29, 1832 in Monogalia Co. VA.

Notes for REV. ALEXANDER SUMMERS:
Alexander was a religious man and in 1814 he and three other men obtain a small parcel of land "for the settlement in which they may live in the religious order for the promotion of the gospel". (The churchs' foundation and graveyard exist today at the New Pisgah Church one half mile from Little Falls in Monongalia County off State Route#73). Alexander Summers went on to become an ordained Methodist Minister in Morgantown Virginia on 19 November 1832. Alexander and Mary Ann Summers then lived in Marion County near Catawba. Mary Ann Died in 1832. It is then believed that Alexander married a Sarah Stansberry but no addition data is available.

Year: 1810 State: Virginia County: Monongalia Page No: 538
Reel no: M252-69 Division: The Division of Monongalia County
Sheet No: 435B Enumerated by: Benjamin Franklin Reader
Transcribed by Mary Louise Lake Roberts USGenWeb,
http://www.rootsweb.com/~census/. Copyright: 2002

			Free White persons													
			Male					Female					Not			
LN	Firstname	Lastname	0-10	10-16	16-25	26-45	45 +	0-10	10-16	16-25	26-45	45 +	Tax	Slv	SNDX	Remark
1	Mapuder	Selby	1	1	1	.	1	3	1	1	.	1	.	.	S410	
2	Wm	Stinson	1	.	.	1	.	.	1	1	.	1	.	2	S352	
3	Rich	Strong	1	.	.	1	.	4	1	.	1	.	.	.	S365	
4	Tho	Stafford	.	.	.	1	.	2	.	1	.	.	.	.	S316	
5	Jno	Stafford, Jr.	2	1	.	1	.	2	1	.	1	.	.	.	S316	
6	Robt.	Stuart	3	1	.	.	1	.	5	1	.	1	.	.	S363	
7	Ch.	Stewert	.	1	2	.	1	1	2	1	.	1	.	.	S363	
8	Jas.	Savier	1	.	.	1	.	.	5	2	.	1	.	.	S160	
9	Henry	Shaver	3	2	1	.	1	1	1	1	.	1	.	.	S160	
10	Alex	Summers	4	2	.	1	.	1	1	.	1	.	.	.	S562	
11	Dav	Seaman	2	1	.	1	.	1	2	.	1	.	.	.	S550	
12	Richd	Smith	3	.	.	1	1	.	1	.	.	.	.	.	S530	
13	Jno.	Snyder	.	.	.	.	1	.	3	.	.	1	.	.	S536	
14	Wm	Snyder	1	1	1	.	1	5	1	.	.	1	.	.	S536	
15	Jno	Seger	1	.	.	1	.	2	.	.	1	.	.	.	S260	
16	Mary	Savier	2	.	.	.	.	.	2	.	1	.	.	.	S160	
17	Dan	Soveins	.	.	.	.	1	.	.	.	2	.	.	.	S152	

18 | Jacob Smith | 1 . . 1 .| 3 3 . 1 .| .| .| S530 |
19 | Wm. Smith | 1 . . 1 .| 1 . . 2 1| .| .| S530 |
20 | Geo. Smith | . 1 . 1 .| 4 1 . 1 .| .| .| S530 |
21 | Gab. Slair | . . 1 . .| 1 . 1 . .| .| .| S460 |
22 | Elij. Slarling | 1 . . . .| 2 1 . 1 .| .| .| S464 |
23 | Selea Sayre | 4 . . . 1| 1 1 . 1 .| .| .| S600 |
===|================================|=======================|======================
=|=====|=====|======|=======

--Census Year: 1800 State: Maryland County: Montgomery Stamped no: 165A
Reel no: M32-11 Division: First Enumerated by: George Magruder

Transcribed by Janice Miles Parker and Proofread by James H. Parker for USGenWeb. Copyright: 2000

===|================================|=======================|===================|====|====
|======|================

| Free White Persons |
| Male | Female |
| 0 10 16 16 26 45 | 0 10 16 26 45 | Not|
LN| Firstname Lastname | 10 16 18 26 45 + | 10 16 26 45 + | Oth| Slv| SNDX | Remarks
===|================================|=======================|===================|====|====
|======|================

1| Jeremiah Lewis | 0 0 2 0 1 | 0 1 1 0 1 | 1 | 0 | L200 | handwritten #44
2| Thomas Lewis | 1 0 0 1 0 | 1 0 0 1 0 | 0 | 0 | L2 0 | abd #224
3| Levy Lewis | 0 0 0 1 0 | 0 0 0 1 0 | 0 | 0 | L200 |
4| James Lawson | 2 0 1 0 0 | 1 0 1 0 0 | 0 | 6 | L250 |
5| George Walker | 1 1 1 1 0 | 1 1 1 1 0 | 0 | 0 | W426 |
6| Zadock Summers | 2 0 0 1 0 | 3 0 0 1 0 | 0 | 2 | S562 |
7| Joshua Purdum | 3 0 0 1 0 | 1 0 0 1 0 | 0 | 0 | P635 |
8| John Ellis | 1 2 0 0 1 | 0 0 2 0 0 | 0 | 0 | E200 |
9| Hezekiah Summers | 0 0 1 1 1 | 0 1 2 1 1 | 1 | 20 | S562 |
10| William Lee | 1 0 0 1 0 | 0 0 0 1 1 | 0 | 0 | L 00 |
11| Garrett T. Lee | 1 1 0 1 0 | 2 0 0 1 0 | 0 | 0 | L000 |
12| John Boyd | 0 0 2 0 1 | 2 3 1 0 1 | 0 | 0 | B300 |
13| Edward King | 2 0 0 1 1 | 1 0 0 1 0 | 0 | 0 | K52 |
14| Charles Harvey | 1 0 0 1 0 | 1 0 1 0 0 | 0 | 0 | H610 |
15| Charles Miles | 3 1 0 1 0 | 3 1 1 1 0 | 1 | 1 | M420 |
16| John King | 0 0 1 0 0 | 0 0 1 0 0 | 0 | 0 | K52 |
17| Joseph Waters | 0 0 0 2 1 | 0 1 0 0 0 | 0 | 8 | W362 |
18| Francis McCater | 2 1 0 1 0 | 2 0 0 1 0 | 0 | 3 | M236 |
19| Edward Jones | 0 0 3 0 1 | 2 4 1 0 1 | 0 | 0 | J520 |
20| Benjamin Burdet | 2 1 3 0 1 | 1 1 2 0 1 | 0 | 0 | B633 |
21| Levin Mobly | 2 1 0 1 0 | 3 2 0 1 0 | 0 | 0 | M140 |
22| Alexander Summers | 3 0 1 0 0 | 1 0 1 0 0 | 0 | 0 | S562 |
===|================================|=======================|===================|====|====
|======|================

-

Children of REV. SUMMERS and MARY VINEGAR are:

i. DAVID SUMMERS[7] (TWIN).
ii. JONATHAN SUMMERS(TWIN).
iii. JAMES SUMMERS.
iv. CHRYSTIANNA SUMMERS.
v. ELIJAH SUMMERS.
vi. REBECCA SUMMERS, m. BAKER.
vii. ELIAS S. SUMMERS.

viii. SARAH SUMMERS.
ix. MARY ANN SUMMERS, m. SWISHER.
x. ELIZABETH SUMMERS, m. SNIDER.
xi. ELISHA SUMMERS.
xii. ALETHA SUMMERS, b. February 01, 1799, Prince George Co, MD; d. April 17, 1849, Preston, WVA; m. PHILLIP HOFFMAN, August 26, 1820, Monongalia Co. VA; b. February 18, 1797, Monongalia Co. VA; d. January 09, 1879, Barbour Co. WVA.

More About ALETHA SUMMERS:
Burial: Mathews Cemetery, Marquess, Preston, VA

Notes for PHILLIP HOFFMAN:
[Brøderbund Family Archive #290, Ed. 1, Census Index: VA, WV, Preston County, 1870 West Virginia Census, Date of Import: Feb 17, 2001, Internal Ref. #1.290.1.16537.1]

Individual: Hoffman, Phillip
Race: W
Age: 73
Birth place: VA
Township: Portland Twp
Microfilm: Roll 1697, Page 155

Obituary Morgantown Post:

Philip Hoffman, father of one of the editors of the Post, died at his residence in Barbour County, WV at 6 o'clock on Thursday evening, January 09, age 82 years, 1 month, 9 days. He was for many years a resident of Monogalia County, and lived in what is the now Clinton District, the place of his nativity, he was the oldest son of John and Sarah Hoffman, who emigrated from Berks County, PA about the year 1795 or 1976, & settled on 'The Old Hoffman Farm' near Smithtown.

Newspaper Clipping: Phillip Hoffman, Father of one of the editors of the Post, died at his residence in Barbour County, West Virginia at 6 o'clock on Thursday evening, January 9th age 82 years, 1 month and 9 days. He was for many years a resident of Monongalia County and lived in what is now Clinton District, the place of his nativity. He was the oldest son of John and Sarah Hoffman, who emigrated from Berks County, Pa. about the year 1795 or 1796, and settled on the "Old Hoffman Farm" near Smithtown. In 1845 or 46 he moved to Preston County where he lived until about 5 years since, when he went to Barbour County. He was married in 1820 to Aletha Summers, daughter of Rev. Alexander Summers, of this county and raised to their majority 10 children, 8 of whom are still living. He leaves 8 children, 56 grandchildren, about 86 great-grandchildren, 3 sisters, and many friends to mourn his loss, but our loss is his gain, and we hope his troubles are over. "

From book "Hoffman Huffman 1741 - 1995" by Patsy Ann Brown

xiii. JOSEPH SUMMERS, b. June 04, 1816, Monogalia Co. VA; d. February 27, 1887; m. JULIA ANN TARLETON, September 01, 1836; b. Abt. 1812; d. 1879.

More About JOSEPH SUMMERS:
Burial: Mt. Zion Cemetery, Marques

More About JULIA ANN TARLETON:
Burial: Mt. Zion Cemetery, Marques

Hezekiah Summers

(Drafted as a minuteman, 17 August 1776)

A true
American Hero

Pension File
R10,304

James R. Bradley
Family Genealogist
STILL SEARCHING THE NEVER ENDING STORY...OUR PAST
5640 Wellfield Rd.
New Port Richey, FL, 34655
727-376-2576
JamesRBradley.com

ALEXANDER SUMMERS

Alexander Summers was born in Maryland on March 9, 1778. He married Mary Ann Vinagar, March 1797, in Frederick County Maryland. He appears on the census of Montgomery County Maryland in 1800 and is in Monongalia County Virginia (West Virginia) by 1810.

Alexander and Mary Ann were the parents of thirteen children according to the Summers Bible record. Mary Ann died February 29, 1832. Alexander married Sarah Stansbury the same year.

Alexander was a Methodist Protestant minister and took out a license to perform marriages in 1836 according to Monongalia County Court records. The names of his children suggest strong Christian affiliation: David and Jonathan who were twins, James, Chrystianna who died at the age of eight months, Elijah, Elisha, Rebecca, Elias, Joseph and Sarah who died at the age of 11 months by drowning in a wash tub of water.

Alexander Summers died April 12, 1847, in Monongalia County.

JANET M. JOHNSON
3105 WENDELL DR.
HASTINGS, NE 68901

HEZEKIAH SUMMERS

Hezekiah Summers was born September 23, 1750 in Prince Georges County Maryland, the son of Dent Summers. He is listed in the Frederick County Maryland Census of 1776, Northwest Hundred:

Hezekiah Summers age 26
Rebacker-32
William Dent-3
Benj (?) 1
Glaz, Charaty age 53
Elennor-23

Although the record does not specifically state it, Rebacker (Rebecca) was most likely his wife. No relationship is stated for Charaty Glaz and Elennor but it is possible they may have been Rebecca's mother and sister.

August 17, 1776, Hezekiah entered service as a Private in the Revólutionary War and served off and on until 1782. His Revolutionary War records indicate he was present at White Plains where the troops joined General Washington and engaged in battle against the British. He also served as a spy, watching the enemy soldiers along the Potomac River and as a guard at the barracks at Fredericktown, Md.

Hezekiah did not own land in Frederick County nor in Montgomery County where he appears on the 1790 and 1800 Census records.

About 1807 Hezekiah and his family moved to Monongalia County Virginia (now West Virginia) where he appears on the census records until 1830.

Monongalia County records do not show a land record for Hezekiah nor a probate record. His Revolutionary War service records where he filed for a pension in 1834 and his widow filed for a Bounty Land Warrant in 1855, provide the most complete records of his life. It includes the date and place of his birth, his experiences as a Revolutionary War soldier and that he resided in Montgomery County Maryland until about 1807 when he came to Monongalia County Virginia. He apparently was widowed and then married Ruth Dauson April 13, 1831. He died in Monongalia County June 7, 1836, at age 85. Ruth Summers, still a widow, applied for a Bounty Land Warrant in 1855. She apparently died January 19, 1866, Monongalia County West Virginia at age 80.

The census records indicate Hezekiah had at least seven children, perhaps four boys and three girls. Without a will or other legal records it is difficult, it not impossible, to determine the names of these children. The two oldest sons ~~were~~ William Dent and Benjamin according to the 1776 census. Benjamin married Verlinda Beckwith October 12, 1798, in Montgomery Count, Maryland. I have no further documentation on Benjamin or William Dent Summers.

J. E. Summers in his letters written in 1936 provide the only documentation (family tradition) that we are descended from Hezekiah...... "My great grandfather Hezekiah was a Revolutionary Soldier..... from the state of Maryland came my great grandfather to West Virginia." Mr. Summers erred, however, and missed a generation by calling Hezekiah his great grandfather.

J. E. Summers states Elias, Elijah, Elisha, Jonathan, David, etc., were the children of Hezekiah. The Summers Bible record, however, names all these children and states they are the children of Alexander Summers. Further evidence that they were not the sons of Hezekiah, but were quite likely his grandchildren, is the age differences. Hezekiah was about age 50 to age 70 when these men were born.

Evidence that Alexander was the son of Hezekiah includes the fact that he resided near to Hezekiah in Montgomery County Maryland in 1800 and next appears residing near to him in Monongalia County Virginia on the 1810 census. Alexander was 28 years younger than Hezekiah.

It is possible these men were also Hezekiah's sons:

John Summers married Mary Ann Hardy, December 8, 1810, Monongalia County West Virginia Hez Summers was surety

Phillip Summers m. Barbara Sower, October 19, 1798, Frederick County Maryland. A Phillip Summers died in Monongalia County West Virginia in 1815 (Inventory dated 30 Sep 1815).

These men resided in Monongalia County by 1820, relationship to Hezekiah unknown: Nathan, Thomas, and William Summers.

The place of burial of Hezekiah Summers is assumed to be Monongalia County West Virginia.

Sources:

Revolutionary War record
1776 Maryland census
Federal census records 1790 to 1830.
J. E. Summers
County marriage and probate records.
Summers Family Bible record

JANET M. JOHNSON
3105 WENDELL DR.
HASTINGS, NE 68901

HEZEKIAH SUMMERS
APPLICATION FOR REVOLUTIONARY WAR PENSION
R10304

Monongalia County
State of Virginia   to Wit

On the 5th day of March 1834, I formally offered **Hezekiah Summers**, a resident of the county and state of aboved, said in his 84th year of age, who being duly sworn according to law before me, *Anthony Smith an acting Justice of the Peace*, in and from the county of Monongalia, in the State of Virginia, an oath on his oath, made the following declaration, in order to obtain the benefit of the provisions make by the act of congress so offered, June 7th, 1832. That **he was drafted the 17th day of August, 1776**, in the County of Montgomery, in the State of Maryland and placed under Capt William Baley, the Regiment was commanded by Col William Beacons, and commanded by Gen James Smallwood, was marched to the white plains, joyned **Gen Washington** where we had an engagement with the enemy, from *thence to Baltimore and he was marching into New Jersey*, the was marched and counter marched and thence he was marched into Pennsylvania and he was discharged in writing on the 19th day of October 1776 at Philadelphia, which discharge he has long since lost and that on the day of September, 1777, he volunteered under Capt George Beal as a spy was called a lookout to guard the Potomack river and served as such, till 18th day of October 1778. That on the 13th day of March 1779, he volunteered under Capt Christopher Kisen, was employed in spying and watching the Potomack river to prevent the enemy from landing till the 25 June 1780. That on the 9th day of may, 1781 he volunteered under Capt John Maurdock and was employed in watching this movement of the enemy till the surrender of Lord Cornwallace, 19th day of October 1781. When he marched to *Hals Fense* to receive the prisoners and Capt James to the barracks at Frederick Town in Maryland was employed in the service as a spy till the 10th day of April, 1782. That he has no documentary evidence and that he knowns of no person whose testimony he procure who can testify to his service and that he was not employed in any civil pursuit during this above tours. He hereby relinquish every claim to a pension or annuity except the present and declares that his name is not on the pension roll of the agency of any state that he was **born on the 23rd day of September 1750** has a record of his age made by the father that he was born in **Prince George's county in the State of Maryland** which record he believes to be true that he was living in Montgomery county the state of Maryland when he was drafted and that when discharged returned home to Montgomery, Prince Georges County, **that he known Gen Washington**, Gen Green, Gen Morgan and seen allmost all the officers during Revolutionary War that he removed to Monongalia county in the state of Virginia, 24 years ago and has resided there ever since.

Hezekiah Summers

Sworn to and subscribed this day and year of our lord before me.
Anthony Smith, J.P.

We, Joseph Shackelford, a clergyman, residing in the county of Monongalia, in the state of Virginia and Robert Henderson residing in the same county and state, he by testify that we are well acquainted with **Hezekiah Summers**, who has subscribed and sworn to this before declaration that we believe him to be on his 84th year of age the he is respected and beloved in the neighborhood where he resides to have been a **soldier in the Revolutionary War** and we concur in that opinion.

Joseph Shackelford
Robert Henderson

(continued) Co NC & sol d there 9 Mar 1839 or 11 Mar 1838 or 1839 & his wid appl there 11 Feb 1854 & in 1854 the only living child of dec'd sol was Elizabeth Boykin who was a daughter by sol's 1st wife (not named), in 1854 a James C. Boykin & Irvin Boykin testified before an H.W. Boykin a JP for Nash Co NC & in 1854 an Alsey Boykin was referred to (no relationships were given), in 1854 a Wiley Grizzell or Grizzill aged 39 & Pidy Morris aged 48 stated they were wid's only "surviving" children

SULSER, William or William Sulcer, VA Line, Jane, W9687, see William Sulcer

SULT, David or David Solt, PA Line, S40537, appl 23 Apr 1818 Union Co PA aged 62, sol enl in Northampton Co PA, in 1820 sol had a wife aged 70 & he referred to 5 sons who "had left him", no names given

SUMERLIN, Winburn or Winburn Summerlin, NC Line, Milly, sol m Milly (--) in Feb 1786 & sol d 24 Apr 1842 & his wid appl 2 Jun 1843 in Wilkes Co NC aged 89, children were; Griffin b 11 Oct 1787, Susanna b 1 Sep 1789, Miles b 16 May 1790, Lazarus b 26 Dec 1792, Hannah b 17 Dec 1794, Thomas b 7 May 1797 & Sarrah b 27 Nov 1799, sol had orig appl in 1832 in Wilkes Co NC, sol was b in 1760 in Bertie Co NC, in 1780 sol went from Wilkes Co NC to Washington Co NC (now in TN) where he enl & later returned to Wilkes Co NC, sol's daughter Susannah Tribell made aff'dt in 1843 in Wilkes Co NC, also shown with the family data was Rufus Sumerlin b 1 Mar 1826 but no kinship was given, an Emily Alspaugh & Susanah Tribell were witnesses to wid's application

SUMMER, George or George A., SC Line, S22001, sol was b 28 Oct 1760 in Lexington Dist SC & he lived there at enl & he always lived there & he appl there 26 Sep 1832, sol had srv under a Capt John A. Summer but no relationship was given, the Rev sol George A. Summer died in Oct 1834

SUMMERFORD, William, SC Line, Piety, W11576, sol was b in Kershaw Dist SC & he lived in York Dist SC at enl & he appl there in 1832 aged 70 yrs, sol m Piety Dabbs in 1811 or 1812 in York Dist SC & sol d there in 1844 & his wid appl 26 Aug 1836 in Monroe Co MS aged 66

SUMMERLIN, Winburn or Winburn Sumerlin, NC Line, Milly, W4346, see Winburn Sumerlin

SUMMERS, David, CT Line, Mary, W2877, sol m Mary Nichols 9 Dec 1779 both were of Fairfield Co CT, sol d 10 Apr 1816, wid appl 27 Aug 1838 Susquehanna Co PA aged 77 a res of New Milford PA, sol lived at North Stratford in Fairfield Co CT at enl

Elizabeth former wid, VA Line, George Lewis, W7218, BLW #26967-160-55 & BLW #108907-160-55, see George Lewis

Farrel, BLW #7832-100-1 Sep 1790 assignee Samuel Cooper, srv as a Pvt in Lamb's Arty (NY)

George, NC Line, Mary, W6606, sol enl in Caswell Co NC, he appl 15 Jun 1818 Fairfax Co VA aged 55, sol m Mary Presgraves 24 Mar 1789 in Fairfax Co VA & sol d there 1 Sep 1838 &his wid appl there 17 Sep 1838 aged 70 & in 1843 she had moved to Loudoun Co VA, in 1820 sol referred to children; Rebecca 28, Daniel 21, Sarah 15 & Mary Ann aged 11, in 1843 Richard H. Summers was of Leesburg VA

Hezekiah, MD Line, Ruth, R10304, BLW #34588-160-55, sol was b 23 Sep 1750 in Prince George Co MD & he lived in Montgomery Co MD at enl, sol appl 27 Mar 1834 Monongalia Co VA, sol m Ruth Dawson 13 Apr 7 Jun 1831 in Monongalia Co VA & sol d there in 1836 & his wid appl 10 May 1855 in Marion Co VA

Horsey, MD Line, S7664, sol was b in Somerset Co MD & he lived there at enl & shortly after the Rev he moved to Accomac Co VA where he was married (wife not named) & he was living there when he appl 12 Sep 1851 aged 89 & sol d in said Co on 25 Feb 1852 leaving no widow but left children; John, Horsey, Mary, Elizabeth, Sally & William Summers

James, NC Line, Lavina or Levina, W2192, BLW #61059-160-55, wid appl 2 Mar 1853 Wilson Co TN aged 75, sol lived in Caswell Co NC at enl & sol m there to Lavina or Levina Gillespie 6 Feb 1803 & their 1st child Lydia was b in Nov 1804, sol d 21 Jan 1820 in Wilson Co TN, on 7 Mar 1786 sol had rec'd 857 acres of of land (grant #193) from the state of NC in Daivdson Co TN on the Red River, on 27 Feb 1861 wid had moved to Saline Co IL to live with her children who had moved there, wid had appl for BLW 16 Feb 1857 in Wilson Co TN

James, VA Line, R10306, sol was b in Jul 1755 in Ireland & he lived in Goochland Co VA at enl & after the Rev he lived in NC & GA, he appl 4 Nov 1833 in Jones Co GA

John, BLW #11718-100-29 Nov 1790 to Frederick Hall adm'r, srv as a Pvt in the MD Line

John, MD Line, Ann, R10303, sol m Ann Claggett 8 Dec 1774 & their children were; Charles Clagget Summers b 7 Sep 1775, Mary b in Sep 1777, John b 24 Nov 1779, Ruth b 17 Mar 1782, Bassil b 11 Sep 1783, Ann b 14 Nov 1785, Joseph b 15 Mar 1789, Solomon b 21 Apr 1792 & William b 1 Oct 1794, sol d 17 Apr 1808, Clagett family data shown; Sarah b 18 Jan 1750, An or Ann or Nancy (sol's wife) b 28 Jun 1753, Hery b 18 Mar 1755, Malinda b 1 Feb 1757, Joh (no n) b 23 Nov 1795, Thomas b 1 Mar 1761 & the father of these children was Charles Clagett & he was b 23 Aug 1729, other Summers family data was; Mary Ann Summers b 2 Apr 1815, Margit Summers b 24 Sep 1816, Solomon Summers b 2 Jan 1819, Jaine Summers b 8 Dec 1822 then James Elfoney b 7 Nov 1826 was shown, William D. Summers b 16 Sep 1829, in 1844 a Zackariah Summers aged 81 was of Iredell Co NC but no relationship was given, sol's sis Tabitha Tomlinson was of Iredell Co NC in 1852, in 1856 an R.A. Summers was of Iredell Co NC but no relationship was given, sol had enl in Montgomery Co MD & near the end of the Rev sol moved to Rowan Co NC, sol & wid had m in Fredericktown MD & sol d 17 Apr 1808 in Iredell Co NC & his wid appl there 24 Jun 1844 aged 91 yrs, wid was dec'd in 1856 (date of death was not given)

John, srv as a Capt in the NC Line, BLW #2094-300-15 Nov 1791, no papers

John, NC & VA Line, S31999, sol was b 20 or 26 May 1762 in Fairfax Co VA & he lived there at enl & he moved with his father (not named) after his 1st service to Caswell Co NC & also enl there & after the Rev he moved to Wilkes Co GA & in 1803 he moved to Clarke Co GA where he appl 20 Nov 1832

John, VA Line, Agnes, W3051, sol was b 26 Jul 1764 & he m Agnes daughter of Charles Bell on 26 Oct 1787 & she was b 10 Feb 1767 & their children were; Susanna b 6 May 1789, Thomas b 21 May 1791, Jesse b 15 Mar 1793, Benjamin b 8 May 1795, Lewey b 19 May 1797, Nancy b 7 Mar 1799, Mason b 6 Feb 1801, Mary b 13 Jan 1805, John, Jr. b 2 Nov 1807 & Emerson B. b 25 Mar 1810, also shown was Mary Green b 22 May 1821, sol was b in Prince William Co VA, sol enl in Frederick Co VA & he appl 3 Sep 1832 Fleming Co KY, sol d 13 Aug 1835 & his wid appl 27 Jul 1846 in Fleming Co KY, a grandson W.I. or W.J. Summers (a son of sol's son Jesse Summers) was of Platte Co MO in 1878

John, VA Line, R10308, sol was b in Mar 1760 in Augusta Co later Rockbridge Co VA & at age of 13 he moved with his parents to Washington Co VA & he enl there then moved to Fayette Co KY then to Clark Co KY then to Green Co KY then to Barren Co KY & in 1812 moved to Warren Co TN & in 1816 moved to Jackson Co AL & he appl 3 Feb 1833 & was still living there on 31 Jul 1837

There are many Summers listed throughout Americas early times. Research tells me that their are many origins of Summers. The English (and there are many), the Dutch and German lines. The names Summers is spelled various way and in some cases I have Summers that changed the spelling on purpose. So Summers, Somers and Summer may all be in the same line. Plus in some cases one line of summers marries into another line of summers. The above is just one of many Summers coat of arms.

JOHN SUMMERS,1st

Your line of Summers are believed to come from England. The first reported Summers in your line was a John Summers. On 18 December 1671, a *Captain John Boddy...having transported 12 persons to Maryland to inhabit*, amongst whom was JOHN SUMMERS, *proved his right to 600 acres of land.*

John Summers was believed to be between 16 and 25 years of age (born about 1650), this being the age of most transported indentured servants. He would have faced a doubtful crossing of the Atlantic. A most dangerous thing at those times, where sickness, on board fires and ship wreaks were only some of the fears. The crossing if it went well would have taken 2 months. Most of the time spent below decks in cramped quarters with little light, sanitation or ventilation. May died of disease on these journeys and John would had to have the true Pioneer spirit to make this trip.

John showed himself to be a ruggard Individualist, by 1682 he was already paying ground rent (tax) on 120 acres of land called ***Pitchcraft.*** It was on the *Westside of the Patuxent River in the freshes*, in Calvert County, later called Prince Georges' County. As most people of the time he was a Planter (Farmer) by trade. He also was active in the community. He testified for a Edward Gold (a Negro) and his freedom in June 1692. He served on Jury duty twice in 1698, and was appointed overseer of the Mount Calvert Hundred (a piece of property). He was married to a Rebecca Dent and had 4 children; *William Summers*, ***John Summers 2nd***, *Sarah Summers* and *Lucy Summers*. He died about 1705 and left his estate to his Wife Rebecca. When she remarried (to a Henry Mackbee in 1708) the estate went to his two sons. Rebecca died about 1711.

JOHN SUMMERS, 2nd

John Summers, 2nd was born in Prince Georges county Maryland about 1685 and like his father he was a Planter. But John Summers the 2nd was a visionary and had a desire to grow with this new land. By 1709 he indentured (brought) his brother Williams' half of Pitchcraft for 1,500 pounds of tobacco. It seems William Summers had some money problems and in 1708 the Sheriff was after him for a owed debt back in 1707 for the sum of 550 pounds of tobacco. It seems he was not at home when the sheriff called. By 1713 John Summers, 2nd married a Mary Moore, daughter of James Moore, Sr. and brought the land adjoining his fathers-in-laws called Moores Adition from a Thomas Clagatt. Moores Adition is 231 acres on the west side of the Patuxent River in the woods and in the fork of Piscataway Branch. John the 2nd and his father-in-law must of got along well because in July 1723 James Moore indentured (sold) a tract of land (35 acres) called Child's Portion to John the 2nd. John the 2nd then deeded the land back to him (James Moore) for "natural affection and loving duty". Besides working a growing farm, he and Mary Moore Summers had 13 children; *John Summers the 3rd, George Summers, William Summers,* ***Dent Summers****, Thomas Summers, Benjamin Summers, James Summers, Joseph Summers, Mary Summers Wheat, Rebeckah Summers King, Rachel Summers Johnson, Ruth Summers Riggs, Jemima Summers Caton*,. All of them out lived him, except James Summers who died in 1761. John and Mary Summers died in 1769.

DENT SUMMERS

The fourth son of John Summers the 2nd, born in Prince Georges county, Maryland in 1727. He grew up on the farm with large extended family of brothers and sisters and aunts and uncles. He married about age 22 (about 1749) to a Mary Ann Claggett. On 18 April 1763 he obtained 100 acres of land called *Joseph's Park*. It was located on the east side of a Rock Creek Branch. When his parents died in 1769, he was willed 50 acres of the *Adition*, a portion laid off at the lower end next to the Wood Yard. He needed this land because he and Mary Ann went on to have 9 children; ***Hezekiah Summers****, Mary Ann Summers Hardy, Sarah Summers White, Paul Summers, James Dent Summers, Zadock Summers, John Summers, Margaret Summers Hoskins* and *William Dent Summers*. Dent Summers was a private, suspicious and bit of a obnoxious man. In 1776 when the new *America* commissioned a census of all its people. Dent Summers told the census taker there was 9 in the family but refused to give their ages. When they came back again to do another census in 1790, he was more corporative and listed his kids along with 5 slaves. In 1802 his wife Mary Ann died and he followed shortly in 1809.

HEZEKIAH SUMMERS

Hezekiah Summers was born in Prince Georges county Maryland on 23 September 1750. He and his brothers work the land and he married a Rebecker Glaz, daughter of John Glaz, on about 1772. Together they had 8 children; *William Dent Summers, Benjamin Summers,* ***Alexander Summers****, John S. Summers, Phillip Summers, Thomas Summers, Margaret Summers* and *Nathan Summers*. Life appeared to be normal but these were not normal time. A nation was being born and Hezekiah soon found himself drafted on 17 August 1776 to fight in the Revolutionary War. He served 4 times in 6 years for a total of two and half years service. He fought in New Jersey, Pennsylvania and was there when Lord Cornwallace surrendered. He stated he personally knew General Washington and was a true Minuteman (enclosed is one of the letters for his pension request). He returned home after the war and was prosperous property owner, planter. He was living in Northwest Hundred, Frederick County, by 1790 (Census) he had 10 slaves. It is believed that Rebecker Glaz Summers died about 1800 and the family was beginning to venture out to find their own lives. Hezekiah Summers children went in many different direction but most went to the western wilderness of Virginia (now West Virginia). Hezekiah moved to Monongalia County Virginia about 1810. It is believed that Hezekiah went west, to be near his children and grandchildren. On 13 April 1831 he married a Ruth Dawson in Monongalia county, Virginia, 30 plus years his younger. Both he and her petitioned the government for his war pension and land grants with no success. He died in 1836 in Monongalia County, Virginia. Ruth Dawson Summers lived on to about 1866.

ALEXANDER SUMMERS

Alexander Summers was born in Prince Georges county Maryland on 9 March 1778. He married a Mary Ann Vinagar from Ireland in Frederick County, Maryland on 25 March 1797. He moved to Monongalia county Virginia about 1807. Together they had 13 children; *David and Jonathan Summers (Twins), Aletha Summers Huffman, James Summers, Chrystianna Summers, Elijah Summers, Elisha Summers, Rebecca Summers Baker, Elias S. Summers, Sarah Summers, Mary Ann Summers Swisher,* ***Joseph Summers*** *and Elizabeth Summers Snider.* Alexander was a religious man and in 1814 he and three other men obtain a small parcel of land "for the settlement in which they may live in the religious order for the promotion of the gospel". (The churchs' foundation and graveyard exist today at the New Pisgah Church one half mile from Little Falls in Monongalia County off State Route # 73). Alexander Summers went on to become an ordained Methodist Minister in Morgantown Virginia on 19 November 1832. Alexander and Mary Ann Summers then lived in Marion county near Catawba. Mary Ann died in 1832. It is then believed that Alexander married a Sarah Stansberry but no addition data is available.

There has been much written and not written about Alexanders' father Hezekiah, I have several records that support Alexander as Hezekiahs' son (letters of J.E. Summers 1936) but there is also other data that argues that point (letter of Mrs. Paul L. Summers 1950). I believe the early documents are more accurate and supportive, but as of this writing NO undisputable evidence has been found.

JOSEPH SUMMERS

Joseph Summers was born 4 June 1816 in Monongalia County, Virginia. Joseph did not follow in his fathers foot steps and become a preach. He had a love for the land and was a farmer. On 1 September 1836 he married Julia Ann Tarleton from Maryland. She was born in 1812 and the daughter of Caleb Tarleton. Together they had seven children; *Alcinda Summers May, Thomas Marshall Summers, Elijah Summers, Alexander Summers, Jr., William Caleb Summers,* ***James Summers*** and *Sarah Elizabeth Summers Wofle\Bomer*. In 1853 we find Joseph and Julia Ann Summers on 164 acres of land that they brought from Mary Ann's brother, Elijah Tarleton in Preston County, near Marques. This place was known as the Summers Place, later the Joe summers place. It is said that Joseph Summers was an honest man in all his dealing and would do no man harm. He was a Christian who attended the Mount Zion church on the hill over looking Marques. One Winter, when Typhoid fever hit the area he died on 27 February 1887. Mary Ann Tarleton Summers had died previous in 1879 and he was laid to rest next to her at the graveyard at the Mount Zion church in Marques. Joseph Summers left his land to be divided between his two sons; William Caleb Summers and James Summers.

JAMES SUMMERS.

James Summers was born 2 July 1850 in Preston County Virginia. He was crippled. probably a form of spina bifida. Letters state he "was crippled in the legs that were drawn crooked by white swelling". He could not straighten them and learned to walk bent on over on his hands and feet, much like an animal. It is said that he used wooden blocks, carrying them in his hands to help him walk bent over. In spite of the handicap, he was very energetic, attended school and was a bright student. His farther even rigged a special saddle for him, so he be able to ride a horse and be more independent.

When he was quite young a man by the name of Braley come to the community to teach music. Braley organized a singing school at the Mt. Zion church which James attended along with his family. James had wanted to attend this singing school but his farther, a man of hard work, had a different view of singing and was against it. Julia his mother also had a different opinion, she helped James attend the school secretly, even sneaking out the horse so he could go and practice. The school developed a choir of sorts that went around to homes and sang for people. James though deprived in one physical aspect excelled in others. Soon he was the leader of the choral group. His farther noticed his sons absence and did some inquiring. When he found out what his son had accomplished, he was truly surprised and then just grinned. After that his farther would help him in any way he could. In time James became a music teacher. He traveled to surrounding counties (Barbour, Randolph, Tucker and Preston counties). James was well liked and it is said the people would travel miles just to hear him sing. He was an industrious man that could work the farm. He could hoe, plant corn, do gardening, milk and feed cows and mow the grass. He was a man of his time, **a survivor**.

It must have been on one of these travels that he met his future bride **Elmira (Almira) Francis Knapp**. On 14 October 1877 he married her at her parents home in Barbour County. They then went and settled on the Summers farm.

James and Elmira had five sons; ***Joseph Willis Summers****, Ira Henson Summers, Charles Robert Summers, John Wesley Summers and an infant that died very young*. In February 1887, his farther died and left him the half the acres of the farm to him. Sadly, 2 months later, on 22 April 1887, James Summers also died of Typhoid. He is buried in the Mt Zion church cemetery, on the hill top, near Marquess in Preston county West Virginia. In 1947 his wife Elmira Francis (fannie) Knapp-Summers-Hurshman died. She is also buried at Mt Zion.

Joseph Willis Summers

Joseph Willis Summers was born February 21, 1879, on the old Summers homestead near the small town of Marquess, Preston County (WV). He attended the local school and spent his early years on the farm

In 1899 he went to Moore (Tucker County) and was employed by W.H. Dasher lumber Company and later by the Chafey company as a edging machine operator (a millwright). Later he worked in a store in Morgantown and became friends with the owner William H. Burke. So much so, that married his 16 year old daughter, *Iva Rebecca Burke* on 18 May 1902 at Montrose in Randolph county. To this Union was born 3 children, *Leroma Blanche Summers,* ***William Clair Summers*** *and Christina Irene Summers.*

In his job as a millwright he went to many places. 1906 he worked for the Tyson & McClure Lumber company and went to Glady and Beverly WV. Then in 1912 he went to Black mountain North Carolina (Near Ashville) for the Pereley & Crockett Lumber company. During this time he became a 32rd degree Mason and sought and found his claim to fame. In that he was very active in many organizations and societies. He was also a vivid genealogist, a member of the Sons of the American Revolution, being a descendent of Adam Arbogast. Adam Arbogast was a colonial soldier, an Indian Spy (today's equivalent of a recon scout). It is evident that he owned land in North Carolina and West Virginia. It is believed and said that he obtained these lands by paying taxes owed by relatives then claiming the land as his own. For these and other deeds he was referred to as the "scoundrel".

In 1919 he came back to Morgantown and purchased property in the Flatts section where he lived with his family and mother. He worked construction until 1925. Later he divorced his wife and continued to live in the Flatts with his mother. From 1925 to 1942 he worked for the city of Morgantown. In 1942 he worked for the University of West Virginia and retired 1 July 1948. He continued to be active in the community until his death on 9 November 1956. He is buried at East Grove Cemetery in Morgantown. In his Will he left $10 to his grandchildren and payed of a loan his son William Clair incurred and left him $10. He left 3 acres of land to the West Virginia University Medical department. To his beloved Mason Lodge he left $100 and bequeathed that his house, land and household items, go the Masons' in order to build another Lodge. In September 1965 they open the new *Joseph Willis Summers Masonic Lodge # 173* at the corner of Windsor Avenue and Burroughs Street in the Suncrest area of Morgantown.

Robert Summers [illegible]

Hezekiah Summers [illegible]

Capt. [illegible]

Col. [illegible]

[illegible] Ma.

Private

[illegible]

War, Revolution

[illegible] appl. for Pen. [illegible]

Va. Re. 1832

Ad. 160 a[illegible] July 11 [illegible]

[illegible]

Thomas G. Walton

[illegible]

Vol. 8-2-165

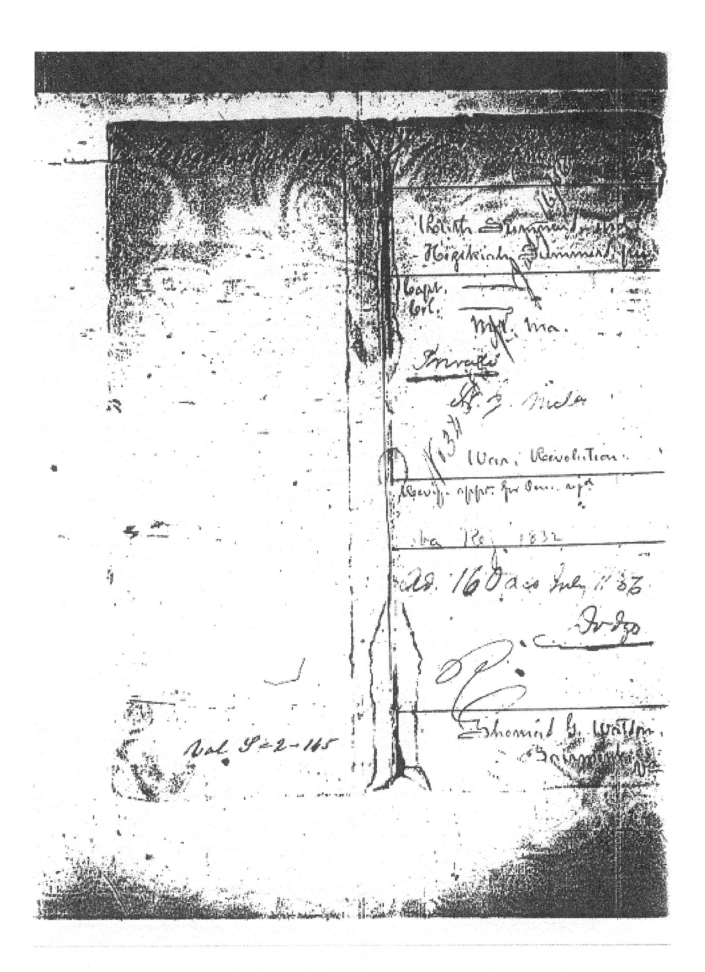

SUMNER:
Ebenezer Sr: b 8-14-1737 CT d 10-12-1 VT m Person Pease Capt CT
Ebenezer: b 4-16-1749 MA d 4-22-1823 MA m Catherine Smith Sgt MA
Edward: b 6-14-1746 MA d 10-28-1829 MA m Elizabeth Clapp PS MA
Ezra: b 8-7-1752 MA d p 1791 m Mrs. Mary Kane Davis Pvt MA
Francis: b c 1750 NC d a 6-10-1807 NC m Lurena --- Pvt CL NC
George: b 4-16-1744 MA d 3-16-1796 MA m Margaret Lewis Pvt MA
Hezekiah: b 8-13-1757 CT d p 1796 m Alethea Barker Pvt MA
Hezekiah: b c 1750 d 1810 VA m X Sol PS VA
Hopestill: b 9-9-1746 MA d 12-25-1826 ME m Mary Rhodes CS MA
Jabez: b 4-2-1759 MA d 2-11-1812 MA m (1)Susanna Withington (2)Elizabeth Gay Cpl CL MA
James: b 12-10-1718 d 8-29-1795 MA m (1)Mary Bigelow (2)Mary Jones PS MA
Jethro: b 3-15-1758 VA d p 4-6-1830 NC m Elizabeth Turner Capt NC
Joel: b 7-31-1761 MA d 4-3-1813 PA m Elizabeth Warren Everett Cpl MA
John: b 1736 CT d 8-6-1804 NY m Mehitable Perry Capt CT
John: b 1747 MA d p 1796 m X Cpl MA
John Jr: b 4-26-1760 MA d 3-19-1839 MA m Hannah Evans Pvt MA PNSR
John Sr: b 8-1-1705 MA d 1787 MA m (1)Susanna Stevens (2)Jedidah Smith PS MA
Joseph: b 1761 d 12-30-1827 GA m Mary Kight Sol GA
Joseph: b 7-29-1760 MA d 12-7-1846 MA m Ruth Legg Pvt MA PNSR
Joseph: b 1-19-1740 CT d 12-9-1824 MA m Lucy Williams PS MA
Joseph: b c 1748 VA d 4- -1795 NC m Martha Philip Sol NC
Robert: b 9-18-1761 CT d 11-19-1845 NY m Jemima Younglove Sgt CT PNSR
Samuel Sr: b 11-13-1695 MA d 2-8-1782 CT m Elizabeth Griffin CS CT
Samuel: b 12-29-1732 MA d 10-11-1813 MA m (1)X (2)Elizabeth Williams PS MA
Seth: b 7-8-1735 MA d 5-2-1814 MA m (1)Elizabeth Davis (2)Mary Gay Capt MA
Shuball: b 11-11-1759 CT d 4-1-1841 NY m Lucy Grover Pvt CT PNSR
Thomas: b --- SC d 12-22-1791 GA m Anna Baker Sol GA
Thomas: b 6-2-1757 MA d 4-19-1825 OH m Elizabeth Holland Pvt MA
William: b 7-9-1757 CT d 11-19-1846 CT m Rebecca Arnold Sol CT
William: b 1-9-1761 CT d 7-21-1850 VT m Saviah Udall Pvt CT
William: b 8-6-1748 MA d 1-30-1836 MA m Mary Pond Lt MA

SUMNEY:
Jacob: b a 1762 PA d 1807 PA m Margaret --- Pvt PA

SUMPTER: SUMTER
George Sr: b --- VA d a 12- -1806 VA m Elizabeth Gross PS VA
John: b 1740 VA d p 12-12-1809 NC m Catherine --- Pvt VA
Thomas: b 12-15-1761/2 VA d 1-15-1846 m Lydia Kirkpatrick Pvt Fif NC PNSR
Thomas: b 8-14-1734 VA d 6-1-1832 SC m Mary Cantey Jameson BGen SC

DAR Read-

2856

SUMPTER: SUMTER
William: b a 1741 VA c 1828 NC m Judi

SUMWALT: see ZUMWALT

SUNDAY:
Adam: b 7-5-1759 PA d 4-14-1855 PA m Ma

SUNDERLAND:
Benjamin: b 1732 MD d 1780-90 MD m Eliz
David: b c 1735 d a 11-7-1809 PA m X PS
Joseph: b 1762 NY d 4-30-1838 PA m Eliz PNSR
Peter: b 1737 PA d 8-1-1827 OH m Cather
Samuel: b 5-4-1752 CT d 7-28-1842 VT m PNSR

SUNDERLIN:
Samuel: b 8-26-1758 NY d p 11-21-1837 P Pvt NY PNSR

SUPLEE: SUPPLEE
Andrew: b 9-13-1734 PA d 1806 PA m (1)Ma (2)Rachel Davis Sol PA
Jacob: b 1759 PA d 3-18-1825 PA m Rebecc
John: b 1730 PA d 1805 PA m Sarah Robert
Peter: b 9-2-1745 PA d 1-24-1778 PA m Su

SUPLER:
John: b 11-3-1757 PA d 6-14-1835 PA m Ra PNSR

SURBER:
Jacob: b 1744 PA d 8-23-1839 OH m (1)Mrs Coffeld (2)Mrs. Barbara (Mayer) Fensle
Joseph: b 1749 VA d a 10- -1825 VA m (1) Ann Stevens Pvt VA

SURFACE: see ZERFASS

SURRATT: SARRATT
John: b c 1763 NC d 9-7-1834 TN m Mary M
John: b 1750-60 WL d a 9-10-1830 SC m Na
Joseph: b --- NC d p 9-1-1801 NC m X CS

SUSONG:
Andrew: b c 1737/8 FR d 1826 TN m Barbar

SUTER: SUDER
John: b 1-16-1744 ST d 11-12-1794 MD m S
John: b 1755 VA d c 1820 VA m Elizabeth

SUTHER:
Samuel: b 5-22-1722 SW d 9-28-1788 SC m

SUTHERLAND: SOUTHERLAND
Alexander: b c 1730 NY d 10-12-1777 NY m NY
Andrew: b 3- -1728 NY d p 9-11-1794 NY m Pvt PS NY
Daniel: b 3- -1753 NC d p 1840 AR m (1) Rysedon (3)Grace Holeman Pvt NC PNSR
Daniel: b 5-9-1755 ST d 1-5-1792 NC m A
Daniel: b 1749 NC d 6-14-1831 NC m --- N
Daniel: b 1745 ST d 8-20-1820 PA m Sarah
David: b 1722 CT d 4-10-1794 NY m Judith
David Jr: b 9-20-1735 NY d 9-6-1799 NY m NY
David: b 8-31-1757 NY d 9-23-1828 NY m L
David Sr: b a 1703 NY d 1778 NY m Mary M
George: b c 1730 d a 6-18-1804 VA m Mary
George: b 8- -1761 ST d a 1-25-1847 VA m Shores (2)Mary Herndon Pvt Drm VA

857

PRINCE GEORGE'S COUNTY, MARYLAND

INDEX TO REGISTER

OF

KING GEORGE'S PARISH

1689 - 1801

PART I

2 SUIT, Nathaniel m. June 24, 1752 to Mary Burch page 349

248 Nathaniel b. March 10, 1756 son Nathaniel & Mary Burch 349

272 Oliver Burch b. August 1, 1773 son of Nathaniel & Mary 359

272 Susanna m. June 27, 1791 to Henry Burch 266

248 Susanna b. December 26, 1770 dau. Nathaniel & Mary Burch 349

277 Susanna b. December 24, 1796 dau. of Oliver B. & Eleanor 394

248 SULAVIN, Charlotte bapt. November 6, 1768 dau. of Daniel & Ann 344

350 Isaac bapt. February 26, 1764 son of Thomas & Judey 322

272 SULOVAN, Judey bapt. April 18, 1762 dau. of Thomas & Judey 305

272 SUMERS, Ann b. March 16, 1761 dau. of George & Elizabeth 306

302 Gorge b. August 26, 1759 son of Gorge & Elizabeth 306

272 SUMMERS, Ann bapt. May 17, 1752 dau. of George & Elizab eth 277

248 Ann bapt. ——1761 dau. of George & Elizabeth 303

2 Ann Verlinder Coxson b. December 6, 1791 dau. of Eleven & Elizabeth 370, 372

352

353 Benjamin b. October 13, 1783 son of Jonathan & Ann 357

389 Grace bapt. July 20, 1766 dau. of Benjamin & Grace 339

355 James b. July 18, 1761 son of James & Mary 303

392 James Dent bapt. ——1761 son of Dent & Mary Ann 303

375 John m. February 27, 1794 to Rebecca Scarce 387

349 John Gwynn b. February 12, 1786 son of Jonathan & Ann 357

349 John Lutten bapt. April 4, 1764 son of Benjamin & Grace 318

349 John Smith b. October 2, 1748 son of John & Mary 271

349 Joseph b. August 31, 1793 son of Paul & Susanna 375

349 Judson b. March 3, 1796 son of Eleven & Elizabeth 401

349 Letisha Lewis b. Sept. 25, 1796 dau. of Nathan & Sarah 401

39. Levin (see Eleven) m. Dec. 31, 1786 to Elizabeth Willcoxon 261
funeral Dec. 15, 1796 398

374 Mary b. January 7, 1750 dau. of John & Mary 271

SUMMERS, Nathaniel b. December 27, 1772 son Josias & Jeremiah 358

Nathaniel m. January 2, 1793 to Sarah Scarce 392

Reason Scarce b. June 7, 1795 son John & Rebecah 393

Thos. Hanson b. August 5, 1793 son of William & Anne 375

William b. May 3, 1792 son of William & Ann 371

William Bowie b. April 7, 1797 son of John & Rebecah 402

SUMMONS, Hanson b. February 24, 1798 son of Joannah 397

SUMMORS, John bapt. May 10, 1767 son of Nathan & Mary 339

SURBELY, William bapt. August 30, 1752 son William & Elizabeth 277

SUTAS, George b. December 3, 1763 bapt. February 19, 1764 son of Thomas & Ester 320, 318

John bapt. December 1, 1765 son of Thomas & Ester 323

SUTTON, Heneretta b. March 29, 1773 dau. William & Elizabeth 356

Henrietta confirmed November 23, 1793 383

John m. October 3, 1746 to Mary Beanes 271

John b. March 5, 1775 son of William & Elizabeth 356

John m. December 21, 1797 to Elizabeth Fenley 390

Mary m. October 27, 1795 to Charles F. Low 389

Mary Elisabeth b. December 19, 174- dau. of John & Mary 271

Sarah Ann b. September 24, 175- dau. of John & Mary 271

William b. May 8, 175- son of John & Mary 271

SWAIN, Eleanor b. September 4, 1772 dau. of Joshua & Alse 358

Elija b. September 10, 1769 son of Josua & Ayls 347

Lucy m. January 20, 1791 to Benjamin Hinniss 266

SWANN, Henritta Sarah b. February 24, 1797 dau. Henry & Lamentius 399

SWAYNE, Joseph Spires m. August 17, 1786 to Amelia Ann Hilton 261

SWEANEY, Drewsila b. March 8, 1761 bapt. September 6, 1761 dau. of Zachariah & Darkus 303

SWEARINGEN, Thos. m. January 7, 1790 to El^{s} Pope 264

INDEX TO REGISTER

PRINCE GEORGE'S PARISH

PRINCE GEORGE'S and MONTGOMERY COUNTIES

MARYLAND

48162,

Compiled by Helen W. Brown, (Mrs. Irvin C.)
Genealogical Records Chairman, Maryland State Society
Daughters of the American Revolution

1961

FOREWORD

This index has been compiled from the original Registers of Prince George's Parish at the Hall of Records in Annapolis, Maryland. The number appearing opposite each name is the page on which the entry may be found in the original records.

In Washington, D.C., copies have been placed at the Daughters of the American Revolution Library, where there is also a microfilm copy, and at the Library of Congress. In Maryland, copies may be seen at the Hall of Records in Annapolis, The Maryland Historical Society in Baltimore, and the Prince George's County Library, Hyattsville, Maryland.

#28-1 Reel 1 Maryland Chur.

The expense of binding has been bourne by the Maryland State Society, Daughters of the American Revolution.

STEWART, WALTER 96
m........12, 1809
Eleanor Gray

STEWART, WILLIAM'S child 100
buried September 5, 1799

STEWART, WM.
father of Levi

STILLINGS, DELILA SPRIGG 176
b. Decmmber 31, 1797
bapt. February 14, 1802
of Joseph and Eleanor

STILLINGS, ELEANOR 176
mother of Joseph Burch 176
" " Ruth Pierce 176
" " Delila Sprigg &
John Sprigg(twins) 176

STILLINGS, JOHN SPRIGG 176
b. December 31, 1797
bapt. February 14, 1802
of Joseph and Eleanor

STILLINGS, JOSEPH BURCH 176
b. January 3, 1792
bapt. February 14, 1802
of Joseph and Eleanor

STILLINGS, JOSEPH
father of Joseph Burch 176
" " Ruth Pierce,
Delila Sprigg and John
Sprigg (twins)

STILLINGS, RUTH PIERCE 176
b. February 1, 1794
bapt. February 14, 1802
of Joseph and Eleanor

STOKER, JOHN 156
father of Marsham 156

STOKER, MARSHAM 167
b. March 1, 1799
of John and Ruth

STOKER, RUTH 167
mother of Marsham

STRODE, MRS. ELIZA 302
took communion
December 28, 1823 about 26 years

SUMMERS, ALETHA 172
b. February 1, 1799
of Alex.r and Mary

SUMMERS, ALEX.R (wife Mary)
father of Aletha 172

SUMMERS, ANN
mother of Mary 159
" " Turesa 172

SUMMERS, ANNA(wife of John)
mother of Caleb Letton 162

SUMMERS, ANNA MARIA 165
b. February 8, 1799
of John L. and AnnaMaria

SUMMERS, ANNA MARIA
mother of Mary Letton 162
" " Anna Maria 165
" " Reubin 175

SUMMERS, CALEB LETTON 162
b. February 27, 1797
bapt. April 30, 1797
of John and Anna

SUMMERS, CLOE
mother of Maryann 174
" " Eliezer 182

SUMMERS, DENT aged 82
buried October 19, 1809 102

SUMMERS, MRS.
wife of Dent 101
buried November 18, 1802

SUMMERS, ELIEZER 182
b. August 15, 1803
bapt. October 2, 1803
of John and Cloe

SUMMERS, JEMIMA 181
b. January 22, 1803
bapt, May 29, 1803
of Paul and Sarah

SUMMERS, JOHN(wife Anna)
father of Caleb Letton 162

SUMMERS, JOHN L.
father of Mary Letton 162
" " Anna Maria 165
" " Reubin 175

SUMMERS, JOHN(wife Cloe)
father of Maryann 174
" " Eliezer 182

SUMMERS, URSULA 166
mother of Mahala

SUMMERS, KITTANN 191
b. April 17, 1810
bapt. August 12, 1810
of Walter W.C. and Sarah

SUMMERS, MAHALA 166
b. July 28, 1798
of Walter and Ursula

SUMMERS, MARY 159
b. June 23, 1792
bapt. August 19, 1792
of Zadok and Ann

SUMMERS, MARY 96
married 1811 Charles Crabb

SUMMERS, MARY(wife Alexander)
mother of Aletha 172

SUMMERS, MARYANN 174
b. February 5, 1801
bapt. June 14, 1801
of John and Cloe

SUMMERS, MARY LETTON 162
b. January 24, 1795
bapt. April 19, 1795
of Jno. L. and AnnaMaria

SUMMERS, PAUL(wife Sarah)
father of Sarah Garner 165
" " Saml. 174
" " Jemima 181

SUMMERS, REUBIN 175
b. August 11, 1801
bapt. October 4, 1801
of John L. and Ann Maria

SUMMERS, SAML. 174
b. October 15, 1800
bt. May 31, 1801
of Paul and Sarah

SUMMERS, SARAH GARNER 165
b. April 12, 1798
of Paul and Sarah

SUMMERS, SARAH
mother of Sarah Garner 165
" " Saml. 174
" " Jemima 181

SUMMERS, SARAH 191
mother of Kittann

SUMMERS, MRS. SUSAN M.
confirmed December 20, 1828
under name of
Miss Susan Johnson 303

SUMMERS, TURESA 172
b. June 27, 1800
of Zadok and Ann

SUMMERS, WALTER 166
father of Mahala

SUMMERS, WALTER W.C.(wife Sarah)
father of Kittann 191

SUMMERS, ZADOK
father of Mary 159
" " Turesa 172

SUSAN (blk) 205
b. 1820
bapt. June 29, 1825
dau. of Celia belonging
to Mrs. Thrift

SUTER, JOHN 102
buried April 27, 1807

SUTER, RUTH wife of James 102
buried April 12, 1806

SWAILS, ANN 182
mother of Ann Wilcoxon

SWAILS, ANN WILCOXON 182
b. February 3, 1803
bapt. October 1, 1803
of Robert and Ann

SWAILS, ROBERT 182
father of Ann Wilcoxon

SWAIN, MR. at Dr. Warfield's
buried July 28, 1803 101

SWAMLY, ELEANOR
child of Jacob 101
buried November 18, 1801

WAR DEPARTMENT,

Pension Office.

Sir:

The evidence in support of your claim under the act of June 7. 1832 has been examined and the papers are herewith returned. The following is a statement of your case in a tabular form. On comparing these papers with the following rules and the subjoined notes you will readily perceive that objections exist which must be removed before a pension can be allowed. The notes and the regulations will shew what is necessary to be done. Those points to which your attention is more particularly directed you will find marked in the margin with a brace (thus: }). You will, when you return your papers to this Department, send this printed letter with them; and you will, by complying with this request, greatly facilitate the investigation of your claim.

A Statement, *shewing the Service of* Hezekiah [illegible]

Period when the service was rendered.	Duration of the claimant's service. Years.	Months.	Days.	Rank of the claimant.	Names and rank of the Field officers under whom he served.	Age at present, and place of abode when he entered the service.	Proof by which the declaration is supported.
1776		2	2	Pri.	Capt Bales Col [illegible]	84 Md.	Traditionary.
1777		1	14	"	Capt G. Beall		
1779	1	3	8	Pri.	Capt Keen		
1781					Capt Murdock Col —		
9 Oct 1781		5	10	Pr.			
10 Apl 1782		5	22	"	do do.		

I am, respectfully,

Your obedient servant

JAMES L. EDWARDS,

Commissioner of Pensions.

No military service excepting [illegible] tradition. Statement not satisfactory,

State of Virginia
Monongalia County } To Wit

On this 27th day of March 1834 personally appeared Hezekiah Summers a resident of the County and State aforesaid in his 84th year of age who being duly sworn according to Law before me Anthony Smith an acting Justice of the peace in and for the County of Monongalia in the State of Virginia and doth on his oath make the following Declaration in order to obtain the benefit of the provisions made by the act of Congress passed June 7th 1832 That he was Drafted the 17th day of August 1776 in the County of Montgomery in the State of Maryland and placed under Capt William Baley the Regiment Was Commanded by Col William Deacons and Commanded by General James Smallwood Was marched to the White plains Joyned Gen Washington Where we had an ingagement with the Enemy from thence he was marched in to New Jersey then was marched and Counter march and from thence he was marched in to Pennsylvania and Was Discharged in Writing on the 19th day of October 1776 at Philidephia Witch Discharg he has long since lost and that on the 4th day of September 1777 he Volunteerd under Capt George Beall as a Spy or What was Called a lookout to gard the Potomack River and Served as sutch till 18th day of october 1778 that on the 13th day of march 1779 he Volunteerd under Capt Christopher Kisen Was imployed in Spying and Watching the Potomack River to prevent the Enemy from landing till the 25th day of June 1780 that on the 9th day of may 1781 he Volunteerd under Capt John Moaredock and was imployed in Watching the movements of the Enemy till the Surrender of Lord Cornwallis 19th day of October 1781 When he was marched to Nols Ferre to Receive the prisoners and helpt gard them to the

to the Barracks at Fredericktown in maryland and
Was inployed in that servis as a gard till the 10 th day of
Apriel 1782 that he has no documentary evidence
and that he knows of no person Whose testimony he can
procure Who can testify to his service and that he was
not inployed in any Civel pursuit during the same
tours He hereby relinquishes every Claim to a pension
or annuity Except the present and declares that his
name is not on the pension roll of the Agency of any
State That He was born on the 23d day of September
1750 has a record of his age made by his Father
that he was born in prince George County in the
State of maryland Witch record he believes to be true
that he Was living in ~~Prince~~ Montgomery ~~George~~ County and State
of maryland When he was Drafted and that When
Discharged returned home to ~~Prince~~ Montgomery ~~George~~ County
[illegible] that he ~~was~~
~~[illegible]~~ known Gen Washington Gen Green Gen morgan
and seen allmost all of the officers during the
Revolution War that he removed to monongalia
County in the State of Virginia
24 Years a go and has resided there Ever since
Since

Hezekiah Summers

Sworn to and subscribed the day and year aforesaid
before me —

Anthony Smith J P

We [illegible] Shackelford — a Clergyman residing in the County
of monongalia in the State of Virginia and
[illegible] residing in the same County and
State hereby Certifies that We are Well acquainted With
Hezekiah Summers Who has subscribed and sworn to
the above Declaration that We believe him to be
in his 84 th year of age that he is reputed and believed
in the neighborhood Where he resides to have been a soldier
of the Revolution — and that We concur in that opinion
[illegible]

INDEX
TO THE
PROBATE RECORDS
OF
PRINCE GEORGE'S COUNTY,
MARYLAND
1696 -1900

Compiled By
The Records Committee
Of The
Prince George's County
Genealogical Society, Inc.

1988

INDEX TO WILLS, ADMINISTRATIONS, AND INVENTORIES

DECEASED	EXECUTOR OR ADMINISTRATOR	DOC	DATE	BOOK	PAGE	FILE	REF
STONESTREET, THOMAS SR	STONESTREET, THOMAS	I	MAR 26 1772	GS	2 193		
STOOPS, ANDREW			JUL 27 1793				X
STOVER, GEORGE			AUG 12 1834				*
STREEKER, ADOLPH			AUG 18 1885			1280	
STREET, ELIZA.	CHURCH, JONATHAN H.	I	JUL 02 1776	GS	2 365		
STREET, ELIZABETH		I	JUL 02 1776	GS	2 365		L
STREET, ELIZABETH	CHURCH, JONATHAN M.	A	JUL 14 1776	JD	1 220		
STREET, ELIZABETH	CHURCH, JONATHAN M.	A	JUL 14 1776	JD	1 220		
STREET, JOHN			JUN 26 1733	BOOK	1 217		
STREETS, ELIZABETH	CHURCH, JONATHAN M.	A	SEP 13 1777	ST	1 009		
STREETS, ELIZABETH	CHURCH, JONATHAN M.	A	SEP 13 1777	ST	1 009		
STRICKLAND, ELEANOR			SEP 10 1872	WAJ	1 492		
STRICKLAND, ELEANOR			SEP 13 1872			0913	
STRICKLAND, JOHN G			JAN 25 1852			0236	
STRICKLAND, WILLIAM E			MAY 11 1868			0777	
STRINGER, FORTUNATE			MAR 22 1794				X
STUART, ISABELLA			NOV 20 1882	WAJJR	1 277		
STUART, JOHN DR.	HODGES, BENJ.	I	JUL 21 1810	TT	1 381		
STUART, MARY				T	1 220		
STUMP, THOMAS		I	AUG 20 1723	TB	1 186		
STUMP, THOMAS			MAY 10 1723	BOOK	1 136		
SUIT, AMELIA R			JUN 23 1900			1767	
SUIT, EDWARD			DEC 09 1850			0158	
SUIT, EDWARD			DEC 09 1850	PC	1 438		
SUIT, FIELDER			FEB 13 1871			0859	
SUIT, JOSIAS			SEP 16 1851			0188	
SUIT, KELITA			JUL 13 1885			1276	
SUIT, KELITA			MAY 19 1875	WAJJR	1 419		
SUIT, LOUISA J			MAY 16 1882	WAJJR	1 251		
SUIT, LOUISA JANE			MAY 16 1882			1184	
SUIT, NATHANIEL			DEC 10 1817				X
SUIT, NATHANIEL			MAY 21 1861	WAJ	1 194		
SUIT, NATHANIEL			MAY 21 1861			0553	
SUIT, NATHANIEL	SUIT, MARY	I	JAN 02 1776	GS	2 388		
SUIT, NATHANIEL	SUIT, MARY	A	JUN 02 1779	ST	1 083		
SUIT, NATHANIEL	SUIT, MARY	A	JUN 02 1779	ST	1 083		
SUIT, RALPH N			SEP 25 1838			4341	
SUIT, REBECCA			FEB 20 1900	JBP	1 630		
SUIT, REBECCA			FEB 20 1900	JBP	1 630		
SUIT, SAMUEL G				WAJJR	1 550		
SUIT, TAYLOR S			OCT 11 1888	WAJJR	1 550		
SUIT, WILLIAM			DEC 08 1870			0849	
SULLIVAN, JOHN			OCT 17 1893			1495	
SUMERS, JOHN			NOV 27 1703	BOOK	1 033		
SUMMER, ALEXANDER			AUG 10 1790	T	1 296		
SUMMERS, CECELIA			SEP 09 1874	WAJJR	1 034		
SUMMERS, CECELIA I			SEP 07 1874			0979	
SUMMERS, ELIZABETH			JAN 08 1868	WAJ	1 382		
SUMMERS, ELIZABETH			JAN 08 1868			0769	
SUMMERS, ELIZABETH			OCT 10 1843	PC	1 226		
SUMMERS, FLORENCE S			FEB 08 1900	WAM	1 117		
SUMMERS, GEORGE			APR 04 1803				X
SUMMERS, GEORGE SR			DEC 16 1795	T	1 371		
SUMMERS, JAMES	SUMMERS, MARY	A	NOV 20 1762	DD	6 373		
SUMMERS, JAMES	SUMMERS, MARY	A	NOV 20 1762	DD	6 373		
SUMMERS, JAMES			FEB 14 1761	BOOK	1 528		
SUMMERS, JOHN			JAN 10 1787				X
SUMMERS, JOHN		I	OCT 30 1707	BB	1 106		
SUMMERS, JOHN	MACKIE, HENRY	A	APR 11 1709	JB	1 045		
SUMMERS, JOHN	RAWLINGS, AARON	I	FEB 02 1787	ST	2 362		
SUMMERS, JOHN	RAWLINGS, AARON	A	AUG 15 1789	ST	1 374		

INDEX TO WILLS, ADMINISTRATIONS, AND INVENTORIES

DECEASED	EXECUTOR OR ADMINISTRATOR	DOC	DATE	BOOK	PAGE	FILE	REF
SUMMERS, JOHN	RAWLINGS, AARON	A	JUL 12 1787	ST	1 313		
SUMMERS, JOHN	SUMMERS, MARY	I	JUN 10 1761	GS	1 129		
SUMMERS, JOHN	MOORE, JOSHUA	A	FEB 10 1788	ST	1 325		
SUMMERS, JOHN	SUMMERS, LYDIA	A	APR 03 1775	JD	1 198		
SUMMERS, JOHN	SUMMERS, JOHN	A	FEB 25 1712	JB	1 068		
SUMMERS, JOHN	MACKBEE, HENRY	A	JUL 20 1708	JB	1 032		
SUMMERS, JOHN	RAWLINGS, AARON	A	JUL 12 1787	ST	1 313		
SUMMERS, JOHN	MOORE, JOSHUA	A	FEB 10 1788	ST	1 325		
SUMMERS, JOHN	SUMMERS, JOHN	A	FEB 25 1712	JB	1 068		
SUMMERS, JOHN	MACKIE, HENRY	A	APR 11 1709	JB	1 045		
SUMMERS, JOHN	RAWLINGS, AARON	A	AUG 15 1789	ST	1 374		
SUMMERS, JOHN	MACKBEE, HENRY	A	JUL 20 1708	JB	1 032		
SUMMERS, JOHN	SUMMERS, LYDIA	A	APR 03 1775	JD	1 198		
SUMMERS, JOHN			NOV 13 1786	T	1 243		
SUMMERS, JOHN F			APR 01 1875			0995	
SUMMERS, JOHN G			OCT 20 1873			0959	
SUMMERS, JOHN JR.	SUMMERS, DORCAS	I	OCT 24 1774	GS	2 303		
SUMMERS, JOHN SR			OCT 09 1769	BOOK	1 619		
SUMMERS, JONATHAN			AUG 08 1820				X
SUMMERS, NATHAN			SEP 22 1843				*
SUMMERS, NATHAN	SUMMERS, NATHAN	A	JUN 28 1791	ST	2 051		
SUMMERS, NATHAN	SUMMERS, NATHAN	A	JUN 28 1791	ST	2 051		
SUMMERS, NATHAN			SEP 19 1843	PC	1 227		
SUMMERS, NATHANIEL			APR 13 1790				X
SUMMERS, NATHANIEL			MAR 31 1784	T	1 185		
SUMMERS, SARAH A			JAN 19 1874			0975	
SUMMERS, WARREN			FEB 16 1864			0660	
SUMMERS, ZADOCK				TT	1 114		
SUMMERS, ZADOCK			APR 06 1815	TT	1 114		
SUMMERS, ZADOK			JUN 27 1815				X
SUMMERSET, THOMAS	MAHALL, THOS.	I	OCT 15 1736	PD	1 345		
SUNDERLAND, RICHARD H			JAN 31 1881			1151	
SURRATT, JOHN H			NOV 18 1862			0593	
SUTTON, JOHN	SUTTON, WM.	I	APR 27 1769	GS	2 134		
SUTTON, JOHN	SUTTON, MARY	A	OCT 20 1770	JD	1 096		
SUTTON, JOHN	SUTTON, MARY	A	OCT 20 1770	JD	1 096		
SUTTON, MARY			JAN 26 1785	T	1 204		
SUTTON, ROBERT			FEB 11 1800				X
SUTTON, ROBERT	SUTTON, JOHN	I	AUG 12 1800	ST	4 031		
SUTTON, ROBERT		I	FEB 21 1800	ST	3 343		
SWAERINGEN, THOMAS	SWEARINGEN, LIDEA	I	JUN 29 1726	TB	1 262		
SWAIN, ANN			DEC 31 1841				*
SWAIN, ANN			DEC 29 1841	PC	1 185		
SWAIN, GABRIEL	SWANN, THOMAS	A	APR 12 1785	JB	1 244		
SWAIN, GABRIEL	SWANN, THOMAS	A	APR 12 1785	JB	1 244		
SWAIN, HENRIETTA			MAR 02 1833	TT	1 514		
SWAIN, HENRY			JUL 10 1822	TT	1 315		
SWAIN, ISAAC	SWAIN, VIRLINDA	A	AUG 04 1808	TT	1 162		
SWAIN, ISAAC	SWAIN, VIRLINDA	A	AUG 04 1808	TT	1 162		
SWAINE, GABIREL	SWAINE, THOS.	I	FEB 11 1783	ST	2 099		
SWAINE, GABRIEL	SWAINE, THOS.	I	FEB 11 1783	ST	2 076		
SWAINE, HENRIETTA			FEB 17 1834				*
SWAINE, HENRY			APR 09 1823				*
SWAINE, ISAAC			JUN 04 1803				X
SWAINE, ISAAC	SWAINE,	I	AUG 09 1803	TT	1 016		
SWAINE, JOHN			SEP 04 1811				X
SWAINE, JOHN			MAR 11 1833				*
SWAINE, JOHN	SWAINE, HENRY	I	DEC 03 1811	TT	1 422		
SWAINE, LUCY			APR 03 1821				*
SWAINE, THOMAS			AUG 18 1787				X
SWANN, ANN			FEB 13 1804	T	1 566		

THE MARYLAND MILITIA IN THE REVOLUTIONARY WAR

by
S. Eugene Clements
and
F. Edward Wright

Class No. 8: Thoms. Holt; Wm. Pegg; Clement Summers; Basil Winsor; John Killehock(?); Jeffrey Magruder; Nacey Waters

A List of the different companies in the lower Battn. of Montgomery county with the different Classes as returned by Coll. John Murdock the 15th of July 1780 -
1st Company: Wm. Bailey, Capt; Hezh. Magruder, 1st Lieut; Stophel Kiser, 2nd do; Josiah Magruder, Ensign
John Busey, 1st Sergt; Isaac Brooke, 2nd do; Richard Magruder, 3; James Slicer 4th Sergt.; Thos. Chapple, 1st Corpl; Hezh. Speak, 2nd do; Saml. King, 3d do Zepah. Burch, 4th
Class No. 1: Wm. Stiles; Hy. Jeans; Robert Thomas; Charles Coats Jones; Zechah. Robertson; Daniel Magruder; George Chapple; Baptist Joy
Class No. 2: Richard C. Clagett; Peter Becraft; Zeckah. Evans; George Harriss; Benjn. Goodrick; Paul Summers; Hezekh. Summers; Philip Kiser
Class No. 3: Thos. McCubbin; Christopher Cochentoffer; John Chapple; Wm. Tucker; John Nichols; Joseph Adkins; Thomas Miles; Aaron Lanham
Class No. 4: George Read; Thomas Clarke; Henry Priest; Baptist Tuttle; Hanson Vermillion; Thos. Greenfield; Saml. Mackettee
Class No. 5: Edward Magruder; Edwd. King; Walter Tucker; Joseph Sprigg Belt; Henry Jones; John Barber; Zephah. Mockbee; Kid: Marcus
Class No. 6: Wm. B. Magruder; Archd. Magruder; Samuel Busey; Saml. Beall Magruder; Benedict Clarke; Zechah. Mockbee; John Graves; Michael Cochentaffer
Class No. 7: Normand B. Magruder; Wm. Steal; Nathan Robertson; John Hawkins; Joshua Shoemaker; Wm. Windham; Robt. Robertson; Benjn. Early; John Madding
Class No. 8: Clement Beall; Charles McHettee(?); Lancelot Crown; Jas. Collins; Nathan Collins; Walter Clagett; Peter Young; Benjn. Madding
2nd Company: Jesse Wilcoxen, Capt; Saml. B. Magruder, 1st Lieut.; Wm. Talbert, 2 do; Richard Blacklock, Ensign; Wm. Clements; 1st Sergt; Alexr. Tucker, 2d do; Ninian Magruder, 3d do; Burch Cheshire, 4th; Daniel Nichols, 1st Corpl.; Benjn Smith Benton, 2d do; Alexr. Wallace, 3rd do; Isaac Ridgeway, 4th do
Class No. 1: Mordecai Boffutt; David Shepone; Wm. T. Chambers; Wm. Moore; Barney Maffatt; Joseph Mitchell; Zechah. Austin
Class No. 2: John Johnson; Wm. Sedgewick; John Sedgewick; Hugh Elder; Nathan Benton; Wm. Wallace; Wm. Collier
Class No. 3: John Clagett; David Oneal; Elisha Williams; Charles Greenfield; Jas. Ball; Edwd. Hughes; John Ferrill
Class No. 4: Leaven Magruder; Benedict Woodard; Richd. Gatton; Jas. Higgins; John Len...(?); Lewis Wilcoxen; Ninn. Riley Junr; Thos. Austin
Class No. 5: Benjn. Gittings; Walter Magruder; Saml. Dyar; Wm. Benton; Chas. Magruder; George Gingle; Richd. Price; Wm. McNear
Class No. 6: Thomas Flint; Thoms. Lewis; Saml. Duckett; John Herring; Moses Deselm; Ninian Willett; James Riley
Class No. 7: Ninian B. Magruder; Baruch Odle; Nathan Clagett; Wm. Lodge; Wm. Willett; Wm. Allnutt; Wm. Tucker
Class No. 8: William Offutt Magruder; Zechah. McCubbin; Edward Adams; James Shearlock; Barton Moore; John Gill; Enoch Magruder

3rd Company: Joseph Magruder, Capt; Joseph White, 1st Lieut; John Marcus; 2nd do; Thos. Scott; Ensign; George H. Offutt, 1st Sergt; Rezin Offutt, 2nd

do; Saml. Clagett, 3rd do; Joseph Clagett, 4 do; Basil Beall, 1st Corpl.; George Viley (?), 2nd do; Zechah. Clagett, 3rd do; Nathan Offutt, 4th do
Class No. 1: Zadok Offutt; Charles Coventry; Henry Childs; Barton Duley; Charles Eeds; James Offutt of Wm.; Henry Downes; John Childs; Henry Vernall
Class No. 2: Hezekiah Offutt; John McCornack; Thos. Clarke; James Flemming; John Barker; Walter Draine; Elias Magruder; Jesse Offutt; Ezekl. Offutt; Leonard Clarke
Class No. 3: John Hetch; John Bogler; David Lowe; George Umble; Wm. L. Davis; Chas. Cradock; Benjn. Bean; Walter Evans; Francis Downing; Nathl. Offutt
Class No. 4: Wm. Jones; Ignatius Speaks; Charles Murphy; Jas. Duley; Wm. Moland; John Offutt; Josiah Harp; John Clarke
Class No. 5: Maccalon Edmonston; Alexr. Offutt; Jacob Tucker; Robert Ridgeway; Hezekh. Clagett; Alexr. Southern; John Hawkins; James Edward Smith; Aaron Rowlen; Alexr. Allen
Class No. 6: Thomas Shields; John Rimington; Wm. Offutt; Thomas Drain; Saml Elliott; Thos. Flint Junr; Philip Murphy; Wm. Harriss
Class No. 7: Richard Roberts; Thos. Offutt Senr; Wm. Gatton; John White; King(?) English; Saml. Jones; Hezekh. Jones; George Culph Junr
Class No. 8: Thomas Offutt Junr; Stephen Jarbo; Charles Jones Millright; Philip Harp; Wm. Davis; Kinsey Beall

4th Company: Thomas Edmonston, Capt.; Edward Wheelor, 1st Lieut; Richard Jones, 2nd do; Jereh. Orme, Ensign; Eli Orme, 1st Sergt; Jonathan Nixon, 2d do; Morris Brashears, 3rd do; Auguston Dunn, 4th do; Tyson Beall, 1st Corpl James Nixon, 2nd Corpl; Wm. Culver, 3rd Corpl; Ninn. Hoskinson, 4th do;
Class No. 1: Robert Willmore; Daniel Lloyd Senr; Charles Chaney; Stephen Lanham; John Selby
Class No. 2: Hugh Nixon; Aaron Orme; Thos. Beall (of Allen); John Cross; Thomas Benson; John Benson
Class No. 3: Thos. Tucker; Richd. Nixon; John Wilmore; Thos. Reynolds
Class No. 4: Lawson Beall; Wm. Kneighton; Francis Ratliff; Philip Orme; Daniel Lloyd; Elisha Hoskinson
Class No. 5: Wm. Ryan; George Wilson (of Wm.); Matthew Fitzgerrald; Jereh. Berry; Henry Clarke; Thomas Trundle
Class No. 6: Wm. Wheelor; Stephen Wilson; Joseph Campbell; Jas. Robinson; Thos. Perry; John Wilson (of Hy.); Chas. Case; Saml. Lloyd
Class No. 7: Saml. Jones; Gabriel Cross; Edward Holland; Thos. Keer; Nathl. Mitchell
Class No. 8: Absalom Bedds; Thos. Willmott; John Beall; George Letman; Joshua Nixon; Richard O Brian; Elias Browning

The List of the different companies in the lower Battn. of Montgomery County. with the different Classes as returned by Coll. John Murdock 15th July 1780 -
5th Company: Saml. Swearingon, Capt; Saml. Beall, 1st Lieut.; Anthony Wilcoxen, 2nd do; George Wilcoxen, Ensign; Baruch Prather, 1st Sergt; Azariah Prather, 2d do; Henry Ferrill, 3rd do; John Wilcoxen, 4th do; Obed Swearingon, 1st Corpl; Azel Butt, 2nd do; Basil Harding, 3rd do; Basil Prather, 4 do
Class No. 1: Edward Beall; Erasmus Perry; Michael Connoly; John Connoly; Basil Gittings; Wm. Richards

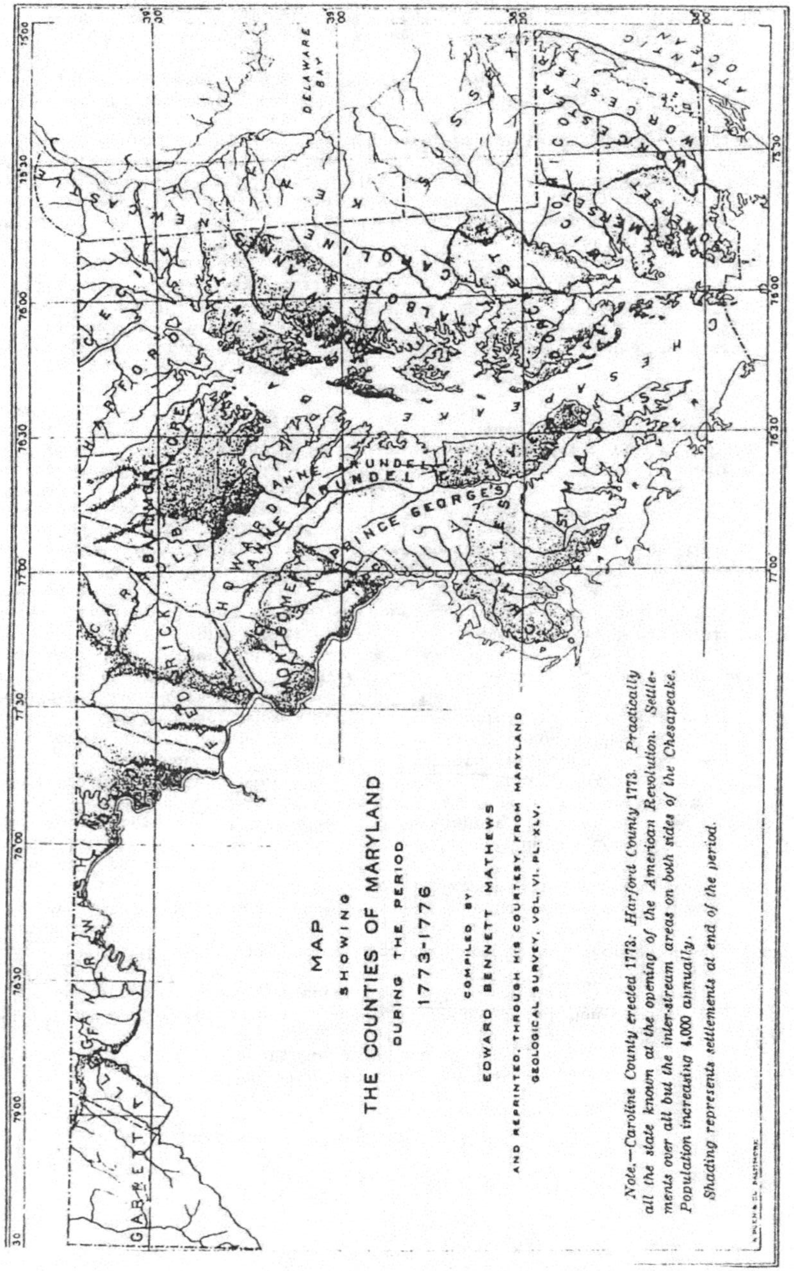

MAP
SHOWING
THE COUNTIES OF MARYLAND
DURING THE PERIOD
1773-1776
COMPILED BY
EDWARD BENNETT MATHEWS
AND REPRINTED, THROUGH HIS COURTESY, FROM MARYLAND
GEOLOGICAL SURVEY, VOL. VI, PL. XLV.
Note.—Caroline County erected 1773; Harford County 1773. Practically all the state known at the opening of the American Revolution. Settlements over all but the inter-stream areas on both sides of the Chesapeake. Population increasing 4,000 annually.
Shading represents settlements at end of the period.

MARYLAND RECORDS

COLONIAL, REVOLUTIONARY, COUNTY AND CHURCH

FROM

ORIGINAL SOURCES

BY

GAIUS MARCUS BRUMBAUGH, M.S., M.D.

Member Maryland Historical Society, Pennsylvania, German Society, American Association for Advancement of Science, National Genealogical Society, American Medical Association, Medical Society of the District of Columbia, Etc.

VOLUME I

Baltimore

GENEALOGICAL PUBLISHING CO., INC.

1985

Stephens, James	Steward, Winifred	Feb. 3, 1787
Stephens, John	Turner, Susannah	Feb. 28, 1798
Stephens, William	Taylor, Ann	Dec. 31, 1785
Stevens, Elizabeth	Gray, Hugh	Aug. 8, 1795
Stevens, William	Tilley, Rebecca	Jan. 15, 1785
Stewart, Ann Eustatia	Watson, Richard	Feb. 19, 1781
Stewart, Ann M.	Winfield, Jonas	Apr. 13, 1781
Stewart, Charles	Calvert, Elizabeth	June 14, 1780
Stewart, Henrietta	Townley, Thomas	Jan. 15, 1782
Stewart, James	Burgess, Massey	Dec. 30, 1790
Stewart, John	Ross, Ariana	Dec. 13, 1791
Steward, Philip	Marshall, Mary	Feb. 26, 1787
Stewart, Philip	Baynes, Mary Fell	Dec. 15, 1792
Steuart, William	Southwell, Pana	Feb. 21, 1778
Stewart, William	Bryan, Jane	June 6, 1783
Steward, Winifred	Stephens, James	Feb. 3, 1787
Stoddert, Benjamin C.	Lowndes, Rebecca	June 7, 1781
Stoddert, Letitia Dent	Dijean, Peter	Jan. 18, 1785
Stoddert, Thomas James	Dent, Cloe Hanson	Sept. 21, 1790
Stone, Ann	Grimes, Charles	Feb. 17, 1787
Stone, Eleanor	Hardey, George	Feb. 7, 1782
Stone, Leonora	Talburt, Nathan	Apr. 19, 1783
Stone, Mary	Taylor, Edward	Jan. 13, 1784
Stone, Mary	Hardey, Noah	Jan. 13, 1794
Stone, Nemiah	Wilson, Sarah	Mch. 3, 1778
Stone, Rachel	Watson, Walter	Oct. 8, 1779
Stonestreet, Buttler E.	Norton, Sarah	Jan. 6, 1778
Stonestreet, Edward	Wright, Margery	May 10, 1780
Stonestreet, Eleanor	Irwin, John	June 2, 1784
Straw, Terrissa	Hall, John Henry	Feb. 22, 1791
Strickland, John	Stallings, Sarah	Feb. 8, 1790
Strickland, Joseph	Page, Verlinda	Jan. 19, 1789
Strickland, Linny	Swain, Isaac	Dec. 28, 1795
Strickland, William	Kidwell, Sarah	Dec. 20, 1784
Stuart, Ariana	Riddle, James	May 8, 1800
Stuart, John	Dove, Mary	Feb. 3, 1790
Suit, John Smith	Scissell, Eleanor	Nov. 28, 1784
Suit, Mary	Edelen, Samuel	Dec. 14, 1787
Suit, Rebecca	Coghlan, Dennis	July 18, 1777
Sullivan, Mary	Lovejoy, Alexander	May 10, 1779
Sullavan, Sarah	Bedder, Thomas	Jan. 8, 1785
Summers, Ann	Fowler, Richard	Jan. 14, 1779

Summers, Ann	Jenkins, Zadock	Jan. 12, 1798
Summers, Anna	Hurley, Salem	Dec. 8, 1784
Summers, Eleven	Wilcoxon, Elizabeth	Dec. 30, 1786
Summers, George	Smith, Jane	May 19, 1787
Summers, Henrietta	Darnall, Gerrard	Nov. 7, 1785
Summers, John	Manley, Elizabeth	Dec. 11, 1785
Summers, John	Scarce, Rebecca	Feb. 26, 1794
Summers, Jonathan	Gwinn, Ann	Dec. 23, 1782
Summers, Nathaniel	Scarce, Sarah	June 2, 1793
Summers, Paul	Ranten, Susannah	Apr. 11, 1789
Summers, Zadock	Jenkins, Mary	Nov. 13, 1794
Summerville, Susannah	Carrington, Leonard	Oct. 22, 1789
Sutherland, Barbara	Anderson, George	Apr. 18, 1788
Sutherland, John	Murray, Margaret	Nov. 30, 1780
Sutton, John	Finly, Elizabeth	Dec. 21, 1797
Sutton, Mary B.	Lowe, Charles F.	Oct. 26, 1795
Swain, Benjamin	Ellecon, Hannah	Feb. 1, 1794
Swain, Elizabeth	Bird, John	Sept. 5, 1788
Swain, Gardiner	Berry, Elizabeth	Jan. 3, 1798
Swain, Isaac	Cassell, Mary	Dec. 24, 1787
Swain, Isaac	Strickland, Linny	Dec. 28, 1795
Swain, John	Harvey, Lucy	Apr. 11, 1797
Swain, Thomas	Smith, Elizabeth	Feb. 17, 1779
Swann, Ann	Compton, Henry T.	Nov. 17, 1797
Swann, Eleanor	Brightwell, John	Sept. 6, 1782
Swann, Henery	Davis, Minty	Jan. 8, 1789
Swan, Jennett	Hawkins, Henry	Dec. 26, 1790
Swann, Letty	Perrie, Francis	Jan. 19, 1798
Swan, Thomas	Cater, Elizabeth	Feb. 11, 1793
Sweeny, Drury	Mitchell, John	May 10, 1788
Sweeney, Lloyd	Walker, Ann	Jan. 10, 1790
Sydebotham, Mary	Shoof, John Thomas	Dec. 18, 1800
Sydebotham, William	Leitch, Margaret	Sept. 23, 1778
Symmes, Elizabeth	Phenix, Thomas	Feb. 26, 1791
Tait, Elizabeth	Boyd, Joseph	Jan. 14, 1800
Talbott, Basil	Lowe, Keziah	June 17, 1788
Talbot, Basil	Wilson, Susannah	July 5, 1800
Talbott, Jesse	Lanham, Mildred	Nov. 12, 1794
Talbott, Lewin	Burch, Elizabeth	Nov. 17, 1794
Talbott, Levin	Jones, Ann	Feb. 11, 1797
Talbott, Salomy	McKenzy, John	Mch. 19, 1794

Street, John, 13 Dec. 1790, Hannah Todd 2 DO
Street, Mansfield, 27 Nov. 1795, Anne Wainwright 2 DO
Street, Mansfield, 23 Sept. 1799, Betsy Wainwright 2 DO
Streets, William, 8 Oct. 1785, Sarah Ross 2 DO
Streett, Thomas, 29 May 1800, Sarah Kennaday 3 HA-29
Streett, William, 15 Dec. 1799, Sarah Cox 3 HA-28
Stretch, Samuel, 13 Oct. 1799, Elizabeth Cook 6 BA
Stricker, John, 30 March 1797, Catherine Wilson 2 HA-349
Strickland, John, 30 June 1793, Alice Perry 1 BA-5
Strickland, Joseph, 22 Jan. 1789, Verlinda Page 2 PG-4
Stricklin, John, 8 Jan. 1781, Eliza Simpson 2 CH-457
Strickling, John, 4 Jan. 1782, Elizabeth Timmons 3 HA-5
Striebech, Christ'r, 9 Jan. 1790, N. Paul 29 BA-1
Strike, Nicholas, 4 Jan. 1794, Eleanor Fann 6 BA
Strike, Nicholas, 2 Jan. 1797, Margaret Phenix 3 BA-341
Stroble, Zachariah, 7 Jan. 1794, Cassandra Ann Amos 3 HA-23
Stroman, John, 8 June 1778, Mary Sitler 11 BA-1
Strong, George, 27 Oct. 1797, Elizabeth Crabbs 4 FR
Strong, Joseph, 1 Nov. 1789, Rachael Hale 11 BA-12
Strong, Joseph, 23 May 1795, Mary Allender 7 BA-2
Strong, Ludwick, 30 Oct. 1785, Mary Hill 11 BA-8
Strongware, Simon, 10 May 1798, Nancy Bishop 2 SO
Strop, Jas., 4 Feb. 1798, Mary Louderman 29 BA-9
Stroud, Thomas, 16 March 1780, Mary Barnhouse 3 HA-1
Stuardt, Lenard, 25 Dec. 1792, Elizab. Perril 2 FR-1168
Stuart, Hugh, 24 Feb. 1795, Margaret Wooden 6 BA
Stuart, Philip, 16 Dec. 1792, Mary Tell Baynes 3 PG-437
Stubbins, Charles, 6 July 1800, Johanna Dye 49 BA-1
Stubbles, Samuel, 20 Sept. 1800, Jane Reanser 3 BA-392
Stubbs, John, 7 April 1794, Sarah Quay 3 BA-285
Stubbs, Joseph, son of Daniel and Ruth, 4th day, 5 mo., 1786, Ruth Pyle, dau. of Moses and Mary 11 SF-210
Stuble, (or Huble), George, Nov. 1799, Cath. Oxx 3 WA-68
Stud, Caspar, 16 Jan. 1787, Margareth Schull 10 BA-188
Studor, Martin, 2 April 1792, Mary Wertenbaker 4 FR
Stull, Adam, 15 April 1788, Elizabeth Ramsbergh 4 FR
Stull, Daniel, 19 Dec. 1789, Mary Beatty 4 FR
Stull, John, 6 May 1790, Margaret Duttero 4 FR
Stull, Lawrence, 11 May 1778, Rebecca Gassaway 4 FR
Stump, Harman, 19 June 1793, Elizabeth Dallam 3 HA-22
Stump, John, 17 Oct. 1779, Cassandra Wilson 5 BA-13
Stump, Joseph, 15 March 1798, Eliz. Bogges 2 FR-1170
4 FR gives the bride's name as Boggass.
Stumpf, George, 29 March 1795, Elis. Walter 3 WA-58
Stuntzer, Henry, 22 May 1796, Elizab. Roth 2 FR-1169
Sturgis, James, 3 Dec. 1799, Caty Purnell Jones 1 WO
Sturgis, John, 24 Jan. 1797, Tabitha Brumbly 1 WO
Sturgis, John, 25 Jan. 1797, Nancy Bishop 1 WO
Sturgis, Levin, 29 Nov. 1799, Nancy Taylor 1 WO
Sturgis, Richard, 18 Dec. 1798, Leah Gunn 1 WO
Sueman, John, 14 May 1791, Margaret Snyder 4 FR
Sueman, Peter, 25 June 1791, Anna Templing 4 FR
Suffrace, Charles, 10 Oct. 1785, Eliz. Liscomb 11 BA-8
Suhman, Adam, 23 Nov. 1790, Cath. Koblentz 2 FR-1168
Suit, Walter, 26 Aug. 1777, Susanna Davis 2 CH-457
Sulavane, Owen, 10 Dec. 1800, Elizabeth Fidamon 2 SF
Sulivan, James B., 9 April 1795, Eliza Ennalls 2 DO
Sulivan, John, 15 Feb. 1791, Elizabeth Collings 6 BA
Sulivane, Joseph, 20 May 1795, Ann Hooper 2 DO
Sullivan, Andrew Moore, 24 March 1798, Araminta Burnham 3 BA-356
Sullivan, Daniel, 15 Oct. 1784, Mary Gray 10 BA-182
Sullivan, Dennis, 8 June 1778, Mary Henderson 11 BA-1
Sullivan, Jeremiah, 5 June 1783, Ann Hoy 11 BA-6
Sullivan, John, 13 April 1788, Rebeckah Widdon 18 BA-1

Sullivan, John P., 13 Oct. 1799, Harriot Linnaway 6 BA
Sullivan, Philip, 21 Sept.? 1781, Ann Shears 3 AA-417
Sullivan, Sylvester, 5 Aug. 1797, Rosanna Hawse 5 MO-114
Sullivan, Thomas, 23 Jan. 1783, Sarah Wood 3 AA-419
Sullivan, Thomas, (c.1791), Jemima Heir 15 BA-4
Sullivan, William, 12 Feb. 1782, Henrietta Wood 3 AA-418
Sullivan, William, 10 Aug. 1799, Mary Harryman 6 BA
Sullivane, Owin, 26 Dec. 1792, Ester Stanton 2 SF
Sullivant, Dennis, 25 Aug. 1782, Martha Griffin 3 AA-418
Sumblin, William, 23 Sept. 1794, Harriot Davis 18 BA-6
Summers, Alex'r, 25 March 1797, Mary Vinagar 4 FR
Summers, Andrew, 19 July 1795, Catherine Harp 6 BA
Summers, Benjamin, 11 Oct. 1798, Virlinder Beckwith 5 MO-115
Summers, Elijah, 11 April 1798, Rachel Shorter 2 DO
Summers, Elijah, 23 Aug. 1799, Betsy Crosswell 2 SO
Summers, James, 20 Jan. 1800, Martha Perry 3 BA-382
Summers, John, 17 Sept. 1778, Elizabeth Spear 11 BA-1
Summers, John, 27 Feb. 1794, Rebecca Scarce 3 PG-439
Summers, John, 12 Feb. 1795, Ann Workman 6 BA
Summers, Levin, 31 Dec. 1786, Elizabeth Willcoxon 3 PG-252
Summers, Nathaniel, 2 Jan. 1793, Sarah Scarce 3 PG-437
Summers, Paul, 14 April 1789, Susanna Ranter 2 PG-4
Summers, Peter, 2 Jan. 1783, Christena Hefner 4 FR
Summers, Philip, 19 Oct. 1798, Barbara Sower 4 FR
Summers, Stephen, 24 July 1787, Elizabeth Summers 1 SO-169
Summers, Thomas, 8 Feb. 1779, Mary Ann Brawney 2 CH-457
Summers, Thomas, of Thos., July 1789, Sophia Ward 1 SO-175
Summers, Thomas, 17 Oct. 1789, Patsy Harris 2 DO
Summers, William, 1 Oct. 1778, Rebecca Jacobs 2 MO-1
Summervill, Henry, 7 Aug. 1789, Priscilla Ball 2 DO
Summerville, Jno., 18 March 1783, Eleanor Malaphant 11 BA-6
Sumwald, George, 17 Oct. 1784, Mary Wort 11 BA-7
Sumwald, Phillip, 8 Jan. 1784, Elizabeth Krebs 10 BA-180
Sunafranck, George, 17 April 1799, Elizabeth Roof 4 FR
Sunday, Matthias, 19 May 1790, Elizabeth Lewis 3 BA-228
Sunderland, Benj'n, 20 July 1788, by Rev. Claggett; Mary Everet 4 AA
Sunpower, Adam, 5 Feb. 1781, Susanna Cronise 4 FR
Super, Joh., 4 April 1796, Elisab. Cart 50 BA-399
Suss, Godfrey, son of John George and Catherine, 16 Nov. 1791, Anna Maria Kramer, dau. of Michael and Elizabeth 5 FR-111
Suss, John George, son of John George and Maria Catherine, 13 Feb. 1781, Maria Barbara Eigenbrod, dau. of John Yost and Eva Maria 5 FR-113
Suss, Paul, son of John George and Catherine, 4 Oct. 1787, Maria Magdalena Beyerle, dau. of Jacob 5 FR-114
Sute, Nath'l, 30 Dec. 1792, Elizab. Grover 2 FR-1169
Suter, Jacob, 25 May 1794, Margaretha Gortner 50 BA-394
Sutfin, William, 21 June 1783, Rachel Owin 4 FR
Sutherland, John, 23 Dec. 1777, Nelly Frazer 2 PG-3
Sutherland, John, 4 Dec. 1780, Margaret Murray 2 PG-5
Sutter, Peter, April 1799, Cath. Urban 3 WA-67
Sutton, Isaac, 2 Nov. 1780, Ann Grimes 11 BA-4
Sutton, John, 21 Dec. 1797, Elizabeth Fenley 3 PG-443
Sutton, Jonathan, 16 Nov. 1791, Sally McCracken 3 HA-21
Sutton, Mathias, 13 Feb. 1799, Sally Dunnock 2 DO
Sutton, Nathan, 9 March 1800, Mary Fossee 6 BA
Sutton, Thos., 20 Jan. 1785, Ann Gotsil 11 BA-8
Swaidner, Adam, 25 March 1797, Eve Lamon 4 FR
Swaidner, Adam, 5 April 1799, Anne Cox 4 FR
Swain, Benjamin, 4 Feb. 1794, Hannah Ellison 3 AA-424
Swain, Jacob, 2 May 1796, Mary Ambrose 4 FR
Swain, Jeremiah, 24 July 1785, Rebecca Herbert 16 BA-3
Swamley, Jacob, 19 Jan. 1799, Eleanor Fulkes 5 MO-115

Swan, George, 13 Dec. 1796, Emmy Redman 2 FR-1169
Swan, Henry, 10 Jan. 1789, by Rev. Claggett; Minty Davis 4 AA
Swan, Joseph, 7 Oct. 1790, Agnes Maxwell 11 BA-13
Swan, Matthew, 7 Sept. 1784, Ann McKean 11 BA-7
Swaney, John, 11 Feb. 1791, Phebe Berrier 4 FR
Swann, Joshua, 26 Dec. 1795, Nancy Helm 6 BA
Swann, Samuel, 7 May 1778, Susannah Punteney 11 BA-1
Swarz, John, 2 Nov. 1784, Mary Elizabeth Sholl 10 BA-182
Swayne, Charles, 14 Dec. 1799, Catherine Gire 4 FR
Swayne, Joseph Spires, 17 Aug. 1786, Amelia Ann Hutton 3 PG-251
Sweadner, Adam, 10 June 1797, Eve Lemmon 4 FR
Swearingen, George, 18 Jan. 1798, Ruth Wilcoxon 6 MO
Swedner, Henry, 27 June 1786, Elizabeth Sensor 4 FR
Sweeny, Loyd, 11 Feb. 1790, Mary Mangun 2 PG-4
Sweeting, John, 28 March 1793, Susanna (Hiser?) 18 BA-5
Sweeting, John, 12 Nov. 1799, Tabitha Bowen 6 BA
Sweeting, Thomas, 14 Nov. 1799, Catherine Wineman 5 BA-13
Sweringen, Thos., 7 Jan. 1790, Els Pope 3 PG-256
Swift, David, 23 Feb. 1796, Lettice Biggs 3 HA-25
7 BA-3 gives the date as 25 Feb. 1796.
Swigett, John, 19th day, 3 mo., 1780, Mary Breeding 2 SF-288
Swiggate, Benjamin, 29 Oct. 1787, Nancy Tregoe 2 DO
Swiggate, James, 30 Nov. 1790, Fama Adams 2 DO
Swindall, Peter, 6 April 1786, Catherine Hisdale 5 BA-13
Swisher, Matthias, 23 Nov. 1796, Catherine Shank 4 FR
Switzer, Jno., 18 Oct. 1798, Patty Kimble 29 BA-9
Switser, Lawrence, 31 Oct. 1797, Sarah Nickey 4 FR
Sydel, Hennrich, May 1799, Mary Weaddle 3 WA-67
Sykes, James, 4 Aug. 1784, Eliza Goldsborough 2 DO
Sylvester, George, 7 Jan. 1798, Rachel Rumage 6 BA
Syme, Nicholas, 25 July 1777, Elizabeth Johnson 2 CH-457
Synnott, Edward, 3 Sept. 1785, Ann Coudren 3 BA-190

Tabbs, Barton, 20 June 1779, Elizabeth Bond 1 CA-2
Tabbs, George C., 17 Feb. 1799, Lucretia Hopewell 4 SM-184
Tabler, Adam, 21 May 1779, Philepeana Yesterday 4 FR
Tabler, Melchor, 7 April 1779, Philipeana Berger 4 FR
Tabler, Michael, 13 April 1783, Catherine Coonce 4 FR
Tabler, Michael, 20 Jan. 1789, Mary Roberts 4 FR
Tabler, Wm., 16 June 1780, Margaret Yesterday 4 FR
Tagert, John, 12 Oct. 1790, Mary Williamson 5 BA-14
Tague, Thomas, 13 July 1793, Rebecca Henley 6 BA
Talbert, John, 19 Oct. 1777, Ann Davis 2 CH-457
Talbot, James, 5 Dec. 1789, Mary Hilton 4 FR
Talbot, John, 17 June 1784, Henrietta Philips 11 BA-7
Talbot, Richard, 20 Aug. 1778, Achsa Wells 11 BA-1
Talbot, Richard, 29 Oct. 1792, by Rev. Dorsey; Rachel Todd 4 AA
Talbot, Thomas, 15 April 1780, Susanna Rhodes 1 CA-3
Talbott, Basil, 19 June 1788, Keziah Lowe 3 PG-254
Talbott, Benjamin, son of John and Mary, 6th day, 10 mo., 1785, Susanna Chandlee, dau. of William and Mary 3 SF
Talbott, Charles, 28 Oct. 1789, Ann Ramsower 4 FR
Talbott, Edmund, 10 Oct. 1780, Elizabeth Parker 3 HA-2
Talbott, James, 5 Jan. 1788, by Rev. Forrest; Ann Poulson 4 AA
Talbott, John, son of John and Mary, 30th day, 12 mo., 1790, Elizabeth Plummer, dau. of Samuel and Mary 3 SF
Talbott, John, 19 Oct. 1796, Sarah Taylor 6 BA
Talbott, Joseph, son of John and Mary, 1st day, 11 mo., 1786, Mary Farquhar, dau. of Allen and Sarah 3 SF
Talbott, Kinsey, son of John and Mary, 21st day, 8 mo., 1800, Deborah Plummer, dau. of Joseph West and Mary 3 SF

Talbott, Paul, 6 March 1791, Sarah Ann Bryan 3 PG-257
Talbott, Thomas, 29 Jan. 1795, Elizabeth Rutledge 1 BA-7
Talbutt, George, 6 Aug. 1778, Mary McDaniel, 2 MO-1
Tall, Anthony, 23 Dec. 1783, Lina Webb 2 DO
Tall, Anthony, 17 April 1800, Nancy Harrington 3 BA-385
Tall, Bruffitt, 13 Feb. 1798, Elizabeth Woodland 2 DO
Tall, Daniel, 17 April 1798, Henney Tall 2 DO
1 DO-39 gives the date as 21 June 1798, and the bride's name as Henrietta.
Tall, John, 25 Oct. 1781, Elizabeth White 2 DO
Tall, John, 1 April 1790, Hagar Havergail 2 DO
Tall, John, 26 Jan. 1795, Henny Frazier 2 DO
Tall, Walter, 25 Nov. 1794, Ann Drill 2 FR-1178
Tall, William, 29 Jan. 1790, Elizabeth Navey 2 DO
Tall, William, 16 Sept. 1799, Sarah Harrington 2 DO
1 DO-40 gives the date as 17 Sept. 1799.
Tall, Young, 1 Feb. 1796, Sarah Lamb. 2 DO
Talley, Ebenezer, 30 May 1794, Margaret Philips 4 FR
Tamplin, Richard, 17 Oct. 1795, Eve Runner 4 FR
Tamplin, William, 20 June 1793, Susanna Gire 4 FR
Tannehill, William, 9 Dec. 1785, Elizabeth Simmons 4 FR
Tanner, Henry, 10 Dec. 1778, Mary Games 1 CA-2
Tanner, Isaac, 11 Nov. 1784, Marg't Reese 11 BA-8
Tanyhill, Leonard, 2 Oct.? 1778, Ann Anly 5 CH-1
Tappan, Abner, 30 Jan. 1792, Elizabeth Stanford 2 DO
Tarlton, Elisha, 18 Aug. 1799, Ann Greenwell 2 SM-138
Tarlton, Ignatius, 9 March 1783, Mary Adams 3 SM-61
Tarlton, Jeremiah, 29 June 1786, Mary Harbert Briscoe 4 FR
Tarman, Benj'n, 8 March 1791, Lettee Fields 3 PG-257
Taron, Wm., 16 July 1797, Susannah Cook 29 BA-8
Tarr, James, 14 Sept. 1799, Mary Skinner 2 DO
Tarr, John, 31 Jan. 1797, Peggy Allen 1 WO
Tarr, Major, 3 Dec. 1799, Betsey Johnson 1 WO
Tarr, Samuel, before 31 Aug. 1796, by Rev. Mills; Rachel Isaac 4 AA
Tarr, William, 22 Sept. 1797, Hannah Guthery 1 WO
Tate, James, 29 Jan. 1782, Elizabeth Coulter 5 BA-14
Tatom, John, 1 March 1797, Temperance Holding 4 KE-72
Tawes, John, March 1782, Catherine Ward 1 SO-174
Taws, John, 27 Aug. 1799, Leah Boston 2 SO
Taylor, Amasa, 1 Jan. 1781, Jemimah Kimble 3 HA-3
Taylor, Aquila, (4 Feb. 1789), Sarah Holland 20 BA-1
Taylor, Aquilla, 6 March 1798, Rachel Knight 4 FR
Taylor, Arthur, 31 July 1798, Polly Lester 1 WO
Taylor, Ezekiel, 14 May 1799, Charity Foxwell 2 SO
Taylor, George, 24 Nov. 1792, Martha Goldsmith 6 BA
Taylor, George, 5 Sept. 1796, Polly Timmons 1 WO
Taylor, Henry, 3 May 1790, Ann Griffith 4 FR
Taylor, Henry H., 30 April 1786, Ann Benneham (or Renneham) 11 BA-9
Taylor, Hezekiah, 20 Oct. 1799, Mary Brown 6 BA
Taylor, Hope, 23 Oct. 1798, Rachel Burnett 1 WO
Taylor, Hugh 13 Sept. 1786, Elizabeth Currey 3 BA-191
Taylor, Ignatius, 13 May 1780, Margaret Jordan 3 SM-58
Taylor, Jacob, 21 March 1799, Sarah Thompson 6 BA
Taylor, James, 7 June 1784, Mary Jones 3 BA-203
3 BA-192 gives the date as 17 June 1784.
Taylor, James, 24 Jan. 1785, Eliza Lucas 11 BA-8
Taylor, James, 13 Oct. 1792, Margaret Murry 3 BA-257
Taylor, James, 26 Aug. 1795, Jane White 3 HA-24
7 BA-2 gives the date as 27 Aug. 1795.
Taylor, James, 11 Dec. 1795, Peggy Aydelott 1 WO
Taylor, James, 6 Nov. 1796, Jemima Coward 6 BA
Taylor, James, 21 Nov. 1797, Elizabeth Reams 6 BA
Taylor, James, 25 Jan. 1800, Sarah Aitkin 3 HA-29
2 HA-351 gives the date as 6 Feb. 1800.

	Age
Clark, Seven	14
Walter	12
Hennerietta	11
Henry, Juner	9
Baless	8
Nancy	7
Lesson	5
Thomson	5
Justson	3
Johnson	1
Negros Joney 50; Maloy 35; Cato 30; Margery 25; Peg 18; Dick 17; Will 15; Anica 15; Mingo 9; Priss 6; Jene 3; Lott 2; Bett 20.	
Larrow, Frances	23
Martha	31
Abraham	10
Elizabeth	8
James	6
George	3
John 6 months old.	
Sarvant Colbo, John	21
Harris, Aaron	30
Mary	26
Sarah	9
Elizabeth	6
Walter	3
Thomas 3 months old.	
Sarvants Camblo, Daniel	20
Knight, John	30
Negros frank 28; Easter 40; Charles 15; Isaac 2.	
Frances, Joseph	34
Elizabeth	28
Lucy	7
Elizabeth	6
Jacob	4

	Age
Frances, Hessa (?)	2
and a Son 4 months old.	
Elemont, Elizabeth	32
Clark, William	26
Honnos (Hennes ?), Cavea	24
Beall, Robert of James	54
Servants Brigges, Richd	22
Mackgyer, Andrew	18
Negro Henne ("female")	27

1776

	Age
Summers, Hezekiah	26
Rebacker	32
William Dent	3
Benjamin (?)	1
Glaz, Charaty	53
Elennor	23
Harwood, Saml	29
Mary Elizth	24
Elizabeth Ann	3
Thomas Noble	2
Mary Ann 2 months old.	
Negros George 60; Lucy 50; Garey 40; Charles 28; Tuba 29; Sarey 21; Janey 19; Bacon 16; Hagea 14; Will 14; Charaty 15; Priss 14; Jack 13; George 8; Nan 8; Jack 5; Lucy 3; Milly 1; John 8 months old, Pag 2 months old—8 black males, 12 black females.	
Beall, Zachariah	33
Rebackah	23
Orasha	2
A Gairl 2 months old.	
Negro Candos	80

	Age
Doxse Elennor	20
Martha	2
Woodard, Frances	63
Weneford	55
Frances	19
Hezekiah	16
Zachariah	13
Sarah	11
Weneford	6
Stallons, Elizabeth	27
Patsa	4
William	1
Stallons, Isaac	66
Ezable	53
Sarah	17
Negros philos 80; Sarah 67; Rachel 30; Ned 15; Jane 12; Sam 10; frank 8; Dick 6.	
Tucker, Martha	32
Catharine	11
Susanna	10
Negro Tamar	3
*Watson, John	42
Sarah	38
John Wright	5½
Sally	2¼
Abington, Elizth	13
Murdock, Martha	25
Servants:	
Dixon, Richard	45
McCoy, Janet	17
Hired for Year:	
McGirtt, James	45
Bannerman, Betsey	54
Negroes, Jack 32; Will 40; Brumley 54; Charles 11;	

	Age
Negroes, Isaac 9—Lucy 29; Sophia 15; Ursula 6.	
Carroll, Daniel	46
Servants:	
Condon, John	25
John	45
Kelly, Tom	16
Kenney	24
Bush	23
Negroes—Joe 28; Deb 28; Tom 10; Kate 8; Bill 4; Babb 3; Henny 1; Rachell 23; Diana 3; Flora 1; Will 18, Roe, Robert, Overseer.—	
Dixon, James	6
Sarah	40
Carroll, Mrs. Ellr	67
Mary	34
Elizth	31
John	40
Negroes—Frank 68; Johnny 28; Tom 36; Johnny 25; Ned 25; Zanga 45; Archy 21; Will 21; Tom 16; Dick 13; Tom 11; Nelly 60; Hanna 20; Pig 45; Nanny 35; Ciss 18; Judith 50; Nanny 18; Nanny 20; Mary 35; Kitt 23; Jett 21; Sue 20; Magg 14; Sall 16; Bett 12; Poll 14; Bett 12; Rose 5; Mary 10; Rachell 7; Nell 1; George 2; Nan 1; Kate 7; Tom 1; Henny 4; Sandy 9; Isaack 25; Isaack 22; Jack 12; Betty 60; Nell 55; Nell 17; Dick 70; Nanny 68—17 black males, 29 black females.	

* At this point a bold, experienced penmanship appears in the original record.

SUMMEY, ELIZABET

PAGE 12,942

COUNTRY UNITED STATES STATE: MARYLAND AS OF MAR 1992

NAME	FATHER / MOTHER OR SPOUSE OR RELATIVE (M=MALE F=FEMALE H=HUSBAND W=WIFE)		TYPE	EVENT DATE	COUNTY, TOWN, PARISH	B	E	S	SOURCE BATCH/FILM No	SOURCE SERIAL SHEET
SUMMEY, ELIZABETH										
SUMMY, ELIZABETH	BENJAMIN MILLER	W	M	27SEP1883	GARRETT, GRANTSVILLE			06JAN1990PV	6000472	34
SUMMY, ELIZABETH ∆∂	BENJAMIN MILLER	W	M	27SEP1883	GARRETT, GRANTSVILLE			25JUL1989PV	F505801	0007
SUMMINS										
SUMMINS, WILLIAM S.	LOUSISA FERGUSON	H	M	23OCT1804	BALTIMORE			20JUN1990JR	M533735	0964
SUMMITT										
SUMWATT, GEORGE HENRY	WM. SUMWATT/	M	C	21NOV1830	BALTIMORE, BALTIMORE, GAY STREET AND COURT HOUSE PLAZA ZION GERMAN LUTHE	01APR1978WA	09JUN1978WA	06JUL1978WA	C507641	5080
SUMMONS , •• SEE SAMMONS										
SUMMORS , •• SEE SUMNER										
SUMMWELL										
SUMMWELL, JOHN	ELEANOR MALLENDER	H	M	18MAR1783	BALTIMORE			29SEP1990LG	M533731	1112
SUMMY , •• SEE SUMMEY										
SUMNER •• SEE ALSO ••										
•• SAMAR	•• SEYMOUR									
•• SIMER										
SUMMERS, MR. ∆∂	PAUL SUMMERS/MISS DENT	M	S	ABT. 1784	ST. MARY	03DEC1988OG	21JAN1989OG	27JAN1989OG	F505661	0020
SUMMERS, MISS ∆∂	PAUL SUMMERS/MISS DENT	F	S	ABT. 1784	ST. MARY	03DEC1988OG	04MAR1989OG	14MAR1989OG	F505661	0020
SUMMERS, MR. ∆∂	PAUL SUMMERS/MISS DENT	M	S	ABT. 1766	ST. MARY	03DEC1988OG	21JAN1999OG	27JAN1989OG	F505661	0020
SUMMERS, MISS ∆∂	PAUL SUMMERS/MISS DENT	F	S	ABT. 1786	ST. MARY	03DEC1988OG	07MAR1989OG	14MAR1989OG	F505661	0020
SUMMERS	BECKWITH	H	M	12OCT1798	MONTGOMERY			15SEP1942SL	A184724	0024
SUMMERS, AARON	JOHN SUMMERS/JEMIMA CULLEN	M	B	16SEP1778	SOMERSET, COVENTRY PARISH	11MAY1943	28JUL1943MT	26SEP1972AL	7126018	32
SUMMERS, AARON	JOHN SUMMERS/JEMIMA CULLEN	M	B	10OCT1778	SOMERSET, REHOBETH, COVENTRY PARISH	11MAY1943	28JUL1943MT	23SEP1976AL	C504731	1763
SUMMERS, AARON	PROVIDENCE SHAW	H	M	19JUL1808	BALTIMORE, BALTIMORE, FIRST METHODIST EPISCOPAL CHURCH			13JUN1990JR	M533736	0390
SUMMERS, AARON	JOHN SUMMERS/MARGARET REBECCA LEATHERMAN	M	B	17NOV1843	FREDERICK, ELLERTON	16MAY1987PV	18AUG1987PV	19AUG1987PV	8704004	30
SUMERS, ABRAHAM	POLLY MOORE	H	M	31DEC1816	SOMERSET			06FEB1973AZ	7208028	93
SUMMERS, ABRAHAM	RACHEL BYRD	H	M	22AUG1820	SOMERSET			06FEB1973AZ	7208028	94
SUMMER, ABRAHAM	CATHARINE MAIN	H	M	12NOV1820	FREDERICK, MIDDLETOWN, LUTHERAN CONGREGATION OF ZION CHURCH			02NOV1978SL	M507591	0056
SUMMERS, ADAM	NANCY HYMES	H	M	11FEB1827	WASHINGTON			20FEB1976OG	7514205	32
SUMMERS, AGNES	FRANK LESLIE JONES	W	M	26MAR1902	GARRETT			10OCT1978OG	7809503	72
SUMMERS, ALETHA ∆∂	ALEXANDER SUMMERS/MARY ANN VINEGAR OR WINEGAR	F	B	01FEB1799	, , OF	28AUG1939	06NOV1939MT	02MAR1990AZ	F511780	0041
SUMMERS, ALETHA ∂	RELATIVE: ISAAC HIGBEE/	F	C	01FEB1799	<MONTG., PRINCE GEORGE>	28AUG1939MT	PRE-1970	PRE-1970	0170422	FILM
SUMMERS, ALETHA	ALEXR. SUMMERS/MARY	F	B	01FEB1799	MONTGOMERY, PRINCE GEORGE PARISH	28AUG1939	06NOV1939MT	27SEP1961SG	7135103	74
SUMMERS, ALETHA	ALEXR. SUMMERS/MARY	F	C	09NOV1800	MONTGOMERY, PRINCE GEORGE PARISH	28AUG1939	06NOV1939MT	30JUN1978OG	C507601	0522
SUMMERS, ALEXANDER ∂	RELATIVE: ISAAC SOMERS HIGBEE/	M	B	ABT. 1773	MONTGOMERY CO.	08SEP1939SL	PRE-1970	PRE-1970	0183581	FILM
SUMMERS, ALEXANDER ∆∂	HEZEKIAH SUMMERS/MRS. REBECCA SUMMERS	M	B	09MAR1778	FREDERICK, , OF	09JUN1960	30SEP1960SL	02MAR1990AZ	F511780	[illegible]
SUMMERS, ALEXANDER	HEZEKIAH SUMMERS/REBECCA GLAZI	M	B	09MAR1778	PRINCE GEORGES	09JUN1960	30SEP1960SL	05NOV1988JR	5001523	[illegible]
SUMMERS, ALEXANDER	MARY ANN VINEGAR OR WINEGAR	H	M	25MAR1797	FREDERICK			CLEARED	5011780	[illegible]
SUMMERS, ALIAS ALIAS OR ELIAS	JOHN SUMMERS/MARGARET REBECCA LEATHERMAN	M	B	31JAN1838	FREDERICK, ELLERTON	16MAY1987PV	18AUG1987PV	19AUG1987PV	8704004	30
SUMMERS, ALICE ∆∂	NATHANIEL SUMMERS/MARY WADE	F	S	ABT. 1837	HANCOCK	03DEC1988OG	16FEB1989OG	14MAR1989OG	F505661	[illegible]
SUMMERS, AMELIA ∂	RELATIVE: FRANKLIN SPENCER/	F	B	22APR1767	SOM., COVENTRY	19MAY1943MT	PRE-1970	PRE-1970	0170425	FILM
SUMMERS, AMELIA	MOSES SUMMERS/PRISCILLA LAWSON	F	B	22APR1767	SOMERSET, COVENTRY PARISH	19MAY1943	02JUL1943MT	06MAR1959SL	7126018	[illegible]
SUMMERS, AMELIA	JONAS NEWCOMER	W	M	13SEP1841	WASHINGTON			22JUL1975LG	7430401	3

∆- ENTRY ALTERED FROM SOURCE; ‡,∂,)-RELATIVES NAMED IN SOURCE. SEE "SYMBOLS" IN INSTRUCTIONS.

A - ADULT CHRISTENING B - BIRTH C - CHRISTENING D - DEATH OR BURIAL ALL OTHERS - MISCELLANEOUS F - BIRTH OR CHRISTENING OF FIRST KNOWN CHILD M - MARRIAGE N - CENSUS W - WILL

Keziah Summers, wid.
Hezekiah Summers, [illegible]

Capt. ——
Col. ——

Md. Mil.

Private

No. 134 [illegible]

War, Revolution.

Rec'd. appr. for Pen. [illegible]

Va. Re. 1832

Ad. 160 acs July 11 86

Judge

Thomas G. Walton
Fairmont, Va.

Vol. S-2-165

~~Acts of July 14, 1862, and March 3, 1873.~~

REJECTED

10,304

P. O.

Hezekiah Summers

Service:

Enlisted: , 18

Discharged: , 18

Application filed: , 18

Alleges:

Re-enlisted:

Attorney:

P. O.

Recognized. Contract.

Cert. of Dis. Searched for , 18

WAR DEPARTMENT,

Pension Office,

Sir:

The evidence in support of your claim under the act of June 7, 1832, has been examined, and the papers are herewith returned. The following is a statement of your case in a tabular form. On comparing these papers with the following rules and the subjoined notes, you will readily perceive that objections exist, which must be removed, before a pension can be allowed. The notes and the regulations will shew what is necessary to be done. Those points to which your attention is more particularly directed, you will find marked in the margin with a brace, (thus: ξ). You will, when you return your papers to this Department, send this printed letter with them: and you will, by compling with this request, greatly facilitate the investigation of your claim.

A Statement, *shewing the Service of* Hezekiah [illegible]

Period when the service was rendered.	Duration of the claimant's service. Years.	Months.	Days.	Rank of the claimant.	Names and rank of the Field officers under whom he served.	Age at present, and place of abode when he entered the service.	Proof by which the declaration is supported.
1776		2	2	Pr.	Capt Briles Col Deacon	84 Md	Traditionary
1777		1	14	"	Capt J. Beall		
+ 1779	1	3	8	Pr.	Capt Kiser		
Nov 9 + 1781				"	Capt Murdock		
to 19 Oct 1781		5	10	Pr.	Col —		
& to 10 Apl 1782		5	22	"	do do		

+ No militia service except on [illegible] Statement not satisfactory,

I am, respectfully,

Your obedient servant,

JAMES L. EDWARDS,

Commissioner of Pensions.

WAR DEPARTMENT

Pension Office,

Sir:

The evidence in support of your claim under the act of June 7, 1832, has been examined, and the papers are herewith returned. The following is a statement of your case in a tabular form. On comparing these papers with the following rules and the subjoined notes, you will readily perceive that objections exist which must be removed, before a pension can be allowed. The notes and the regulations will shew what is necessary to be done. Those points to which your attention is more particularly directed, you will find marked in the margin with a brace, (thus: {). You will, when you return your papers to this Department, send this printed letter with them; and you will, by compling with this request, greatly facilitate the investigation of your claim.

A Statement, *shewing the Service of* Hezekiah [illegible]

Period when the service was rendered.	Duration of the claimant's service. Years.	Months.	Days.	Rank of the claimant.	Names and rank of the Field officers under whom he served.	Age at present, and place of abode when he entered the service.	Proof by which the declaration is supported.
1776		2	2	Pr.	Capt Bailey Col Deacon	84 Md	Traditionary
1777		1	14	"	Capt J. Beall		
+ 1779	1	3	8	Pr.	Capt Kiser		
Nov 9 + 1781				"	Capt Murdock Col —		
to 19 Oct 1781		5	10	Pr.			
5 to 10 Apl 1782		5	22	"	do do		

I am, respectfully,

Your obedient servant,

JAMES L. EDWARDS,

Commissioner of Pensions.

+ [illegible] exceptions [illegible] statement not [illegible]

Virginia Marion County ss.

On this 10 day of May AD one thousand eight hundred and fifty five personally appeared before the undersigned a justice of the peace within and for the county and State aforesaid Ruth Summers aged years a resident of said County and State, who being duly sworn according to law declares that she is the widow of Hezekiah Summers deceased who was a private soldier of the United States in the ~~war~~ of the revolutionary war with Great Britain, that her said husband she thinks served in the Maryland Militia but she does not know in what company or regiment or the names of the officers thereof, nor the length of his term of service, but alleges that it was over fourteen days, and that he was honorably discharged; that her said husband made application in his lifetime for a Pension which was rejected or suspended as she has been informed in consequence of there not being a sufficient length of term of service established to entitle him to a Pension under the law then in force.

She makes this declaration & she further declares she was married to said Hezekiah Summers in Monongalia County Virginia on the 13 day of April AD 1831 by one Thomas Parrill a minister of the

[illegible] of said County and State, who being [illegible]
duly sworn according to law declares that she
is the widow of Hezekiah Simmons [illegible]
who was a private soldier of the United
States in the [illegible] of the revolutionary war
with Great Britain, that her said husband
she thinks served in the Maryland Militia
but she does not know in which company
or regiment or the names of the officers
thereof, nor the length of his term of service,
but alleges that it was over fourteen days,
and that he was honorably discharged;
that her said husband made application
in his lifetime for a Pension which was
rejected or suspended as she has been informed in consequence of there not being
a sufficient length of term of service established to entitle him to a Pension under
the law then in force.

She makes this declaration & she further declares she was married to said Hezekiah Simmons in Monongalia County
Virginia on the 13th day of April AD 1831 by one
Thomas Pennell a minister of the
methodist church, that her name before
her said marriage was Ruth Dawson
that her said husband died at Monongalia County Virginia about the [illegible]

she is entitled under the act of 3 March 1853, and for proof of the service of her said husband she refers to his application for a pension and the proof therewith filed or referred to

Ruth her mark Summers

We Allen Holland of Monongalia County and John Malot of Marion County Virginia upon our oaths declare that ~~the foregoing decl~~ Ruth Summers made her mark to, and acknowledged the foregoing declaration in our presence, and that we believe from the appearance, ~~statements~~ and from our own personal knowledge of the applicant that she is the identical person she represents herself to be.

We also further state upon our oaths aforesaid, that we were present at the marriage of said applicant to the said Hezekiah Summers about the 13 day of April AD 1831, and that said Hezekiah Summers died in Monongalia County Virginia about the 7 day of June 1836, leaving the said Ruth his widow who is still a widow

Allen Holland
John Malot

day of June 1836, that she is now a
widow, that there is no record of her said
marriage, that she is aware of—

She makes this declaration for the purpose of obtaining the bounty land to which
she is entitled under the act of 3 March
1855; and for proof of the service of
her said husband she refers to his application for a pension and the proof
therewith filed or referred to.

Ruth her mark Summers

We Allen Holland of Monongalia
County and John Malot of Marion
County Virginia upon our oaths declare that
~~the foregoing that~~ Ruth Summers made
her mark to, and acknowledged the foregoing
declaration in our presence, and that we
believe from the appearance, ~~statements~~
and from our own personal knowledge
of the applicant that she is the identical
person she represents herself to be.

We also further state upon our oaths
aforesaid, that we were present at the
marriage of said applicant to the said
Elizabeth Summers about the 13 day
of April AD 1831, and that said Elizabeth Summers resided in Monong—

The foregoing declaration and affidavit were sworn to and subscribed before me on the day and year above written, and I certify that I know the affiants to be credible persons, that the claimant is the person she represents herself to be and that I have no interest in this claim.

Jacob Swisher Jr J.P

I Thomas L. Boggess clerk of the County court of Marion County Virginia certify in the State of Virginia certify that Jacob Swisher Jr. esqr who hath given the preceding certificate is a justice of the peace in and for the said county, and that the foregoing signature purporting to be his is genuine,

witness my hand and the Seal of said court, this 18 day of May 1855

Thomas L. Boggess

Fairmont Va
May 27 1856

Dear Sir

I desire the application of Ruth Summers No 142.986 for bounty lands under the act 3 March 1855 re examined, as I think she is now entitled to bounty Land under the provisions of the act of 14 May 1856. For evidence of service of her husband Hezekiah Summers I refer you to his application for a Pension and evidence therewith filed, which is also referred to in her declaration—

Very Respectfully
Yours &c
J. G. Watson

Palatine 1st Month 1853

James E. Heath

Dear Sir

Margaret Summers the only child living of Hezekiah Summers who was a revolutionary Soldier (probably of the Maryland line) received a letter a few weeks since from S. W. Knight. (likely a claim agent) concerning her right to receive money from the government on the account of her fathers services and desiring that she should execute to him a power of attorney to prosecute the claim for a contingent fee of 6

This lady is very poor and on the point if she has any thing coming it would be well to save it all for her, and for this purpose I desire you to have the Pension papers of Hezekiah Summers examined and see what proof is wanting and communicate to me.

From Knights letter I learn the H Summers papers are on file there please have this attended to

Respectfully
your friend

T. G. Haymond

P.S. H. Summers (17 years) has been dead 16 or 15 years

Hezekiah Summers Applicant

I the undersigned Hezekiah Summers
At the requisition of the Secretary of war give the following narrative of my aged Revolutionary Services to Wit— I was born in the year 1750—

[illegible] Sometime during the war of the Revolution I can't tell in what year— I volunteered in Maryland under Capt George Bell and was with him on the potomac three 3 weeks. there were three Battalions in the expedition under Col. Murdock— the whole were discharged after being in service for three weeks only—

Some time after this I can't tell how long nor in what year. I was drafted and marched from Montgomery County under Capt. William Baley, to Baltimore, then to New Jersey ("but dont remember the place) I was in the expedition for three months. Genl. Smallwood commanded—

after the last mentioned tour I was one month at Fredericktown guarding the Prisoners— and this ends my services. Mr Copelan wrote my declaration I told him the same I now tell. I agreed to give him 2/3 the amount drawn. In Witness of all which I hereto subscribe my name. Nov. 14. 1834.

Witness
W. Singleton

Hezekiah Summers

A Copy
D W. Singleton
Nov. 30 1834

[illegible]

Monongalia County } To Wit

On this 18th day of June 1834 personally appeared before me Hezekiah Summers a resident of the County and State aforesaid in his 84 th year of age Who being duly Sworn according to Law before me ~~Anthony Smith~~ Jacob J. Wagner an acting Justice of the peace in and for the County of monongalia in the State of Virginia and doth on his oath make the following amended Declaration in order to obtain the benefit of the provisions made by the act of Congress passed June 7th 1832 that he was Drafted the 17th day of August 1776 in the County of Montgomery in the State of maryland and placed under Capt William Baley and served a tour of two month and two days and that in 1777 he served a tour of one month and forteen days under Capt George Beall and that in 1779 he served a tour of more than ~~[illegible]~~ month as a Volunteer in the ~~[illegible]~~ garding and Spying a long the potomack river to prevent the Enemy from landing that his Calls onto Said Service were so frequent that it is impossible for him now to recollect the several periods at Which they Were made or the precise length of time but he is Confident that he was not less then a nine months in actual Service under Capt or Lieut Christopher Tuber and [illegible] [illegible] Volunteer under Capt or Colo John [illegible] [illegible] a minit man Watching the [illegible] [illegible] [illegible] was not less than [illegible] the State of Virginia and doth on his oath make the following merged Declaration in order to obtain the benefit of the provisions made by the act of Congress passed June 7th 1832 that he was Drafted the 17th day of August 1776 in the County of Montgomery in the State of Maryland and placed under Capt William Baley and served a tour of two month and two days and that in 1777 he served a tour of one month and forteen days under Capt George Beale and that in 1779 he served a tour of more then ~~three~~ month as a Volunteer in the ~~..... .....~~ garding and Spying along the potamack river to prevent the Enemy from landing that his Calls unto Said Service were so frequent that it is impossible for him now to recollect the several periods at Which they Were made or the precise lenth of tim but he is Confident that he was not less then a Nine months in actual Services under Capt or lieut Christopher Tiser and that in 1781 he Volunteerd under Capt or Colo John Moredock and was imployed as a minit man Watching the movement of the Enemy as stated a bove and Was not less then three month in actual Services and that it may be that he is mistaken as to the length of time he helpt gard the presiners at Fredrick Town in Maryland but knows he was under Capt ... ... John Moredock and that he is Confident that the Company did not leave Fredrick Town till 9th or 10th of ... 1782 and Was not Dicharged till after that

... of [illegible] ... or an annuity except the present and he declares that he is not on the pension roll of any agency in any state or territory and personally appeared before me the undersigned Justice of the peace Hezekiah Summers who being duly sworn deposeth and saith that by reason of old age and the consequent loss of memory he cannot swear positively as to the precise length of his services but according to the best of his recollection he served not less than the period mentioned and that in all of his tours he served as a private a boue and ... Soldier

Hezekiah Summers

Jacob J Wagner

and I ~~Anthony Smith~~ Justice of the peace in and for the County of Monongalia in the State of Virginia do Certify that the Applicant Was duly sworn to this his amended Declaration on the 15th day of June 1834

J. J. Wagner J.P.

of Monongalia Co

I Thomas P. Ray, clerk of the County court of Monongalia in the state of Virginia do certify that Jacob J Wagner esq. is a Justice of the peace in and for said county and that the above signature purporting to be his is genuine. In testimony whereof I have hereunto signed my name and affixed the seal of said court this 19th of June A.D. 1834

Thos P. Ray

And I Anthony Smith a Justice of the Peace in
and for the County of Monongalia in the State of Virginia
do hereby declare my opinion after the investigation of the
matter and after puting the interrogatories perscribed
by the War Department that the above named
applicant was a Revolutionary Soldier and served as he
states and I further certify that Joseph Shackelford who has
signed the preceding Certificat is a Clergyman resident in the County of Monongalia in the State of
Virginia and that Robert Henderson who has also
signed the same is a credible person and that
thier Statement is entitled to credit And I do
further certify that Hezekiah Summers the present
applicant is unable to appear in open Court by reason
old age and bodily infirmity to make this his
Declaration Sworn and subscribed to the day and
year aforesaid

Anthony Smith J P

Virginia

I Thomas P. Ray clerk of the County court of Monongalia do certify that Anthony Smith esq: is a Justice of the peace in and for said county, and that the foregoing signatures purporting to be his is genuine. In testimony whereof I have hereunto signed my name and affixed the seal of said court this 12th of May 1834

#45 1800 Census

XXXXXXXXX

Montgomery County
1st District

Name	White Males: Under 10 yrs (I)	10 & under 16 (II)	16 & under 26 (III)	26 & under 45 (IV)	45 yrs & over (V)	White Females: Under 10 yrs (I)	10 & under 16 (II)	16 & under 26 (III)	26 & under 45 (IV)	45 yrs & over (V)	Other free per's (VI)	Slaves (VII)
John Bear	1	2	1	-	1	3	-	-	-	1	-	-
Elizabeth Duvall	2	-	-	1	-	1	-	-	1	-	-	-
John Poole	2	-	-	1	-	1	-	-	-	-	-	-
Richard Jones	4	-	-	1	-	2	-	-	1	-	-	-
Jeremiah Watkins	1	1	2	-	1	1	-	2	-	1	-	4
Nicholas Watkins	3	2	0	1	-	3	-	-	1	-	-	-
Joseph Watkins	-	-	-	1	-	-	-	-	-	-	-	-
Jacob Lizaer	2	1	-	1	-	2	2	1	1	1	-	-
Jeremiah Lewis	-	-	2	-	1	-	1	1	-	1	1	-
Thomas Lewis	1	-	-	1	-	1	-	-	1	-	-	-
Levy Lewis	-	-	-	1	-	-	-	-	1	-	-	-
James Lawson	2	-	1	-	-	1	-	1	-	-	-	6
George Walker	1	1	1	1	-	1	1	1	1	-	-	-
Zadock Summers	2	-	-	1	-	3	-	-	1	-	-	2
Joshua Purdom	3	-	-	1	-	1	-	-	1	-	-	-
John Ellis	1	2	-	-	1	-	-	2	-	-	-	-
Hezekiah Summers b 1750	-	-	Ben 1	Will 1	1	-	Marg 1	2	0	1	1	20
William Lee	1	-	-	1	-	-	-	-	1	1	-	-
Garret F. Lee	1	1	-	1	-	2	-	-	1	-	-	-
John Boyd	-	-	2	-	1	2	3	1	-	1	-	-
Edward King	2	-	-	1	1	1	-	-	1	-	-	-
Total												

* Record damaged and illegible

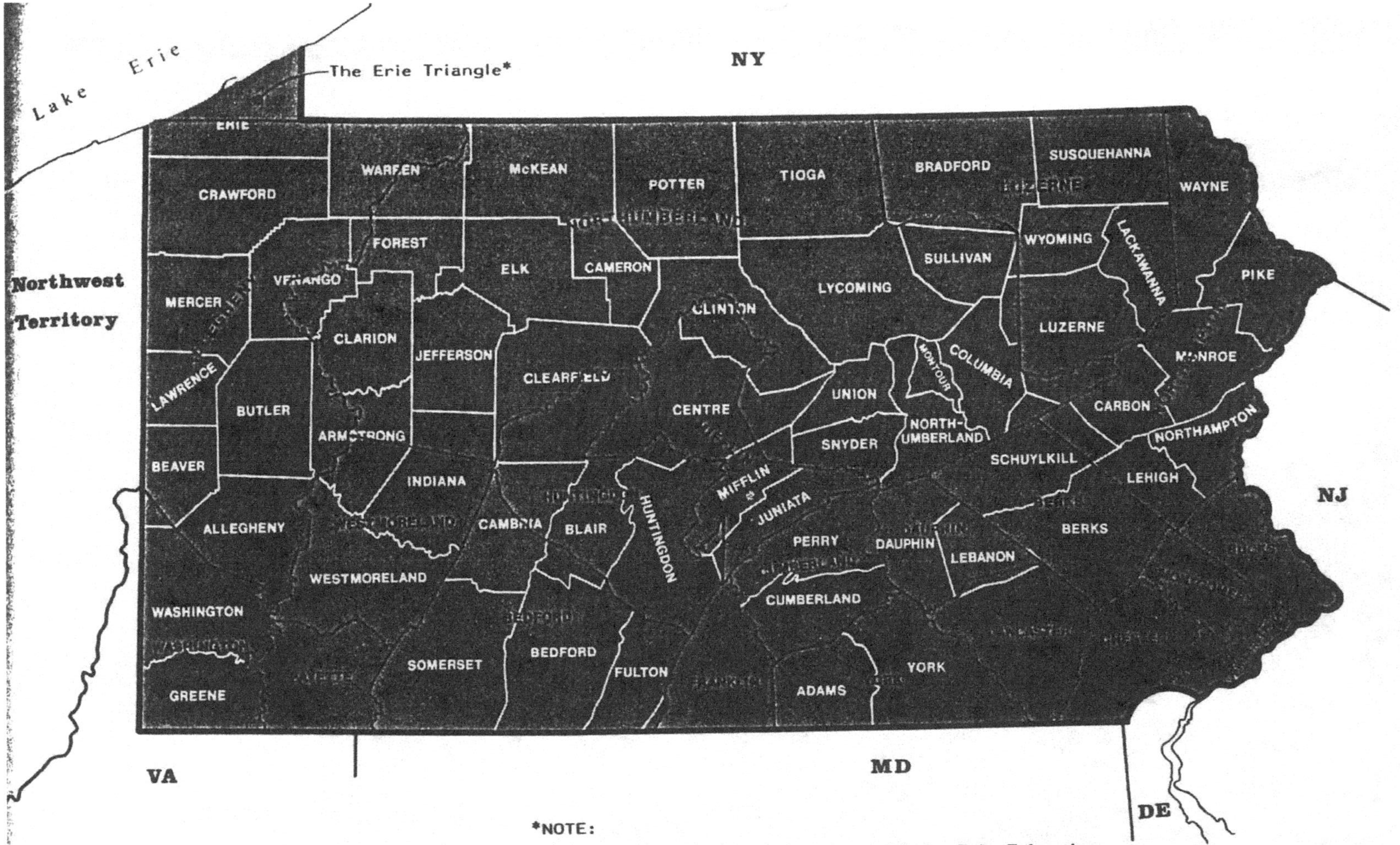

*NOTE:

Although the federal government sold the Erie Triangle to Pennsylvania by patent in 1792, Pennsylvania had purchased the land from Indians in 1789. The Triangle was added to Allegheny County in 1792.

CENSUS AVAILABILITY

Federal census extant for all counties

MAP GUIDE TO THE U.S. FEDERAL CENSUSES, 1790-1920 by William Thorndale and William Dollarhide.

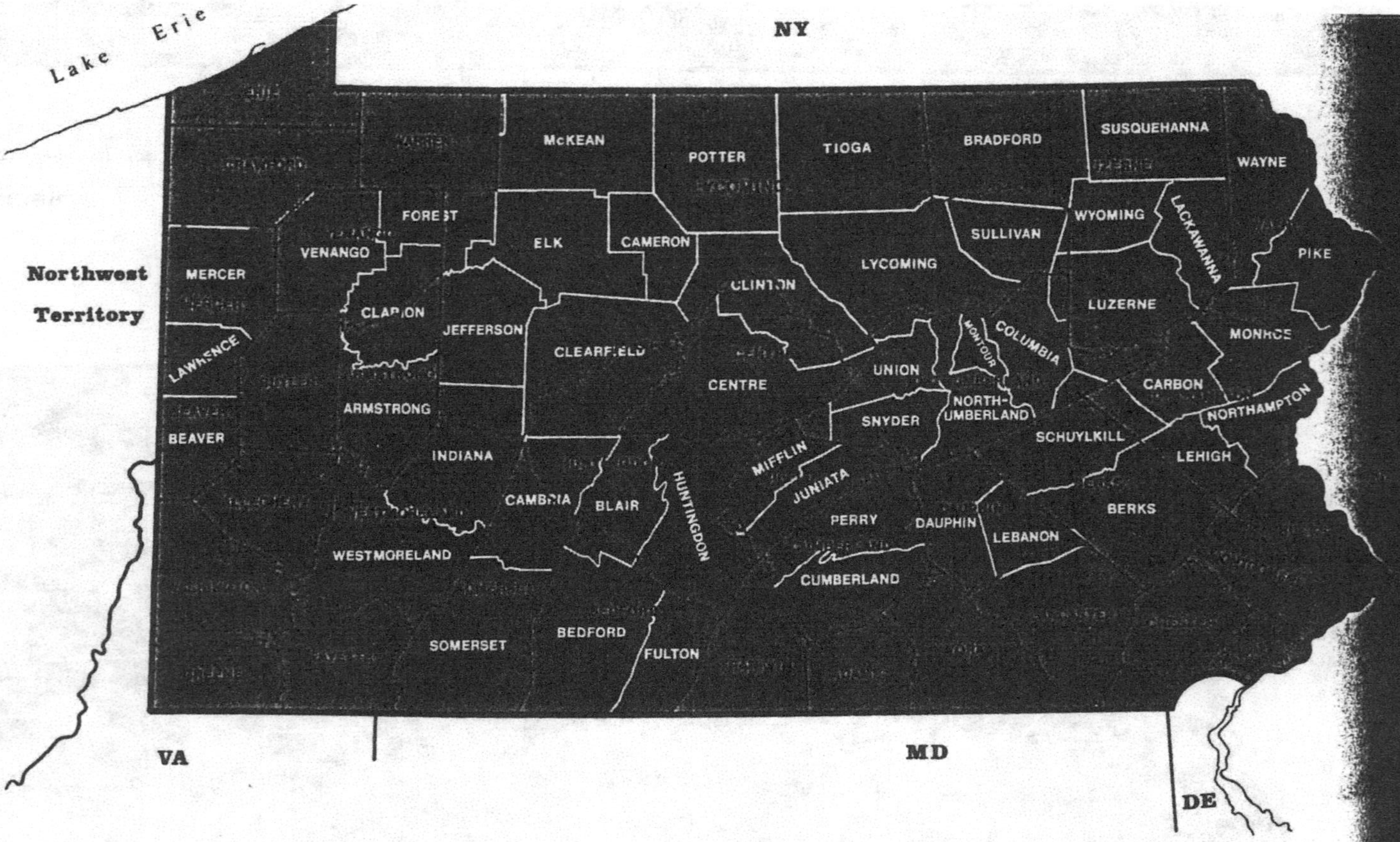

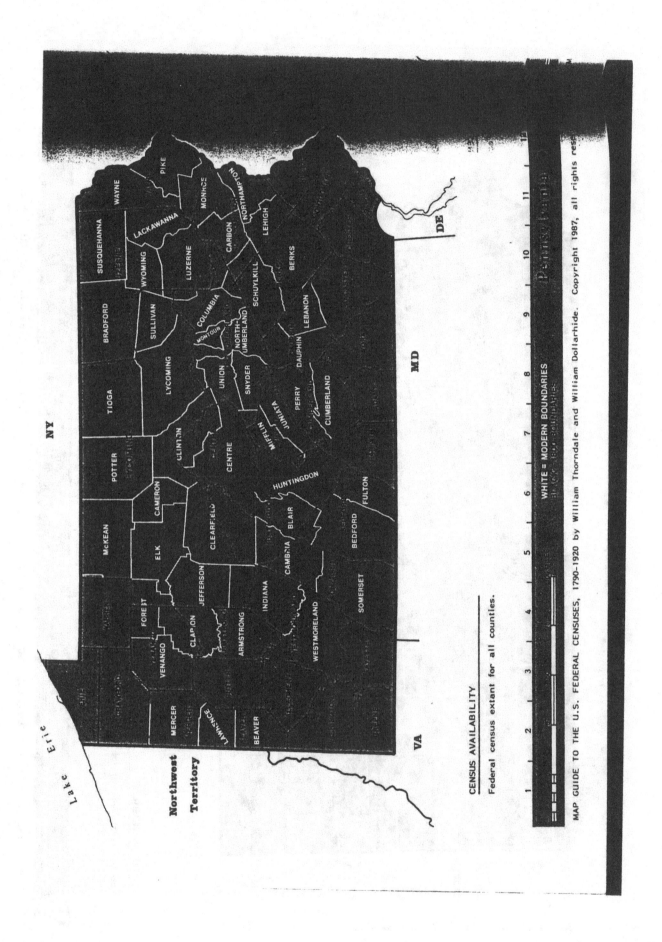

CENSUS AVAILABILITY

Federal census extant for all counties.

1 2 3 4 5 6 7 8 9 10 11 12

WHITE = MODERN BOUNDARIES

MAP GUIDE TO THE U.S. FEDERAL CENSUSES, 1790-1920 by William Thorndale and William Dollarhide.

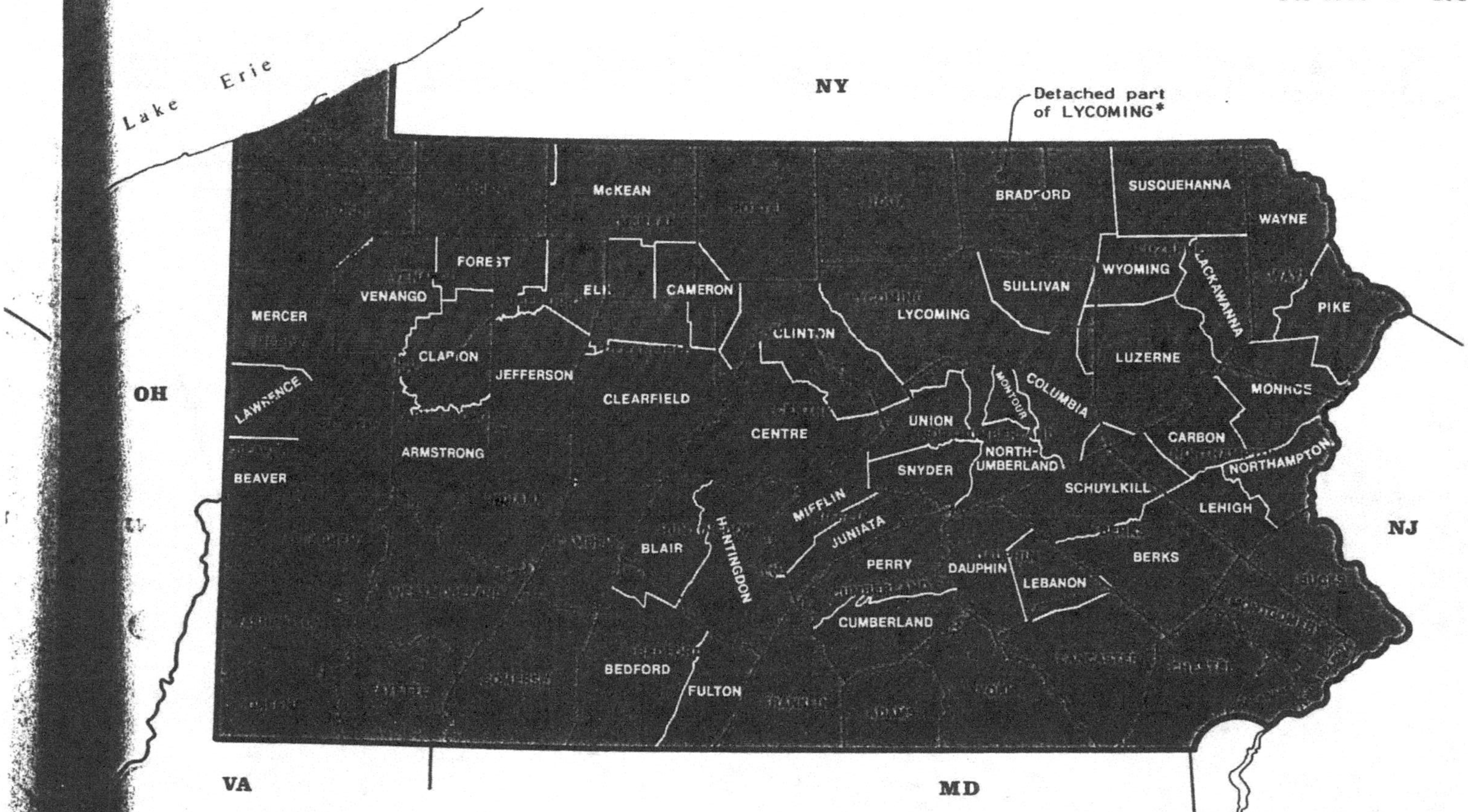

*NOTE:

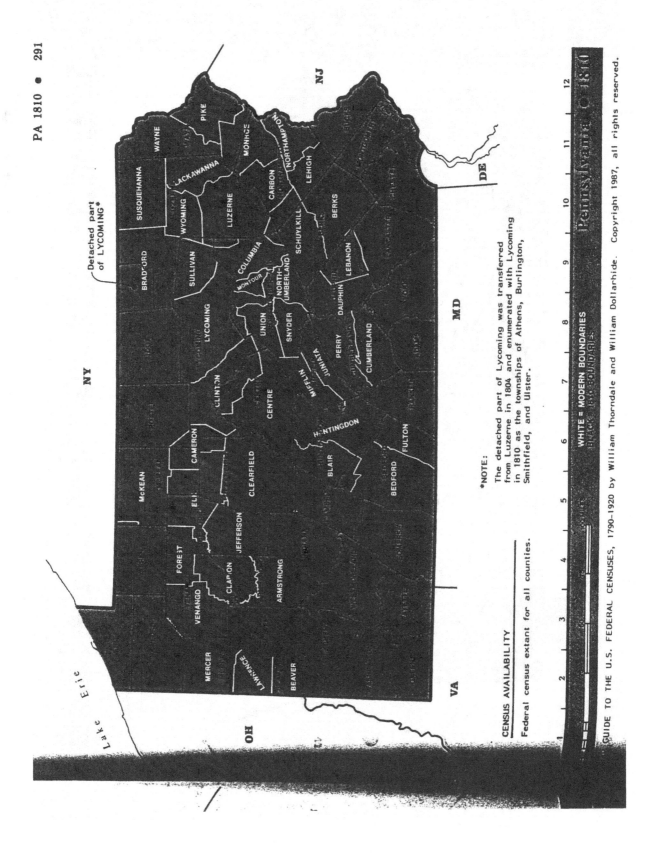

The detached part of Lycoming was transferred from Luzerne in 1804 and enumerated with Lycoming in 1810 as the townships of Athens, Burlington, Smithfield, and Ulster.

CENSUS AVAILABILITY

Federal census extant for all counties.

1 2 3 4 5 6 7 8 9 10 11 12

WHITE = MODERN BOUNDARIES
BLACK = 1810 BOUNDARIES

Pennsylvania • 1810

GUIDE TO THE U.S. FEDERAL CENSUSES, 1790-1920 by William Thorndale and William Dollarhide.

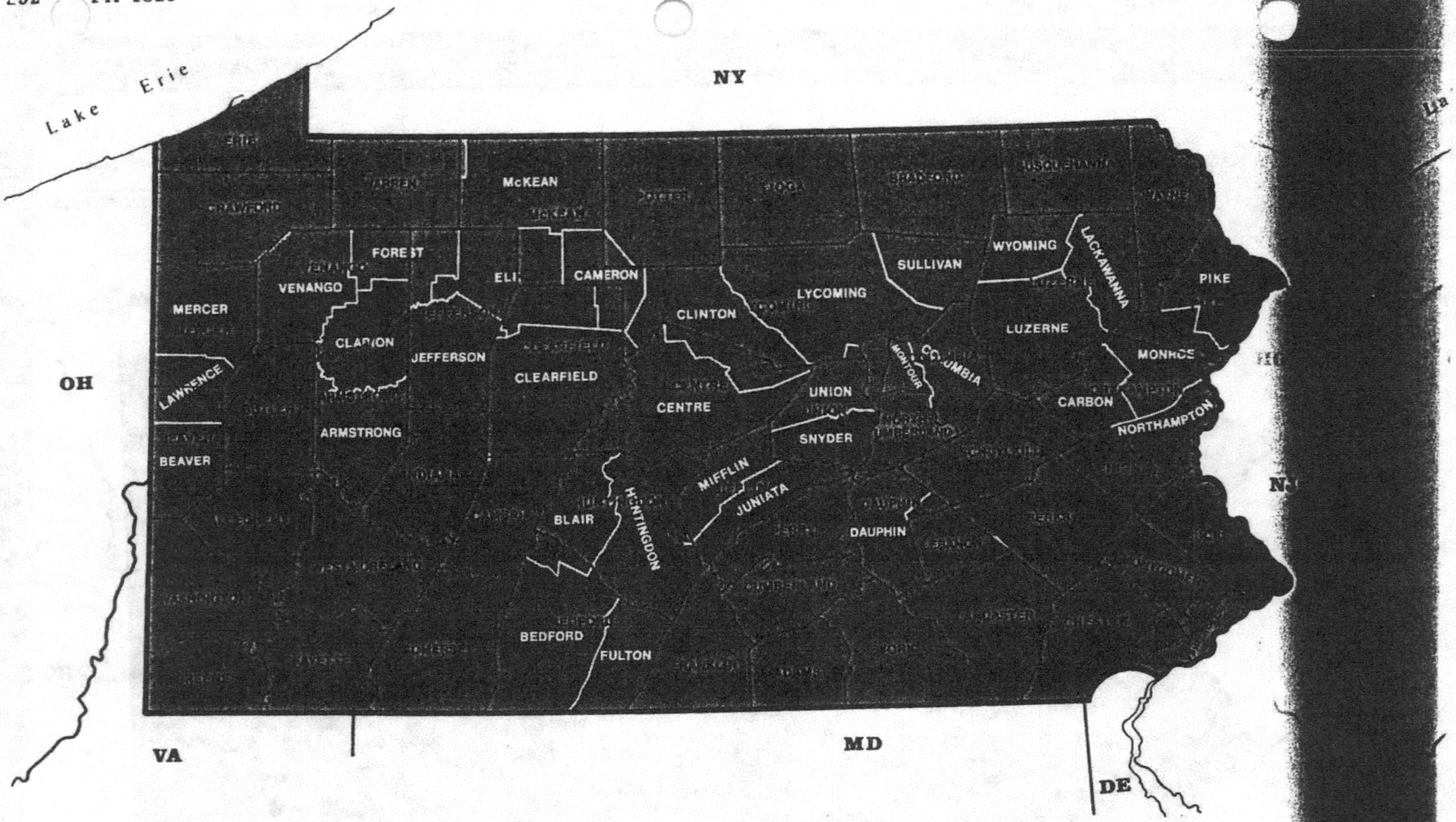

CENSUS AVAILABILITY

Federal census extant for all counties.

MAP GUIDE TO THE U.S. FEDERAL CENSUSES, 1790–1920 by William Thorndale and William Dollarhide.

Michael DeBolt

and His Descendants

by One of Them

Ella M. (Doggett) Hostetler

1926

Clipper Press, Shelton, Nebraska

ELLA M. (DOGGETT) HOSTETLER

Michael DeBolt came to America according to Rupp's list of early Pennsylvania Settlers (page 135) the 3rd of September, 1739, on the ship, "Robert and Alice," with Walter Goodman, Commander, from Rotterdam.

Michael DeBolt was descended from the French Huguenots, and it is more than likely that the severe persecutions of his ancestors caused him and a brother to seek a country of freedom.

On landing in Philadelphia, he at once took the oath of allegience to America. His signature, very well written in doing so, has been preserved and filed with many others in the Old Records Department of the Pennsylvania State Library at Harrisburg. I sought a copy of it and secured it through the courtesy of the librarian and the clerk.

It is not positively known where Michael DeBolt was located during the interval between his arrival in 1739 and his application for surveying his land in 1773. Judge Veech in his history said, "it is likely that Michael DeBolt and others took 'Squatters Rights' at first."

Another history states, "the French were different from most of the other early Pennsylvania emigrants who arrived, from the fact that they were eager to get away from the city as speedily as possible, and push on into the interior, in the wilderness to establish homes."

Tradition gives it that he was in the locality where he is later known to have lived as early as 1768. He may have been there earlier.

Some people living in Masontown, Pennsylvania, today by the name of DeBolt say in their childhood the name was pronounced as if spelled "Tiebolt," and from that fact, and the following account I am inclined to believe he was there much earlier than 1768. Henning's Statutes at Large, Vol. 8., page 127, for 1764 to '73 of Agusta county, Virginia, (which included part of southwestern Pennsylvania at that time) in its record of Robert

Brackenride's company of militia in 1758 states, "Michael Tiebolt was paid ten pounds," but does not specify what for. Part of the article reads, "and they (the commissioners) shall pay any claims that may be produced to them, for provisions furnished the volunteers, and captains on their return from Pittsburg to the Virginia Colony."

As this route would be almost directly in line with where it is known he later lived, and too, from the fact that he is said to have always lived on neighborly and friendly relations with the Indians, I am inclined to believe he lived there at that time, and provided provisions for the soldiers, rather than that he served as a soldier.

By trade he was a gunsmith.

A warrant for a patent to land was issued to Michael DeBolt in Philadelphia in these words, "1st April, 1773, The Hon. Richard Penn, Esquire, (who was the youngest son of William Penn), Lieutenant Governor of the late Province of Pennsylvania, by virtue of certain powers, granted to Michael DeBolt to be surveyed, one hundred acres of land on Catt's Run, on the east side of the Monongahela river subject to the purchase money, and so forth.

This tract of land was called "St. Michaels" in the patent. It is in German township, and in the present Fayette county. Before it was called Fayette, it was Bedford. German township and Fayette county were organized at the same time in 1787. "His Excellency, Benjamin Franklin, Esqr., who was President of the Supreme Executive Council of Pennsylvania," signed the patent in clear, even, and excellent writing, the 25th day of October, 1787, and in the twelfth year of the Commonwealth of Pennsylvania.

A copy of the above is recorded in Patent Book "P," Vol. 11, Page 318, in the Department of Internal Affairs of Pennsylvania, at Harrisburg, and the original parchment or patent is in the possession of a bank cashier in Masontown, who says he will never part with it, and regards it as he would his very life.

His father bought the Michael DeBolt farm and there he was born more than fifty years ago. The farm is still the property of his brother and himself. The patent had been left in a desk and thrown out with "other rubbish." He found it, secreted it and kept the knowledge of it even from his brothers for many years. He loves it because it is old and at one time of great value; he loves it because it was his find; there are no family ties binding it to him, yet he fairly worships it. He was a stranger to me when I went to his bank to make some inquiry about the farm. I gave him some information about it he had not known. He became interested and told me if I would call there later he would show me some old historic papers. I went and he handed me the patent of my ancestors. I did not know it was in existence and the sensations I experienced in holding in my hand that parchment which had been handled by so many of my ancestors can never be described, nor even understood, except by one placed in a similar position.

Last year I called on the cashier again. I had copied the copy of the patent at Harrisburg, but I wanted to copy the original, for in the copy Benjamin Franklin's signature was typed. In the original it was written by his own hand. I wanted to copy that and was given the privilege, but being a stranger to him, he took great precautions lest his precious document might run off. I copied it at a desk in an outer office enclosed by a railing which has a gate with a spring lock. After I was seated and ready for work the locked gate was well tested as to its strength. It was a laughing matter to me, and yet it was the strongest proof he could have given of his loyalty to our old family heirloom and I am indeed grateful that he has preserved it. It could not have been better preserved in any other hands.

What is now Fayette county, Pennsylvania, was in early times the French and Indian battleground. Pennsylvania, Maryland and Virginia all claimed it, and in that county George Washington lost his first and only battle, at Fort Necessity.

About the time the patent was granted, Michael DeBolt sold the one hundred acres it covered to George DeBolt of what relation we do not know.

I have copied in the Court House at Uniontown, Pennsylvania, the county seat of Fayette, every record bearing on any of my ancestors there I could find. Among them the maps of the surveys made of their lands, and wish they might all be included in this sketch.

Michael DeBolt's son, Michael DeBolt, Jr., was granted a patent by the Commonwealth of Pennsylvania, the 14th of September, 1796, to two hundred and ninety-four acres of land in a tract called "Clear Springs" which he was to hold in trust for his father's heirs.

Michael DeBolt, Sr., died about 1795. His minor children only are mentioned in the county records. His wife's name was not found. Possibly she died first as the records for the year 1796, in the Orphan's Court names as minor children, Catherine, who later married George Mason and lived in Allegheny county; Michael, Jr., who was born in 1774; Madaline, or as she was often called Micklin, who married William Ecklson and lived in Beaver county, and Mary. In 1800 Michael DeBolt, Jr., was made administrator of his father's estate and the court records show that he paid to each heir one hundred and thirteen pounds and ten shillings.

Michael DeBolt, Jr., married Abalona Yeager—a German lady—the daughter of Joseph Yeager, who was a Revolutionary soldier and one of the very early settlers of Springhill township in Fayette county. All county records concerning him show him to have been a man of means, of good sound business judgment and a man of affairs.

He was one of the trustees in purchasing the land for the Lutheran church and cemetery near Masontown. This church is said to have been one of the very first churches erected west of the Allegheny mountains.

JOSEPH YEAGER
Revolutionary Soldier

Descendants—Ella M. (Doggett) Hostetler (right) and Goldie (Mrs. Wayne) Darrall (left).

Joseph Yeager lived to the age of 98 years. He was born in 1740 and died in 1838. He is buried in the cemetery he helped to locate. His grave is fittingly marked with a tombstone which is yet in fairly good condition. It probably was placed there soon after his death. He died in the home of his son-in-law, Michael DeBolt, in a two-story red brick house, very common in those days in that country. Today it is well preserved and is about a half mile, "as the crow flies," from Masontown.

Michael DeBolt and his wife, Abalona (Yeager) DeBolt, were the parents of a large family. Joseph married a Ralphsnider; Catherine married a Shuck; Eva married a Stone and Mary (my grandmother) married Squire Huffman; Rosina, who was baptized in 1811 and married William Altman on whose farm we are informed the town of Wauseon, Ohio, was located; Naomi married John Newcommer; Elizabeth married a Sangston; George is not recorded as married; Henry married Elizabeth Richey September 18, 1834; Solomon born 1816, died 1819, and John born 1803 died in six days.

Some Masontown people talk of what they have heard of the hospitality of Michael DeBolt's home.

Michael DeBolt was an industrious, big-hearted farmer, never so happy as with his family about him and as many more as could gather in.

Near the home he built a great barn, and much of the timber in it was of walnut and other valuable woods. An orchard was planted above the house and nearby was a very large spring of clear, sparkling water, and a spring house close by. The first time I visited the spring tears rained from my eyes as I went down the steps and thought of the many times my mother's pattering feet as a child had passed that way, for it was there she and her sister lived after they were motherless. Then there must have been trees all about them; now there are none, save in the orchard.

On my last visit—1925—I found the wind had secured sufficient sweep over those naked hills to blow down the famous old barn, and in taking the coal from under the land in this one of the richest coal fields of the United States, the surface had dropped sufficiently to cause the great spring to entirely disappear, and now the owners have had to pipe lines from the town for water.

When Henry, the youngest son of Michael DeBolt, was in business in Masontown, he signed a contract with the builders of the National Pike to supply the workers through Fayette county with all the pork needed to feed them. The demand was too great. He lost all he had in trying to meet his contract. Then his father was taxed to the utmost to assist him, and finally signed his name as security for him. With the usual result, the wrecking of a home and all earthly possessions.

The National Pike was begun in 1811 and completed in 1818, and from that time until 1852 it was the one great highway over which passed the bulk of trade and travel and also the mails between the east and the west.

It was in 1843 that the final crash came to the DeBolt family and the security debt had to be paid. Michael DeBolt left the home of his ancestor—the only home he had ever known—and the only home of his own he was ever to know, and with his family and his son, Henry, and his family, they went away entirely empty-handed, leaving even the spoons, knives and forks. He said they were justly another's and the long-prized patent was left in the desk.

A veil has kindly been drawn over their departure, which hides it entirely from our view. We were too young to be told of these things when our mother died, and we did not come in touch with any of the family again until my first visit to Masontown in 1918, and now I love it so much I go there every year. We have no knowledge of how the exiles reached Adams county, Ohio, and the little country place calley "Tranquility."

It was considered too great a burden to care for both children longer under the circumstances, so before they left Pennsylvania, my mother was sent to an aunt in northern Ohio. She was compelled to bear burdens she was unaccustomed to, and beyond her strength. She was found one day at a spring where her aunt had sent her to do the family washing. The country was still a wilderness, abounding in wolves. She was overcome with fear. Mr. James Sparks, a friend of Michael DeBolt, and who formerly lived in Fayette county, Pennsylvania, discovered her in this plight, and picked her up, placed her behind him on his horse and took her to her grandparents in southern Ohio. Then he and his wife, who had no children, took her to their own home. She lived with them until her marriage, giving and receiving the affection of a real daughter. She was married from their home, the "Denny House," in Hillboro, Ohio, June 20, 1855.

Henry DeBolt remained with his parents in Adams county, Ohio, for ten years, then moved with his family to Holt county, Missouri.

Michael DeBolt was sixty-nine years of age when he left his only home and like his Huguenot ancestors, he started out from Pennsylvania he hardly knew where, but remained in Ohio with his wife and granddaughter, Eva, after his son's departure. Eva died in 1854 and Michael, who had given up all for the sake of honor, followed her in 1859. Henry returned for his mother and took her to his home in Missouri. She died October 21, 1861, and is buried there in Fairview graveyard. How scattered this once happy family were at last!

For many years I had a great desire to find the graves of this honorable and kind old man and my aunt, his granddaughter, and in 1919 the way was made for me to do so. I had never heard their graves were marked, but I found them side by side with two pretty white marble tombstones (white after all these years) under a large maple tree near the church in the "Tranquility" churchyard in Adams county, Ohio.

The inscription on one reads:

Michael DeBolt
Died May 21, 1859
Aged 85 yrs.
& 9 ds.

On the other:

Eva E.
Daughter
Squire and Mary Huffman
Died
April 10, 1854
Aged 21 Years
11 m's and 3 ds.

It is my belief that my mother had the two stones placed

at those graves.

My grandmother, Mary DeBolt, was born March 24, 1809. Married Squire Huffman March 19, 1829. She died February 16, 1833, and is buried in the Lutheran cemetery at Masontown, Pennsylvania, beside her two young brothers, and not far from her grandfather, Joseph Yeager. She left two young daughters, Mary Ellen (my mother), and Eva Elizabeth, a babe.

The inscription on her tombstone reads:

In Memory of Mary Huffman, Consort of Squire Huffman
Daughter of Michael and Abalona DeBolt
Who departed this life February 16, 1833
Aged 23 years, 10 months and 22 days
Death is a debt to nature due, which I have paid,
and so must you.

My mother, Mary Ellen Huffman, was born July 13, 1830. She married Cary Armstead Doggett June 20, 1855, in Hillsboro, Ohio. She died April 7, 1866, and is buried in the Hillsboro cemetery. She left two children, Martha Luella Doggett, born August 25, 1856; Charles Brownell Doggett born January 26, 1858, who died May 13, 1874, and is buried beside our mother.

Before my brother, Charlie, reached the age of 14, he had chiseled (under instructions) on a block of marble the flag of the United States. It is well done and one of my most treasured possessions. Ill health prevented him from doing more. He died at the age of 17. He had blue eyes, and fine features. His hair like his disposition was full of the sunshine color. He had the quiet dignity of our mother and was a student.

Martha Luella Doggett (always called Ella) married Max A. Hostetler, September 21, 1880. There are no children and their residence since marriage has been Shelton, Nebraska.

Our mother's father, Squire Huffman, was the grandson of a Revolutionary soldier, John Huffman, of Bedford county, later Fayette. Bedford county then embraced all of southwestern Pennsylvania. In 1773 Westmorland county was erected from it and in 1787 Fayette county. The official tax rolls of Bedford county for 1773 shows that John Huffman was one of the early settlers, and there as early as 1772. Judge Veech in his history, "The Monongahela of Old" also mentions him as one of the first settlers. Squire Huffman died from cholera at Port Hudson, Louisiana, about 1850.

Our father, Cary Armstead Doggett, was born April 23, 1827, in Hillsboro, Ohio, in his father's log tavern, called "The Eagle," one of the first built in the town, and twenty-nine years later his daughter, Ella, was born on the same location, but in a new brick building called "The Ellicott House."

Cary Armstead Doggett died at Hyde, Colorado, June 22, 1887, in a railroad town located on his land. He is buried there. He was in the Mexican War as a sergeant through 1846-47. In the Civil War he was a first lieutenant in the First Ohio Volunteer Cavalry. His captain and friend was Martin Buck of Hillsboro.

Cary Armstead Doggett's father, Armstead Doggett, served as a non-commissioned officer in the War of 1812 under two enlistments from Culpeper county, Virginia. He is buried in Hillsboro, Ohio, on my father's burial lot. Armstead's father, James Doggett, was a soldier in the Revolutionary War from Virginia and James' father, "George Doggett, Planter," was commissioned a lieutenant in 1741 in Orange county, Virginia.

As the last living member of Michael DeBolt, Sr. and Michael DeBolt, Jr., through my grandmother, Mary (DeBolt) Huffman's branch of that family, I have written out this history of honorable Huguenot descendents. It may interest other branches of the family and be the means of reuniting them, but my main purpose has been to give to history these facts as far as I have been able to find them and above all to give due credit to these two courageous men who had their place in the history-making of this country.

—15—

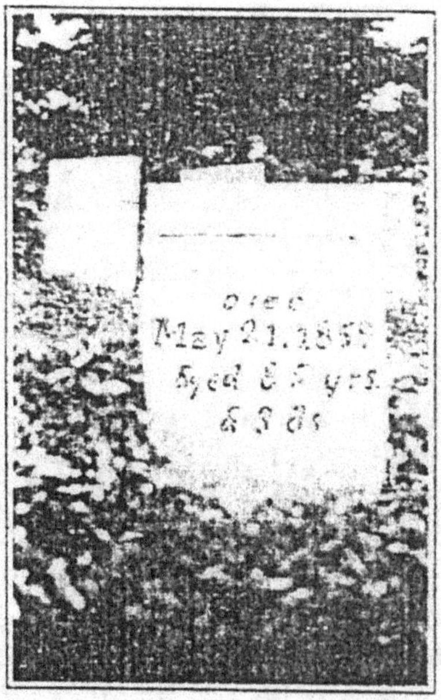

MY MOTHER

MARY ELLEN (HUFFMAN) DOGGETT

Through whom I inherited ancestry to the Michael DeBolt family, and, as I knew her, for nine and one-half years until she was called to her Heavenly home in 1866.

The memory of her is as strong today as though the sixty years intervening had been but yesterday.

She was only 36 years of age at the time she left us. She was as fine in appearance as she was in character, and though we were only children, we looked upon our mother with just pride and admiration.

She was, perhaps, about five feet and seven inches tall, and in health weighed 150 pounds. She was straight. She had black hair and brown eyes, eyes that always seemed to look deep down into our own as if to read our inmost thoughts. We knew then; I know it today, that they spoke as nothing else could to us her desire to have us be all that she wished in goodness, kindness and loving obedience. I am sure she was never once disappointed in my brother. He was like her in all things and always made her happy, while I never knowingly was disrespectful to her, I caused her grief by running away, by climbing trees and falling from them, often being badly hurt and engaging in boys' games.

She lived ahead of her time in many ways, in the thoughts she expressed, the things she did and her study not common in those days, particularly the study of medicine which she took up before she became a homemaker that she might be able to care properly for her household.

She was absolutely fearless in entering a home where there was disease of any nature and once when smallpox came in the home of a friend across the alley, she sent us children to relatives in the country and went to that home and cared for her friend until she was well.

She seemed proof against disease herself. It was only at the last when lung trouble attacked her from watching by many bedsides that she was forced to yield.

No home had been poor enough to keep her away, if the need was there.

She was especially tender and kind to elderly people, her early childhood had been spent with them and she had learned to take upon herself responsibilities and keep her heart atune with joy and cheer that they might be made happier.

In one thing, I am like my mother. In her hearty laughing she always cried.

She was married in 1855 and soon after that the whole country was torn asunder by events leading to the Civil War in 1861. We lived near the "border" in southern Ohio, causing problems not found generally. With her three-year-old baby son, Charlie, in her arms and me, not yet five years old, clinging to her skirt, we stood on the depot platform and waved goodbye to our father as he went off to war as a first lieutenant in the First Ohio Volunteer Cavalry.

In 1862 he was with General Grant at Corinth, Mississippi. Water conditions were bad. He contracted typhoid fever and was sent to Louisville, Kentucky, and our mother went to him, taking a supply of fresh linen. She nursed him back to health and when he was able to be moved, took him home. When he was well he was appointed deputy provost marshal and served until the close of the war.

Our mother was intensely patriotic and that spirit helped her over many rough places during those dark days.

Many women brought their letters from the battle fronts to her to be deciphered and read. Many came to her for information, for she kept well informed. To others she gave food, clothing and consolation.

If she had stronger sympathy with one class of unfortunates than another, it was for the motherless children and many were comforted in their last hours by her promise to try to provide homes for their children. This she did in a number of cases. That was before there were many public children's homes in this country.

In religion, our mother was a devoted member of the Baptist church. Her church and her Bible were her staffs of life.

She was my father's second wife, but the family of his first wife's father, Squire William Richards (of whom there were none superior in southern Ohio), took her at once to their hearts and homes as their very own. The affection shown between them brings happiness to me today. It was always beautiful to see and is beautiful to remember.

They were devoted to each other at all times and when she left us they took us children to their home for a time. Many of them have "passed on" but there is a "tie that binds" for all time to those who are left.

Our mother did very beautiful sewing by hand. She never owned a sewing machine and when she made her wedding dress, a pearl-colored silk, it was all made by hand. The forms in the back of the bodice (which I now have) were as neatly stitched as any machine today could do it.

When Thanksgiving Day came, she neatly folded her work in her basket and rested as she did on Sunday.

She often taught us children lessons for life through the stories she told. One day while she was so engaged our father passed through the room and while he did not stop nor make any comment, I considered it a great intrusion. We were so intent in listening to her that I resented his appearance at all, being much like him; he evidently understood my look of resentment, smiled and passed on into another room, carefully closing the door after him. He knew he had no place in that hallowed spot just then. He knew what we did not know and I wonder now if he did not pass through to see how our mother's strength was holding out.

One of her stories that day made a deep impression on my life. Street lamps were not yet common and she pictured elderly people, some crippled, some infirm, trying to find their way about on dark nights, over rough and uneven streets with no light to aid or guide them. That picture caused me great sympathy and distress. Our home had inside shutters and she said to us "always leave the upper shutters open at night to light the way for old people," and to this day, in spite of electric lights along our streets, I invariably try to have the light shine out from our home for a time every evening, in memory of her wishes.

The moral of another story was, no matter how uncouth or rough looking a person may appear, they may be thoroughly good at heart, so she told us not to mistreat such a person, and especially, not to fear them. I do not recall her telling us stories again. I think it was the last time she was able to be up.

I know now, though, she was so cheery and bright that day with us that she knew the parting time was near, and so with the courage of her Huguenot ancestors, the DeBolts, she was trying to prepare us to carry on, and be unafraid.

The greatest blessing in life is the noble character of a good Christian mother, and such was our mother.

ELLA M. (DOGGETT) HOSTETLER.

9731 Oak Hill Road
Woodsboro, Maryland
21798-9714

Dear Friends and Family,

Rosemary and I are happy to be able to fulfill our lifelong goal to write our book on the roots of the Summers Family. We would not have accomplished it without the help of family, friends, and all those happy, cheerful, and helpful librarians. My interest began as a child when my Aunt Jeannette O'Neill Jackson, an employee at the Daughters of the American Revolution in Washington, was encouraged by her friends to find an ancestor. As a Camp Fire Girl I made a 'Family Tree' Folder ...hand-painted tree in the centerfold with the few ancestors I knew.

I am a born 'Washingtonian'. William O'Neale arrived there in 1794. John Summers managed his tobacco plantation on the road to Marlboro just ouside of Washington and owned many slaves. I have a Christmas card my grandpa sent in 1935. He wrote.."Come visit me and hear our new radio!" If I knew than...

Today, John Summers II's tobacco plantation is part of Andrews Air Force Base, our "President's Own!" When driving around the beltway on I-95, at Pennsylvania Avenue [Maryland Route #4] one travels through the lands of my ancestor Nathan Summers...fifth generation...Nathan, Nathan, John, John, John. East on Pennsylvania Avenue there is a curve in the road. The home and family cemetery was there on the old Marlboro Pike. I passed that way many times as a child. I learned about this two years after the firemen practiced burning the neglected house. The family gravestones have been moved to a nearby church cemetery! John Summers III and John II lived down the old road where 'Andrews Air Force Base' is today. John Summers I's plantation was just over the railroad tracks five miles east.

My brother has taught me to use and value the computer. We visit weekly and continue to add documented members of our Summers' family. I received the following with a book order...

"I have my ancestor to an Anna Maria Summers who married Thomas Markland. He was born in Prince George's County and the family settled in Hamilton County, Ohio." Easy! She was the daughter of Benjamin, son of John II, son of John I.

If you will send your family line...birth, marriage, and death for each generation including your own...with the known sources...beginning with yourself to the last generation you know, we may have another Summers line to share! Please enclose a self-addressed stamped envelope!

We have a great heritage! I hope this book will preserve our past for generations to come and help others to find their beginnings in our great country.

Affectionately,

THE FIRST THREE GENERATIONS
of
JOHN SUMMERS
of
PRINCE GEORGE'S COUNTY, MARYLAND

by Rosemary B. Dodd and Helen Summers Holweck

The records abstracted from those held at the Maryland State Archives
are published with the permission of the Maryland State Archivist.

Table of Contents

Preface

This monograph incorporates the known material about the earliest three generations of the John Summers family of Prince George's County, Maryland. It is presented as a tool for studying succeeding generations. That part of Calvert County where the Summers lived became Prince George's County in 1696. The early Prince George's records are available as well as various parish materials. The records of early Calvert County are extinct, but state records for this period exist.

The first Summers generations are identified in the state records as "planters," tillers of the rich virgin land of Maryland. Many of the third generation began to leave Prince George's County (county established in 1696), first for the Frederick area (county established in 1748) and particularly that part which became Montgomery County (established in 1776). After the death of John Summers II, some of these members of the third generation moved from Maryland to Pennsylvania, Virginia, and the Carolinas. Records indicate this generation married in Maryland and when they moved, their children usually moved with them. Their inventories were modest, but they identified their land.

An Act of the Maryland Assembly enacted February 5, 1777, required the Oath of Fidelity and Support be taken by all citizens especially all holding positions of trust, all voting at any election, and all transacting business in Maryland, and thus is another type of census. It is likely that there are other records of this nature not included in Brumbaugh. The authors have used the *1776 MD Census* when possible; the Census is complete for Prince George's, Frederick, and Montgomery Counties but as with other Census, the absence of a name does not mean the individual was not in the State at that time.

There are a number of references on colonial Maryland. Life in early Maryland is discussed in *Maryland at the Beginning* by Carr, Menard, and Peddicord. The conditions of the plantation is covered in Newman's *The Flowering of the Palatinate*.

There are other Summers in the same time frame, but the authors have determined no connection between these and the John Summers family of Prince George's County. A brief resumé of other Summers will appear following the body of the monograph.

The following abbreviations are used in the body of the material:

b = born
bapt = baptised
m = married
d = died
dau = daughter
decd = deceased
/ = folio
MD = Maryland
MSA = Maryland State Archives
Index 56 = Rent Rolls-Index to Owner
Index 58 = Debt Books-Index to Owners of Tracts
LWT = Last Will and Testament
PG = Prince George's County, Maryland

The words **Senior** and **Junior** have not been indexed because of the varying uses of those words.

The LAND RECORDS, WILLS, and INVENTORIES are found in the Maryland State Archives, 350 Rowe Boulevard, Annapolis, Maryland 21401. The WILLS have been copied verbatim, including original spelling. Researchers, however, are encouraged to consult the original documents for their own interpretation and meaning.

The authors express their thanks to the staff of the Maryland State Archives for their helpfulness. The authors also wish to recognize the contribution of Letha Summers for sharing her study of George Summers and Sergio Dunlap for her research of Jemima Summers Caton.

The authors welcome correspondence about the presented material. Correspondence should be directed to: Helen S. Holweck, 9731 Oak Hill Road, Woodsboro, Maryland 21798-9714.

Helen Summers Holweck

MAPS

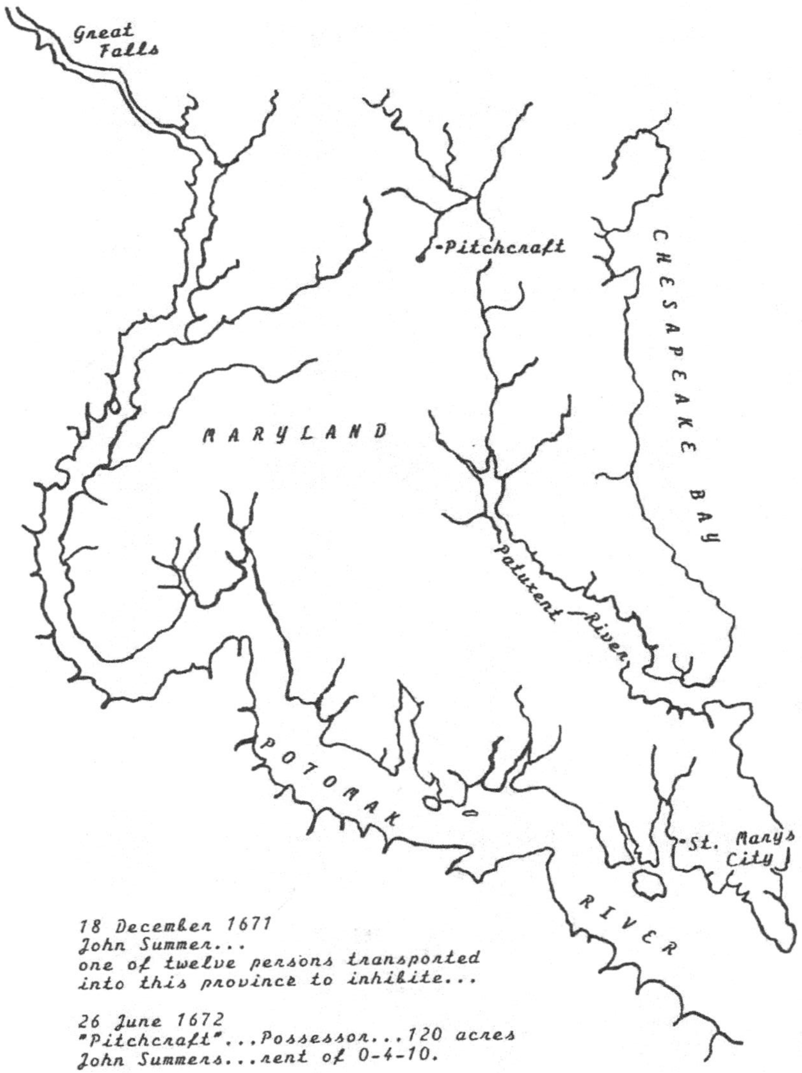

18 December 1671
John Summer...
one of twelve persons transported
into this province to inhibite...

26 June 1672
"Pitchcraft"...Possessor...120 acres
John Summers...rent of 0-4-10.

Prince George's County, Maryland,
east of Washington, D.C. and
west of the Patuxent River.

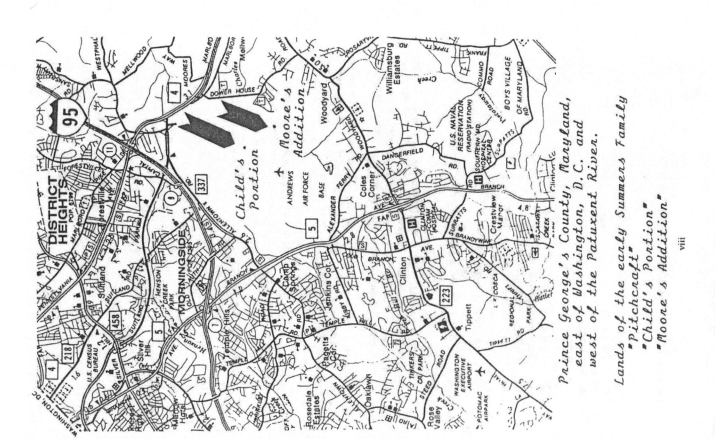

Lands of the early Summers Family
"Pitchcraft"
"Child's Portion"
"Moore's Addition"

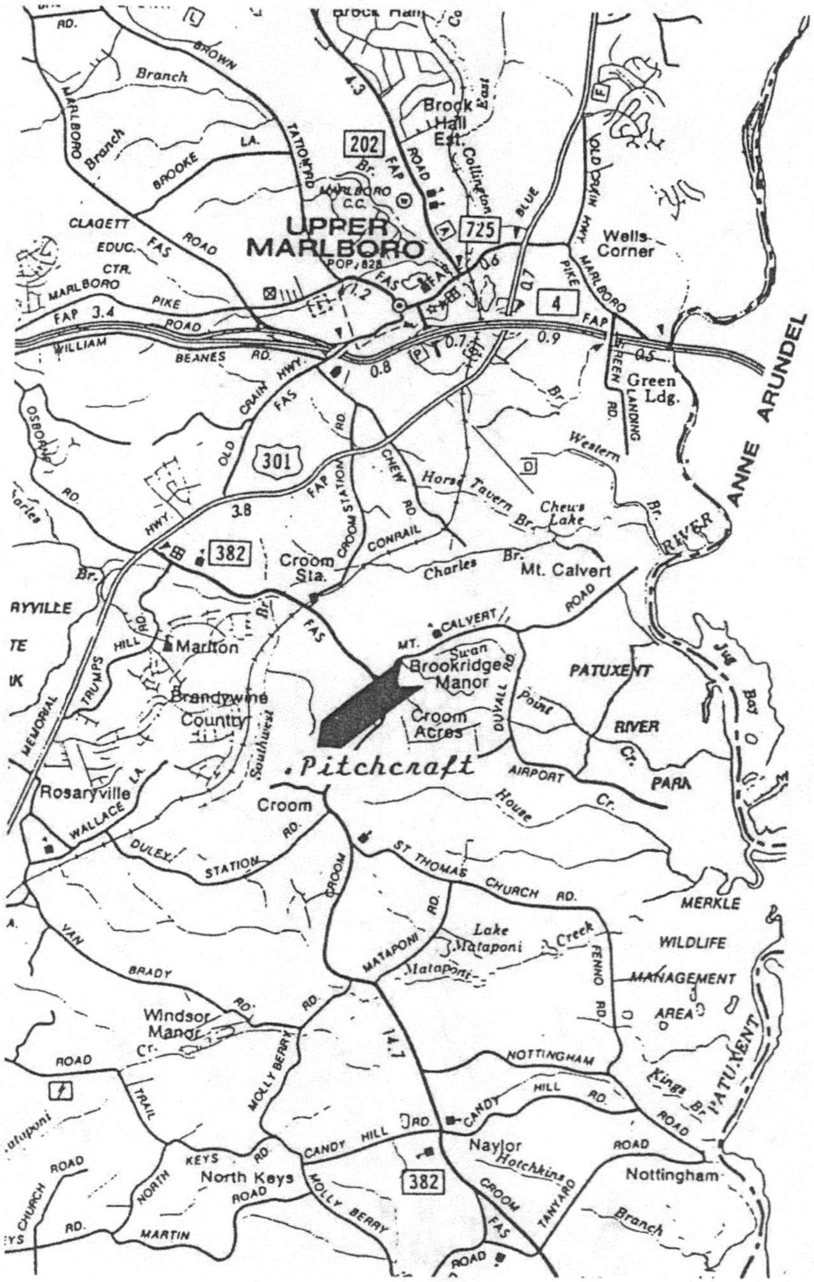

Lands of the Early Generations
of the Summers Family
on
Andrews Air Force Base, Maryland

1-"Child's Portion"...On the west side Patuxent River in the freshes and in the forks of Piscataway Branch.

2-"Moore's Addition"...on the west side of the Patuxent River in the fork of the Piscataway Branch.

3-"Outlett"...in a small branch that falls into Darnalls mill branch.

4-"His Lordships Kindness"...on the west side of the main branch of the Piscataway.

5-"Friendship"...on the East side of a small branch that runs into the Tinkers Branch.

6-"Poorman's Industry"...upon a knole at the head of the Tinkers Branch.

7-"Covert"...in a fork of a branch called Hensons Branch.

Location of Lands of John Summers II and
his Father-in-Law, James Moore
and Related Families

Now the President's Airport!
Andrews Air Force Base, Maryland

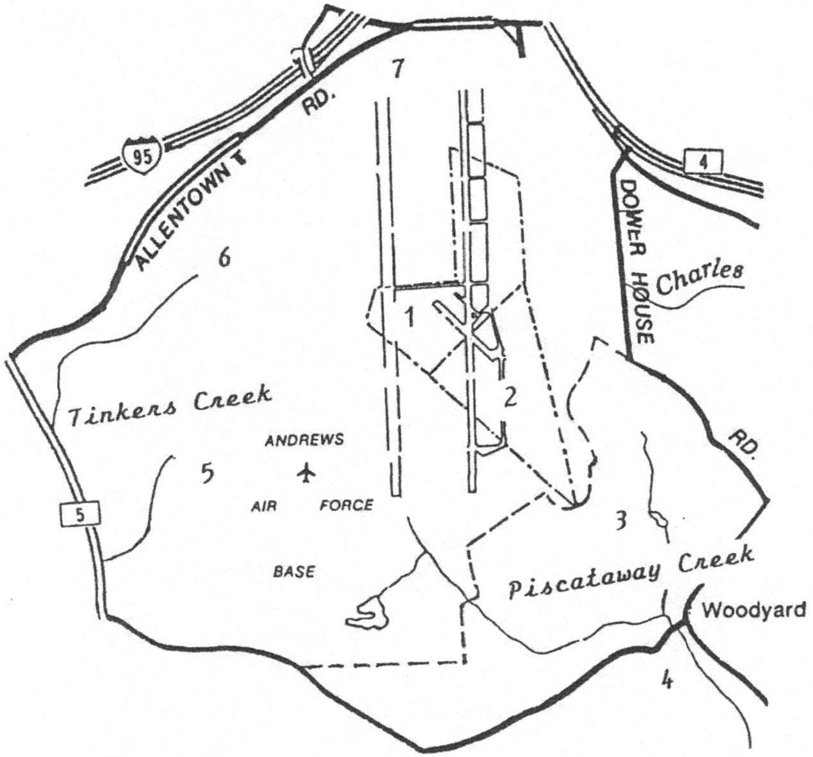

Major runways of Andrews Air Force Base are on the lands of "Child's Portion"...227 acres patented in 1694 and "Moore's Addition"...231 acres patented in 1691!

— — — = lands of Andrews Air Force Base **not** along a road.
— · — = lands of "Child's Portion" and "Moore's Addition"
= lands of related families

More Lands of the Early Generations
of the Summers Family
in Maryland

"Bradford's Rest"...on the east side of Rock Creek.

"Dann"...in a branch of Potomac River called Rock Creek branch, and on the West side near the forks of the said branch.

"Friends Advice"...near the head of a small branch on the East side that falls into Little Sineca.

"Gum Spring"...near ye draught of a branch called Oxon and near a cluster of Pines.

"Holding Spring"...on the bank of a spring that runs into Dry Seneca.

"Joseph Parke"...East side of a Rock Creek Branch, side ye Southernmost bound tree of his own Land called Hermitage.

"Saulsberry Plains"...near the head of a glade that falls into branch of Sennecca known as Cabin Branch.

"Strawberry Patch"...on the north side of a hill in the fork of Buck Lodge Branch.

"Sugarlands"...of Frederick County.

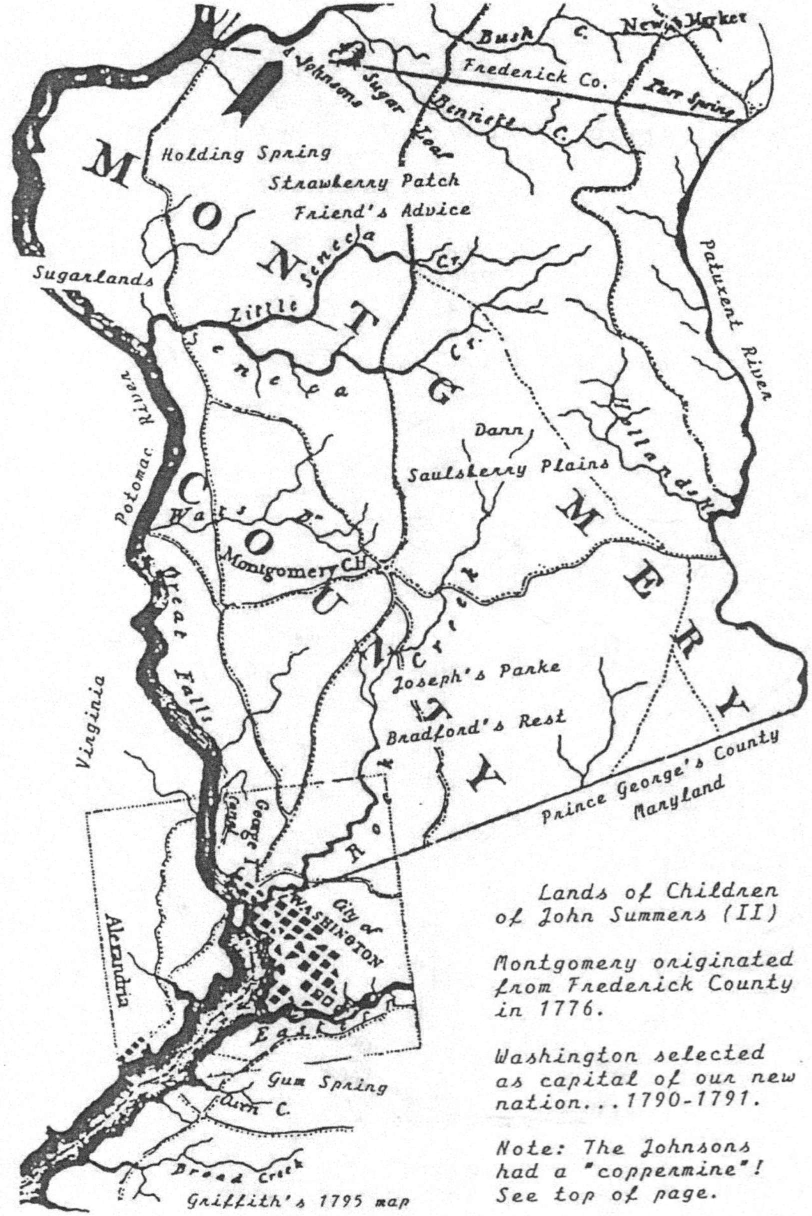

Lands of Children
of John Summers (II)

Montgomery originated from Frederick County in 1776.

Washington selected as capital of our new nation...1790-1791.

Note: The Johnsons had a "coppermine"! See top of page.

Map References

General Highway Map, Prince Georges County, Maryland. Prepared by the Department of Transportation, State Highway Administration, in cooperation with the U.S. Department of Transportation, Federal Highway Administration, 1990.

Griffith, Dennis. Map of Maryland. 1795. Original and copies at the Library of Congress, Washington, D.C.

Hienton, Louise Joyner. Prince George's Heritage: Sidelights on the Early History of Prince George's County, Maryland from 1696 to 1800. Map. The Maryland Historical Society. 1972.

Maryland. Geological Survey. Map of Prince George's County and District of Columbia showing the geological formations. In co-operation with U.S. Geological Survey. [Annapolis] 1911. Original and copies at the Library of Congress, Washington, D.C.

This map was used to transpose the Land Patents..."Child's Portion" and "Moore's Addition".

GENERATION I

John Summers

ARRIVAL

18 Dec 1671 Captain **John Boddy** proved his right to 600 acres of land for having transported 12 persons to Maryland among whom was **John Summer**. *Prince George's Land Patents 16*/394

Remarks: The records do not indicate the place of embarkation. This was the time Virginians, particularly Quakers and Puritans, were moving into Maryland. But with the **Summers'** activity in the parishes of the Church of England, it seems likely they arrived from England. The usual age for being transported as indentured was between 16 and 25 years.

PROPERTY

26 Jun 1672 PICH CROFT was surveyed lying in Calvert County Maryland on the west side of the Patuxent River in the woods south of "Croome", east of "Toogood" (Towgood) and southeast of "Timberly", 400 acres, for **Edward Fitzherbert**. *Prince George's Land (Certificate) 17*/311

26 Jun 1672 PITCHCRAFT survey for **Ed Fitzherbert**. Possessors: 280 acres **Henry Darnall**; 120 acres **John Summers** .... rent of £0.4.10. *Rent (tax) Roll Prince George's Land 4*/322

7 Jun 1680 **John Summers** of Calvert County demands his right to fifty acres of land due to him for his time of Service performed in this Province. Legally proved this day. On the same day **John Summers** sells unto **William Cocks** of St. Maris County all his right to said fifty acres of land. *Prince George's Land (Patents) WC#2*/173-174

1682 **Henry Brent** of Calvert County claims the right to Pitchcroft as **Edward Fitzherbert**, late of this province, failed to meet the conditions of the Plantations. **Edward Fitzherbert** "quitt and forfitted right" to claim. On this record the name **"Summers"** is written in the margin under Pitchcroft. *Prince George's Land (Patents) CB#2* /474-475

Remarks: Immigrant **John Summers** was transported to Maryland in December 1671, and by June 1672 was paying "ground rent" (tax) on 120 acres of land called Pitchcraft in Calvert, later Prince George's,

County. The importance of his claiming land in 1680, although it appears he had possessed land earlier, may relate to the right of suffrage as established by Charles, Lord Baltimore, in 1680: no one could vote who did not own 50 acres. (Ellis, Edward S. *History of the United States Vol I*/254)

CIVIL ACTIVITIES

6 Jun 1692 Sheriff of Calvert County to issue summons for **John Somers** to attend next court to testify re Edward Gold a negro (and) his freedom. (*Maryland Archives 13*/336)

Mar 1697/98 Impanelled as Juror. (Smith, Joseph H. and Philip A. Crowl, *Court Records of Prince Georges County, MD 1696-1699*/325)

Mar 1697/98 Defendant against **Josias Towgood**. (Ibid /333-34)

Mar 1697/98 "desires his marke be recorded viz. crop under keele and slitt in the right eare and cropp and under keele on the left ear". (Ibid /348)

28 Jun 1698 Impanelled on jury. (Ibid /356)

Nov 1698 "the marke J of **JOHN SUMERS**" (Ibid /389)

Sep 1699 **John Summers** and **John Henry** be overseers of Mount Calvert Hundred. (Ibid /547)

Remarks: **John Summers** was involved in the civil activities of the day by such examples as serving on the jury and as overseer of Mount Calvert Hundred.

LAST WILL and TESTAMENT

Prince George's Co. Prerogative Wills 12/110-111

"In the Name of God amen The first day of March in ye yeare of our Lord 1703.
I **John Sumers** Being Sick and Weake in body but in sound and perfect memory Thanks be to God for ye same I Doe make and ordain this my Last will and Testamt. first I give my Soule to Almighty God and body to ye Earth whereof it was made and to be decently Buried my Exx hereafter named-
First I make my Loving wife **Rebacca Sumers** my hole and sole Exx of my hole Estate During her natural Life Excpt She Should marry and then She shall be putt to her third part of the whole Estate.
Secondly I give my well beloved Daughter **Sary Westly** a Gray mare Branded with S and her increase to her and her heires forever and also I Give unto her two cows at ye day of her Marriage and their increase to her and her heires forever-
Thirdly I give my well beloved Grandson **John Street** a mare fole and her increase to him and his heires forever. I give my well beloved son **Jno Sumers** a young mare and her increase to him and his heirs forever
I give **Saml** Westly a mare fole and her increase to him and his heires foreverand after my wifes decds my Land to be equally to be divided between my two sons **Wm Sumers** and **Jno Sumers** -and to them and their heires forever and also my personall Estate to be equally devided amongst all my children and my wife **Rebaccah Sumers** to be my hole Exx of this my Last will and testamt Revoking all others- former wills and testamts thereby as Witness my hand and Seale ye day and yeare above written

Jno (S) Sumers"

Witnessed by **Fra: Pile**
Tho: Underwood
Hen: Boteler

WILL probated by 27 Nov. 1705

INVENTORY

30 Oct 1707 Goods and Chattells of **John Summers**, late of Prince Georges County, deceased. Appraised by **David Small** and **Christopher Bean**. £07.13.00 *Prince George's Co Inven BB1* /106

ADMIN...TRATION ACCOUNTS

20 Jul 1708 Account of **Henry Mackbee** and **Rebecca**, his wife, Executrix of LWT of **John Summers**, late of Prince Georges County. £104.15.00 *Prince George's Co Acct JB1/32-33*

11 Apr 1709 Account of **Henry Mackie** and **Rebbecca**, his wife, Executrix of **John Summers**, late of Prince George's County, deceased. £104.15.00 *Prince George's Co Acct JB1/45-46*

25 Feb 1711/12 Additional Account of **John Summers**, Surviving Executor of **John Summers**, late of Prince George's County, deceased. £1.19.3 *Prince George's Co Acct JB1/68-69*

Remarks: His wife **Rebecca** by his LWT was appointed sole executrix. By 1708 she had married **Henry Mackbee (Mackie)** and apparently was dead by 1711/12 when **John Summers**, as "surviving executor", presented an additional account of his father's estate. No WILL, INVENTORY, or ACCOUNT has been found for either **Rebecca Mackbee (Mackie)** or **Henry Mackbee (Mackie)**.

According to the WILL of **John Sumers**, his property was to be divided between his two sons after the death of his wife. Since the division of Pitchcraft between **William** and **John** took place in 1709, but not "enrolled" until 1713, it appears to reaffirm that **Rebecca** had died ca 1711/12. (For these citations, see GENERATION II.)

Generation II

Westly / Groom, Sara - By 1703, date of father's WILL, **Sara** was likely a widow, but her father anticipated her marriage (i.e. in his LWT she is to be given two cows at the day of her marriage). By 1707 she was the wife of **Richard Groom** when he and wife **Sarah** complained that **"Wm Sumers**, late of Prince George's Co. the 28th day of March 1707........stood justly indebted unto the said **Sarah** when she was also then called **Sarah Westly** for the sum of 550 lbs. of tobacco" *Prince George's Co. Court Records D i/*10.

No WILL, INVENTORY, or ACCOUNT has been found for **Sara Groom(e)**. There are entries identifying **Richard Groom** as a witness to various Indentures with the last being 1714. There is a 1734 WILL for a **Richard Groome** Prince George's Co., but there is no data that connects the two generations or two families. (See Generation III)

Remarks: It is probable that **Sara's** first husband was **Samuel Westly** because **Westly** is the name in her father's WILL and **Sarah Westly**, Administrator and Executrix of **Samuel Westly**, gave bond 25 Oct 1700 Prince George's (*Testamentary Proceedings Liber 18B* folio 73). In Smith and Crowl's *Prince George's Court Records* there is the following entry "**John Paine** sonn of **John Paine** about seven year old by his Fathers consent is bound to serve **Samuell Westly** untill he arrive to twenty one years of age...." Nov. Court 1696 p. 59. Also in *Prince George's Inventories Liber 20*/138 is the Inventory of Estate of **Samuel Westley** late of Prince George's Co. taken by **Richd Marsham** and **Thomas Greenfeild** Oct. 29, 1700.

Street, ______ - nothing further known about this daughter. The fact that she is not named in her father's WILL would indicate that she predeceased him.

Summers, William- presumed the elder son since he was mentioned first in father's WILL.

*Prince George's Co. Court Record (1708/06-1710/16) D i/*10 describes the legal action **Sarah Westly Grooms** and husband **Richard Grooms** took against **William**, "late of Prince George's Co., planter", because he did not repay the 550 lbs. tobacco in 1707. In the same Court Record folio 50 is the entry that two of her majesties agents were unable to locate the defendent and that they left a copy of the declaration and account at the house where he last lived.

In the August Court 1708 the Sheriff of PG Co. was ordered to attach the goods and chattel of **William Sumers** for the debt.

It was in 1709 that **William** sold his part of Pitchcroft to his brother **John**. That Indenture was witnessed by **Richard Groom**. *Prince George's Land Records Bk E* folio 199.

Remarks: There appear to be several **William Summers** in this time frame in the state of Maryland; records are located in Charles County, Calvert County and Baltimore County.

There was a **William Summers**, Charles County, surety for the Administrative Bond of **Ellinor Wakelin**, Administrator of **Charles Wakelin** 5 September 1709 (*Testamentary Proceedings Liber 21* folio 194). There is a **William Summers'** Inventory, *Charles Co. Liber I/*68 dated 17 May 1716 totalling £12.01.04. *Charles Co. Register of Wills 1708-1738 Liber 7*/147 gives the Account of **William Summers**, with **Mary Summers** Adm, dated March 21, 1718.

Violetta Summers, Baltimore County, by her renunciation dated 13 May 1718, assigns her right of Administration for her deceased husband **William Sumers'** estate to **Francis Street** dated 7 August 1719 (*Testamentary Proceedings Liber 23* folio 281). The *Baltimore Co. Accounts. Liber 2*/343, of 1719 is the record of **Francis Streets** adm. of **William Summers**, late of Baltimore Co., decd; but no relationship has been established from that document.

And there is in Calvert County an Inventory for William Summers 1746 (*Testamentary Proceedings Liber 32* folio 16), and a *Calvert Co. Account Liber 25*/88 of **Thomas Ireland, Jun.**, Adm. of **Wm Summers**, late of Calvert Co., dated June 29, 1747.

Summers, John - b ca 1685, Maryland. He was an adult in 1703 when his father wrote his WILL.

m by 1713 to **Mary Moore** (_____ - d after 1769), daughter of **James Moore, Sr.** and his wife **Mary**. *Prince George's Land Records Liber E*/185 " Indenture 10 July 1713 between **John Summers** of Prince George's Co. plantor and **Arthur Neale** ... a parcell of land being part of greater tract called Pitchcroft on westside Patuxent River in the freshes of the River" 120 acres. **Mary Summers** acknowledged the deed.

d by 9 Oct. 1769 in Prince George's Co., date WILL was probated

Prince George's Land Records 1710-1716 Liber E /21 contains an entry of July 26, 1710 of a bill to be paid **Hezekiah Burley** for £20.07.00. Signed **John ( ) Summers**. On back is note "for Mr. **Arden Careton** merchant in London".

Remarks: By 1710, **John Summers** was participating in business affairs. It is assumed that he could have been around 25 years of age then, so his birth was probably ca 1685, and thus likely he was born in Maryland.

Census:

1719 Taxable List, Piscattaway Hundred, Prince George's Co., lists **John Summers**. (*Calendar of Maryland State Papers No. 1, The Black Books*/164)

1733 Prince George's County List of Taxables in Upper Piscattaway Hundred lists **John Summers**. (Ibid page 268)

PROPERTY:

Pitchcroft- *Prince George's Co. Land Records Liber E*/199 Indenture 2 Sept 1709 between **Wm Somers**, Prince George's Co planter, and **John Somers** same co. planter.....sell all rights title and interest in parcel of land called Pitchcroft, "lying on westside of **Patuxent River** in the freshes". Consideration was 1,500 lbs. tobacco. Witnessed by **John Marklin** and **Richard Groom**. *Prince George's Land Records Book E old Series 5*/284 records the above Indenture with the notation "enrolled Oct. 21, 1713". Pitchcroft was sold to **Arthur Neale** 10 July 1713. *Prince George's Land Records Liber E*/185

Moors Adition- *Prince George's Land Records Liber E*/197 Indenture 1 Aug. 1713 between **Thos Clagatt** of Prince George's Co. and **John Somers** for tract called Moors Adition west side Patuxent River in the woods and in the fork of Piscataway Branch adjacent to part of parcel surveyed for **James Moore** called Child's Portion laid out for 231 acres. Enrolled Oct 21, 1713. Survey for Moore's Addition is dated 16 February 1694 (Prince George's Land Rent-tax 4/316). **Thos Clagett** had purchased Moores Adition from **James Moore** 28 Aug. 1712. At the death of **Mary Moore Summers**, the lower portion next to the Woodyard was bequeathed to son **Dent** and the rest to son **Benjamin**.

Child's Portion- *Prince George's Co. Land Records I*/546 Indenture between **James Moore, Sen.**, of Prince George's Co. and son-in-law **John Summers** of same county also planter for "natural affection and fatherly love" a tract of 35 acres called Child's Portion. July 20, 1723. Remarks: on the same day **John Summers** "for natural affection and loving duty" deeded to father-in-law **James Moore Sen**. 35 acres of a tract called Addition. *Prince George's Co. Land Records I*/457.

The Certificate for Child's Portion (*Prince George's Land Records B 23*/242) for **James Moore** was dated 1694 for 227 acres. By virtue of warrant of 500 acres granted to **Thomas Moore** of Calvert Co. bearing date 22 Aug. 1694 on west side of Patomac River, in the woods and in the freshes of the said river and in the forks of a branch called Piscattaway and next adjoining parcel surveyed for Col. **Ninian Beale** called Maidens Dowery. Original survey 11 July 1671, Calvert Co. Prince George's Land Rent Tax 4/362.

LAST WILL and TESTAMENT *Prince George's WILL Liber 37*/ 334-336

" In the Name of God Amen I **John Summers Sen.** of Prince Georges County being mindful of the uncertainty of Human Life and of perfect mind memory and understanding Doe make Ordain and Constitute this to be my Last Will & Testament in manner and form following / that is to say First I give and bequeath unto my loving Wife **Mary Summers** all the Land and

Plantation where I now live called Addition during her natural Life and after her Decease I give and bequeath fifty acres of the Tract of Land aforesaid to be laid off at the Lower end next to the Wood Yard unto my son **Dent Summers** his Heirs and Assigns forever I also give and bequeath all the remaining part of the said Tract of Land where I now dwell called Addition unto my son **Benjamin Summers** his heirs and assigns forever. And as for any Personal Estate which it has pleased God to Bless me with I give and bequeath unto my Loving Wife **Mary Summers** during her life and after her Decease I give and bequeath my Negro Man Charles unto my Daughter **Rebeckah King** and all the remaining part of my Estate after my wife's Decease to be equally Divided among my Children namely **John Summers, George Summers, William Summers, Dent Summers, Thomas Summers, Benjamin Summers, Joseph Summers, Mary Wheat, Rebeckah King, Rachel Johnson, Ruth Riggs,** and **Jemima Caton** and doe Constitute and appoint my Loving Wife **Mary Summers** my whole and Sole Executrix of this my Last Will and Testament and doe Revoke disanul and make void all other Wills by me heretofore made In Witness whereof I have hereunto sett my hand and Seal this ___ day of August Anno Dom. 1763

John (£) Summers Sen."

Witnessed by **Nath: Magruder**
Mord: Mitchell
James Moore son of **Benjamin**
John King Jun.

Probate dated 9 October 1769. Ibid p 335

Remarks: Of the thirteen known children of **John** and **Mary Moore Summers**, all lived into adulthood and only one (**James**) predeceased his parents. It appears that the children moved from Prince George's County into Frederick County, and then to other points, but did not leave Maryland until after their father's death. (There are records in other states of five of the 13 children.)

The records give no information about the death of **Mary Moore Summers**, but she is not listed in the *1776 MD Census*.

Note: George Alfred Townsend in his *Washington, Outside and Inside* published in 1874, page 706, describes the Woodyard in connection with the 1814 approach of British Troops "The Wood-yard stands at the source of Piscataway Creek and near by the ground is marshy. An old mill, mill-race and a couple of deserted barns are within a few furlongs distance in an old sleeping field. The aspect of the place is dismal except that a large dwelling surveys a part of the scenery from a moundy hill above the deep dell of the stream".

Westly/Groome, Sara, descendants

A **Samuel Westly** was alive in 1703 when he was left a bequeath in the WILL of **John Summers** (1703). The relationship was not identified. **Samuel Westly** is not listed in *Prince George's Co. Index to Wills, Administrations and Inventories (1696-1900)*.

An Administrative Bond for a **Samuel Westly** was filed March 1, 1720, Prince George's County by **Stephen Jeremaiy**, his Administrator (*Testamentary Proceedings Liber 24* folio 310) with an Inventory August 27, 1721 (*Testamentary Proceedings Liber 25* folio 24).

Prince George's Co. Will Liber 21 /244 records the WILL of a **Richard Groome** dated April 25, 1734, listing his children (all named Groome). His daughters are named Rebecca and Sarah. They were bequeathed "after their mother's decease" the 150 acres where "I now live and that they take care of my son **Samuel** to keep him after his mother's decease". His wife was named **Amy _____ Groome**. The witnesses were **John Orme, Peter Knight, Philip Ward** and **Matthew Watson**. The WILL was proved Sept. 27, 1734.

Remarks: The names of Rebecca and Sarah could indicate his mother was **Sarah Summers**.

Street, __________, descendants

A **John Street**, grandson of **John Summers**, was alive in 1703 when he was left a bequeath in his grandfather's WILL. There are no proved descendents.

A **John Street** assigns all right, title, claim and demand of, in and to the Administration of his deceased father's **Francis Street's** estate to **Richard Gist**, merchant, date 31 August 1719, Baltimore Co. (*Testamentary Proceedings Liber 24* folio 92). The Inventory of a **Francis Street** is dated Jan 16, 1719, Baltimore Co. with Appraiser **George Ogg**, Jr. and **Edward Robarts**. Creditors are **Joshua Howard** and **Kathrin Talbott**. (Skinner, V. L. Jr., *Abstracts of the Inventories of the Prerogative Court of Maryland 1718-1720*).

Baltimore Co. Accts 1719 Liber 2 /343 records the account of **Francis Streets** admministrator of **William Summers**, late of Baltimore Co.

Prince George's Co. Wills 1733 Box 4, folder 43, records the nuncupative WILL of a **John Street**. **Andrew Tawnohill** made oath that a certain **John Street** late of Prince George's Co. deceased on his death bed said that **George Beall** might have care of his son **Francis**. Administration of **George Beall** is recorded in *Liber CC Baltimore Co. No.3* /746.

Summers, William - no known descedents

Summers, John (II) - Descendants in order as listed in father's WILL, except for **James** who predeceased his father, with genealogical information following.

John Summers (III)

George Summers

William Summers

Dent Summers

Thomas Summers

Benjamin Summers

Joseph Summers

Mary Summers Wheat

Rebeckah Summers King

Rachel Summers Johnson

Ruth Summers Riggs

Jemina Summers Caton

James Summers

John Summers (III)
b before 1722 (see brother **George**), Prince George's Co.
m (1) **Mary Moore** by 2 Oct. 1748, date of birth of son John
(2) **Elizabeth** _________ d post 1786
d by 30 Nov 1786, date WILL proved. Inventory 10 Jan 1787 (*Prince George's Co. Inventory Liber ST 2* /362)

Census:
1733, Prince George's County, List of Taxables in Upper Piscattaway Hundred includes **John Summers** Jun. (III). *Calendar of Maryland States Papers No. 1, The Black Books*/268
1776 Maryland Census does not list a **John Summers**.
1790 Maryland Census lists **Elizabeth Summers** in Prince George's Co. as 1 female and 4 slaves.

Property:
Addition as referenced in his WILL, which had become Summers' property during the life of his father.
Child's Portion as referenced in his WILL, which had become Summers' property during the time of his father.
Covert purchased 1752. *Prince George's Land Liber PP* (pp 1-175) /13 contains the Indenture dated 4 April 1752 between **Benonie Price**, Prince George's taylor, and **John Summers** Jun for parcel called Covert, laid out for 100 acres; witnessed by **John Hepburn** and **Nathaniel Offutt**. This property is not referenced in his WILL. Covert was located in the fork of Hensons Branch; original grant was 406 acres; survey is dated 6 May 1715 (Prince George's Rent-tax 4/410).
The Outlet which he purchased in 1772. *Prince George's Land Records Liber BB 3* /13, 14, 15 contains Indenture dated 6 April 1772 between **John Hepburn**, Prince George's Co., Esq., and **John Summers**, Prince George's Co., for tract of 168 acres "all that part of tract called the outlet by a small branch that falls into the Woodyard Mill branch formerly called Mr. **Darnall**'s Mill branch". Survey for The Outlett is dated 28 March 1723 for 250 acres (Prince George's Rent-tax 4/457).

Military:
A **John Summers** of PG Co. signed the Oath of Fidelity as #102 (Brumbaugh *Revolutionary Records of Maryland*/10).

WILL *Prince George's Co. WILL Liber T 1/243*

Dated 11 Nov 1786

"In the Name of God Amen I **John Summers** of Prince George's County in the State of Maryland Planter being weak in Body but of perfect mind and memory thanks be given unto God and calling unto mind the mortality of my Body knowing that it is appointed for all men once to die do make and ordain this my last Will and Testament Principally I give and recommend my Soul into the hands of God that gave it and my Body to be buried in decent Christian burial at the discretion of my Executors and as touching such worldly estate as it hath pleased Almighty God to bless me with in this life I give devise and dispose of in the following manner and form

I give and bequeath unto my grandson **Zadock Summers** one hundred acres of land where I now have a Quarter to him and his heirs forever Imprimis

Item I give and bequeath unto my loving son **Josias Summers** all the remaining part of that tract or parcel or parcels of land at my Quarter called outlet Addition and Childs Portion after giving to my grandson **Zadock Summers** one hundred acres of said land which may be any part of it that my son **Josias Summers** pleases to him and his heirs forever

Item I give and bequeath unto my loving son **Nathan Summers** two hundred seventy and five pounds nineteen shillings and five pence farthing specie currency which is in the hands of Mr. **Tilghman Hilliary** and for which I have his Bond. To be paid as soon after my decease as it can be recovered to him and his heirs

Item I give and bequeath unto my youngest son **Levan Summers** fifteen pounds a year during his natural life to be paid him annually by my Executors out of the Income of the Plantation whereon I now live But should Reformation of Life take place in him and his conduct be amemded on the judgment of his Friends and Neighbors I give and bequeath unto my son **Levan Summers** half of the land whereon I now live to him and his heirs.

I give and bequeath unto my loving wife and my grandson **Nathan Summers** the other half of the land whereon I now live together with all the houses and improvements on it to be jointly possessed by them during the life of my wife **Elizabeth Summers** and only during her widowhood and at her decease or marriage my will and desire is that the said land be sold and equally divided among my three sons **Nathan**, **Josias** and **Levan Summers**

All the residue and remaining part of my estate I give to be divided equally among my children and wife who by contract is to have a child's part, namely **Nathan Summers**, **Josias Summers**, **Levan Summers**, **Mary Rawlins**, **Elizabeth Wigfield**, **Henrietta Darnall**, **Anna Hurley** and **Elizabeth Summers**

And lastly I constitute and appoint **Aron Rawlins** and **Nathan Summers** my Executors of this my last Will and Testament and do revoke disannull and make void all other Wills by me heretofore made. In Witness whereof I have hereunto set my hand and seal this eighteenth day of November one thousand seven hundred and eighty-six."

John Summers

Witnessed by **Joseph Messenger**
John Osbourn
John Darcey

Probated Nov 30, 1786

Children of **John** and **Mary Moore Summers**:

John Summers b 2 Oct 1748 (*King George's Parish Births 1689-1801* Part I p 129); m **Dorcus** ___________; d by 24 August 1774 when **Dorcas Summers** presented her Administrative Bond with **Benjamin Moore, Sr.**, and **James Moore, Sr.**, her sureties (Testamentary Proceedings Liber 46 folio 72). (*Prince George's Co. Inventory Bk 118* /264). This meant he predeceased his father. Had signed the Oath of Fidelity as #17 (Brumbaugh Opus Cit Vol. II/306).

Mary Summers b Jan 7, 1750 (*Prince George's Co., MD, Piscataway or St. John's Parish Index to Register* /214); m **Ar(r)on Rawlin(gs)** by 1784. There are 2 **Aaron Rawlings** in the *1790 MD Census*. One in Montgomery Co. with 2 males over 16 yrs, 1 under 16 yrs. and 2 females. The other in Frederick Co. with 3 males over 16 yrs, 3 under 16, and 6 females.

Nathaniel Summers d ca 1784 (*Prince George's Will Bk T 1* /185) WILL dated 3 Feb 1784; proved Mar 31, 1784. He leaves bequeaths to sister **Mary Rawlins**, brother **Nathan**, brother **Josias**, sister **Henrietta**, sister **Naomnah**, brother **Levin**; brother **Levin** is sole executor; WILL witnessed by **William Moodie** and **Jarat Darnall**. No wife or children are mentioned.

Josias(h) Summers m **Jeremiah** ________ by Dec 27, 1772 (birth of son **Nathaniel)** *Piscataway* Opus Cit /214. Signed the Oath of Fidelity as # 128 (Brumbaugh Opus Cit Vol.II/307). *1790 MD Census* lists a **Josias** in Prince George's Co. with 3 males over 16, 2 under 16, 4 females and 6 slaves.

Nathan Summers m **Mary** _____ by May 10, 1767 (Bapt. of son **John)** *Piscataway* Opus Cit /339. Signed Oath of Fidelity as # 79 (Brumbaugh Opus Cit Vol.II/306). *1790 MD Census* lists him with 1 male over 16, 1 under 16, 2 females and 2 slaves.

Levin(e) (Eleven) Summers m (2) **Elizabeth Wilcoxon** 31 Dec. 1786 (*Piscataway* Opus Cit /214). *1790 MD Census* lists him with 1 male over 16, 2 males under 16, 1 female and 1 slave. d ca 15 Dec. 1796 (date of funeral) *Piscataway* /214.

Henrietta Summers m **Gerrard (Jarrett) Darnall** (1757-1826) 7 Nov 1785, Prince George's Co. (Brumbaugh, G. M. *Maryland Records* Vol. I /157) *1790 MD Census* lists him with 1 male over 16 yrs, 1 under 16, 4 females, and 5 slaves. Family moved to Tennessee in 1817. Is listed in *1820 Tennessee Census*, Sumner Co., with a husband, wife and child. (Files of Avlyn D. Conley)

Namonah Summers listed in WILL of brother **Nathaniel** in 1784, but not in WILL of father in 1786, so she probably predeceased her father.

Children of **John** and **Elizabeth** ______ **Summers**

Elizabeth Summers m ________ **Wigfield**

Anna Summers m **Joseph Hurley**. An **Anna Summers** m **Salem Hurley**, license Prince George's Co. dated Dec 8, 1784 (Brumbaugh Opus Cit Vol I /126)

Note: *Prince George's Co. Deed Book JJ 2*/319-323 records the Indentures between **Josias Summers** and **Nathan Summers**, son of **Nathan**, and **Levin Summers** and **Nathan**, son of **Nathan**, for the property left by **John Summers**, father of **Josias** and **Levin**, and grandfather of said **Nathan**, which parcel is on the site of Andrews Air Force Base, Prince George's Co., near Washington, DC. In 1843 at the death of **Nathan**, son of **Nathan** and grandson of **John**, the Summers family tobacco plantation was divided among his nine children, each receiving about 150 acres and several slaves. The plantation was located where Andrews Air Force Base is today, near the current intersection of I-95 and Pennsylvania Avenue.

The Summers-Marshall Family Cemetery caused the curve in Pennsylvania Avenue east of I-95 interchange. Four tombstones in 1959 were moved to Epiphany Episcopal Cemetery in Forestville, MD.

George Summers (Sumers)

b ca 1722 (Brumbaugh *Maryland Records Vol I* /15 "Prince George's Co. Census 1776")

m **Elizabeth Talbot** by May 17, 1752, date of bapt of daughter **Ann** (*Piscataway* Opus Cit p 213). *Prince George's Land Liber 2 i* (1774-1780), folio 567, records a Deed of Gift Jan 27, 1779 from **"Ann Talbot** (widow of **Paul Talbot)** Prince George's Co. for love and affection to my kind son-in-law **George Summers** and his family one Negro man named Frank one feather bed with all its furniture and a cow". Deed dated 20 Jan 1779.

d by 16 Dec. 1795, date WILL proved (*Prince George's Lib TI* /371-2)

Census:

MD 1776 Census of St. John's and Prince George's Parish, PG Co. lists

Summers, George, age 54
George Jr., age 17
Paul, age 10
Elizabeth, age 54
Ann, age 22
Virlinda, age 15

MD 1783 Assessment lists a **George Summers** in Sugarland, Montgomery Co.

1790 MD Census lists **George Summers** in PG Co., with 1 male over 16 yrs, 2 under 16 yrs, 1 female and 4 slaves.

Property:

Prince George's Land Bk NN /7 contains the March 26, 1752, Indenture between **Benedict Calvert**, Esq. of City of Annapolis and **George Summers** of Prince George's Co. planter for a "grant to farm" that parcel in Prince George Co., part of tract of His Lordship's Kindness, bordered by land of **Henry Darnall** Esq., containing 100 acres; to have for the natural life of **George Summers** and natural life of **Elizabeth**, wife of **George** and the natural life of **Jonathan**, son of **George**. Original survey of "His Lordships Kindness" is dated 29 February 1703 (Prince George's Rent-tax 4/322), located on west side of main branch of the Piscattaway, and included 7,000 acres.

Military:

A **Geo: Summers** is listed in Montgomery Co., Upper Battalion (Clements, S Eugene and F. Edward Wright *The Maryland Militia in the Revolutionary War* /193). This is a 1778 list of all free male inhabitants in the County between the age of 16 and 50 years.

W (*Prince George's MD WILLS T1 /371-372*)

"In the Name of God Amen I **George Summers** of Maryland in Prince George's County planter Being of perfect mind and memory and Calling to mind and duty considering the uncertainty of human life make this my last Will and Testament first and principally I commit my soul unto the hands of my blessd maker trusting in his Mercies and in the Merits of my dear Redeemer for the demission of all my sins my Body I commit to the earth to be decently buried as to my temporal Estate I Bequeath and dissolve it in the following manners Imprimis.

I bequeath to my two Daughters namely **Anna** and **Ann** one Negro woman and half her increase from this date to be equally divided between them and one room in my dwelling house during their single life also each of them a feather bed and furniture bedstead and cord a cow and calf a sow and pigs a ewe and lamb and the two first choices of my horses to them and their forever the other half of the aforesaid Negro womans increase I Bequeath to my five Children Namely **Maryann Jonathan Quillah Verlinnder and George** the residue and remainder of my Estate with all other properties of what kindsoever to be appertaining I give devise and Bequeath to my son **Paul** whom I constitute and appoint the whole and sole Executor of this my last Will and Testament after the decease of my wife **Elizabeth** I do hereby revoke Disallow and Disannul all former Bequeaths and legasses by me heretofore in anywise left or made Declaiming Ratifying and confirming this and no other to be my last Will and Testament in witness whereof I have hereunto set my hand and seal this twenty first Day of March anna domini one thousand seven hundred and ninety one."

George Summers Sen.

Witnessed: **Henry Harvey** and **John H. Willson**

Proved: December 16th 1795

Children of **George** and **Elizabeth Talbot Summers**:

Jonathan Summers b by 1752 (Indenture *Prince George's Liber NN*), marriage license 23 Dec. 1782 Prince George's Co. to **Ann Gwinn** (Brumbaugh Opus Cit Vol I p 157). *1790 MD Census* lists him in Prince George's Co. with 1 male over 16 yrs, 2 under 16, 1 female and 5 slaves.

Ann Summers bapt May 17, 1752 (*Piscataway* Opus Cit p 213). Apparently died early because a second daughter was named **Ann**.

Velinder Summers b 2 June 1754 Prince George's Co (per Letha Summers)

George Summers, Jr. bapt. Aug. 26, 1759 (*Piscataway* Cit p 213); marriage license **Jane Smith** 19 May 1787 (Brumbaugh Opus Cit Vol I p 157). *1790 MD Census* lists him in Prince George's Co. with 1 male over 16 yrs., 2 under 16, 1 female and 4 slaves. Died Oct 1811, Washington Co., Ky. (Papers of Letha Summers)

Ann Summers bapt. March 16, 1761 (*Piscataway* /213) not married 1791, date of father's Will

Paul Summers b 30 Aug 1763; marriage license to **Susanna Ranten** 11 Mar 1789 (Brumbaugh Opus Cit Vol 1 p 146); m (2) **Sarah Huley** 1801 (per Letha Summers). *1790 MD Census* lists him in Montgomery Co. with 1 male over 16 yrs, 1 under, and 4 females.

Anna Summers single in 1791 when father wrote WILL

Quillah Summers, born after 1776 (not listed in that Census), single in 1791 when F wrote his WILL

Mary Ann Summers listed in father's Will as one of his eight children. (Is she one of the Anns or another child?)

William Summers

b 22 April 1726, Prince George's Co. (Miller, Mildred *Carolina Summers* /90)

m (1) 10 Feb. 1745 (Ibid) **Mary Wheat** (20 Sept 1727-6 Dec 1797) (Petrucelli, Katherine Sanford *The Heritage of Rowan Co., NC*). She appears to be the daughter of **William** and **Amy Wall Wheat**. *Prince George's Land Records Liber RR* /142 records the following "**Mary Wall** of Prince George's Co. for natural love and affection I bear to my beloved grandchildren **Mary Summers** wife of **William Summers William Wheat Jun** and **Sarah Nabis** wife of **John Nabis** after my decease and the decease of my daughter **Amy Wheat** all the estate, property and Interest except my negro man Thane which I give to granddaughter **Mary Summers** to be equally divided among my said grandchildren.......**William Wheat** husband of said **Amy** shall have no property after her decease". Dated 10 July 1761.

LWT of **William Wheat** bequeaths to daughter **Mary Wheat**, wife of **William Summers**, one negro woman named Chloe and her child Sam and "all belonging to me" and appoints them his Executors. Dated 7 Jan 1767; proved 18 March 1767. *Frederick Will Bk A/287*

LWT of **William Wheat** is dated 16 April 1767 (*Testamentary Proceedings Vol 42*/107). In the June Court of that year **William Summers** is identified as the Executor of the WILL of **William Wheat** (Ibid /155).

Petrucelli (Opus Cit, p 600) identifies **Mary Wheat Summers** as the daughter of **William** and **Sarah Pardue Wheat**.(?)

m (2) **Cassandra Ellis**, dau of **Samuel Ellis** (Montgomery Historical Society)

d post 4 June 1799, date WILL written, Iredell Co., NC

Census:

1760 List of Sundry Inhabitants of All Saints, Frederick Co. includes **William Summers**. *Calendar of Maryland States Papers No. 1, The Black Books*/966

1776 MD Census lists 2 **William Summers** in Lower Potomack Hundred, Frederick Co., both aged 25 yrs.

MD Assessment of 1783 lists **William** in Montgomery Co., Sugarland

NC 1790 Census lists **William** in Salisbury District, Iredell Co. with 1 male over 16 yrs, 1 under 16, 1 female and 9 slaves. There is also a **William** in Salisbury District, Rowan Co. with 2 males over 16 yrs, 3 under 16, and 3 females. This is more likely **William, Jr**.

Property:

Strawberry Patch, 50 acres, Frederick Co. (now Montgomery Co.) on north side of a hill in the fork of Buck Lodge Branch. Original survey 20 August 1740 (MSA Patent PT 2/294). From 1745 to 1773 listed in MSA Index to Owners of Tracts.

Resurvey on strawberry Patch 1759, 180 acres (MSA *Patent LG #E* /573), (Certificate *BC & GS #12* /115)

Resurvey Wolf's Cow, 8 acres, on south side of a small branch called Buck Lodge that runs into the middle Sinaca. Indenture dated 15 Dec 1767 between **Philip Holt** and **William Summers**, Frederick Co., planter. *Frederick Land Bk L*/130. Original patent dated 12 September 1760 MSA *BC&GS 14*/48.

Resurvey on the Wolf's Cow, 50 acres, part of first and second resurvey. Indenture dated 20 October 1773 between **Joseph Newton Chiswell** and **William Summers**, Frederick Co., planter. *Frederick Land Bk U*/105

Wheat's purchase, 100 acres, by a spring by side of Buck Lodge branch. Indenture dated 20 October 1773 between **Solomon Simpson** and **William Summers**, Frederick Co., planter. *Frederick Land Bk U*/117. Original patent to William Wheat for 100 acres on 18 March 1746.

Montgomery Co. Land Bk A/561 records the Indenture dated 18 Sept 1780 of **William Summers** to **James Hawkins**, Prince George's Co. **William** is now seized of 4 tracts viz Wheat's purchase orginally patented to **William Wheat** for 100 acres on 18 March 1746, Resurvey on Strawberry Patch orginially granted to **William Summers** for 180 acres 24 Jan. 1755, 8 acres part of second Resurvey on Woolf's Cow, 50 acres part of second Resurvey on Woolf's Cow- 2nd resurvey for **Philip Holt**, Jun., dated 25 July 1767, who by Deed Liber S folio 130 and 131 Frederick Co. dated 15 Dec 1767 conveyed to **William Summers** the 8 acres and by Deed Liber N folio 9A, Frederick Co dated 15 Nov 1769 conveyed the 50 acres to **Joseph Newton Chiswell** and **Chiswell** by deed Liber U folio 105, Frederick Co., dated 20 Oct. 1773 transferred the 50 acres to **William Summers**. This Indenture includes the 4 tracts. **Mary**, wife of **William** released her dower.

resurvey on Brandy (*Montomery Co. MD Land Bk A1* /606, contains the Indenture 30 Oct. 1780 between **Samuel Blackmore**, Montgomery Co., planter and **William Summers**, afsd co., for a tract called the resurvey on Brandy containing 491 acres; recorded March 12, 1781)

resurvey on Brandy (*Montgomery Co. MD Land Bk B* /192) contains the Indenture 6 Dec. 1783 between **William Summers** of Montgomery Co. planter, and **Charles Cowley** of Anne Arundel Co. for that tract in Montgomery Co. which **Robert Peter** sold to **Samuel Blackmore** then Frederick Co. **Blackmore** conveyed same to **William Summers** which land is called resurvey on Brandy containing 491 acres. **Mary** wife of **William** released her dower. Recorded 20 Feb. 1784)

The earliest record so far in NC is 1789 "adj. **William Summers** land on Hunting Creek". (Coulter, Shirley, Edis Purdy and Lois Schneider *Iredell County NC Deed Abstracts Vol I Books A & B* /15).

Iredell Co., NC, **William Summers** purchased 160 acres 12 Nov 1792 from **James Scott**. (Coulter, Shirley, Edie Purdy and Lois Schneider *Minutes of the Court of Pleas and Quarter Sessions* /49)

Deed of **Will Summers** to **Isaiah Hurley** for 150 acres dated Jan 15, 1790. Recorded 1794 (Ibid /74)

Deed proved 1798 of **William Summers** and wife to **David Caldwell** for 155 acres dated 15 Aug 1798. (Ibid /132)

Note: **William Summers** appears to have moved from Montgomery County, Maryland, to Iredell County, North Carolina, in the mid to late 1780s.

Military:

William Summers, Sen is listed as #103 as taking the Oath of Fidelity 1778, Montgomery Co., and **William, Jun** as #105, (Brumbaugh Opus Cit *Revolutionary Records of Maryland*/10).

William Summers Sen and **Jun** are listed in the Upper Battalion, Montgomery Co. Militia. (Clements and Wright Opus Cit /193)

Civic Activities:

William Summers is listed on the Jury, Iredell Co., NC, during the years of 1789, 1790 and 1791. He was a Grand Juror in 1794. (Coulter, et al *Court of Pleas*)

WILL *Iredell Co., NC, WILLS 1787 - 1917, WILL BK I No 138*, /205; duplicate in *WILL BK 1A* /28

"In the name of God Amen this the fourth day of June in the year of our Lord one thousand seven hundred and ninety nine. **I Wm Summers** of the County of Iredell and State of North Carolina being aged and weak in body but of sound mind and perfect memory and calling to mind the mortality of my body and knowing that it is appointed once for all men to die, do make and ordain this my last will and testament that is to say

Principaly and first of all. I resign my soul to God who gave it and my body to be buried in a desent manner at the discretion of my Executors and touching such worldly things where with it hath pleased God to bless me with in this life, I give and disposed of in the following manner and form.

Viz. I give unto my daughter **Amey Howard** ten pounds and no more of my estate.

Item I give unto my son **John Summers** three hundred acres of land that was conveyed to him by **Alexander Read** and no more of my Estate.

Item I give unto my daughter **Linney Summers** ten pounds and no more of my Estate.

Item I give unto my dauter **Biney Belt** but ten pounds and no more of my Estate.

Item I give unto my son **Wm Summers** negro Matt also one hundred acres of land bein a part of the tract that was conveyed the aforesaid **Alexr Read** unto **John Summers**.

I give unto my dauter **Mary Jacob** one negroe boy Isac.

Item I give unto my dauter **Darkey Jacob** negroe Sam.

Item I give unto my dauter **Bithe Tombelson** negroe little George.

Item I give unto my beloved wife **Cassandra** negroe boy James one negro girl nancy two beds and furniture one set cups and saucers one glass tumbler one grey mare foal one large trunk. I also give unto my beloved wife one hundred acres of land including the plantation whereon my son **Basil** now lives during her natural life or widowhood.

I give unto the heirs of my son **Thomas** decd twenty shillings and no more of my Estate.

Item I give unto my grandson **William Jacobs Summers** five pounds in money and four head of sheep.

I give unto my son **Basil Summers** my home plantation including an entry of fifty acres that is joining it and at the death or marriage of my beloved wife to have that hundred acres that he now lives on to him his heirs assigns forever. I also give unto him my negroes big George and Sall, one dish, one waggon with her gears and horse rocks.

Item I also give to my daughter **Bitha Tomlinson** negro boy Ned.

Item I leave all the rest and residue of my estate both real and personal to be sold and all of my just debts to be paid with the legacees by this will made and the balance to be equally divided between my beloved wife **Cassandra**, my son **William**, my dauter **Mary Jacobs**, my dauter **Darkey Jacobs**, my dauter **Betha Tombelson** and my son **Basil Summers**.

Last of all I order and ordain my son **Basil Summers** and my trusty friend **Burgess Gaither** executors to this my last will and testament, revoking and disanuling all wills heretofore by me made. In witness whereof I have hereunto set my hand and sele the day and year above in the presants of

Joseph Alhen

Horatio Beall **Wilm (his mark) Summers"**

Children of **William** and **Mary Wheat Summers**

Anney(Amy) Summers b May 11, 1746 (Miller Opus Cit p 90); m **William Howard** ca 1785 (Montgomery Co. Historical Society Vertical File)

John Summers b March 7, 1746 (Ibid); m Dec 8, 1774, Fredericktown, MD, to **Ann Claggett** (b June 28, 1753, dau of **Charles**), served in American Revolution, Montgomery Co. MD militia as sergent, 2nd Lieut and later Capt. A **John Summers** purchased 203 acres, westside of Rocky Creek 13 May 1796 (Coulter, et al Opus Cit *Deed Abstracts* /82). He died Apr 17, 1806, Iredell Co., NC (Montgomery Historical Society)

Linney Summers unmarried in 1799

Biney Summers m _______ **Belt** by 1799

William Summers b ca 1751. *1776 MD Census* lists him in Frederick Co. Lower Potomack Hundred, (Brubaugh Vol I Opus Cit /186; m **Rebecca Jacob** Oct 1, 1778 Montgomery Co.; witnessed in 1792 Rowan Co., NC, deed of **William Howard**, husband of sister **Amy** (Montgomery Historical Society). Indenture to **William Jr.** for 160 acres on each side of Rockey Creek of South Yadkin River (Coulter, et al *Iredell Deed Bk* /481-482). Deed 1790 of **William Jr.** of Rowan Co to **Isaiah Hurley** 150 acres, Little and Hunting Creek (*Iredell Deed Bk B* /184-185); **William Jr.** of Rowan Co. to **Thomas Stroud** 25 3/4 acres on Little Creek, waters of South Yadkin (*Iredell Deed Bk B* /561-2); **William, Jr.**, of Rowan Co. to **Richard Kent** 50 acres on waters of hunting and Little Creek (*Iredell Deed Bk B* /581-82)

Mary Summers b 1750; m **Edward Jacob(s)** Oct 28, 1779, Montgomery Co. (Brumbaugh Vol II Opus Cit /519); moved to Iredell Co., NC 1781; d 1806 Wilson Co (Montgomery Historical Society)

Darkus (Dorcas, Darkey) Summers b 1753 (Montgomery Historical Society); m **Zacharius Jacob(s)** Aug 5, 1779, Montgomery Co. (Brumbaugh Opus Cit /519)

Bitha (Bertha, Tabitha, Tabithey) b 12 Aug 1770; m by 1799 **John Tombelson (Tomlinson)**, who was born in Frederick Co., MD and migrated with his parents to Rowan Co, NC, later Iredell Co. (Petrucelli Opus Cit /600). In 1852 she gave a deposition re brother John's Revolutionary activities. (Summers, Coite *Somers* /22)

Basil Summers m **Ann Ellis** (dau of **Samuel Ellis**) Feb. 12, 1788 Rowan Co., NC; WILL recorded Apr 8, 1824, Iredell Co. (Montgomery Historical Society) A **Barsil Summers** is listed in *NC 1800 Census*, Iredell Co.)

Thomas Summers d by 1799. Father's WILL mentioned **Thomas'** heirs.

Note: **Rebecca, Edward** and **Zachariah Jacobs** were children of **Jeremiah Jacob** (b 1712-17) and **Rachel Gaither**, dau of **Edward Gaither**. (Montgomery Co. Historical Society)

Wheat researchers will be interested in the listing of **William Wheat** as taxable in Mattapany Hundred, Prince George's Co., 1733, and a Freeholder in Frederick Co., 1751. (*Calendar of Maryland States Papers, No. 1, The Black Books*/276 and 703) **William**, Jr., is listed in All Saints Parish, Frederick Co., 1756 and as an Inhabitant of the Parish

of All Saints, Fredercik Co., 1760. (Ibid pages 864 and 966) The **Joseph Wheat** listed as taxable in Upper Piscattaway Hundred 1733 (Ibid/268) may or may not be the Freeholder in Frederick Co., 1751 (Ibid /705), and may or may not be the **Joseph Wheat** on the PG Land (Rent-tax) 4/272 for the land called Wheat's Choice, 53 acres on Buck Lodge Branch, surveyed 19 May 1748. It is noted that **William Wheat** had property called Wheat's Purchase, 100 acres on Buck Lodge Branch (Prince George's Land (Rent-tax) 4/267), patented 10 Mar 1746.

Dent Summers
b 1727 (Jones, Genevieve Broome *Children, Meet Your Ancestors* /150)
m to **Mary Ann** ________ by 1754, baptism of daughter **Sarah** (Opus Cit *Index to King George Parish* /287). The funeral of **Mary Ann Summers** was Nov 18th 1802 (Brumbaugh Vol II Opus Cit /569)
d by 3 Dec. 1809 (date WILL probated)

Census:
MD 1776 Census identified **Dent Summers** as living in the North West Hundred, Frederick County. He said there were 9 in the family, but refused to give their ages. (Brumbaugh Vol I Opus Cit /232)
MD Assessment of 1783, Montgomery Co., lists **Dent Summers** in Lower Newfoundland Hundred.
1790 MD Census lists **Dent Summers** in Montgomery Co. with 3 males over 16 yrs, 1 female and 5 slaves.
1800 MD Census lists **Dent Summers** in Frederick Co with 1 male over 45 yrs, 1 female over 45 yrs, and 2 slaves.

Military:
None identified.

Property:
Joseph's Park, 100 acres, Lease and Assignment, dated April 18, 1763, between **Thomas Nichols** and **Dent Summers** *Frederick Co Land Bk H/*657. Land located east side of a Rock Creek Branch; original survey 20 May 1689 (Prince George's Rent-tax 4/383.
50 acres "off the lower end next to the Woodyard", part of Moore's Addition, via father's LWT 9 October 1769 (*Prince George's Co. MD WILLS* 37/334).

WILL *Montgomery Co. WILL Liber G/*1

"In the Name of God Amen the last Will and Testament of **Dent Summers** of Frederick County in the State of Maryland made in sound and disposing mind and memory this Twenty eighth day of September in the year of our Lord Eighteen hundred and two. In the first place I recommend my Spirit to the hands of God that gave it and my body to my Executors hereafter to be named to be by them decently buried and as to my worldly Goods I dispose of them in the following manner to wit,
Item I give and bequeath to my son **Hezekiah Summers** a correl Mare and a Sider Cask which he has now in possession for his full part of my Estate and nomore I give and bequeath to my Daughter **Maryan Hardey** and my Daughter **Sarah White** also to my sons **Paul Summers James Summers Zadock Summers** and **John Summers** also my Daughter **Margaret Hoskins** the moneys due me from my son **Walter Dent Summers** and to be equally divided amongst them. Each of them receiving one seventh part thereof to them their Heirs or Assigns for their full parts of my Estate and no more and if payment should be refused by my son **Walter Dent Summers**, when demanded by my Executors here after Named they are hereby empowered to bring soot recover the said monneys due and pay the same as in this bequeath stated.
Item I further give and bequeath to my son **Zadock Summers** and the Heirs of his Body for ever all the residue of my Estate of every kind whatever.
I give and bequeath to my son **Walter Dent Summers** one Shilling for his full part of my Estate and no more.
Lastly I appoint my beloved sons **Hezekiah Summers** and **Zadock Summers** my Executors to this my last Will and Testament with full powers to Execute the same revoking and disannulling all former wills whatever. In Witness whereof I hereunto affixed my hand and seal
Dent Summers"

Witnessed by **Willm Morsell, Philn Griffith, William Morsell Jun**.

Probated 3 December 1809 Montgomery Co.

Children of **Dent** and **Mary Ann** ______ **Summers**
Hezekiah Summers age 26 in 1776 (Brumbaugh, Opus Cit /232). He was living then in Northwest Hundred, Frederick Co. with wife **Rebacker** age 32, **William Dent** age 3, and **Benjamin** (?) age 1. He was a private in the Maryland Militia, and his widow applied for a pension (Newman, Harry Wright *Maryland Revolutionary Records*). In *1790 MD Census* he was listed in Montgomery Co. with 2 males over 16 yrs, 3 under 16 years, 4 females and 10 slaves.
Maryan Summers m ________ **Hardey**
Sarah Summers bapt 23 Sept 1754 (*King George* Opus Cit p 306); m ________ **White**
Paul Summers
James Dent Summers bapt 1761 (*Piscataway* Opus Cit p 214. *1790 MD Census* lists him in Anne Arundel Co. with 1 male over 16 years, 1 under 16 and 2 females.
Zadock Summers
John Summers
Margaret Summers m ______ **Hoskins**
Walter Dent Summers

Thomas Summers

b Prince George's Co, MD

m to **Rachel Talbot**, daughter of **Joseph** and **Mary Berckhead Talbot**, by 1754. (Ref. Deed re son George.)

d by 1799, Iredell Co., NC (Coulter, et al *Minutes of Court* /145 references the estate of **Thomas Summers** decd, dated 21 Aug 1799). Letters of Administration were to **Solomon Summers** and **George Summers** who gave bond with **Bazil Summers** and **Henry Cligate** Securities. (Ibid)

Census:

1733 List of Taxables Lower Part of Piscattaway Hundred, Prince George's Co., lists a **Thomas Summers**. *Calendar of Maryland States Papers, No. 1, The Black Books*/270

1776 MD Census lists a **Thomas Summers**, aged 25, in Georgetown Hundred, Frederick Co. This is likely the son of **Thomas** and **Rachel**.

1783 MD Assessmnt lists **Rachel, Dent John** and **Thomas Summers** in Linganore, Montgomery Co.

1787 Bedford Co., VA, Personal Property Tax List "A" includes **Summers, Paul T** (taxable for 1 horse and 4 cattle), **Thomas** (not taxable), **Zacharias** (taxable for 1 male over 16 and under 21 and 1 horse (not tithable)), **Rachel** (taxable for 1 male over 16 and under 21, 1 horse and 1 cattle (not tithable))

1790 VA Census does not list any of the preceeding persons.

1790 NC Census lists a **Thomas Summers** in Salisbury Dis, Iredell Co. with 1 male over 16 yrs., 2 under 16 yrs. and 2 females.

In that Census another **Thomas Summers** is listed in Salisbury District, Rowan Co., with 2 males over 16 yrs, 3 under 16 yrs and 5 females. This would appear to be the son.

Property:

His Lordship's Kindness. *Prince George's Land Bk NN*/261 contains the "grant to farm" dated 29 May 1754 between **Benedict Calvert** of City of Annapolis and **Thomas Summers**, Prince George's planter, for that tract, being part of His Lordship's Kindness, bounded by **Thomas Taylor**'s line containing 116 acres, for natural life of **Thomas Summers**, natural life of **Rachel Summers** his wife and the natural life of **George Summers**, son of **Thomas**. Witnessed by **Geo Stewart, Richd Dorsey**.

Prince George's Land Records Liber RR/116 contains the request of **John Stone** to have the following assignment recorded Feb. 28, 1761: PG Co. "I **Thomas Summers**, planter, have assigned to **John Stone** all my right title and estate of and into the within _______ lands and premises." Dated 13 Feb. 1761.

Joseph's Park. *Frederick Land Bk H*/201 records Lease dated 12 June 1762 between **Daniel Carroll** and **Thomas Summers**, Frederick Co. planter, grant to farm that part of tract called Joseph's Park, east side of Rock Creek, laid out for 103 1/2 acres, during natural life of **Thomas**, and of **Rachel** his wife, and natural life of **George**, son of **Thomas**.

Iredell Co., NC Deed Bk B/766-767, records Indenture 18 July, 1797 when **Thomas** sold to **Wilson Turner** 133 acres on Third Creek, part of the tract granted to **Thomas** by NC State.

Iredell Co 22 Aug 1797 **Humphrey Becket Tomblinson** sold to **Thos Summers** 100 acres. (Coulter, et al *Minutes of Court*/117). This does not indicate whether father or son.

Military:

Thomas Summers, Sen., and **Thomas Summers** are listed in Montgomery Co., Upper Battalion (Militia Lists of Daus of Founders and Patriots, held by MD Historical Society).

A **Thomas Summers** is listed under Patriot Oaths of Fidelity and Support 1778, Montgomery Co. #104 (Brumbaugh Opus Cit *Revolutionary Records*/10)

A **Thomas Summers** had rank of Private, Infantry, 6th Co., 2nd MD Reg., commanded by Col Tho Price Sept 9, 1778.

Civic Activities:

A **Thomas Summers** served on the Iredell County, NC, Jury 1790, 1792, 1793, 1796 and 1797. (Coulter, et al Opus Cit *Minutes of Court*)

WILL- none located. The earliest Iredell County Estate Record for a **Thomas** is dated 1851, so does not refer to this **Thomas**.

Children of **Thomas** and **Rachel Talbot Summers**

George Summers b by 29 May 1754 in MD (Indenture in *Prince George's Land Bk NN* /261); purchased 154 acres Iredell Co., NC Oct 15, 1798 from **David Baggarly** (*Iredell Deed Bk C* /321)

Thomas Summers b ca 1751 (was probably the **Thomas** in the 1776 Census).

John Dent Summers bapt 13 July 1754 (*King George's Parish* /306)

Paul Talbutt Summers bapt Jan. 1762 (*Prince George's Parish*, Prince George's Co.) m **Sarah Bruce** 1789, Bedford Co., VA (Miller Opus Cit p 91). Bought land in 1798 on Fifth Creek, Iredell Co. (Miller p 18)

Zachariah Summers b 1763 (Miller Opus Cit p 91) consent of mother **Rachel** for marriage of her son to **Sarah Dawson**, Bedford Co.,

VA, March 1, 1786. Father **Thomas** signed as teste. (Ibid). Purchased land on Fifth Creek, Iredell Co. (Ibid p 22)

Benjamin Summers (b 1772, MD; d 1829, buried Iredell Co., NC, according to booklet "Genealogy of Benjamin Summer and His Descendents", compiled 1903 and located in Montgomery Co. Historical Society, MD); m **Verlinda Lovelace**; bought 127 acres on South Yadkin, Iredell Co. in 1799 (*Iredell Co., NC, Deed Bk C /463*). *NC 1800 Census* lists a **Benjamin** in Iredell Co.

Other information:

A **Thomas (X) Summers** is witness to the WILL of **Benjamin Gaither** probated 1788, Iredell Co. NC. (Linn, Mrs. Stahle, Jr. *Abstracts of WILLS and Estate Records of Rowan Co., NC 1753-1805 /37*)

A **Thomas Summers** (with written signature) witnessed the WILL of **Joseph Orten(s)** 1807, Iredell Co., NC

Benjamin Summers
b ca 1737 (*DAR Patriot Index*), Prince George's Co
m **Grace Letton**, daughter of **Caleb** and **Grace Letton** by 20 January 1762, birth of daughter **Mary**
d ca 1783, Washington Co. PA. No Will on file. Appraisal of Inventory made 28 July 1783.

Census:

1776 MD Census does not list a **Benjamin Summers** as head of a household.

Property:

Addition - that part inherited from father via LWT 9 October 1769 *Prince George's MD WILLS 37/334*

The Resurvey on Friends' Advice, containing 135 acres; second Resurvey of the Wolf's Cow, containing 17 acres; Salisbury planes at head of glade that falls into Cabin branch, containing 50 acres; Summer's Chance, near line of Resurvey on John's Delight, containing 15 acres. Indenture dated 27 September 1771 between **Joseph Summers** of province of North Carolina and **Benjamin Summers** for these four tracts in Frederick Co. *Frederick Land Bk O pp 347-709/608*

Summer's Lot patented to **Benjamin Summers** in 1777, for 191 1/2 acres in Frederick Co. (MSA *BC & GS #51 /460*) *Montgomerty Co. Land Bk A/572* contains Indenture 21 Oct. 1780 between **Benjamin Summers**, Montgomery Co. planter, and **William Wilcoxon** of the same for all that tract being part of a tract known as Summer's Lott bordered by Salsbury plains laid out for 191 and 1/2 acres; and all that parcel being part of tract called second resurvey on Wolf's Cow containing 17 acres; also that tract called Salisbury Plains near head of glade that falls into branch of Sennecca known as Cabin branch containing 50 acres; also that tract called Summers Chance bounded by Johns Delight laid out for 15 acres. Release of dower signed by **Grace Summers**. Recorded Oct. 22, 1780.

Remarks: It would appear that with the selling of this property in Maryland in 1780 that **Benjamin** was moving his family about that time to Pennsylvania.

Because of the confusion over state lines for PA/VA/MD, other early deeds to **Benjamin Summers** were not located; however **John Litton Summers** patented them for the heirs of Benjamin: 300 acres on Pigeon Creek patent issued Sept 15, 1787 and 302 acres called John's Hard Travels patented Apr 7, 1788.

Military:

Benjamin Summers signed Patriots' Oaths of Fidelity and Support, 1778, Montgomery Co. # 458 (Brumbaugh Opus Cit *Rev Records* /5)

Benjamin Summers listed as Ensign, Patriotic Service, MD PA (*DAR Patriotic Index*)

WILL - none has been found in Maryland or Pennsylvania

Children of **Benjamin** and **Grace Letton Summers** as listed in *Orphans Court Book A-1*/34, Washington Co. PA, at time of partitioning the land, north fork of Pidgeon Creek, containing 550 acres, (with the personalized comments from the sources cited) 1786

Caleb Summers identified as the oldest son, m **Rachel Crawford**, Mar 2, 1780, Montgomery Co. MD (Brumbaugh Vol II Opus Cit /520)

Mary Summers bapt 20 Jan 1762 (*Prince George's Parish* Opus Cit p 262)

John Lutten (Litton, Letton) Summers bapt April 4, 1764 (*Piscataway Parish* Opus Cit p 214); m **Anna Moriah** (*Washington Co. PA Deed Book 1 E* /148 1790). Died June 15, 1802; gravestone 4 miles from Rockville in "Willow Tree" graveyard on westside of Rock Creek (Ridgely, Helen *Historic Graves of Maryland* /174)

Grace Summers bapt July 20, 1766 (*Piscataway Parish* Opus Cit /339), listed in distribution dated Feb. 7, 1786, but not in partitioning (brother **John** bought **Grace**'s lot).

William Burton Summers was by Oct 1790 in Montgomery Co., MD (*Washington Co., PA Deed Bk 1-E* /148); by Nov 19, 1790 his address was Ohio Co. VA (*Washington Co. PA Deed Bk 1-I* /43)

Benjamin Summers identified as of Montgomery Co. MD Oct. 24, 1792 (*Washington Co., PA Deed Bk 1-I* /520) and as of Bullet Co. KY April 28, 1798 (*Washington Co., PA Deed Bk 1-O* /254). *Montgomery Co. Land Records Liber E* /10 records the certificate appointing **Benjamin** as Deputy Sheriff Dec 10th 1791.

Anna Maria Summers- listed as minor at time of father's decease; m **Thomas Markland** of Ohio Co., VA by Aug 30, 1791, *Montgomery Co. MD Deed Book 221* /566

Michael Summers- listed as minor at time of father's decease

Noah Summers- listed as minor at time of father's decease; of Jefferson Co., KY, Nov. 9, 1802 (*Washington Co., PA Deed Bk 1-S* /386)

Thomas Dent Summers- listed as minor at time of father's decease, of Boone Co., KY Nov. 9, 1802 (*Washington Co., PA Deed Bk 1-S* /386)

Joseph Summers

b ca 1730, Prince George's Co., Maryland

m **Eleanor Clary**, daughter of **Daniel** and **Eleanor Deveron Clary**, by 1756 (birth of son William).

d by 16 January 1809, date WILL probated, Newberry, SC

Census:

1790 SC Census does not include a Joseph Summers.

1800 SC Census, Newberry District, lists him with 1 male over 45 yrs., 1 female between 16 and 26 yrs, 1 female between 26 and 45 yrs, and 1 slave.

Property:

The Resurvey on Friend's Advice, 135 acres, Indenture dated March 17, 1763, between **Elisha Williams** and **Joseph Summers**, planter. *Frederick Land Bk H*/309-310. Original patent dated 3 January 1760 describes it as near the head of small branch on east side that falls into Little Sineca. *BC&GS 14*/80

Summers Chance, 15 acres, patented 22 Feb 1764. Warrant issued 2 Sept 1763. *BC&GS 27*/215). Patent *BC&GS 23*/390

Saulsbury Plain on the Seneca, 50 acres, near head of glade that falls into Cabin branch of the Sennecca. Indenture dated 13 November 1764, between **Nicholas Maccubbin** and **Joseph Summers**, planter. *Frederick Land Bk J pp 1036-1401*/1042

Second Resurvey on Wolf's Cow, 17 acres, Indenture dated 15 December 1767 between **Philip Holt** and **Joseph Summers**, planter. *Frederick Land Bk L*/131

Resurvey on Friend's Advice, Second Resurvey on the Wolf's Cow, Salisbury plains, and Summers' Chance sold to **Benjamin Summers** 27 September 1771. *Frederick Land BK O*, 608-609

Indenture 2 Aug 1774, District of Ninety-Six, Newberry Co., SC, between **Robert Yealdall** and **Joseph Summers** of Bush River for 300 acres between Broad and Saluda Rivers, on branch of Bush River call Palmetto. *Newberry Co Deed BK D*/272-3

Indenture 12 March 1788 between **Joseph Summers**, Ninety-Six District, SC, to **Ghiles (Giles) Chapman**, of same district for 125 acres. *Newberry Co. Deed Bk A*/673

Indenture for 166 acres in Edgefield Co., SC, on Big Creek 28 September 1792 from **Aaron Booth** to **Joseph Summers** (Hendrix, G. Lee Corley *Edgefield Co. Abstracts of Deeds Books 1 -12 Vol I*/114)

Indenture dated July 15, 1806, from **Joseph Summers** to **John Summers** for 126 acres on Palmetto branch of Bush River, part of tract conveyed to **Joseph** by **Robert Yeldall**. *Newberry Deed Bk H*/295

Note: Using the land records, it is determined that Joseph Summers migrated from MD to SC between 1771 and 1774. Migrating about the same time was Joseph's father-in-law, Daniel Clary, and his family.

Military:
None identified.

Note: Joseph is listed as a member of the Bush River Quaker Monthly Meeting in 1775 (Medlin, William *Quaker Families of South Carolina & Georgia*/71). The usual history is that he was the leader of a group of Dunkers who migrated from MD to SC (Pope, Thomas H. *The History of Newberry Co.* Vol I/82). This congregation later became Universalists. (Ibid).

Civil Activities:
Joseph Summers served on the Petit Jury, Newberry County, February Term, 1796. (Holcomb, Brent H. *Newbery County, SC Minutes of the County Court 1785-1798*/259)

WILL *Newberry Co., SC WILL Bk Vol 2, Book E*/7, 8

Dated 3 Feb. 1802. Probated 16 Jan. 1809

"In the Name of God Amen.
I, **Joseph Summers**, of the District of Newberry in the State of South Carolina, planter, being weak in Body but of perfect Mind and Memory, thanks be to God, therefore calling to Mind the mortality of my Body and knowing that it is appointed for all men to die do make and ordain this my last Will and Testament. That is to say principally and first of all, I give and recommend my Soul to the hands of the Almighty God that gave it and for my Body I recommend it to the earth to be intered at the discretion of my Executors. And as touching such worldly Estate wherewith it hath pleased God to bless me in this life, I give and dispose of the same in the following manner and form. That is to say first of all it is my will and I do hereby order that all my just debts be paid.
I Devise and Bequeath unto my well beloved son, **William Summers**, one hundred and thirty-five acres of land laid out to him on which he now lives to him and his heirs and assigns forever.
I Give, Devise and Bequeath unto my beloved son, **John Summers**, one hundred acres of land laid off to him adjoining my son, **William Summers'** land, to him, his heirs and assigns forever.
I give, devise and bequeath to my beloved son, **Jesse Summers**, one hundred and sixty-six acres of land on Big Creek in Edgefield District to him, his heirs and assigns forever.
I give, devise and bequeath to my four sons, to wit **William**, **John**, **James** and **Jesse Summers** all my land lying on the waters of Edisto to be equally divided between them.

I give, devise and bequeath to the heirs of my daughter, **Ellenor Waters**, deceased, one cow and calf each.
I give and bequeath to the heirs of my daughter, **Cassandra Riggs**, if any there be five shillings.
I also give and bequeath to my dear and well-beloved wife, **Elinor**, all the plantation or tract of land whereon I now live with all the rest of my moveable estate during her natural life, and after her death the said tract of land to be divided between my three daughters, **Mary Chapman**, **Ann Wells**, and **Dorcas Summers**, in the following manner or proportion that is to say to **Mary Chapman** the one fourth part thereof, to **Ann Wells** the one fourth part thereof, and to **Dorcas Summers** the remaining two fourths, and the remaining part of my moveable estate to be equally divided between all my sons and daughters now living that is to say **William Summers**, **James Summers**, **John Summers**, and **Jesse Summers**, **Mary Chapman**, **Ann Wells** and **Dorcas Summers**.
I do hereby constitute make and ordain my beloved son, **John Summers**, Executor of this my Last Will and Testament, and I do hereby utterly disallow, revoke, and disannul all and every former Testaments Wills Legacies Bequests and Executors by me in any way before this time named willed and bequeathed ratifying and confirming this and no other to be my Last Will and Testament. In Witness whereof I have hereto set my hand and seal this Third day of February in the year of our Lord one thousand and eight hundred and two in the twenty sixth year of American Independence.

Joseph Summers"

Witnesses: **P.B. Waters**
Sme. Summers
John Summers

Children of **Joseph** and **Eleanor Clary Summers**
William Summers b 10 Aug 1756 in MD; m 1777 to **Susannah Teague**; d 12 Oct 1823, buried in Chapman-Summers Cemetery ("Old Dunker") Newberry Co., SC. (Bible of Robert Summer, Senora, GA; and *Newberry County Cemeteries Vol I*/113). In 1809 he was one of the original trustees of the Newberry Academy (Pope Opus Cit p 216). *1790 SC Census* lists him in Newberry Co., with 1 male over 16 yrs, 4 under 16 yrs, and 4 females.
Mary Summers b 10 Oct 1758 in MD; m 14 Sept 1775 to **Giles Chapman**; d 15 Oct 1813, buried in Chapman-Summers Cemetery ("Old Dunker"), Newberry, SC. *Newberry County Cemeteries Vol I*/113. *1790 SC Census* lists Giles Chapman in Newberry Co., with 2 males over 16 yrs, 4 under 16 yrs, and 4 females.
John Summers b 29 June 1763 in MD; m **Rosanna Waters**; d 22 Mar 1836, Newberry Co., SC. *Newberry County Cemeteries Vol I*/113.

1790 SC Census lists **John Summers**, Newberry Co., with 1 male over 16 yrs, 1 female, and 4 slaves.

Ruth Summers bapt Dec 6, 1765 MD *Prince George's Parish* Opus Cit p 277) It appears she died early.

Jesse Summers b 1775, Newberry Co; m **Sarah Coate**; d ca 1837, Charles Co., AL. WILL probated January 11, 1837.

James Summers b unk; m **Elizabeth** ____; d ca 1826, Edgefield Co. SC. WILL probated Aug 1826.

Ellenor (Nelly) Summers b unk; m **Thomas W Waters** in SC; d prior 1802, date her father wrote his WILL. *1790 SC Census* lists Thos W Waters in Newberry District with 1 male over 16 yrs, 4 females, and 6 slaves.

Cassandra Summers b unk; m _____ **Riggs**; d prior 1802, date her father wrote his Will.

Ann (Anne) Summers b unk; m **James Wells**; d Edgefield District, SC

Dorcas Summers b unk; m **Griffin Coleman** post 1802 (father's WILL uses maiden name); d 20 March 1837, Newberry Co., SC. *Newberry Co. Will Book M*/526-531

Mary Summers
b probably Prince George's Co
m **John Wheat (II)** by 1728, date of birth of daughter **Sarah** (*Piscataway* Opus Cit)
d unknown (In the *1776 MD Census* she is not listed in household of **John Wheat**)

Census:

1733 Prince George's Co. lists **John Wheat** (II) as taxable in Upper Piscattaway Hundred, along with **Francis Wheat** and **Joseph Wheat**. *Calendar of Maryland States Papers, No. 1, The Black Books*/268

1776 MD Census lists a **John Wheat** in St. John's and Prince George's Parishes, Prince George's Co., with **John** aged 43, other males ages 12, 9, 7, 1; and the oldest female, **Mary**, aged 11 and other female aged 5; and 1 negro female slave age 19. This would appear to be the son of **John** and **Mary Wheat**, born 11/18/1730.

1790 MD Census lists a **John Wheat** in Prince George's Co. with 3 white males 16 yrs. and over, 3 white males under 16 yrs, 4 females and 2 slaves. This also appears to be the son of **John** and **Mary Summers Wheat**.

1800 MD Census lists a **John Wheat** in Prince George's Co. with 1 male between 10 and 16 yrs, 1 male between 16 and 26 years, 1n female between 10 and 16 years, and 2 females betweem 16 and 26 yrs. This is perhaps **John**, grandson of **Mary Summers** and **John Wheat,** but does not agree with the *1776 MD Census.*

Property:

Friendship Addition, 25 acres, patented to **John Wheat** 26 February 1753 (*GS #1*/213), lying between tract called Friendship and tract called Addison's Purchase on north side of a small branch that runs into Tinkers branch. Patented to **Meredith Davis** 12 Sept 1712 *Prince George's Land Bk PL 7*/566.

Resurvey on Friendship was granted to **John Wheat, Sen.** dated 22 July 1760 for a parcel called Friendship originally granted 10 November 1730 to **Meredith Davis** for 100 acres. The Resurvey contains 103 1/2 acres. (*Prince George's Land AM 1*/304)

Friendship Second Addition, 357 acres, patented to **John Wheat, Sen.**, 29 September 1762, Prince George's Co. (*BC&GS 17*/181 and *BC&GS 19*/4)

Military:

John Wheat took the Patriots' Oath of Fidelity and Support 1778, Montgomery Co., #134 (Brumbaugh Opus Cit *Revolutionary Records of MD*/2).

Civil Activities:

A **John Wheat** was a Grand Juror, Prince George's Co., Loyal Civil Services 1780, p 32, and 1782, p 35 (Ibid)

WILL - none has been found

Children of **John** and **Mary Summers Wheat**

Sarah Wheat - b 4 May 1728 (Piscataway Opus Cit)

John Wheat, Jr.- b ca 1730 (Piscataway Opus Cit p 258). His children may be

Mary Wheat- b ca 1764/5, according to 1776 Census. (Brumbaugh *Maryland Records* Opus Cit/140 lists a Mary Wheat m to Thomas B. Moreland Oct. 17, 1799, Prince George's Co. "Marriage Licenses 1777-1801")

Sarah Wheat baptized Oct. 24, 1765 (*Piscataway* Opus Cit p 335)

Joseph Wheat baptized Aug. 7, 1768 (Ibid p 336) In the *1790 MD Census* there is a **Joseph Wheat**, Montgomery Co., with 1 male over 16 yrs, 1 under 16, 2 females and 3 slaves.

son- b ca 1769, according to *1776 MD Census*

daughter - b ca 1771, according to *1776 MD Census*

Thomas Wheat baptized Feb. 15, 1774 (*Piscataway* Opus Cit p 355)

In the *1790 Census* is a **Hezekiah Wheat**, Montgomery Co., with 1 male over 16 yrs, 4 under 16, and 5 females.

Remarks: *Prince George's Inventory and Accounts Liber 32C/* 150 records inventory of estate of **John Wheate** decd. Appraisal by **John Boone** and **Thomas Blanford** 20 Sept. 1711 with the Inventory/Administration dated 1712 *Prince George's Co. JB1* 090 and *JB1* 080. Although there is no proved relationship between the two **John Wheats**, there are no other **John Wheats** in this time frame and place and no later WILL, Inventory or Accounts has been located for any **John Wheat**. Thus **John Wheat** (II) was born before 1712, which places **Mary Summers** as one of the older children. The **John Wheat** baptized 11/18/1730 would be the son of **John** and **Mary Summers Wheat** and thus **John** (III).

In the *Wheat Genealogy Vol I* by Silas C. Wheat, there is a discussion of **Francis Wheat** of Maryland and his descendants.

Rebeckah Summers

b probably Prince George's Co.

m **John King**, ca 1738

d prior to 1789 (not mentioned in husband's WILL of that date)

Census:

1733 List of Taxables lists two **John King**, one in Western Branch Hundred, Prince George's Co.; and the other in Lower Part of Piscattaway Hundred, Prince George's Co. (Opus Cit Black Books/263, 270)

MD Census of 1776 lists three **John King** in St. John's and Prince George's Parishes, PG Co. (Brumbaugh Opus Cit Vol I) The most likely to be husband of **Rebeckah Summers** is a **John King**, age 74 and only male in household, with the oldest female being **Mary** age 29 yrs, and other females ages 18 and 16. A second is a **John King** aged 38, with a son aged 7, the oldest female's being **Eleanore** aged 39 and other females ages 12, 13, 11, 9, 5, and 1. The third **John King** is aged 25, with sons ages 16 and 11, with the oldest female's being **Kersey** aged 20 and other females ages 14, 9, and 7.

More conclusive would appear to be the listing in the *1776 Census* North West Hundred, Frederick Co., of **Edward King**, aged 36, with **Edward**, Jr, aged 2, and **Rebackah** aged 34, **Elizabeth** aged 13, **Sarah** aged 12, **Mary** aged 9, **Charity** aged 7, and **Rebackah** aged 5 months.

MD Assessment of 1783 lists two **John King** in Montgomery Co.; one in Lower Newfoundland Hundred, as is an **Edward King** and the other in Linganore.

Military:

A **John King** took Patriots' Oaths of Fidelity and Support, as # 435 in Montgomery Co, 1778 (Brumbaugh Opus Cit *Revolutionary Records*/5)

A **John King** is listed in Montgomery Co. 1st Co. Lower Bn, (Clements and Wright Opus Cit p 198) and a **John King** is listed in 7th Co. Class No 3, Montgomery Co. (Ibid p 206).

Property:

none identified

WILL *Prince George's Will Bk T1/286*

"In the Name of God Amen I **John King** of Prince Georges County planter being sick and weak but of perfect mind and memory thanks be given un to God, calling unto mind the mortality of my body and knowing that it is appointed for all Men once to die do make and Ordain this my last Will and Testament. That is to say principally and first of all I give and recommend my soul unto the hand of Almighty God that gave it, and my Body to the Earth to be buried in decent Christian burial at the discretion of my Executor nothing doubtin but at the General resurection I shall receive the same again by the mighty power of God and as touching such worldly Estate wherewith it hathe pleased God to bless me with in this Life I give devise and dispose of the same in the following manner and form

First I will and bequeath unto **Elizabeth Darcey** and **John King** my beloved daughter and son all my goods and chattles now in the Possession of my Son **Benjm King** living near the sugar lands in Frederick County Viz. one mare and saddle, seven head of cattle, two large pewter dishes and three basons one bed and bed furniture, two bedsteads, two chests three heads of sheep, one pair of spoon moulds, one irone pot and one pair of pot hooks. Likewise all my movable effects.

Also I will and bequeath unto the rest of my beloved sons and daughters in the manner and form following unto my Sons **Edward** and **Wilm King** I give and bequeath one shilling sterling each

Likewise my Daughter **Mary Peacock** and my Son **Thomas King** I will and bequeath one shilling each.

I also will and bequeath unto my beloved son **Benjn King** and my beloved Daughter **Rebeccah Viemullion** one shilling sterling each.

I likewise constitute and ordain **John Darcey** and **Elizabeth Darcey** the sole Executors of this my last Will and Testament and I do hereby revoke and Disannul all and every other former Testaments, Wills, Legacies, bequests and Executors by me in amywise before named willed and bequeathed ratifying and confirming this and no other to be my last Will and Testament. In Witness whereof I have hereunto set my hand and Seal this eighteenth Day of December in the year of our Lord one thousand seven hundred and eighty nine. **John (X) King Sen"**

Witnessed by **Joseph Burgess, Josias Moore, Jesse Moore**

Proved January 12th 1790

Children of **John** and **Rebeccah Summers King** as listed in father's WILL

Elizabeth, b ca 1753, m **John Darcey**. *1776 MD Census* lists a **John Dorsey**, age 39, Prince George's Co., with other males 14, 12, 2 and with females **Elizabeth** age 23, other females ages 7 and 4. No **John** or **Elizabeth Darcey** is in *MD 1790 Census*, but there is a **John Dorsey** in Montgomery Co. with 1 male over 16 yrs., 1 under 16 yrs., and 1 female.

John King, b ca 1738. A **John King** was a Pvt. in the Maryland Line, and received a Federal Bounty Grant of 100 acres in Apr 28, 1791

(Newman, Opus Cit p 31). *1790 MD Census*, Prince George's Co., lists a **John King** with 3 males over 16 and 4 females. WILL in *Prince George's Will Bk TT1*/166-167, dated 19 July 1812, for a **John King**, Sen. It lists bequeathes to granddaughter **Elenor Grimes**, daughter **Anne King** and **Mary Mullican** children. **Thomas Mullican** to settle his affairs. Proved January 31st 1816.

Edward King, b ca 1740. *MD 1776 Census*, North West hundred, Frederick Co., lists **Edward King**, age 36, **Rebeckah** age 34, **Elizabeth** age 13, **Sarah** age 12, **Mary** age 9, **Charity** age 7, **Benjamin** age 4, **Edward Jr**. age 2 and **Rebeckah** age 5 months. In the same Census (1776) in St. John's and Prince George's Parishes, Prince George's Co., is an **Edward King**, age 48, with males ages 5 and 1, with the oldest female **Ann**, age 30 and other females ages 13, 10, 6 and 3. An **Edward King** is listed in Montgomery Co., *1790 MD Census*, with 3 males over 16 yrs., 2 under 16 and 4 females.

William King. No **William King** is listed in the *1776 MD Census*. A **William King** is listed in Montgomery County, *1790 MD Census*, with 4 males over 16 yrs, 3 males under 16 and 6 females. A **William King** is listed as a Pvt. in the Maryland Line and received a Federal Bounty Grant of 100 acres, May 4, 1797 (Newman Opus Cit p 31).

Mary King, b ca 1747, m ______ **Peacock** after 1776 Census, but before father wrote his WILL in 1790. *MD 1790 Census* lists a **John Peacock**, Prince George's Co., with 1 male over 16, 1 under, no females, and 1 slave.

Thomas King. A **Thomas King** is listed in Anne Arundel Co. in the *MD 1776 Census*, All Hallows Parish, with 1 white female and 1 white child; this **Thomas King** and **Sarah** are parents of **Rachel** b 31 July 1774 and **Sarah** born 25 Feb 1776 (Wright, F. Edward *Anne Arundel County Church Records of the 17th and 18th Centuries*). **Thomas King, Sr.** and **Jr**, are listed in Prince George's Co., *1790 MD Census*. A **Thomas King** served as Pvt. in the Maryland Line and received a Federal Bounty Grant of 100 acres, dated May 4, 1797 (Newman Ibid p 31).

Benjamin King. A **Benjamin** took the Oath of Fidelity, PG Co., 1776 (Brumbaugh *Maryland Records* Vol II p 308). A **Benjamin** is listed in Montgomery Co., *1790 MD Census* with 2 males over 16 yrs, 2 under 16, 4 females and 4 slaves.

Rebeccah King, b ca 1758 (*MD 1776 Census*) m ________ **Virmillien**. *1790 MD Census* lists **Edward, Giles** and **John Vermillian** in Prince George's Co.

Female born ca 1760 or another female age 16 in household 1776 according to *1776 MD Census*.

Note: Although there is no proven connection, the following records will be of interest to those researching the King family.

Calvert Co. Will Liber 25/225 records the WILL of **John King** of Calvert Co. 26 Nov. 1745. It identifies sons **Ignatius**, **Thomas**, and **Samuel** and wife as **Sarah**.

John King, in Skinner's *Abstracts of Inventories 1766-1769*, lists his Inventory Feb. 27, 1769, Charles Co., mentions "Chanman's Purchase" (200 acres); next of kin is **Anne Gray** and **Catharine King Gray**. Administrators are **Henry Moore** and **Benedict Hamilton**.

Rachel Summers
b 1720, Prince George's Co. (Miller, opus cit p 1)
m **Benjamin Johnson** by 1743, birth of daughter **Mary Ann** (Ibid p 79)
d after 1800 (is listed in Montgomery Co in *1800 MD Census*)

Census:

1733 list of Taxables, Upper Piscattaway Hundred, Prince George's Co., includes a **Benjamin Johnson** and a **James Johnson**. (Opus Cit. The Black Books/268)

1776 Census of MD does not list a **Benjamin Johnson**

1783 MD Assessment lists **Benjamin Johnson Sr.** and **Jr.** in Linganore, Montgomery Co.

1790 MD Census lists **Benjamin Johnson** (probably senior) in Montgomery Co. with 2 males over 16 yrs, 1 under 16, 2 females and 7 slaves.

1800 MD Census lists **Rachel Johnson**, Montgomery Co.

1810 MD Census lists several "R. Johnson" with no given names.

Property:

Bradford's Rest. Indenture dated 27 Oct 1755 between **Daniel Clary** and **Eleanor** his wife and **Mary Brown** and **William Deveron Clary** of Frederick Co on the one part and **Benjamin Johnson** of Prince George's Co. planter for tract called Bradford Rest in Frederick Co containing 121 acres. Witnessed by **David Lynn**, **Charles Jones**. Recorded Nov 20, 1755. *Frederick Co. Land Liber E*/904. This Indenture is rerecorded in *Frederick Co Land Bk F*/529 when **William Clary**, now of age, acknowledges the sale. Original patent was to John Bradford, Jr.

Venture, 50 acres, Frederick Co., bounded by a tract of land called Dry Spring. Patented to **Benjamin Johnson** 1774. Survey 8 December 1774. (*BC&GS 48*/257 and *BC&GS* 51/6)

Bradford's Rest. Indenture July 10, 1780 between **Benjamin Johnson** of Montgomery Co. planter and **Thomas Swearingon**, Montgomery Co. planter, a tract part of Bradford's Rest, east side of Rock Creek containing 230 acres. **Rachall** signed release of dower. Deed recorded July 18th 1780. *Montgomery Land Bk A*/530

Military:

Benjamin Johnson took Patriots' Oaths of Fidelity and Support, Prince George's Co. (Brumbaugh *Maryland Records* Opus Cit Vol II/290)

DAR Patriot Index lists **Benjamin Johnson** b ca 1718 d ca 1-10-1795; Patriotic Service MD.

"In the name of God Amen I **Benjamin Johnson** of Montgomery County and State of Maryland being thru the abundant mercy of God tho week in body yet of sound and perfect understanding and memory do constitute and appoint this my last will and testament and desire it to be received by all as such. Imprimus. I most humbly bequest my Soul to God my maker beseaching his most gracious of it thu the all suffcient merit to Redeemer Jesus Christ who gave himself to be an atonement for my sins and able to save to the ultimate all that come to God by him for mercy in this hope and confidence I render up my Soul with comfort humbly beseeching the most blessed and glorious trinity one God most holy most gracious and merciful to prepare me for the time of my dissolution and there to take me to him self into that peace and rest and incomparable felicity which he has prepared for those that love and fear his holy name Amen blessed be God. Imprimus I give my body to the earth from whence it was taken in full assurance of its resurrection from thence at the last day as for my burial I desire it may be decent without pomp or state at the discretion of my executors hereafter named who I doubt not will manage it with all required prudence. As to my worldly estate I will and positively order that all my just debts be paid.

Item I give and bequeath to my son **Benjamin Johnson** one shilling sterling.

Item I give and bequeath to my son **John Johnson** one shilling sterling.

Item I give and bequeath to my son **Jonothan Johnson** one shiling sterling.

Item I give and bequeath to my daughter **Mary Ann Johnson** now called **Tall** one shilling sterling.

Item I give and bequeath to my daughter **Elizabeth Harriss** one shilling sterling.

Item I give and bequeath to my daughter **Rachell Willman** one shilling sterling.

Item I give and bequeath to my daughter **Lurana Mullikin** one shilling sterling.

Item I give and bequeath **Jemina Ryan** heirs one shilling sterling.

Item I give and bequeath to my son **James Johnson** heirs one shilling sterling.

Item I give and bequeath to my son **Josius Johnson**'s heirs one shilling sterling

Item I give all the rest of my estate to my beloved wife **Rachel Johnson** for and during her natural life and after her decease I give and bequeath to my son **Samuel Johnson** one negro girl named Dinah to him his heirs and assigns forever. Item I give order and bequeath to my son **Resin Johnson** his heirs and assigns for ever after the death of his mother all the remainder of my property be it of what nature or kind soever except that in case my negro woman Tender should hereafter have another child then

and in such case my will is that the same shall go and desend to my son **Jonathan Johnson** his heirs and assigns forever And lastly I do nominate constitute and appoint my sons **Samuel** and **Resin Johnson** my executors to this my last will and testament In witness whereof I have hereunto set my hand and seal this twenty fifth day of August one thousand seven hundred and eighty eight. **Benjamin (Ɨ) Johnson"**

Witnessed by **John L. Summers, John Dent Summers, John Nicholson.**

Proved 10 January 1795

Children of **Benjamin** and **Rachel Summers Johnson** as listed in father's WILL

Benjamin Johnson b 1740, MD (Hege, Katherine *From Maryland to Buck Shoals, the Johnson Family*). *1790 MD Census* lists 2 **Benjamins** in Montgomery Co.; this likely is father and son. **Benjamin, Jr.**, is listed as owning "Rich Bottom alias Birch Bottom (Buck Bottom)" from 1769 thru 1773. (MSA Index 58). There is an Indenture of lease and release for a **Benjamin Johnson**, Frederick Co., silversmith, and **Susannah** his wife, late called **Susanna Franckenfeldt**, for tract called Rocky Creek, dated 17 April 1771 (*Frederick Co Land Bk O pp 1-346*/343); it has not been determined if this is the son of **Rachel** and **Benjamin Johnson**. Died 1818, Iredell Co., NC; his WILL references his wife as Cassandra (Hege Opus Cit).

John Johnson. In *1790 MD Census* 2 **John** are listed in Frederick Co. and 2 in Montgomery Co.

Jonathan Johnson b ca 1755, Montgomery Co., MD (Records of Louise Terrill, Pryor, OR). A **Jonathan Johnson** m **Mary Summers** Oct 10, 1779, Montgomery Co. (Brumbaugh Opus Cit Vol II/519). *1790 MD Census* lists a **Jonathan** in Anne Arundel Co. Died ca 1799, Fayette Co., KY; WILL probated Fayette Co., KY WILL Bk E, 74, dated Aug 20, 1819 (Terrill).

Mary Ann Johnson m **Arthur Thomas Taul** (4/12/1749-2/24/1812). *1776 MD Census* lists an **Arthur Tall**, age 28, **Benjamin** age 4, **Pentacast** age 3, and **Maryann** age 33, in Frederick County Hundred, now Montgomery Co. **Arthur Thomas Taul** is listed as performing Patriotic Service in MD (*DAR Patriots Index Edition 1966*). Neither **Taul** nor **Tall** is listed in *1790 MD Census*.

Elizabeth Johnson m ________ **Harris**. An **Elizabeth Harris** is listed in *1790 MD Census* in Frederick Co.

Rachell Johnson m ________ **Williman**

Lurana Johnson m ________ **Milliken**

Jemima Johnson m ________ **Ryan**. Died prior to date father wrote his WILL (1788)

James Johnson m ______ **Elizabeth**. Purchased 100 acres of tract called The Resurvey on Friend's Advice by Indenture from **Elisha Williams**, dated 12 March 1763. (*Frederick Land Bk H*/308). **Elizabeth Johnson**, widow and relict of **James Johnson**, late of Frederick Co., decd, quits claim to all manner of dower rights; recorded 16 March 1767 at request of **Benjamin Johnson**. (*Frederick Land Bk K*/996). **Benjamin Johnson** was Adminstrator of estate of **James Johnson** Frederick Co. March 4, 1768 (*Frederick Co. Inventory Liber 96*/305). Creditors are listed as **Charles Caton** and **Joseph Summers**. Next of kin are listed as **Charles Caton** and **Adam Fisher**. This **James** was probably the son of **Benjamin** because at the time father wrote his WILL (1788), he referred to the "heirs" of son **James**. Inventory for **James Johnson** in Frederick Co., Sept 26, 1768 (MSA *Testamentary Proceedings Vol 43*/97).

Josias Johnson died prior to date father wrote his WILL (1788)

Resin Johnson. No **Resin** is listed in *1790 MD Census*.

Samuel Johnson. A **Samuel** is listed in Montgomery Co. in *1790 MD Census*, with 2 males over 16 years, 3 under 16 years, 3 females, and 3 slaves.

Note: Researchers of **Benjamin Johnson** may be interested in the Indenture (*Prince George's Land Bk PP*/8) dated 13 Oct. 1749 between **Joseph Johnson** and **Benjamin Johnson**, Prince George's Co. planters, and **Edmund Castile**, Prince George's planter. Original grant 10 Dec. 1714 to **Robert Johnson**, Prince George Co., for tract called Poor Man's industry, at head of Tinkir's Branch, laid out for 100 acres. **Robert Johnson** by LWT dated 14 May 1717 bequeathed the land to his sons **Joseph** and **Benjamin**.

Ruth Summers

b probably Prince George's Co.

m **Edmund Riggs**, son of **James** and **Elizabeth Riggs** (Riggs, John Beverley *The Riggs Family of Maryland*/492), after 1742 (birth of son by Riggs' first wife **Mary Brooke Riggs**)

d after 1790 and before 1800 (listed in *1790 MD Census*, Montgomery Co., but not in *1800 MD Census*)

Census:

1733 List of Taxables in New Scotland Hundred, Prince George's Co., includes **Edmund Riggs**. (Opus Cit. The Black Books/275)

1758-59 Vestrymen, Churchwardens and Freeholders, Prince George Parish, Prince George's Co., lists Edmund Riggs. (Ibid page 942)

1776 MD Census lists no **Edmond Riggs**, but does list a **James Riggs**, age 35, Frederick Co. Lower Potomac Hundred, with a **Robert Riggs** age 13, a **Basil Riggs**, age 21, a **Mary Riggs**, age 27, a **Maxemelia Riggs**, age 7 and a **Mary Riggs** age 4.

1783 MD Assessment lists **Edmund Riggs** in Linganore, Montgomery Co.

1790 MD Census lists **Ruth Riggs** in Montgomery Co. with 2 white males 16 yrs and over and 3 females.

1800 MD Census does not list **Ruth Riggs**.

Military:

Edmond Riggs served as Private in French and Indian War (1757-58). ("Maryland Historical Magazine" Vol IX p 271)

Property:

Dann - Lease April 3, 1750, between **Lucy Brooke** of Prince George's Co and **Edmond Riggs** of Frederick Co. one messuage, tenement and tract of land, part of large tract called Dann in Frederick Co., corner of a parcel belonging to **Charles Brooke**, laid out for 100 acres for natural life of **Edmond**, **Mary** his wife and **James** their son. Witnessed by **John Hepburn** and **R. Brooke**. *Frederick Land Bk B*/155. Original patent dated 16 February 1694 to **Thomas Brooks**, lying on the west side of a branch of the Potomac River called Rock Creek branch, near the forks of the branch, bounded by land of **William Joseph**, Esq. (*Prince George's Land B 27*/23) Holding Spring, 100 acres, Frederick Co. (now Montgomery) Indenture dated 10 Sept 1767, between **William Coats**, Frederick Co., and **Edmond Riggs**, Frederick Co., for all the tract on dry Sineca called Holding Spring. *Frederick Land Bk L*/37. **Edmond Riggs** is listed as owning Holding Spring from 1769 to 1773 (MSA Index to Owners).

John's Delight, 82 1/2 acres, Frederick Co. Indenture 18 November 1772 between **John Harriss**, Frederick Co., and **Edmond Riggs**, same county, for part of tract called John's Delight and known by name of Green Bryar. *Frederick Land Bk P,pp 342-699*/487. This Indenture is rerecorded in *Frederick Land Bk V*/305, dated 10 May 1774, giving the name as Green Briar, and containing 84 acres.

Albany, tract containing 15 1/2 acres, lying "at" land called holding spring, purchased by **Ruth Riggs**, Executrix of **Edmund Riggs**, Montgomery Co., from **Charles Clagett**, dated 13 Jan 1790. (*Montgomery Land Records Liber D*/361)

WILL *Montgomery Co. Will Book B i*/132

"In the Name of God Amen I **Edmund Riggs** of the County of Montgomery and Province of Maryland considering the uncertainty of this mortal life and blessed with sound mind and memory Thanks be given to God for the same, therefore I do make and ordain this to be my last Will and Testament Viz:

First and principally I recommend my body to the Earth to be decently buried at the discretion of my Executors in a christian like manner Nothin doubting but at the general Resurrection to receive the same again by the Mighty power of God, and my soul to God that gave it _______ and as touching what worldly Estate it hath pleased God to bless me with I give and bequeath the same in the following manner

Imprimis: It is my will and I do ordain that all my just debts be paid and satisfied.

Item-I give and bequeath unto my beloved wife **Ruth Riggs** all my Real and Personal Estate during her natural life or while she remains my widow she making no waste of the same but to the best of her skill and understanding keep things together for the good of her children and after her Decease the whole both Real and Personal to be sold at public Action.

Item - I give unto my beloved son **James Riggs** eight pounds current money of this province

I give and bequeath unto my beloved daughter **Elizabeth Leech** eight pounds of like currency

I give and bequeath unto my beloved Daughter **Verlender Caton** eight pounds do

I give and bequeath unto my beloved son **Greenbrier Riggs** eight pounds

I give and bequeath unto my beloved son **John Riggs** eight pounds

And as touching the Remainder or Residue of my Estate after the above legatees is satisfied, the same to be equally divided amongst the rest of the children that are then living

And Lastly I do will and ordain my beloved wife **Ruth Riggs** and my Beloved son **James Riggs** Executors of this my last will and testament. Revoking and disannulling all former wills by me made whereunto I have set my hand and seal the Twenty forth Day of November One thousand seven hundrend Eighty Three.

Edmund Riggs"

Witnessed by **Newton Chiswell, Charles Clagett, Lawrence Owen**.

Proved April 11th 1784

Inventory:

Nov 2, 1798. Signed by **Sarah Riggs** and **Eleanor Reid** as next of kin. (Riggs, Opus Cit p 492)

Nov 5, 1798. An additional Inventory signed by **Edmond Riggs, Jr.** (Ibid)

Children: (as listed in WILL)

Child of **Edmond** and **Mary Brooke Riggs**

James Riggs (9/15/1742 - 2/22/1815) m **Mary Johnson** (Ibid)

Children of **Edmond** and **Ruth Summers Riggs**

Elizabeth Riggs m **Thomas Leech** (Ibid)

Verlinder Riggs m **John Caton** 11-7-1781, Montgomery Co. (Ibid)

Greenbury Riggs m **Ann Hardy** (license dated 1/25/1781). He is listed in Montgomery Co., Upper BN, 3rd Co. MD Militia in the Revolutionary War (Clements and Wright Opus Cit p 193). d 1844.

John Summers Riggs b 5 Oct. 1760. Tradition says he was drowned (Riggs Opus Cit p 492). A **John Riggs** is listed in Montgomery Co., 6th Co., Upper BN (Clements and Wright Ibid p 194).

"the rest of the children"

Note: John Beverly Riggs in his *The Riggs Family of Maryland*, published in 1939, lists additional children as follows:

Samuel Riggs, b Jan 20, 1765, moved to KY. A **Samuel Riggs** is listed in Montgomery Co. 7th Co., Upper BN (p 195) and another is listed in Montgomery Co. 4th Co., Middle BN (Clements and Wright Opus Cit p 196)

Rosewell Riggs

Edmond Riggs, Jr. m May 23, 1799 in St. Peter's Parish, Montgomery Co., to **Jane Willson**

Note: *Prince George's Co. WILLS Liber 24*/10 contains the WILL of **James Riggs, Sen.**, dated 21 Aug. 1744. He leaves to wife **Elizabeth** "everything except a feather bed and furniture and a brendle cow heifer during her natural life" and after her decease to be divided among his children **James Riggs**, **John Riggs**, **Edmond Riggs**, **Sarah Riggs**, and **Jane Cramphin**. Refer to the WILL for other details.

Jemina Summers
b probably PG Co
m **Charles Caton (Keaton, Cayton)** (b 20 Aug 1733, son of **John Keaton** and **Elizabeth**) by Dec. 1758, date son **John** was born Piscataway Parish, Prince George's Co.
d prior Nov. 1814 Rowan Co., NC (is not mentioned in husband's WILL of that date)

Census:
1776 MD Census lists no **Charles Caton**
1783 MD Assessment, Montgomery Co., lists no **Caton**.
1790 NC Census lists **Charles Caiton** in Salisbury Dis, Rowan Co., with 3 males of 16 yrs and over, 1 male under 16 yrs, and 4 females.
1800 NC Census lists **Charles Caiton**, Rowan Co., 1 male between 6 and 16 yrs, 1 male between 26 and 45 yrs, and 1 male over 45 yrs., with 1 female over 45 yrs.

Property:
The Resurvey on Friends Advice, Frederick Co., 100 acres. Indenture 12 March 1763 between **Elisha Williams** and **Charles Caton**, Frederick Co., planter, for all that tract of a greater tract called the Resurvey on Friends Advice. *Frederick Land Bk H*/310
Resurvey on Friends Advice, Montgomery Co., 100 acres. Indenture dated 27 October 1780 from **Charles Caton**, Montgomery Co., to **Walter Beall** for all that part of the tract, adjoining lands of **William Wilcoxen** and **Thomas Cramphin, Sen.**, which was conveyed to **Charles Caton** by **Elisha Williams** *Montgomery Co Deed BK A*/582.
Rowan Co., NC, Land BK 55/110, grant to **Charles Caton, Jr.**, dated 4 November 1784 for 150 acres in forks of Yadkin River. (Was this father or son?)
Charles Caton owned property on Hunting Creek, Iredell Co., NC 1794 (*Iredell Co., NC, Deed Bk B*/191-192)
Charles Caton received a grant for 300 acres on waters of Rockey Creek 18 Aug. 1796 (Ibid p 448)

Military:
Charles Caton took Oath of Fidelity and Support Required for Civil Officers, Montgomery Co. 1780-1782 (Brumbaugh Opus Cit *Revolutionary Records of MD*/11)
Chas. Caton is listed in Montgomery Co. Upper Battalion, 3rd Co. 1777 (Clements and Wright Opus Cit p 193)

WILL *Rowan Co. WILL Bk G*/389-390
"In the name of God Amen. I **Charles Caton Sen** of the County of Rowan and state of North Carolina being in good health and in perfect mind and memory thanks be unto God, Calling into mind the Mortality of my Body and Knowing it is appointed for all men to die I do this Second day of November Anno Domini One

Thousand Eight Hundred and Fourteen make and ordain this my last will and Testament (Viz) Principally and first of all I give and recommend my Soul into the hands of Almighty God that gave it and my body I recommend to the Earth to be Buried according to the directions of my Executors hereafter names, Nothing doubting but at the General Resurrection I shall receive the Same again by the mighty power of God and as touching such worldly estate as it has pleased God to bless me with in this life I give and devise and dispose of in the following manner,-
First of all my will and desire is that all my lawfull debts should be paid.
Item. I give and Bequesth unto my Son **John Caton** Twenty dollars
Item. I give and Bequeath unto my Son **Charles Caton** One Hundred dollars.
Item. I give and Bequeath unto my Son **Jesse Caton** Ten Shillings
Item. I give and Bequeath to my Son **George Dent Caton** Ten Shillings
Item. I give and Bequeath unto my Son **Benjamin Caton** Ten Shillings
Item. I give and Bequeath unto my daughter **Mary Felps** One Hundred dollars
Item. I give and Bequeath un to my daughter **Jemima Hill** One Hundred dollars
Item.I give and Bequeath unto my daughter **Rebecca Ridgway** Two Hundred dollars
Item. I give and Bequeath to my daughter **Elizabeth Ridgway** Two Hundred dollars
Item. I give and Bequeath unto my Son **William Caton** Ten Shillings
Item. I give and Bequeath unto my daughter **Ann Orrel** after the other Legatees is paid their legacies and is paid to them by my said daughter **Ann Orrel** out of the Estate Movable left in their on her hands, and if not paid out of the movable or personal estate, it shall be raised out of my land which I die possessed with. Now if she or any Other person for her will pay off the legatees, their part of the estate left them in this my last will and Testament, at my death, then in that case my will and desire is to give all my Land to my daughter **Ann Orrell** if not my Will and desire is their legacies shall be raised by the sale of my lands, used in this case I nominate and appoint my Son **Charles Caton** to ask for and receive of **Ann Orrel** the amount of his own legacy left him, also all the legacies left each of my children and if paid when demanded, then my son **Charles** must give as Speay information to call on him for their legacies as possible, and when paid he shall be clear but liable until paid. Should my Daughter **Ann Orrel** fail in paying up those legacies when demanded immediately after my decease by my Son **Charles Caton** I then and in that case appoint my Son **Charles Caton** and give him full power and all Lawful authority to Sell all my lands which I die possessed of and to convey the Title of the said lands to the purchaser as fully as I could have done in that while living, and thereby raise the money due each legatee So that each Legatee my receive his part or her part as soon as he can make himself ready to settle with them. And for the trouble, and for the natural love I bear for him as one of my children I give and Bequeath unto my Son **Charles Caton** Fifty dollars over and above the first Gift of the within One Hundred dollars. I also give unto my Son **Charles Caton** all the money, all Bonds, notes, accounts assignments and also all my wearable Cloaths, which I die possessed with which is my Will and desire he Should be possessed with Immediately after my decease,-

I appoint **James Orrel** Executor to pay all my lawful debts out of the estate or movable property, delivered in his hands for that and other purposes, I appoint him Executor to this my last will and Testament I **Charles Caton Sen**. do this Fourth day of November the year our Lord Christ 1814 publish and proclaim this to be my last Will and Testament as witness whereof I have this day above mentioned, Signed Sealed and Acknowledged the Same in the presence of us who in our presence and the presence of each other have witnessed the same.

Charles Caton"

Attest **Nath. Peebles**

Jos. Douthil

N. Peebles

Alpha Peebles Probated 1815

Children of **Charles** and **Jemina Summers Caton**

John Caton bapt. Dec 7, 1758 (*Piscataway* Opus Cit p 301), m **Susannah** ________ (Dunlap Opus Cit); a **John** is in Rowan Co., *1800 NC Census* with 3 males between 10 and 16 yrs, 1 between 16 and 26 yrs, and 1 between 26 and 45 yrs, with 12 female under 10 , 2 between 16 and 26 and 1 between 26 and 45.

Jesse(y) Caton bapt. April 20, 1762 (*Piscataway* Opus Cit p 306); m 20 Jan 1787 to **Esther Sparks**, Rowan Co. (Holcomb, Brent *Marriages of Rowan Co., NC 1753-1868*/70). A **Jesse Caton** and **Elizabeth Orrel** were married 26 Jan 1813, with **Edgar Orrel** bondsman and **John March Sr**. witness (Ibid). Died Warren Co., MO prior 1854.

Charles Caton m **Rebecca Weyatt** 27 Feb 1810, Rowan Co, NC, with **John Stinchcomb** bondsman and **John March Sr.**, witness (Holcomb Opus Cit p 70). A second **Charles Caton** is listed in *1800 NC Census*, Rowan Co. with 10 males under 10 yrs, 2 between 10 and 16 yrs, 1 between 16 and 26, and 1 45 and over, with 1 female under 10 yrs, 2 between 10 and 16, 2 between 16 and 26 and 1 45 yrs and over. This would seem to indicate the 1810 marriage was a second one.

George Dent Caton m **Nancy Hurley**, 19 Nov 1789, Rowan Co., NC (Dunlap). Died 13 Jun 1852 (Ibid).

Benjamin Caton m **Betsey Bundridge** 2 Apr 1806, Clark Co., KY (Ibid)

Mary Caton m **John Felps (Phelps)** 30 Jan 1786, Rowan Co., NC (Holcomb Opus Cit p 129)

Jemima Caton m **Jacob Hill** 14 Dec. 1790, Stokes Co., NC (Dunlap)

Rebecca Caton m ________ **Ridgway**, according to father's Will.

Elizabeth Caton m **Samuel Ridgway**, 22 Apr 1799 (Dunlap Opus Cit)

William Caton m **Cynthya Smith** 7 Nov 1803 with **Thomas Smith** bondsman and **A.L. Osborn**, D.C., witness (Holcomb Opus Cit p 70)

Ann Caton m (1) **Jonas Sparks** 15 Oct 1796 (2) **James Orrell** (Dunlap Opus Cit)

Note: Mrs. Dunlap also lists a daughter **Jane Caton** who married an **Orrell**. This daughter is not listed in father's Will dated 1814.

James Summers

b probably Prince George's Co.

m **Mary** ______ by 1746, baptism of daughter Survina Prince George's Co. (*King George Index* opus cit p 270)

d by 14 Feb 1761, date WILL probated

Property:

Gum Spring Enlarged, Prince George's Co., near a branch called Oxon, 569 acres is patented to **James Summers** 1760. (*BC & GS 16*/307) Original survey 6 March 1718.

MSA Index 58 (Owners of tracts of land in Prince George's Co.) lists **James Summers** as owning Gumspring, Green Spring Enlarged from 1753 thru 1772.

25 Jan. 1753, living in Prince George's Co. near Eastern Branch of Potowmack **James Summers** reports a runaway convict servant. (Green, Karen Mauer "The Maryland Gazette 1727-1761" p 115)

WILL *Prince George's Will Bk I*/528

"In the name of God Amen the eighth day of January in the year of our Lord 1761. I **James Summers** of Prince George's County being verey sick and weak in Body but of perfect mind and memory Thanks be given unto God for the same and calling to Mind the Mortality of my Body and knowing That it is appointed for all Men to Die Do make and ordain this my Last Will and Testament That is for to say Principally and first of all I give and Recommend my Sole into the Hands of God that gave it and for my Body I Recommend it to the Earth to be Buried in a Christian like and Decent Manner at the Discretion of my Executors nothing doubting But at the General Resurection I shall Receive the Same again By the Mighty Power of God and as Touching My Worldly Estate which it hath Pleased God for to Bless me with in this Life

I give Devise and Dispose of the Same in the Manner and form following That is to say in the first place I give and Bequeath to my Dear and well beloved Wife **Mary Summers** all my Moveable Estate which it hath been Pleas'd God for to Bless me with Till the Day of marriage and then to be Equally Divided Among my five Children

I give and bequeath to my Dear and well Beloved Daughter **Sabine Summers** That part of the Land where **William Locker** settled Containing Seventy Acres

And to my Daughter **Mary Summers** Seventy Acres lying next to Philip Evans

and likewise my Daughter **Vilinda Summers** Seventy Acres lying next to Philip Evans

and to my Daughter **Rebekah Summers** Seventy Acres lying in Barnaba Branch and one Hundred ten and a half acres which if my Wife Should be with Child and Should bring a Boy That Hundred and ten and half Acres to belong to him

and my Daughter **Ann Summers** to have to the Value of the Seventy Acres of Land Made up in household Stuff Stock or Money and if the Child which we expect she is now going with should be a Daughter then that Hundred and ten and a half Acres of Land to be equally Divided Between my Daughter **Ann Summers** & it and then my Daughter **Ann** to have only her Equal part of the Household stuff and Moveables and further I Disallow Disannull and Revoke all and every other former Wills and Testaments By me in any Wise before this time Named Willed and Bequeathed Ratifying and Confirming this and no other to be my last Will and Testament In Witness whereof I have Sat my hand and Seal This Day and Year above Written.

James Summers"

Witnessed by **John Summers, Jun.**
Josiah Wilcoxen
Robt St Clare

Proved 14 Febry 1761. On same day widow **Mary Summers** declared she would not accept the bequeath made by husband, but claimed the widow's share. **Mary Summers**, widow, Executrix with **John Summers**, Jr., and **Dent Summers** of Prince George's Co. her sureties (*Testamentary Proceedings Liber 38* folio 87).

Inventory:
Prince George's Inventory GS 1/129,130 made 14 April 1761 totalled £125.19.11.

Accounts:
Prince George's Accts Liber 48/380. **Mary Summers**, exec of LWT of **James**, late of Prince George's, planter. Dated 1762.
1770 Prince George's Guardian Bonds/280 dated 20 March 1770 **Nathaniel Macgruder** and **John Osbourn** appointed to view lands and plantations left by **James Summers**, decd.
Find 1 dwelling 20 X 16 feet with 8 ft shed and under frame much rotten 1 old logg kitchen 20 X 16. Tobacco House 32 ft. by 22 much decayed. 1 log corn house. 1 apple orchard with 130 trees-many decayed. 1 parcel of scrub peach and cherry trees. Fencing in bad repair. Annual value to be £5.

Children of **James** and **Mary** ________ **Summers**
Sabina bapt 24 Oct. 1746 (*King George* Opus Cit p 289)
Mary bapt 11 Jan. 1751 (Ibid)
Virlinda bapt 11 July 1753 (Ibid)
Rebekah
Ann
James bapt 18 July 1761 (*Piscataway* Opus Cit 214) (He would have been the unborn listed in father's WILL)

POSTSCRIPT

Other Summers of the same time frame, place or name

Summers, John "service 1674. Of Kent Co." Skordas *The Early Settlers of Maryland*, p 448
There are similar names of Thomas (Dorchester Co.) and Benjamin (Somerset Co), but no connection has been found between these families and those of the western shore.

Summers, John - survey 22 June 1703 for Littleton, in fork of Patuxent River, 280 acres, Index Roll 56, Anne Arundel Co. John and Elizabeth were parents of John b 3 Nov 1695 and Robert b 7 Nov 1697, All Hallow's Parish (Wright, F. Edward, *AA CO. CHURCH RECORDS of 17th and 18th Centuries*, p 2 and 4). This John born in 1695 is unlikely to be handling business affairs in 1710 (*Prince George's Land Bk E*/21).

Summers, John - WILL and Testamentary Bond, Baltimore Co., 23 January 1758 by David Carlisle and Richard Williams, his Executors (*Testamentary Proceedings Liber 37*, folio 22). Administrative Bond and Additional Account of David Carlisle and Edward Williams 7 August 1760 (*Testamentary Proceedings Liber 38* folio 17).

Summers, John, ancestor of Judge Lewis Summers, West Virginia Historical Magazine Vol. 3/229, is identified as having been "born in Maryland in 1687", but gives no location or source of the information.

Summers, John of Alexandria, Virginia, is identified as living to be 103 years old, and having been born in Maryland.

Summers, Mary - Oct. 1699 Court, Prince George's Co., MD "It is ordered that Mary Thought be bound to serve John Summers till this November coming come twelve months in consideration the said John Summers to finde and allow her meat, drink, lodging and apparrell to keep her warm" Smith, Joseph H. and Philip A. Crowl *Court Records of Prince George's County, MD 1696-1699* /554

Summers, Michael - servant boy to Richard Edwards Ibid p 184

Summers, Peter - Prince George's Co. 1706 (*Testamentary Proceedings Liber 19C* folio 129)

Sumers, Sara- Sumers, male Sept 1697 A233. Petition of Hannah Edwards "your petitioner having had a child of Sarah Sumer and bred it up from its infancy as my own child and as I am informed that sais Sumers now Sarah Smart unjustly intends to take this child from me without any consideration et al ...... Anthony Smart". Although John Summers of Prince George's Co. had a daughter named Sarah, by

1703 she was a widow Westly and had not likely been married five years previously to Anthony Smart.

Summers, Robert - (see John I) Josias Towgood demands Capias against Robert Summers. Debt 2466: warrant to arrest and return- same case. March 1697/8 Court Ibid 322

Summers, Thomas - administrator of estate of Vincent Langford, St. Mary's Co., 26 November 1718 (*Testamentary Proceedings Liber 23* folio 295,402).

There are also the "German Summers" of the Frederick area. By 1764 a John Summers of Frederick Town, cordwinder, was buying land. The authors have determined no relationship between the "English Summers" of this monograth and the "German Summers" who by mid-1700 had arrived in the Frederick area.

Bibliography

________ *Genealogy of Benjamin Summers and His Descendants*

________ *King George's Parish Births 1689-1801*

________ *Prince George's County Maryland, Piscataway or St. John's Parish Index to Register*

Abrams, George Carter, Editor *Newberry County South Carolina Cemeteries Volume One*

Brown, Helen W. *Index to Register Prince George's Parish Prince George's and Montgomery Counties Maryland*

Brumbaugh, Gaius Marcus *Maryland Records Vol I & II*

Brumbaugh, Gaius Marcus *Revolutionary War Records Maryland*

Carr, Lois Green, Russell R. Menard, Louis Peddicord *Maryland at the Beginning*

Clements, S. Eugene and F. Edward Wright *The Maryland Militia in the Revolutionary War*

Coulter, Shirley, Edie Purdy and Lois Schneider *Iredell Co., NC, Deed Abstracts Vol I 1788-1797*

Coulter, Shirley, Edie Purdy and Lois Schneider *Minutes of the Court of Pleas Iredell Co. 1789-1800*

DAR *Patriot Index*

Ellis, Edward S. *History of the United States Vol I*

Hege, Katherine *From Maryland to Buck Shoals, the Johnson Family*

Hendrix, G Lee Corley *Edgefield Co. SC Abstracts of Deeds Books 1 - 12*

Holcomb, Brent H. *Marriages of Rowan Co., NC 1753-1868*

Holcomb, Brent H. *Newberry County, South Carolina, Minutes of the County Court 1785-1798*

Jones, Genevieve Broome *Children, Meet your Ancestors*

Linn, Mrs. Stahle *Abstracts of Wills and Estate Records of Rowan Co., NC 1753-1805*

Medlin, William *Quaker Families of South Carolina and Georgia*

Miller, Mildred *Carolina Summers*

Newman, Harry Wright *The Flowering of the Palatinate*

Newman, Harry Wright *Maryland Revolutionary Records*

Petrucelli, Katherine Sanford *The Heritage of Rowan Co., NC Vol I*

Pope, Thomas H. *The History of Newberry County Vol I*

Prince George's County Genealogical Society *Index to Wills, Administrations and Inventories 1696-1900*

Ridgely, Helen *Historic Graves of Maryland*

Riggs, John Beverly *The Riggs Family of Maryland*

Skinner, V.L. *Abstracts of the Inventories of the Prerogative Court of Maryland 1718-1720 and 1766-1769*

Skordas, Gust *The Early Settlers of Maryland*

Smith, Joseph H. and Philip A Crowl *Court Records of Prince George's County, Maryland 1696-1699*

Summers, Loite *Somers*
Summers, John L. *My Family History*
Townsend, George Alfred *Washington, Outside and Inside*
Wheat, Silas C. *Wheat Genealogy Vol I*
Wright, F. Edward *Anne Arundel County Church Records of the 17th and 18th Centuries*

INDEX

—T—

—U—

—V—

—W—

—Y—

GENERATION 6 FAMILY NO.

ANCESTOR ALEXANDER ANCESTRAL LINE SUMMERS

Son of And [ ]

Born 3-9-1778 At Md. Baptized

Died 4-12-1847 At MONONGALIA CO. Va. Buried At LITTLE FALLS MONONGALIA CO. W. Va.

Married 3-25-1797 At FREDERICKS CO. Md. By

Wife MARY ANN VINEGAR Other Husbands

Born 4-15-1776 At IRELAND Baptized

Died 12-29-1832 At MONONGALIA CO. Va. Buried At LITTLE FALLS MONONGALIA CO. W. Va.

Dau. Of And [ ]

Other Marriages 2 SARAH STANSBERRY B: 1791 M: D:
DAU OF: STEPHEN STANSBERRY

Occupation

Residence

Civil and Military Service

Reference Data
Name, Vol., and Page:

NAME OF CHILD / NAME OF WIFE OR HUSBAND	DATE AND BIRTHPLACE CHILD / WIFE OR HUSBAND	MARRIAGE DATE / PARENTS	DEATH DATE / PLACE
NO. DAVID SUMMERS	3-26-1797	8-20-1821	4-19-1866
PHOEBE WILLIAMS		SARAH FAIRCHILDS	
RACHAEL SATERFIELD		HENRY WILLIAMS	
NO. JONATHAN SUMMERS	3-26-1797	5-7-1821 1-31-1839	4-2-1875
MARGARET TRICKETT	2-11-1801	MARGARET JOSEPH TRICKETT	
CATHERINE MAY		GEORGE MAY	
NO. ALETHA SUMMERS	2-1-1799	11-26-1820	4-17-1849
PHILLIP HOFFMAN	1798	SARAH GOODWIN JOHN HOFFMAN	1877
NO. JAMES SUMMERS	10-22-1800	6-24-1824	8-9-1842
MARY BARNETT		DRUSILLA	
NO. CHRYSTINNA SUMMERS	12-23-1802		8- -1803
NO. ELIJAH SUMMERS	6-16-1804	6-19-1828	5-22-1877
SUSANNAH BARNETT	1810	SUSANNAH WILLIAM BARNETT	12-8-1875
NO. ELISHA SUMMERS	2-16-1806	6-12-1828	8-31-1886
MARTHA STEELE	2-5-1809	MARGARET ROBINSON JOHN STEELE	12-25-1882

NAME OF CHILD NAME OF WIFE OR HUSBAND	DATE AND BIRTHPLACE CHILD WIFE OR HUSBAND	MARRIAGE DATE PARENTS	DEATH DATE CHILD PLACE W. OR H.
NO.			
REBECCA SUMMERS	11-6-1807	9-27-1846	1-22-1887
BENJIMAN BARKER	1-21-1807	SARAH SCOTT AARON BARKER	10-1-1879
NO.			
ELIAS SUMMERS	11-16-1809	1-1-1835	11-16-1884
MIRANDA WILSON	1814	HANNAH CAMP THOMAS WILSON	1901
NO.			
SARAH SUMMERS	8-7-1811		7- -1812
NO.			
MARY ANNE SUMMERS	9-1-1813	1-18-1836	3-10-1837
MORGAN SWISHER	3-16-1812	DRUSILLA MORGAN JACOB SWISHER	
NO.			
JOSEPH SUMMERS	6-4-1816	9-1-1836	2-2-1887
JULIA TARLETON	1-1-1812	MARGARET BEAN CALEB TARLETON	6-4-1879
NO.			
ELIZABETH SUMMERS	6-8-1821	10-13-1849	2-25-1900
SAMUEL B.SNIDER	8-3-1805	ELIZABETH COTTEN DAVID SNIDER	3-30-1872
NO.			

Biographical Data Ancestor

Biographical Data Wife of Ancestor

Additional Remarks Interesting Sidelights Family Migrations Will Data Civil Offices Held War Records

Dates Verified in Vital Records are Check Marked

COMPILED BY Norma Conrad DATE Aug 1981

Family History No. 10 CHEDWATO SERVICE Box 746 Burlington, Vt. PRINTED U.S.A. COPYRIGHT 1951

Rte 1 Box 131, Harrisville, WV 26362

SUMMERS PAGES

M. Davis
431 E. Haltern
Glendora, CA 91740

Su1 Will - William T. Summers, 1836 (054.801.12)
Su2 Genealogy or Family Tree of Benjamin Summers and his descendants for Four Generations, Nov. 1903
Su3 Carolina Summers, p. 1-7, 78-81 (xerox pages)
Su4 Notes on William Summers will, 1799
Su5 Notes on register of St. John's or Piscataway Parish, Prince George, MD 1701-1805
Su6 Notes on Johnston of Caskieben Cremond and Caiesmell, p. 251, Lorand V. Johnson, p. 251
Su7 Carolina Summers (book - with other genealogy books)
Su8 MD Marriage Records, p. 288 - John, Lazarus, Mary Summers
Su9 Power of Attorney, Gift and Misc. Deeds in Iredell Co. - Vol. XI, #2 Jan Iredell Co. Tracks
Su10 ALLISON Graveyard, Statesville, Margaret consort of Benjamin Summers, Vol. XI, #2 Jan, Iredell Co. Tracks
Su11 Benjamin Summers m. Isabel Wale, Old Somerset on the Eastern Shores of MD, p. 459 and notes from other pages re other Summers family members
Su12 Notes from 1800 Iredell Co., Census
Su13 "Children Meet Your Ancestors", Genevieve Brown Jones, West Point, [illegible]
p. 147-151a - The Summers Family
Su14 Notes from Early Settlers of MD
Su15 Notes from GSICNC, v. 6, #4 and v. 6, #4
Su16 Notes from Deeds #548907 - Iredell Co.
Su17 Notes from Massachusetts Magazine Marriage and Death Notices, 17[illegible]-1791, J. Stevens
Su18 VA Land Records, p. 417 - Abstracts frm Stafford Co. VA Deed Book 1722-[illegible]
Su19 Notes from MD Rev. Records, Newman - Misc. Records
Su20 Notes from VA Co. Records, v. 7, Misc. Records 1565-17[illegible] [illegible] Wills [illegible] Adm. 1637-1800
Su21 Census of 1776 - MD Records, v. 1, p. 1[illegible], 77, 191
Su22 Will - John Summers, Sr. - Aug. 1763
Su23 Will Abstracts - James, 1761; Nathaniel, 17[illegible]; George, [illegible]
Su24 Letter Dunlop re Jemima and Charles Oaten
Su25 Misc. Dent family information
Su26 VA Historical Index, p. 829
Su27 Index of MD Colonial Wills, 1634-1777

On your family sheet, where is copy of Mary [illegible] and William's marriage date? Can we help each other? I also have attached other info not on above list.

Mary Davis

Dear Betty,

Thanks oh so much for the info. I really appreciate it very much. Enclosed you will find my sheets. I recently switched computer programs I went from Family Ties to Family Orgins. I am still in the process of putting in all info sources etc.

I sent the info on the Moores that I have. The abreviation & Prefers to the Prodigy BB. My ID # is CKSM18B if you have access to it. Due to rate increases my husband & I are going to get off of Prodigy & go to Genie. Do you belong to any bulletin services?

On Prodigy I came across a Mrs. Hammonds, a descendant of Alexander Summers thru Joseph. She had not gone any further than Alexander Summers.

The address on the computer sheets is our house address. We are in the process of selling our house. I have all genealogy material sent to my husbands office so I know I'll get it. If you ever want to call give a call to 1800 453 8735 and leave word with my husband, Dennis & I will get back. I work up there part time.

Do you know if there are any pictures around of Alexander's kids or of him? I found a picture of someone in another line that was made in the 1840's. I assume it's a painting of which the photo was made.

Susannah Huffman dau of Phillip Hoffman & Aletha Summers was md to Solomon Barr. I have his picture but not one of his wife, Susannah.

Keep in touch. Enclosed is a check. Thanks again.

Marla Powell
1021 N. 6th
Monroe, LA 71201
1-800-453-8735

HOMELIFE
TOPIC: GENEALOGY RESOURCES
TIME: 09/19 1:32 PM

TO: DARLA POWELL (CKSM18B)
FROM: WANDA CHUDEUSZ (VHBS47A)
SUBJECT: MD SURNAMES

Darla, I have something that may mean something. Tell me what you think.
Folio 456 . Deed of Gift, 20 Jul 1723; enrolled 20 Jul 1723.
From: James Moore Sr, planter of Prince George County
To: John Summers, Son in Law, planteer of P G County.
Part of a tract of land called CHILD'S PORTION in Prince Georges Co containing 35 Acres; one coined piece of silver>> called six pence paid before ensealing.
/s/ John Summers (mark & seal)
Wit: Joseph Belt, Thomas Sprigg
(No signature of James Moore Sr. and no acknowledgement.
(Also this one which could or could not be the same John, as the name would be pronounced the same.)

Folio 284 . Indenture 1 Aug 1713.
From: Thomas Clagett of Prince Georges County
To: John Somers
for 40L land called MOORE'S ADDITION in Prince Georges >> County on the west side of the Patuxent in the fork of Piscataway Branch adjoining land surveyed for James Moore called CHILDS PORTION; contaning 231 acres of land.
Signed: Tho Clagett (seal)
Witnessed: Tho Sprigg, J. Gerard
Memo: Mry Clegett, wife of Thomas, acknowledges deed.
Becasue this property is next to the property given to Summers, I think it is the same person.
folio 284 . Indenture 02 Sep 1709
From: William Somers, planter of Prince Georges County
To: John Somers, planter of Prince Georges County. >>>
For 1500 pounds of tobacco " all my right, title and interest" of a tractof land called PITCHCROFT in the fresheson the west side of the Patuxent River.
Signed: William Somers (mark & seal)
witnessed: John Maklin (mark), Richd Groom.

I think that your John Summers must have married a daughter of my James Moore. as he was listed as his son in law. How do you like that. Tell me what you think of this. Wanda

PRODIGY(R) interactive personal service 09/19/92 9:58 PM

HOMELIFE
TOPIC: GENEALOGY RESOURCES
TIME: 09/18 1:12 PM

TO: DARLA POWELL (CKSM18B)
FROM: WAYNE DAWSON (RPGT89B)
SUBJECT: MD: -LAND DEEDS

Darla - John Summers witnessed a deed in Prince George's Co, MD on 24 March 1696. From Mary Yate of Anne Arundel Co, widow and Samuel Magruder of PG Co, planter. For Turkey Cock Branch on the western branch of the Patuxent River, part of the tract "The Vale of Benjamin".
Folio 69, Exchange, 26 July 1710 From John Summers to Hezekiah Bursers to Robert Corm, a 30 day bill of exchange. Then 20 July 1708, Henry Mackie and Rebecca, executors of John Summers, dec'd paid out debts on his estate of 104.15 pounds.
Folio 129, Will of Beorge Billingsly of Churcketuck of Upper Norfolk, VA, 21 Dec 1681, witnessed by James Summers.
Folio 269, Indenture, 10 July 1713 From John Summers, planter of PG Co to Arthur Neale, planter of PG Co, a parcel of the greater tract called Pitchercroft (Pitchcroft?) on the west side of the Patuxent River in PG Co, 120 acres. Witnessed: R. Bradly, Henry Calvert. Memo: 10 July 1713, John Summers and Mary his wife acknowledged deed.
John Summer's plantation was adjacent to Castell in a deed dated 25 April 1719.
Folio 456, Deed of Gift, 20 July 1723, enrolled 20 July 1723. From: James Moore, Sr., planter of PG Co. To: John Summers, son-in-law, planter of PG Co. Part of a tract of land called Child's Portion in PG Co containing 35 acres. one coined piece of silver called six pence paid before ensealing. Wit: Joseph Belt, Thomas Sprigg. No signature of James Moore, Sr. and no acknowldegment.
Folio 465. Freights entered and published in 1722. Among others, John Sumner, Commander of the ship Restoration sets his said vessel to freight at 7 pounds/ ton. The name is Sumners, not Summers in this abstract.
Folio 715, enrolled, 3 March 1725. Debts of John Medcalfe to satisfy the Justices claims according to the Act of Assembly. John Summer among many others.

That's the last mention between 1696 and 1726 IN PG Co.

Wayne in CA

Preface

About three years ago, I was given an assignment that has proved to be not only interesting but has been a challenge. I have used many sources and have tried to document when possible; however, I have found it necessary to use some family tradition when it was not contradictory to the results of research. The purpose of the book is partly to record some of these family traditions.

Some problems have been solved but not to my complete satisfaction. Other questions remain to be answered. Conclusions have been made from the best evidence available. Further research will change some of these conclusions and will strengthen others. It is hoped that readers will share information with us. Possibly such information and further research will bring forth a second and more complete edition in the future.

No attempt was made to complete all lines, because this book is, for the most part, about the Carolina Summers and their allied families and the local history around their homes.

The purpose of this edition is to give descendants in other areas a picture of what life was like in Iredell County for their ancestors. For readers who are not descendants, we hope the story will be interesting to you. I am in no way related to any of these families, but I have found Summers folks and their kin to be most interesting.

Wills and letters have been copied using the original spelling, which, needless to say, is not always conventional.

It is hoped that researchers will find the code numbers used in the genealogy helpful. With a little practice it can be used with ease. John Summers, Sr. was given the number 1; his son, Thomas, is listed as the sixth child, thus his code is 1.6. His first child becomes 1.61 or the third generation from John. By removing the last number on the right, it is easy to find the parent using his code number.

New information or corrections may be sent to me at Route 2, Box 128, Stony Point, N. C. 28678. Books will be available from me or Thomas Alexander Summers, Jr., 5820 Washington Ave., Houston, Texas 77007

Special thanks to all who have contributed to the research and writing of this history. Fear of omission and lack of space will not permit naming all who have made contributions in so many ways.

Mildred J. Miller, C.G.
July, 1980

Carolina Summers

ONE

§§§§§§§§§§§§§§§§§

The Summers-Lovelace Family In Maryland

See notes. I don't agree.

The progenitor of the North Carolina Summers family was John Summers, Sr., who was born in Anne Arundel County, Maryland on November 3, 1695. There is strong consensus that he was the son of Benjamin Summers, who immigrated to Northampton County, Virginia in 1655 and died in Somerset County, Maryland between 1709 and December, 1715. Benjamin was first married to Isabel Wale on March 26, 1667; his second marriage was to Deborah Woolridge on April 18, 1676; and his third marriage was to Mary

Much of this information was taken from the book, *Old Somerset on the Eastern Shore of Maryland*, by Clayton Torrence, 1935. Benjamin and his first wife had three children: Benjamin, William, and another child. He and his second wife had four children: Thomas, John, Elizabeth, and Ann.

There are others who say that John Summers, Sr. was the son of John Summers, whose will was proved in Prince George's County, Maryland on November 27, 1705. He named his wife, Rebecca, and two sons, William and John; a daughter, Sary or Lucy; and a daughter who married John Street. Sary is mentioned with her son, Samuel Westly, in her father's will. The will of Samuel Westly[1] named his wife, Lucy, and a son, Samuel.

John Summers, Sr., the progenitor of the North Carolina family, married Mary Moore, daughter of James Moore of Prince George's County. John Summers conveyed land to "my well beloved father-in-law, James Moore, Sr."[2] The will was executed in August, 1763 and proved October 9, 1769. Mary Moore Summers died June 11, 1769; both she and her husband are buried in Prince George's County.

John and Mary Summers had 13 children, all born in Prince George's County. John, the first named in his father's will, married Frances
in Prince George's County where he died on November 22, 1786. A son, George, is named, but there is no further information about him. William was born on April 22, 1726 and married Mary Wheat on February 10, 1745 in his native county before moving to Iredell County, N.C. just after the Revolution-

ary War. Further information will be given about his family in the genealogy. Their son, Dent, died in Frederick County, Maryland about 1809. Thomas moved to Bedford County, Virginia, where several of his children married before moving to Iredell County and settling near their uncle, William Summers, who had preceded their arrival.

Benjamin, another son of John and Mary Summers, was born about 1737 in Prince George's County where he married Grace Letton on December 31, 1742. They later moved to Washington County, Pennsylvania, where they died. According to information compiled by Van A. Stilley, attorney of Washington, D. C., they had ten children:

1. Caleb married Rachel Crawford and lived in Jefferson County, Kentucky.
2. Mary, born January 20, 1762, married Jonathan Johnson on October 10, 1779 and lived in Fayette County, Kentucky.
3. John Letton, born May 12, 1764, married Anna Maria Letton and died in Montgomery County in June 1802.
4. Grace, no further information.
5. Anna Maria married Thomas Markland, died in Hamilton County, Ohio June 9, 1832.
6. William Burton, born July 22, 1768, married Mary Craven on May 3, 1792 in Nelson County, Kentucky, died in Nelson County on September 9, 1808.
7. Benjamin, born June 12, 1771, married Volinda Beckwith on October 11, 1798 in Montgomery County, died in Bullitt County, Kentucky, August 6, 1844. Their other three children were Michael, Noah, and Thomas Dent.

Joseph, son of John and Mary Summers, married Eleanor Clary, Prince Georges' Parish Records of Montgomery County, Maryland records the birth of one of their daughters on December 6, 1765. They moved to Newberry County, South Carolina and appear on the 1800 census in that county. Joseph, also, had land in Lexington County, South Carolina. Extensive research has been done on this line by descendants of Joseph and Eleanor. The results of this research reveal that they had the following seven children:

1. William 1756-1832 married in 1777 Susannah Teague.
2. Mary 1758-1813 married in 1775 Giles Chapman.
3. James 1760-1836 married in 1781 Elizabeth
4. John 1763-1840 married in 1786 Rosanna Waters.
5. Ruth born 1765.
6. Jesse 1775-1837 married Sarah Coate.
7. Hezekiah 1780-1823 married Helen

Further research in the South Carolina records would provide further information about the descendants of Joseph and Eleanor Clary Summers.

The seventh child named in John Summers' will was a son, Joseph (above). Next were daughters, Mary, who married John Wheat; Rebeckah, who married John King, Jr.; Rachel, who married Benjamin Johnson; Ruth, who married Edmond Riggs; and Jemima, who married Charles Caton.

The Summers family in Maryland was an old established family in the colony. The *Early Settlers Index* gives the following immigrants; all came into

the colony in the latter part of the 1600's:

Thomas Somers, transported 1667 (Book 11, page 229)
Benjamin Somers and wife, service, 1675 (Book 15, page 319)
John Summer, transported, 1671 (Book 16, page 394)
Robert Summers, transported, 1665 (Book 9, page 304)
Robert Summer, transported, 1678 (Book 15, page 574)
Ann Summers, transported, 1674 (Book 18, page 24)
John Summers, of Kent County, service, 1674 (Book 18, page 267)
Mary Summers, transported, 1669 (Book 15, page 422)
Oliver Summers, transported, 1675 (Book 18, page 280)
Roger Summers, transported, 1665 (Book 9, pages 470 and 478)
(Book 9, page 304)

Will of John Summers
Executed August, 1763
Proved 9 October 1769

Prince Georges County, Md., Liber 37, Folio 334

In the name of God Amen. I John Summers, Sen. of Prince Georges' County being mindful of the uncertainty of human life and of perfect mind memory and understanding do make ordain and constitute this to be my last will & testament in manner and form following, that is to say, First I give and bequeath unto my loving wife Mary Summers all the land and plantation where I now live called Addition during her natural life and after her decease I give and bequeath fifty acres of the Tract of Land aforesaid to be laid off at the lower end next to the woodyard unto my son Dent Summers and his heirs and assigns forever. I also give and bequeath all the remaining part of the said tract of land where I now dwell called Addition unto my son Benjamin Summers his heirs and assigns forever. And as for my personal estate which it has pleased God to bless me with I give and bequeath unto my loving wife Mary Summers during her life and after her decease I give and bequeath my Negro man Charles unto my daughter Rebeckah King and all the remaining part of my estate after my wife's decease to be equally divided among my children namely John Summers, George Summers, William Summers, Dent Summers, Thomas Summers, Benjamin Summers, Joseph Summers, Mary Wheat, Rebeckah King, Rachel Johnson, Ruth Riggs, and Jemina Caton, and do constitute and appoint my loving wife Mary Summers my whold and sole executrix of this my last will and testament & do rovoke disanul and make void all other wills by me heretofore made. In witness where of I have hereunto sett my hand and seal this day of August Anno Domini 1763.

his
John x Summers, Senr.
mark

Signed sealed acknowledged & declared to be his last will and testament in presence of Nath. Magruder, Mord. Mitchell, James Moore son of Benjamin, John King, Junr.

EIGHT

§§§§§§§§§§§§§§§§§

Summers Genealogy

1\. John Summers, Sr., born November 3, 1695, died January 13, 1769 in Prince Georges' County, Maryland, married Mary Moore (ca 1696 — June 11, 1796), daughter of James Moore, Sr.[1] They had the following children:[2]

1.1 John died Prince George's County November 22, 1786.

1.2 James died 1761.[3]

1.3 George married Elizabeth ________, died 1795.[4]

1.4 William, born April 22, 1726, married Mary Wheat in Prince George's County February 10, 1745, died in Iredell County, North Carolina.[5]

1.5 Dent, born 1727, died 1809 in Frederick County, Md., married Mary Ann________.[6]

1.6 Thomas (See Chapter III, also page 91.)

1.7 Benjamin married Grace Letton, born December 31, 1742, died in Washington County, Pennsylvania. He was an ensign, Capt. James Craven's 5th Battn., Washington County, Pennsylvania Militia, 1782.[7] They had the following children:[8]

1.71 Caleb married Rachel Crawford, March 2, 1780 in Montgomery County, Maryland.

1.72 Mary, born January 20, 1762, married Jonathan Johnson, son of Benjamin and Rachel Summers Johnson, October 10, 1779, in Montgomery County, Md., died in Fayette County, Kentucky.

1.73 John, born May 12, 1764, married Anna Maria Letton, died June, 1802 in Montgomery County, Maryland.

1.74 Grace, baptized July 30, 1766, Prince George's County, Maryland.

1.75 Anna Maria, married Thomas Markland, died June 9, 1832 in Hamilton County, Ohio.

1.76 William Burton, born July 22, 1768, married Mary Craven May 3, 1792 in Nelson County, Kentucky, died there on September 9, 1808.

1.77 Benjamin, born June 12, 1771, married Volinda Beckwith on October 11, 1798 (or 1796) in Montgomery County, Maryland, died Bullitt County, Kentucky, August 6, 1844.

1.78 Michael married Mary McAdams, April 3, 1795, Nelson Co. Ky.

1.79 Noah

1.7A Thomas Dent died 1826, Bullitt Co., Ky. married Mary Ann

1.8 Joseph, born Prince George's County, Maryland, married in 1755, Eleanor Clary. Some sources give a second wife, also named Eleanor, who was the daughter of Major Thomas W. Waters. (Ref. "Chapman-Pug Genealogy", page 108, by Minnie May Pugh). Joseph Summers, said to be a Quaker preacher, moved from Maryland to Newberry County, South Carolina about 1760 and settled on Bush River. According to his will recorded in Will Book E, page 5, proved and recorded January 16, 1809, he had the following children:

1.81 William died 1816, married Susannah Teague.

1.82 John married Rosannah Walters died ca 1836.

1.83 Jesse married Sarah Coate.

1.84 James died 1826.

1.85 Ellenor married ________Waters.

1.86 Cassandra married ________Reggs.

1.87 Mary married Rev. Giles Chapman.

1.88 Ann married ________Wells.

1.89 Darcus

For further information about this family, see "Chapman-Pugh Genealogy", pages 108-109, with a complete genealogy of Mary Summers and Giles Chapman given in this book. The preceding may not be completely accurate as it is not taken from primary sources, and should be used only as a guide for further research.

1.9 Rebecca married John King, Jr.

1.A Mary married John Wheat.

1.B Rachel, married Benjamin Johnson. His will was proved in Montgomery County, Maryland, January 10, 1795.[9] They had the following children:[10]

1.B1 Benjamin

1.B2 John

1.B3 Mary Ann, born August 5, 1743, married Arthur Thomas Taul.

1.B4 Elizabeth married ________ Harris.

1.B5 Rachel married ________ Wilman.

1.B6 Lurania married ________ Milliken.

1.B7 Jemima married ________ Ryan.

1.B8 James

1.B9 Josiah

1.BA Samuel married Agnes Wilson.

1.BB Resin

1.BC Jonathan, born ca 1755, married Mary Summers, daughter of Benjamin and Grace Letton Summers (#1.7), died in 1799 in Fayette County, Kentucky.

1.C Ruth married Edmond Riggs.

1.D Jemima married Charles Caton (some say Clagett)

Many of the dates used in compiling information about the family of John Summers was taken from the records of Van A. Stilley, Washington, D. C., Mr. and Mrs. Luther H. Kelly, Jr., Houma, Louisana, Mrs. Judy Somers, Wichita, Kansas, and Mrs. Claude Maxwell, Vandalia, Missouri.

William Summers, Sr.

1.4 William Summers, Sr., son of John and Mary Moore Summers, was born April 22, 1726 in Prince George's County, Maryland. He married Mary Wheat (September 20, 1727 — December 6, 1797), daughter of William and Amia Semosters Wheat, on February 10, 1745. His will is recorded in Iredell County, North Carolina and is dated June 4, 1799. They had the following children:[11]

1.41 Amey (or Anna), born May 11, 1746, married William Howard. It is believed that she married a second time to Allen Clagett on February 18, 1817 in Woodford County, Kentucky.

1.42 John, born March 7, 1749, married Ann Clagett December 8, 1774 in Frederick County, Maryland and died April 17, 1808. She was born June 28, 1753, daughter of Charles Clagett, who was born August 23, 1729. John served in the Revolutionary War. His will is recorded in Iredell County Will Book 1, page 17. They had the following children:[12]

1.421 Charles Clagett, born September 7, 1775.

1.422 Mary Ann, born September 15, 1777, married Robert Lazenby, died February 17, 1847.

1.423 John, born November 24, 1779, married Rebecca Baggarly, died March, 1850. They had the following children:[13]

1.4231 George Washington, married ________. Children:

1.42311 Nancy

1.42312 Mary

1.42313 William Solomon

1.42314 Sarah Roxanna

1.42315 George Clagett

1.42316 Francis Marion

1.42317 Charles Ross

1.4232 Solomon, born 1819, settled Floyd Co., Georgia.

1.4233 Nancy (1818-1880) married Joshua L. Lazenby, lived Iredell County.

1.4234 Alphonse (or Alpheus) lived Floyd Co., Georgia.

1.424 Ruth, born March 17, 1782, died August 6, 1819, may be buried Bethany.

1.425 Basil, born September 11, 1783, married Polly Lazenby, daughter of Thomas Lazenby.

1.426 Ann, born November 14, 1785.

1.427 Joseph, born March 15, 1789, died December 25, 1849, married Mary Dobbins, daughter of John Dobbins; they are buried at Bethany Presbyterian Church in Iredell County, N. C.

1.428 Solomon, born April 21, 1792, died October 25, 1860, married Susanna Tomlinson, daughter of John and Tabitha Summers, and is buried at Mt. Bethel Methodist Church in Iredell County.

1.429 William C., born October 1, 1794, died February 11, 1853, married Sara Ward, buried Bethany Church.

§§§

1.43 Thomas, born November 20, 1752, married Salome ________. He died 1799. John McGuinn was appointed guardian to Jesse, orphan of Thomas Summers in the February term of court in 1803. The division of the land of Thomas is found in Iredell County Deed Book L, page 588, naming his wife, Salome, and children, Thomas, Jesse, and Linney as heirs. The will of Salome Summers which was a verbal will, told to Nancy Bell and Rachel Summers, can be found in Iredell County Will Book 2, dated May 12, 1829. She named the same children that were named in the estate settlement of her husband.

1.44 Linney, born June 17, 1755.

1.45 William, Jr., born January 27, 1757, married first on October 1, 1778 in Montgomery County, Maryland, Rebecca Jacobs, married 2nd Verlinda Brandon [14] and third, Nancy Reid on June 19, 1816. (Note: some say that his second marriage was to Malinda Clagett, daughter of Henry.)

1.46 Mary, born October 25, 1759, married October 28, 1799 in Montgomery County, Maryland. Edward Gaither Jacobs, son of Jeremiah and Rachel Gaither Jacobs. [15]

1.47 Dorcas, born February 20, 1762, married Zachariah Jacobs, August 5, 1779. [16] He was the brother of Edward Gaither Jacobs.

1.48 Sabrina, born August 19, 1765, married Benjamin Belt. [17]

1.49 Basil, born May 16, 1769, died June 27, 1824, married Ann Ellis (May 16, 1769 — April 27, 1827) daughter of Samuel Ellis. [18]
According to Basil's will recorded in Iredell County Will Book 2, page 17, their children were:

1.491 Mary, born November 1, 1790, died 1865, married ________ Massey.

1.492 Rebecca, born September 1, 1792, married ________ Jacobs.

1.493 William, born January 7, 1795.

1.494 Greenberry, born January 11, 1797

1.495 Matilda, born January 12, 1799, died February 21, 1894, married February 7, 1826 Basil Tomlinson, son of John and Tabitha Summers, Tomlinson. They are buried at Tabor Presbyterian Church. Among their children were John and Noah Tomlinson.

1.496 Ann, born June 21, 1801.

1.497 Eliza, born September 21, 1803, married ________ Ellis.

1.4A Tabitha, born August 12, 1770, died 1858, married John Tomlinson.

William Summers, Sr. married a second time. [19] His second marriage was to Cassandra Ellis, born November 17, 1779, daughter of Samuel Ellis. [20] Her second marriage was to John Tomlinson. [21]

1.425 Basil Summers, born September 11, 1783, son of John and Ann Clagett Summers married Polly Lazenby, daughter of Thomas Lazenby. [22] He moved his family from their home in east Iredell County, south of the south fork of Fifth Creek, to a branch of Little Rocky Creek, just northeast of Snow Creek Church, where he operated a mill. His will, written September 19, 1848, is recorded in Iredell County Will Book 3, page 155, and was proved in the November term of court in 1860. Members of his family were members of Snow Creek Methodist Church. They had the following children:

1.4251 Asa, born May 11, 1810, died January 23, 1901, married Emeline Potts, daughter of James and Sarah Potts; they had no children. Asa is buried at Concord Presbyterian Church in Iredell County with his wife and the Potts family. Their graves are marked by an unusually large monument with the tall, slender marble columns reaching toward the sky resting on a base made like a stairway. It was erected at the request of Emeline Potts Summers as requested in her will. It covers the graves of her entire family — Mother, Father, brothers and sisters. Asa is not mentioned in Basil's will; however, he is listed as Basil's son by Dr. P. F. Laugenhour in his histories and genealogies found in *The Sentinel*, a Statesville newspaper printed at the turn of the century and for a number of years thereafter.

1.4252 John Franklin Summers (1805-1855) married Elizabeth Ward, daughter of Samuel Ward. Their home was north of Providence Church in Iredell County. No wife is named in John Franklin's will written in 1848, indicating that she died prior to 1848. Their children were: [23]

1.42521 Jane married Lafayette Brandon. [24] They had children Ada and Octa.

1.42522 Sarah

1.42523 N. Columbus, born February 14, 1841, died March 9, 1930, buried at New Hope Baptist Church in north Iredell, married S. A. Turner on February 3, 1870. [25]

1.42524 Samuel

1.42525 Emma Frances

1.42526 Preston Basil born August 6, 1849, died January 4, 1909, married on December 6, 1877, [26] Mary Tomlinson, born February 10, 1851, died January 10, 1930, buried Bethany Church.

1.42527 William F., born December 20, 1854, died April 2, 1882, buried Bethany Church.

1.42528 Cecilia (Cilla), born September 12, 1852, died July 27, 1939, buried Bethany Church. [27]

1.42529 Arabella, born ca 1857.

1.4253 Thomas W., born 1811, worked as a miller.

1.4254 Robert Harrison, born about 1812.

1.4255 Mary Ann, born about 1813.

1.4256 Elizabeth, born about 1814.

1.4257 Sarah Emeline, [28] born about 1815

1.4258 .Lucy,[29] born about 1816

1.4259 Melissa, born about 1817.

1.425A Basil Pinkney, born ca 1822, a teacher.

1.4256 Elizabeth Summers, daughter of Basil Summers, was born about 1814.

1.42561 Thomas Summers, born May 6, 1839, was the son of Elizabeth Summers.[30] His wife, Margaret Elizabeth Guy, whom he married on February 5, 1867,[31] was the daughter of Hial and Margaret Morrison Guy. She was born August 15, 1848 near Liberty Hill in Iredell County. Both of them died in 1918; Thomas, known as "Devil Tom", preceded his wife in death by one month on March 3, 1918. Margaret died on April 28, 1918. Children:[32]

1. Hattie

2. Rufus W., born November 3, 1869, married Tecorah Walker on July 2, 1891.[33] Born September 22, 1870, she was the daughter of William and Mary Angeline Sharpe Walker. Their children:[34]

(1) Guy born May 27, 1892, died June, 1948, married Grace Marshall.

(2) Roy born April 24, 1896, married February 26, 1925, Zula Gwaltney, born November 22, 1903.

(3) Katy born September 5, 1898, married Robert Honeycutt.

(4) Amos born April 5, 1902, married Dora

(5) Jack born October 14, 1904.

(6) Pete born September 15, 1906, married October 27, 1927 Mabel Virginia Kenny, born November 22, 1910.

(7) Grover, born December 10, 1908.

(8) Carrie born November 9, 1910, married Oscar Bryant.

(9) Dock, born June 5, 1912, married Florence

3. John

4. Walter Alvin, born 1881, died 1956.

5. Minnie, born April 9, 1871, died June 17, 1961, married September 9, 1888, William Henry Gill, born 1860 in Georgia, son of Thomas and Molly Tomlin Gill of Iredell County. The Gills lived in Georgia for several years and later returned to their home at Olin. Minnie Summers' second marriage was to A. C. McHargue, no issue. Children of Minnie and William Henry Gill:

(1) William Lester

(2) Henry

(3) John Guy

(4) Thomas Grady

(5) Etta

(6) Margaret (Mag)

(7) Willie Mae

(8) Robert Young Gill married Eva E. Mayberry. Their son, William Thomas Gill, married Fae Carol Gerard of Jamestown, New York. They have the following children: Richard Mathew, William Mark, Michael David, Linda Sue, Robert Gerard and Thomas Paul (indentical twins), John Franklin, and Nicholas Lee. Robert Gill's second marriage was to Grace Anderson.

6. Emma married first Gus Davidson, second Charlie Summers. A son, Blake Summers, married Georgia Abernathy, no issue.

7. Essie married Lee Brown.

8. Joe E. (1889 — 1960) married Mamie Ann Reavis, their children are: Joe Summers, Sr. married Nellie Johnson; James Thomas married Joy L. Stone; and Robert Shelton married Katherine Webster.

9. William Harrison, born April 5, 1868, died May 24, 1931, on October 1, 1888, married Telura Walker, born November 22, 1868, died June 17, 1934, daughter of William A. and Mary Angeline Walker. Lived in Texas. Children:[35]

(1) Floyd P., born November 24, 1889, died December 6, 1943, married June 19, 1910 Nellie Brown.

(2) Franklin Walker, born July 6, 1892, died January 27, 1961, married in May, 1913 Alma Berry.

(3) Julius V., born April 24, 1894, died August 9, 1964, married September 1, 1923 Ethel Reavis.

(4) Thomas S., born December 12, 1898, died December 30, 1969, married June 14, 1924, Hazel Cole.

(5) William J., born July 16, 1903, died January 17, 1905.

(6) Stella, born April 8, 1906, married May 29, 1926 H. C. (Bob) Nicks, born June 29, 1892, died May 13, 1975.

10. Margaret Matilda, born October 10, 1876, died November 22, 1954.

§§§

1.427 Joseph Summers, son of John and Ann Clagett Summers, born March 15, 1798, died December 25, 1849, married Mary Dobbins (1794 —

1853); they are buried at Bethany Church. His will is recorded in Iredell County, Will Book 3, page 41. They had the following children:

1.4271 Mary Ann, born April 2, 1815, married William Moore, moved to Burke County, North Carolina.

1.4272 Margaret, born September 24, 1816, married George Reid (1807 — 1882), son of David Reid. No children.

1.4273 Solomon, born January 2, 1819.

1.4274 Jaine, born December 8, 1822.

1.4275 James Elfoney, born November 7, 1826, died August 30, 1861 in the Civil War, buried Bethany Presbyterian Church.

1.4276 William D., born September 16, 1829, never married. He was a well known Register of Deed in Iredell County from 1870 to 1886. His personality and accomplishments are described in the many items about him that appeared in *The Landmark* during his long and colorful career. Several selected ones appear here:

August 8, 1874. "Next Monday Billy Summers will give a watermelon feast. The melons have been ordered from Charleston; the ladies — unmarried — are requested to meet at the Register's office at 10 o'clock."

December 25, 1885. "The results of the act of the legislature requiring the registration of deeds was in evidence. 'The people are piling old deeds in for registration. Register Summers reports there are now 500 deeds in the courthouse to be registered. It is like court week there now all the time."

July 3, 1885. From the personals: "Register of Deeds Billy Summers was off last week on another courting expedition. It was our purpose to administer the estate and take possession of his office the next time he went away, but he got back before anyone had time to take out letters."

December 9, 1886. "In the retirement of W. D. Summers, Esq., from the office of Register of Deeds, the county has lost one of the most efficient and obliging officers it ever had. Every man in the county knows Billy Summers, and he retires from the office which he filled so well for fifteen years with the good will of everybody."

October 17, 1899. "Mr. William D. Summers, for about 17 years register of deeds of Iredell County and up to 13 years ago a resident of Statesville, died at Marion Thursday morning. Mr. Summers was never married and he has now no very close relatives in the county."

1.428 Solomon Summers, born April 21, 1792, died October 25, 1860, son of John and Ann Clagett Summers, married Susanna Tomlinson, born April 10, 1797, died January 26, 1892, daughter of John and Tabitha Summer Tomlinson. They are buried at Mt. Bethel Methodist Church in Iredell County. According to the census records and Dr. Laugenour's articles in *The Sentinel*, they had the following children:

1.4281 John died in the Civil War. No children.

1.4282 Humphrey, born ca 1828; in 1860, he is listed as a farmer with property valued at $18,000, died Civil War May 13, 1863.

1.4283 Tabitha A., born February 4, 1833, died October 5, 1921, never married.

1.4284 Nancy, born February 4, 1833, married James Melvin Holmes on Aug. 11, 1853.

1.4285 Robert O., born October 2, 1835, died May 3, 1863 in Battle of Chancellorsville. He was in Company G, 4th Reg.

1.4286 Jane Olivia, born about 1838, married J. William Albea, born August 17, 1836, died September 3, 1908, buried Mt. Bethel Methodist Church.

1.4287 Lucy, born ca 1840, married David Gaither.

1.4288 Lamira C., born October 28, 1830, died September 14, 1898, married Wilson Tomlinson, born April 19, 1826, died June 30, 1902.

§§§

1.429 William C. Summers, born October 1, 1794, died February 11, 1853, son of John and Ann Clagett Summers, married Sarah Ward. He owned a mill on the north prong of Fifth Creek, where Andrew Caldwell owned a grist mill in 1800. By 1860 when Summers owned it, only corn was ground there. William C. Summers is buried at Bethany Presbyterian Church. As listed in Iredell Deed Book 1, page 76, in the division of the William C. Summers Land, their children were:

1.4291 Elizabeth A.

1.4292 Margaret C.

1.4293 John W.

1.4294 Sarah A.

1.4295 William E.

1.4296 Noah S.

1.4297 Mary J.

1.4298 Joseph L.

1.45 William Summers, Jr., born January 27, 1757, son of William and Mary Wheat Summers, married first, Rebecca Jacobs, on October 1, 1778, in

Montgomery County, Maryland. She was the daughter of Jerimiah and Rachel Gaither Jacobs.[36] His second marriage appears to be to a woman named Verlinda for in 1798, William Summers, Jr. and wife, Verlinda, deeded property to David Caldwell.[37] According to the Swann papers, she may have been Verlinda Brandon. Others say that his second wife was Malinda Clagett, daughter of Henry. No information has been found to completely determine who is right. According to many descendants of this family, William married a third time to Nancy Reid, daughter of Alexander and Susanna Reid on June 19, 1816. In his will, found in Book 2, page 229, written April 29, 1841, Alexander Reid, Jr. names his daughter, Nancy Summers; however, he did not identify her husband. According to Mr. Floyd Gaither, Rebecca Jacobs Summers died shortly after the birth of their son, William Jacobs Summers and according to information compiled by him, William Summers, Jr. had at least six children in addition to William Jacobs. His children, including his son by his first wife, were as follows:

1.451 William Jacobs, born June 17, 1779, died September 28, 1836.

1.452 William F., born October 27, 1820, died 1836.

1.453 Basil, born April 23, 1822, died 1864.

1.454 Pinkney, born April 11, 1824, married Jane C. (Jenie) Nesbit, born October 8, 1826, died November 15, 1921. Children:[38]

1.4541 William, born about 1845

1.4542 Robena born about 1849

1.4543 Laura born about 1852

1.4544 Junius born about 1856

1.4545 Cynthia Adline, born February 4, 1857, married Rufus F. Sharpe, on September 22, 1881.

1.4546 Nancy Clementine (1861 — 1943) married Thomas Newton D. Payne.

1.4547 Mary born about 1862

1.4548 James born about 1865

1.4549 Thomas born about 1873

1.454A Victoria born about 1868

1.454B John Augustus born October 28, 1873, died January 16, 1946

(Note: There is not any definite proof that this Pinkney is the son of William Summers, Jr.; however, he is the only one of several Pinkney Summers that fits here.)

1.455 Amanda Melvina, born September 11, 1826, died 1848.

1.456 Gassaway Wilson, born April 22, 1828, died 1848, married Mary ________. He was a blacksmith at Olin. They had children: John W., Amanda C., Martin S., and possibly others.[39]

1.457 John Norris, born January 28, 1830, died 1876.

§§§

1.451 William Jacobs Summers, born June 17, 1779, died September 28, 1836 in Iredell County, North Carolina, is buried at Snow Creek Methodist Church. He signed his will "William J." and his tombstone inscription is "William I."; therefore it is believed that his name may have been William Ivy Jacobs Summers. His will is recorded in Will Book 2, page 162 in Iredell County; it was written June 7, 1836. In land transactions between William and his grandfather, William Summers, Sr. and his father, William Summers, Jr., he was always referred to as William Jacobs or William J. Summers.

In 1840, William S. Caldwell and Harriet Saunders of Coosa County, Alabama sold 4 tracts of land totaling 3074 acres of land to Joseph Caldwell for only $500 with 1260 acres of this land subject to the dower of Elvira Summers.[40] The same day, Elvira Summers, relinquished all dower rights of said land to Joseph Caldwell for $100. Elvira is believed to have been the second wife of William Jacobs Summers, and furthermore, it is believed that she was the widow of David Caldwell[41] and the daughter of William and Catherine Reese Sharpe.[42] This belief is based on the fact that David Caldwell died in 1819 and the fact that the land being sold is a part of the speculation land of David Caldwell, the Osbornes, and the Sharpes.

According to the descendants of William J. Summers, his first wife was Anne Lovelace, daughter of Charles and Catherine Beall Lovelace and sister of Verlinda Lovelace, who married Benjamin Summers, a cousin of William Jacobs Summers. The will of Charles Lovelace, found in Book 1, page 5 of the Iredell County records, names a daughter, Linney Summers (Benjamin's wife, Verlinda); he, also, referred to his daughter, Anne, and if she was married at the time, he did not give her husband's name. The will was written October 8, 1796 and as the first child of William is believed to be Alvin, who was born in 1808, it is most likely that Anne had not married at the time that her father's will was written. Children of William J. and Anne Lovelace Summers were:

1.4511 Alvin, born February 29, 1808, died August 23, 1904, buried at Snow Creek. He married Rachel Louisa Lawrence, born September 18, 1813, died June 27, 1898. She was the daughter of John and Elizabeth

Beall Lawrence who were members of Snow Creek Methodist Church. She also was a granddaughter of Adam and Rachel McLelland Lawrence. Alvin owned a mill north of Statesville. Their children as taken from the 1850 and 1860 Iredell County Census were:

1.45111 William Ivy, born December 6, 1832, died Sept. 28, 1842.

1.45112 John Quincy, born June 14, 1834, died Oct. 21, 1899, married Delia Lillian Tomlin.

1.45113 Elizabeth Anne, born May 7, 1836, died August 5, 1917, married John Norton.

1.45114 Louisa Jane, born September 1838, died October 22, 1921, married N. Franklin Hartness, born March 19, 1835, died March 6, 1914, buried Pisgah Methodist Church, Iredell County.

1.45115 Lilas Isabella, born June 22, 1840, died September 29, 1924, married on April 18, 1867, James Y. Millsaps.

1.45116 Thomas Bell, born June 11, 1842, died May 31, 1862, killed Battle of Seven Pines and buried in the battlefield. He served in Company C, Fourth N. C. Volunteers.

1.45117 Dublin Lawrence, born October 11, died July 21, 1924, married Bettie Johnson, said to have moved to Eddy, Texas.

1.45118 Christiana Caroline, born January 17, 1845, died August 13, 1918, never married.

1.45119 Alfred Nelson Tomlin, born September 13, 1848, died May 23, 1934, married on November 20, 1878 Clarissa Elizabeth King, born 1856, died December 22, 1933, daughter of Richard F. King, buried Snow Creek.

1.4511A Eliza Adeline, born May 12, 1850, died July 11, 1932.

1.4511B William Alvin, born May 8, 1855, died February 28, 1940, married on May 8, 1890 Catherine Campbell, duaghter of Dr. Robert and Mary King Campbell. He served as sheriff of Iredell County.

1.4512 Rebecca married John Murchinson.

1.4513 Lillis married Jeremiah Johnson, son of Asa and Sarah Lovelace Johnson and moved to Alabama.[44]

1.4514 Thomas married Anne Allison in 1844 and lived at the Chipley place. Their children were:

1.45151 Mary, born October 27, 1845

1.45142 Delia, born July 12, 1848

1.45143 A son, born November 7, 1850

1.4515 Alfred died in Rutherford County, Tennessee, possibly married Lucinda Summers, daughter of William and granddaughter of George in Rutherford County.

1.4516 Malinda

1.4517 Greenberry married Lydia Emaline Johnson, daughter of Benjamin (Jr.) and Mary Johnson, who was born February 3, 1817. They moved to Cherokee County, Texas.

Thomas Summers

1.6 Thomas Summers, son of John Summers, Sr. and Mary Moore,[46] was born in Prince Georges County, Maryland. He married Rachel Talbot,[47] daughter of Joseph and Mary Berckhead Talbot. They left Maryland and went to Bedford County, Virginia, where two of their sons married before their final movement to Iredell County, North Carolina.[48] No doubt, they had other children; however, no record is available at this time except for the following four sons. Thomas may have lived in Rowan County and then moved to Iredell County to live with one of his sons.[49] He may be buried at Bethany Presbyterian Church. The following are the four known children of Thomas and Rachel Talbot Summers:

1.61 Paul Taulbot, born January, 1762, married Sarah Bruce, daughter of Celina Bruce, on May 26, 1789 in Bedford County, Virginia.[50] They moved to Iredell County where Paul bought a tract of land on Fifth Creek in 1797.[51] He is listed as a landowner in the Tax List of 1800, he was a resident of Iredell when the census was taken in 1810. According to tradition he moved to Tennessee; there is no proof given to substantiate this. There is some evidence that he went back to Maryland. He has no known descendants in Iredell County. There is part of an estate settlement at the N. C. Dept. of Archives in Raleigh for Summers, dated 1820. Only one page of this estate settlement is extant, page 1, and it gave the widow, Sarah, her year's provision.

1.62 George Summers came to Iredell County where he bought a track of land of 153 acres on the South Yadkin River.[52] He was also listed as a land owner in 1800 and is listed on the census of that year. No further information has been found in Iredell County about this family. Tradition says that he also went to Tennessee, no proof is given.

1.63 Zachariah Summers

1.64 Benjamin Summers (See page 95)

§§§

1.63 Zachariah Summers, born 1763, married in March, 1786, Sarah Dawson, daughter of John and Susanna Dawson, in Bedford County,

LINEAGE CHART

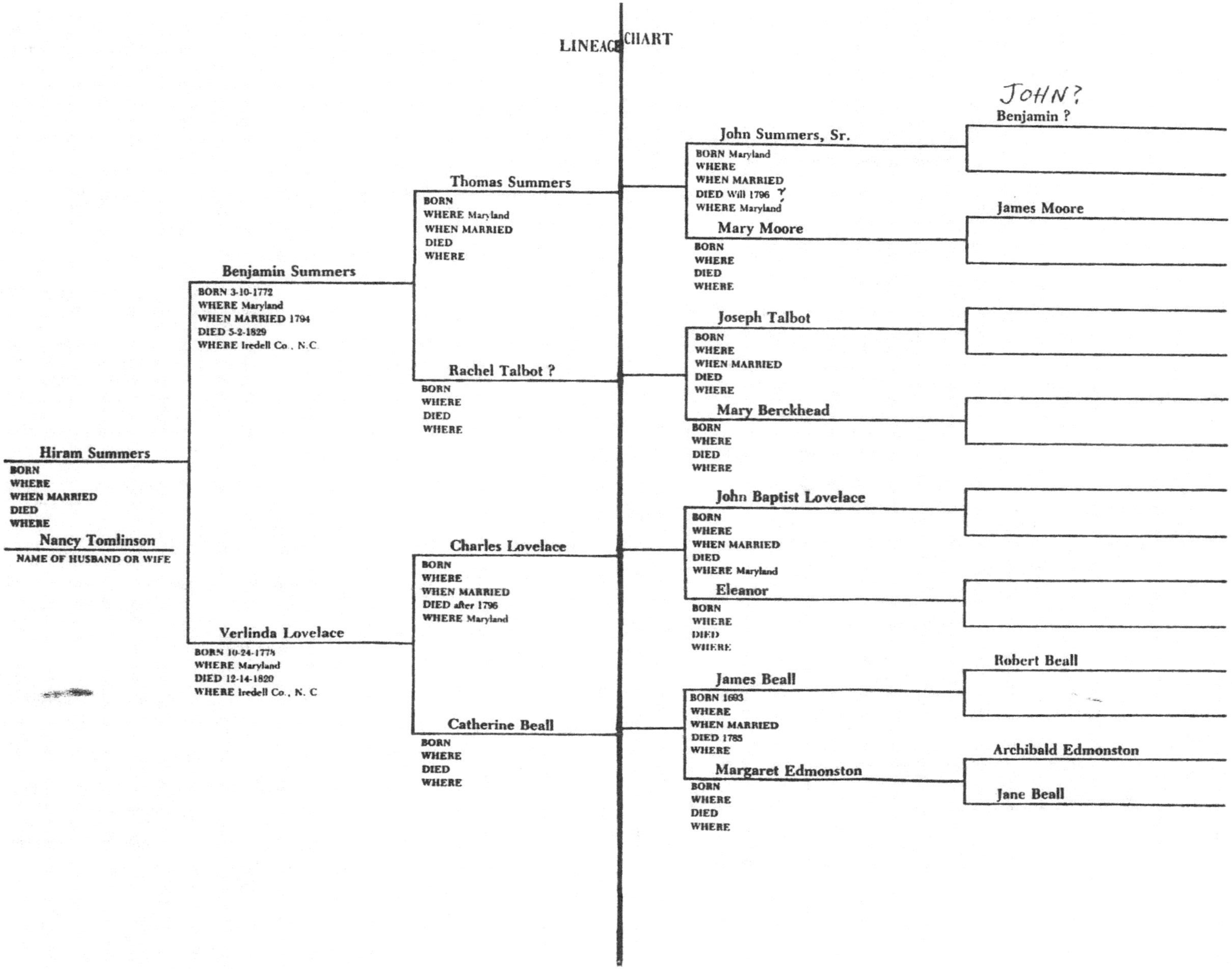

CHAPTER I
FOOTNOTES

1. Prince George's County, Md., Will Book 12, page 10
2. Prince George's County, Deed Book 1, page 457
3. Ibid., Liber. 33, Folio 322
4. Charles County Deeds, Liber. Z, No. 2 Folio 81, Hall of Records, Annapolis, Md.
5. Ibid., Liber. L, No. 3, Folio 430
6. Ibid., Liber. V, No. 3, Folio 446
7. Ibid.
8. Rowan County Wills, Book A, page 233
9. Iredell County Wills, Book 1, page 5

CHAPTER II
FOOTNOTES

1. Lewis Graveyard, Iredell County, N. C.
2. Iredell County Deeds
3. E. F. Rockwell, *The Carolina Watchman*, published at Salisbury, N. C.

CHAPTER III
FOOTNOTES

1. Iredell County Deeds
2. Bedford County, Va. Marriage Bonds
3. Ibid.
4. Iredell County Deeds, Book B, page 647
5. 1800 Iredell County Tax List
6. Iredell County Deeds, Book C., page 321
7. Iredell County Estate Records, State Archives, Raleigh, N. C.
8. Iredell County Deeds, Book B, page 55
9. Thomas E. Swann Papers, on microfilm at State Archives, Raleigh, N. C. (Hereafter cited Swann Papers)
10. Ibid.
11. Iredell County Deeds, Book C, page 463
12. Ibid., Book G, page 530

CHAPTER IV
FOOTNOTES

1. Alvin Howard Summers, *Genealogy of the Descendants of Benjamin Summers*, 1905 (Hereafter cited Summers Genealogy) Note: this book was used only as a guide. Many additions have been made possible by further research. Some changes have been made. The Author.
2. Swann Papers
3. Iredell County Wills, Book 2, page 77
4. Federal Census, Caldwell County, 1850 (Hereafter cited Census)
5. John D. Summers Land Division, Iredell County Deeds
6. Mrs. Vallie Hatchett Raymond, Statesville, N. C.
7. Most of the information about Charles L. Summers came from various news items in *The Landmark*, a newspaper published in Statesville, N. C. (Hereafter cited *The Landmark*)
8. Stony Point Cemetery, Stony Point, N. C. (Hereafter cited Stony Point Cemetery)
9. Methodist Church Records, Alexander County Library, Taylorsville, N. C.
10. Ibid.
11. Ibid.
12. *The Landmark*
13. Alexander Circuit, Methodist Church

CHAPTER V
FOOTNOTES

1. Bethany Church Cemetery, Iredell County, N. C. (Hereafter cited Bethany Cemetery)
2. Iredell County Marriage Index
3. Personal knowledge of author.
4. Iredell County Record of Accounts, Vol. 1 & 2, December 20, 1872, microfilm
5. Summers Family Records
6. Snow Creek Church Records
7. Iredell County tradition
8. John Hill Summers
9. Iredell County Deeds, Book 4, page 230

CHAPTER VI
FOOTNOTES

1. Homer M. Keever, *Iredell — Piedmont County*, (1976), page 79
2. Land Grants, Anson and Rowan County, Land Grant Office, Raleigh, N. C.
3. William Sharpe, Map of Fourth Creek Congregation, 1773 (Hereafter cited Map of Fourth Creek Congregation)
4. Rowan County Land Entry 581, Land Grant Office
5. Iredell County Deeds, Book A, page 292
6. Rowan County Land Grant 70
7. Iredell County Deeds, Book G, page 150
8. Ibid., Book L, page 383, Snow Creek Methodist Episcopal Church Records
9. Webber Family Records, Irene Weber, Statesville, N. C.
10. Iredell County Deeds, Book J., page 294½
11. Iredell County Census, 1860
12. Iredell County Deeds, Book 4, page 406
13. Mildred J. Miller, *John Sharpe, Rev. Soldier*, (1976), pages 79-80
14. Iredell County Deeds, Book 56, page 198
15. Ibid., Book 4, page 230
16. Bethany Church Records
17. Snow Creek Methodist Episcopal Church Records

CHAPTER VII
FOOTNOTES

1. Map of Fourth Creek Congregation
2. Iredell County Deeds, Book R, page 28
3. Information from Mrs. Thomas E. Swann, a descendant of Wesley Privette.
4. Ibid.
5. Ibid.
6. Ibid.

CHAPTER VIII
FOOTNOTES

1. Prince George's County, Md., Deeds, Book 1, page 1, page 457
2. Prince George's County Wills, Liber. 37, Folio 334

3. Ibid., Book 1, page 528
4. Ibid., Liber T1, Folio 371
5. Iredell County Wills, Book 1, page 205
6. Montgomery Co., Md. Wills, Liber G, Folio 1
7. *Pennsylvania Archives* 6th Series, Vol. 2, page 219
8. Estate Settlements, Washington County, Penn.
9. Montgomery County, Md. Wills, Liber. C. Folio 151
10. Ibid.
11. Iredell County Wills, Book 1, page 205
12. Entries from Prayer Book of John and Ann Summers (A copy is included in his Pension Application for Revolutionary War Service)
13. Swann Papers
14. Ibid.
15. Ibid.
16. Ibid.
17. Ibid.
18. Iredell County Wills, Book 1, page 98
19. Ibid., Book 1, page 205
20. Ibid., Book 1, page 98
21. Swann Papers
22. Ibid.
23. Iredell County Census
24. Swann Papers
25. Iredell County Vital Statistics, Book 16, page 98 (Hereafter cited Vital Statistics)
26. Iredell County Marriage Index
27. Vital Statistics, Book 25, page 361
28. Iredell County Wills, Book 6, page 1
29. Ibid., Book 6
30. Vital Statistics, Vol 4A, pages 22 and 149, Iredell Will Book 6, page 1, and Book 6, page 3
31. Iredell County Marriage Index
32. Mrs. Fae G. Gill, Statesville, N. C.
33. Iredell County Marriages
34. Mildred J. Miller, *Major Amos Sharpe*
35. Bible of Telura Walker Summers
36. Swann Papers
37. Iredell County Deeds, Book C, page 335
38. Iredell County Census, 1850 and 1860
39. Swann Papers
40. Elvira Summers of Coosa County, Ala. to James Caldwell, William S. Caldwell, and Harriet Saunders of Coosa County to Joseph Caldwell, Oct. 19, 1840, Deed Book 1, page 9-10, Iredell County, N. C.
41. Will of David Caldwell, Iredell County, N. C.
42. Iredell County Wills, Book 1A, page 13
43. Information about the Alvin Summers family is from W. A. Summers as told to his daughter, Rachel Summers Solomonson
44. Iredell County Wills, Book 3, page 1
45. Swann Papers, Iredell County Census (1850), and Panthea Sharpe Allison Papers
46. Prince George's County, Md. Wills, Liber 37, Folio 331
47. Prince George's Parish Records of Montgomery County, Md., page 262 (Hereafter cited Prince George's Parish Records)
48. Dennis and Smith, *Marriage Bonds of Bedford County, Virginia 1755-1800*, Genealogical Publishing Co., Inc., Reprinted 1976 (hereafter cited Bedford County Marriage Records)

49. Rowan County Census (N. C.) 1790, Iredell County Census 1800, Rowan County Court Minutes, 1786
50. Bedford County Marriage Records
51. Iredell County Deeds, Book B, page 647
52. Ibid., Book C, page 321
53. Bedford County Marriages
54. Iredell County Deeds, Book B, page 55
55. Swann Papers
56. Lewis Graveyard, Iredell County
57. Iredell County Equity Court (1849-1852)
58. *Western Carolinian*, newspaper published in Salisbury, N. C.
59. Iredell County Deeds, (Sale of lands of Zachariah Summers on Third Creek), Book 1, page 30
60. Iredell County Equity Court (1849)
61. Iredell County Deeds, Book Y, page 572
52. Ibid.
63. Rev. Samuel Harris Stevenson, *Stevenson Family*, 2nd Edition, page 204
64. Obituary of H. C. Summers, *The Landmark*
65. Abner Rufus Summers family records
66. Will of Charles Lovelace, Iredell County
67. Ibid., Benjamin Summers
68. Iredell County Wills, Book 2, page 77
69. Swann Paper (Jacobs file)
70. Iredell County Wills, Book 2, page 86
71. Summers Genealogy
72. Bethany Church Cemetery
73. Bethany Church Records, Family records
74. Information about this family from obituary of James Albert Summers, *The Landmark*
75. Family records
76. Information supplied by individual families
77. Information about Sidney C. Summers family was supplied by Myrtle Summers, Independence, Missouri
78. Ibid., John Franklin Summers
79. Swann Papers
80. Stony Point Methodist Church Cemetery
81. Summers Genealogy, Alexander Census, 1850
82. Ibid.
83. Mrs. Vallie Hatchett Raymond, Statesville, N.C.
84. Ibid.
85. *The Landmark*
86. Obituary of John N. Summers, *The Landmark*
87. Iredell County Census Records and Tax List
88. Iredell County Deeds, Book S, page 46
89. Swann Papers
90. Ibid.
91. Iredell County Census, 1850
92. Swann Papers
93. Iredell County Deeds, Book N, page 428
94. Ibid., Book S, page 108
95. John A. White Bible
96. Ibid., Iredell County Census Records
97. Mildred J. Miller, *John Sharpe, Rev. Soldier* (1976)

Box 325
Alma, NE 68920
Dec. 5, 1980

Betty I. Jones
P.O. Box 1203
Globe, AZ 85501

Dear Betty,

In reference to your ancestor, Elias Summers, listed in Computerized Roots Cellar, Genealogical Helper, July-August 1980, I have the following:

(Author, my great uncle Jonah Elbert Summers, born in West Virginia and died in Platte County Nebraska, 1937.) "Hezekiah Summers married _____ Fairchild and came to WV from Maryland. He had the following children: Elias, Elijah, Elisha, Jonathan, Joseph, James, David (my direct ancestor) and three daughters whose first names I do not know but who married Phillip Huffman, a Snyder, and a Barker. Elias and Elijah left Monongalia going to what is now Doddridge and Ritchie Counties about 1835 when the county was but thinly settled. There they were forced to meet the needs of primitive settlers of those days. Neighbors were distant and few. They builded their cabins to meet their needs and raised their families to meet those loneliness of all settlers."

This was written from memory not long before Uncle Bert died.

Further research by me showed Hezekiah Summers was born 23 Sep 1750 in Prince Georges County MD, lived in Frederick Co MD in 1776, Montgomery Co MD in 1790 and came to WV in 1807. He was a Revolutionary War Soldier. I believe he had three wives. Wife #1 Rebecca, married about 1772, known children William Dent and Benjamin. (MD Records, Brumbaugh), I am sure they had several more children. Wife #2 _______ Fairchild named by J.E. Summers. Wife #3 Ruth Dauson, married 13 Apr 1831. Hez Summers died 7 Jun 1836 in Monongalia Co. (Source Rev War Records)

Does this sound like your family line? If so, I have more information on the Summers family, including of MD 1800-1700. I would like to exchange information.

I have never been able to find a will on Hez Summers. One thing puzzles me, Hez would have been 50-65 years old at the time the children named by Bert were born. It is possible Rebecca died and he married a much younger woman and raised another family. But I have wondered if Bert missed a generation and Hez was the <u>grandfather</u> of the ten children including Elias and David. David was born about 1800. J.E. Summers was David's grandson. Can you help me on this?

Sincerely,

Janet M. Johnson

Janet M. Johnson

Box 325
Alma, NE 68920
22 Jan 1981

Betty Jones
P.O. Box 1203
Globe AZ 85501

Dear Betty,

Thank you so much for your reply to my letter. Yes, we do have the same family. As I stated in my first letter, I believe J.E. Summers (Bert) missed a generation when he named Hezekiah as the father of those children, when he appears instead to be the grandfather.

The 1810 census Monongalia Co. VA names Hezekiah (over 45) and Alexander, age 26-44. Hezekiah and Alexander were in Montgomery Co. MD in 1800,

The will you have of David Summers, Taylor Co., 1866, is Alexander and Mary Ann's son. According to Bert "David Summers m. Phoebe Williams and they had the following children (he then names all the children listed in the will plus James who died young.) Phoebe died about 1845, David then married a widow, Rachel Reed Van Gilder, and moved to Taylor County.

The Hezekiah named in David's will is my g.g. grandfather who came to Nebraska and he is also Bert's father. Bert wrote that he remembered being at his grandfather David's home when he died. Henry, listed as deceased in the will died in the Civil War.

Bert recorded his family history in 1936-1937 when he was about 77 years old, he died Oct 1937. He didn't do any research, but simply recorded what he remembered about his family from his youth in West Virginia.

I have tried to find proof of what he wrote through searching census, land, and probate records, etc. He appears to have been quite accurate about David.

He says Hezekiah was a Revolutionary War soldier in Maryland before he came to WV. I have the Rev. War record of Hez which shows this to be correct, also census records of him in MD and WV.

I have searched quite a bit for a will of Hezekiah and haven't found anything. The closest thing I have of evidence that he belonged as a direct descendent would be Bert's word, eventhough he named him as David's father.

Since Bert's father, Hezekiah, was obviously named after the first Hezekiah, he perhaps had a better memory of him than of Alexander. Family pride in the fact Hez served in the Revolutionary War probably also was a reason his name was remembered.

Bert says"Hezekiah m. _______ Fairchild which is where the Irish comes from" I notice on the information you sent me that Elias claimed his mother was born in Ireland according to the 1880 census. Bert is, in effect, saying David's mother was a Fairchild, since his mother was actually married to Alexander, this could be a clue to Mary Ann's maiden name.

I have about 18 pages of information on the Summers family of Maryland dating back to the late 1600s. It would cost me about $3 to have copies made and mailed to you which I would do if you are interested. It includes some wills, land records, Hez's Revolutionary War Records, and some pages from a book on the Summers family by Genevieve Jones of West Point, GA, 1976, "Children, Meet your Ancestors".

Sincerely,

Janet

Janet M. Johnson
(Mrs. Jerry C. Johnson)

Box 325
Alma, NE 68920
16 Apr 1981

Dear Betty,

Thank you for the information you sent me on different Summers families. I especially was interested in the one about Elijah Summers who settled in the Monongalia Valley in 1783. I wonder if and how he may fit in the picture.

You asked why I think Hezekiah is Alexander's father and if I had proof. No, I have no proof, such as a will which states such. I am trying to put two and two together and am probably coming up with an answer of five.

1. It is family tradition: Bert Summers recorded during the 1930s that Hezekiah Summers of Maryland served in the Revolutionary War and was injured in a battle. He moved to Monongalia County WV. (Bert recorded what his father told him or he remembered. He did not do research such as we are doing.)

a. The Rev. War record of Hez Summers obtained from the Archives coincides with this story and states he moved to WV in 1807.

b. Census records coincide with this: Hezekiah was in Montgomery Co MD in 1790 and 1800 and not there in 1810. He was, however, in Monongalia Co WV in 1810. I have looked for, but have not as yet run across any other Hezekiah Summers of that generation.

2. Bert claimed Hezekiah as a grandfather, Bert's father was evidently named after this Hezekiah.

3. Bert stated his grandfather was David Summers who married Phoebe Williams in Monongalia County WV and named the following children: Sarah, Rhoda, Alexander, Hezekiah, David, John A., William, Joseph, James and Henry. He stated he later moved to Taylor County WV and died about 1865.

a. Census and marriage records coincide with this. David's will was recorded in Taylor County in 1866

b. Notice that David named his boys apparently after himself, his father, grandfather, and John Summers is believed to perhaps be the immigrant of this line and John was a popular Summers name in Maryland. I believe Hezekiah may have had a son named John Summers, (John Summers m. Mary Ann Hardy, 8 Dec 1810, Monongalia Co., Hezekiah was surety). James was also a popular

Maryland Summers name, David had a brother named James. Hezekiah, the Rev. War Soldier, had a brother James and John, an uncle William and Joseph. Phoebe's father's name was Henry.

c. Although first names do not show proof of relationship, it does appear David named several of his sons after different relatives, including Hezekiah.

4. Alexander and Hez appeared to come from Montgomery Co MD to Monongalia Co WV together.

1790 Census, Montgomery Co MD-Alexander doesn't appear-unmarried

1800 Census " " -

John Summers	pg 18	age 26-45			
Wm "		over 45			
Paul "		over 45			
Zadock "	pg 14	26-45			
Hezekiah"	pg 44	over 45	00111	012111	20
Alexander "	pg 44	16-26	30100	101000	0

The first five men could all be brothers, sons of Dent. Alexander and Hez appear on the same page so apparently lived near each other.

1810 Montgomery Co Alex and Hez do not appear

1810 Monongalia Co VA:

Alexander Summers	42010	11010	00
Hezekiah Summers	11001	02001	00

1820 Monongalia Co VA

Hezekiah Summers	pg 81	East Division
Alexander Summers	pg 84	East Division
John Summers	pg 58	West Division
Thomas Summers	pg 56	West Division
Wm Summers	pg 56	West Division

I do not know who John, Thomas, or Wm were, they were all about Alexander's age.

5. Bert named David's brothers accurately, named his sister's married names but couldn't remember their given names, he made no mention of the two girls who died in infancy and Maryann Swisher who died in 1837. He was fairly accurate in locating their counties of residence and stated he remembered meeting several of them (the three youngest men). Incidently, did you know there's a Summers Methodist Church in Monongalia Co, Jonathan and his wife donated the land for it.

a. The problem: Bert named Hezekiah as father of David and his brothers and sisters instead of Alexander. Long before I heard from you and of the Bible record, this had puzzled me. From later census records on these children I could tell Hez would have been 50-70 years of age when these children were born. Not impossible if his first wife died and he remarried a young woman. But census records for 1800-1820 never showed him having this age of children in his household, at least not this many.

Before seeing the Bible record I was trying to find evidence that David was perhaps a younger son, and some or most of those other children such as Elisha and Elias were his nephews or cousins, rather than brothers. It never occurred to me to use the approach that Hez was his grandfather instead of his father. When I do that, the household of Alexander has the correct number of children, but of course I still do not know the content of the household of Hez (as to whether these are all children in later years or if he has grandchildren and/or married children residing with him)

b. I speculate that Bert recalled Hezekiah's name as a grandfather because the story had been passed down in the family that he was a Rev. War soldier. This was probably a source of pride. I do not know if Bert's statement that Hez was injured in a battle is fact or just an embellishment added somewhere along the years in the story telling to make the story more exciting. The fact that Bert's father was also named Hezekiah is no doubt a factor, he may have been proud of who he was apparently named after.

Bert was born in 1860, thirteen years after Alexander died, Bert wrote his Summers history when he was about 75 years old. I think it is possible he just didn't recall Alexander's name. Since he didn't include dates and ages it probably didn't occur to him he had lost a generation in the telling of his story.

I am not sure of what to do with the information that Hezekiah married an Irish woman named Fairchild. Since MaryAnn turned out to be a Vinagar (a bit of a strange name, does it sound Irish to you?) perhaps it was Hezekiah who married a Fairchild. Perhaps, even the Fairchild name will show up on Bert's mother's side of the family, the Stansburys. He wrote some very helpful information on that line also.

So, I have written quite a lot, you are the only person I have come across who would be working on this generation of Summers, (have corresponded with many who are working on the same line in earlier years in MD which I could fill you in on, in a later letter.)

I would really like to hear yourargument either for or against Hezekiah as a direct descendant. I do not mean to sound as if I have it figured out correctly and would really welcome another point of view.

Your letter arrived just a few days after I had had major surgery (hysterectomy) and I am a little slow in answering because I just hadn't had the energy to write letters until recently.

page 4

I am looking forward to hearing from you again. If we put our heads together maybe we can find some proof of who was Alexander's father. Did Alexander leave a will, do you have any documentation as to when he became a minister and of his ministry?

Sincerely,

Janet

Janet M. Johnson

	Source
David Summers	
Born: 26 Mar 1797 Maryland	Bible record
Marriage #1 Phoebe Williams, 20 Aug 1821	Morongalia CO WV
Children: Sarah Ann m. Elias Jones	
Rhoda (never married)	
Alexander m. Anna Frum 16 Jun 1848	"
Hezekiah	
b. 14 May 1829	
m. Sarah Starsbury, 20 Feb 1849	"
d. 3 Sep 1904	
buried Platte Co Nebraska	
Henry	
b. 22 Mar 1831	
m. 11 May 1851, Irena Moran	
d. 20 Jan 1863, Civil War	
David m. Francis	
John A. m. Elizabeth S. Wolf, 15 Jan 1852	Marion Co WV
William m. Nancy	
Joseph	
James, died young	

Sources were Jonah Elbert Summers, the will of David and cemetery records

Phoebe died in Monongalia County WV before 1850. David then married Rachel Reed Van Gilder, a widow. They did not have any children. They are listed in the 1850 Marion County WV census. David Summers bought 172 acres on White Day Creek in Taylor Co WV, 27 Sep 1859

The will of David Summers was written 9 Apr 1866, and proved 14 May 1866, recorded in Will Book one, page xxxx 94, Taylor Co WV

David's son Hezekiah came to Nebraska with his family during the 1880s. Among their children were Jonah Elbert Summers, who recorded the family history I have referred to, and Lucy Ellen Summers Moran, my great grandmother.

A large number of youth had become active when the church began to have summer pastors. This may have given part of the impetus to building a church basement. Begun in 1947, this major project was to require much labor for many years. It was finally completed in the 1950s. The full basement provided opportunities for social and class room functions as well as greater comfort. A furnace and eventually rest rooms were added once the basement was completed.

The desire for improvements continued, however. The church was covered with shingles in 1956, and payments were made in 1958 toward new pews. In 1959, the council decided to add new class rooms at the back of the sanctuary.

The years from 1947 until the 1960s were a period of intense concentration on the remodeling and improving of the church plant. The various projects served to develop new leadership and to express deep commitment on the part of the members to the church and its work.

The Poling Family.

The Poling name is found from the earliest times in the Shiloh Church, and the family has made a significant contribution to the life of the Church.

Several Poling ministers have served the church, e.g., Russell Poling, Godfrey J. Poling, and Henry O. Poling. Of these, Henry O. Poling is best known, having served more then three decades as minister and pastor of the Shiloh Church. Henry O. Poling was a son of W. Bucklew and Catherine Bolner Poling. Born March 22, 1902, he was married on June 17, 1926, to Beatrice Coffman, a daughter of George H. and Hattie E. Ekis Coffman. She survives him. Rev. Poling's grandparents were Reason and Margaret Bolner Poling and Henry and Julie Ann Auvil Bolner.

H. O. served the church first as a deacon and then as a minister, being elected to that office on Sept. 17, 1938. He was a free minister and supported himself by working on his farm and serving as a locomotive engineer on the B. and O. Railroad for forty-six years. His ministry was an active one, not only locally but in the Brotherhood at large. He served as Trustee of Bridgewater College for two terms and was on the Standing Committee of Annual Conference six times. His ministerial service included over 100 weddings, 350 funerals, and unnumbered sermons preached over a period of more than 40 years.

The Polings are parents of five children: 1) Robert who married Susan Nester; 2) Betty Lew who married Rev. Byron M. Flory; 3) Joseph who married Pauline Hovatter; 4) Catherine who married Donald Poling, and 5) Henrietta who married David Ball.

The Shahan Family.

Of Irish extraction, the father of Elder George Emory Shahan, first settled in Delaware, moving to Tucker County before the formation of the state of West Virginia. Born Feb. 29, 1830, and died June 29, 1891, George Washington Shahan was married to Louisa Marian Huffman who was born June 25, 1835, and died Apr. 30, 1885 (Dora Shahan correspondence).

The family lived near Rowlesburg for some years before moving near St. George in Tucker County. There the family lived within the boundary of the Union Chapel (Bull Run) branch of the Shiloh Congregation.

The children of George W. and Louisa Shahan number sixteen, including several who died in infancy. 1) Aletha E., born Aug. 3, 1850; 2) William Francis, born Dec. 22, 1852, who married Michel Nester; 3) John Wesley, born July 20, 1854; 4) Sarah Minerva, born Oct. 20, 1856, who married T. Walt Poling; 5) Christina Leverna, born May 16, 1858, and died 1933, who married David Hovatter (1853-1929); 6) Mary Catherine, born June 21, 1860, died Dec. 15, 1941, who married Martin Poling; 7) Cyrena Margaret, born Sept. 8, 1862, who married Isaac (Doc) Poling; 8) George Emory, born Oct. 9, 1864, and died Dec. 18, 1966, and who married Cora Jane Hovatter, who died Mar. 26, 1948; 9) Richard Jefferson, born Feb. 18, 1867, and died May 13,1954, who married Joannah Beavers; 10) Olive Jeanette, born Mar. 27, 1868, and died in 1902, who married Tom Bohon; 11) Elijah S., born July 13, 1872; 12) Caroline J., born June 10,

1874, and died Aug. 26, 1951, who married Da
born May 5, 1880, and died Dec. 14, 1947, wh
July 4, 1882, who married first, Max Dunlap, se

The eighth child, George Emor
Shahan, manifested special talents an
an early interest in religion. He bega
a vigorous study the Bible while still i
his teens, soon mastering larg
portions by memory. His obituar
states that he began preaching at th
age of fifteen, which would have bee
around 1879. The year after hi
marriage in 1891 to Cora Jan
Hovatter, he was ordained to th
ministry. He was advanced as an Elde
in 1904 and thereupon given charge o
the Shiloh Congregation, a position h
held until 1907.

He continued his labor for th
church at Union Chapel, serving a
one of the ministers of that branc
until his transfer to the Grafto
Brethren Church which later becam
the Grace Brethren Church. He wa
called as pastor of the Grafton Church
a service which he fulfilled for man
years. He gave up this work in 194
and moved to Clarksburg where he wa
retired.

Most of his life he served in the
and carpentering. Before moving fro
tract of land, some of which was purc
the land was sold during an economi

Bro. Shahan was a man of high
loved by his fourteen children, most
impact on his family and those with

A member of the National Fello
member of that organization at the ti
still occasionally preached in the last
occasion when he preached at the Gra
the age of 100. His ministerial work

The Ball Family.

The Ball family was associated at
It appears that their association with
of Elder Daniel Leatherman in Ma
Catherine who was a daughter of El
of George Custer were Paul and Sarah
families migrated to Somerset and Fa
owned land in Turkeyfoot Twp. in Son
lived in the Georges Creek Congrega
Mack held a funeral for a young dau

Shiloh Congregation called two n
and George M. Isaac Ball, of conserv

1874, and died Aug. 26, 1951, who married Daniel K. Hebb; 13) and 14) stillborn twins; 15) David C., born May 5, 1880, and died Dec. 14, 1947, who married Martha R. Annon; and 16) Louisa C. V., born July 4, 1882, who married first, Max Dunlap, second, Sam Austin, and third, Arthur J. Spare.

The eighth child, George Emory Shahan, manifested special talents and an early interest in religion. He began a vigorous study the Bible while still in his teens, soon mastering large portions by memory. His obituary states that he began preaching at the age of fifteen, which would have been around 1879. The year after his marriage in 1891 to Cora Jane Hovatter, he was ordained to the ministry. He was advanced as an Elder in 1904 and thereupon given charge of the Shiloh Congregation, a position he held until 1907.

Elder G. Emory Shahan
Taken at age 100

He continued his labor for the church at Union Chapel, serving as one of the ministers of that branch until his transfer to the Grafton Brethren Church which later became the Grace Brethren Church. He was called as pastor of the Grafton Church, a service which he fulfilled for many years. He gave up this work in 1940 and moved to Clarksburg where he was retired.

Most of his life he served in the free ministry, supporting his family by farming and carpentering. Before moving from Tucker County, he had accumulated a large tract of land, some of which was purchased for as little as $1.65 per acre. Most of the land was sold during an economic depression, and little gain was realized.

Bro. Shahan was a man of high character and devotion. Much respected and loved by his fourteen children, most of whom are now deceased, he left a strong impact on his family and those with whom he worked.

A member of the National Fellowship of Brethren Ministers, he was the oldest member of that organization at the time of his death at the age of 102 in 1966. He still occasionally preached in the last decade of his life. Many will remember the occasion when he preached at the Grafton and Shiloh Churches after he had passed the age of 100. His ministerial work was greatly appreciated and respected.

The Ball Family.

The Ball family was associated at an early time with the Shiloh Congregation. It appears that their association with the Brethren goes back to the congregation of Elder Daniel Leatherman in Maryland. George Custer (1765-1829) married Catherine who was a daughter of Elder Leatherman (Gleim, 22-23). The parents of George Custer were Paul and Sarah Martha Ball Custer. Many members of these families migrated to Somerset and Fayette Counties in Pennsylvania. William Ball owned land in Turkeyfoot Twp. in Somerset County in 1834. Relatives of Isaac Ball lived in the Georges Creek Congregation of Fayette County. In 1864, Elder Jacob Mack held a funeral for a young daughter of Zachariah and Sister Lydia Ball.

Shiloh Congregation called two members of the Ball family as ministers, Isaac and George M. Isaac Ball, of conservative bent, united with the Old Order German

Descendants of Christina L. Shahan

Generation No. 1

1. CHRISTINA L.[3] SHAHAN *(GEORGE WASHINGTON[2], GEORGE[1])[1]* was born May 16, 1858 in Sinclair, WV, and died February 02, 1933 in Tucker Co.,WV. She married DAVID T. HOVATTER[1] December 23, 1877 in Hannahsville, Tucker Co. WVA[1], son of DAVID HOVATTER and SARAH THOMPSON. He was born June 15, 1853 in Kesson, WV[1], and died October 31, 1929 in Tucker Co.,VA now WV.

Notes for DAVID T. HOVATTER:
1880 Census Place: Licking, Tucker, West Virginia
Source:FHL Film 1255414 National Archives Film T9-1414 Page 378A
Relation Sex Marr RaceAgeBirthplace
D. C. HOVATTER SelfM M W 25 VA
Occ:Laborer Fa: VA Mo: VA
Chrystena L. HOVATTER WifeFM W 22 VA
Occ:Keeping House Fa: VA Mo: VA
Charles HOVATTER Son M SW 1 WV
Fa: VA Mo: VA
Lilley C. HOVATTEROtherFSW 1MWV
Fa: VA Mo: VA

Barbour County Cities, Towns and Settlements
Kasson

According to an account found in Barbour County West Virginiapublished by the Barbour County Historical Society in 1979 Kasson, in Cove District, was first named Danville after the first settler Dan Highly. The hill he lived on, overlooking Kasson is still known as Highly Hill. Mr. Highly raised mulberry trees to feed his silkworms and produced silk thread was put on spools and shipped to Baltimore.

Danville was given the name Kasson because there was another WV Post Office called Danville. The first letter was mailed to a man named Kasson. The first Post Office was establised in 1862. Carr Bishop was the first postmaster. After him, Marion Newman, 1884; Lewis Coffman, 1904; George Coffman served from 1908 till his death in 1930. Hattie Coffman, his wife and two sons, Hayse & George Sherwood took it over until 1937 when Rachel Wilson Ball served till her death.

In the early days of Kasson the community included:
Stores:
Jack Bishop in 1870, John and Ed Compton, 1875; Marion Newman, 1880; Daniel J. Nester, 1890 and Lewis Coffman.

Blacksmith Shops:
David Hovatter, 1860; Ben Ekis in 1864; Albert Loar in 1891; and Lewis Coffman who learned the trade from his uncles Mike and Lige Coffman who had shops in Valley Furnace, Belington and Elkins. His first shop was near West Point

Churches:
The Kasson United Methodist Church, built in 1898. Daniel Nestor and Daniel Lohr were overseers.
The Church of the Brethren, David Hovatter had the Communion and Love Feast in his house, this was the

beginning of the Shiloh Church of the Brethren which was organized in 1845 about 1 ½ miles from Kasson.

More About DAVID T. HOVATTER:
Burial: Preston Co. WV

Children of CHRISTINA SHAHAN and DAVID HOVATTER are:

2. i. CHARLES E.[4] HOVATTER, b. October 11, 1878.
   ii. LELLIE C. HOVATTER[1], b. April 18, 1880[1]; m. JOHN PATRICK BURNS; b. July 20, 1877; d. 1950.
3. iii. WILBERT F. HOVATTER, b. April 01, 1882, Preston Co. WV; d. August 19, 1969, Greene Co. Miss..
4. iv. IRA J. HOVATTER, b. April 17, 1885; d. July 1968.
5. v. MARY L. HOVATTER, b. March 07, 1887.
6. vi. GEORGE E. HOVATTER, b. February 15, 1889.
   vii. LLOYD A. HOVATTER[1], b. June 29, 1891[1]; m. LULU STERRINGER.
   viii. MAUDIE P. HOVATTER[1], b. July 21, 1893[1]; m. SAMUEL DUMIRE.
7. ix. ARLIE DAVID HOVATTER, b. August 15, 1895, WVA; d. December 1977.
   x. BOYD E. HOVATTER[1], b. September 24, 1897[1,2]; d. August 1980[2]; m. HILDA DAVIS.

More About BOYD E. HOVATTER:
Fact 5: Social Security #: 234-03-1597[2]
Fact 6: Issued in: West Virginia[2]
Fact 7: Residence code: Alabama[2]
Fact 8: Last residence ZIP: 36584[2]

Generation No. 2

2. CHARLES E.[4] HOVATTER *(CHRISTINA L.[3] SHAHAN, GEORGE WASHINGTON[2], GEORGE[1])*[3] was born October 11, 1878[3]. He married ELLA AGNICE BURNS, daughter of JOHN BURNS and SARAH DAVIS. She was born March 07, 1883.

Children of CHARLES HOVATTER and ELLA BURNS are:

i. CLAUDENE ELWOOD[5] HOVATTER, m. ARIETTA SHOCKLEY.
ii. ELSTON GERALD HOVATTER, m. MYRA E. HOWARD.
iii. CHARLES WOODROW WILSON HOVATTER, m. MADELINE KAUSCH.

Notes for CHARLES WOODROW WILSON HOVATTER:
Picture on page 102 in book "Generations from Hoffman to Hovatter"

iv. WANDA LORRAINE HOVATTER, m. ALBERT H. HEARN.
v. EARL GAY HOVATTER, b. January 06, 1912; d. August 08, 1934.
vi. THOMAS DAVID HOVATTER, b. June 02, 1908; m. ELSIE AMBROSIO.
vii. ELMER DALLAS HOVATTER, b. August 24, 1902; d. June 13, 1970; m. JESSIE B. NOCE, Bet. 1919 - 1950; b. Bet. 1898 - 1917; d. Bet. 1919 - 1992.
viii. ETTA IVES HOVATTER, m. EARL C. CATHEL.
ix. DELBERT RAY HOVATTER, b. November 22, 1904; d. November 1974; m. BARBARA CHANDLER.
x. LEODA PEARL HOVATTER.
xi. ORA MARIE HOVATTER, b. April 03, 1914; d. April 16, 1937; m. HERBERT FUES, SR.
xii. ELFORD HAROLD HOVATTER, b. May 03, 1924; d. May 03, 1924.

3. WILBERT F.[4] HOVATTER *(CHRISTINA L.[3] SHAHAN, GEORGE WASHINGTON[2], GEORGE[1])*[3] was born April 01, 1882 in Preston Co. WV[3], and died August 19, 1969 in Greene Co. Miss.[3]. He married HATTIE LEE JONES[3] February 18, 1903 in Greene Co. Miss.[3], daughter of ENOCH JONES and MARY SMITH. She was born October 06, 1885 in Greene Co, Miss.[3], and died October 09, 1969 in Greene Co, Miss.[3].

Notes for WILBERT F. HOVATTER:
87 years old 4 months and 18 days at time of death

More About WILBERT F. HOVATTER:

Burial: Stateline, MS
Social Security Number: Pennslyvania[3]

Notes for HATTIE LEE JONES:
84 years old and 3 days at time of death
Pictures on pages 106, 107 108 in book "Generations of Hoffman to Hovatter"

More About HATTIE LEE JONES:
Burial: Stateline, MS
Fact 5: Social Security #: 177-14-7342[4]
Fact 6: Issued in: Pennsylvania[4]
Fact 7: Residence code: Mississippi[4]
Fact 8: Last residence ZIP: 39451[4]

Children of WILBERT HOVATTER and HATTIE JONES are:

i. EULA[5] HOVATTER[5], b. December 14, 1903, Greene Co, Miss.[5]; d. October 24, 1937, WVA[5]; m. (1) SAMUEL LINTON[5]; m. (2) HOPE WATSON.

Notes for EULA HOVATTER:
picture on pages 93 in book "Generations of Hoffman to Hovatter"

ii. ODIE HOVATTER[5], b. October 27, 1905[5]; d. December 03, 1905[5].

More About ODIE HOVATTER:
Burial: Slay Cemetary

iii. WILBERTIE VALENTINE HOVATTER[5], b. February 14, 1908, Greene Co, Miss.[5]; d. September 23, 1987[6,7,7,8,9]; m. (1) HAZEL DELL CLEVENGER[10]; b. June 07, 1907[11,12]; d. November 06, 1988[13,14,15]; m. (2) RUBY BARNETT; b. July 16, 1915.

Notes for WILBERTIE VALENTINE HOVATTER:
Bertie and Hazel had broke up and he met Ruby. Ruby became pregnant with his daughter Rosalie. Hazel decided that they should try to make another go of their marriage, so he left Ruby and went back to Hazel. There is some speculation about when he knew about Ruby's pregnancy. When he found out about his daughter Rosalie he acknowledged her as his child as he did his other children.
Died of Cancer.

Pictures on pages 93, 94, 95 in book "Generations of Hoffman to Hovatter"

More About WILBERTIE VALENTINE HOVATTER:
Social Security Number: 232-05-5326[16]

iv. BOYD HOVATTER[16], b. August 10, 1910, Greene Co, Miss. re: Family Bible[16]; d. February 1975[17,18,19].

Notes for BOYD HOVATTER:
picture on page 93 in book "Generations of Hoffman to Hovatter"

More About BOYD HOVATTER:
Burial: Egg Harbor, NJ
Social Security Number: 560-07-8262[19]

v. FLOYD HOVATTER[19], b. March 19, 1913[19]; d. March 21, 1913[19].

vi. LOIS HOVATTER[19], b. November 19, 1914, Greene Co, Miss.[19]; d. May 30, 1983, Lower Bank, NJ[19]; m. THOMAS MANCUSO[19,20,21], September 23, 1935, Croydon, PA[22]; b. December 31, 1912, Italy; d. May 27, 1985, St. Petersburg, FL[22,23].

Notes for LOIS HOVATTER:
Married Sept. 23, 1935
Pictures on pages 96, 97 98, 100 in book "Generations of Hoffman to Hovatter"

More About LOIS HOVATTER:
Burial: Egg Harbor City, NJ[24]

Social Security Number: 177-14-8410[24]

More About THOMAS MANCUSO:
Burial: Clearwater FL[24,25]

vii. HATTIE ALMALEE HOVATTER, b. October 06, 1917.
viii. AUBREY HOVATTER[26], b. September 27, 1920[26].
ix. DESSIE HOVATTER[26], b. September 07, 1921, Preston Co. VA[26]; d. January 21, 2001, Las Vegas, NV; m. (1) EDGAR THOM[26], October 16, 1941, Trenton, NJ[26]; b. October 23, 1922[27,27,27,27,27,27,27,27,27,28]; d. January 1982[29,29,29,29,29,29,29,29,29,30]; m. (2) WILLIAM F. PUTNAM, June 26, 1960, Trenton, NJ; b. September 10, 1932; d. March 29, 2002, Las Vegas, NV.

Notes for DESSIE HOVATTER:
Pictures of Dessie Hovatter and more information on pages 98, 99 in book "Generation from Hoffman to Hovatter"

More About EDGAR THOM:
Adoption: [31,32]
Residence: Residence code: New Jersey[33,34]
Social Security Number: Social Security #: 154-12-8658[35,36]

Notes for WILLIAM F. PUTNAM:

Subj: Re: a short note
Date: 03/29/2002 1:34:39 PM Eastern Standard Time
From: P1AND2
To: JSutton639

E-mail dated 3-29-02
Hi Joyce,

It's Robin and Rick--responding from Dad's e-mail. We are at his house taking care of things. This is a hell of a thing to relay via e-mail, but we tried the phone numbers we found for you and Bob and got no answer, so I apologize in advance, but need to let you know.

Wednesday I couldn't get a hold of Dad, and grew concerned when his phone just kept ringing. So Rick and I drove in and we found him; he had fallen in the bathroom and was unconsious. We summoned paramedics and they took him to Valley Hospital. He passed away this morning around 6:30. He never regained consiousness. Rick, Bill and I like to think he had little or no pain, and know for sure he is in a better place now....probably with Mom :).

I know he wanted you to have Mom's albums....there are also a lot of pictures...I'd like for you to have anything you want. Please let me know.

We are still in the midst of arrangements and will let you know what is going on when we have more info.

Again I'm sorry to relay this via reply e-mail, but wanted you to know....Can I ask a favor pls...you knew a lot of Mom and Dad's e-mail buddies...would you be able to let them know about Dad for us pls, we'd really appreciate it.

Thanks.

Robin

William Putnam

William F. Putnam, 69, died March 29 in a local hospital.
He was born Sept. 10, 1932, in Port Henry, N.Y. A Navy veteran of the Korean and Vietnam wars, he was a corrections officer and a 22-year resident of Las Vegas.
He is survived by his son, William; and daughter, Robin Walker, both of Indian Springs; and five grandchildren.
Services are private. Davis Funeral Home-Charleston handled arrangements.

x. VERNON HOVATTER[36,37], b. February 26, 1924, West Virgina[38]; d. January 03, 1996, San Angelo, Texas[39,40,40,40,40,40,40,40,40,40,41].

Notes for VERNON HOVATTER:
Picture on page 101 in book "Generations from Hoffman to Hovatter"

More About VERNON HOVATTER:
Social Security Number: new Jersey[41]

xi. KENNETH GENE HOVATTER[41], b. October 31, 1927, west virginia Re: Family Bible[41]; d. March 06, 1983[41].

Notes for KENNETH GENE HOVATTER:
Picture on pages 100 in book "Generations from Hoffman to Hovatter"

More About KENNETH GENE HOVATTER:
Social Security Number: 587-56-1847[41]

4. IRA J.[4] HOVATTER *(CHRISTINA L.[3] SHAHAN, GEORGE WASHINGTON[2], GEORGE[1])*[41] was born April 17, 1885[41,42], and died July 1968[42]. He married DESSIE THOMAS.

More About IRA J. HOVATTER:
Social Security Number: 232-22-9008

Child of IRA HOVATTER and DESSIE THOMAS is:
i. NINA[5] HOVATTER.

5. MARY L.[4] HOVATTER *(CHRISTINA L.[3] SHAHAN, GEORGE WASHINGTON[2], GEORGE[1])*[43] was born March 07, 1887[43]. She married ANDREW JACKSON BROWN February 18, 1903 in Greene Co MS. He was born February 04, 1877, and died February 04, 1932.

Notes for MARY L. HOVATTER:

The information I received from Tracy had Fruitville listed in it but from Marriages in MS it seems that there was a double wedding, hers and her brother Wilbert. Both were married same day, same county and State. Greene Co. MS in Leakesville.

Children of MARY HOVATTER and ANDREW BROWN are:
i. ANDREW C.[5] BROWN, b. January 29, 1904; d. July 28, 1975; m. MILDRED FORTNEY.
ii. ALBERT LEROY BROWN, b. January 23, 1908; d. Abt. May 12, 1994; m. MARIE MIZELL.
iii. RUBY BROWN, b. September 02, 1908; m. BRYAN HOVATTER; d. 1996.
iv. WILBER JACKSON BROWN, b. December 04, 1912; d. December 04, 1912.

More About WILBER JACKSON BROWN:
Burial: Fruitdale Cemetary

v. HOMER JENNINGS BROWN, b. July 07, 1914; d. July 17, 1972; m. MARY MYRTLE DEESE OR DEES, December 26, 1932; b. February 28, 1918; d. May 08, 1989.

Notes for HOMER JENNINGS BROWN:
Worked in sawmill.
died of a heart attack

More About HOMER JENNINGS BROWN:
Burial: Fruitdale Cemetary

Notes for MARY MYRTLE DEESE OR DEES:

Died of Lou gerrings

More About MARY MYRTLE DEESE OR DEES:
Burial: Fruitdale Cemetary

vi. DELBERT JENNINGS BROWN, b. April 19, 1917; d. February 02, 1998.
vii. WILLIAM HENRY BROWN, b. July 23, 1920.
viii. NELLIE MAE BROWN BROWN, b. November 23, 1923.
ix. DAVID ELMER BROWN, b. November 04, 1926; d. February 10, 1929.

6. GEORGE E.[4] HOVATTER *(CHRISTINA L.[3] SHAHAN, GEORGE WASHINGTON[2], GEORGE[1])*[43] was born February 15, 1889[43]. He married CECIL MAY BURNS.

Notes for CECIL MAY BURNS:
There is a possibility that the spelling of her name was different. May have been Cecilia or another variation.

Children of GEORGE HOVATTER and CECIL BURNS are:
i. ERNEST RAY[5] HOVATTER, b. July 25, 1916; m. (1) MILDRED KINTER; m. (2) EVELYN ?; m. (3) FRANCIS BOYER.
ii. VIOLET MILDRED HOVATTER, b. June 1915; m. FRED BAIOCCHI; d. 1987.
iii. VELMA ARIZONIA HOVATTER, b. October 1917.

Notes for VELMA ARIZONIA HOVATTER:
Was a Major in the Army. She adopted her sister Mary Children and raised them as her own. Whe passed away in Aniston Ala in 1999 her daughter Jean and son Larry still live on the farm there.

iv. BERYL HOVATTER, m. PAGE EVANS.
v. MARY ELIZABETH HOVATTER, b. 1923; m. (1) MR. PERT; m. (2) LEONARD BLACKMON.

Notes for MARY ELIZABETH HOVATTER:
She had four Children. Her husband abused her and she divorced him. Her father took her home to Grafton where she moved in with grandma. Aunt Velma came in from a tour in Greenland and took her mom Cecil and mary and all four kids with her to Texas to live. She ended up raising the four children and taking care of her mother until she passed away in the late 1970's. Mary Elizabeth remarried Leonard Blackmon and remained in the San Antonio area. They now live in Schertz, Texas

vi. DARRELL HOVATTER, m. SHIRLEE.

7. ARLIE DAVID[4] HOVATTER *(CHRISTINA L.[3] SHAHAN, GEORGE WASHINGTON[2], GEORGE[1])*[43] was born August 15, 1895 in WVA[43], and died December 1977[44,45]. He married LAURA POLING.

Notes for ARLIE DAVID HOVATTER:
[Broderbund Family Archive #110, Vol. 1 A-K, Ed. 7, Social Security Death Index: U.S., Date of Import: Jul 3, 2001, Internal Ref. #1.111.7.127438.120]

Individual: Hovatter, Arlie
Social Security #: 705-10-2282
Issued in: Railroad Board

Birth date: Aug 15, 1895
Death date: Dec 1977

Residence code: West Virginia

ZIP Code of last known residence: 26354
Primary location associated with this ZIP Code:

Grafton, West Virginia

More About ARLIE DAVID HOVATTER:
Fact 1: Issued in: Railroad Board[45]
Fact 2: Residence code: West Virginia[45]
Fact 3: Last residence ZIP: 26354[45]
Fact 6: Issued in: Railroad Board[46]
Fact 7: Residence code: West Virginia[46]
Fact 8: Last residence ZIP: 26354[46]
Social Security Number: Social Security #: 705-10-2282[46,47]

Child of ARLIE HOVATTER and LAURA POLING is:
i. LESTER[5] HOVATTER.

Endnotes

1. Mancuso.FTW, Date of Import: Sep 6, 2000.
2. Genealogy.com, Family Archive #110, Social Security Death Index: U.S. Ed. 9, Social Security Death Index, Release date: April 10, 2000, Internal Ref. #1.111.9.122873.66.
3. Mancuso.FTW, Date of Import: Sep 6, 2000.
4. Genealogy.com, Family Archive #110, Social Security Death Index: U.S. Ed. 9, Social Security Death Index, Release date: April 10, 2000, Internal Ref. #1.111.9.122873.123.
5. Mancuso.FTW, Date of Import: Sep 6, 2000.
6. Broderbund Family Archive #110, Vol. 1, Ed. 7, Social Security Death Index: U.S., Date of Import: May 20, 2000, Internal Ref. #1.111.7.127439.53
7. Broderbund Family Archive #110, Vol. 1, Ed. 7, Social Security Death Index: U.S., Date of Import: May 21, 2000, Internal Ref. #1.111.7.127439.53
8. Mancuso.FTW, Date of Import: Sep 6, 2000.
9. Genealogy.com, Family Archive #110, Social Security Death Index: U.S. Ed. 9, Social Security Death Index, Release date: April 10, 2000, Internal Ref. #1.111.9.122873.201.
10. Mancuso.FTW, Date of Import: Sep 6, 2000.
11. Broderbund Family Archive #110, Vol. 1, Ed. 7, Social Security Death Index: U.S., Date of Import: May 20, 2000, Internal Ref. #1.111.7.127438.181
12. Mancuso.FTW, Date of Import: Sep 6, 2000.
13. Broderbund Family Archive #110, Vol. 1, Ed. 7, Social Security Death Index: U.S., Date of Import: May 20, 2000, Internal Ref. #1.111.7.127438.182
14. Mancuso.FTW, Date of Import: Sep 6, 2000.
15. Genealogy.com, Family Archive #110, Social Security Death Index: U.S. Ed. 9, Social Security Death Index, Release date: April 10, 2000, Internal Ref. #1.111.9.122873.125.
16. Mancuso.FTW, Date of Import: Sep 6, 2000.
17. Broderbund Family Archive #110, Vol. 1, Ed. 7, Social Security Death Index: U.S., Date of Import: May 20, 2000, Internal Ref. #1.111.7.127438.126
18. Broderbund Family Archive #110, Vol. 1, Ed. 7, Social Security Death Index: U.S., Date of Import: May 21, 2000, Internal Ref. #1.111.7.127438.126
19. Mancuso.FTW, Date of Import: Sep 6, 2000.
20. Genealogy.com, Family Archive #110, Social Security Death Index: U.S. Ed. 9, Social Security Death Index, Release date: April 10, 2000.
21. Mancuso Cramer Sutton.FTW, Date of Import: Jun 25, 2001.
22. Mancuso.FTW, Date of Import: Sep 6, 2000.
23. Mancuso Cramer Sutton.FTW, Date of Import: Jun 25, 2001.
24. Mancuso.FTW, Date of Import: Sep 6, 2000.
25. Mancuso Cramer Sutton.FTW, Date of Import: Jun 25, 2001.
26. Mancuso.FTW, Date of Import: Sep 6, 2000.
27. Broderbund Family Archive #110, Vol. 2, Ed. 7, Social Security Death Index: U.S., Date of Import: May 20, 2000, Internal Ref. #1.112.7.120056.133
28. Mancuso.FTW, Date of Import: Sep 6, 2000.
29. Broderbund Family Archive #110, Vol. 2, Ed. 7, Social Security Death Index: U.S., Date of Import: May 20, 2000, Internal Ref. #1.112.7.120056.133

Christina Shahan Hovatter

Hand made

underside of quilt

Descendants of Johan Heinrich Hochwarter

1 Johan Heinrich Hochwarter 1678 - 1763
.... +Anna Maria Zeilnerin 1686 - 1749
.... 2 Anna Margaretha Hohwerter 1702 -
.... 2 John Jacob Hohwerter 1703/04 -
.... 2 Johann Valentin Hohwerter 1710 - 1747/48
.... +Anna Christina Huettenmeyer 1709 - 1760
.... 3 Philipp Nikel Hohwerter 1736 - 1768
.... +Elisabeth Schiffler
.... 3 Johan Michael Hohwerter 1738 - 1787
.... +Maria Catherine Pidgeon
.... 4 George Hovatter
.... 4 Unknown Hovatter
.... 4 Christopher Hovatter 1762 - 1859
.... +Catherine Spendgler 1764 - 1859
.... 5 Sara Jane Hovatter 1790 -
.... +Peter Wilt 1790 -
.... 6 Peter Wilt 1819 -
.... +Catherine Wilson 1819 -
.... 7 Mary M. Wilt 1840 -
.... 7 John H. Wilt 1841 -
.... 7 Abigail Wilt 1843 -
.... 7 George K. Wilt 1846 -
.... 7 Wilson Wilt 1848 -
.... 7 Sarah Jane Wilt 1851 -
.... 7 Vilena (Violena) Wilt 1855 -
.... 7 Thomas Wilt Wilt 1856 -
.... 7 Anzina Wilt 1857 -
.... 5 Jacob Hovatter 1796 - 1810
.... 5 George Michael Hovatter 1799 - 1875
.... +Barbara Shroyer 1791 - 1847
.... 6 Jacob Hovatter
.... 6 David Hovatter 1821 - 1840
.... 6 Melker Hovatter 1826 - 1900
.... +Susanna Lohr 1834 -
.... 7 George M. Hovatter 1854 -
.... 7 Catherine Hovatter 1857 -
.... 7 Mary Ann Hovatter 1862 -
.... 7 James W. Hovatter 1868 -
.... 7 Waitman L. Hovatter 1874 -
.... *2nd Wife of George Michael Hovatter:
.... +Catharine Lohr 1811 - 1879
.... 5 Elizabeth Hovatter 1801 - 1859
.... 5 John Hovatter 1803 - 1863
.... +Nancy Hardin 1821 - 1906
.... 5 Andrew Hovatter 1804 -
.... +Elizabeth Wilson 1802 -
.... 6 Elizabeth Hovatter 1832 -
.... 6 Jackson Hovatter 1834 -
.... 6 Bassil Hovatter 1837 -
.... 6 Andrew Jacob Hovatter 1840 -
.... +Elizabeth Satterfield
.... 5 Henry Hovatter 1806 -
.... +Rachel Kittle 1811 -
.... 6 John J. Hovatter
.... 6 Lousia Hovatter
.... 6 Isaac Hovatter 1832 -
.... 6 Christopher Hovatter 1835 -
.... 6 Harriet Hovatter 1838 -
.... 6 Jacob Hovatter 1840 -
.... 6 Virginia Hovatter 1843 -
.... 5 David Hovatter 1810 - 1881
.... +Sarah Ann Thompson
.... 6 Cora Jane Hovatter 1876 - 1948
.... +George Emery Shahan 1864 - 1966
.... 7 Walter Brown Shahan
.... 7 Agnes Shahan 1892 - 1986
.... 7 Minnie Pearl Shahan 1894 - 1959
.... 7 Donna Jane Shahan 1896 - 1972
.... 7 Mary Elizabeth Shahan 1897 - 1918
.... 7 Daisy Virginia Shahan 1899 - 1978
.... 7 Flora Shahan 1904 - 1904
.... 7 Dora Shahan 1904 -
.... 7 Charles Lee Shahan 1907 - 1971
.... 7 Cora Louise Shahan 1908 - 1987
.... +Floyd Edward Sayre

7 Ruby Bessie Shahan 1910 -
7 Georgia Oletha Shahan 1912 - 1975
7 Lillian Ann Shahan 1916 -
7 Victoria Arabelle Shahan 1919 -
6 Henry Hovatter
+Ozella Lipscomb
6 John Hovatter
6 Hezekiah Hovatter 1836 - 1900
+?
7 Olive V. Hovatter 1872 -
7 Igerby A. Hovatter 1873 -
7 Elias Hovatter 1875 -
+?
8 Leatha L. Hovatter
8 Clide Hovatter
8 Danny Hovatter
8 Cecil B. Hovatter
8 Donna A. Hovatter
8 William H. Hovatter
6 Malinai Jane Hovatter 1839 -
6 Susan Hovatter 1841 -
6 Michael Hovatter 1844 -
6 Benjamin Hovatter 1847 -
6 Andrew Hovatter 1849 -
6 David T. Hovatter 1853 - 1929
+Christina L. Shahan 1858 - 1933
7 Charles E. Hovatter 1878 -
+Ella Agnice Burns 1883 -
8 Claudene Elwood Hovatter
+Arietta Shockley
8 Elston Gerald Hovatter
+Myra E. Howard
8 Charles Woodrow Wilson Hovatter
+Madeline Kausch
8 Wanda Lorraine Hovatter
+Albert H. Hearn
8 Earl Gay Hovatter 1912 - 1934
8 Thomas David Hovatter 1908 -
+Elsie Ambrosio
9 Timothy Hovatter
8 Elmer Dallas Hovatter 1902 - 1970
+Jessie B. Noce 1898 - 1919
8 Etta Ives Hovatter
+Earl C. Cathel
8 Delbert Ray Hovatter 1904 - 1974
+Barbara Chandler
9 Barbara Lindsay Hovatter 1944 - 1968
9 Sandra Lee Hovatter 1946 -
+James Moore
9 Martha Jean Hovatter 1953 -
+Kenneth Speer - 1988
10 Barbara Anne Speer 1974 -
10 Donald Ray Speer 1977 -
*2nd Husband of Martha Jean Hovatter:
+Charles Reno
8 Leoda Pearl Hovatter
8 Ora Marie Hovatter 1914 - 1937
+Herbert Fues, Sr
8 Elford Harold Hovatter 1924 - 1924
7 Lellie C. Hovatter 1880 -
+John Patrick Burns 1877 - 1950
7 Wilbert F. Hovatter 1882 - 1969
+Hattie Lee Jones 1885 - 1969
8 Eula Hovatter 1903 - 1937
+Samuel Linton
9 Voncile Linton
*2nd Husband of Eula Hovatter:
+Hope Watson
9 Junior Lee Watson
9 Francis Watson
9 Joyce Watson
8 Odie Hovatter 1905 - 1905
8 Wilbertie Valentine Hovatter 1908 - 1987
+Hazel Dell Clevenger 1907 - 1988
9 Marjorie Hovatter 1927 -
9 Dolores Hovatter 1929 -
9 Berta Jayne Hovatter 1938 - 1988

.... +Harold Snyder
.... 10 Pam Snyder 1959 -
.... 11 Brian Snyder 1976 -
.... *2nd Husband of Berta Jayne Hovatter:
.... +Thomas Moser 1930 -
.... 10 Thomas Moser 1969 -
.... *Partner of Wilbertie Valentine Hovatter:
.... +Ruby Barnett 1915 -
.... 9 Rosalie J. Hovatter 1932 -
.... +Charley Jenkins
.... *2nd Husband of Rosalie J. Hovatter:
.... +David Faulknier
.... 8 Boyd Hovatter 1910 - 1975
.... 8 Floyd Hovatter 1913 - 1913
.... 8 Lois Hovatter 1914 - 1983
.... +Thomas Mancuso 1912 - 1985
.... 9 Joyce F.. Mancuso 1934 -
.... +Robert Thomas Sutton 1932 -
.... 10 Dolores Lea Sutton 1958 -
.... 10 Susan Joyce Sutton 1964 -
.... +Christopher Keating
.... 11 Christopher Keating Jr.
.... 11 Benjamin Keating
.... 10 Bobbi Lynn Sutton 1968 -
.... +Karl Frank Chase
.... 11 Shawn Joseph Chase 1995 -
.... 11 Samantha Joyce Chase 1997 -
.... *Partner of Bobbi Lynn Sutton:
.... +Mr. McHenry
.... 11 Dani-Lynn McHenry 2006 -
.... 9 Patrina Mancuso 1937 - 1937
.... 8 Hattie Almalee Hovatter 1917 -
.... 8 Aubrey Hovatter 1920 -
.... 8 Dessie Hovatter 1921 - 2001
.... +Edgar Thom 1922 - 1982
.... 9 Dennis Thom 1949 - 1971
.... *2nd Husband of Dessie Hovatter:
.... +William F. Putnam 1932 - 2002
.... 9 Robin Putnam 1963 -
.... +Edison Richard Walker
.... 10 Stephen Randall Walker 1987 -
.... 10 Jaren Dawn Walker 1993 -
.... 9 William F. Putnam 2 1966 -
.... +Bernetta Graham 1970 -
.... 10 William F. Putnam 3 1990 -
.... 10 Olivia Lucille Putnam 1997 -
.... 8 Vernon Hovatter 1924 - 1996
.... 8 Kenneth Gene Hovatter 1927 - 1983
.... 7 Ira J. Hovatter 1885 - 1968
.... +Dessie Thomas
.... 8 Nina Hovatter
.... 7 Mary L. Hovatter 1887 -
.... +Andrew Jackson Brown 1877 - 1932
.... 8 Andrew C. Brown 1904 - 1975
.... +Mildred Fortney
.... 9 Donald Brown
.... 9 Keith Brown
.... 9 Larraine Brown
.... 9 Swanee Brown
.... 9 Frank Brown
.... 9 Paul Brown
.... 8 Albert Leroy Brown 1908 - 1994
.... +Marie Mizell
.... 8 Ruby Brown 1908 -
.... +Bryan Hovatter - 1996
.... 9 William Hovatter
.... 9 Prudence Hovatter
.... 8 Wilber Jackson Brown 1912 - 1912
.... 8 Homer Jennings Brown 1914 - 1972
.... +Mary Myrtle Deese or Dees 1918 - 1989
.... 9 Cecile Leota Brown 1934 - 1937
.... 9 Andrew Jennings Brown 1937 - 1994
.... +Jackine Lou Tallet
.... 9 Homer Ray Brown 1938 -
.... +Anna Cecelia Stevens
.... 10 Tracy Lee Brown 1966 -
.... 8 Delbert Jennings Brown 1917 - 1998

8 William Henry Brown 1920 -
8 Nellie Mae Brown Brown 1923 -
8 David Elmer Brown 1926 - 1929
7 George E. Hovatter 1889 -
+Cecil May Burns
8 Ernest Ray Hovatter 1916 -
+Mildred Kinter
9 Gary Ray Hovatter 1949 -
+Linda Hunnicut
10 Health Hovatter
10 Heather Hovatter
+Anthony Galvez
11 Daniel Galvez
11 Rebecca Galvez
11 Allisa Galvez
9 Vickie Lynn Hovatter 1954 -
+William Claypool 1949 -
10 Daniel Claypool 1978 -
10 Kevin Claypool 1981 -
*2nd Wife of Ernest Ray Hovatter:
+Evelyn ?
9 Patti Ann Hovatter
+? Smith
*3rd Wife of Ernest Ray Hovatter:
+Francis Boyer
9 Francis Lee Hovatter
8 Violet Mildred Hovatter 1915 -
+Fred Baiocchi - 1987
9 Yvonne Baiocchi
8 Velma Arizonia Hovatter 1917 -
8 Beryl Hovatter
+Page Evans
9 Male Child Evans
8 Mary Elizabeth Hovatter 1923 -
+Mr. Pert
9 Jean Pert
9 Larry Pert
9 unknown Pert
*2nd Husband of Mary Elizabeth Hovatter:
+Leonard Blackmon
8 Darrell Hovatter
+Shirlee
9 Donna Hovatter
9 Kathy Hovatter
7 Lloyd A. Hovatter 1891 -
+Lulu Sterringer
7 Maudie P. Hovatter 1893 -
+Samuel Dumire
7 Arlie David Hovatter 1895 - 1977
+Laura Poling
8 Lester Hovatter
7 Boyd E. Hovatter 1897 - 1980
+Hilda Davis
6 Elizabeth Hovatter 1861 -
+Max K. Shahan 1859 -
6 Ingaby Hovatter 1863 -
+Andrew J. Ball 1860 -
5 William Hovatter 1816 -
+Clarissa Kittle
6 George M. Hovatter
+Mary Jane Nestor
6 Isaac Hovatter 1854 -
+Emily C. Lipscomb 1860 -
6 Henry B. Hovatter 1856 -
+Jennie Belle
6 Catherine Hovatter 1851 -
+David A. Loughry 1850 -
7 [2] Mary E. Loughry 1871 -
+[1] Jacob Hovatter 1862 -
6 [1] Jacob Hovatter 1862 -
+[2] Mary E. Loughry 1871 -
4 Anna Maria Howerter/ Hovatter 1766 -
+Jacob Haller 1769 - 1807
4 Anna Hovatter 1768 -
4 Maria Magdalina Hohwerter/ Hovatter 1770 -
4 Anna Margaretha Howerter/ Hovatter 1774 -
4 Michael Howerter Hovatter 1775 - 1793

.... 4 Jacob Hovatter 1777 -
.... 4 Anna Catharina Howerter/ Hovatter 1782 -
.... 3 Maria Margaretha Hohwerter 1739/40 -
.... 3 Johan Adam Hohwerter 1742 - 1819
.... +Catherine Krohn 1748 - 1819
.... 4 Hienrich Hohwerter 1768 - 1838
.... 4 Johan Adam Hohwerter 1769 - 1847
.... 4 Johan Peter Hohwerter 1772 - 1862
.... 4 Catherine Hohwerter 1775 -
.... 4 Salome Hohwerter 1776 - 1797
.... 4 Sarah Hohwerter 1778 -
.... 4 Maria Elizabeth Hohwerter 1778 - 1818
.... +Spies
.... 4 Christina Hohwerter 1780 - 1848
.... 4 Susanne Hohwerter 1782 - 1850
.... 4 Johannes Hohwerter 1783 - 1790
.... 4 Anna Maria Hohwerter 1786 - 1860
.... 3 Johann George Hohwerter 1743/44 - 1835
.... +Magdalena (Molly) Schiffer 1750 - 1834
.... 4 George Hohwerter
.... 4 Christian Hohwerter 1772 -
.... +Julianna Carmony
.... 5 Johannes Howerter
.... +Nancy Weirich
.... 6 Henry Hovarter
.... +Catherine Hartman
.... 7 Emanuel Hovarter
.... +Lucinda Reamer
.... 8 Paul Hovarter 1907 - 1968
.... +Delores Beaty 1916 - 1972
.... 9 Sharon Hovarter 1938 -
.... +William Wilcox
.... 9 Dale Robert Hovarter 1948 -
.... 4 unknown Hohwerter 1773 -
.... 4 unknown Hohwerter 1785 -
.... 4 unknown Hohwerter 1787 -
.... 4 William Hohwerter 1790 -
.... 4 Unknown Hohwerter 1800 -
.... 3 Valentin Hohwerter 1746 -
.... 3 Elisabeth Hohwerter 1747/48 - 1761
.... 2 Johan George Hohwerter 1712 -
.... +Barbara Brada
.... 2 Anna Barbara Hohwerter 1714 -
.... +Johann Peter Morion

Descendants of Johan Heinrich Hochwarter

1 Johan Heinrich Hochwarter 1678 - 1763
+Anna Maria Zeilnerin 1686 - 1749
2 Anna Margaretha Hohwerter 1702 -
2 John Jacob Hohwerter 1703/04 -
2 Johann Valentin Hohwerter 1710 - 1747/48
+Anna Christina Huettenmeyer 1709 - 1760
3 Philipp Nikel Hohwerter 1736 - 1768
+Elisabeth Schiffler
3 Johan Michael Hohwerter 1738 - 1787
+Maria Catherine Pidgeon
4 George Hovatter
4 Unknown Hovatter
4 Christopher Hovatter 1762 - 1859
+Catherine Spendgler 1764 - 1859
5 Sara Jane Hovatter 1790 -
+Peter Wilt 1790 -
6 Peter Wilt 1819 -
+Catherine Wilson 1819 -
7 Mary M. Wilt 1840 -
7 John H. Wilt 1841 -
7 Abigail Wilt 1843 -
7 George K. Wilt 1846 -
7 Wilson Wilt 1848 -
7 Sarah Jane Wilt 1851 -
7 Vilena (Violena) Wilt 1855 -
7 Thomas Wilt Wilt 1856 -
7 Anzina Wilt 1857 -
5 Jacob Hovatter 1796 - 1810
5 George Michael Hovatter 1799 - 1875
+Barbara Shroyer 1791 - 1847
6 Jacob Hovatter
6 David Hovatter 1821 - 1840
6 Melker Hovatter 1826 - 1900
+Susanna Lohr 1834 -
7 George M. Hovatter 1854 -
7 Catherine Hovatter 1857 -
7 Mary Ann Hovatter 1862 -
7 James W. Hovatter 1868 -
7 Waitman L. Hovatter 1874 -
*2nd Wife of George Michael Hovatter:
+Catharine Lohr 1811 - 1879
5 Elizabeth Hovatter 1801 - 1859
5 John Hovatter 1803 - 1863
+Nancy Hardin 1821 - 1906
5 Andrew Hovatter 1804 -
+Elizabeth Wilson 1802 -
6 Elizabeth Hovatter 1832 -
6 Jackson Hovatter 1834 -
6 Bassil Hovatter 1837 -
6 Andrew Jacob Hovatter 1840 -
+Elizabeth Satterfield
5 Henry Hovatter 1806 -
+Rachel Kittle 1811 -
6 John J. Hovatter
6 Lousia Hovatter
6 Isaac Hovatter 1832 -
6 Christopher Hovatter 1835 -
6 Harriet Hovatter 1838 -
6 Jacob Hovatter 1840 -
6 Virginia Hovatter 1843 -
5 David Hovatter 1810 - 1881
+Sarah Ann Thompson
6 Cora Jane Hovatter 1876 - 1948
+George Emery Shahan 1864 - 1966
7 Walter Brown Shahan
7 Agnes Shahan 1892 - 1986
7 Minnie Pearl Shahan 1894 - 1959
7 Donna Jane Shahan 1896 - 1972
7 Mary Elizabeth Shahan 1897 - 1918
7 Daisy Virginia Shahan 1899 - 1978
7 Flora Shahan 1904 - 1904
7 Dora Shahan 1904 -
7 Charles Lee Shahan 1907 - 1971
7 Cora Louise Shahan 1908 - 1987
+Floyd Edward Sayre

7 Ruby Bessie Shahan 1910 -
7 Georgia Oletha Shahan 1912 - 1975
7 Lillian Ann Shahan 1916 -
7 Victoria Arabelle Shahan 1919 -
6 Henry Hovatter
+Ozella Lipscomb
6 John Hovatter
6 Hezekiah Hovatter 1836 - 1900
+?
7 Olive V. Hovatter 1872 -
7 Igerby A. Hovatter 1873 -
7 Elias Hovatter 1875 -
+?
8 Leatha L. Hovatter
8 Clide Hovatter
8 Danny Hovatter
8 Cecil B. Hovatter
8 Donna A. Hovatter
8 William H. Hovatter
6 Malinai Jane Hovatter 1839 -
6 Susan Hovatter 1841 -
6 Michael Hovatter 1844 -
6 Benjamin Hovatter 1847 -
6 Andrew Hovatter 1849 -
6 David T. Hovatter 1853 - 1929
+Christina L. Shahan 1858 - 1933
7 Charles E. Hovatter 1878 -
+Ella Agnice Burns 1883 -
8 Claudene Elwood Hovatter
+Arietta Shockley
8 Elston Gerald Hovatter
+Myra E. Howard
8 Charles Woodrow Wilson Hovatter
+Madeline Kausch
8 Wanda Lorraine Hovatter
+Albert H. Hearn
8 Earl Gay Hovatter 1912 - 1934
8 Thomas David Hovatter 1908 -
+Elsie Ambrosio
9 Timothy Hovatter
8 Elmer Dallas Hovatter 1902 - 1970
+Jessie B. Noce 1898 - 1919
8 Etta Ives Hovatter
+Earl C. Cathel
8 Delbert Ray Hovatter 1904 - 1974
+Barbara Chandler
9 Barbara Lindsay Hovatter 1944 - 1968
9 Sandra Lee Hovatter 1946 -
+James Moore
9 Martha Jean Hovatter 1953 -
+Kenneth Speer - 1988
10 Barbara Anne Speer 1974 -
10 Donald Ray Speer 1977 -
*2nd Husband of Martha Jean Hovatter:
+Charles Reno
8 Leoda Pearl Hovatter
8 Ora Marie Hovatter 1914 - 1937
+Herbert Fues, Sr
8 Elford Harold Hovatter 1924 - 1924
7 Lellie C. Hovatter 1880 -
+John Patrick Burns 1877 - 1950
7 Wilbert F. Hovatter 1882 - 1969
+Hattie Lee Jones 1885 - 1969
8 Eula Hovatter 1903 - 1937
+Samuel Linton
9 Voncile Linton
*2nd Husband of Eula Hovatter:
+Hope Watson
9 Junior Lee Watson
9 Francis Watson
9 Joyce Watson
8 Odie Hovatter 1905 - 1905
8 Wilbertie Valentine Hovatter 1908 - 1987
+Hazel Dell Clevenger 1907 - 1988
9 Marjorie Hovatter 1927 -
9 Dolores Hovatter 1929 -
9 Berta Jayne Hovatter 1938 - 1988

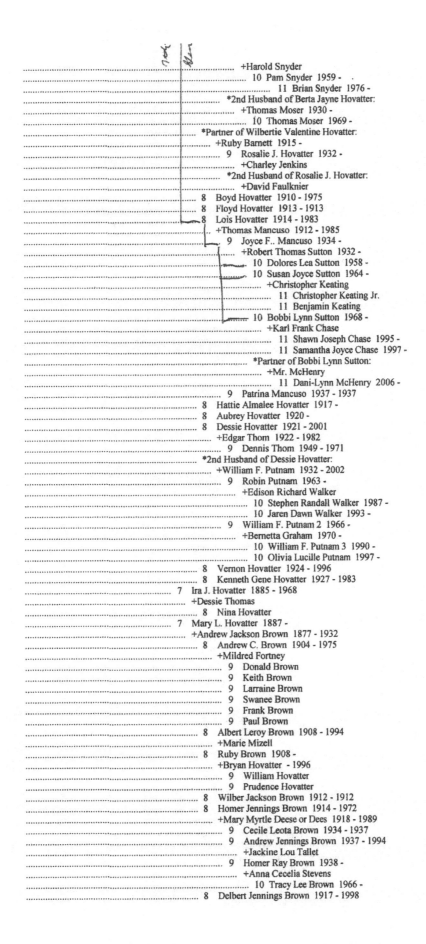

+Harold Snyder
10 Pam Snyder 1959 -
11 Brian Snyder 1976 -
*2nd Husband of Berta Jayne Hovatter:
+Thomas Moser 1930 -
10 Thomas Moser 1969 -
*Partner of Wilbertie Valentine Hovatter:
+Ruby Barnett 1915 -
9 Rosalie J. Hovatter 1932 -
+Charley Jenkins
*2nd Husband of Rosalie J. Hovatter:
+David Faulknier
8 Boyd Hovatter 1910 - 1975
8 Floyd Hovatter 1913 - 1913
8 Lois Hovatter 1914 - 1983
+Thomas Mancuso 1912 - 1985
9 Joyce F.. Mancuso 1934 -
+Robert Thomas Sutton 1932 -
10 Dolores Lea Sutton 1958 -
10 Susan Joyce Sutton 1964 -
+Christopher Keating
11 Christopher Keating Jr.
11 Benjamin Keating
10 Bobbi Lynn Sutton 1968 -
+Karl Frank Chase
11 Shawn Joseph Chase 1995 -
11 Samantha Joyce Chase 1997 -
*Partner of Bobbi Lynn Sutton:
+Mr. McHenry
11 Dani-Lynn McHenry 2006 -
9 Patrina Mancuso 1937 - 1937
8 Hattie Almalee Hovatter 1917 -
8 Aubrey Hovatter 1920 -
8 Dessie Hovatter 1921 - 2001
+Edgar Thom 1922 - 1982
9 Dennis Thom 1949 - 1971
*2nd Husband of Dessie Hovatter:
+William F. Putnam 1932 - 2002
9 Robin Putnam 1963 -
+Edison Richard Walker
10 Stephen Randall Walker 1987 -
10 Jaren Dawn Walker 1993 -
9 William F. Putnam 2 1966 -
+Bernetta Graham 1970 -
10 William F. Putnam 3 1990 -
10 Olivia Lucille Putnam 1997 -
8 Vernon Hovatter 1924 - 1996
8 Kenneth Gene Hovatter 1927 - 1983
7 Ira J. Hovatter 1885 - 1968
+Dessie Thomas
8 Nina Hovatter
7 Mary L. Hovatter 1887 -
+Andrew Jackson Brown 1877 - 1932
8 Andrew C. Brown 1904 - 1975
+Mildred Fortney
9 Donald Brown
9 Keith Brown
9 Larraine Brown
9 Swanee Brown
9 Frank Brown
9 Paul Brown
8 Albert Leroy Brown 1908 - 1994
+Marie Mizell
8 Ruby Brown 1908 -
+Bryan Hovatter - 1996
9 William Hovatter
9 Prudence Hovatter
8 Wilber Jackson Brown 1912 - 1912
8 Homer Jennings Brown 1914 - 1972
+Mary Myrtle Deese or Dees 1918 - 1989
9 Cecile Leota Brown 1934 - 1937
9 Andrew Jennings Brown 1937 - 1994
+Jackine Lou Tallet
9 Homer Ray Brown 1938 -
+Anna Cecelia Stevens
10 Tracy Lee Brown 1966 -
8 Delbert Jennings Brown 1917 - 1998

8 William Henry Brown 1920 -
8 Nellie Mae Brown Brown 1923 -
8 David Elmer Brown 1926 - 1929
7 George E. Hovatter 1889 -
+Cecil May Burns
8 Ernest Ray Hovatter 1916 -
+Mildred Kinter
9 Gary Ray Hovatter 1949 -
+Linda Hunnicut
10 Health Hovatter
10 Heather Hovatter
+Anthony Galvez
11 Daniel Galvez
11 Rebecca Galvez
11 Allisa Galvez
9 Vickie Lynn Hovatter 1954 -
+William Claypool 1949 -
10 Daniel Claypool 1978 -
10 Kevin Claypool 1981 -
*2nd Wife of Ernest Ray Hovatter:
+Evelyn ?
9 Patti Ann Hovatter
+? Smith
*3rd Wife of Ernest Ray Hovatter:
+Francis Boyer
9 Francis Lee Hovatter
8 Violet Mildred Hovatter 1915 -
+Fred Baiocchi - 1987
9 Yvonne Baiocchi
8 Velma Arizonia Hovatter 1917 -
8 Beryl Hovatter
+Page Evans
9 Male Child Evans
8 Mary Elizabeth Hovatter 1923 -
+Mr. Pert
9 Jean Pert
9 Larry Pert
9 unknown Pert
*2nd Husband of Mary Elizabeth Hovatter:
+Leonard Blackmon
8 Darrell Hovatter
+Shirlee
9 Donna Hovatter
9 Kathy Hovatter
7 Lloyd A. Hovatter 1891 -
+Lulu Sterringer
7 Maudie P. Hovatter 1893 -
+Samuel Dumire
7 Arlie David Hovatter 1895 - 1977
+Laura Poling
8 Lester Hovatter
7 Boyd E. Hovatter 1897 - 1980
+Hilda Davis
6 Elizabeth Hovatter 1861 -
+Max K. Shahan 1859 -
6 Ingaby Hovatter 1863 -
+Andrew J. Ball 1860 -
5 William Hovatter 1816 -
+Clarissa Kittle
6 George M. Hovatter
+Mary Jane Nestor
6 Isaac Hovatter 1854 -
+Emily C. Lipscomb 1860 -
6 Henry B. Hovatter 1856 -
+Jennie Belle
6 Catherine Hovatter 1851 -
+David A. Loughry 1850 -
7 [2] Mary E. Loughry 1871 -
+[1] Jacob Hovatter 1862 -
6 [1] Jacob Hovatter 1862 -
+[2] Mary E. Loughry 1871 -
4 Anna Maria Howerter/ Hovatter 1766 -
+Jacob Haller 1769 - 1807
4 Anna Hovatter 1768 -
4 Maria Magdalina Hohwerter/ Hovatter 1770 -
4 Anna Margaretha Howerter/ Hovatter 1774 -
4 Michael Howerter Hovatter 1775 - 1793

.... 4 Jacob Hovatter 1777 -
.... 4 Anna Catharina Howerter/ Hovatter 1782 -
.... 3 Maria Margaretha Hohwerter 1739/40 -
.... 3 Johan Adam Hohwerter 1742 - 1819
.... +Catherine Krohn 1748 - 1819
.... 4 Hienrich Hohwerter 1768 - 1838
.... 4 Johan Adam Hohwerter 1769 - 1847
.... 4 Johan Peter Hohwerter 1772 - 1862
.... 4 Catherine Hohwerter 1775 -
.... 4 Salome Hohwerter 1776 - 1797
.... 4 Sarah Hohwerter 1778 -
.... 4 Maria Elizabeth Hohwerter 1778 - 1818
.... +Spies
.... 4 Christina Hohwerter 1780 - 1848
.... 4 Susanne Hohwerter 1782 - 1850
.... 4 Johannes Hohwerter 1783 - 1790
.... 4 Anna Maria Hohwerter 1786 - 1860
.... 3 Johann George Hohwerter 1743/44 - 1835
.... +Magdalena (Molly) Schiffer 1750 - 1834
.... 4 George Hohwerter
.... 4 Christian Hohwerter 1772 -
.... +Julianna Carmony
.... 5 Johannes Howerter
.... +Nancy Weirich
.... 6 Henry Hovarter
.... +Catherine Hartman
.... 7 Emanuel Hovarter
.... +Lucinda Reamer
.... 8 Paul Hovarter 1907 - 1968
.... +Delores Beaty 1916 - 1972
.... 9 Sharon Hovarter 1938 -
.... +William Wilcox
.... 9 Dale Robert Hovarter 1948 -
.... 4 unknown Hohwerter 1773 -
.... 4 unknown Hohwerter 1785 -
.... 4 unknown Hohwerter 1787 -
.... 4 William Hohwerter 1790 -
.... 4 Unknown Hohwerter 1800 -
.... 3 Valentin Hohwerter 1746 -
.... 3 Elisabeth Hohwerter 1747/48 - 1761
.... 2 Johan George Hohwerter 1712 -
.... +Barbara Brada
.... 2 Anna Barbara Hohwerter 1714 -
.... +Johann Peter Morion

Descendants of Johan Heinrich Hochwarter

Generation No. 1

1. JOHAN HEINRICH[1] HOCHWARTER was born 1678 in Switzerland, and died May 25, 1763 in Thaleischweiler, Zweibrucken, Germany. He married ANNA MARIA ZEILNERIN Abt. 1701 in Evangelisch, Marnheim, Pfalz, Bayern. She was born Abt. 1686 in Switzerland, and died August 30, 1749 in Thaleischweiler, Zweibrucken, Germany.

Notes for JOHAN HEINRICH HOCHWARTER:

Notes for Johan Heinrich HOCHWARTER:

sent to me from Sharon Wilcox.
From information received from Tim Conrad. (The info on Johan Heinrich Hochwaerter and family)
Johan Heinrich HOCHWARTER (also spelled HOCHWAERTER) was born in Germany died in Thaleischweiler, Zweibrucken, Germany. He married before 1710 in Germany.
The information on Christian and Juliana Howerter was gotten from Quitophilia Hill church records, Old Jerusalem cemetary records, IGI (index from LDS), and various records from Lebanon Co., PA.
John and Nancy (Weirich) Hovarter records are from various sources, including DeKalb Co. IN History, cemetary records at Fairfield Center cemetary, DeKalb co., IN, census records, Wayne co., OH wills, and many other family members and researchers who are researching these same families.
The information on Henry Hovarter family came in large part from my own research, which included the records from the family Bible which the William Hovarter family has, and personal interviews with family members of the William Hovarter family in Burr Oak Michigan and with my Aunt Nina Barnett who has been a really great help. Ron Hovarter contributed much of the Reinoehl information. I also received information from George W. Page.
I have also received more information on the Hochwaerter, Howerter, Hovatter, Hovarter family from Edgar Hovarter of Oklahoma in February 2000. He had much information from Ghlee Howerter, Cuba, Illinois. Ghlee had hired a researcher in Germany to research the family. Edgar has the original documents that Ghlee received from the German researcher. This included church records, and other documents. The researcher was archivist, Dr. Eager. He was an archivist at Speyer, Germany.
Some of the various spellings of the name were:
Hohwerder, Hochwerter, Huberter, Howarter, Hoberter, Howarter, Oberter, Howerter, Hochwerder, Hovarter, Hochwarter, Hoverter, Hovater, Hobarter, Hovatter, and Hochwaerter.

The earliest known ancestor (as of Feb. 2000), Heinrich Hochwaerter, was born about 1678 possibly in Switzerland. Proof: Research done on the Howerter Family by Ghlee Howerter. Heinrich died 25 May 1763 in Thaleisweiler, Germany. Proof was the Lutheran Church Record...(Edgar Hovarter has the copy of this record). Heinrich Hochwaerter was a baker.

Transcript from the Lutheran Church Register of the Parish of Thaleischweiler:
Book # 2, Deaths, year 1763
Number 16: Heinrich Howereter
widow; former spouse A. Maria
died May 25, Saturday, and is buried here.
85 years old.
This is certified by:
Johann Peter Morion, the daughter's husband and
Anna Barbara Morion, daughter (handsign)

Notes for ANNA MARIA ZEILNERIN:
Notes for Anna Maria ZEILNERIN:
Transcript from the Lutheran Church Register of the Parish of Thaleischweiler:
Book # 4, year 1749
13. A. Maria, Heinrich Howerter, wife of this citizen, died on August 30 and was buried on the 31st.
63 years old.
This is certified by:
Heinrich Howerter, spouse
Johan Georg Howerter, son
Anna Barbara (initialed), daughter

This information was given to me by:
William L. Powell
609 Brier Drive
Olathe, Kansas 66061
He received it from Ghlee Hovarter who had hired a researcher in Germany to research the Howerter family.

More About Anna Maria ZEILNERIN:
Burial: 31 August 1749, Thaleischweiler, Zweibrucken, Germany

The above information was sent to me by Sharon Wilcox.

More About ANNA MARIA ZEILNERIN:
Burial: August 31, 1749

Children of JOHAN HOCHWARTER and ANNA ZEILNERIN are:

i. ANNA MARGARETHA[2] HOHWERTER, b. Abt. 1702.
ii. JOHN JACOB HOHWERTER, b. February 17, 1703/04, Evangelisch, Marnhiem, Pfalz, Bayern.
2. iii. JOHANN VALENTIN HOHWERTER, b. Abt. 1710, Thaleischweiler, Zweibrucken, Pfalz, Germany; d. February 28, 1747/48, Montgomery, New Hanover.
iv. JOHAN GEORGE HOHWERTER, b. Abt. 1712, Thaleischweiler, Zweibrucken, Germany; m. BARBARA BRADA, Germany.

Notes for JOHAN GEORGE HOHWERTER:
Notes for Johan George HOHWERDER:
George served in the military in Germany. He was a Corporal of the Greniader Guard of Pirmasens.
Information from Ghlee Howerter of Cuba, Illinois who had research done in Germany by a professional researcher.

v. ANNA BARBARA HOHWERTER, b. 1714; m. JOHANN PETER MORION, Germany.

Generation No. 2

2. JOHANN VALENTIN[2] HOHWERTER *(JOHAN HEINRICH[1] HOCHWARTER)* was born Abt. 1710 in Thaleischweiler, Zweibrucken, Pfalz, Germany, and died February 28, 1747/48 in Montgomery, New Hanover. He married ANNA CHRISTINA HUETTENMEYER October 18, 1736 in Thaleiscweiler, Zweibrucken, Germany, daughter of LORENTZ HUETTENMEYER and SUSANNA MUGLER. She was born 1709 in Neuensten, Hohenlohe, Germany, and died 1760 in New Hanover, Montgomery Co. PA.

Notes for JOHANN VALENTIN HOHWERTER:
Notes for Johann Valentin (Sr.) HOHWERDER:
see Gen. Soc. of PA,XII :3, pg, 231.
Sent to me from Sharon Wilcox
He immigrated on 12 October 1741from Thaleschweler, Germany to PA sailing from Rotterdam on the ship "Friendship". He died in Chester Co. PA, and is buried in Falckner Swamp Church, cemetary, New Hanover Twp.

Montgomery Co. PA. He was a baker by trade.
Note: there are several variable spellings on the surname.
Information on Valetin can be found in Pennsylvania German Pioneers, by Ralph Beaver Strassburger, LLD., Vol. 1, 1727-1775, page 307.
He signed Oath of Allegiance to Crown 12 October 1741, and his signature is recorded in Pennsylvania Pioneers by Strasburger. Tradition has it that they settled near Hummelstown, PA. He was one of the Palatines imported in the ship "Friendship". Proof may be found on pages 148-149 of " A collection of Upwards of Thirty Thousand Names of German, Swiss, Dutch and French, and Other Immigrants in PA from 1727-1776 by Prof. I. Daniel Rupp, Baltimore Genealogical Publishing Co., 1965.

He was age 31. Proof: Penn. German Pioneers, by Ralph Beaver Strassburger, LLD, Vol. 1, 1727-1775. Second Printing, Gen. Pub. Co. Baltimore 1975. [age 307, list 86a.

His death was recorded in the New Hanover Lutheran Church records, New Hanover, PA. Valentin, resided in Heimestelle Pfalz Kaiserlautern, Germany. Although it has not been documented, the records, his marriage and taufsheins, (baptisimal records) of there children were all included in the archives of the Lutheran Church at Speyer, Germany. These records atate that he was the local baker and his wife was the daughter of Lorentz Huttenmeyer, the high Count of Neuenstein in the Hohenlohischen district. Valentin and his wife lived in this area is supported by the fact that numerous passengers on the ship to America were from this same area. His name was lissted as Valentin Hochwarter in one reference and also as Valentin Huberter in another. They came to America with three children.

Ship Friendship date is 10/12/1741

More About Johann Valentin (Sr.) HOHWERDER:
Burial: Falckner Swamp Church Cemetery, New Hanover Twp., Montgomery Co., PA

Notes for ANNA CHRISTINA HUETTENMEYER:
Notes for Anna Christina HUETTENMEYER:
Anna immigrated from Germany with her husband, on 12 October 1741 to PA ("Friendship") Her name can be found in Meiser's burial records.

A copy of the PA German Church records, Gen. Publ. Co. 1983, Vol 1, Montgomery Co. PA, Trappe Augustus Evangelical Lutheran Church pages 352,353,355,360 shows the her name as Anna Christina.

Anna Christina's christening record was 8 May 1709 in Neuenstein, Jagstkreis, Wuerttemberg

Marriage Notes for Johann HOHWERDER and Anna HUETTENMEYER:
Transcript from the Lutheran Church Register of the Parish of Thaleischweiler:
Marriages: year 1736

Johann Valentin Hochwarter, bachelor baker
son of Johann Heinrich Hochwarter,
married today, 18 October
A. Christina, daughter of Lorentz Huttenmeyer, from Neuenstein
under jurisdiction of the high count of Hohenlohe.

The above information was given to me by:
William L. Powell
609 Brier Drive
Olathe, Kansas 66061
He received it from Ghlee Howerter.

The above information was sent to me Sharon Wilcox.

More About ANNA CHRISTINA HUETTENMEYER:
Burial: Falckner Swamp Church

Children of JOHANN HOHWERTER and ANNA HUETTENMEYER are:

i. PHILIPP NIKEL[3] HOHWERTER, b. October 1736, Thaleischweiler, Zweibrucken, Germany; d. Aft. 1768, Pa; m. ELISABETH SCHIFFLER, December 06, 1768, Reading, Berks Co. PA.

Notes for PHILIPP NIKEL HOHWERTER:
Notes for Philipp Nikel HOHWERDER:
from Bulletin of Historical Society of Montgomer Co., PA, Vol 30, No. 3, Fall 1996: Owen Evans Records (servants).
pg 233. 28 November 1748. Nicholas Howerter unto Jacob Lonacre to serve him 8 years and 11 months, and said Jacob to pay unto his mother Ann Howerter or her exers sum of 20 shillings every year (9 pounds during his life) and master to pay his servant 6 pounds when free, 2 sote (suit) of apparel and a new hoe ax mall and wedges.
(Note: if the dates are correct Nicholas would have only been 12 years old at this time. This was after his father's death and his mother probably did not have the money to support her children.)
Some records have his name as Phillip Nikel and some Phillip Nicholas.

Transcript from the Lutheran Church Register of the Parish of Thaleischweiler (Germany):
Book # 4, page 10 year 1736
32. Phillip Nicol. born August 24th
The father is Valentin Hochwarther, local baker,
the mother is Anna Christina:
baptism was on the August 28 (22nd Sunday after Trinity)
witnesses:
1. Nicolaus Weber, local
2. Ott Phillip Geyer, bachelor schoolmaster from Mabweiler
3. Maria Catherina Weberin, housekeeper of Mattias Dielen, local
Signed: Valentin Hohwerder, father of the child
Michael Weber, witness
Ott Phillip Geyer, witness
Maria Catherine Weberin, godmother (hand sign)

The above transcript was given to me by:
William L. Powell
609 Brier Drive
Olathe, Kansas 66061
He received it from Ghlee Howerter.

The above information was given to me by Sharon Wilcox.

Notes for ELISABETH SCHIFFLER:
Notes for Elisabeth SCHIFFLER:
Her last name has been spelled Schiffer in some records.

Marriage Notes for Philipp HOHWERDER and Elisabeth SCHIFFLER:
They were married by Rev. Waldschmidt

3. ii. JOHAN MICHAEL HOHWERTER, b. August 28, 1738, Thaleischweiler, Zweibrucken, Germany; d. July 11, 1787, Frederick Co. MD.

iii. MARIA MARGARETHA HOHWERTER, b. January 21, 1739/40, Thaleischweiler, Zweibrucken, Germany.

Notes for MARIA MARGARETHA HOHWERTER:
Notes for Maria Margaretha HOHWERDER:
Transcript from the Lutheran Church Register of the Parish of Thaleischweiler;
Book # 4, page 66, page 1740 (Baptism book)
1. Maria Margaretha
born January 21.
The father is Johan Valentine Hochwarther, the local baker,
the mother is A. Christina, brought her for baptism on the 24th.
Witnesses, Johann Philipp Diel, local resident and taylor master
2. Rosina Maria Wandelina, current pastor here,
3. Anna Margaretha, wife of the local miller, Johann Leonhardt Flosser.
This is certified by Johann Phillip Diehl,
Valentin Hohwerder, the father of the child,

Rosina Wandelina Maria Rauschin.

The above information was given to me by:
William L. Powell
609 Brier Drive
Olathe, Kansas 66061
He got the information from Ghlee Hovarter, another researcher who had hired a researcher in Germany to research the family.

The above information was sent to me by Sharon Wilcox.

4. iv. JOHAN ADAM HOHWERTER, b. September 02, 1742, Chester Co. PA; d. December 06, 1819, Upper Mahoney Twp, Northumberland Co. PA.
5. v. JOHANN GEORGE HOHWERTER, b. February 02, 1743/44, Chester Co. PA; d. July 26, 1835, Annville, Lebanon Co. PA.
vi. VALENTIN HOHWERTER, b. April 20, 1746, New Hanover, Montgomery Co. Pa.

Notes for VALENTIN HOHWERTER:
Notes for Valentine (Jr.) HOHWERDER:
He was baptized on 11 October 1746 in Falckner Swamp church, New Hanover Twp., Montgomery Co. PA. Some records have his name spelled Valentin. He owned land in 1770 in PA. Deed Abstract book A-M 1729-1770, 7 July 1777. He served in the military in Lancaster Co., PA. Master roll of 2nd class 3d Battle Lancaster Co. Mil's on a tour of duty at Lancaster for the purpose of guard of British prisoners. The person who served their tour was private Valentine Hovarter, Lancaster co., 21 August 1781.
(Penn. Archives 5 Ser., Vol. 7 page 249)

vii. ELISABETH HOHWERTER, b. January 25, 1747/48, New Hanover, Montgomery Co. Pa; d. Aft. 1761, Pa.

Notes for ELISABETH HOHWERTER:
Notes for Elisabeth HOHWERDER:
It appears that Elisabeth's father passed away shortly after she was born. She was baptized on 14 March 1748 in Falckner Swamp Church, New Hanover Twp., Montgomery Co. PA. She was confirmed on 1 June 1760 in Augustus Evangelical Lutheran Church, Trappe, New Providence Twp. Montgomery Co. PA.

Generation No. 3

3. JOHAN MICHAEL[3] HOHWERTER *(JOHANN VALENTIN[2], JOHAN HEINRICH[1] HOCHWARTER)* was born August 28, 1738 in Thaleischweiler, Zweibrucken, Germany, and died July 11, 1787 in Frederick Co. MD. He married MARIA CATHERINE PIDGEON July 02, 1764 in Swedes Church, Phila. PA.

Notes for JOHAN MICHAEL HOHWERTER:
Notes for Johan Michael HOHWERDER:
sent to me from Sharon Wilcox
The last name of this family is spelled Hochwaerter on many of the early records including the records in Germany.
Michael emigrated from Germany on 12 October 1741 along with his father and mother. He resided in or near Elizabethtown, Lancaster Co., PA. Where the birth of his daughter, Maria Magdalena is recorded in the church there as a baptism 4 November 1770. The records of Anna Margaretha, Michael, Jacob, and Anna Catherina are found in the Evangelical Lutheran church records. Also in the church records is the marriage of Margaretha Hochwaerther to Heinrich Cox, and the death of Michael Sr. and Jr. Michael Sr. died of high fever the 11th of July 1787(midnight) at the age of 49 years. He signed a will on 11 July 1787 in Frederick Co., Maryland. From LDS Files #014019, Frederick Co., Maryland wills - 1783-1794, pages 246-247.

(his will reads as follows:)
In the Name of God Amen. I Michael Hohwairte of Frederick County and State of Maryland being now in a

sick and weakly condition; tho of perfect mind and memory (praised be God for it)., Do make and ordain this my Last Will and Testament; That is to say: After my Debts are all Paid, My will and desire is that my Beloved Wife Catharina have and possess the full third third part of my Estate, real and personal during her Natural Life is to say, her Residence in the house during her life. The remaining two thirds to be equally divided among my eight children, equal parts. Moreover I will and desire that my house and lott shall be enjoyed and possessed by such one of my children (after their Mother's decease) as shall be able to satisfy their Brother or Sisters for their prospective shares, but if none of them shall be able, then it shall be sold to the Greatest Advantage and the return or price thereof equally shared among them as aforementioned. And I do hereby nominate and appoint my beloved wife Catharine sole Executrix of this my Last Will and Testament which alone I do ratify and confirm as such revoking and disannulling all former Wills, Legaoies, and bequests by me heretofore make left or Bequeaths. In Witness whereof I have hereunto set my hand Seal this Eleventh day of July ammo Dmini Seventeen hundred and eighty-seven.

Signed, sealed pronounced and declared by the Testator
in our presence who subscribed their names in his presence and in that of each other
Christian Geimert
Henry Cronise
Edward Salmon

Michael Hohwairte
(his mark)

Frederick County, Maryland August 11, 1787

Then came Catharine Hohwairter and make Oath that the aforegoing Instrument of Writing is the True and whole will and testament of Michael Hohwairter Late of Frederick County Deceased that hath come to her hands and possession and that she doth not know of any other.

George Murdock Reg.

Then came Christian Geimert and Henry Cronise two of the Subscribing witnesses to the aforegoing Last will and testament of Michael Hohwairter late of Frederick County deceased and make oath that they did see the testator therein named sign and seal this will that they heard him publish, pronounce and declare the same to be his Last Will and Testament that at the time of his so doing he was the best of their apprehension of a sound and disposing mind memory and understanding that they respectively subscribed their names as witnesses to this will in the presence and at the request of the testator and that they did also see Edward Salmon the other subscribing Witness wign his name as witness thereto in the presence and at the request of the Testator and all in the presence of each other.

George Murdock, Reg.

He is buried in Gods Acre Cemetery, Maryland.
This couple had 2 sons and a daughter who died young. They had a total of 11 children, 5 boys and 6 girls.

The following is a transcript from the Lutheran Church Register of the Parish of Thaleischweiler (Germany):
Book # 4, page 41, year 1738
No. 23 Johann MIchel was born on the 28th of August by A. Christina, wife of Valentin Hochwarter, the baker, and was baptized on the 1st of September.
Witnesses: Johann Lenhardt Flosser, bachelor, miller & doctor in Schriessheim, born in Heydelberg, Palatinate.
2. Michael Ehregott Rausch, pastor; 3. A. Margaretha Peter Matthils, daughter of resident miller here, former unwed daughter, witness to marriage of above mentioned
Johann Leonhardt Flosser
Valentine Hohwerder, father of the child
Michael Ehregott Rausch, witness
Johann Leonhardt Flosser, witness
Anna Margaretha Mattilin, godmother

The above church information from Germany was given to me by:

William L. Powell
609 Brier Drive
Olathe, Kansas 66061
He originally received the information from Ghlee Howerter.

More About Johan Michael HOHWERDER:
Burial: 12 July 1787, Frederick, Maryland, Gods Acre Cemetery

More About JOHAN MICHAEL HOHWERTER:
Burial: Gods Acre Cemetery MD

Notes for MARIA CATHERINE PIDGEON:
Notes for Maria Catharine PIDGEON:
Maria may have been a widow and Pidgeon may not have been her maiden name.

Children of JOHAN HOHWERTER and MARIA PIDGEON are:

i. GEORGE[4] HOVATTER.
ii. UNKNOWN HOVATTER.
6. iii. CHRISTOPHER HOVATTER, b. May 12, 1762, Pa; d. September 12, 1859, Barbour Co. WVA.
iv. ANNA MARIA HOWERTER/ HOVATTER, b. 1766, Lancaster Co., PA; m. JACOB HALLER, May 09, 1790, Frederick Co., Maryland; b. January 11, 1769, Frederick Co. MD; d. May 12, 1807, Frederick Co. MD.

Notes for ANNA MARIA HOWERTER/ HOVATTER:
Notes for Anna Maria HOWERTER:
Anna was baptized on 13 April 1783 in Frederick Co., Maryland. From LDS Film # 139333. She was confirmed at the Evangelical Lutheran Church.

Notes for JACOB HALLER:
More About Jacob HALLER:
Burial: 13 May 1807, God's acre Cemetery, Evangelical Lutheran Church, Frederick Co. MD

Marriage Notes for Anna HOWERTER and Jacob HALLER:
Witnesses: Michael Haller, Maria Hochwaerter, Johannes Theodore Peter, Georg Kaufmann.

More About JACOB HALLER:
Burial: May 13, 1807, Gods Acre Cemetery MD

v. ANNA HOVATTER, b. 1768, Lancaster Co., PA.
vi. MARIA MAGDALINA HOHWERTER/ HOVATTER, b. August 19, 1770, Lancaster Co., PA.
vii. ANNA MARGARETHA HOWERTER/ HOVATTER, b. March 13, 1774.
viii. MICHAEL HOWERTER HOVATTER, b. December 01, 1775, Frederick Co. MD; d. April 12, 1793, Frederick Co. MD.

Notes for MICHAEL HOWERTER HOVATTER:
Notes for Michael HOWERTER:
Michael was baptized on 8 April 1776. Frederick Co., Maryland. Baptism was at Evangelical Lutheran Church with Georg Michael Haller and his wife Maria Dorothea as his sponsors. He died on 12 April 1793 in Frederick Co., Maryland. His death notice was written as follows:
1793 April 12, Friday - Son of Mihhail Hochwaeter and his wife Catharina, Born 1 Dec 1775. For four and one half years he was an apprentice with Mr. Thomas Hickman in order to learn Shoemaker, Hand work. He died of an infection April 11 at 1:30 P.M. aged 17years 4 months 10 days.

ix. JACOB HOVATTER, b. September 17, 1777, Frederick Co. MD.
x. ANNA CATHARINA HOWERTER/ HOVATTER, b. December 19, 1782, Frederick Co. MD.

Notes for ANNA CATHARINA HOWERTER/ HOVATTER:
Notes for Anna Catharina HOWERTER:
Anna was baptized on 19 October 1783 in Frederick Co., Maryland, Evangelical Lutheran Church with Anna Catharina Ilgnern (?) as sponsor

4. JOHAN ADAM[3] HOHWERTER *(JOHANN VALENTIN[2], JOHAN HEINRICH[1] HOCHWARTER)* was born September 02, 1742 in Chester Co. PA, and died December 06, 1819 in Upper Mahoney Twp, Northumberland Co. PA. He married CATHERINE KROHN April 30, 1764 in Mertz Church, Rockland Twp, Berks Co. PA, daughter of MARTIN KROHN. She was born December 12, 1748 in Germany, and died April 23, 1819 in Upper Mahoney Twp, Northumberland Co. PA.

Notes for JOHAN ADAM HOHWERTER:
Notes for Johan Adam HOHWERDER:
Johan Adam was baptized on 3 October 1742 in Augustus Evangelical lutheran Church, Trappe, New Providence Twp., Montgomery Co., PA. Trappe Records Faulkner Swamp Church by Balentin Kraft, minister. Sponsors were Johan Adam Kunzel, Anna Dorthea Widrigin. (This area of Montogomery Co., was then a part of Chester Co. His tombstone says he was born in Chester Co.) He took the U.S. Oath on 5 May 1778 in Macungie Twp., Lehigh Co., PA. He served in the military on 10 May 1780 in Ens, Rev. War, 1st Bn, 8th Co., Berks Co., Militia (PAA 5:5, 168). He bought land in 1784 in Longswamp Twp., Berks Co., PA (51 A, 40 p, deed 11:75). He bought land on 16 January 1784 in Longswamp Twp., Berks Co. PA (95 A, 171p, deed 11:73) He sold land on 3 March 1792 in Longswamp Twp., Berks Co., PA (84 A, 98p, deed 12:321?) He entered an agreement on 23 March 1792 in Longswamp Twp., Berks co., PA (deed 12:468) He migrated about 1795 to Upper Mahoney Twp., Northumberland Co., PA. He sold land on 3 April 1795 in Longswamp twp., Berks Co., PA (14 A, deed 14:293 and 15:199) He bought land on 10 April 1795 in Upper Mahoney Twp., Northumberland Co., PA (deed 2:171) , He sold land 6 April 1812 in Upper Mahoney Twp., Northumberland Co., PA (deed R:99). He was a farmer, cordwainer (shoemaker), grist miller, saw miller. 1st Bn Berks County Militia, 8th Co., Ensign (PAA 5:5, 168 10 May 1780. He was listed in the book "Soldiers of the Revolution" by Maurer, page 162, as Ensign Adam Howarter, 8th Company, 1st Battalion; PA Archives, 5th Series, Captain Richstein's Company.

Some say he was a Hessian soldier joining USA, but it is the strong belief of others that he was born in Chester Co., PA.

Johan Adam Hohwerder and his wife, Catherine, had ten children, all christened in the Longswamp Church.

US Oath 56:212
DAR application 761461 (via son Heinrich)

A will signed November 29th,1819, by Adam Howerter, Saldin Paul and Peter Yoder, states "I, the Subscriber acknowledge that this is my earnest will, that my two sons Adam and Peter Howerter as Administers shall divide all my goods amongst my Children in equal parts. After my death they shall let all my loose goods be appraised, and made vendue and make the money in equal shares except what my burying expenses are. They shall be paid before hand, but Elizabeth or her children shall have her share, and that shall also be divided amongst them in equal shares. She has yet to receive L28.0,6 till she has received one hundred Pounds but this would be my wish, that none of my children should go to Law, which I sign with my hand by witness and seal."
Also, part of this is Adam's agreement with his son Peter in Deed R:99. It mentions the exchange of the plantation for care in Adam's (and his wife's) old age. In settling the financials, Adam mentions Adam "to give of his children one hundred pounds while he lives". . and goes on to mention splitting the remainder amongst the rest of the children.

More About Johan Adam HOHWERDER:
Burial: Howerter's Church Cemetery, Upper Mahoney Twp., Northumberland Co., PA

The above information was sent to me by Sharon Wilcox.

Notes for CATHERINE KROHN:

Notes for Catherine KROHN:
She was baptized and confirmed at Lehigh Church 25 April 1785, although it is said that she was born in Europe.

More About Catherine KROHN:
Burial: Howerter's church Cemetery, Upper Mahoney Twp., Northumberland Co., PA

More About CATHERINE KROHN:
Burial: Upper Mahoney Twp, Northumberland Co. PA

Children of JOHAN HOHWERTER and CATHERINE KROHN are:

- i. HIENRICH[4] HOHWERTER, b. January 27, 1768; d. May 13, 1838, Berks Co. PA.
- ii. JOHAN ADAM HOHWERTER, b. August 24, 1769, Berks Co. PA; d. April 14, 1847, Northumberland Co. PA.
- iii. JOHAN PETER HOHWERTER, b. November 04, 1772, Berks Co. PA; d. May 06, 1862, Upper Mahoney Twp, Northumberland Co. PA.
- iv. CATHERINE HOHWERTER, b. March 29, 1775.
- v. SALOME HOHWERTER, b. September 27, 1776, Berks Co. PA; d. 1797.
- vi. SARAH HOHWERTER, b. 1778.
- vii. MARIA ELIZABETH HOHWERTER, b. July 27, 1778, Berks Co. PA; d. Aft. 1818; m. MR. SPIES.
- viii. CHRISTINA HOHWERTER, b. 1780, Berks Co. PA; d. 1848.
- ix. SUSANNE HOHWERTER, b. March 30, 1782; d. 1850, Coal Twp. Northumberland, PA.
- x. JOHANNES HOHWERTER, b. May 31, 1783, Berks Co. PA; d. Bef. 1790, Longswamp Twp. Berks PA.
- xi. ANNA MARIA HOHWERTER, b. August 08, 1786, Berks Co. PA; d. February 11, 1860, Northumberland Co. PA.

5. JOHANN GEORGE[3] HOHWERTER *(JOHANN VALENTIN[2], JOHAN HEINRICH[1] HOCHWARTER)* was born February 02, 1743/44 in Chester Co. PA, and died July 26, 1835 in Annville, Lebanon Co. PA. He married MAGDALENA (MOLLY) SCHIFFER Abt. 1770 in Lancaster, PA, daughter of GEORGE SCHIFFER. She was born Abt. 1750, and died 1834 in Annville, Lebanon Co. PA.

Children of JOHANN HOHWERTER and MAGDALENA SCHIFFER are:

- i. GEORGE[4] HOHWERTER.
- 7. ii. CHRISTIAN HOHWERTER, b. April 12, 1772.
- iii. UNKNOWN HOHWERTER, b. Abt. 1773.
- iv. UNKNOWN HOHWERTER, b. 1785.
- v. UNKNOWN HOHWERTER, b. 1787.
- vi. WILLIAM HOHWERTER, b. Abt. 1790.
- vii. UNKNOWN HOHWERTER, b. Abt. 1800.

Generation No. 4

6. CHRISTOPHER[4] HOVATTER *(JOHAN MICHAEL[3] HOHWERTER, JOHANN VALENTIN[2], JOHAN HEINRICH[1] HOCHWARTER)* was born May 12, 1762 in Pa, and died September 12, 1859 in Barbour Co. WVA. He married CATHERINE SPENDGLER 1795 in PA.. She was born Bet. 1764 - 1769 in Pa, and died 1859 in Barbour Co. WVA.

Notes for CHRISTOPHER HOVATTER:
A variation of the name is Howerter, Christopher is shown with both spellings.

Children of CHRISTOPHER HOVATTER and CATHERINE SPENDGLER are:

- 8. i. SARA JANE[5] HOVATTER, b. Bet. 1790 - 1798.
- ii. JACOB HOVATTER, b. November 02, 1796, Frederick Co. MD; d. Bef. 1810.
- 9. iii. GEORGE MICHAEL HOVATTER, b. October 05, 1799, Frederick Co. MD; d. January 31, 1875.
- iv. ELIZABETH HOVATTER, b. 1801, Pa; d. July 23, 1859.
- v. JOHN HOVATTER, b. October 08, 1803, Fayette Co. Pa; d. September 08, 1863; m. NANCY HARDIN, February 02, 1860; b. April 07, 1821, Mongalia Co. VA; d. July 09, 1906.

  Notes for JOHN HOVATTER:
  There is reference that John Hovatter was married the first time before 1860. Nancy Hardin was his second wife.

Notes for NANCY HARDIN:
There is reference that Nancy Hardin was widowed and Hardin was her married name, also that she is the second wife of John Hovatter.

10. vi. ANDREW HOVATTER, b. 1804, va.
11. vii. HENRY HOVATTER, b. 1806.
12. viii. DAVID HOVATTER, b. 1810, Barbour co.; d. 1881.
13. ix. WILLIAM HOVATTER, b. 1816.

7. CHRISTIAN^4 HOHWERTER *(JOHANN GEORGE^3, JOHANN VALENTIN^2, JOHAN HEINRICH^1 HOCHWARTER)* was born April 12, 1772. He married JULIANNA CARMONY.

Child of CHRISTIAN HOHWERTER and JULIANNA CARMONY is:
14. i. JOHANNES^5 HOWERTER.

Generation No. 5

8. SARA JANE^5 HOVATTER *(CHRISTOPHER^4, JOHAN MICHAEL^3 HOHWERTER, JOHANN VALENTIN^2, JOHAN HEINRICH^1 HOCHWARTER)* was born Bet. 1790 - 1798. She married PETER WILT. He was born Bet. 1790 - 1799 in MD.

Child of SARA HOVATTER and PETER WILT is:
15. i. PETER^6 WILT, b. 1819.

9. GEORGE MICHAEL^5 HOVATTER *(CHRISTOPHER^4, JOHAN MICHAEL^3 HOHWERTER, JOHANN VALENTIN^2, JOHAN HEINRICH^1 HOCHWARTER)* was born October 05, 1799 in Frederick Co. MD, and died January 31, 1875. He married (1) BARBARA SHROYER March 09, 1824. She was born December 12, 1791, and died December 07, 1847. He married (2) CATHARINE LOHR August 21, 1847 in Barbour Co.. She was born November 26, 1811 in Rockingham Co. VA, and died May 16, 1879.

Notes for GEORGE MICHAEL HOVATTER:
Was also known as George Michael Hovatter.

Children of GEORGE HOVATTER and BARBARA SHROYER are:
i. JACOB^6 HOVATTER.
ii. DAVID HOVATTER, b. Abt. 1821; d. Abt. 1840.
16. iii. MELKER HOVATTER, b. January 15, 1826, Randolph Co. Va; d. 1900, Barbour Co. WVA.

10. ANDREW^5 HOVATTER *(CHRISTOPHER^4, JOHAN MICHAEL^3 HOHWERTER, JOHANN VALENTIN^2, JOHAN HEINRICH^1 HOCHWARTER)* was born 1804 in va. He married ELIZABETH WILSON August 31, 1821. She was born Abt. 1802.

Children of ANDREW HOVATTER and ELIZABETH WILSON are:
i. ELIZABETH^6 HOVATTER, b. Abt. 1832.
ii. JACKSON HOVATTER, b. Abt. 1834.
iii. BASSIL HOVATTER, b. Abt. 1837.
iv. ANDREW JACOB HOVATTER, b. Abt. 1840; m. ELIZABETH SATTERFIELD, July 15, 1867.

11. HENRY^5 HOVATTER *(CHRISTOPHER^4, JOHAN MICHAEL^3 HOHWERTER, JOHANN VALENTIN^2, JOHAN HEINRICH^1 HOCHWARTER)* was born 1806. He married RACHEL KITTLE August 08, 1831 in Randolph Co. WVA (VA). She was born Abt. 1811.

Marriage Notes for HENRY HOVATTER and RACHEL KITTLE:
Another noted marriage date is May 8, 1831, posslibly a 5 and 8 could be mistaken.

Children of HENRY HOVATTER and RACHEL KITTLE are:

i. JOHN J.[6] HOVATTER.
ii. LOUSIA HOVATTER.
iii. ISAAC HOVATTER, b. Abt. 1832.
iv. CHRISTOPHER HOVATTER, b. Abt. 1835.
v. HARRIET HOVATTER, b. October 13, 1838.
vi. JACOB HOVATTER, b. Abt. 1840.
vii. VIRGINIA HOVATTER, b. Abt. 1843.

12. DAVID[5] HOVATTER *(CHRISTOPHER[4], JOHAN MICHAEL[3] HOHWERTER, JOHANN VALENTIN[2], JOHAN HEINRICH[1] HOCHWARTER)[1]* was born 1810 in Barbour co., and died 1881. He married SARAH ANN THOMPSON September 14, 1835 in Randolph Co. WVA, daughter of HESAKIAH THOMPSON.

Children of DAVID HOVATTER and SARAH THOMPSON are:
17. i. CORA JANE[6] HOVATTER, b. October 05, 1876, Tucker Wv; d. March 28, 1948, Clarksburg, Harrison, WV.
ii. HENRY HOVATTER, m. OZELLA LIPSCOMB, August 27, 1871, Tucker Co. WVA.
iii. JOHN HOVATTER.
18. iv. HEZEKIAH HOVATTER, b. 1836, Randolph Co. Va; d. 1900.
v. MALINAI JANE HOVATTER, b. 1839.
vi. SUSAN HOVATTER, b. 1841.
vii. MICHAEL HOVATTER, b. 1844.
viii. BENJAMIN HOVATTER, b. 1847.
ix. ANDREW HOVATTER, b. 1849.
19. x. DAVID T. HOVATTER, b. June 15, 1853, Kesson, WV; d. October 31, 1929, Tucker Co.,VA now WV.
xi. ELIZABETH HOVATTER, b. Abt. 1861; m. MAX K. SHAHAN, November 19, 1880, Tucker Co. WVA; b. Abt. 1859.
xii. INGABY HOVATTER, b. Abt. 1863; m. ANDREW J. BALL, March 23, 1883, Tucker Co. WVA; b. Abt. 1860.

13. WILLIAM[5] HOVATTER *(CHRISTOPHER[4], JOHAN MICHAEL[3] HOHWERTER, JOHANN VALENTIN[2], JOHAN HEINRICH[1] HOCHWARTER)* was born 1816. He married CLARISSA KITTLE.

Notes for CLARISSA KITTLE:
Better known as Clara.

Children of WILLIAM HOVATTER and CLARISSA KITTLE are:
i. GEORGE M.[6] HOVATTER, m. MARY JANE NESTOR, December 10, 1868.
ii. ISAAC HOVATTER, b. Abt. 1854; m. EMILY C. LIPSCOMB, December 10, 1880; b. Abt. 1860.
iii. HENRY B. HOVATTER, b. Abt. 1856; m. JENNIE BELLE, September 02, 1882.

Notes for JENNIE BELLE:
Listed in WV Marriage as Jennie Belle Herman

20. iv. CATHERINE HOVATTER, b. Abt. 1851.
v. JACOB HOVATTER, b. 1862; m. MARY E. LOUGHRY; b. 1871.

14. JOHANNES[5] HOWERTER *(CHRISTIAN[4] HOHWERTER, JOHANN GEORGE[3], JOHANN VALENTIN[2], JOHAN HEINRICH[1] HOCHWARTER)* He married NANCY WEIRICH.

Child of JOHANNES HOWERTER and NANCY WEIRICH is:
21. i. HENRY[6] HOVARTER.

Generation No. 6

15. PETER[6] WILT *(SARA JANE[5] HOVATTER, CHRISTOPHER[4], JOHAN MICHAEL[3] HOHWERTER, JOHANN VALENTIN[2], JOHAN HEINRICH[1] HOCHWARTER)* was born 1819. He married CATHERINE WILSON 1839. She was born 1819.

Children of PETER WILT and CATHERINE WILSON are:
i. MARY M.[7] WILT, b. February 12, 1840.

>>>> acknowledge those who
>>>> put their life on the line and esp. recognize who
>>>> made the ultimate call to
>>>> duty.
>>>>
>>>> perhaps you are related to a former classmate of
>>>> mine- Scotty Hovatter.
>>>> Scotty was a great guy who helped me going through
>>>> some awkward teen years
>>>> at Parsons.
>>>> mary on the mtn.top
>>>> ----- Original Message -----
>>>> From: <hskids@mikrotec.com>
>>>> To: <wvtucker@rootsweb.com>
>>>> Sent: Wednesday, August 22, 2007 8:19 AM
>>>> Subject: [WVTUCKER] Sheriff O. Gay Hovatter
>>>>
>>>>
>>>> > It is good to see messages on the Tucker County
>>>> site. I want to share a
>>>> > little history regarding a former Sheriff and
>>>> distant relative of mine by
>>>> > pasting this from a website,
>>>> http://www.odmp.org/officer.php?oid=6736
>>>> >
>>>> > Perhaps others are connected to the Hovatter
>>>> family. My connection was
>>>> > through my Grandmother, Mary E. (Ball) Skidmore
>>>> and her Mother, Inaby or
>>>> > Ingeby (Hovatter) Ball. Sheriff Hovatter was her
>>>> Nephew.
>>>> >
>>>> > Thanks, Harry
>>>> >
>>>> >
>>>>
>>> --
>>>> >
>>>> > Sheriff O. Gay Hovatter
>>>> > Tucker County Sheriff's Department
>>>> > West Virginia
>>>> > End of Watch: Monday, September 9, 1946
>>>> >
>>>> > Biographical Info
>>>> > Age: Not available
>>>> > Tour of Duty: Not available
>>>> > Badge Number: Not available
>>>> >
>>>> > Incident Details
>>>> > Cause of Death: Gunfire
>>>> > Date of Incident: Monday, September 9, 1946
>>>> > Weapon Used: Officer's handgun
>>>> > Suspect Info: Executed
>>>> >
>>>> > Sheriff O. Gay Hovatter and Sergeant Joseph Horne,
>>>> of the West Virginia
>>>> > State Police, were shot and killed while arresting
>>>> a man for stealing a
>>>> > coal truck.
>>>> >
>>>> > The officers had served the arrest warrant at the
>>>> man's home and

Ray, You probably didn't mean this David, but as a point of interest, David Hovatter and Sarah Ann (Thompson) Hovatter were the GrandParents of Orpha GAY Hovatter, the slain Sheriff. Gay's parents were John and Mary (Guthrie) Hovatter. I found the following obituary of a Son of Gay Hovatter's on the World Connect Website.

Harry

Donald H. Hovatter

Donald H. Hovatter, age 74, of Lewisburg, died Sunday, January 13, 2002, in Greenbrier Valley Medical Center following an extended illnes
Born March 9, 1927, at Auvil, Tucker County, he was the son of the late O. G. and Grace Grindstaff Hovatter.
A brother, Alan G. Hovatter, also preceded him in death in 200
Mr. Hovatter was a member of the Parkersburg Lutheran Church, and a member of the Lewisburg Lions Club.
He served his country twice, in the U. S. Navy as a Gunner's Mate, Third Class, in World War II, and in the U. S. Air Force as Second Lieutenant, stationed at Patrick Air Force Base in Florida, during the Korean War. He was employed by the U. S. Forest Service as a fire watcher in Tucker County after discharge from the Navy.
A graduate of Potomac State College, he also received a degree in accounting from West Virginia University. Following employment by Price Waterhouse Accounting and Burroughs Corporation, he went with the National Radio Astronomy Observatory at Green Bank, retiring following 26 years of service.
Survivors include his wife of 46 years, Jona Hovatter, of Lewisburg; two daughters, Donna Jo Hinkle, of Lewisburg, and Peggy Ann Hovatter, of McCurdysville; six grandsons; two sisters, Mary Margaret Backoff, of Maryland, and Helen Shafer, of Parsons.
Graveside services will be at 1 p.m. Saturday at the Parsons Cemetery.

> Mary,
> Did I ask you before was sheriff Hovatter related to David Hovatter
> that
> used to live at Bull Run? Ray Harlow
> ----- Original Message -----
> From: "mary" <mamullenax@frontiernet.net>
> To: <wvtucker@rootsweb.com>
> Sent: Sunday, October 28, 2007 9:20 PM
> Subject: Re: [WVTUCKER] Sheriff O. Gay Hovatter
>
>
>> still here in tucker county near parsons. expecting frost tonight.
>> take care
>> ----- Original Message -----
>> From: "Art Grady" <gradya3@yahoo.com>
>> To: <wvtucker@rootsweb.com>
>> Sent: Sunday, October 28, 2007 8:26 AM
>> Subject: Re: [WVTUCKER] Sheriff O. Gay Hovatter
>>
>>
>>> Are you still near Parsons?
>>>
>>> Art Grady
>>>
>>> --- mary <mamullenax@frontiernet.net> wrote:
>>>
>>>> thx for sharing your story of sheriff hovatter.
>>>> so much for sleepy little small towns. It is good to

ii. JOHN H. WILT, b. July 11, 1841.
iii. ABIGAIL WILT, b. November 22, 1843.
iv. GEORGE K. WILT, b. February 1846.
v. WILSON WILT, b. 1848.
vi. SARAH JANE WILT, b. 1851.
vii. VILENA (VIOLENA) WILT, b. 1855.
viii. THOMAS WILT WILT, b. 1856.
ix. ANZINA WILT, b. 1857.

16. MELKER[6] HOVATTER *(GEORGE MICHAEL[5], CHRISTOPHER[4], JOHAN MICHAEL[3] HOHWERTER, JOHANN VALENTIN[2], JOHAN HEINRICH[1] HOCHWARTER)* was born January 15, 1826 in Randolph Co. Va, and died 1900 in Barbour Co. WVA. He married SUSANNA LOHR Abt. 1853 in Barbour Co.. She was born Abt. 1834.

Notes for MELKER HOVATTER:
Other Spelling on Melker Hovatter is Melkes Hovatter.

Children of MELKER HOVATTER and SUSANNA LOHR are:
i. GEORGE M.[7] HOVATTER, b. Abt. 1854, WVa.
ii. CATHERINE HOVATTER, b. Abt. 1857, WVa.
iii. MARY ANN HOVATTER, b. Abt. 1862, WVa.
iv. JAMES W. HOVATTER, b. Abt. 1868, WVa.
v. WAITMAN L. HOVATTER, b. Abt. 1874, WVa.

17. CORA JANE[6] HOVATTER *(DAVID[5], CHRISTOPHER[4], JOHAN MICHAEL[3] HOHWERTER, JOHANN VALENTIN[2], JOHAN HEINRICH[1] HOCHWARTER)* was born October 05, 1876 in Tucker Wv, and died March 28, 1948 in Clarksburg, Harrison, WV. She married REV. GEORGE EMERY SHAHAN April 30, 1891 in Tucker Co. WVA, son of GEORGE SHAHAN and LOUISA HOFFMAN. He was born October 09, 1864 in Rowlesburg, Preston WVA, and died December 18, 1966 in Clarksburg, Harrison, WVA.

Notes for REV. GEORGE EMERY SHAHAN:
Notes for REV. GEORGE EMERY SHAHAN:
[For Jo Ann.FTW]

[AAA NewOne.FTW]

[WFT3719_Vol10.FTW]

There is a picture of Elder G. Emory Shahan at age 100 on page 621 of "Alleghany Passage: Churches and Families" by Emmert F. Bittinger, and the following biography:

"The family lived near Rowlesburg for some years before moving near St. George in Tucker County. There the family lived within the boundary of the Union Chapel (Bull Run) branch of the Shiloh Congregation.

"The eighth child, George Emory Shahan, manifested special talents and an early interest in religion. He bagan a vigorous study [of] the Bible while still in his teens, soon mastering large portions by memory. His obiturary states that he began preaching at age fifteen, which would have been around 1879. The year after his marriage in 1891 to Cora Jane Hovatter, he was ordained to the ministry. He was advanced as an Elder in 1904 and thereupon given charge of the Shiloh Congregation, a position he held until 1907.

"He continued his labor for the Church at Union Chapel, serving as one of the ministers of that branch until his transfer to the Grafton Brethren Church which later became the Grace Brethren Church. He was called as pastor of the Grafton Church, a service which he fufilled for many years. He gave up this work in 1940 and moved to Clarksburg where he has retired.

"Most of his life he served in the free ministry, supporting his family by farming and carpentering. Before moving to Tucker County, he had accumulated a large tract of land, some of which was purchased for as little as $1.65 per acre. Most of the land was sold during an economic depression, and little gain was realized.

"Bro. Shahan was a man of high character and devotion. Much respected and loved by his fourteen children, ost of whom are now deceased, he left a strong impact on his family and those with whom he worked.

"A member of the National Fellowship of Brethren Ministers, he was the oldest member of that organization at the time of his death at the age of 102 in 1966. He still occasionally preached in the last decade of his life. Many will remember the occasion when he preached at the Grafton and Shiloh Churches after he had passed the age of 100. His ministerial work was greatly appreciated and respected."

More About REV. GEORGE EMERY SHAHAN:
Burial: Unknown, Clarksburg, WV2416,2417

Children of CORA HOVATTER and GEORGE SHAHAN are:

- i. WALTER BROWN[7] SHAHAN.
- ii. AGNES SHAHAN, b. October 29, 1892, St. George, Tucker, W; d. September 03, 1986, Clarksburg, Harrison,WVA.
- iii. MINNIE PEARL SHAHAN, b. June 04, 1894, St. George, Tucker, W; d. November 19, 1959.
- iv. DONNA JANE SHAHAN, b. January 29, 1896, St. George, Tucker, WVA; d. January 24, 1972, Kingswood, Preston, WVA.
- v. MARY ELIZABETH SHAHAN, b. September 23, 1897, Hannasville, Tucker, WV; d. November 01, 1918, Hannasville, Tucker, WV.
- vi. DAISY VIRGINIA SHAHAN, b. June 25, 1899, St. George, Tucker, W; d. December 07, 1978, Clarksburg, Harrison, WV.
- vii. FLORA SHAHAN, b. February 07, 1904, Hannasville, Tucker, WV; d. February 07, 1904, Hannasville, Tucker, WV.
- viii. DORA SHAHAN, b. February 07, 1904.
- ix. CHARLES LEE SHAHAN, b. February 1907, Hovatter, Preston, WV; d. May 21, 1971, Clarksburg, Harrison, WV.
- x. CORA LOUISE SHAHAN, b. December 12, 1908, St. George, Tucker, W; d. June 22, 1987, St. Petersburg, FL; m. FLOYD EDWARD SAYRE, January 31, 1931, Clarksburg, Harrison, WV.
- xi. RUBY BESSIE SHAHAN, b. September 14, 1910, St. George, Tucker, W.
- xii. GEORGIA OLETHA SHAHAN, b. December 24, 1912, St. George, Tucker, W; d. July 12, 1975, Clarksburg, Harrison, WV.
- xiii. LILLIAN ANN SHAHAN, b. March 31, 1916, St. George, Tucker, W.
- xiv. VICTORIA ARABELLE SHAHAN, b. February 04, 1919, St. George, Tucker, W.

18. HEZEKIAH[6] HOVATTER *(DAVID[5], CHRISTOPHER[4], JOHAN MICHAEL[3] HOHWERTER, JOHANN VALENTIN[2], JOHAN HEINRICH[1] HOCHWARTER)* was born 1836 in Randolph Co. Va, and died 1900. He married ? Abt. 1881.

Children of HEZEKIAH HOVATTER and ? are:

- i. OLIVE V.[7] HOVATTER, b. Abt. 1872.
- ii. IGERBY A. HOVATTER, b. Abt. 1873.
- 22. iii. ELIAS HOVATTER, b. Abt. 1875.

19. DAVID T.[6] HOVATTER *(DAVID[5], CHRISTOPHER[4], JOHAN MICHAEL[3] HOHWERTER, JOHANN VALENTIN[2], JOHAN HEINRICH[1] HOCHWARTER)[1]* was born June 15, 1853 in Kesson, WV[1], and died October 31, 1929 in Tucker Co.,VA now WV. He married CHRISTINA L. SHAHAN[1] December 23, 1877 in Hannahsville, Tucker Co. WVA[1], daughter of GEORGE SHAHAN and LOUISA HOFFMAN. She was born May 16, 1858 in Sinclair, WV, and died February 02, 1933 in Tucker Co.,WV.

Notes for DAVID T. HOVATTER:

1880 Census Place: Licking, Tucker, West Virginia
Source:FHL Film 1255414 National Archives Film T9-1414 Page 378A
Relation Sex Marr RaceAge Birthplace
D. C. HOVATTER SelfM M W 25 VA
Occ:Laborer Fa: VA Mo: VA
Chrystena L. HOVATTER WifeFM W 22 VA
Occ:Keeping House Fa: VA Mo: VA
Charles HOVATTER Son M SW 1 WV
Fa: VA Mo: VA

Lilley C. HOVATTEROtherFSW 1MWV
Fa: VA Mo: VA

Barbour County Cities, Towns and Settlements
Kasson

According to an account found in Barbour County West Virginiapublished by the Barbour County Historical Society in 1979 Kasson, in Cove District, was first named Danville after the first settler Dan Highly. The hill he lived on, overlooking Kasson is still known as Highly Hill. Mr. Highly raised mulberry trees to feed his silkworms and produced silk thread was put on spools and shipped to Baltimore.

Danville was given the name Kasson because there was another WV Post Office called Danville. The first letter was mailed to a man named Kasson. The first Post Office was establised in 1862. Carr Bishop was the first postmaster. After him, Marion Newman, 1884; Lewis Coffman, 1904; George Coffman served from 1908 till his death in 1930. Hattie Coffman, his wife and two sons, Hayse & George Sherwood took it over until 1937 when Rachel Wilson Ball served till her death.

In the early days of Kasson the community included:
Stores:
Jack Bishop in 1870, John and Ed Compton, 1875; Marion Newman, 1880; Daniel J. Nester, 1890 and Lewis Coffman.

Blacksmith Shops:
David Hovatter, 1860; Ben Ekis in 1864; Albert Loar in 1891; and Lewis Coffman who learned the trade from his uncles Mike and Lige Coffman who had shops in Valley Furnace, Belington and Elkins. His first shop was near West Point

Churches:
The Kasson United Methodist Church, built in 1898. Daniel Nestor and Daniel Lohr were overseers.
The Church of the Brethren, David Hovatter had the Communion and Love Feast in his house, this was the beginning of the Shiloh Church of the Brethren which was organized in 1845 about 1 ½ miles from Kasson.

More About DAVID T. HOVATTER:
Burial: Preston Co. WV

Children of DAVID HOVATTER and CHRISTINA SHAHAN are:

23. i. CHARLES E.[7] HOVATTER, b. October 11, 1878.
ii. LELLIE C. HOVATTER[1], b. April 18, 1880[1]; m. JOHN PATRICK BURNS; b. July 20, 1877; d. 1950.
24. iii. WILBERT F. HOVATTER, b. April 01, 1882, Preston Co. WV; d. August 19, 1969, Greene Co. Miss..
25. iv. IRA J. HOVATTER, b. April 17, 1885; d. July 1968.
26. v. MARY L. HOVATTER, b. March 07, 1887.
27. vi. GEORGE E. HOVATTER, b. February 15, 1889.
vii. LLOYD A. HOVATTER[1], b. June 29, 1891[1]; m. LULU STERRINGER.
viii. MAUDIE P. HOVATTER[1], b. July 21, 1893[1]; m. SAMUEL DUMIRE.
28. ix. ARLIE DAVID HOVATTER, b. August 15, 1895, WVA; d. December 1977.
x. BOYD E. HOVATTER[1], b. September 24, 1897[1,2]; d. August 1980[2]; m. HILDA DAVIS.

More About BOYD E. HOVATTER:
Fact 5: Social Security #: 234-03-1597[2]
Fact 6: Issued in: West Virginia[2]
Fact 7: Residence code: Alabama[2]
Fact 8: Last residence ZIP: 36584[2]

20. CATHERINE[6] HOVATTER *(WILLIAM[5], CHRISTOPHER[4], JOHAN MICHAEL[3] HOHWERTER, JOHANN VALENTIN[2], JOHAN HEINRICH[1] HOCHWARTER)* was born Abt. 1851. She married DAVID A. LOUGHRY November 30, 1882, son of WILLIAM LOUGHRY. He was born Abt. 1850.

Child of CATHERINE HOVATTER and DAVID LOUGHRY is:
i. MARY E.[7] LOUGHRY, b. 1871; m. JACOB HOVATTER; b. 1862.

21. HENRY[6] HOVARTER *(JOHANNES[5] HOWERTER, CHRISTIAN[4] HOHWERTER, JOHANN GEORGE[3], JOHANN VALENTIN[2], JOHAN HEINRICH[1] HOCHWARTER)* He married CATHERINE HARTMAN.

Child of HENRY HOVARTER and CATHERINE HARTMAN is:
29. i. EMANUEL[7] HOVARTER.

Generation No. 7

22. ELIAS[7] HOVATTER *(HEZEKIAH[6], DAVID[5], CHRISTOPHER[4], JOHAN MICHAEL[3] HOHWERTER, JOHANN VALENTIN[2], JOHAN HEINRICH[1] HOCHWARTER)* was born Abt. 1875. He married ? Abt. 1903 in Licking Twp, Tucker Co. WV.

Children of ELIAS HOVATTER and ? are:
i. LEATHA L.[8] HOVATTER.
ii. CLIDE HOVATTER.
iii. DANNY HOVATTER.
iv. CECIL B. HOVATTER.
v. DONNA A. HOVATTER.
vi. WILLIAM H. HOVATTER.

23. CHARLES E.[7] HOVATTER *(DAVID T.[6], DAVID[5], CHRISTOPHER[4], JOHAN MICHAEL[3] HOHWERTER, JOHANN VALENTIN[2], JOHAN HEINRICH[1] HOCHWARTER)*[3] was born October 11, 1878[3]. He married ELLA AGNICE BURNS, daughter of JOHN BURNS and SARAH DAVIS. She was born March 07, 1883.

Children of CHARLES HOVATTER and ELLA BURNS are:
i. CLAUDENE ELWOOD[8] HOVATTER, m. ARIETTA SHOCKLEY.
ii. ELSTON GERALD HOVATTER, m. MYRA E. HOWARD.
iii. CHARLES WOODROW WILSON HOVATTER, m. MADELINE KAUSCH.

Notes for CHARLES WOODROW WILSON HOVATTER:
Picture on page 102 in book "Generations from Hoffman to Hovatter"

iv. WANDA LORRAINE HOVATTER, m. ALBERT H. HEARN.
v. EARL GAY HOVATTER, b. January 06, 1912; d. August 08, 1934.
30. vi. THOMAS DAVID HOVATTER, b. June 02, 1908.
vii. ELMER DALLAS HOVATTER, b. August 24, 1902; d. June 13, 1970; m. JESSIE B. NOCE, Bet. 1919 - 1950; b. Bet. 1898 - 1917; d. Bet. 1919 - 1992.
viii. ETTA IVES HOVATTER, m. EARL C. CATHEL.
31. ix. DELBERT RAY HOVATTER, b. November 22, 1904; d. November 1974.
x. LEODA PEARL HOVATTER.
xi. ORA MARIE HOVATTER, b. April 03, 1914; d. April 16, 1937; m. HERBERT FUES, SR.
xii. ELFORD HAROLD HOVATTER, b. May 03, 1924; d. May 03, 1924.

24. WILBERT F.[7] HOVATTER *(DAVID T.[6], DAVID[5], CHRISTOPHER[4], JOHAN MICHAEL[3] HOHWERTER, JOHANN VALENTIN[2], JOHAN HEINRICH[1] HOCHWARTER)*[3] was born April 01, 1882 in Preston Co. WV[3], and died August 19, 1969 in Greene Co. Miss.[3]. He married HATTIE LEE JONES[3] February 18, 1903 in Greene Co. Miss.[3], daughter of ENOCH JONES and MARY SMITH. She was born October 06, 1885 in Greene Co, Miss.[3], and died October 09, 1969 in Greene Co, Miss.[3].

Notes for WILBERT F. HOVATTER:
87 years old 4 months and 18 days at time of death

More About WILBERT F. HOVATTER:
Burial: Stateline, MS
Social Security Number: Pennslyvania[3]

Notes for HATTIE LEE JONES:
84 years old and 3 days at time of death
Pictures on pages 106, 107 108 in book "Generations of Hoffman to Hovatter"

More About HATTIE LEE JONES:
Burial: Stateline, MS
Fact 5: Social Security #: 177-14-7342[4]
Fact 6: Issued in: Pennsylvania[4]
Fact 7: Residence code: Mississippi[4]
Fact 8: Last residence ZIP: 39451[4]

Children of WILBERT HOVATTER and HATTIE JONES are:

32. i. EULA[8] HOVATTER, b. December 14, 1903, Greene Co, Miss.; d. October 24, 1937, WVA.

ii. ODIE HOVATTER[5], b. October 27, 1905[5]; d. December 03, 1905[5].

More About ODIE HOVATTER:
Burial: Slay Cemetary

33. iii. WILBERTIE VALENTINE HOVATTER, b. February 14, 1908, Greene Co, Miss.; d. September 23, 1987.

iv. BOYD HOVATTER[5], b. August 10, 1910, Greene Co, Miss. re: Family Bible[5]; d. February 1975[6,7,8].

Notes for BOYD HOVATTER:
picture on page 93 in book "Generations of Hoffman to Hovatter"

More About BOYD HOVATTER:
Burial: Egg Harbor, NJ
Social Security Number: 560-07-8262[8]

v. FLOYD HOVATTER[8], b. March 19, 1913[8]; d. March 21, 1913[8].

34. vi. LOIS HOVATTER, b. November 19, 1914, Greene Co, Miss.; d. May 30, 1983, Lower Bank, NJ.

vii. HATTIE ALMALEE HOVATTER, b. October 06, 1917.

viii. AUBREY HOVATTER[8], b. September 27, 1920[8].

35. ix. DESSIE HOVATTER, b. September 07, 1921, Preston Co. VA; d. January 21, 2001, Las Vegas, NV.

x. VERNON HOVATTER[8,9], b. February 26, 1924, West Virgina[10]; d. January 03, 1996, San Angelo, Texas[11,12,12,12,12,12,12,12,12,13].

Notes for VERNON HOVATTER:
Picture on page 101 in book "Generations from Hoffman to Hovatter"

More About VERNON HOVATTER:
Social Security Number: new Jersey[13]

xi. KENNETH GENE HOVATTER[13], b. October 31, 1927, west virginia Re: Family Bible[13]; d. March 06, 1983[13].

Notes for KENNETH GENE HOVATTER:
Picture on pages 100 in book "Generations from Hoffman to Hovatter"

More About KENNETH GENE HOVATTER:
Social Security Number: 587-56-1847[13]

25. IRA J.[7] HOVATTER *(DAVID T.[6], DAVID[5], CHRISTOPHER[4], JOHAN MICHAEL[3] HOHWERTER, JOHANN VALENTIN[2], JOHAN HEINRICH[1] HOCHWARTER)*[13] was born April 17, 1885[13,14], and died July 1968[14]. He married DESSIE

THOMAS.

More About IRA J. HOVATTER:
Social Security Number: 232-22-9008

Child of IRA HOVATTER and DESSIE THOMAS is:
i. NINA[8] HOVATTER.

26. MARY L.[7] HOVATTER *(DAVID T.[6], DAVID[5], CHRISTOPHER[4], JOHAN MICHAEL[3] HOHWERTER, JOHANN VALENTIN[2], JOHAN HEINRICH[1] HOCHWARTER)[15]* was born March 07, 1887[15]. She married ANDREW JACKSON BROWN February 18, 1903 in Greene Co MS. He was born February 04, 1877, and died February 04, 1932.

Notes for MARY L. HOVATTER:

The information I received from Tracy had Fruitville listed in it but from Marriages in MS it seems that there was a double wedding, hers and her brother Wilbert. Both were married same day, same county and State. Greene Co. MS in Leakesville.

Children of MARY HOVATTER and ANDREW BROWN are:
36. i. ANDREW C.[8] BROWN, b. January 29, 1904; d. July 28, 1975.
ii. ALBERT LEROY BROWN, b. January 23, 1908; d. Abt. May 12, 1994; m. MARIE MIZELL.
37. iii. RUBY BROWN, b. September 02, 1908.
iv. WILBER JACKSON BROWN, b. December 04, 1912; d. December 04, 1912.

More About WILBER JACKSON BROWN:
Burial: Fruitdale Cemetary

38. v. HOMER JENNINGS BROWN, b. July 07, 1914; d. July 17, 1972.
vi. DELBERT JENNINGS BROWN, b. April 19, 1917; d. February 02, 1998.
vii. WILLIAM HENRY BROWN, b. July 23, 1920.
viii. NELLIE MAE BROWN BROWN, b. November 23, 1923.
ix. DAVID ELMER BROWN, b. November 04, 1926; d. February 10, 1929.

27. GEORGE E.[7] HOVATTER *(DAVID T.[6], DAVID[5], CHRISTOPHER[4], JOHAN MICHAEL[3] HOHWERTER, JOHANN VALENTIN[2], JOHAN HEINRICH[1] HOCHWARTER)[15]* was born February 15, 1889[15]. He married CECIL MAY BURNS.

Notes for CECIL MAY BURNS:
There is a possibility that the spelling of her name was different. May have been Cecilia or another variation.

Children of GEORGE HOVATTER and CECIL BURNS are:
39. i. ERNEST RAY[8] HOVATTER, b. July 25, 1916.
40. ii. VIOLET MILDRED HOVATTER, b. June 1915.
iii. VELMA ARIZONIA HOVATTER, b. October 1917.

Notes for VELMA ARIZONIA HOVATTER:
Was a Major in the Army. She adopted her sister Mary Children and raised them as her own. Whe passed away in Aniston Ala in 1999 her daughter Jean and son Larry still live on the farm there.

41. iv. BERYL HOVATTER.
42. v. MARY ELIZABETH HOVATTER, b. 1923.
43. vi. DARRELL HOVATTER.

28. ARLIE DAVID[7] HOVATTER *(DAVID T.[6], DAVID[5], CHRISTOPHER[4], JOHAN MICHAEL[3] HOHWERTER, JOHANN VALENTIN[2], JOHAN HEINRICH[1] HOCHWARTER)[15]* was born August 15, 1895 in WVA[15], and died December 1977[16,17]. He married LAURA POLING.

Notes for ARLIE DAVID HOVATTER:
[Broderbund Family Archive #110, Vol. 1 A-K, Ed. 7, Social Security Death Index: U.S., Date of Import: Jul 3, 2001, Internal Ref. #1.111.7.127438.120]

Individual: Hovatter, Arlie
Social Security #: 705-10-2282
Issued in: Railroad Board

Birth date: Aug 15, 1895
Death date: Dec 1977

Residence code: West Virginia

ZIP Code of last known residence: 26354
Primary location associated with this ZIP Code:

Grafton, West Virginia

More About ARLIE DAVID HOVATTER:
Fact 1: Issued in: Railroad Board[17]
Fact 2: Residence code: West Virginia[17]
Fact 3: Last residence ZIP: 26354[17]
Fact 6: Issued in: Railroad Board[18]
Fact 7: Residence code: West Virginia[18]
Fact 8: Last residence ZIP: 26354[18]
Social Security Number: Social Security #: 705-10-2282[18,19]

Child of ARLIE HOVATTER and LAURA POLING is:
i. LESTER[8] HOVATTER.

29. EMANUEL[7] HOVARTER *(HENRY[6], JOHANNES[5] HOWERTER, CHRISTIAN[4] HOHWERTER, JOHANN GEORGE[3], JOHANN VALENTIN[2], JOHAN HEINRICH[1] HOCHWARTER)* He married LUCINDA REAMER.

Child of EMANUEL HOVARTER and LUCINDA REAMER is:
44. i. PAUL[8] HOVARTER, b. January 04, 1907; d. May 11, 1968.

Generation No. 8

30. THOMAS DAVID[8] HOVATTER *(CHARLES E.[7], DAVID T.[6], DAVID[5], CHRISTOPHER[4], JOHAN MICHAEL[3] HOHWERTER, JOHANN VALENTIN[2], JOHAN HEINRICH[1] HOCHWARTER)* was born June 02, 1908. He married ELSIE AMBROSIO.

Child of THOMAS HOVATTER and ELSIE AMBROSIO is:
i. TIMOTHY[9] HOVATTER.

31. DELBERT RAY[8] HOVATTER *(CHARLES E.[7], DAVID T.[6], DAVID[5], CHRISTOPHER[4], JOHAN MICHAEL[3] HOHWERTER, JOHANN VALENTIN[2], JOHAN HEINRICH[1] HOCHWARTER)* was born November 22, 1904, and died November 1974. He married BARBARA CHANDLER.

Children of DELBERT HOVATTER and BARBARA CHANDLER are:
i. BARBARA LINDSAY[9] HOVATTER, b. February 02, 1944; d. June 29, 1968.
ii. SANDRA LEE HOVATTER, b. December 31, 1946; m. JAMES MOORE, 1977.

45. iii. MARTHA JEAN HOVATTER, b. July 17, 1953.

32. EULA[8] HOVATTER *(WILBERT F.[7], DAVID T.[6], DAVID[5], CHRISTOPHER[4], JOHAN MICHAEL[3] HOHWERTER, JOHANN VALENTIN[2], JOHAN HEINRICH[1] HOCHWARTER)*[20] was born December 14, 1903 in Greene Co, Miss.[20], and died October 24, 1937 in WVA[20]. She married (1) SAMUEL LINTON[20]. She married (2) HOPE WATSON.

Notes for EULA HOVATTER:
picture on pages 93 in book "Generations of Hoffman to Hovatter"

Child of EULA HOVATTER and SAMUEL LINTON is:
i. VONCILE[9] LINTON[20].

Children of EULA HOVATTER and HOPE WATSON are:
ii. JUNIOR LEE[9] WATSON.
iii. FRANCIS WATSON.
iv. JOYCE WATSON.

33. WILBERTIE VALENTINE[8] HOVATTER *(WILBERT F.[7], DAVID T.[6], DAVID[5], CHRISTOPHER[4], JOHAN MICHAEL[3] HOHWERTER, JOHANN VALENTIN[2], JOHAN HEINRICH[1] HOCHWARTER)*[20] was born February 14, 1908 in Greene Co, Miss.[20], and died September 23, 1987[21,22,22,23,24]. He married (1) HAZEL DELL CLEVENGER[25]. She was born June 07, 1907[26,27], and died November 06, 1988[28,29,30]. He met (2) RUBY BARNETT, daughter of MARSHALL BARNETT and ADA GREENLIEF. She was born July 16, 1915.

Notes for WILBERTIE VALENTINE HOVATTER:
Bertie and Hazel had broke up and he met Ruby. Ruby became pregnant with his daughter Rosalie. Hazel decided that they should try to make another go of their marriage, so he left Ruby and went back to Hazel. There is some speculation about when he knew about Ruby's pregnancy. When he found out about his daughter Rosalie he acknowledged her as his child as he did his other children.
Died of Cancer.

Pictures on pages 93, 94, 95 in book "Generations of Hoffman to Hovatter"

More About WILBERTIE VALENTINE HOVATTER:
Social Security Number: 232-05-5326[31]

Children of WILBERTIE HOVATTER and HAZEL CLEVENGER are:
i. MARJORIE[9] HOVATTER, b. August 10, 1927.
ii. DOLORES HOVATTER, b. May 02, 1929.
46. iii. BERTA JAYNE HOVATTER, b. August 17, 1938; d. January 16, 1988.

Child of WILBERTIE HOVATTER and RUBY BARNETT is:
iv. ROSALIE J.[9] HOVATTER, b. December 14, 1932; m. (1) CHARLEY JENKINS; m. (2) DAVID FAULKNIER.

Notes for ROSALIE J. HOVATTER:
Joyce i was not on record at all Bertie went in to the lawer office and sign affidaved that i was his to get me a birth certficall of these people around here that is Hovatters are relation to Bertie im glad Patty sent you the stuff my scaner isent hook up im just glad i got the putor Patty is Dave niece she is so good to me have you heard any more a bout Bill Well ill let you go all my Love tell Bob hello for me Rosalie

34. LOIS[8] HOVATTER *(WILBERT F.[7], DAVID T.[6], DAVID[5], CHRISTOPHER[4], JOHAN MICHAEL[3] HOHWERTER, JOHANN VALENTIN[2], JOHAN HEINRICH[1] HOCHWARTER)*[31] was born November 19, 1914 in Greene Co, Miss.[31], and died May 30, 1983 in Lower Bank, NJ[31]. She married THOMAS MANCUSO[31,32,33] September 23, 1935 in Croydon, PA[34], son of VITO MANCUSO and PATRINA TUMBARELLO. He was born December 31, 1912 in Italy, and died May 27, 1985 in St. Petersburg, FL[34,35].

Notes for LOIS HOVATTER:
Married Sept. 23, 1935
Pictures on pages 96, 97 98, 100 in book "Generations of Hoffman to Hovatter"

More About LOIS HOVATTER:
Burial: Egg Harbor City, NJ[36]
Social Security Number: 177-14-8410[36]

More About THOMAS MANCUSO:
Burial: Clearwater FL[36,37]

Children of LOIS HOVATTER and THOMAS MANCUSO are:
47. i. JOYCE F..[9] MANCUSO, b. May 11, 1934, Bristol, PA.
ii. PATRINA MANCUSO, b. Abt. 1937; d. Abt. 1937.

35. DESSIE[8] HOVATTER *(WILBERT F.[7], DAVID T.[6], DAVID[5], CHRISTOPHER[4], JOHAN MICHAEL[3] HOHWERTER, JOHANN VALENTIN[2], JOHAN HEINRICH[1] HOCHWARTER)*[38] was born September 07, 1921 in Preston Co. VA[38], and died January 21, 2001 in Las Vegas, NV. She married (1) EDGAR THOM[38] October 16, 1941 in Trenton, NJ[38], son of GUSTOV THOM and SARAH. He was born October 23, 1922[39,39,39,39,39,39,39,39,40], and died January 1982[41,41,41,41,41,41,41,41,42]. She married (2) WILLIAM F. PUTNAM June 26, 1960 in Trenton, NJ, son of HOWARD PUTNAM and DOROTHY RIDDLE. He was born September 10, 1932, and died March 29, 2002 in Las Vegas, NV.

Notes for DESSIE HOVATTER:
Pictures of Dessie Hovatter and more information on pages 98, 99 in book "Generation from Hoffman to Hovatter"

More About EDGAR THOM:
Adoption: [43,44]
Residence: Residence code: New Jersey[45,46]
Social Security Number: Social Security #: 154-12-8658[47,48]

Notes for WILLIAM F. PUTNAM:

Subj: Re: a short note
Date: 03/29/2002 1:34:39 PM Eastern Standard Time
From: P1AND2
To: JSutton639

E-mail dated 3-29-02
Hi Joyce,

It's Robin and Rick--responding from Dad's e-mail. We are at his house taking care of things. This is a hell of a thing to relay via e-mail, but we tried the phone numbers we found for you and Bob and got no answer, so I apologize in advance, but need to let you know.

Wednesday I couldn't get a hold of Dad, and grew concerned when his phone just kept ringing. So Rick and I drove in and we found him; he had fallen in the bathroom and was unconsious. We summoned paramedics and they took him to Valley Hospital. He passed away this morning around 6:30. He never regained consiousness. Rick, Bill and I like to think he had little or no pain, and know for sure he is in a better place now....probably with

Mom :).

I know he wanted you to have Mom's albums....there are also a lot of pictures...I'd like for you to have anything you want. Please let me know.

We are still in the midst of arrangements and will let you know what is going on when we have more info.

Again I'm sorry to relay this via reply e-mail, but wanted you to know....Can I ask a favor pls...you knew a lot of Mom and Dad's e-mail buddies...would you be able to let them know about Dad for us pls, we'd really appreciate it.

Thanks.

Robin

William Putnam

William F. Putnam, 69, died March 29 in a local hospital.
He was born Sept. 10, 1932, in Port Henry, N.Y. A Navy veteran of the Korean and Vietnam wars, he was a corrections officer and a 22-year resident of Las Vegas.
He is survived by his son, William; and daughter, Robin Walker, both of Indian Springs; and five grandchildren.
Services are private. Davis Funeral Home-Charleston handled arrangements.

Child of DESSIE HOVATTER and EDGAR THOM is:

i. DENNIS[9] THOM[48], b. September 17, 1949[49,49,49,49,49,49,49,49,49,49,49,49,50]; d. March 1971[51,51,51,51,52].

More About DENNIS THOM:
Social Security Number: Social Security #: 570-84-6960[53,54]

Children of DESSIE HOVATTER and WILLIAM PUTNAM are:

48. ii. ROBIN[9] PUTNAM, b. April 17, 1963.
49. iii. WILLIAM F. PUTNAM 2, b. August 19, 1966.

36. ANDREW C.[8] BROWN *(MARY L.[7] HOVATTER, DAVID T.[6], DAVID[5], CHRISTOPHER[4], JOHAN MICHAEL[3] HOHWERTER, JOHANN VALENTIN[2], JOHAN HEINRICH[1] HOCHWARTER)* was born January 29, 1904, and died July 28, 1975. He married MILDRED FORTNEY.

Children of ANDREW BROWN and MILDRED FORTNEY are:

i. DONALD[9] BROWN.
ii. KEITH BROWN.
iii. LARRAINE BROWN.
iv. SWANEE BROWN.
v. FRANK BROWN.
vi. PAUL BROWN.

37. RUBY[8] BROWN *(MARY L.[7] HOVATTER, DAVID T.[6], DAVID[5], CHRISTOPHER[4], JOHAN MICHAEL[3] HOHWERTER, JOHANN VALENTIN[2], JOHAN HEINRICH[1] HOCHWARTER)* was born September 02, 1908. She married BRYAN HOVATTER. He died 1996.

Children of RUBY BROWN and BRYAN HOVATTER are:

i. WILLIAM[9] HOVATTER.
ii. PRUDENCE HOVATTER.

38. HOMER JENNINGS[8] BROWN *(MARY L.[7] HOVATTER, DAVID T.[6], DAVID[5], CHRISTOPHER[4], JOHAN MICHAEL[3] HOHWERTER, JOHANN VALENTIN[2], JOHAN HEINRICH[1] HOCHWARTER)* was born July 07, 1914, and died July 17, 1972. He married MARY MYRTLE DEESE OR DEES December 26, 1932. She was born February 28, 1918, and died May 08, 1989.

Notes for HOMER JENNINGS BROWN:
Worked in sawmill.
died of a heart attack

More About HOMER JENNINGS BROWN:
Burial: Fruitdale Cemetary

Notes for MARY MYRTLE DEESE OR DEES:
Died of Lou gerrings

More About MARY MYRTLE DEESE OR DEES:
Burial: Fruitdale Cemetary

Children of HOMER BROWN and MARY DEES are:

i. CECILE LEOTA[9] BROWN, b. December 12, 1934; d. May 1937.

Notes for CECILE LEOTA BROWN:
died of Brights discease

More About CECILE LEOTA BROWN:
Burial: Fruitdale Cemetary

ii. ANDREW JENNINGS BROWN, b. May 20, 1937; d. April 03, 1994; m. JACKINE LOU TALLET, February 14, 1969.

Notes for ANDREW JENNINGS BROWN:
Died of Lymphoma

50. iii. HOMER RAY BROWN, b. July 07, 1938.

39. ERNEST RAY[8] HOVATTER *(GEORGE E.[7], DAVID T.[6], DAVID[5], CHRISTOPHER[4], JOHAN MICHAEL[3] HOHWERTER, JOHANN VALENTIN[2], JOHAN HEINRICH[1] HOCHWARTER)* was born July 25, 1916. He married (1) MILDRED KINTER. He married (2) EVELYN ?. He married (3) FRANCIS BOYER.

Children of ERNEST HOVATTER and MILDRED KINTER are:

51. i. GARY RAY[9] HOVATTER, b. March 12, 1949.
52. ii. VICKIE LYNN HOVATTER, b. July 21, 1954, Grafton, WV.

Child of ERNEST HOVATTER and EVELYN ? is:

iii. PATTI ANN[9] HOVATTER, m. ? SMITH.

Child of ERNEST HOVATTER and FRANCIS BOYER is:

iv. FRANCIS LEE[9] HOVATTER.

40. VIOLET MILDRED[8] HOVATTER *(GEORGE E.[7], DAVID T.[6], DAVID[5], CHRISTOPHER[4], JOHAN MICHAEL[3] HOHWERTER, JOHANN VALENTIN[2], JOHAN HEINRICH[1] HOCHWARTER)* was born June 1915. She married FRED BAIOCCHI. He died 1987.

Child of VIOLET HOVATTER and FRED BAIOCCHI is:

i. YVONNE[9] BAIOCCHI.

41. BERYL^{8} HOVATTER *(GEORGE E.^{7}, DAVID T.^{6}, DAVID^{5}, CHRISTOPHER^{4}, JOHAN MICHAEL^{3} HOHWERTER, JOHANN VALENTIN^{2}, JOHAN HEINRICH^{1} HOCHWARTER)* She married PAGE EVANS.

Child of BERYL HOVATTER and PAGE EVANS is:

i. MALE CHILD^{9} EVANS.

42. MARY ELIZABETH^{8} HOVATTER *(GEORGE E.^{7}, DAVID T.^{6}, DAVID^{5}, CHRISTOPHER^{4}, JOHAN MICHAEL^{3} HOHWERTER, JOHANN VALENTIN^{2}, JOHAN HEINRICH^{1} HOCHWARTER)* was born 1923. She married (1) MR. PERT. She married (2) LEONARD BLACKMON.

Notes for MARY ELIZABETH HOVATTER:
She had four Children. Her husband abused her and she divorced him. Her father took her home to Grafton where she moved in with grandma. Aunt Velma came in from a tour in Greenland and took her mom Cecil and mary and all four kids with her to Texas to live. She ended up raising the four children and taking care of her mother until she passed away in the late 1970's. Mary Elizabeth remarried Leonard Blackmon and remained in the San Antonio area. They now live in Schertz, Texas

Children of MARY HOVATTER and MR. PERT are:

i. JEAN^{9} PERT.
ii. LARRY PERT.
iii. UNKNOWN PERT.

43. DARRELL^{8} HOVATTER *(GEORGE E.^{7}, DAVID T.^{6}, DAVID^{5}, CHRISTOPHER^{4}, JOHAN MICHAEL^{3} HOHWERTER, JOHANN VALENTIN^{2}, JOHAN HEINRICH^{1} HOCHWARTER)* He married SHIRLEE.

Children of DARRELL HOVATTER and SHIRLEE are:

i. DONNA^{9} HOVATTER.
ii. KATHY HOVATTER.

44. PAUL^{8} HOVARTER *(EMANUEL^{7}, HENRY^{6}, JOHANNES^{5} HOWERTER, CHRISTIAN^{4} HOHWERTER, JOHANN GEORGE^{3}, JOHANN VALENTIN^{2}, JOHAN HEINRICH^{1} HOCHWARTER)* was born January 04, 1907, and died May 11, 1968. He married DELORES BEATY January 13, 1934. She was born January 07, 1916, and died February 27, 1972.

Children of PAUL HOVARTER and DELORES BEATY are:

i. SHARON^{9} HOVARTER, b. April 13, 1938; m. WILLIAM WILCOX.
ii. DALE ROBERT HOVARTER, b. August 01, 1948.

Generation No. 9

45. MARTHA JEAN^{9} HOVATTER *(DELBERT RAY^{8}, CHARLES E.^{7}, DAVID T.^{6}, DAVID^{5}, CHRISTOPHER^{4}, JOHAN MICHAEL^{3} HOHWERTER, JOHANN VALENTIN^{2}, JOHAN HEINRICH^{1} HOCHWARTER)* was born July 17, 1953. She married (1) KENNETH SPEER 1971. He died November 15, 1988. She married (2) CHARLES RENO December 31, 1998.

Children of MARTHA HOVATTER and KENNETH SPEER are:

i. BARBARA ANNE^{10} SPEER, b. September 15, 1974.
ii. DONALD RAY SPEER, b. March 05, 1977.

46. BERTA JAYNE^{9} HOVATTER *(WILBERTIE VALENTINE^{8}, WILBERT F.^{7}, DAVID T.^{6}, DAVID^{5}, CHRISTOPHER^{4}, JOHAN MICHAEL^{3} HOHWERTER, JOHANN VALENTIN^{2}, JOHAN HEINRICH^{1} HOCHWARTER)* was born August 17, 1938, and died January 16, 1988. She married (1) HAROLD SNYDER. She married (2) THOMAS MOSER. He was born March 29, 1930.

Notes for BERTA JAYNE HOVATTER:
Died of Cancer.

Child of BERTA HOVATTER and HAROLD SNYDER is:
53. i. PAM^{10} SNYDER, b. April 18, 1959.

Child of BERTA HOVATTER and THOMAS MOSER is:
ii. THOMAS^{10} MOSER, b. August 07, 1969.

47. JOYCE F..^{9} MANCUSO *(LOIS^{8} HOVATTER, WILBERT F.^{7}, DAVID T.^{6}, DAVID^{5}, CHRISTOPHER^{4}, JOHAN MICHAEL^{3} HOHWERTER, JOHANN VALENTIN^{2}, JOHAN HEINRICH^{1} HOCHWARTER)* was born May 11, 1934 in Bristol, PA. She married ROBERT THOMAS SUTTON[54] October 19, 1957 in Pomona, NJ[54], son of ROBERT SUTTON and DORA WATSON. He was born December 07, 1932 in Atlantic City, NJ[54].

Notes for JOYCE F.. MANCUSO:
DAR member number 831198, installed Oct. 16, 2004

Notes for ROBERT THOMAS SUTTON:
Bob was born on a Wednesday. His wife Joyce was born on a Friday two years later, each year their bithdays fall on the same day of the week.

Children of JOYCE MANCUSO and ROBERT SUTTON are:
i. DOLORES LEA^{10} SUTTON[54], b. September 24, 1958[54].
54. ii. SUSAN JOYCE SUTTON, b. December 01, 1964.
55. iii. BOBBI LYNN SUTTON, b. November 09, 1968.

48. ROBIN^{9} PUTNAM *(DESSIE^{8} HOVATTER, WILBERT F.^{7}, DAVID T.^{6}, DAVID^{5}, CHRISTOPHER^{4}, JOHAN MICHAEL^{3} HOHWERTER, JOHANN VALENTIN^{2}, JOHAN HEINRICH^{1} HOCHWARTER)* was born April 17, 1963. She married EDISON RICHARD WALKER November 19, 1986 in Las Vegas, NV, son of EDISON WALKER and VIVIAN.

Children of ROBIN PUTNAM and EDISON WALKER are:
i. STEPHEN RANDALL^{10} WALKER, b. July 04, 1987.
ii. JAREN DAWN WALKER, b. December 06, 1993.

49. WILLIAM F. PUTNAM^{9} 2 *(DESSIE^{8} HOVATTER, WILBERT F.^{7}, DAVID T.^{6}, DAVID^{5}, CHRISTOPHER^{4}, JOHAN MICHAEL^{3} HOHWERTER, JOHANN VALENTIN^{2}, JOHAN HEINRICH^{1} HOCHWARTER)* was born August 19, 1966. He married BERNETTA GRAHAM December 28, 1989 in Las Vegas, NV, daughter of DONALD GRAHAM and LINDA NELSON. She was born November 03, 1970.

Children of WILLIAM 2 and BERNETTA GRAHAM are:
i. WILLIAM F. PUTNAM^{10} 3, b. June 30, 1990.
ii. OLIVIA LUCILLE PUTNAM, b. February 26, 1997.

50. HOMER RAY^{9} BROWN *(HOMER JENNINGS^{8}, MARY L.^{7} HOVATTER, DAVID T.^{6}, DAVID^{5}, CHRISTOPHER^{4}, JOHAN MICHAEL^{3} HOHWERTER, JOHANN VALENTIN^{2}, JOHAN HEINRICH^{1} HOCHWARTER)* was born July 07, 1938. He married ANNA CECELIA STEVENS October 22, 1960.

Child of HOMER BROWN and ANNA STEVENS is:
i. TRACY LEE^{10} BROWN, b. October 30, 1966.

Notes for TRACY LEE BROWN:
Tracy and daughter on page 103 in book "Generations of Hoffman to Hovatter"

51. GARY RAY[9] HOVATTER *(ERNEST RAY[8], GEORGE E.[7], DAVID T.[6], DAVID[5], CHRISTOPHER[4], JOHAN MICHAEL[3] HOHWERTER, JOHANN VALENTIN[2], JOHAN HEINRICH[1] HOCHWARTER)* was born March 12, 1949. He married LINDA HUNNICUT.

Children of GARY HOVATTER and LINDA HUNNICUT are:

i. HEALTH[10] HOVATTER.

56. ii. HEATHER HOVATTER.

52. VICKIE LYNN[9] HOVATTER *(ERNEST RAY[8], GEORGE E.[7], DAVID T.[6], DAVID[5], CHRISTOPHER[4], JOHAN MICHAEL[3] HOHWERTER, JOHANN VALENTIN[2], JOHAN HEINRICH[1] HOCHWARTER)* was born July 21, 1954 in Grafton, WV. She married WILLIAM CLAYPOOL. He was born 1949 in Austin, TX.

Children of VICKIE HOVATTER and WILLIAM CLAYPOOL are:

i. DANIEL[10] CLAYPOOL, b. September 11, 1978.

ii. KEVIN CLAYPOOL, b. 1981.

Generation No. 10

53. PAM[10] SNYDER *(BERTA JAYNE[9] HOVATTER, WILBERTIE VALENTINE[8], WILBERT F.[7], DAVID T.[6], DAVID[5], CHRISTOPHER[4], JOHAN MICHAEL[3] HOHWERTER, JOHANN VALENTIN[2], JOHAN HEINRICH[1] HOCHWARTER)* was born April 18, 1959.

Notes for PAM SNYDER:
Pam had a lot of problems so she let her mother, Berta Jayne legally adopt Brian.

Child of PAM SNYDER is:

i. BRIAN[11] SNYDER, b. March 26, 1976.

54. SUSAN JOYCE[10] SUTTON *(JOYCE F..[9] MANCUSO, LOIS[8] HOVATTER, WILBERT F.[7], DAVID T.[6], DAVID[5], CHRISTOPHER[4], JOHAN MICHAEL[3] HOHWERTER, JOHANN VALENTIN[2], JOHAN HEINRICH[1] HOCHWARTER)*[54] was born December 01, 1964[54]. She married CHRISTOPHER KEATING[54], son of WILTON KEATING and MARGUERITE TOTH.

Notes for SUSAN JOYCE SUTTON:
DAR member number 831199

Children of SUSAN SUTTON and CHRISTOPHER KEATING are:

i. CHRISTOPHER KEATING[11] JR.[54].

ii. BENJAMIN KEATING[54].

55. BOBBI LYNN[10] SUTTON *(JOYCE F..[9] MANCUSO, LOIS[8] HOVATTER, WILBERT F.[7], DAVID T.[6], DAVID[5], CHRISTOPHER[4], JOHAN MICHAEL[3] HOHWERTER, JOHANN VALENTIN[2], JOHAN HEINRICH[1] HOCHWARTER)*[54] was born November 09, 1968[54]. She married (1) KARL FRANK CHASE[54]. She met (2) MR. MCHENRY.

Notes for BOBBI LYNN SUTTON:
DAR member number 831200, installed Oct. 16, 2004

Children of BOBBI SUTTON and KARL CHASE are:

i. SHAWN JOSEPH[11] CHASE[54], b. March 14, 1995[54].

ii. SAMANTHA JOYCE CHASE[54], b. April 06, 1997[54].

Child of BOBBI SUTTON and MR. MCHENRY is:

iii. DANI-LYNN[11] MCHENRY, b. June 08, 2006.

Chase Sr. Obit

Press of Atlantic City - ObituariesJavascript Menu by Deluxe-Menu.com
Your browser either doesn't support JavaScript or it is disabled. Read our help page to enable JavaScript in order for this site to operate properly.

Karl F. "Gaggy" Chase Sr.

CHASE, KARL, F., SR. "Gaggy", 64 - of Little Egg Harbor Twp, (formerly of Galloway Twp.), passed away on Tuesday, June 19, 2007. He was born in Camden, became a union carpenter with carpenter local of South Florida. He is survived by his mother, Gertrude Chase; his sisters, Joan Whittly and Sandra Kauffman; his brothers, Mark Chase (Carol), and George Chase (Glenda); his children, Kelly Fiallas, Karl Chase, Jr., Kenneth Scott Chase, Kim, Karen; his grandchildren, Shawn Chase, Samantha Chase, Matthew Fiallas, Priscilla Fiallas; step-daughters, Wendy, Dawn, and Cheryl and their children. His Memorial Service will be 2:00 PM, Sunday, June 24, 2007 at Wimberg Funeral Home, 211 E. Great Creek Rd., Galloway Twp., (609-641-0001). For directions and/or condolences, please visit www.wimbergfuneralhome.com In lieu of flowers, donations may be made to Samaritan Hospice, 5 Eves Dr., Suite 300, Marlton, NJ 08053.

Published in The Press of Atlantic City on 6/21/2007.
Guest Book • Flowers • Gift Shop • Charities

Printer-friendly version   E-mail to a friend

Today's The Press of Atlantic City obituaries

Questions about obituaries or Guest Books?
Contact Legacy.com • Terms of use

obituaries nationwide

Karl F. Chase, Sr.

56. HEATHER[10] HOVATTER *(GARY RAY[9], ERNEST RAY[8], GEORGE E.[7], DAVID T.[6], DAVID[5], CHRISTOPHER[4], JOHAN MICHAEL[3] HOHWERTER, JOHANN VALENTIN[2], JOHAN HEINRICH[1] HOCHWARTER)* She married ANTHONY GALVEZ.

Children of HEATHER HOVATTER and ANTHONY GALVEZ are:

i. DANIEL[11] GALVEZ.
ii. REBECCA GALVEZ.
iii. ALLISA GALVEZ.

Endnotes

1. Mancuso.FTW, Date of Import: Sep 6, 2000.
2. Genealogy.com, Family Archive #110, Social Security Death Index: U.S. Ed. 9, Social Security Death Index, Release date: April 10, 2000, Internal Ref. #1.111.9.122873.66.
3. Mancuso.FTW, Date of Import: Sep 6, 2000.
4. Genealogy.com, Family Archive #110, Social Security Death Index: U.S. Ed. 9, Social Security Death Index, Release date: April 10, 2000, Internal Ref. #1.111.9.122873.123.
5. Mancuso.FTW, Date of Import: Sep 6, 2000.
6. Broderbund Family Archive #110, Vol. 1, Ed. 7, Social Security Death Index: U.S., Date of Import: May 20, 2000, Internal Ref. #1.111.7.127438.126
7. Broderbund Family Archive #110, Vol. 1, Ed. 7, Social Security Death Index: U.S., Date of Import: May 21, 2000, Internal Ref. #1.111.7.127438.126
8. Mancuso.FTW, Date of Import: Sep 6, 2000.
9. Genealogy.com, Family Archive #110, Social Security Death Index: U.S. Ed. 9, Social Security Death Index, Release date: April 10, 2000.
10. Mancuso.FTW, Date of Import: Sep 6, 2000.
11. Broderbund Family Archive #110, Vol. 1, Ed. 7, Social Security Death Index: U.S., Date of Import: May 20, 2000, Internal Ref. #1.111.7.127439.43
12. Broderbund Family Archive #110, Vol. 1, Ed. 7, Social Security Death Index: U.S., Date of Import: May 21, 2000, Internal Ref. #1.111.7.127439.43
13. Mancuso.FTW, Date of Import: Sep 6, 2000.
14. Genealogy.com, Family Archive #110, Social Security Death Index: U.S. Ed. 9, Social Security Death Index, Release date: April 10, 2000, Internal Ref. #1.111.9.122873.131.
15. Mancuso.FTW, Date of Import: Sep 6, 2000.
16. Genealogy.com, Family Archive #110, Social Security Death Index: U.S. Ed. 9, Social Security Death Index, Release date: April 10, 2000, Internal Ref. #1.111.9.122873.61.
17. Broderbund Family Archive #110, Vol. 1, Ed. 7, Social Security Death Index: U.S., Date of Import: Jul 3, 2001, Internal Ref. #1.111.7.127438.120
18. Genealogy.com, Family Archive #110, Social Security Death Index: U.S. Ed. 9, Social Security Death Index, Release date: April 10, 2000, Internal Ref. #1.111.9.122873.61.
19. Broderbund Family Archive #110, Vol. 1, Ed. 7, Social Security Death Index: U.S., Date of Import: Jul 3, 2001, Internal Ref. #1.111.7.127438.120
20. Mancuso.FTW, Date of Import: Sep 6, 2000.
21. Broderbund Family Archive #110, Vol. 1, Ed. 7, Social Security Death Index: U.S., Date of Import: May 20, 2000, Internal Ref. #1.111.7.127439.53
22. Broderbund Family Archive #110, Vol. 1, Ed. 7, Social Security Death Index: U.S., Date of Import: May 21, 2000, Internal Ref. #1.111.7.127439.53
23. Mancuso.FTW, Date of Import: Sep 6, 2000.
24. Genealogy.com, Family Archive #110, Social Security Death Index: U.S. Ed. 9, Social Security Death Index, Release date: April 10, 2000, Internal Ref. #1.111.9.122873.201.
25. Mancuso.FTW, Date of Import: Sep 6, 2000.
26. Broderbund Family Archive #110, Vol. 1, Ed. 7, Social Security Death Index: U.S., Date of Import: May 20, 2000, Internal Ref. #1.111.7.127438.181
27. Mancuso.FTW, Date of Import: Sep 6, 2000.
28. Broderbund Family Archive #110, Vol. 1, Ed. 7, Social Security Death Index: U.S., Date of Import: May 20, 2000, Internal Ref. #1.111.7.127438.182
29. Mancuso.FTW, Date of Import: Sep 6, 2000.
30. Genealogy.com, Family Archive #110, Social Security Death Index: U.S. Ed. 9, Social Security Death Index, Release date: April 10, 2000, Internal Ref. #1.111.9.122873.125.
31. Mancuso.FTW, Date of Import: Sep 6, 2000.
32. Genealogy.com, Family Archive #110, Social Security Death Index: U.S. Ed. 9, Social Security Death Index, Release date: April 10, 2000.

David Hovatter

Eula and Sam

Boyd and Bertie

Vernon Hovatter

Kenneth Gene Hovatter

Hattie Lee Jones Hovatter

Lois and Dessie

Mary Lavina Hovatter

Woodrow Wilson Hovatter

Hovatter Air Hero

Staff Sergeant Woodrow W. Hovatter, who resided at 40 Reeger Avenue, while an employe of the Eastern Aircraft Corporation, has taken part in 25 combat bombing operations as ball turret gunner on a Flying Fortress of the Eighth A. A. F. His ship is the Fortress "Gremlin Gus."

Holder of the Distinguished Flying Cross, and the Air Medal with three Oak Leaf Clusters, he also has the Purple Heart for injuries suffered when his ship crashed in England after bombing a submarine base near Bordeaux. He took part in the bombing of the ball bearing factory near Regensburg, when the fleet of bombers continued on to Africa. His pilot reports that Hovatter was unusual in his cooperation with the other gunners, tracking enemy planes as they came in and calling their position to the men on the other guns. Hovatter was also assistant radio operator.

Article on Woodrow Wilson

Descendants of Big Shoe-make

1 Big Shoe-make
.... 2 Mary Shumate 1820 - 1892
.... +John Smith
.... 3 James Aaron Smith 1852 -
.... 3 Mary A. Smith 1855 - 1911
.... +George A. Powell
.... *2nd Husband of Mary A. Smith:
.... +Enoch Jones 1822 - 1903
.... 4 Mary Powell Jones 1873 -
.... 4 James Powell Jones 1876 -
.... 4 Hattie Lee Jones 1885 - 1969
.... +Wilbert F. Hovatter 1882 - 1969
.... 5 Eula Hovatter 1903 - 1937
.... +Samuel Linton
.... 6 Voncile Linton
.... *2nd Husband of Eula Hovatter:
.... +Hope Watson
.... 6 Junior Lee Watson
.... 6 Francis Watson
.... 6 Joyce Watson
.... 5 Odie Hovatter 1905 - 1905
.... 5 Wilbertie Valentine Hovatter 1908 - 1987
.... +Hazel Dell Clevenger 1907 - 1988
.... 6 Marjorie Hovatter 1927 -
.... 6 Dolores Hovatter 1929 -
.... 6 Berta Jayne Hovatter 1938 - 1988
.... +Harold Snyder
.... 7 Pam Snyder 1959 -
.... 8 Brian Snyder 1976 -
.... *2nd Husband of Berta Jayne Hovatter:
.... +Thomas Moser 1930 -
.... 7 Thomas Moser 1969 -
.... *Partner of Wilbertie Valentine Hovatter:
.... +Ruby Barnett 1915 -
.... 6 Rosalie J. Hovatter 1932 -
.... +Charley Jenkins
.... *2nd Husband of Rosalie J. Hovatter:
.... +David Faulknier
.... 5 Boyd Hovatter 1910 - 1975
.... 5 Floyd Hovatter 1913 - 1913
.... 5 Lois Hovatter 1914 - 1983
.... +Thomas Mancuso 1912 - 1985
.... 6 Joyce F.. Mancuso 1934 -
.... +Robert Thomas Sutton 1932 -
.... 7 Dolores Lea Sutton 1958 -
.... 7 Susan Joyce Sutton 1964 -
.... +Christopher Keating
.... 8 Christopher Keating Jr.
.... 8 Benjamin Keating
.... 7 Bobbi Lynn Sutton 1968 -
.... +Karl Frank Chase
.... 8 Shawn Joseph Chase 1995 -
.... 8 Samantha Joyce Chase 1997 -
.... *Partner of Bobbi Lynn Sutton:
.... +Mr. McHenry
.... 8 Dani-Lynn McHenry 2006 -
.... 6 Patrina Mancuso 1937 - 1937
.... 5 Hattie Almalee Hovatter 1917 -
.... 5 Aubrey Hovatter 1920 -
.... 5 Dessie Hovatter 1921 - 2001
.... +Edgar Thom 1922 - 1982
.... 6 Dennis Thom 1949 - 1971
.... *2nd Husband of Dessie Hovatter:
.... +William F. Putnam 1932 - 2002
.... 6 Robin Putnam 1963 -
.... +Edison Richard Walker
.... 7 Stephen Randall Walker 1987 -
.... 7 Jaren Dawn Walker 1993 -
.... 6 William F. Putnam 2 1966 -
.... +Bernetta Graham 1970 -
.... 7 William F. Putnam 3 1990 -
.... 7 Olivia Lucille Putnam 1997 -
.... 5 Vernon Hovatter 1924 - 1996
.... 5 Kenneth Gene Hovatter 1927 - 1983
.... 4 Jessie Jones 1888 -

.... 4 Chester Jones 1890 -
.... 4 Julius Jones 1892 -
.... 3 Michael Franklin Smith 1856 -
.... 3 M. J. Smith 1862 -
.... 3 Joel D .Smith 1866 -

Descendants of John Smith

Generation No. 1

1. JOHN[1] SMITH[1] was born in AL[1]. He married MARY SHUMATE[1], daughter of BIG SHOE-MAKE. She was born January 01, 1820 in S.C.[1], and died August 07, 1892 in Greene Co, Miss.[1].

Notes for JOHN SMITH:
The story handed down to me was that my g-g-grandmother Mary Shumate, was married to John Smith and that he signed a treaty and was on the indian side.
There is a treaty dated July 1, 1861 called the:
Articles of Confederation entered into between Musgogees, Siminoles, Choctaws and Chickasaws and the Confederate States of America.
His name is listed as a signer.

More About MARY SHUMATE:
Burial: Slay Cemetary[1]

Children of JOHN SMITH and MARY SHUMATE are:

- i. JAMES AARON[2] SMITH[1], b. Abt. 1852, MS[1].
- 2. ii. MARY A. SMITH, b. October 10, 1855, Al; d. October 05, 1911, Greene Co, Miss..
- iii. MICHAEL FRANKLIN SMITH[1], b. April 08, 1856, AL[1].
- iv. M. J. SMITH[1], b. Abt. 1862, AL[1].
- v. JOEL D .SMITH[1], b. September 1866, AL[1].

Generation No. 2

2. MARY A.[2] SMITH *(JOHN[1])*[1] was born October 10, 1855 in Al[1], and died October 05, 1911 in Greene Co, Miss.[1]. She married (1) GEORGE A. POWELL. She married (2) ENOCH JONES[1] September 30, 1880 in Greene Co. Miss.[1], son of WILLIAM JONES and ELIZABETH PHELPS. He was born February 23, 1822 in Dallas County, AL[1], and died July 24, 1903 in Greene co. Ms[1].

Notes for MARY A. SMITH:
Mary Ann was 1/2 Choctaw Indian

More About MARY A. SMITH:
Burial: Slay Cemetary[1]

More About ENOCH JONES:
Burial: Slay cemetary

Children of MARY SMITH and ENOCH JONES are:

- i. MARY POWELL[3] JONES[1], b. July 01, 1873[1].
- ii. JAMES POWELL JONES[1], b. February 22, 1876[1].
- iii. HATTIE LEE JONES[1], b. October 06, 1885, Greene Co, Miss.[1]; d. October 09, 1969, Greene Co, Miss.[1]; m. WILBERT F. HOVATTER[1], February 18, 1903, Greene Co. Miss.[1]; b. April 01, 1882, Preston Co. WV[1]; d. August 19, 1969, Greene Co. Miss.[1].

  Notes for HATTIE LEE JONES:
  84 years old and 3 days at time of death
  Pictures on pages 106, 107 108 in book "Generations of Hoffman to Hovatter"

  More About HATTIE LEE JONES:
  Burial: Stateline, MS

Fact 5: Social Security #: 177-14-7342[2]
Fact 6: Issued in: Pennsylvania[2]
Fact 7: Residence code: Mississippi[2]
Fact 8: Last residence ZIP: 39451[2]

Notes for WILBERT F. HOVATTER:
87 years old 4 months and 18 days at time of death

More About WILBERT F. HOVATTER:
Burial: Stateline, MS
Social Security Number: Pennslyvania[3]

iv. JESSIE JONES[3], b. February 08, 1888[3].
v. CHESTER JONES[3], b. March 04, 1890[3].
vi. JULIUS JONES[3], b. April 10, 1892[3].

Endnotes

1. Mancuso.FTW, Date of Import: Sep 6, 2000.
2. Genealogy.com, Family Archive #110, Social Security Death Index: U.S. Ed. 9, Social Security Death Index, Release date: April 10, 2000, Internal Ref. #1.111.9.122873.123.
3. Mancuso.FTW, Date of Import: Sep 6, 2000.

Descendants of Enoch Jones

Generation No. 1

1. ENOCH[2] JONES *(WILLIAM NATHANIEL[1])*[1] was born February 23, 1822 in Dallas County, AL[1], and died July 24, 1903 in Greene co. Ms[1]. He married (1) SUSAN ABNEY[1] September 01, 1842 in Neshoba County, MS[1]. She was born November 18, 1827 in Hinds Co. MS[1], and died November 16, 1876. He married (2) ROSE GORDON 1878. He married (3) MARY A. SMITH[1] September 30, 1880 in Greene Co. Miss.[1], daughter of JOHN SMITH and MARY SHUMATE. She was born October 10, 1855 in Al[1], and died October 05, 1911 in Greene Co, Miss.[1].

More About ENOCH JONES:
Burial: Slay cemetary

More About SUSAN ABNEY:
Burial: Slay Cemetary

Notes for MARY A. SMITH:
Mary Ann was 1/2 Choctaw Indian

More About MARY A. SMITH:
Burial: Slay Cemetary[1]

Children of ENOCH JONES and SUSAN ABNEY are:

i. DORTHEA SARAH[3] JONES[1], b. March 28, 1843[1].
ii. SARAH E. JONES[1], b. November 03, 1843[1].
iii. WILLIAM JOSEPH JONES[1], b. January 23, 1847[1].
iv. MARTHA MATILDA JONES[1], b. December 29, 1848[1].
v. ENOCH ROBERT JONES[1], b. December 18, 1850[1].
vi. JOHN C. JONES[1], b. November 13, 1852[1]; d. 1927.

More About JOHN C. JONES:
Burial: Slay Cemetary

vii. JESSE NELSON JONES[1], b. April 14, 1855[1].
viii. ANNA E. JONES[1], b. July 24, 1857[1].
ix. MARGARET EMILY JONES[1], b. May 04, 1859[1].
x. THOMAS JEFFERSON JONES[1], b. September 18, 1861[1].
xi. SUSAN LOUISA JONES[1], b. August 09, 1864[1].

Children of ENOCH JONES and MARY SMITH are:

xii. MARY POWELL[3] JONES[1], b. July 01, 1873[1].
xiii. JAMES POWELL JONES[1], b. February 22, 1876[1].
xiv. HATTIE LEE JONES[1], b. October 06, 1885, Greene Co, Miss.[1]; d. October 09, 1969, Greene Co, Miss.[1]; m. WILBERT F. HOVATTER[1], February 18, 1903, Greene Co. Miss.[1]; b. April 01, 1882, Preston Co. WV[1]; d. August 19, 1969, Greene Co. Miss.[1].

Notes for HATTIE LEE JONES:
84 years old and 3 days at time of death
Pictures on pages 106, 107 108 in book "Generations of Hoffman to Hovatter"

More About HATTIE LEE JONES:
Burial: Stateline, MS
Fact 5: Social Security #: 177-14-7342[2]
Fact 6: Issued in: Pennsylvania[2]
Fact 7: Residence code: Mississippi[2]

Fact 8: Last residence ZIP: 39451[2]

Notes for WILBERT F. HOVATTER:
87 years old 4 months and 18 days at time of death

More About WILBERT F. HOVATTER:
Burial: Stateline, MS
Social Security Number: Pennslyvania[3]

xv. JESSIE JONES[3], b. February 08, 1888[3].
xvi. CHESTER JONES[3], b. March 04, 1890[3].
xvii. JULIUS JONES[3], b. April 10, 1892[3].

Endnotes

1. Mancuso.FTW, Date of Import: Sep 6, 2000.
2. Genealogy.com, Family Archive #110, Social Security Death Index: U.S. Ed. 9, Social Security Death Index, Release date: April 10, 2000, Internal Ref. #1.111.9.122873.123.
3. Mancuso.FTW, Date of Import: Sep 6, 2000.

MARY ANN SMITH/JONES
DAUGHTER OF
JOHN SMITH/ MARY SHUMATE/SMITH

Mary Ann Smith/Jones purse and knoll from a buttonwood tree that was used as a tooth cleaning device

Descendants of Moses Phelps

Generation No. 1

1. MOSES[1] PHELPS[1].

Child of MOSES PHELPS is:

2. i. ENOCH S.[2] PHELPS, b. 1775, Tyrell, NC; d. 1848.

Generation No. 2

2. ENOCH S.[2] PHELPS *(MOSES[1])*[1] was born 1775 in Tyrell, NC[1], and died 1848[1]. He married MARY SPRUILL[1]. She was born 1780 in SC or NC[1].

Child of ENOCH PHELPS and MARY SPRUILL is:

3. i. ELIZABETH[3] PHELPS, b. 1799, Edgefield,S.C.; d. April 27, 1863, Beech Springs, Neshoba County, MS.

Generation No. 3

3. ELIZABETH[3] PHELPS *(ENOCH S.[2], MOSES[1])*[1] was born 1799 in Edgefield,S.C.[1], and died April 27, 1863 in Beech Springs, Neshoba County, MS. She married WILLIAM NATHANIEL JONES[1] Bet. 1818 - 1819 in Edgefield District, S.C.. He was born 1795 in S.C.[1], and died Bet. 1856 - 1857 in Beech Springs, Neshoba County, MS.

Children of ELIZABETH PHELPS and WILLIAM JONES are:

i. MARY[4] JONES, b. Abt. 1820; d. Aft. 1820, Texas; m. JAMES J. JONES, 1839, Neshoba County, Ms; b. 1811, S.C.; d. Bet. 1859 - 1860, Neshoba County, MS.

ii. ENOCH JONES[1], b. February 23, 1822, Dallas County, AL[1]; d. July 24, 1903, Greene co. Ms[1]; m. (1) SUSAN ABNEY[1], September 01, 1842, Neshoba County, MS[1]; b. November 18, 1827, Hinds Co. MS[1]; d. November 16, 1876; m. (2) ROSE GORDON, 1878; m. (3) MARY A. SMITH[1], September 30, 1880, Greene Co. Miss.[1]; b. October 10, 1855, Al[1]; d. October 05, 1911, Greene Co, Miss.[1].

More About ENOCH JONES:
Burial: Slay cemetary

More About SUSAN ABNEY:
Burial: Slay Cemetary

Notes for MARY A. SMITH:
Mary Ann was 1/2 Choctaw Indian

More About MARY A. SMITH:
Burial: Slay Cemetary[1]

iii. ELIZABETH ANN JONES, b. Abt. 1823.
iv. SON JONES, b. Abt. 1825.
v. FERRABA ROSANNE JONES, b. December 27, 1826.
vi. SON JONES, b. Abt. 1828.
vii. DAUGHTER JONES, b. Abt. 1830.
viii. D. R. HULDA JONES, b. September 23, 1833.
ix. MARGARET EMILY JONES, b. February 09, 1835.
x. W. JOHN JONES, b. Abt. 1839.
xi. JULIA E. C. JONES, b. July 30, 1842.

Descendants of William Nathaniel Jones

Generation No. 1

1. WILLIAM NATHANIEL[1] JONES[1] was born 1795 in S.C.[1], and died Bet. 1856 - 1857 in Beech Springs, Neshoba County, MS. He married ELIZABETH PHELPS[1] Bet. 1818 - 1819 in Edgefield District, S.C., daughter of ENOCH PHELPS and MARY SPRUILL. She was born 1799 in Edgefield,S.C.[1], and died April 27, 1863 in Beech Springs, Neshoba County, MS.

Children of WILLIAM JONES and ELIZABETH PHELPS are:

2. i. MARY[2] JONES, b. Abt. 1820; d. Aft. 1820, Texas.
3. ii. ENOCH JONES, b. February 23, 1822, Dallas County, AL; d. July 24, 1903, Greene co. Ms.
iii. ELIZABETH ANN JONES, b. Abt. 1823.
iv. SON JONES, b. Abt. 1825.
v. FERRABA ROSANNE JONES, b. December 27, 1826.
vi. SON JONES, b. Abt. 1828.
vii. DAUGHTER JONES, b. Abt. 1830.
viii. D. R. HULDA JONES, b. September 23, 1833.
ix. MARGARET EMILY JONES, b. February 09, 1835.
x. W. JOHN JONES, b. Abt. 1839.
xi. JULIA E. C. JONES, b. July 30, 1842.

Generation No. 2

2. MARY[2] JONES *(WILLIAM NATHANIEL[1])* was born Abt. 1820, and died Aft. 1820 in Texas. She married JAMES J. JONES 1839 in Neshoba County, Ms. He was born 1811 in S.C., and died Bet. 1859 - 1860 in Neshoba County, MS.

Children of MARY JONES and JAMES JONES are:

i. JOSEPHINE[3] JONES, b. 1840.
ii. MARGARET A. JONES, b. 1842.
iii. WILLIAM B. JONES, b. 1844.
iv. GEORGE P. JONES, b. 1846.
v. SARAH ELIZABETH JONES, b. March 01, 1848.
vi. SUSAN A. JONES, b. 1851.
vii. MARY J. JONES, b. 1853.
viii. JAMES J JONES. JR, b. 1855.
ix. JOHN E. JONES, b. 1858.
x. WILLIAM T. B. JONES, b. 1860.

3. ENOCH[2] JONES *(WILLIAM NATHANIEL[1])*[1] was born February 23, 1822 in Dallas County, AL[1], and died July 24, 1903 in Greene co. Ms[1]. He married (1) SUSAN ABNEY[1] September 01, 1842 in Neshoba County, MS[1]. She was born November 18, 1827 in Hinds Co. MS[1], and died November 16, 1876. He married (2) ROSE GORDON 1878. He married (3) MARY A. SMITH[1] September 30, 1880 in Greene Co. Miss.[1], daughter of JOHN SMITH and MARY SHUMATE. She was born October 10, 1855 in Al[1], and died October 05, 1911 in Greene Co, Miss.[1].

More About ENOCH JONES:
Burial: Slay cemetary

More About SUSAN ABNEY:
Burial: Slay Cemetary

Notes for MARY A. SMITH:
Mary Ann was 1/2 Choctaw Indian

More About MARY A. SMITH:
Burial: Slay Cemetary[1]

Children of ENOCH JONES and SUSAN ABNEY are:

i. DORTHEA SARAH[3] JONES[1], b. March 28, 1843[1].
ii. SARAH E. JONES[1], b. November 03, 1843[1].
iii. WILLIAM JOSEPH JONES[1], b. January 23, 1847[1].
iv. MARTHA MATILDA JONES[1], b. December 29, 1848[1].
v. ENOCH ROBERT JONES[1], b. December 18, 1850[1].
vi. JOHN C. JONES[1], b. November 13, 1852[1]; d. 1927.

More About JOHN C. JONES:
Burial: Slay Cemetary

vii. JESSE NELSON JONES[1], b. April 14, 1855[1].
viii. ANNA E. JONES[1], b. July 24, 1857[1].
ix. MARGARET EMILY JONES[1], b. May 04, 1859[1].
x. THOMAS JEFFERSON JONES[1], b. September 18, 1861[1].
xi. SUSAN LOUISA JONES[1], b. August 09, 1864[1].

Children of ENOCH JONES and MARY SMITH are:

xii. MARY POWELL[3] JONES[1], b. July 01, 1873[1].
xiii. JAMES POWELL JONES[1], b. February 22, 1876[1].
xiv. HATTIE LEE JONES[1], b. October 06, 1885, Greene Co, Miss.[1]; d. October 09, 1969, Greene Co, Miss.[1]; m. WILBERT F. HOVATTER[1], February 18, 1903, Greene Co. Miss.[1]; b. April 01, 1882, Preston Co. WV[1]; d. August 19, 1969, Greene Co. Miss.[1].

Notes for HATTIE LEE JONES:
84 years old and 3 days at time of death
Pictures on pages 106, 107 108 in book "Generations of Hoffman to Hovatter"

More About HATTIE LEE JONES:
Burial: Stateline, MS
Fact 5: Social Security #: 177-14-7342[2]
Fact 6: Issued in: Pennsylvania[2]
Fact 7: Residence code: Mississippi[2]
Fact 8: Last residence ZIP: 39451[2]

Notes for WILBERT F. HOVATTER:
87 years old 4 months and 18 days at time of death

More About WILBERT F. HOVATTER:
Burial: Stateline, MS
Social Security Number: Pennslyvania[3]

xv. JESSIE JONES[3], b. February 08, 1888[3].
xvi. CHESTER JONES[3], b. March 04, 1890[3].
xvii. JULIUS JONES[3], b. April 10, 1892[3].

Endnotes

1. Mancuso.FTW, Date of Import: Sep 6, 2000.
2. Genealogy.com, Family Archive #110, Social Security Death Index: U.S. Ed. 9, Social Security Death Index, Release date: April 10, 2000, Internal Ref. #1.111.9.122873.123.
3. Mancuso.FTW, Date of Import: Sep 6, 2000.

MARY SMITH BORN JAN. 1st 1820
ENOCH S. JONES BORN FEB 22 1822
MARY A. JONES BORN OCT 10, 1855

Children of Mary Smith / Powell
Mary E. Powell Born June 1st, 1873
James Powell Born Feb. 22, 1876

Children of Mary Smith / Enoch Jones
Enoch Jones Born April 13th 1881
Minnie Drucilla Jones Born Aug. 23, 1883
Hattie L. Jones Born Oct. 6, 1885
Jessie Jones Born Feb. 5, 1888
Chester Grover Cleveland (Bud) Jones
Born March 4, 1890

Julius Brown (Jule) Jones
Born April 10, 1892

MARY SMITH DIED AUG 7th 1892

Enoch died July 24, 1903
Mary A. died May 5th, 1911
2 Childred Enoch Jones Nov. 4th 1881
Minnie Jones died May 5th 1884

Mississippi Department of Archives and History

Archives and Library Division

Post Office Box 571 • Jackson, Mississippi 39205-0571 •Telephone 601-359-6876

Reference #: R40235

Dear Mrs. Sutton:

You will find a response to your inquiry in the statement(s) checked below. We do not keep copies of this correspondence. If it is necessary to write again, please return this form and any related correspondence.

1. ☒ Enclosed is a quotation sheet for the information we have located. Prepayment is required.

2. ☐ We have checked the sources listed on the second page and have been unable to find the information you requested.

3. ☐ We are unable to comply with your request because the source material ☐ has not been processed, ☐ has not been cataloged, ☐ does not circulate, ☐ includes a publisher's note which prohibits photocopying, ☐ is too fragile to photocopy, ☐ will not photocopy clearly.

4. ☐ No official birth and death records were kept by the State of Mississippi until November 1912. Prior to that time, census records can be used to determine the birth year. All birth records since 1912 and death records from 1944 to present are in the custody of the State Board of Health, Vital Records Section, P. O. Box 1700, Jackson, MS 39205.

5. ☐ Enclosed is a list of persons who do research here should you need further assistance.

6. ☐ The library search room is open Mondays 9:00-5:00, T-F, 8:00-5:00, and on Saturdays, 8:00-1:00. The library is closed on state holidays.

7. ☒ other: We searched and were unable to locate an obituary for your great grandmother. We searched for a marriage record for Enoch and Mary A. Jones. The marriage soundex (on microfilm) listed that they were married on September 30, 1880. The Greene County Marriage Records (1875-1910) book lists that they married on September 27, 1880.

#098
15^{00}
40235

D
R
try for obit

October 16, 2001

Jones
J520

MDAH
P.O. Box 571
Jackson, MS 39205

To Whom it may Concern:

I have been researching my family and have hit a brick wall. It may well be that you have some information in the obituaries ~~or marriage~~ records that can be of help to me.

(Leakesville)
Bathwell, Sand Hill, Piave, Neely, Hillman

My great grandfather was Enoch Jones from Greene Co. MS. I have a lot of information on him but have not been able to get much on my great grandmother, his third wife. Mary A. Smith/Jones, she died Oct. 5, 1911, buried in Slay Cemetery, MS., also her mother, Mary Smith, died Aug. 7,1892. She is also buried in Slay Cemetery. If there is any information on file that might have their parents name on it I would appreciate getting it. Leakesville newspaper not published in 1892

Enoch and Mary A. Jones were married Sept. 1880, either on the 27th or 30th. There might be some information about her parents in the marriage records. Enclosed is a check for $15.00 for research. Please let me know if you were able to complete the research for that amount, I will send another $15.00 if needed.

Thank you,

Joyce Sutton

Joyce Sutton
2074 River Road
Egg Harbor, NJ 08215

609-965-2476

Greene County Herald
Leakesville, Greene Co, MS.
Nov. 25, 1910 - Dec. 22, 191
(np 0471)

Obituary not found

Greene Co. Marriage Records (1875-1910) Book says E.S. Jones and Mary A. Powell married on Sept. 27, 1880.

Marriages Prior To 1926
MDAH roll number: mr26
Enoch S. Jones and Mary A. Powell were married on Sept. 30TH 1880 in Greene County.
Book —, Page 200

200

STATE OF MISSISSIPPI,

GREENE COUNTY.

Know All Men by these Presents.

That we, Enoch S Jones Principal and Joseph Robinson

Surety, are held and firmly bound unto the State of Mississippi, in the sum of One Hundred Dollars lawful money of the said State, for which payment well and truly to be made, we bind ourselves, our heirs, executors, and administrators, each and every one of us and them, jointly and severally, firmly by these presents.

Sealed with our Seals, and dated this the 27th day of September, Eighteen Hundred and Eighty-

The Condition of this Obligation is such, That, Whereas, a MARRIAGE is intended shortly to be celebrated between the above bound E. S. Jones and Mary A Pearce, now if there is no lawful cause to obstruct the said Marriage, then this obligation to be void, otherwise to remain in full force and virtue

ATTEST:

Clerk.

E S Jones (SEAL)

Joseph Robinson (SEAL)

THE STATE OF MISSISSIPPI,
GREENE COUNTY.

I, , do solemnly swear that I am twenty-one years old, and that , whom I wish to marry, is eighteen years old. So help me God

Subscribed and Sworn to Before Me, this day of A. D. 188

Clerk.

D. C.

THE STATE OF MISSISSIPPI,
GREENE COUNTY.

To any Judge, Minister, Justice, or other person lawfully authorized to solemnize the rites of Matrimony:

You are Hereby Authorised to celebrate the RITES OF MATRIMONY between [illegible] and Joseph Robinson of said County. And you are hereby required to transmit to the undersigned, Clerk of the Circuit Court of said County, or his successors in office, a CERTIFICATE OF THE MARRIAGE of said parties within six months after celebration of the same.

Herein fail not, under the penalty in such cases made and provided.

Given Under my Hand and Official Seal, This the 27 day of September A. D. 1880

W. E. [illegible] Clerk.

D. C.

Circuit Court Greene County.

By Virtue of a License from the Clerk of the Circuit Court of Greene County, I have this day joined in the HOLY STATE OF MATRIMONY, Enoch S Jones and Mary A Pearce

GIVEN UNDER MY HAND, this the 30th day of September 1880

L. C. [illegible]

J. P.

Filed 188

DISTRICT # 2 - 1870 United States Census, Greene County, MS

H Fam	Name	A-S-R	Occupation	Real	Pers.	Birth
1-1	Robertson, J. J.	55mw	Farmer	200	450	SC
	Robertson, Harriett	33fw	keeping house			FL
	Robertson, Jane	18fw	at home			MS
	Robertson, Berry	16mw	at home			MS
	Robertson, Elizabeth	4fw	at home			MS
	Robertson, Ransom	4mw	at home			MS
	Robertson, Mary	3fw	at home			MS
	Robertson, John	2mw	at home			MS
	Robertson, George	8/12mw	at home			MS
2-2	Kittrell, David	40mw	Farmer	200	250	MS
	Kittrell, Margaret	36fw	keeping house			MS
	Kittrell, Jane	12fw	at home			MS
	Kittrell, John	11mw	at home			MS
	Kittrell, Margaret	10fw	at home			MS
	Kittrell, Mary	3fw	at home			MS
	Kittrell, David	1mw	at home			MS
3-3	Jones, E. S.	48mw	Farmer	1600	600	AL
1st Wife —	Jones, Susan	42fw	keeping house			MS
	Jones, Martha	21fw	at home			MS
	Jones, Rob't E.	19mw	works in farm			MS
	Jones, J. C.	17mw	works in farm			MS
	Jones, J. M.	15mw	at home			MS
	Jones, N. E.	12mw	at home			MS
	Jones, Margaret	11fw	at home			MS
	Jones, Thomas J.	9mw	at home			MS
	Jones, Susan	5fw	at home			MS
4-4	Hood, J. R.	36mw	Ret. merchant		3000	GA
	Hood, Mary C.	26fw	keeping house			AL
	Hood, Nora	1fw	at home			AL
	Miles, Laura	15fw	seamstress			AL
	Howel, E. R.	30mw	clerk in ret. store			AL
5-5	Byrd, Jesse	23mw	Ret merchant		800	MS
	Byrd, Lizzie	22fw	keeping house			MS
	Byrd, Sidney, A.	1mw	at home			MS
6-6	Harris, Mary	67fw	keeping house			NC
	Harris, B. F.	24mw	Ret. merchant		800	MS
	Harris, John	21mw	Carpenter			MS
	Harris, Osburn	19mw	at home			MS
	Posey, H. M.	27mw	Clerk in ret. store			AL
7-7	Packer, George	60mm	Carpenter			SC
	Packer, Minnie	34fm	keeping house			AL
	Packer, M. W.	14mm	at home			AL
	Packer, Ripley	11mm	at home			AL
	Packer, Lisbon	9mm	at home			AL
	Packer, Sam'l	3mm	at home			AL
8-8	Grishom, John	54mw	Miller	5000	5000	SC
	Grishom, Joseph	24mw	Clerk in saw mill			SC
	Grishom, Mary	20fw	keeping house			FL
9-9	McInnis, Benj	75mb	without occupation			SC
	McInnis, Sofa	50fb	keeping house			SC
	McInnis, Tobe	25mb	cuts cross ties			MS
10-10	Marshal, J. L.	48mw	Farmer	300	500	MS
	Marshal, D. M.	34fw	keeping house			MS
	Marshal, Jane	18fw	at home			MS
	Marshal, Edward	16mw	at home			MS
	Marshal, William	14mw	at home			MS

<HTML><FONT SIZE=3 PTSIZE=10>Subj: <B>(no subject)</FONT><FON
T SIZE=3 PTSIZE=10></B>
Date: 07/27/2000 1:56:36 AM Eastern Daylight Time
From: JSutton639
To: JSutton639
</FONT><FONT SIZE=3 PTSIZE=10>

ID: I105322
Name: Enoch Sprewell JONES
Given Name: Enoch Sprewell
Surname: JONES
Sex: M
Birth: 23 FEB 1822 in AL
Death: 20 JUL 1903 in Stateline,MS (Greene)
Burial: JUL 1903 Slay Cemetery (Ernest Guy Cem),Stateline,MS
Note:
Enoch was a also a goldsmith and a cup he made still exists in the
 family.
Tombstone at Slay Cemetery (now known as Ernesy Guy Cemetery) in<B
R>
Stateline, MS (Greene). 1850 Newton Co, MS census p194. 1870 Green
e Co,
MS census p102. 1880 Greene Co, MS census ed136 st5, beat 5-Statel
ine, MS
hh#37/38. 1900 Greene Co, MS census, Avera precinct, ed19 hh#27/29
.
Assorted census records for children. Will of Enoch S. JONES dated
 27 Feb
1884, Greene Co, MS. Enoch S. & Susan ABNEY JONES family Bible pag
es.
Probate records, Neshoba Co, MS, for Enoch's parents William & Eli
zabeth
JONES. 1819-1849 Abstradex of MS Free & Accepted Masons book. LDS<
BR>
records. Greene & Wayne Co, MS cemetery books. Assorted family rec
ords &
photos. Who Married Whom in Greene Co, MS & Who Married Whom in Wa
yne Co,
MS both books by Strickland. Assorted MS land and probate records.

</HTML>

BEAT # 2 - 1880 United States Census, Greene County, MS

Some Spelling errors:
*Johns-Jones ——— see 37-38
Rize-Reese
Kitheral Kitteral Kittrell
McClarron-McLaurin
Stinton-Stinson;
Pain-Payne
Daves-Davis

H Fam	Name	Race Sex	Age		Relation Occup		State	
BEAT # 2								
17-18	Walle, July B.	W F	28		H keeper MS	MS	GA	
	Oliv C.	W F	4	Dau		MS	MS	MS
	J. C.	W	M	3	Son		MS	MS
18-19	Smith, C. P.	W M	27		Farmer	MS	MS	MS
	C. E.	W F	27	Wife	H keeper FL	FL	FL	
	Louella	W F	1	Dau		MS	MS	FL
	Adelia	W F	3/12	Dau		MS	MS	FL
19-20	Ezell E. L.	W M	54		Farmer	Ga	SC	SC
	Margaret	W F	51	Wife	H keeper MS	MS	NC	
	M. Jane	W F	24	Dau	A home	MS	MS	MS?
	N. Jane	W F	21	Dau	At home	MS	MS	MS
	M. C.	W F	18	Dau	At home	MS	MS	MS
	Susanna	W F	13	Dau	At home	MS	MS	MS
	E. L.	W N	11	Son	At home	MS	MS	MS
20-21	Morgan, Eph.	W M	59		Farmer	MS	SC	RI?
	America	W F	42	Wife	H keeper MS	MS	MS	
	J. W.	W M	20	Son	Farms	MS	MS	MS
	Clarissa	W F	15	Dau	At home	MS	MS	MS
	Rufus	W M	2	Son		MS	MS	MS
21-22	Lankford, J.A.	W M	40	Farmer		MS	GA	NC
	H. C.	W F	43	Wife	H keeper MS	SC	SC	
	J. E.	W	M	17	Son At home		MS	Ga
	D. C.	W M	14	Son	At home	MS	GA	SC
	Isabelle A.	W F	12	Dau	At home	MS	GA	SC
22-23	Robertson, J.J.	W M	66		Farmer	SC	SC	SC
	Harriett	W F	'38	Wife	H keeping	FL	GA	GA
	Elizabeth	W F	16	Dau	At home	MS	SC	FL
	R. C.	W M	14	Son	At home	MS	SC	FL
	Marie	W F	13	Dau	At home	MS	SC	FL
	John	W M	12	Son	At home	MS	SC	FL
	G. L.	W M	10	Son	At home	MS	SC	FL
	H. E.	W F	8	Dau	At home	MS	SC	FL
	S.R.	W	M	6	Son At home		MS	SC
	Juda	W F	5	Dau	At home	MS	SC	FL
	Joe	W	M	2	Son At home		MS	SC
23-24	*Rize, Sara W	F	40		H keeper FL	GA	GA	
	John	W M	24	Son	Farm laborer	FL	GA	GA
	A. E.	W F	23	Dau	At home	MS	GA	FL
	M. E.	W F	19	Dau	At home	MS	GA	FL
	George	W M	11	Son	At home	MS	GA	FL
24-25	Avera, S.W.	W M	27	Farmer		MS	MS	MS
	E.	W F	22	Wife	H keeper LA	MD	MD	
	Marion	W M	2	Son	At home	MS	MS	LA
	William	W M	1	Son		MS	MS	LA
	Walle Georg	B M	18		Servant	MS	MS	MS

	M. J.	W F	13	Dau	At home	MS	MS	MS
	D. C. U	W M	11	Son	At home	MS	MS	MS
	M. L.	W F	8	Dau		MS	MS	MS
	A. D.	W M	5	Son		MS	MS	MS
	S. E.	W M	4	Son		MS	MS	MS
	F. F.	W M	3	Son		MS	MS	MS
	Julius	W M	2	Son		MS	MS	MS
	Joseph	W M	1/12	Son		MS	MS	MS
	Abslom	W M	53	Brother	Farm Labor	MS	NC	NC
37-38	*Johns E. S.	W M	58		Farmer	AL	SC	SC
	Smith, Mary	W F	59	Border		SC	SC	SC
	Powell, Mary A.	W F	26	H keeper	H.keeper AL	MS	SC	
	Mary E.	W F	7	Dau		AL	Al	AL
	J. F.	W	M	4	Son		AL	AL
38-39	Smith, James	W M	28		Farmer	MS	SC	SC
	A. M	W F	24	Wife		AL	AL	AL
	M. A.	W F	3	Dau		MS	MS	AL
	Emmaline	W F	2	Dau		AL	MS	AL
	Caroline	W F	1/12	Dau		MS	MS	AL
39-40	Norsworthy G.	W M	27		Farmer	MS	MS	MS
	Ann	W	F	23	Wife		MS	AL
	Elizabeth	W F	2	Dau		MS	MS	MS
	Fredrick	W M	21	Brother		MS	MS	MS
40-41	Robertson, Jos.	W M	71		Farmer	SC	SC	SC
	Ann	W F	53	Wife	H keeper MS	SC	SC	
	W. B.	W M	20	Son	Farm Labor	MS	SC	NC
	Sara	W	F	18	Dau At home		MS	SC
	J. A	W M	16	Son	At home	MS	SC	NC
	R. T.	W M	13	Son	At home	MS	MS	MS
41-42	Robertson, Jn.	W M	73		Farmer	SC	SC	SC
	C. A.	W F	73	Wife	H keeper SC	NC	NC	
43	Davis, Luu	B F	25	Servant		MS	MS	MS
	Martha	B F	12	Dau		MS	MS	MS
	Jain	B F	9	Dau		MS	MS	MS
	Lenard	B M	7	Son		MS	MS	MS
	M--	B M	5	Son		MS	MS	MS
42-44	Kitteral, C. R.	W F	52		H Keeper MS	NC	NC	
	Thomas	W M	20		Farmer	MS	MS	MS
	M. O.	W F	18	Dau	At home	MS	MS	MS
43-45	Kitherall, A. S.	W M	24		Farmer	MS	MS	MS
	M. M.	W F	22	Wife	H keeper MS	MS	MS	
	Denny	W M	1	Son		MS	MS	MS
44-46	Mills, G. J	W M	20		Labor in FarmMS	MS	MS	
	D. R.	W M	18		Labor in FarmMS	MS	MS	
	*Johns, P. J.	W M	18		Labor in FarmMS	MS	MS	
45-47	*McClarron, E.	W F	63	H keeper	MS	SC	SC	
	Daniel	W M	24	Son	Farmer	MS	SC	MS
	Sara	W	F	38	Dau At home		MS	SC
	McClendon, A.	W F	10	Orphan	At home	MS	MS	MS
46-48	Mills, M. J.	W M	25		Farmer	AL	AL	AL
	Elizabeth	W F	36	Wife	H keeper MS	SC	MS	
	L. M.	W F	4	Dau		MS	AL	MS
	G. A.	W F	2	Dau		MS	AL	MS
47-49	Mills, James	B M	25		Laborer	MS	MS	MS
	Caroline	B F	23	Wife	H keeper MS	MS	MS	
48-50	McCann, Joe	B M	50	Laborer		MS	MS	MS
	Chante?	B F	40	Wife	H keeper NC	NC	NC	
49-51	Green, Harriett	B F	30?		Labor	MS	MS	MS
	Molly	B F	16	Dau	At home	MS	MS	MS
	Janes	B F	7	Dau		MS	MS	MS
	Thomas	B M	5	Son		MS	MS	MS
	Henderson, C.	B F	12	Border		MS	MS	MS
50-52	McCann, Tom	B M	30	Labor in Farm		AL	AL	AL
	Hester	B F	28	Wife	H keeper MS	MS	MS	
	Tom	B M	13	Son	at home	MS	MS	MS
	David	B M	11	Son	At home	MS	MS	MS

Mary A. - mother soon to be 2nd wife. —

Mary A. Powell / Jones
daughter of John Smith and Mary Shumate / Smith

HATTIE JONES- HWATTER

MARY ANN SMITH/JONES
DAUGHTER OF
JOHN SMITH/ MARY
SHUMATE/SMITH

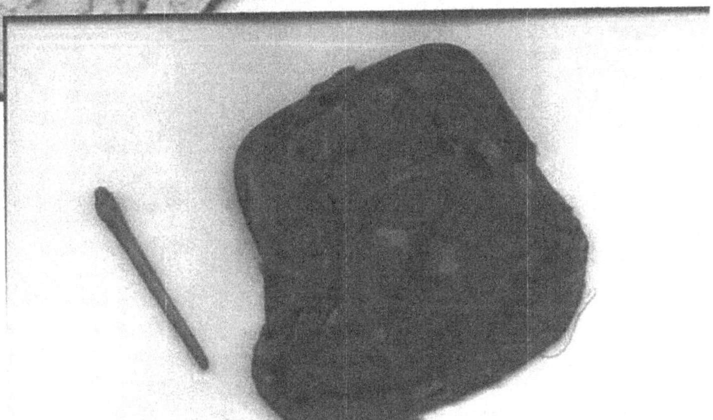

Mary Ann Smith/Jones purse and knoll from a buttonwood tree that was used as a tooth cleaning device

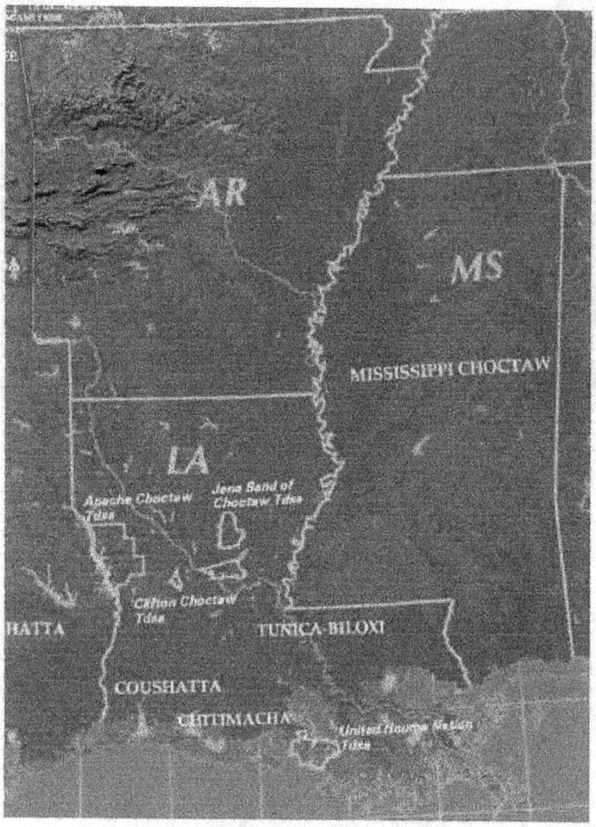
AR
MS
MISSISSIPPI CHOCTAW
LA
Apache Choctaw Tdsa
Jena Band of Choctaw Tdsa
Clifton Choctaw Tdsa
HATTA
TUNICA-BILOXI
COUSHATTA
CHITIMACHA
United Houma Nation Tdsa

Jacqueline A. Matte * 1714 Kestwick Circle * Birmingham, AL 35226

9/2/2005

Ms. Joyce F. Sutton
2074 River Road
Egg Harbor, NJ 08215

Dear Ms. Sutton:

The MOWA Choctaw Indians in Alabama need your help. As someone who purchased our book, *They Say the Wind is Red: The Alabama Choctaw Lost in Their Own Land*, you are familiar with the history of the MOWA Band of Choctaw Indians.

As you know we have been fighting for federal recognition for almost a quarter century. I am enclosing an article written by Cedric Sunray, a MOWA Choctaw, published in *Native American Times*, July 27, 2005. It will bring you up to date on our current situation.

Congressman Jo Bonner, 1st District, Alabama has introduced a bill **HR 3526, "MOWA Band of Choctaw Indians of Alabama Recognition Act." 109th Congress: 1st Session** We are asking your support in getting our bill passed in Congress. Please send a letter or e-mail to your U. S. Representative and Senator in support of passage of this bill.

You can get e-mail addresses or mailing addresses on Internet by going to http://matte.accessgenealogy.com and click on Members of Congress, Members of House, and Members of Committee on Resources. The Committee on Resources will be the first to review our Bill HR 3526. The Bill has to pass this committee before it will go to the full house. If any of these members are in your state, please send a letter asking them to support HR 3526.

If you don't use a computer, look in the blue pages of your telephone directory under U. S. Government, then Congress. Your Senators and Representatives will be listed there with addresses.

This is our last chance for federal recognition. We need your help now.

Sincerely,

Jacqueline A. Matte

Jacqueline Anderson Matte
Tribal Historian & Author of
They Say the Wind is Red

JACQUELINE A. MATTE
1714 Kestwick Circle
Birmingham, AL 35226
205-822-3701
jackiematte@charter.net
http://matte.accessgenealogy.com

Phone: 205-822-3701 * e-mail: jackiematte@charter.net

1831 year

Page 48

No. :

Names of Indians owning farms.	No. of acres cultivated.	Entire No. of the family.	Males over 16 years.	Males and females under 10 years.
Ishtonakhopaii	3	7	2	1
Shapha (widow)	1½	6	2	3
Tashkahimilta	4	8	1	3
Samuel Mosely	2	4	1	2
Sholashhoma	5	6	1	2
Paiimataha	23	18	5	4
Onarke (widow of Tishohikabi)	....	1	....	....
Tihekabi	12	12	2	4
Okchanakahoma	....	8	2	1
Kashonnishtikabi	4	4	1	2
Yoshohika	....	5	1	3
Anderson	4	4	1	2
Capt. Nahomastibi	8	7	1	3
David Wainer	....	2	1	....
Poshochcya	3	6	1	2
Tishoa:hahbi	5	7	1	1
Holahtoklabi	6	10	2	3
Big Meat	6	7	1	3
Loui Lucas	8	7	2	3
Big Shoe-make (possibly father to Mary Shumate/Smith)	12	4	2	1
Sakitabi	....	7	2	3
Sayakasbi	12	6	3	2
Simon Peter	30	4	2	1
Louie		8	3	2
Tuscona, (widow of Parahukala)	7	2	1	1
John Cammels	4	3	1	1
Atonahacho	....	5	1	3
Capt. Hopaiahoma	12	16	3	6
Kashonachabi	....	10	3	3
Ittalohnochi	5	4	1	2
[redacted]	....	[redacted]	[redacted]	[redacted]

Tushkimaiyubi	2	3	1	....
Malitayo	3	4	2	....
Tishohimitta	1½	5	1	3
Shaphemastabi	10	8	2	8
Lokatonabi	3	10	1	5

Subj:	**Re: (no subject)**
Date:	10/10/2001 6:26:18 PM Eastern Daylight Time
From:	*dustyc@microgear.net (Dusty)*
To:	*JSutton639@aol.com*

Since your Mary Smith was still in Mississippi in 1892, then she didn't remove to Indian Territory after the treaty of 1830. Unfortunately, the Choctaws are one tribe that doesn't have very many records before they went to Oklahoma in the middle 1800s.

On the 1831 Armstrong Roll done in Miss. and Ala., there is a "Big Shoemake" listed. He lived "Chickasawhay River, east side" according to land records. that river runs through extreme southeastern Mississippi near the Alabama border. He had 4 members in his family, but there are no records of their names. There were 2 males over 16 and 1 child under 10 in 1831. Shumate/Shumake is a common name among the Mississippi Choctaws today. It's possible your Mary was a descendant of his.

There is a Truman Smith listed with 480 acres in Greenwood Leflore's district in the 1831 List of Claims. There is a William Smith listed as a "white man" livng on the Chickasawhay river, Emoklashatown. A Freeman Smith is listed as living in the"Yazoo Valley" with 480 acres in 1831. The last treaty with the Choctaws was signed in 1830, but I don't see Big Shumake's name on the list of those who signed it.

This is all the information I can find on these surnames. Good luck in your research.

dusty

----- Original Message -----
From: JSutton639@aol.com
To: dustyc@microgear.net
Sent: Wednesday, October 10, 2001 2:43 PM
Subject: Re: (no subject)

I am trying to find out who my Great, great grandfather was. I have two very common names in my family, Smith and Jones and Smith married Jones.
My G-G Grandmother was Mary Smith Possible maiden name Shumate
Born Jan 1, 1820 in AL
Died Aug 7, 1892 in MS,
One of her children was my G-Grandmother,
Mary Ann Smith Powell/Jones
Born Oct. 10, 1855 in AL
Died Oct. 5, 1911 In MS

She married Enoch Jones in 1880, she is mentioned in Ben Stricklands book of Who Married Who as his third wife. She had two children from her previous marriage to
Mr. Powell and six children by Enoch Jones.

She is listed on the Census of 1880 as his house keeper and her mother as a border. They must have married soon after the census was taken.

I have been told that my G-Grandmother was 1/2 Choctaw Indian by her daughter, Hattie Jones/Hovatter, my grandmother, and that there was money from land due to them. I am not interested in the land money nor am I trying to be enrolled although I would feel privileged if I were. I would like to find out if there is a record of who my
G-G-Grandfather was. I was told that he did sign a treaty and that he was on the Indian side.

All my relatives are buried in Slay Cemetery, Greene Co. MS, this is also recorded in one of Ben Stricklands books.

ARTICLES OF CONFEDERATION ENTERED INTO BETWEEN MUSCOGEES, SEMINOLES, CHOCTAWS AND CHICKASAWS AND THE CONFEDERATE STATES OF AMERICA

July 1, 1861

Whereas the dissolution of the Federal Union under which the government of the United States existed, had absolved the Muscogee, Seminole, Choctaw and Chickasaw Nation of Indians from allegiance to any foreign government whatever, that by the providence of God, the current of events has left them free and independent to form such alliances as may ensure their own safety, promote general welfare, provide for the common defense, establish justice, insure domestic tranquility, as may to them seem best and retain unimpaired their Tribal or National rights, titles and interest in and to the country which they now respectively hold; Therefore Articles of Confederation and perpetual union are hereby entered into by and between the Muscogee, Seminole, Choctaw and Chickasaw Indians by their commissioners in convention, held at North Fork in the country of the Muscogee, on the first day of July, A.D. 1861.

Article 1. We agree that such Tribe or Nation, party to this act of Confederation, shall retain its sovereignty, freedom and independence and jurisdiction and constitutional rights not expressly delegated to the Grand Council of the United Nations of the Indian Territory to be composed of any members from each Tribe or Nation, and the title of their laws shall be "Be it enacted by the Grand Council of the United Nations of the Indian Territory."

Article 2. It is further agreed that the four Tribes or Nations herein mentioned have severally entered into a firm league and friendship with the each other for their common defense, the security of their liberties and their mutual and general welfare, and bind themselves to apart each other against all force offered to or attacks that might be made upon any or all of them, or account of their sovereignty independence country or any other positions whatsoever, and for the convenient management of the general interest and welfare of the Confederate Tribes or Nations, it is hereby determined that delegates shall be annually elected in such manner as the Council or Legislation or each Tribe or Nation shall direct, to meet in the Grand Council at North Fork, on the first Monday of September of every year, provided, however, that first meeting of the Grand Council of United Nations shall be on the first of December A.D. 1861 and should provide further that the Council or Legislation of each Nation shall have approved of the Articles of Confederation, and due notice shall have been first given by the Executive Authority of each Nation to the other.

Article 3. It is also agreed to that the Principal Chief or Governor of each Tribe or Nation, party to this Confederation shall all attend the meetings of Grand Council of the United Nations and give such information of the state of affairs in their respective districts or country, and recommend any measures they may desire necessary to the Grand Council for their consideration. A majority of Chiefs or Governors signing any bills, resolutions or acts which may be passed by the Grand Council it shall become the force of a law, as if all the Chiefs or Governors of the Confederation had approved and signed the same.

Article 4. In case any of the Principal Chiefs or Governors of the several Nations or Tribes herein mentioned, be indisposed or unable to attend the meetings of the delegates; he shall have the power to appoint one in his place to perform the duties required of the Principal Chief or Governor during the session of the Grand Council; also, either of the Chiefs or Governors shall have the privilege of convening the Grand Council, should he deem the consideration of affairs among his people require it, by giving due notice of the time to other Chiefs or Governors.

Article 5. When vacancies happens or the Grand Council from the Tribes or Nations herein Confederated, the Executive Authority thereof shall fill the vacancies by appointments.

Article 6. The Grand Council shall choose their President and other officers and make such needful bills for the government of the House, as they may deem proper and necessary, and shall be the judges of the election returns and the qualifications of its members; and a majority of delegates shall constitute a quorum to do business but a smaller number may adjourn from day to day until five days shall have transpired when they shall adjourn sine die.

Article 7. Each Nation or Tribe may give such compensation to each of their respective members as they may think best to allow.

Article 8. Any other Nation or Tribe of Indians, not a party of this Compact, may be admitted into this Confederacy by conforming to the foregoing Articles of Confederation, and with the consent of the Grand Council.

Article 9. It is further agreed and understood, that, for the mutual protection and safety of the Nations or Tribes parties to this Compact the right of way to all forces of the Confederate States of America through our territory is hereby granted.

Article 10. The Grand Council shall have power to call on each of the Nations or Tribes herein confederated, to furnish any number of troops to repel invasion by a foreign enemy, or to suppress insurrections under such regulations and measures as they may deem necessary to adopt.

Article 11. It is further agreed that such Nations or Tribes, parties to this Compact shall be bound to abide by the determinations or acts passed by the Grand Council in pursuance of the powers herein granted.

Article 12. It is also agreed that whenever two-thirds of the members of the Grand Council desire to amend or change any part of the foregoing Articles of Confederation, they shall make amendments or change the same in such manner as they may think proper.

Article 13. That when any one of the Nations or Tribes herein confederated become dissatisfied and desire to withdraw from the same, they shall give their reasons in writing, and be required to give notice of their intention to the Grand Council which shall have power to absolve them from all obligations of the Compact. Whereas, it is highly necessary that the right of way and free passage through the several districts or country of the Muscogee, Seminole, Choctaw, and Chickasaw Nations of Indians be granted forthwith to all forces or troops which may desire to make their march through any of the Districts or countries aforesaid, in order to repel the invading forces of Abraham Lincoln, therefore

Be it resolved by the Commissioners in convention assembled, that the right of way and free passage be and is hereby granted to all forces of the Confederate States of America, as well as to the forces of any Nation or Tribe who may desire to march their forces through to any part of the Indian Territory to repel the invading forces of abolition hands under Abraham Lincoln, whose army is now approaching our position.

This resolution to be in full force and effect from and after its passage.

R.K. Pone

President of the Convention

Attest:

Geo. W. Harkins, Sr. Secretary

Seminole Commissioners: Muscogee Commissioners:

Pahsocya hola, his x mark, George M. Steadather,

Pasbunnucko chi, his x mark, Louis McIntosh,

James M.L. Smith,

Choctaw Commissioners: Samuel Chekele,

Forbis Leflore, D.W. McIntosh,

Sampson Folsom, George W. Walker,

William Bryant, Leon Burnett,

Alfred Wade, John Smith

James Riley,

McKee King, *Chickasaw Commissioners:*

William King, Edmund Pickins,

Rufus Folsom, Asha Letubbee, his x mark,

Allen Wright, William Frazier, his x mark,

William Pitchlynn, Chun shepher Columbus, his x mark,

S.P. Turnbull, James Gamble,

Winchester Colbert,

John E. Hudson,

Joel E. Kemp

John M. Johnson,

Holmes Colbert,

W. Colbert,

Samuel Colbert,

James A. McClish,

William Kemp,

Martin N. Allen,

A. Alexander.

RESOLUTION OF THE CHOCTAW NATION

FEBRUARY 7, 1861

Resolutions expressing the feelings and sentiments of the General Council of the Choctaw Nation in reference to the political disagreement existing between the Northern and Southern States of the American Union.

February 7, 1861

Resolved by the General Council of the Choctaw Nation assembled, That we view with deep regret and great solicitude the present unhappy political disagreement between the Northern and Southern States of the American Union, tending to a permanent dissolution of the Union and the disturbance of the various important relations existing with that

Government by treaty stipulations and international laws, and portending much injury to the Choctaw government and people.

Resolved further, That we must express the earnest desire and ready hope entertained by the entire Choctaw people, that any and all political disturbances agitating and dividing the people of the various States may be honorably and speedily adjusted; and the example and blessing, and fostering care of their General Government, and the many and friendly social ties existing with their people, continue for the enlightenment in moral and good government and prosperity in the material concerns of life to our whole population.

Resolved further, That in the event a permanent dissolution of the American Union takes place, our many relations with the General Government must cease, and we shall be left to follow the natural affections, education, institutions, and interests of our people, which indissolubly bind us in every way to the destiny of our neighbors and brethren of the Southern States, upon whom we are confident we can rely for the preservation of our rights of life, liberty, and property, and the continuance of many acts of friendship, general counsel, and material support.

Resolved further, That we desire to assure our immediate neighbors, the people of Arkansas and Texas, of our determination to observe the amicable relations in every way so long existing between us, and the firm reliance we have, amid any disturbances with other States, the rights and feelings so sacred to us will remain respected by them and be protected from the encroachments of others.

Resolved further, That his excellency the principal chief be requested to inclose, with an appropriate communication from himself, a copy of these resolutions to the governors of the Southern States, with the request that they be laid before the State convention of each State, as many as have assembled at the date of their reception, and that in such as have not they be published in the newspapers of the State.

Resolved, That these resolutions take effect and be in force from and after their passage.

Approved February 7, 1861.

Descendants of Moses Phelps

Generation No. 1

1. MOSES[1] PHELPS[1].

Child of MOSES PHELPS is:
2. i. ENOCH S.[2] PHELPS, b. 1775, Tyrell, NC; d. 1848.

Generation No. 2

2. ENOCH S.[2] PHELPS *(MOSES[1])*[1] was born 1775 in Tyrell, NC[1], and died 1848[1]. He married MARY SPRUILL[1]. She was born 1780 in SC or NC[1].

Child of ENOCH PHELPS and MARY SPRUILL is:
3. i. ELIZABETH[3] PHELPS, b. 1799, Edgefield,S.C.; d. April 27, 1863, Beech Springs, Neshoba County, MS.

Generation No. 3

3. ELIZABETH[3] PHELPS *(ENOCH S.[2], MOSES[1])*[1] was born 1799 in Edgefield,S.C.[1], and died April 27, 1863 in Beech Springs, Neshoba County, MS. She married WILLIAM NATHANIEL JONES[1] Bet. 1818 - 1819 in Edgefield District, S.C.. He was born 1795 in S.C.[1], and died Bet. 1856 - 1857 in Beech Springs, Neshoba County, MS.

Children of ELIZABETH PHELPS and WILLIAM JONES are:

i. MARY[4] JONES, b. Abt. 1820; d. Aft. 1820, Texas; m. JAMES J. JONES, 1839, Neshoba County, Ms; b. 1811, S.C.; d. Bet. 1859 - 1860, Neshoba County, MS.

ii. ENOCH JONES[1], b. February 23, 1822, Dallas County, AL[1]; d. July 24, 1903, Greene co. Ms[1]; m. (1) SUSAN ABNEY[1], September 01, 1842, Neshoba County, MS[1]; b. November 18, 1827, Hinds Co. MS[1]; d. November 16, 1876; m. (2) ROSE GORDON, 1878; m. (3) MARY A. SMITH[1], September 30, 1880, Greene Co. Miss.[1]; b. October 10, 1855, Al[1]; d. October 05, 1911, Greene Co, Miss.[1].

More About ENOCH JONES:
Burial: Slay cemetary

More About SUSAN ABNEY:
Burial: Slay Cemetary

Notes for MARY A. SMITH:
Mary Ann was 1/2 Choctaw Indian

More About MARY A. SMITH:
Burial: Slay Cemetary[1]

iii. ELIZABETH ANN JONES, b. Abt. 1823.
iv. SON JONES, b. Abt. 1825.
v. FERRABA ROSANNE JONES, b. December 27, 1826.
vi. SON JONES, b. Abt. 1828.
vii. DAUGHTER JONES, b. Abt. 1830.
viii. D. R. HULDA JONES, b. September 23, 1833.
ix. MARGARET EMILY JONES, b. February 09, 1835.
x. W. JOHN JONES, b. Abt. 1839.
xi. JULIA E. C. JONES, b. July 30, 1842.

Descendants of William Nathaniel Jones

Generation No. 1

1. WILLIAM NATHANIEL[1] JONES[/] was born 1795 in S.C.[/], and died Bet. 1856 - 1857 in Beech Springs, Neshoba County, MS. He married ELIZABETH PHELPS[/] Bet. 1818 - 1819 in Edgefield District, S.C., daughter of ENOCH PHELPS and MARY SPRUILL. She was born 1799 in Edgefield,S.C.[/], and died April 27, 1863 in Beech Springs, Neshoba County, MS.

Children of WILLIAM JONES and ELIZABETH PHELPS are:

2. i. MARY[2] JONES, b. Abt. 1820; d. Aft. 1820, Texas.
3. ii. ENOCH JONES, b. February 23, 1822, Dallas County, AL; d. July 24, 1903, Greene co. Ms.
iii. ELIZABETH ANN JONES, b. Abt. 1823.
iv. SON JONES, b. Abt. 1825.
v. FERRABA ROSANNE JONES, b. December 27, 1826.
vi. SON JONES, b. Abt. 1828.
vii. DAUGHTER JONES, b. Abt. 1830.
viii. D. R. HULDA JONES, b. September 23, 1833.
ix. MARGARET EMILY JONES, b. February 09, 1835.
x. W. JOHN JONES, b. Abt. 1839.
xi. JULIA E. C. JONES, b. July 30, 1842.

Generation No. 2

2. MARY[2] JONES *(WILLIAM NATHANIEL[1])* was born Abt. 1820, and died Aft. 1820 in Texas. She married JAMES J. JONES 1839 in Neshoba County, Ms. He was born 1811 in S.C., and died Bet. 1859 - 1860 in Neshoba County, MS.

Children of MARY JONES and JAMES JONES are:

i. JOSEPHINE[3] JONES, b. 1840.
ii. MARGARET A. JONES, b. 1842.
iii. WILLIAM B. JONES, b. 1844.
iv. GEORGE P. JONES, b. 1846.
v. SARAH ELIZABETH JONES, b. March 01, 1848.
vi. SUSAN A. JONES, b. 1851.
vii. MARY J. JONES, b. 1853.
viii. JAMES J JONES. JR, b. 1855.
ix. JOHN E. JONES, b. 1858.
x. WILLIAM T. B. JONES, b. 1860.

3. ENOCH[2] JONES *(WILLIAM NATHANIEL[1])*[/] was born February 23, 1822 in Dallas County, AL[/], and died July 24, 1903 in Greene co. Ms[/]. He married (1) SUSAN ABNEY[/] September 01, 1842 in Neshoba County, MS[/]. She was born November 18, 1827 in Hinds Co. MS[/], and died November 16, 1876. He married (2) ROSE GORDON 1878. He married (3) MARY A. SMITH[/] September 30, 1880 in Greene Co. Miss.[/], daughter of JOHN SMITH and MARY SHUMATE. She was born October 10, 1855 in Al[/], and died October 05, 1911 in Greene Co, Miss.[/].

More About ENOCH JONES:
Burial: Slay cemetary

More About SUSAN ABNEY:
Burial: Slay Cemetary

Notes for MARY A. SMITH:
Mary Ann was 1/2 Choctaw Indian

More About MARY A. SMITH:
Burial: Slay Cemetary[1]

Children of ENOCH JONES and SUSAN ABNEY are:

i. DORTHEA SARAH[3] JONES[1], b. March 28, 1843[1].
ii. SARAH E. JONES[1], b. November 03, 1843[1].
iii. WILLIAM JOSEPH JONES[1], b. January 23, 1847[1].
iv. MARTHA MATILDA JONES[1], b. December 29, 1848[1].
v. ENOCH ROBERT JONES[1], b. December 18, 1850[1].
vi. JOHN C. JONES[1], b. November 13, 1852[1]; d. 1927.

More About JOHN C. JONES:
Burial: Slay Cemetary

vii. JESSE NELSON JONES[1], b. April 14, 1855[1].
viii. ANNA E. JONES[1], b. July 24, 1857[1].
ix. MARGARET EMILY JONES[1], b. May 04, 1859[1].
x. THOMAS JEFFERSON JONES[1], b. September 18, 1861[1].
xi. SUSAN LOUISA JONES[1], b. August 09, 1864[1].

Children of ENOCH JONES and MARY SMITH are:

xii. MARY POWELL[3] JONES[1], b. July 01, 1873[1].
xiii. JAMES POWELL JONES[1], b. February 22, 1876[1].
xiv. HATTIE LEE JONES[1], b. October 06, 1885, Greene Co, Miss.[1]; d. October 09, 1969, Greene Co, Miss.[1]; m. WILBERT F. HOVATTER[1], February 18, 1903, Greene Co. Miss.[1]; b. April 01, 1882, Preston Co. WV[1]; d. August 19, 1969, Greene Co. Miss.[1].

Notes for HATTIE LEE JONES:
84 years old and 3 days at time of death
Pictures on pages 106, 107 108 in book "Generations of Hoffman to Hovatter"

More About HATTIE LEE JONES:
Burial: Stateline, MS
Fact 5: Social Security #: 177-14-7342[2]
Fact 6: Issued in: Pennsylvania[2]
Fact 7: Residence code: Mississippi[2]
Fact 8: Last residence ZIP: 39451[2]

Notes for WILBERT F. HOVATTER:
87 years old 4 months and 18 days at time of death

More About WILBERT F. HOVATTER:
Burial: Stateline, MS
Social Security Number: Pennslyvania[3]

xv. JESSIE JONES[3], b. February 08, 1888[3].
xvi. CHESTER JONES[3], b. March 04, 1890[3].
xvii. JULIUS JONES[3], b. April 10, 1892[3].

Endnotes

1. Mancuso.FTW, Date of Import: Sep 6, 2000.
2. Genealogy.com, Family Archive #110, Social Security Death Index: U.S. Ed. 9, Social Security Death Index, Release date: April 10, 2000, Internal Ref. #1.111.9.122873.123.
3. Mancuso.FTW, Date of Import: Sep 6, 2000.

Scrapbook of Hattie Lee Jones

Hattie Lee Jones Hovatter

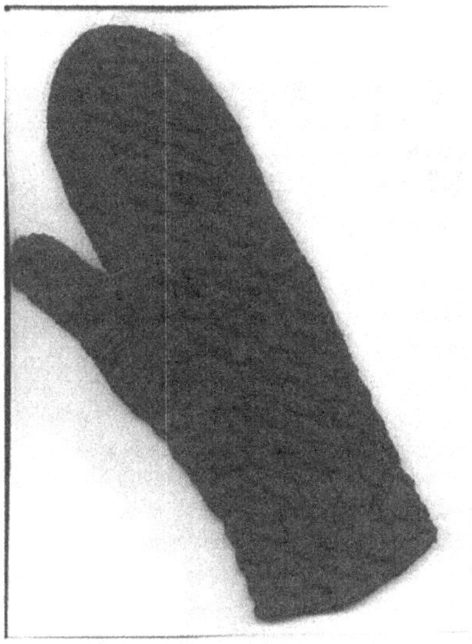

Hatties Mitten

Hattie

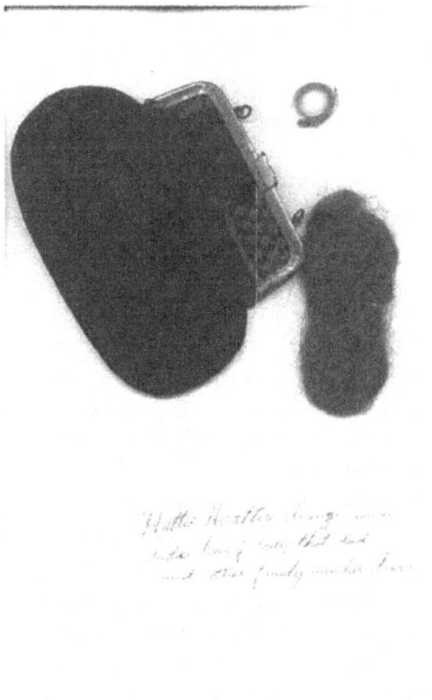

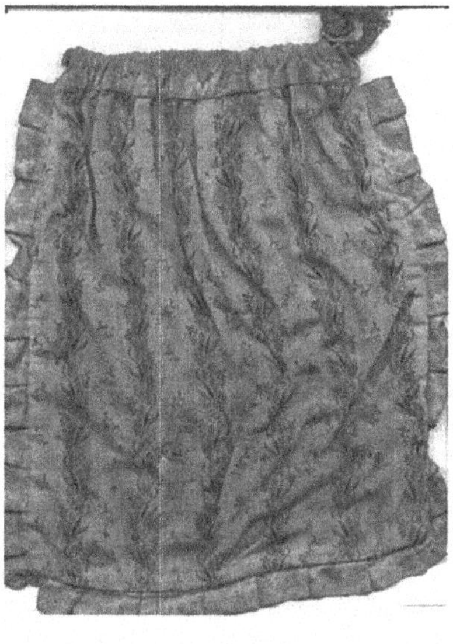

Hatties's drawstring purse

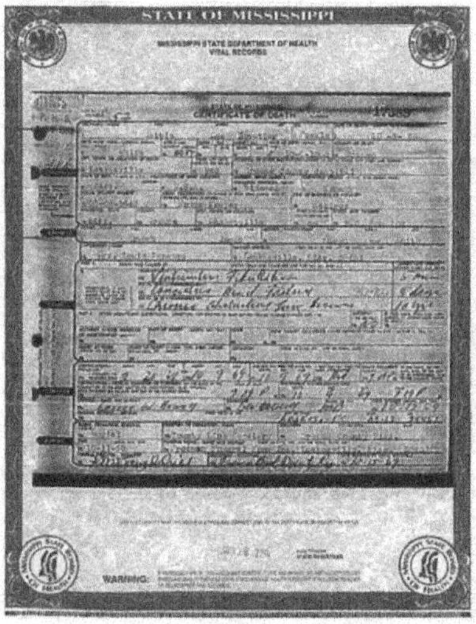

STATE OF MISSISSIPPI

MISSISSIPPI STATE DEPARTMENT OF HEALTH
VITAL RECORDS

CERTIFICATE OF DEATH

WARNING:

Hatties Death Certificate

Descendants of David T. Hovatter

Generation No. 1

1. DAVID T.[6] HOVATTER *(DAVID[5], CHRISTOPHER[4], JOHAN MICHAEL[3] HOHWERTER, JOHANN VALENTIN[2], JOHAN HEINRICH[1] HOCHWARTER)[1]* was born June 15, 1853 in Kesson, WV[1], and died October 31, 1929 in Tucker Co.,VA now WV. He married CHRISTINA L. SHAHAN[1] December 23, 1877 in Hannahsville, Tucker Co. WVA[1], daughter of GEORGE SHAHAN and LOUISA HOFFMAN. She was born May 16, 1858 in Sinclair, WV, and died February 02, 1933 in Tucker Co.,WV.

Notes for DAVID T. HOVATTER:
1880 Census Place: Licking, Tucker, West Virginia
Source:FHL Film 1255414 National Archives Film T9-1414 Page 378A
Relation Sex Marr RaceAgeBirthplace
D. C. HOVATTER SelfM M W 25 VA
Occ:Laborer Fa: VA Mo: VA
Chrystena L. HOVATTER WifeFM W 22 VA
Occ:Keeping House Fa: VA Mo: VA
Charles HOVATTER Son M SW 1 WV
Fa: VA Mo: VA
Lilley C. HOVATTEROtherFSW 1MWV
Fa: VA Mo: VA

Barbour County Cities, Towns and Settlements
Kasson

According to an account found in Barbour County West Virginiapublished by the Barbour County Historical Society in 1979 Kasson, in Cove District, was first named Danville after the first settler Dan Highly. The hill he lived on, overlooking Kasson is still known as Highly Hill. Mr. Highly raised mulberry trees to feed his silkworms and produced silk thread was put on spools and shipped to Baltimore.

Danville was given the name Kasson because there was another WV Post Office called Danville. The first letter was mailed to a man named Kasson. The first Post Office was establised in 1862. Carr Bishop was the first postmaster. After him, Marion Newman, 1884; Lewis Coffman, 1904; George Coffman served from 1908 till his death in 1930. Hattie Coffman, his wife and two sons, Hayse & George Sherwood took it over until 1937 when Rachel Wilson Ball served till her death.

In the early days of Kasson the community included:
Stores:
Jack Bishop in 1870, John and Ed Compton, 1875; Marion Newman, 1880; Daniel J. Nester, 1890 and Lewis Coffman.

Blacksmith Shops:
David Hovatter, 1860; Ben Ekis in 1864; Albert Loar in 1891; and Lewis Coffman who learned the trade from his uncles Mike and Lige Coffman who had shops in Valley Furnace, Belington and Elkins. His first shop was near West Point

Churches:
The Kasson United Methodist Church, built in 1898. Daniel Nestor and Daniel Lohr were overseers.

The Church of the Brethren, David Hovatter had the Communion and Love Feast in his house, this was the beginning of the Shiloh Church of the Brethren which was organized in 1845 about 1 ½ miles from Kasson.

More About DAVID T. HOVATTER:
Burial: Preston Co. WV

Children of DAVID HOVATTER and CHRISTINA SHAHAN are:

2. i. CHARLES E.[7] HOVATTER, b. October 11, 1878.
   ii. LELLIE C. HOVATTER[1], b. April 18, 1880[1]; m. JOHN PATRICK BURNS; b. July 20, 1877; d. 1950.
3. iii. WILBERT F. HOVATTER, b. April 01, 1882, Preston Co. WV; d. August 19, 1969, Greene Co. Miss..
4. iv. IRA J. HOVATTER, b. April 17, 1885; d. July 1968.
5. v. MARY L. HOVATTER, b. March 07, 1887.
6. vi. GEORGE E. HOVATTER, b. February 15, 1889.
   vii. LLOYD A. HOVATTER[1], b. June 29, 1891[1]; m. LULU STERRINGER.
   viii. MAUDIE P. HOVATTER[1], b. July 21, 1893[1]; m. SAMUEL DUMIRE.
7. ix. ARLIE DAVID HOVATTER, b. August 15, 1895, WVA; d. December 1977.
   x. BOYD E. HOVATTER[1], b. September 24, 1897[1,2]; d. August 1980[2]; m. HILDA DAVIS.

   More About BOYD E. HOVATTER:
   Fact 5: Social Security #: 234-03-1597[2]
   Fact 6: Issued in: West Virginia[2]
   Fact 7: Residence code: Alabama[2]
   Fact 8: Last residence ZIP: 36584[2]

Generation No. 2

2. CHARLES E.[7] HOVATTER *(DAVID T.[6], DAVID[5], CHRISTOPHER[4], JOHAN MICHAEL[3] HOHWERTER, JOHANN VALENTIN[2], JOHAN HEINRICH[1] HOCHWARTER)[3]* was born October 11, 1878[3]. He married ELLA AGNICE BURNS, daughter of JOHN BURNS and SARAH DAVIS. She was born March 07, 1883.

Children of CHARLES HOVATTER and ELLA BURNS are:

   i. CLAUDENE ELWOOD[8] HOVATTER, m. ARIETTA SHOCKLEY.
   ii. ELSTON GERALD HOVATTER, m. MYRA E. HOWARD.
   iii. CHARLES WOODROW WILSON HOVATTER, m. MADELINE KAUSCH.

   Notes for CHARLES WOODROW WILSON HOVATTER:
   Picture on page 102 in book "Generations from Hoffman to Hovatter"

   iv. WANDA LORRAINE HOVATTER, m. ALBERT H. HEARN.
   v. EARL GAY HOVATTER, b. January 06, 1912; d. August 08, 1934.
   vi. THOMAS DAVID HOVATTER, b. June 02, 1908; m. ELSIE AMBROSIO.
   vii. ELMER DALLAS HOVATTER, b. August 24, 1902; d. June 13, 1970; m. JESSIE B. NOCE, Bet. 1919 - 1950; b. Bet. 1898 - 1917; d. Bet. 1919 - 1992.
   viii. ETTA IVES HOVATTER, m. EARL C. CATHEL.
   ix. DELBERT RAY HOVATTER, b. November 22, 1904; d. November 1974; m. BARBARA CHANDLER.
   x. LEODA PEARL HOVATTER.
   xi. ORA MARIE HOVATTER, b. April 03, 1914; d. April 16, 1937; m. HERBERT FUES, SR.
   xii. ELFORD HAROLD HOVATTER, b. May 03, 1924; d. May 03, 1924.

3. WILBERT F.[7] HOVATTER *(DAVID T.[6], DAVID[5], CHRISTOPHER[4], JOHAN MICHAEL[3] HOHWERTER, JOHANN VALENTIN[2], JOHAN HEINRICH[1] HOCHWARTER)[3]* was born April 01, 1882 in Preston Co. WV[3], and died August 19, 1969 in Greene Co. Miss.[3]. He married HATTIE LEE JONES[3] February 18, 1903 in Greene Co. Miss.[3], daughter of ENOCH JONES and MARY SMITH. She was born October 06, 1885 in Greene Co, Miss.[3], and died October 09, 1969 in Greene Co, Miss.[3].

Notes for WILBERT F. HOVATTER:
87 years old 4 months and 18 days at time of death

More About WILBERT F. HOVATTER:
Burial: Stateline, MS
Social Security Number: Pennslyvania[3]

Notes for HATTIE LEE JONES:
84 years old and 3 days at time of death
Pictures on pages 106, 107 108 in book "Generations of Hoffman to Hovatter"

More About HATTIE LEE JONES:
Burial: Stateline, MS
Fact 5: Social Security #: 177-14-7342[4]
Fact 6: Issued in: Pennsylvania[4]
Fact 7: Residence code: Mississippi[4]
Fact 8: Last residence ZIP: 39451[4]

Children of WILBERT HOVATTER and HATTIE JONES are:

i. EULA[8] HOVATTER[5], b. December 14, 1903, Greene Co, Miss.[5]; d. October 24, 1937, WVA[5]; m. (1) SAMUEL LINTON[5]; m. (2) HOPE WATSON.

Notes for EULA HOVATTER:
picture on pages 93 in book "Generations of Hoffman to Hovatter"

ii. ODIE HOVATTER[5], b. October 27, 1905[5]; d. December 03, 1905[5].

More About ODIE HOVATTER:
Burial: Slay Cemetary

iii. WILBERTIE VALENTINE HOVATTER[5], b. February 14, 1908, Greene Co, Miss.[5]; d. September 23, 1987[6,7,7,8,9]; m. (1) HAZEL DELL CLEVENGER[10]; b. June 07, 1907[11,12]; d. November 06, 1988[13,14,15]; m. (2) RUBY BARNETT; b. July 16, 1915.

Notes for WILBERTIE VALENTINE HOVATTER:
Bertie and Hazel had broke up and he met Ruby. Ruby became pregnant with his daughter Rosalie. Hazel decided that they should try to make another go of their marriage, so he left Ruby and went back to Hazel. There is some speculation about when he knew about Ruby's pregnancy. When he found out about his daughter Rosalie he acknowledged her as his child as he did his other children.
Died of Cancer.

Pictures on pages 93, 94, 95 in book "Generations of Hoffman to Hovatter"

More About WILBERTIE VALENTINE HOVATTER:
Social Security Number: 232-05-5326[16]

iv. BOYD HOVATTER[16], b. August 10, 1910, Greene Co, Miss. re: Family Bible[16]; d. February 1975[17,18,19].

Notes for BOYD HOVATTER:
picture on page 93 in book "Generations of Hoffman to Hovatter"

More About BOYD HOVATTER:
Burial: Egg Harbor, NJ
Social Security Number: 560-07-8262[19]

v. FLOYD HOVATTER[19], b. March 19, 1913[19]; d. March 21, 1913[19].

vi. LOIS HOVATTER[19], b. November 19, 1914, Greene Co, Miss.[19]; d. May 30, 1983, Lower Bank, NJ[19]; m. THOMAS MANCUSO[19,20,21], September 23, 1935, Croydon, PA[22]; b. December 31, 1912, Italy; d. May 27, 1985, St. Petersburg, FL[22,23].

Notes for LOIS HOVATTER:
Married Sept. 23, 1935
Pictures on pages 96, 97 98, 100 in book "Generations of Hoffman to Hovatter"

More About LOIS HOVATTER:
Burial: Egg Harbor City, NJ[24]
Social Security Number: 177-14-8410[24]

More About THOMAS MANCUSO:
Burial: Clearwater FL[24,25]

vii. HATTIE ALMALEE HOVATTER, b. October 06, 1917.
viii. AUBREY HOVATTER[26], b. September 27, 1920[26].
ix. DESSIE HOVATTER[26], b. September 07, 1921, Preston Co. VA[26]; d. January 21, 2001, Las Vegas, NV; m. (1) EDGAR THOM[26], October 16, 1941, Trenton, NJ[26]; b. October 23, 1922[27,27,27,27,27,27,27,27,27,28]; d. January 1982[29,29,29,29,29,29,29,29,29,30]; m. (2) WILLIAM F. PUTNAM, June 26, 1960, Trenton, NJ; b. September 10, 1932; d. March 29, 2002, Las Vegas, NV.

Notes for DESSIE HOVATTER:
Pictures of Dessie Hovatter and more information on pages 98, 99 in book "Generation from Hoffman to Hovatter"

More About EDGAR THOM:
Adoption: [31,32]
Residence: Residence code: New Jersey[33,34]
Social Security Number: Social Security #: 154-12-8658[35,36]

Notes for WILLIAM F. PUTNAM:

Subj: Re: a short note
Date: 03/29/2002 1:34:39 PM Eastern Standard Time
From: P1AND2
To: JSutton639

E-mail dated 3-29-02
Hi Joyce,

It's Robin and Rick--responding from Dad's e-mail. We are at his house taking care of things. This is a hell of a thing to relay via e-mail, but we tried the phone numbers we found for you and Bob and got no answer, so I apologize in advance, but need to let you know.

Wednesday I couldn't get a hold of Dad, and grew concerned when his phone just kept ringing. So Rick and I drove in and we found him; he had fallen in the bathroom and was unconsious. We summoned paramedics and they took him to Valley Hospital. He passed away this morning around 6:30. He never regained consiousness. Rick, Bill and I like to think he had little or no pain, and know for sure he is in a better place now....probably with Mom :).

I know he wanted you to have Mom's albums....there are also a lot of pictures...I'd like for you to have anything you want. Please let me know.

We are still in the midst of arrangements and will let you know what is going on when we have more info.

Again I'm sorry to relay this via reply e-mail, but wanted you to know....Can I ask a favor pls...you knew a lot of Mom and Dad's e-mail buddies...would you be able to let them know about Dad for us pls, we'd really appreciate it.

Thanks.

Robin

William Putnam

William F. Putnam, 69, died March 29 in a local hospital.
He was born Sept. 10, 1932, in Port Henry, N.Y. A Navy veteran of the Korean and Vietnam wars, he was a corrections officer and a 22-year resident of Las Vegas.
He is survived by his son, William; and daughter, Robin Walker, both of Indian Springs; and five grandchildren.

Services are private. Davis Funeral Home-Charleston handled arrangements.

x. VERNON HOVATTER[36,37], b. February 26, 1924, West Virgina[38]; d. January 03, 1996, San Angelo, Texas[39,40,40,40,40,40,40,40,40,41].

Notes for VERNON HOVATTER:
Picture on page 101 in book "Generations from Hoffman to Hovatter"

More About VERNON HOVATTER:
Social Security Number: new Jersey[41]

xi. KENNETH GENE HOVATTER[41], b. October 31, 1927, west virginia Re: Family Bible[41]; d. March 06, 1983[41].

Notes for KENNETH GENE HOVATTER:
Picture on pages 100 in book "Generations from Hoffman to Hovatter"

More About KENNETH GENE HOVATTER:
Social Security Number: 587-56-1847[41]

4. IRA J.[7] HOVATTER *(DAVID T.[6], DAVID[5], CHRISTOPHER[4], JOHAN MICHAEL[3] HOHWERTER, JOHANN VALENTIN[2], JOHAN HEINRICH[1] HOCHWARTER)*[41] was born April 17, 1885[41,42], and died July 1968[42]. He married DESSIE THOMAS.

More About IRA J. HOVATTER:
Social Security Number: 232-22-9008

Child of IRA HOVATTER and DESSIE THOMAS is:
i. NINA[8] HOVATTER.

5. MARY L.[7] HOVATTER *(DAVID T.[6], DAVID[5], CHRISTOPHER[4], JOHAN MICHAEL[3] HOHWERTER, JOHANN VALENTIN[2], JOHAN HEINRICH[1] HOCHWARTER)*[43] was born March 07, 1887[43]. She married ANDREW JACKSON BROWN February 18, 1903 in Greene Co MS. He was born February 04, 1877, and died February 04, 1932.

Notes for MARY L. HOVATTER:

The information I received from Tracy had Fruitville listed in it but from Marriages in MS it seems that there was a double wedding, hers and her brother Wilbert. Both were married same day, same county and State. Greene Co. MS in Leakesville.

Children of MARY HOVATTER and ANDREW BROWN are:
i. ANDREW C.[8] BROWN, b. January 29, 1904; d. July 28, 1975; m. MILDRED FORTNEY.
ii. ALBERT LEROY BROWN, b. January 23, 1908; d. Abt. May 12, 1994; m. MARIE MIZELL.
iii. RUBY BROWN, b. September 02, 1908; m. BRYAN HOVATTER; d. 1996.
iv. WILBER JACKSON BROWN, b. December 04, 1912; d. December 04, 1912.

More About WILBER JACKSON BROWN:
Burial: Fruitdale Cemetary

v. HOMER JENNINGS BROWN, b. July 07, 1914; d. July 17, 1972; m. MARY MYRTLE DEESE OR DEES, December 26, 1932; b. February 28, 1918; d. May 08, 1989.

Notes for HOMER JENNINGS BROWN:
Worked in sawmill.
died of a heart attack

More About HOMER JENNINGS BROWN:

Scrapbook of Christina L. Shahan

David & Christina Hovatter

Christina Shahan Hovatter

Hand made

underside of quilt

Scrapbook of Charles Woodrow Wilson Hovatter

W. W. Hovatter

Woodrow Wilson Hovatter

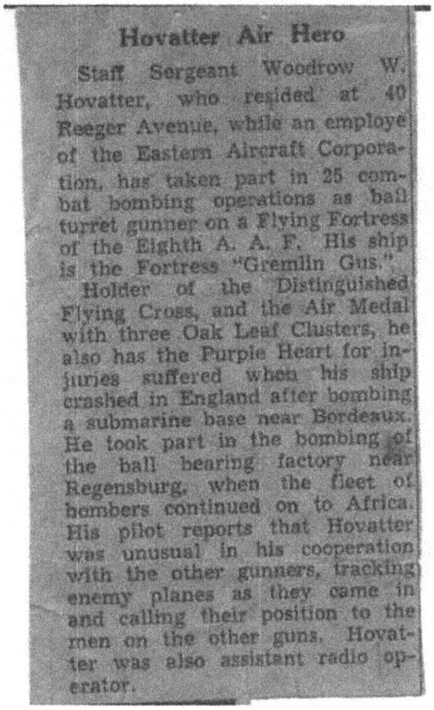

Hovatter Air Hero

Staff Sergeant Woodrow W. Hovatter, who resided at 40 Reeger Avenue, while an employe of the Eastern Aircraft Corporation, has taken part in 25 combat bombing operations as ball turret gunner on a Flying Fortress of the Eighth A. A. F. His ship is the Fortress "Gremlin Gus."

Holder of the Distinguished Flying Cross, and the Air Medal with three Oak Leaf Clusters, he also has the Purple Heart for injuries suffered when his ship crashed in England after bombing a submarine base near Bordeaux. He took part in the bombing of the ball bearing factory near Regensburg, when the fleet of bombers continued on to Africa. His pilot reports that Hovatter was unusual in his cooperation with the other gunners, tracking enemy planes as they came in and calling their position to the men on the other guns. Hovatter was also assistant radio operator.

Article on Woodrow Wilson

Scrapbook of Mary L. Hovatter

Mary Lavina Hovatter

Burial: Fruitdale Cemetary

Notes for MARY MYRTLE DEESE OR DEES:
Died of Lou gerrings

More About MARY MYRTLE DEESE OR DEES:
Burial: Fruitdale Cemetary

vi. DELBERT JENNINGS BROWN, b. April 19, 1917; d. February 02, 1998.
vii. WILLIAM HENRY BROWN, b. July 23, 1920.
viii. NELLIE MAE BROWN BROWN, b. November 23, 1923.
ix. DAVID ELMER BROWN, b. November 04, 1926; d. February 10, 1929.

6. GEORGE E.[7] HOVATTER *(DAVID T.[6], DAVID[5], CHRISTOPHER[4], JOHAN MICHAEL[3] HOHWERTER, JOHANN VALENTIN[2], JOHAN HEINRICH[1] HOCHWARTER)*[43] was born February 15, 1889[43]. He married CECIL MAY BURNS.

Notes for CECIL MAY BURNS:
There is a possibility that the spelling of her name was different. May have been Cecilia or another variation.

Children of GEORGE HOVATTER and CECIL BURNS are:

i. ERNEST RAY[8] HOVATTER, b. July 25, 1916; m. (1) MILDRED KINTER; m. (2) EVELYN ?; m. (3) FRANCIS BOYER.
ii. VIOLET MILDRED HOVATTER, b. June 1915; m. FRED BAIOCCHI; d. 1987.
iii. VELMA ARIZONIA HOVATTER, b. October 1917.

Notes for VELMA ARIZONIA HOVATTER:
Was a Major in the Army. She adopted her sister Mary Children and raised them as her own. Whe passed away in Aniston Ala in 1999 her daughter Jean and son Larry still live on the farm there.

iv. BERYL HOVATTER, m. PAGE EVANS.
v. MARY ELIZABETH HOVATTER, b. 1923; m. (1) MR. PERT; m. (2) LEONARD BLACKMON.

Notes for MARY ELIZABETH HOVATTER:
She had four Children. Her husband abused her and she divorced him. Her father took her home to Grafton where she moved in with grandma. Aunt Velma came in from a tour in Greenland and took her mom Cecil and mary and all four kids with her to Texas to live. She ended up raising the four children and taking care of her mother until she passed away in the late 1970's. Mary Elizabeth remarried Leonard Blackmon and remained in the San Antonio area. They now live in Schertz, Texas

vi. DARRELL HOVATTER, m. SHIRLEE.

7. ARLIE DAVID[7] HOVATTER *(DAVID T.[6], DAVID[5], CHRISTOPHER[4], JOHAN MICHAEL[3] HOHWERTER, JOHANN VALENTIN[2], JOHAN HEINRICH[1] HOCHWARTER)*[43] was born August 15, 1895 in WVA[43], and died December 1977[44,45]. He married LAURA POLING.

Notes for ARLIE DAVID HOVATTER:
[Broderbund Family Archive #110, Vol. 1 A-K, Ed. 7, Social Security Death Index: U.S., Date of Import: Jul 3, 2001, Internal Ref. #1.111.7.127438.120]

Individual: Hovatter, Arlie
Social Security #: 705-10-2282
Issued in: Railroad Board

Birth date: Aug 15, 1895
Death date: Dec 1977

Residence code: West Virginia

ZIP Code of last known residence: 26354
Primary location associated with this ZIP Code:

Grafton, West Virginia

More About ARLIE DAVID HOVATTER:
Fact 1: Issued in: Railroad Board[45]
Fact 2: Residence code: West Virginia[45]
Fact 3: Last residence ZIP: 26354[45]
Fact 6: Issued in: Railroad Board[46]
Fact 7: Residence code: West Virginia[46]
Fact 8: Last residence ZIP: 26354[46]
Social Security Number: Social Security #: 705-10-2282[46,47]

Child of ARLIE HOVATTER and LAURA POLING is:
i. LESTER[8] HOVATTER.

Endnotes

1. Mancuso.FTW, Date of Import: Sep 6, 2000.
2. Genealogy.com, Family Archive #110, Social Security Death Index: U.S. Ed. 9, Social Security Death Index, Release date: April 10, 2000, Internal Ref. #1.111.9.122873.66.
3. Mancuso.FTW, Date of Import: Sep 6, 2000.
4. Genealogy.com, Family Archive #110, Social Security Death Index: U.S. Ed. 9, Social Security Death Index, Release date: April 10, 2000, Internal Ref. #1.111.9.122873.123.
5. Mancuso.FTW, Date of Import: Sep 6, 2000.
6. Broderbund Family Archive #110, Vol. 1, Ed. 7, Social Security Death Index: U.S., Date of Import: May 20, 2000, Internal Ref. #1.111.7.127439.53
7. Broderbund Family Archive #110, Vol. 1, Ed. 7, Social Security Death Index: U.S., Date of Import: May 21, 2000, Internal Ref. #1.111.7.127439.53
8. Mancuso.FTW, Date of Import: Sep 6, 2000.
9. Genealogy.com, Family Archive #110, Social Security Death Index: U.S. Ed. 9, Social Security Death Index, Release date: April 10, 2000, Internal Ref. #1.111.9.122873.201.
10. Mancuso.FTW, Date of Import: Sep 6, 2000.
11. Broderbund Family Archive #110, Vol. 1, Ed. 7, Social Security Death Index: U.S., Date of Import: May 20, 2000, Internal Ref. #1.111.7.127438.181
12. Mancuso.FTW, Date of Import: Sep 6, 2000.
13. Broderbund Family Archive #110, Vol. 1, Ed. 7, Social Security Death Index: U.S., Date of Import: May 20, 2000, Internal Ref. #1.111.7.127438.182
14. Mancuso.FTW, Date of Import: Sep 6, 2000.
15. Genealogy.com, Family Archive #110, Social Security Death Index: U.S. Ed. 9, Social Security Death Index, Release date: April 10, 2000, Internal Ref. #1.111.9.122873.125.
16. Mancuso.FTW, Date of Import: Sep 6, 2000.
17. Broderbund Family Archive #110, Vol. 1, Ed. 7, Social Security Death Index: U.S., Date of Import: May 20, 2000, Internal Ref. #1.111.7.127438.126
18. Broderbund Family Archive #110, Vol. 1, Ed. 7, Social Security Death Index: U.S., Date of Import: May 21, 2000, Internal Ref. #1.111.7.127438.126
19. Mancuso.FTW, Date of Import: Sep 6, 2000.
20. Genealogy.com, Family Archive #110, Social Security Death Index: U.S. Ed. 9, Social Security Death Index, Release date: April 10, 2000.
21. Mancuso Cramer Sutton.FTW, Date of Import: Jun 25, 2001.
22. Mancuso.FTW, Date of Import: Sep 6, 2000.
23. Mancuso Cramer Sutton.FTW, Date of Import: Jun 25, 2001.
24. Mancuso.FTW, Date of Import: Sep 6, 2000.
25. Mancuso Cramer Sutton.FTW, Date of Import: Jun 25, 2001.
26. Mancuso.FTW, Date of Import: Sep 6, 2000.
27. Broderbund Family Archive #110, Vol. 2, Ed. 7, Social Security Death Index: U.S., Date of Import: May 20, 2000,

David & Tena Hovatter

DAVID T. HOVATTER IS SON OF DAVID HOVATTER. TENA IS DAUGHTER OF BULL SHAHAN AND LOUISA MARION HOFFMAN.

DAVID LOST HIS EYE TO CANCER AND HAD A GLASS EYE

David Hovatter

D. T. Hovatter &
Tena Shahan (Christina)

TUCKER COUNTY, WEST VIRGINIA MARRIAGES
1856 - 1887

Taken from the marriage book in Tucker county courthouse.

Date	Groom	Bride	Groom's Parents	Bride's Parents
Jan. 6, 1856	Andrew Stump	Harriet Loughry	John C. & Mary Stump	Delia Loughry
Nov. 13, 1856	Washington Parsons	Martha (Bond) Long	Abraham & Emily Parsons	William & Martha Bond
Jan. 9, 1857	Columbus Wolford	Mary Flanagan	John & Fanny Wolford	William & Anna Flanagan
Feb. 8, 1857	Daniel H. Sell	Rebecca E. White	Henry & Rebecca Sell	John P. & Mary M. White
Feb 18, 1857	John William Dumire	Margaret Catherine Gray	Daniel & Delia Dumire	John P. & Margaret Gray
Mar. 19, 1857	William T. Flanagan	Virginia Lambert	William & Anna Flanagan	James B. & Susanna Lambert
Apr. 16, 1857	Jacob Motes	Sarah Everetts	Basil & Priscilla Motes	George & Anna Everetts
Apr. 30, 1857	Isaac Watts	Emily Bonner	Philip & Elizabeth Watts	Catherine Bonner
May 25, 1857	Joshua Martin Robinson	Louisa Jane Dumire	John O. & Rebecca Robinson	Charles & Ruth Dumire
June 18, 1857	Anson Carr	Phoebe Jane Roy	Abner & Elizabeth Carr	Joseph & Elizabeth Roy
Sept. 10, 1857	Mathias Pennington	Elizabeth Anna Johnson	Solomon A. & Virginia	Robert & Margaret Johnson
Sept. 13, 1857	Joseph J. Long	Elizabeth Stump	James & Barbara Long	John C. & Mary Stump
Nov. 12, 1857	Madison G. Lambert	Elizabeth J. Fansler	James B. & Susanna Lambert	Jacob & Anna Fansler
Nov. 12, 1857	Samuel D. Kalar	Mary Gray	Susanna Kalar	John P. & Margaret Gray
Dec. 24, 1857	Elias B. Lipscomb	Mary Ellen Wiles	Fieldan & Jane Lipscomb	Christian & Elizabeth Wiles

Oct. 4, 1877	D.H. Spessert, 36	Fannie Mason, 31	George Spessert	Thomas M. Mason
Oct. 25, 1877	William F. Shaffer, 23	Mary A. Evans, 26	Fred Shaffer	William Evans
Oct. 25, 1877	Samuel Poling, 24	Ida J. Phillips, 15	David Poling	Hiram Phillips
Nov. 1, 1877	John Mitchell, 23	Sarah Virginia Pitzer, 21	William Mitchell	Henson P. Pitzer
Nov. 1, 1877	Thomas D. Poling, 21	Sarah M. Shahan, 21	Reason Poling	George W. Shahan
Nov. 3, 1877	Sampson Roy Fansler, 21	Martha I. Dumire, 37	Solomon & Catherine Fansler	George & Sarah Dumire
Nov...., 1877	James P. Porter, 27	Amanda M. Goff, 24	Jacob & Rachel Porter	John R. & Eunice Goff
Nov. 20, 1877	William Davis	M.E. Miller	Joseph Davis	John M. Miller
Nov. 21, 1877	C.W. Lansberry, 23	Henrietta E. Kisner, 16	Abraham Lansberry	Samuel Kisner
Nov...1877	J.H. Roy, 23	Sarah A. Carr, 18	------	Enos Carr
Nov. 29, 1877	John W. Shaver, 25	Rebecca Jane Phillips, 23	Adam Shaver	Jackson Phillips
Dec. 2, 1877	George W. Long, 22	Catherine E. Nestor, 22	William E. & Mary E. Long	Jacob & E. Nestor
Dec. 2, 1877	M.J. Bonner, 22	M.E. Bonner, 19	Arch & E. Bonner	Solomon & JaneBonner
Dec. 6, 1877	James W. Johnson, 27	Anne E. Long, 21	Martin & Mary Johnson	William E. & Mary E. Long
Dec. 20, 1877	J.A. Summerfield, 20	S.A. Carr, 22	George W. Summerfield	James & Jemima Carr
Dec. 23, 1877	D.T. Hovatter, 22	T.L. Shahan, 21	D. & S.A. Hovatter	G. & L.M. Shahan
Jan. 3, 1878	Samuel H. James, 24	Cordelia Hebb, 17	Isaac S. & Nancy M. James	William & Margaret Hebb
Feb. 2, 1878	James R. Raines, 27	Martha Cooper, 25	William Raines	--------
Mar. 20, 1878	J.T. Mason, 34	Catherine Hart, 21	Thomas M. Mason	John B. & M. Hart
Apr. 7, 1878	R.T. Griffith, 38	Alice Duckworth, 22	Hillery & Elizabeth	Griffith
Apr. 8, 1878	Isaac Poling, 56	Osa (Phillips) Poling, 44	Richard & Rachel Poling	Jacob & Catherine Phillips
Apr. 18, 1878	William E. Bonner, 23	Mary E. Hedrick, 19	------	------

Mississippi

Connections

Edited & Revised Marriages Greene Co., Ms. Index - HI

[redacted]

NOTE:
These marriages have been edited and revised from the origninal Marriage Index from Greene Co., Ms.
Some of the individuals had other marriages and are linked to them, even across county lines.
Click on HELP button above and then select Marriage Help for editing notes, and codes used, & how you can help.

HADDOX, George W	HUTTO, Frances Elizabeth	1880 Febru
HADLEY, James	LONG, Sarah	1882 Octob
HAGGER, Charles	ANDERSON, Mary	1900 Decem
HAIRE, Nicholas	HOLLIMAN, Silla	1901 Janua
HALBROOK(HEATHCOCK),W(m.)A(ndrew)	LANE, Theodona ("Docia")	1887 Octob
HALL, James	, Mary	1877 April
HALL, W(illiam) R(ichard)	BALL, Ena	1906 Decem
HAM, E(lon) T	TURNER, L(ouvenia) A	1906 March
HAM, J S	WALLACE, Lelia	1901 May,0
HAMERICK, T(aylor) L(aphate)	ODOM, Lena	1905 May,2
HAMILTON, John	GILBERT, Lanna	1882 Janua
HAMPSTEAD(HEMPSTEAD),S(am.)D(avid)	EUBANKS, Ella (Ellen Louvenia)	1891 April
HAMRICK, B(enjamin) F(ranklin) Dr	SMITH, M(ary) Estelle	1880 April
HAMRICK, James P	SMITH-[DOUGLAS], Judy(Julia)	1878 May,1
HANCOCK, Ellis	MACK, Sophia	1896 Septe
HANCOCK, John	STINSON, Martha	1904 Decem
HANK, W R	ELLIOTT, Argent (E.)	1901 March
HARDY, William	HARRIS, Missouri	1896 July,
HARE, A E	MILLER, Rose Anna	1892 Octob
HARE, N	MILLER, Mary	1877 July,
HARE(HAM), W J	FREEMAN[BRADLEY], M(ary) E(liz.) Mrs	1882 Decem
HARRINGTON,(Grover)Cleveland	BRELAND, Queenie (Victoria)	1909 May,2
NOTE: The above HARRINGTON may be	HERRINGTON	
HARRIS, Charlie	WILLIAMS, Lula Mrs	1906 March
HARRIS, Dock	WILLIAMS, Mary	1901 June,
HARRIS, J W	ROGERS, Buner	1888 Octob
HARRIS, James	HARRIS, Gracie	1907 July,

HOOKS, Manuel	EVERITT, Clara	1906 Septe
HOPE, Morris	MARSHALL, Rosa	1907 May,1
HOPKINS, A	BROWN, Mozella	1908 June,
HOPKINS, H W	BRAZILLE, Julia	1892 Augus
HORN, Henderson	SINGLETON, Lula Mrs	1906 June,
HORN, John	CHAMBISS, Millie	1894 Octob
HOUSE, Jackson	WOODARD, Helen	1882 Febru
HOVALTER, M L	BROWN, A J	1903 Febru
~~HOVALTER(HOVATTER), W(~~illiam~~ Albert) F~~	~~JONES, H(attie) L~~	~~1903 Febru~~
HOWARD, Albert R	CURRY, Martha L	1896 Septe
HOWARD, Boney	GODIN, Fannybelle	1906 April
HOWARD, Bony	HARRISON, Mary Celia	1908 July,
HOWARD, C E	DAVIS, Emma	1909 Janua
HOWARD, C E	HOWARD, Jennie Mrs	1903 Septe
HOWARD, Dennis	WELBORN, Julia	1908 July,
HOWARD, Ellis	HILL, Emma	1909 June,
HOWARD, L J	REECE, Mary	1888 June,
HOWELL, John T	MILLER, Ellen	1902 July,
HOWELL, Walter	RICE, Florence	1904 Septe
HUBBARD, Richard	MICHLE, Ada	1894 Octob
HUBBARD, Peter	TATUM, Eliza	1899 Decem
HUDSON, Green	SHEPARD, Alberta	1906 April
HUFF, Will	RHODES, Jessie	1909 Augus
HUGGER, Annie	HUGGER, Moses	1905 Septe
HUGGER, Minna	ANDERSON, Jack	1880 March
HUGGER, Moses	HUGGER, Annie	1905 Septe
HUGGER, Prince	LAWRENCE, Martha	1889 July,
HUGGER, Prince	ROBERTS, Nancy	1904 May,1
HUGGINS, Albert (A.)	RAINWATER, Lottie	1905 Decem
HUGGINS, (Daniel) Dennis	HYATT, Hattie	1908 May,0
HUGGINS, Edward	EASLEY, Victoria	1877 Augus
HUGGINS, J E	WEBBER, Louvenice	1881 Augus
HUNT, C(harles) A	GOLMAN, Bertha (M.)	1908 March
HUNTER, Charlie	KING, Alma	1904 May,2
HUNTER, Frank	GRICE, Laura	1905 Augus
HUNTER, Norris	WILLIAMS, Maria	1893 Febru
HUTTER, Willis	WALLEY, Caroline	1892 April
HUTTO, J(ohn N.)	BREWER, Harriet J	1894 Decem
ICKWOOD, James	HAWKINS, June	1889 April
INGRAM, J R	DOWNEY, R J	1880 Novem
IRKWOOD, James	OXNER, Pattie (S.)	1908 Novem
ISAAC, James	LONG, Nelly Mrs	1879 Septe
IVEY, Gus	JOHNSON, Diana	1906 Novem
IVEY, James	BLACKLEDGE, Sallie Ann	1904 Febru

Return to Main Page

Return to Main Marriage Index

Greene Co., Ms. Index

- A - B - C - D - E - F - G - HI - J - K - L - Mc - MNO - PQ - R - S - TUV - WXYZ

Certificate of Birth

STATE OF WEST VIRGINIA,
COUNTY OF PRESTON, TO-WIT:

I, Nancy Reckart, Clerk of the County Commission in and for said County and State (the same being a Court of Record), also, the Custodian of the Birth Records, do hereby certify that the Birth Records disclose the following:

Name: Wilbert Francis Hovatter

Date of Birth: April 1, 1882 Sex: Male

Father's Name: David Hovatter

Mother's Maiden Name: (Tena) Terra Laverna Shahan

Born in said County and State as more fully shown by the Records of Births in my office in Birth Register

No. 1868-84, Page H-25, Line No. 9.

Date of Recordation 3/4/42.

Given under my hand and official seal this the 14th day of November, 2001.

NANCY RECKART, Clerk

By ________________, Deputy

Descendants of Wilbert F. Hovatter

Generation No. 1

1. WILBERT F.[7] HOVATTER *(DAVID T.[6], DAVID[5], CHRISTOPHER[4], JOHAN MICHAEL[3] HOHWERTER, JOHANN VALENTIN[2], JOHAN HEINRICH[1] HOCHWARTER)*[1] was born April 01, 1882 in Preston Co. WV[1], and died August 19, 1969 in Greene Co. Miss.[1]. He married HATTIE LEE JONES[1] February 18, 1903 in Greene Co. Miss.[1], daughter of ENOCH JONES and MARY SMITH. She was born October 06, 1885 in Greene Co, Miss.[1], and died October 09, 1969 in Greene Co, Miss.[1].

Notes for WILBERT F. HOVATTER:
87 years old 4 months and 18 days at time of death

More About WILBERT F. HOVATTER:
Burial: Stateline, MS
Social Security Number: Pennslyvania[1]

Notes for HATTIE LEE JONES:
84 years old and 3 days at time of death
Pictures on pages 106, 107 108 in book "Generations of Hoffman to Hovatter"

More About HATTIE LEE JONES:
Burial: Stateline, MS
Fact 5: Social Security #: 177-14-7342[2]
Fact 6: Issued in: Pennsylvania[2]
Fact 7: Residence code: Mississippi[2]
Fact 8: Last residence ZIP: 39451[2]

Children of WILBERT HOVATTER and HATTIE JONES are:

2. i. EULA[8] HOVATTER, b. December 14, 1903, Greene Co, Miss.; d. October 24, 1937, WVA.

ii. ODIE HOVATTER[3], b. October 27, 1905[3]; d. December 03, 1905[3].

More About ODIE HOVATTER:
Burial: Slay Cemetary

3. iii. WILBERTIE VALENTINE HOVATTER, b. February 14, 1908, Greene Co, Miss.; d. September 23, 1987.

iv. BOYD HOVATTER[3], b. August 10, 1910, Greene Co, Miss. re: Family Bible[3]; d. February 1975[4,5,6].

Notes for BOYD HOVATTER:
picture on page 93 in book "Generations of Hoffman to Hovatter"

More About BOYD HOVATTER:
Burial: Egg Harbor, NJ
Social Security Number: 560-07-8262[6]

v. FLOYD HOVATTER[6], b. March 19, 1913[6]; d. March 21, 1913[6].

4. vi. LOIS HOVATTER, b. November 19, 1914, Greene Co, Miss.; d. May 30, 1983, Lower Bank, NJ.

vii. HATTIE ALMALEE HOVATTER, b. October 06, 1917.

viii. AUBREY HOVATTER[6], b. September 27, 1920[6].

5. ix. DESSIE HOVATTER, b. September 07, 1921, Preston Co. VA; d. January 21, 2001, Las Vegas, NV.

x. VERNON HOVATTER[6,7], b. February 26, 1924, West Virgina[8]; d. January 03, 1996, San Angelo, Texas[9,10,10,10,10,10,10,10,10,11].

Notes for VERNON HOVATTER:
Picture on page 101 in book "Generations from Hoffman to Hovatter"

More About VERNON HOVATTER:
Social Security Number: new Jersey[11]

xi. KENNETH GENE HOVATTER[11], b. October 31, 1927, west virginia Re: Family Bible[11]; d. March 06, 1983[11].

Notes for KENNETH GENE HOVATTER:
Picture on pages 100 in book "Generations from Hoffman to Hovatter"

More About KENNETH GENE HOVATTER:
Social Security Number: 587-56-1847[11]

Generation No. 2

2. EULA[8] HOVATTER *(WILBERT F.[7], DAVID T.[6], DAVID[5], CHRISTOPHER[4], JOHAN MICHAEL[3] HOHWERTER, JOHANN VALENTIN[2], JOHAN HEINRICH[1] HOCHWARTER)*[11] was born December 14, 1903 in Greene Co, Miss.[11], and died October 24, 1937 in WVA[11]. She married (1) SAMUEL LINTON[11]. She married (2) HOPE WATSON.

Notes for EULA HOVATTER:
picture on pages 93 in book "Generations of Hoffman to Hovatter"

Child of EULA HOVATTER and SAMUEL LINTON is:
i. VONCILE[9] LINTON[11].

Children of EULA HOVATTER and HOPE WATSON are:
ii. JUNIOR LEE[9] WATSON.
iii. FRANCIS WATSON.
iv. JOYCE WATSON.

3. WILBERTIE VALENTINE[8] HOVATTER *(WILBERT F.[7], DAVID T.[6], DAVID[5], CHRISTOPHER[4], JOHAN MICHAEL[3] HOHWERTER, JOHANN VALENTIN[2], JOHAN HEINRICH[1] HOCHWARTER)*[11] was born February 14, 1908 in Greene Co, Miss.[11], and died September 23, 1987[12,13,13,14,15]. He married (1) HAZEL DELL CLEVENGER[16]. She was born June 07, 1907[17,18], and died November 06, 1988[19,20,21]. He met (2) RUBY BARNETT, daughter of MARSHALL BARNETT and ADA GREENLIEF. She was born July 16, 1915.

Notes for WILBERTIE VALENTINE HOVATTER:
Bertie and Hazel had broke up and he met Ruby. Ruby became pregnant with his daughter Rosalie. Hazel decided that they should try to make another go of their marriage, so he left Ruby and went back to Hazel. There is some speculation about when he knew about Ruby's pregnancy. When he found out about his daughter Rosalie he acknowledged her as his child as he did his other children.
Died of Cancer.

Pictures on pages 93, 94, 95 in book "Generations of Hoffman to Hovatter"

More About WILBERTIE VALENTINE HOVATTER:
Social Security Number: 232-05-5326[22]

Children of WILBERTIE HOVATTER and HAZEL CLEVENGER are:
i. MARJORIE[9] HOVATTER, b. August 10, 1927.
ii. DOLORES HOVATTER, b. May 02, 1929.
iii. BERTA JAYNE HOVATTER, b. August 17, 1938; d. January 16, 1988; m. (1) HAROLD SNYDER; m. (2) THOMAS MOSER; b. March 29, 1930.

Notes for BERTA JAYNE HOVATTER:
Died of Cancer.

Child of WILBERTIE HOVATTER and RUBY BARNETT is:

iv. ROSALIE J.[9] HOVATTER, b. December 14, 1932; m. (1) CHARLEY JENKINS; m. (2) DAVID FAULKNIER.

Notes for ROSALIE J. HOVATTER:
Joyce i was not on record at all Bertie went in to the lawer office and sign affidaved that i was his to get me a birth certficall of these people around here that is Hovatters are relation to Bertie im glad Patty sent you the stuff my scaner isent hook up im just glad i got the putor Patty is Dave niece she is so good to me have you heard any more a bout Bill Well ill let you go all my Love tell Bob hello for me Rosalie

4. LOIS[8] HOVATTER *(WILBERT F.[7], DAVID T.[6], DAVID[5], CHRISTOPHER[4], JOHAN MICHAEL[3] HOHWERTER, JOHANN VALENTIN[2], JOHAN HEINRICH[1] HOCHWARTER)*[22] was born November 19, 1914 in Greene Co, Miss.[22], and died May 30, 1983 in Lower Bank, NJ[22]. She married THOMAS MANCUSO[22,23,24] September 23, 1935 in Croydon, PA[25], son of VITO MANCUSO and PATRINA TUMBARELLO. He was born December 31, 1912 in Italy, and died May 27, 1985 in St. Petersburg, FL[25,26].

Notes for LOIS HOVATTER:
Married Sept. 23, 1935
Pictures on pages 96, 97 98, 100 in book "Generations of Hoffman to Hovatter"

More About LOIS HOVATTER:
Burial: Egg Harbor City, NJ[27]
Social Security Number: 177-14-8410[27]

More About THOMAS MANCUSO:
Burial: Clearwater FL[27,28]

Children of LOIS HOVATTER and THOMAS MANCUSO are:

i. JOYCE F..[9] MANCUSO, b. May 11, 1934, Bristol, PA; m. ROBERT THOMAS SUTTON[29], October 19, 1957, Pomona, NJ[29]; b. December 07, 1932, Atlantic City, NJ[29].

Notes for JOYCE F.. MANCUSO:
DAR member number 831198, installed Oct. 16, 2004

Notes for ROBERT THOMAS SUTTON:
Bob was born on a Wednesday. His wife Joyce was born on a Friday two years later, each year their bithdays fall on the same day of the week.

ii. PATRINA MANCUSO, b. Abt. 1937; d. Abt. 1937.

5. DESSIE[8] HOVATTER *(WILBERT F.[7], DAVID T.[6], DAVID[5], CHRISTOPHER[4], JOHAN MICHAEL[3] HOHWERTER, JOHANN VALENTIN[2], JOHAN HEINRICH[1] HOCHWARTER)*[29] was born September 07, 1921 in Preston Co. VA[29], and died January 21, 2001 in Las Vegas, NV. She married (1) EDGAR THOM[29] October 16, 1941 in Trenton, NJ[29], son of GUSTOV THOM and SARAH. He was born October 23, 1922[30,30,30,30,30,30,30,30,31], and died January 1982[32,32,32,32,32,32,32,32,33]. She married (2) WILLIAM F. PUTNAM June 26, 1960 in Trenton, NJ, son of HOWARD PUTNAM and DOROTHY RIDDLE. He was born September 10, 1932, and died March 29, 2002 in Las Vegas, NV.

Notes for DESSIE HOVATTER:
Pictures of Dessie Hovatter and more information on pages 98, 99 in book "Generation from Hoffman to Hovatter"

More About EDGAR THOM:

Adoption: [34,35]
Residence: Residence code: New Jersey[36,37]
Social Security Number: Social Security #: 154-12-8658[38,39]

Notes for WILLIAM F. PUTNAM:

Subj: Re: a short note
Date: 03/29/2002 1:34:39 PM Eastern Standard Time
From: P1AND2
To: JSutton639

E-mail dated 3-29-02
Hi Joyce,

It's Robin and Rick--responding from Dad's e-mail. We are at his house taking care of things. This is a hell of a thing to relay via e-mail, but we tried the phone numbers we found for you and Bob and got no answer, so I apologize in advance, but need to let you know.

Wednesday I couldn't get a hold of Dad, and grew concerned when his phone just kept ringing. So Rick and I drove in and we found him; he had fallen in the bathroom and was unconsious. We summoned paramedics and they took him to Valley Hospital. He passed away this morning around 6:30. He never regained consiousness. Rick, Bill and I like to think he had little or no pain, and know for sure he is in a better place now....probably with Mom :).

I know he wanted you to have Mom's albums....there are also a lot of pictures...I'd like for you to have anything you want. Please let me know.

We are still in the midst of arrangements and will let you know what is going on when we have more info.

Again I'm sorry to relay this via reply e-mail, but wanted you to know....Can I ask a favor pls...you knew a lot of Mom and Dad's e-mail buddies...would you be able to let them know about Dad for us pls, we'd really appreciate it.

Thanks.

Robin

William Putnam

William F. Putnam, 69, died March 29 in a local hospital.
He was born Sept. 10, 1932, in Port Henry, N.Y. A Navy veteran of the Korean and Vietnam wars, he was a corrections officer and a 22-year resident of Las Vegas.
He is survived by his son, William; and daughter, Robin Walker, both of Indian Springs; and five grandchildren. Services are private. Davis Funeral Home-Charleston handled arrangements.

Child of DESSIE HOVATTER and EDGAR THOM is:

i. DENNIS[9] THOM[39], b. September 17, 1949[40,40,40,40,40,40,40,40,40,40,40,40,41]; d. March 1971[42,42,42,42,43].

More About DENNIS THOM:
Social Security Number: Social Security #: 570-84-6960[44,45]

Children of DESSIE HOVATTER and WILLIAM PUTNAM are:

ii. ROBIN[9] PUTNAM, b. April 17, 1963; m. EDISON RICHARD WALKER, November 19, 1986, Las Vegas, NV.
iii. WILLIAM F. PUTNAM 2, b. August 19, 1966; m. BERNETTA GRAHAM, December 28, 1989, Las Vegas, NV;

Scrapbook of Wilbert F. Hovatter

Wilbert Hovatter

Hattie Lee Jones Hovatter

company visiting

Hattie and Wilbert

Wilbert Hovatter

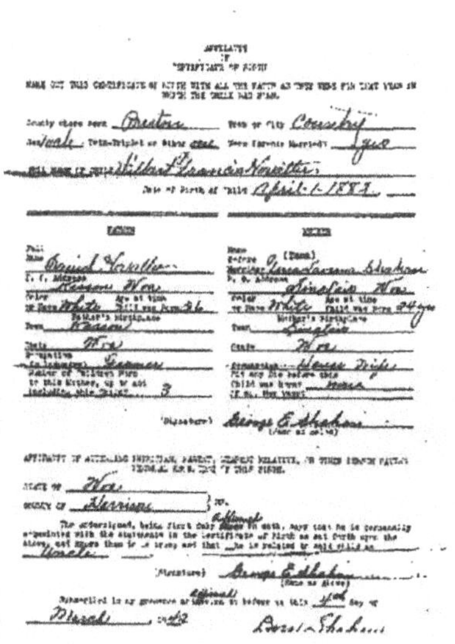

Preston — Country
male — one — Yes
White — Wva — Farmer
White — Wva — House Wife
George E. Shahan
Wva
Harrison
Uncle
George E. Shahan
March

Afidavit of Wilberts Birth

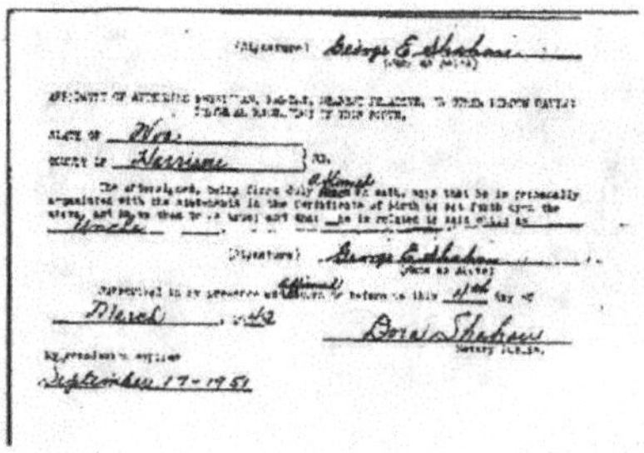

(Signature)

STATE OF W.Va.

COUNTY OF Harrison

(Signature)

March

September 17-1951

afidavit

Wilbert, Hazel and Bertie

Hovatter Family Picture

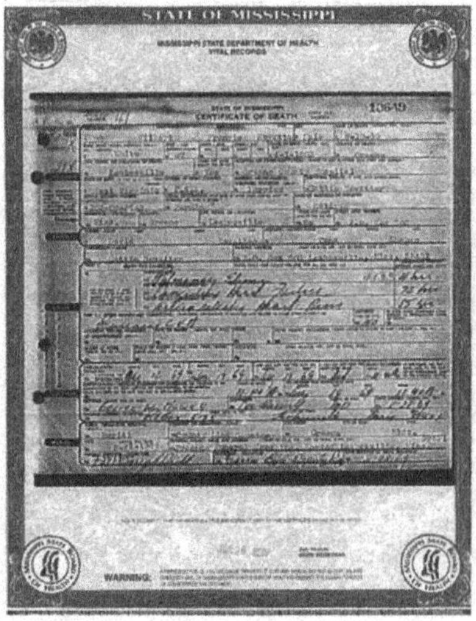

STATE OF MISSISSIPPI

MISSISSIPPI STATE DEPARTMENT OF HEALTH

VITAL RECORDS

CERTIFICATE OF DEATH

WARNING:

Wilbert's Death Certificate

Bertie

Bertie

Boyd and Bertie

Bertie and Hazel

Bertie

Bertie

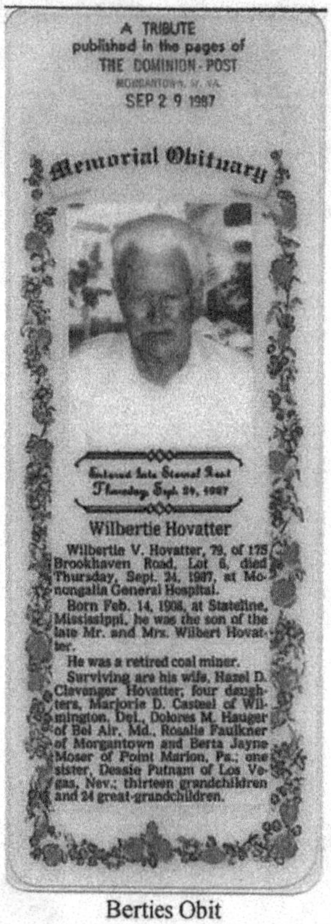

A TRIBUTE
published in the pages of
THE DOMINION-POST
MORGANTOWN, W. VA.
SEP 2 9 1987

Memorial Obituary

Entered Into Eternal Rest
Thursday, Sept. 24, 1987

Wilbertie Hovatter

Wilbertie V. Hovatter, 79, of 175 Brookhaven Road, Lot 6, died Thursday, Sept. 24, 1987, at Monongalia General Hospital.

Born Feb. 14, 1908, at Stateline, Mississippi, he was the son of the late Mr. and Mrs. Wilbert Hovatter.

He was a retired coal miner.

Surviving are his wife, Hazel D. Clevenger Hovatter; four daughters, Marjorie D. Casteel of Wilmington, Del., Dolores M. Hauger of Bel Air, Md., Rosalie Faulkner of Morgantown and Berta Jayne Moser of Point Marion, Pa.; one sister, Dessie Putnam of Los Vegas, Nev.; thirteen grandchildren and 24 great-grandchildren.

Berties Obit

Scrapbook of Berta Jayne Hovatter

Berta Jane and Dolores Hovatter

Descendants of Lois Hovatter

Generation No. 1

1. Lois[8] Hovatter *(Wilbert F.[7], David T.[6], David[5], Christopher[4], Johan Michael[3] Hohwerter, Johann Valentin[2], Johan Heinrich[1] Hochwarter)[1]* was born November 19, 1914 in Greene Co, Miss.[1], and died May 30, 1983 in Lower Bank, NJ[1]. She married Thomas Mancuso[1,2,3] September 23, 1935 in Croydon, PA[4], son of Vito Mancuso and Patrina Tumbarello. He was born December 31, 1912 in Italy, and died May 27, 1985 in St. Petersburg, FL[4,5].

Notes for Lois Hovatter:
Married Sept. 23, 1935
Pictures on pages 96, 97 98, 100 in book "Generations of Hoffman to Hovatter"

More About Lois Hovatter:
Burial: Egg Harbor City, NJ[6]
Social Security Number: 177-14-8410[6]

More About Thomas Mancuso:
Burial: Clearwater FL[6,7]

Children of Lois Hovatter and Thomas Mancuso are:
2. i. Joyce F..[9] Mancuso, b. May 11, 1934, Bristol, PA.
ii. Patrina Mancuso, b. Abt. 1937; d. Abt. 1937.

Generation No. 2

2. Joyce F..[9] Mancuso *(Lois[8] Hovatter, Wilbert F.[7], David T.[6], David[5], Christopher[4], Johan Michael[3] Hohwerter, Johann Valentin[2], Johan Heinrich[1] Hochwarter)* was born May 11, 1934 in Bristol, PA. She married Robert Thomas Sutton[8] October 19, 1957 in Pomona, NJ[8], son of Robert Sutton and Dora Watson. He was born December 07, 1932 in Atlantic City, NJ[8].

Notes for Joyce F.. Mancuso:
DAR member number 831198, installed Oct. 16, 2004

Notes for Robert Thomas Sutton:
Bob was born on a Wednesday. His wife Joyce was born on a Friday two years later, each year their bithdays fall on the same day of the week.

Children of Joyce Mancuso and Robert Sutton are:
i. Dolores Lea[10] Sutton[8], b. September 24, 1958[8].
3. ii. Susan Joyce Sutton, b. December 01, 1964.
4. iii. Bobbi Lynn Sutton, b. November 09, 1968.

Generation No. 3

3. Susan Joyce[10] Sutton *(Joyce F..[9] Mancuso, Lois[8] Hovatter, Wilbert F.[7], David T.[6], David[5], Christopher[4], Johan Michael[3] Hohwerter, Johann Valentin[2], Johan Heinrich[1] Hochwarter)[8]* was born December 01, 1964[8]. She married Christopher Keating[8], son of Wilton Keating and Marguerite Toth.

Notes for Susan Joyce Sutton:
DAR member number 831199

Children of SUSAN SUTTON and CHRISTOPHER KEATING are:

i. CHRISTOPHER KEATING[11] JR.[8].

ii. BENJAMIN KEATING[8].

4. BOBBI LYNN[10] SUTTON *(JOYCE F..[9] MANCUSO, LOIS[8] HOVATTER, WILBERT F.[7], DAVID T.[6], DAVID[5], CHRISTOPHER[4], JOHAN MICHAEL[3] HOHWERTER, JOHANN VALENTIN[2], JOHAN HEINRICH[1] HOCHWARTER)*[8] was born November 09, 1968[8]. She married (1) KARL FRANK CHASE[8]. She met (2) MR. MCHENRY.

Notes for BOBBI LYNN SUTTON:
DAR member number 831200, installed Oct. 16, 2004

Children of BOBBI SUTTON and KARL CHASE are:

i. SHAWN JOSEPH[11] CHASE[8], b. March 14, 1995[8].

ii. SAMANTHA JOYCE CHASE[8], b. April 06, 1997[8].

Child of BOBBI SUTTON and MR. MCHENRY is:

iii. DANI-LYNN[11] MCHENRY, b. June 08, 2006.

Endnotes

1. Mancuso.FTW, Date of Import: Sep 6, 2000.
2. Genealogy.com, Family Archive #110, Social Security Death Index: U.S. Ed. 9, Social Security Death Index, Release date: April 10, 2000.
3. Mancuso Cramer Sutton.FTW, Date of Import: Jun 25, 2001.
4. Mancuso.FTW, Date of Import: Sep 6, 2000.
5. Mancuso Cramer Sutton.FTW, Date of Import: Jun 25, 2001.
6. Mancuso.FTW, Date of Import: Sep 6, 2000.
7. Mancuso Cramer Sutton.FTW, Date of Import: Jun 25, 2001.
8. Mancuso.FTW, Date of Import: Sep 6, 2000.

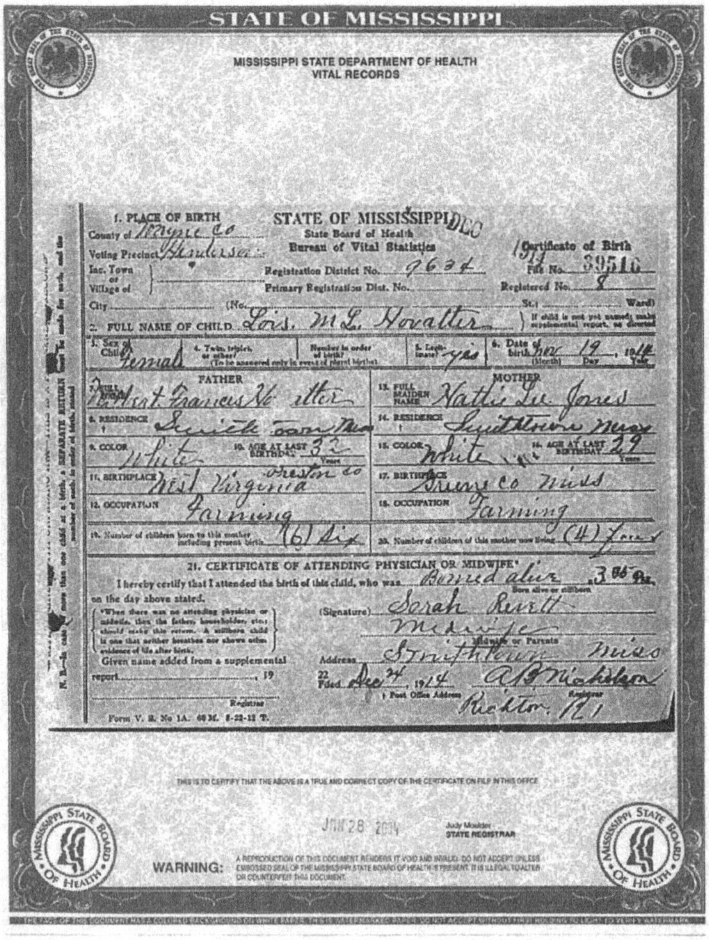

STATE OF MISSISSIPPI

MISSISSIPPI STATE DEPARTMENT OF HEALTH
VITAL RECORDS

1. PLACE OF BIRTH
County of Wayne Co
Voting Precinct Henderson
Inc. Town or Village of
City (No. St. Ward)

STATE OF MISSISSIPPI
State Board of Health
Bureau of Vital Statistics
Registration District No. 9634
Primary Registration Dist. No.

Certificate of Birth
File No. 39516
Registered No. 8

2. FULL NAME OF CHILD Lois, M.L. Hovatter
If child is not yet named, make supplemental report, as directed

3. Sex of Child Female
4. Twin, triplet, or other (To be answered only in event of plural births)
Number in order of birth?
5. Legitimate? yes
6. Date of birth Nov 19, 1914 (Month) (Day) (Year)

FATHER	MOTHER
7. FULL NAME Robert Francis Hovatter	13. FULL MAIDEN NAME Hattie Lee Jones
8. RESIDENCE Smith Town Miss	14. RESIDENCE Smithtown Miss
9. COLOR White; 10. AGE AT LAST BIRTHDAY 32 Years	15. COLOR White; 16. AGE AT LAST BIRTHDAY 29 Years
11. BIRTHPLACE West Virginia Preston co	17. BIRTHPLACE Greene Co Miss
12. OCCUPATION Farming	18. OCCUPATION Farming
19. Number of children born to this mother including present birth (6) Six	20. Number of children of this mother now living (4) four

21. CERTIFICATE OF ATTENDING PHYSICIAN OR MIDWIFE*
I hereby certify that I attended the birth of this child, who was Borned alive at 3 05 a.m. on the day above stated. (Born alive or stillborn)

*When there was no attending physician or midwife, then the father, householder, etc., should make this return. A stillborn child is one that neither breathes nor shows other evidence of life after birth.

(Signature) Sarah Revett
Midwife (Midwife or Parents)
Address Smithtown Miss

Given name added from a supplemental report, 19
Registrar

22 Filed Dec 24, 1914 A.B. Michelson Registrar
Post Office Address Richton R1

Form V. S. No 1A. 60 M. 5-22-13 T.

THIS IS TO CERTIFY THAT THE ABOVE IS A TRUE AND CORRECT COPY OF THE CERTIFICATE ON FILE IN THIS OFFICE

JAN 28 2014

Judy Moulder
STATE REGISTRAR

WARNING: A REPRODUCTION OF THIS DOCUMENT RENDERS IT VOID AND INVALID. DO NOT ACCEPT UNLESS EMBOSSED SEAL OF THE MISSISSIPPI STATE BOARD OF HEALTH IS PRESENT. IT IS ILLEGAL TO ALTER OR COUNTERFEIT THIS DOCUMENT.

Birth Certificate

Lois

Lois

Tommy & Lois Mancuso

Tommy and Joyce

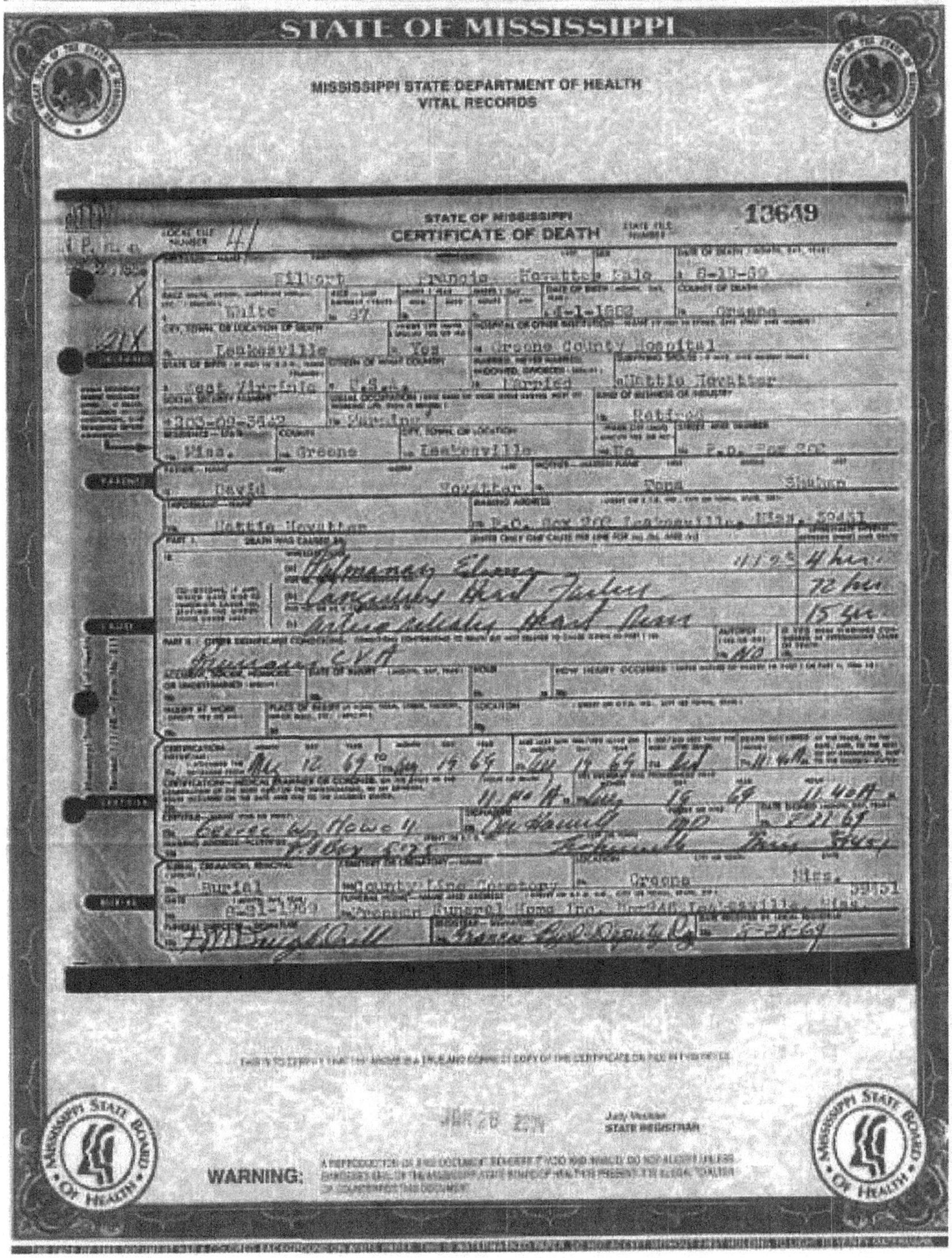

STATE OF MISSISSIPPI

MISSISSIPPI STATE DEPARTMENT OF HEALTH
VITAL RECORDS

STATE OF MISSISSIPPI
CERTIFICATE OF DEATH

13649

Local file number: 41

Gilbert Francis Hovatter Male 8-19-69

White 87 8-1-1882 Greene

Leakesville Yes Greene County Hospital

West Virginia U.S.A. Married Hattie Hovatter

303-09-3542 Farming Retired

Miss. Greene Leakesville No P.O. Box 202

Father: David Hovatter

Mother: Dona Shuhan

Informant: Hattie Hovatter P.O. Box 202 Leakesville, Miss. 39451

Part I. Death was caused by:

(a) Pulmonary Edema 4 hrs.

(b) Congestive Heart Failure 72 hrs.

(c) Arteriosclerotic Heart Disease 15 yrs.

Part II. Other significant conditions: Previous CVA

Autopsy: No

Certification: Aug 12 69 to Aug 19 69; Aug 19 69; 11:40 A

11:40 A Aug 19 69 11:40 A

Certifier: Cecil W. Howell MD 8-21-69

P.O. Box 575 Leakesville Miss 39451

Burial County Line Cemetery Greene Miss.

8-21-1969 Freeman Funeral Home Inc. Box 245 Leakesville, Miss.

Funeral director: [illegible]

Registrar: Greene Co. ... Deputy Clerk 8-28-69

THIS IS TO CERTIFY THAT THE ABOVE IS A TRUE AND CORRECT COPY OF THE CERTIFICATE ON FILE IN THIS OFFICE

JAN 20 2011

Judy Moulder
STATE REGISTRAR

WARNING: A REPRODUCTION OF THIS DOCUMENT RENDERS IT VOID AND INVALID. DO NOT ACCEPT UNLESS EMBOSSED SEAL OF THE MISSISSIPPI STATE BOARD OF HEALTH IS PRESENT. IT IS ILLEGAL TO ALTER OR COUNTERFEIT THIS DOCUMENT.

STATE OF MISSISSIPPI

MISSISSIPPI STATE DEPARTMENT OF HEALTH
VITAL RECORDS

STATE OF MISSISSIPPI
CERTIFICATE OF DEATH

Local File Number: 52

State File Number: 17383

Deceased—Name: Hattie Lou Hovatter | Sex: Female | Date of Death: 10-9-69

Race: White | Age: 85 | Date of Birth: 10-6-1884 | County of Death: Greene

City, Town, or Location of Death: Leakesville | Inside City Limits: Yes | Hospital or Other Institution: Greene County Hospital

State of Birth: Miss. | Citizen of What Country: U.S.A. | Married, Never Married, Widowed, Divorced: Widowed | Surviving Spouse: None

Social Security Number: 403-09-3643 | Usual Occupation: House Keeper | Kind of Business or Industry: Retired

Residence—State: Miss. | County: Greene | City, Town, or Location: Leakesville | Inside City Limits: No | Street and Number: P.O. Box

Father—Name: Enoch Jones | Mother—Maiden Name: Mary Smith

Informant—Name: Mrs. Louis Fancuss | Mailing Address: Leakesville, Miss. 39451

Part I. Death was caused by:

(a) Ventricular Fibrillation — 5 min

(b) Congestive Heart Failure — 3 days

(c) Chronic Obstructive Lung Disease — 18 yrs

Autopsy: No

Certification—Physician: 3 21 69 — 10 9 69 — 10 9 69 — 7:19 P

7:29 P — 10 9 69 — 7:19 P

Certifier—Name: George W. Howey | Signature: [signature] MD | Date Signed: 10-15-69

Mailing Address: Leakesville, Miss. 39451

Burial, Cremation, Removal: Burial | Cemetery or Crematory—Name: County Line Cemetery | Location: Greene County Miss.

Date: 10-11-69 | Funeral Home—Name and Address: Freeman Funeral Home Inc. Leakesville, Miss. 39451

Funeral Director—Signature: [signature] | Registrar—Signature: Greene Cty. Deputy Reg. | Date Received by Local Registrar: 10-15-69

THIS IS TO CERTIFY THAT THE ABOVE IS A TRUE AND CORRECT COPY OF THE CERTIFICATE ON FILE IN THIS OFFICE.

JAN 28 2011

Judy Moulder
STATE REGISTRAR

MISSISSIPPI STATE BOARD OF HEALTH

WARNING: A REPRODUCTION OF THIS DOCUMENT RENDERS IT VOID AND INVALID. DO NOT ACCEPT UNLESS EMBOSSED SEAL OF THE MISSISSIPPI STATE BOARD OF HEALTH IS PRESENT. IT IS ILLEGAL TO ALTER OR COUNTERFEIT THIS DOCUMENT.

WARNING: Do not accept this copy unless the raised seal of the Township of Waterford is affixed hereon.

TOWNSHIP OF WATERFORD, CAMDEN COUNTY, N. J.
OFFICE OF REGISTRAR OF VITAL STATISTICS

This is to certify that the following is a true copy of a record filed in this Department.

Registrar of Vital Statistics

NEW JERSEY STATE DEPARTMENT OF HEALTH
CERTIFICATE OF DEATH

1. NAME OF DECEASED (First) (Middle) (Last): LOIS MANCUSI
2. DATE OF DEATH: 5/30/83
3a. PLACE OF DEATH (City, Town): Hammonton
3b. County: Atlantic
4a. Residence (No. and St.): Box 192D
4b. City or Town: Egg Harbor
5a. Name of Hospital or Institution (If not either, give No. and St.): Kessler Memorial Hospital
4c. County: Burlington
4d. State: N.J.
4e. Zip Code: 08215
4f. Inside City Limits: Yes ☐ No
5b. If Hospital or Institution, check correct box: DOA ☐ Inpatient ☐ Emergency ☐ Other
6. Marital Status: 1 ☐ Single 2 ☐ Married 3 Widowed 4 ☐ Divorced ☐ Separated
7a. Was Deceased ever in U.S. Military (If "Yes" enter War and Dates): ☐ Yes No
7b. War: —
7c. Date From: To:
8. Sex: F
9. Date of Birth: 11-19-1914
10. Age Last Birthday: 68
11a. Under "1" Year: MONTHS DAYS
11b. Under "1" Day: HOURS MINUTES
12a. Birthplace (State or Foreign Country): Mississippi
12b. Citizen of what Country: U.S.A
13. Surviving Spouse (If Wife, Maiden Name): None
14. Social Security Number: 177-14-8410
15. Race: White ☐ American Indian ☐ Other (Specify) ☐ Black
16. Ethnic Origin: ☐ Puerto Rican ☐ Mexican ☐ Italian ☐ Cuban ☐ German Other (Specify): AMERICAN
17. Name and Address of Last Employer: —
18. Usual Occupation (Kind of work done most of Life - even if retired):
19. Kind of Business or Industry: Homemaker
20. NAME OF FATHER (First) (Middle) (Last): Wilbert Houatter
21. MAIDEN NAME OF MOTHER (First) (Middle) (Last): Hattie Jones
21a. Name of Informant: Joyce Sutton
21b. Relationship: Daughter
21c. Number and Street: Box 242
21d. City or Town: Egg Harbor
21e. State: N.J.
22a. Disposition: ☐ Burial ☐ Removal Cremation ☐ Other
22b. Name of Cemetery or Crematory: LeRoy P. Wooster Crematory
22c. City or Town: Atco
22d. State: N.J.
23a. Name and Address of Funeral Home: LeRoy P. Wooster Funeral Home Atco, N.J.
23b. Signature of Funeral Director:
23c. N.J. License No.: 2824
24a. Signature of Registrar:
24b. Date received by Registrar: 6-1-83
25a. Name and Address of Certifier ☐ Attending Phys. Med. Exam.: DANTE A. RAGASA M.D. 175 MADISON AVE, MT. HOLLY, N.J. 08060
25b. To the best of my knowledge, death occurred at time, date and place, due to cause(s) stated. Signature:
25c. Date Signed: 5/31/83
26a. Hour of Death:
26b. Pronounced Dead: 8:00 Am. 5/30/83
27a. PART I Immediate Cause (Enter only one cause per line for (a), (b), and (c). Please print)
a. Cardiorespiratory failure
Due to or as a consequence of
b. Chronic alcoholic liver & brain disease
Due to or as a consequence of
c.
Interval between onset and death
27d. If female, was she pregnant at death or any time 90 days prior to death? ☐ Yes No
PART II Other significant conditions: conditions contributing to death but not related to cause in PART I
28. Was Autopsy performed? ☐ Yes No
29. Was case referred to Medical Examiner? ☐ Yes ☐ No
30. Death due to: Accident ☐ Suicide ☐ Homicide ☐ Undetermined ☐ Pending Investigation ☐ Other
31a. Describe how injury occurred
31b. Date of Injury
31c. Hour of Injury
31d. Injury at Work: Yes No
31e. Place of Injury: Home Farm Street Factory Office Building Other
31f. Location (No. and St.)
31g. City or Town
31h. State

STATE OF MISSISSIPPI

MISSISSIPPI STATE DEPARTMENT OF HEALTH
VITAL RECORDS

1. PLACE OF BIRTH

County of Wayne co

Voting Precinct Henderson

Inc. Town or Village of

City (No. St. Ward)

STATE OF MISSISSIPPI DEC

State Board of Health

Bureau of Vital Statistics

1914 Certificate of Birth

Registration District No. 9634 File No. 39516

Primary Registration Dist. No. Registered No. 8

2. FULL NAME OF CHILD Lois M L Hovatter (If child is not yet named; make supplemental report, as directed)

3. Sex of Child Female | 4. Twin, triplet, or other? | Number in order of birth? (To be answered only in event of plural births) | 5. Legitimate? yes | 6. Date of birth Nov 19, 1914 (Month) Day Year

FATHER	MOTHER
7. FULL NAME Herbert Francis Hovatter	13. FULL MAIDEN NAME Hattie Lee Jones
8. RESIDENCE Smith town Miss	14. RESIDENCE Smithtown Miss
9. COLOR White — 10. AGE AT LAST BIRTHDAY 32 Years	15. COLOR White — 16. AGE AT LAST BIRTHDAY 29 Years
11. BIRTHPLACE West Virginia Preston co	17. BIRTHPLACE Greene co Miss
12. OCCUPATION Farming	18. OCCUPATION Farming
19. Number of children born to this mother including present birth (6) Six	20. Number of children of this mother now living (4) Four

21. CERTIFICATE OF ATTENDING PHYSICIAN OR MIDWIFE*

I hereby certify that I attended the birth of this child, who was Borned alive (Born alive or stillborn) at 3 05 P.M., on the day above stated.

*When there was no attending physician or midwife, then the father, householder, etc., should make this return. A stillborn child is one that neither breathes nor shows other evidence of life after birth.

(Signature) Sarah Revett

Midwife (Midwife or Parents)

Address Smithtown Miss

Given name added from a supplemental report........, 19 ...... Registrar

Filed Dec 22 4, 1914 A B Nicholson Registrar

† Post Office Address Richton R1

Form V. S. No 1A. 60 M. 8-22-12 T.

N. B.—In case more than one child at a birth, a SEPARATE RETURN must be made for each, and the number of each, in order of birth, stated

THIS IS TO CERTIFY THAT THE ABOVE IS A TRUE AND CORRECT COPY OF THE CERTIFICATE ON FILE IN THIS OFFCE

JAN 28 2004

Judy Moulder
STATE REGISTRAR

MISSISSIPPI STATE BOARD OF HEALTH

WARNING: A REPRODUCTION OF THIS DOCUMENT RENDERS IT VOID AND INVALID. DO NOT ACCEPT UNLESS EMBOSSED SEAL OF THE MISSISSIPPI STATE BOARD OF HEALTH IS PRESENT. IT IS ILLEGAL TO ALTER OR COUNTERFEIT THIS DOCUMENT.

TELEPHONE
(609) 965-0081
FAX
(609) 965-0715

500 LONDON AVENUE
EGG HARBOR CITY, NEW JERSEY 08215

City of Egg Harbor

New Jersey

CITY CLERK'S OFFICE

December 17, 2003

Mrs. Joyce Sutton
2074 River Road
Egg Harbor City, New Jersey 08215

Dear Mrs. Sutton:

As per your request, the following people are buried in the Egg Harbor City Cemetery:

Section "Y", Row 14, Grave 48
[illegible]
Kenneth Gene Hovatter (ashes)
Lois Mancuso (ashes)

If there is any more information needed, please feel free to contact me.

Very truly yours,

CITY OF EGG HARBOR CITY,

Lillian DuBow, RMC
City Clerk

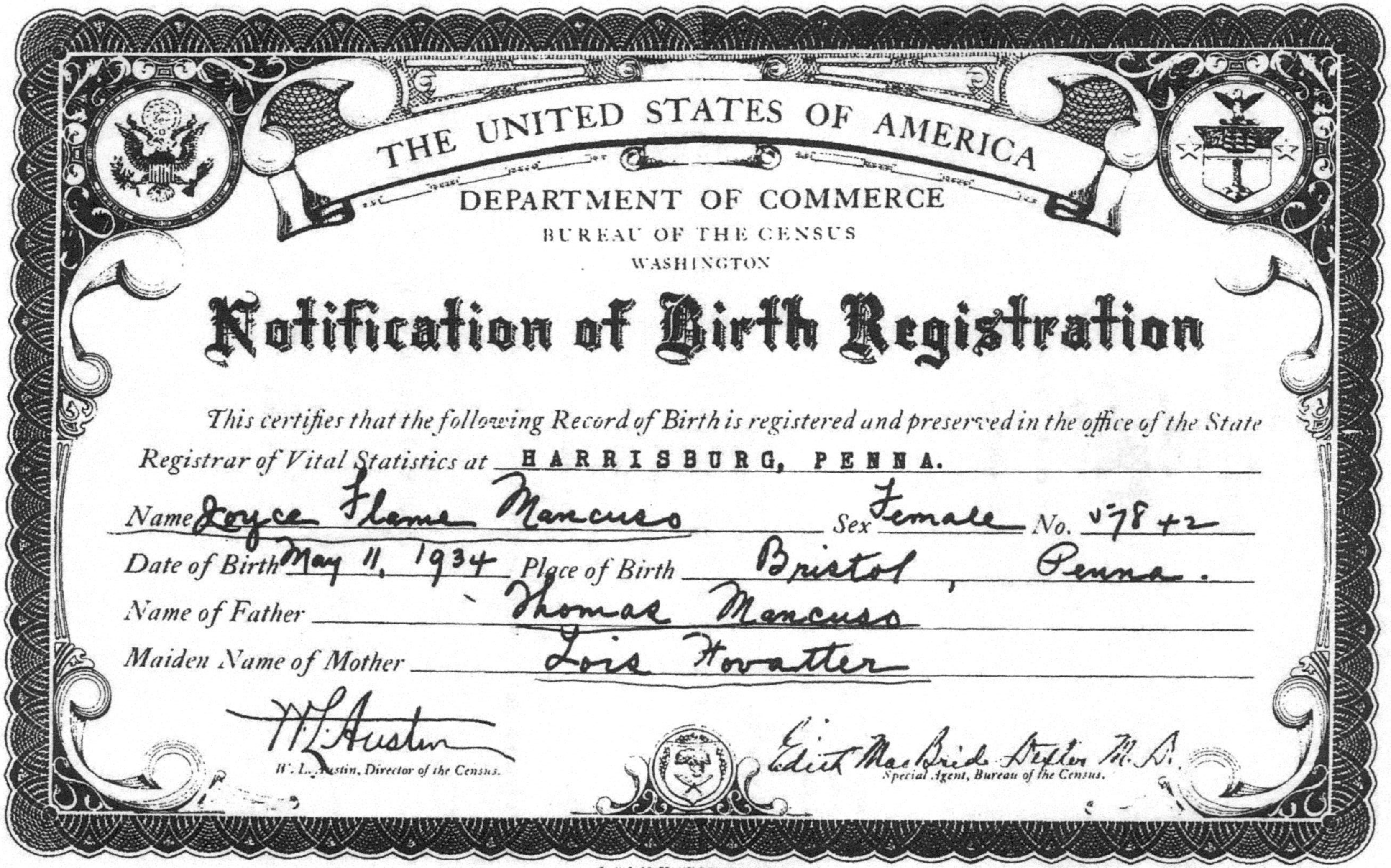

THE UNITED STATES OF AMERICA

DEPARTMENT OF COMMERCE

BUREAU OF THE CENSUS

WASHINGTON

Notification of Birth Registration

This certifies that the following Record of Birth is registered and preserved in the office of the State Registrar of Vital Statistics at HARRISBURG, PENNA.

Name Joyce Flame Mancuso *Sex* Female *No.* V7842

Date of Birth May 11, 1934 *Place of Birth* Bristol, Penna.

Name of Father Thomas Mancuso

Maiden Name of Mother Lois Howatter

W. L. Austin

W. L. Austin, Director of the Census.

Edith MacBride Dexter M.D.

Special Agent, Bureau of the Census.

O U S GOVERNMENT PRINTING OFFICE 1938

NEW JERSEY STATE DEPARTMENT OF HEALTH
TRENTON, N. J.

August 1, 1974
(Date)

THIS IS TO CERTIFY THAT THE FOLLOWING IS A TRUE COPY OF A RECORD FILED IN THIS DEPARTMENT

L. Merton Dayboll — State Registrar of Vital Statistics

Joanne E. Finley M.D. — State Commissioner of Health

WARNING: DO NOT ACCEPT THIS COPY UNLESS THE RAISED SEAL OF THE STATE DEPARTMENT OF HEALTH IS AFFIXED HEREON.

M9415

PLACE OF BIRTH — STATE DEPARTMENT OF HEALTH — BUREAU OF VITAL STATISTICS

County Allentown State New Jersey Registered No. 110

Township or Borough Allentown Ally Hospital St. 3-4 Ward

FULL NAME OF CHILD Robert Thomas Sutton

Sex Male | If plural births: Twin, triplet, or other; Number, in order of birth | Premature; Full term yes | Legitimate? yes | Date of birth Dec - 7 1932

FATHER: Full Name Robert C Sutton; Residence New Gretna N J; Color or Race white; Age at last birthday 26; Birthplace USA; Trade, profession, or particular kind of work done Labor; Industry or business in which work was done

MOTHER: Full Maiden Name Dora Watson; Residence (Mail Address) New Gretna N J; Color or Race white; Age at last birthday 17; Birthplace New Jersey; Trade, profession, or particular kind of work done Housewife; Industry or business in which work was done; Date (month and year) last engaged in this work; Total time (years) spent in this work

What Preventive for Ophthalmia Neonatorum was used? 25% Argyrol

Number of children of this mother (at time of this birth and including this child): Born alive and now living 1; Born alive but now dead 0; Stillborn 0

I hereby certify that I attended the birth of this child, who was born alive on the date above stated at 9:15 A.M.

(Signature) Jos Polancy M.D. (Physician or Midwife.)

Date

Address

Given name added from a supplemental report, 19...... Registrar.

Received 12/12, 1932 [illegible] Local Registrar

THIS CERTIFIES

that on the 19th day of Oct. in the year of our Lord 57

Robert T Sutton of New Gretna NJ.

and Joyce Mancuso of [illegible] Bank NJ.

were by me united in

HOLY MATRIMONY

at Pomona

Galloway Twp.

According to the Ordinance of God and the laws of New Jersey

Witnesses

Lawrence G. Rose

Marjorie S Rose

[illegible]

Pastor.

Municipal Mag.

Galloway Twp.

You are far within the
mark, if you say —

That all the blues of the sky,
all the greens of the forests,
all the splendor of the deserts,
all the might of the mountains,
and all the mistery of the oceans,
put together have not affected
this woman, as has her only
contribution for ever having
lived, a daughter.

Written by
Louis M. Mancuso
December — 1964

Tuesday – AM.
Nov 12 –

Dear Joyce –
– I guess this is a personal letter – you are very much on my mind and I can't sleep – so I'll just talk to you – nothing very special – Once I read that we live and die – never once having said the things we want to say – rather – the things people want or expect us to say. – Maybe you've heard it – so I'll tell you again about the day you were born – I guess I gave you some bad habits – you slept like a doll all day and then about eleven o'clock at night – you awakened – I

decided it was really going to happen—but I didn't say anything until the family got up at five thirty—Mrs. Johnson from across the street came in about seven or eight—She had had four children and of course Mom had eleven—Now for the next two or three hours I heard how it wasn't nothing at all—Mom said she had never even grunted hard with hers—this was pretty confusing since she had used my birth sort of like a lever when she was mad—It was usually about the same thing about how she had gone down into the valley of death—the pain—the suffering to bring me into this world etc—Well as you can imagine—for the rest of the day — I kept waiting for things to get so bad — I'd start climbing the walls — Mom said walk between pains so I did — and every time I could get by my self — I'd talk to you — you were a pretty good listener — for about five minutes at a time — then I would shut up while you went into your pantomime — It was more than clear that you were tired of waiting around but I couldn't quite figure out who was supposed to make the first move — so I waited and then you waited — By five thirty in the afternoon your calls had got down to three minutes and I supposed being a thrifty little girl you would keep an eye on the over charge — which you did —

~~IIII~~ Thursday AM

I wish we had a phone so I could call you - The nearest one is about two miles away - So on the day you were born - Mom had about ten soap opera's that she listened to on the Radio - and as always on Friday They build up suspence so you listen again on Monday - Mom almost ran her self to death not to miss anything - Radio or me - There was "David Harum M.D." He always had a near death patient on his hands - "Ma Perkins" a widower seemed to feed the entire town where she lived - "My Gal Sunday" a poor little orphan found by two very rich old prospectors + now in love with a rich titled Englishman -

##

"Mary and Bob" Don Ameche played the part of Bob who was a wife cheater & I loved listening to his voice — "Back Stage Wife" a story about a handsome actor named Larry Noble — and I guess from all the sobs going on & a very ugly wife, but very angelic all of them put together was about like "General Hospital" today — In the evening there were such programs as "Little Orphan Annie" "Jack Armstrong" "John Henry" "Missing Persons" "Gang Busters" "Duffy's Tavern" "Henry Aldrich" "The Shadow" "Green Hornet" "Floyd Gibbons" "Walter Winchell" "Lowell Thomas" & of course "Amos & Andy" — most of the programs were fifteen minutes a few were thirty — Anyway they all had Themes or some tricks announcement — We had a real nice console type Majestic which had a beautiful sound — It was always high and it's bass carried to all the rooms — I think I knew the time by the programs that were on — Dad used to love to hold a baby and rock — and this rocking chair had its own personal creak — I could hear how it hurried up real fast — some time slowing down until I could hardly hear — some time it would stop and then I would listen and wait for it to get going again — how in with all this I tried to understand what the Doctor or Mom was saying — They didn't agree on how a woman was to have a baby — having a baby two different ways is quite a thing. If you just end up laying there and let Nature take its course — Mom would say "Push down hard, the baby is almost born" Then the Doctor would decide not yet and push you back in — You and me didn't have much to say or do about anything — For the first time in my life — everything was crystal clear in sight and sound and is so yet to-day — It went like this —

Mom: It is almost over Lois.
Lois: unmhhhhh unhhhh —
Doc: easy Lois — just a second —
Rocking chair — creak creak creak —
Radio — is Lowell Thomas for Sonoco —
Rocking chair: — creak —
Lois: Unmmhhhhh —
Doc: This time — I think —

Lois: Umhhhhhhh —
Radio: Amos and Andy —
Rocking chair: creak
Joyce: Yahhhhhh — yah yah
Lois: Let me see her —
Doc: Lay down — you have the rest
of your life to look at her —
Joyce: yah yah yak —
Rocking chair
Radio: Was brought you, Amos & Andy
Lois: Well what do you know — ?
Mom: What do you think she weighs?
Doc: about three and a half pounds.
Mom: Looks weight about five & a half —
Joyce: yah yak
Lois: Well nothing's missing —
Radio: Stay tuned for
Rocking chair — creak creak creak creak creak
Incredible pleasure — I did it
& boy what a day it was —
first Mom

Letter my mother wrote to me when Bobbi Lynn was born

Tuesday 16

Dear Family:

Received your letter yesterday and it was wonderful to hear I have another granddaughter — I love her name — the sound of it is kind of flirty and yet soft and gentle — and a very heavenly birthday gift — I cant wait to see her — and well now I have some one to share the Scorpio sign with — I dont think it is as beautiful as Dolores and Susans and yet people born at this time have so much going for them — It is the only occult sign and every one I have met has been

far above average (not me) They
are Intelligent, aggressive, blunt,
sarcastic and lack of diplomacy.
We are dreamy, slow to anger
but hold grudges. We should
be good in the arts, also as
Doctors and builders — We
are watery and Fruitful and
very feminine — I wish all
the good things for her always —
The enclosures are nothing —
I was upset a little and I
couldn't sleep — so like I
said — I talked to you —
I must close now as
Boyd is going into town and
I can get this mailed — I
love you all dearly and I
am as ever

Just Mom

Tell Dolores I will write to her as soon as I can - and I loved her letter and the picture she drew.

Descendants of Egnasio Thomas Tumbarello

1 Egnasio Thomas Tumbarello
.. +Susanna La Fata
.... 2 Patrina Tumbarello
.... +Vito Mancuso
.... 3 Angelina Mancuso
.... +Anthony Bono
.... 3 Sarah Mancuso 1907 - 2001
.... +Samuel Farina
.... 3 Ada Mancuso
.... +Henry Roach
.... 3 Yolanda Mancuso 1918 - 2005
.... +Joseph Buzzatto
.... 4 Joseph Buzzatto
.... 5 Alicia Buzzatto
.... 5 Brett Buzzatto
.... 5 Jodi Buzzatto
.... 3 Alfred Mancuso
.... 3 Joseph Mancuso 1909 - 1980
.... 3 Thomas Mancuso 1912 - 1985
.... +Lois Hovatter 1914 - 1983
.... 4 Joyce E. Mancuso 1934 -
.... +Robert Thomas Sutton 1932 -
.... 5 Dolores Lea Sutton 1958 -
.... 5 Susan Joyce Sutton 1964 -
.... +Christopher Keating
.... 6 Christopher Keating Jr.
.... 6 Benjamin Keating
.... 5 Bobbi Lynn Sutton 1968 -
.... +Karl Frank Chase
.... 6 Shawn Joseph Chase 1995 -
.... 6 Samantha Joyce Chase 1997 -
.... *Partner of Bobbi Lynn Sutton:
.... +Mr. McHenry
.... 6 Dani-Lynn McHenry 2006 -
.... 4 Patrina Mancuso 1937 - 1937
.... 2 Theresa Tumbarello
.... 2 Martino Tumbarello

Descendants of Egnasio Thomas Tumbarello

Generation No. 1

1. EGNASIO THOMAS[1] TUMBARELLO was born in Italy. He married SUSANNA LA FATA. She was born in Italy.

Children of EGNASIO TUMBARELLO and SUSANNA LA FATA are:

2. i. PATRINA[2] TUMBARELLO, b. Italy; d. Bristol, PA.
   ii. THERESA TUMBARELLO.
   iii. MARTINO TUMBARELLO.

Generation No. 2

2. PATRINA[2] TUMBARELLO *(EGNASIO THOMAS[1])*[1] was born in Italy[1], and died in Bristol, PA[1]. She married VITO MANCUSO[1] in Italy. He was born in Italy[1], and died in Bristol, PA[1].

Children of PATRINA TUMBARELLO and VITO MANCUSO are:

   i. ANGELINA[3] MANCUSO, m. ANTHONY BONO.
   ii. SARAH MANCUSO, b. 1907, Italy; d. July 24, 2001, Briston Pa; m. SAMUEL FARINA.

      More About SARAH MANCUSO:
      Burial: July 28, 2001, St. Mark Cemetery Bristol, Pa.

   iii. ADA MANCUSO, m. HENRY ROACH.
3. iv. YOLANDA MANCUSO, b. March 03, 1918, Bristol, PA; d. September 13, 2005, Orlando, FL.
   v. ALFRED MANCUSO.
   vi. JOSEPH MANCUSO[2], b. February 24, 1909[3]; d. December 1980[3].

      Notes for JOSEPH MANCUSO:
      [Genealogy.com, Family Archive #110, Vol. 2 L-Z, Ed. 9, Social Security Death Index: U.S., Date of Import: Dec 30, 2000, Internal Ref. #1.112.9.18355.107]

      Individual: Mancuso, Joseph
      Social Security #: 181-22-4236
      Issued in: Pennsylvania

      Birth date: Feb 24, 1909
      Death date: Dec 1980

      Residence code: Pennsylvania

      ZIP Code of last known residence: 19007
      Location associated with this ZIP Code:

      Bristol, Pennsylvania

      ZIP Code where death benefit payment was sent: 19047
      Location associated with this ZIP Code:

      Langhorne, Pennsylvania

      More About JOSEPH MANCUSO:
      Fact 5: Social Security #: 181-22-4236[3]

Fact 6: Issued in: Pennsylvania[3]
Fact 7: Residence code: Pennsylvania[3]
Fact 8: Death benefit payment ZIP: 19047[3]

4. vii. THOMAS MANCUSO, b. December 31, 1912, Italy; d. May 27, 1985, St. Petersburg, FL.

Generation No. 3

3. YOLANDA[3] MANCUSO *(PATRINA[2] TUMBARELLO, EGNASIO THOMAS[1])* was born March 03, 1918 in Bristol, PA, and died September 13, 2005 in Orlando, FL. She married JOSEPH BUZZATTO.

Child of YOLANDA MANCUSO and JOSEPH BUZZATTO is:
5. i. JOSEPH[4] BUZZATTO.

4. THOMAS[3] MANCUSO *(PATRINA[2] TUMBARELLO, EGNASIO THOMAS[1])*[4,5,6] was born December 31, 1912 in Italy, and died May 27, 1985 in St. Petersburg, FL[7,8]. He married LOIS HOVATTER[9] September 23, 1935 in Croydon, PA[9], daughter of WILBERT HOVATTER and HATTIE JONES. She was born November 19, 1914 in Greene Co, Miss.[9], and died May 30, 1983 in Lower Bank, NJ[9].

More About THOMAS MANCUSO:
Burial: Clearwater FL[9,10]

Notes for LOIS HOVATTER:
Married Sept. 23, 1935
Pictures on pages 96, 97 98, 100 in book "Generations of Hoffman to Hovatter"

More About LOIS HOVATTER:
Burial: Egg Harbor City, NJ[11]
Social Security Number: 177-14-8410[11]

Children of THOMAS MANCUSO and LOIS HOVATTER are:
6. i. JOYCE F..[4] MANCUSO, b. May 11, 1934, Bristol, PA.
ii. PATRINA MANCUSO, b. Abt. 1937; d. Abt. 1937.

Generation No. 4

5. JOSEPH[4] BUZZATTO *(YOLANDA[3] MANCUSO, PATRINA[2] TUMBARELLO, EGNASIO THOMAS[1])*

Children of JOSEPH BUZZATTO are:
i. ALICIA[5] BUZZATTO.
ii. BRETT BUZZATTO.
iii. JODI BUZZATTO.

6. JOYCE F..[4] MANCUSO *(THOMAS[3], PATRINA[2] TUMBARELLO, EGNASIO THOMAS[1])* was born May 11, 1934 in Bristol, PA. She married ROBERT THOMAS SUTTON[11] October 19, 1957 in Pomona, NJ[11], son of ROBERT SUTTON and DORA WATSON. He was born December 07, 1932 in Atlantic City, NJ[11].

Notes for JOYCE F.. MANCUSO:
DAR member number 831198, installed Oct. 16, 2004

Notes for ROBERT THOMAS SUTTON:
Bob was born on a Wednesday. His wife Joyce was born on a Friday two years later, each year their bithdays fall on the same day of the week.

Children of JOYCE MANCUSO and ROBERT SUTTON are:

i. DOLORES LEA[5] SUTTON[11], b. September 24, 1958[11].
ii. SUSAN JOYCE SUTTON[11], b. December 01, 1964[11]; m. CHRISTOPHER KEATING[11].

Notes for SUSAN JOYCE SUTTON:
DAR member number 831199

iii. BOBBI LYNN SUTTON[11], b. November 09, 1968[11]; m. (1) KARL FRANK CHASE[11]; m. (2) MR. MCHENRY.

Notes for BOBBI LYNN SUTTON:
DAR member number 831200, installed Oct. 16, 2004

Endnotes

1. Mancuso.FTW, Date of Import: Sep 6, 2000.
2. Genealogy.com, Family Archive #110, Social Security Death Index: U.S. Ed. 9, Social Security Death Index, Release date: April 10, 2000.
3. Genealogy.com, Family Archive #110, Social Security Death Index: U.S. Ed. 9, Social Security Death Index, Release date: April 10, 2000, Internal Ref. #1.112.9.18355.107.
4. Mancuso.FTW, Date of Import: Sep 6, 2000.
5. Genealogy.com, Family Archive #110, Social Security Death Index: U.S. Ed. 9, Social Security Death Index, Release date: April 10, 2000.
6. Mancuso Cramer Sutton.FTW, Date of Import: Jun 25, 2001.
7. Mancuso.FTW, Date of Import: Sep 6, 2000.
8. Mancuso Cramer Sutton.FTW, Date of Import: Jun 25, 2001.
9. Mancuso.FTW, Date of Import: Sep 6, 2000.
10. Mancuso Cramer Sutton.FTW, Date of Import: Jun 25, 2001.
11. Mancuso.FTW, Date of Import: Sep 6, 2000.

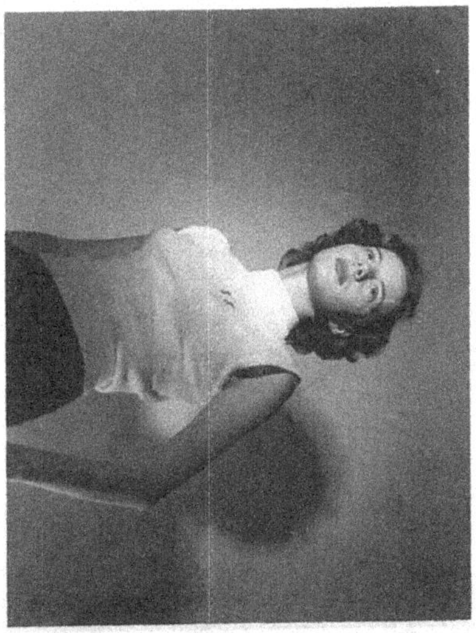

Joyce's 7th grade

Tommy - hair dressing school

Lois Hovatter/Mancuso

Tommy Mancuso

Yolanda & Joe

Sarah Farina

Bristol Boro Resident

Sarah Farina (nee Mancuso), age 94, of Bristol, Pa., died on Tuesday, July 24, 2001, at the Temple Lower Bucks Hospital.

Born in Italy, she was a resident of Bristol Boro for the past 89 years. She was a retired employee of Philco Corp. and Mancuso Bakery formerly in Bristol Boro.

She is the sister of the late Angelina Bono, Alfred, Thomas and Joseph Mancuso. She is the widow of the late Samuel Farina. She is survived by her sisters, Yolanda Buzzalto of Orlando and Ida Roach of Doylestown; and several nieces and nephews.

Relatives and friends are invited to call on Saturday 8:30-9:30 a.m. at the Galzerano Funeral Home, 430 Radcliffe Street in Bristol. Mass of Christian burial will be celebrated 10 a.m. at the St. Ann Church. Interment will follow in St. Mark Cemetery. There will be no evening calling hours.

83 rd birthday

July 12, 1985

THOMAS MANCUSO (Cremains)

Niche 4, Tier K, Corridor F, Complex I

1912

1985

MANCUSO, THOMAS, 72, of 446 87th Ave. N, died Sunday (May 26, 1985) at University General Hospital, Seminole. Born in Italy, he came here in 1975 from Bristol, Pa. and was a self-employed painter. He was a Catholic. Survivors include a daughter Joyce Sutton, Lower Bank, N.J.; three sisters, Sarah Farina, Bristol, Ida Roach and Yolanda Bussatta of Orlando, and three grandchildren. Robert D. Easter Funeral Home, Gulfport.

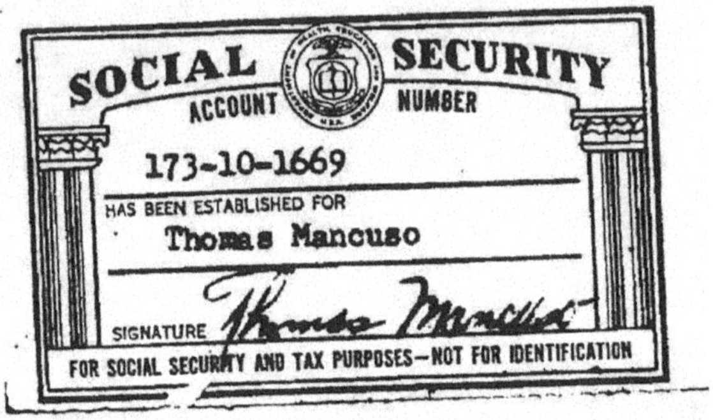

SOCIAL SECURITY
ACCOUNT NUMBER
173-10-1669
HAS BEEN ESTABLISHED FOR
Thomas Mancuso
SIGNATURE Thomas Mancuso
FOR SOCIAL SECURITY AND TAX PURPOSES—NOT FOR IDENTIFICATION

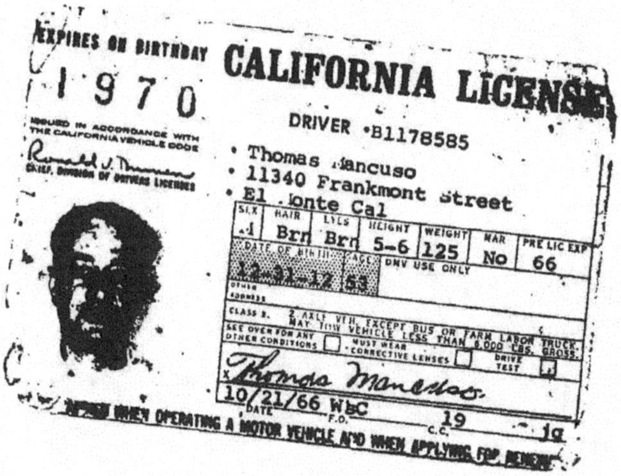

EXPIRES ON BIRTHDAY
1970
CALIFORNIA LICENSE
DRIVER B1178585
ISSUED IN ACCORDANCE WITH THE CALIFORNIA VEHICLE CODE
Ronald J. Thomas
CHIEF, DIVISION OF DRIVERS LICENSES
Thomas .ancuso
11340 Frankmont Street
El .onte Cal

SEX	HAIR	EYES	HEIGHT	WEIGHT	MAR	PRE LIC EXP
M	Brn	Brn	5-6	125	No	66

DATE OF BIRTH 12-31-12 AGE 53 DMV USE ONLY
OTHER ADDRESS
CLASS 3. 2 AXLE VEH. EXCEPT BUS OR FARM LABOR TRUCK. MAY TOW VEHICLE LESS THAN 6,000 LBS. GROSS.
SEE OVER FOR ANY OTHER CONDITIONS
MUST WEAR CORRECTIVE LENSES
DRIVE TEST
X Thomas Mancuso
10/21/66 WBC
DATE F.O. 19 C.C. jg
[illegible] WHEN OPERATING A MOTOR VEHICLE AND WHEN APPLYING FOR RENEWAL

CERTIFICATE OF DEATH
FLORIDA

LOCAL FILE NO.

DECEDENT—NAME (First, Middle, Last): 1. Thomas Mancuso	SEX: 2. Male	DATE OF DEATH (Mo. Day, Yr.): May 26, 1985
RACE: 4. White	AGE—Last Birthday (Yrs): 5a. 72	DATE OF BIRTH (Mo. Day, Yr.): December 31, 1912
COUNTY OF DEATH: 7a. Pinellas	CITY, TOWN OR LOCATION OF DEATH: 7b. Seminole	HOSPITAL OR OTHER INSTITUTION: 7c. University General Hospital
IF HOSP OR INST (Indicate DOA, OP/Emer. Rm., Inpatient (Specify)): 7d. Inpatient	STATE OF BIRTH (If not in U.S.A., name country): 8. Italy	CITIZEN OF WHAT COUNTRY: 9. U.S.A.
MARRIED, NEVER MARRIED, WIDOWED, DIVORCED (Specify): 10. Widowed	SURVIVING SPOUSE (If wife, give maiden name): 11. ————————	SOCIAL SECURITY NUMBER: 12. 173-10-1669
USUAL OCCUPATION: 13a. Painter	KIND OF BUSINESS OR INDUSTRY: 13b. Building	
RESIDENCE—STATE: 14a. Florida	COUNTY: 14b. Pinellas	CITY, TOWN OR LOCATION: 14c. St. Petersburg
STREET AND NUMBER: 14d. 446-87th. Ave. No.	INSIDE CITY LIMITS (Specify Yes or No): 14e. Yes	
FATHER—NAME: 15. Vito Mancuso	MOTHER—MAIDEN NAME: 16. Petrina Tumbrello	
INFORMANT—NAME: 17a. Mrs. Joyce Sutton	MAILING ADDRESS: 17b. RR#2 Box 254, Egg Harbor, New Jersey 08215	
BURIAL, CREMATION, REMOVAL, OTHER (Specify): 18a. Cremation	CEMETERY OR CREMATORY: 18b. Southeastern Crematorium Service Inc.	LOCATION: Clearwater, Florida
FUNERAL DIRECTOR—(Signature): 19a. Robert D. Easter	FUNERAL HOME: 19b. Robert D. Easter Funeral Home,	ADDRESS: 5730-15th. Ave. So. Gulfport, Florida 33707
20a. To the best of my knowledge, death occurred at the time, date and place and due to the cause(s) stated. (Signature and Title): E.R. DeLucia, DO	DATE SIGNED: 20b. 5-30-85	HOUR OF DEATH: 20c. 11:25 A. M
NAME OF ATTENDING PHYSICIAN IF OTHER THAN CERTIFIER: 20d.	21a. On the basis of examination and/or investigation, in my opinion death occurred at the time, date and place and due to the cause(s) stated. (Signature and Title):	DATE SIGNED: 21b. HOUR OF DEATH: 21c. M
PRONOUNCED DEAD (Mo. Day, Yr.): 21d. ON	PRONOUNCED DEAD (Hour): 21e. AT M	
NAME AND ADDRESS OF CERTIFIER: 22. Dr. E.R. DeLucia D.O., 1262-9th. St. No., St. Petersburg, Fla.		
REGISTRAR (Signature): 23a. David L. Fleischer 5-30-85 Lab	DATE RECEIVED BY REGISTRAR: 23b. May 30, 1985	

24. IMMEDIATE CAUSE	Interval between onset and death
PART I (a) Resporatory Failure	3 Days
DUE TO, OR AS A CONSEQUENCE OF: (b) Adenocarcinoma, Left Lung	6 Months
DUE TO, OR AS A CONSEQUENCE OF: (c)	

PART II OTHER SIGNIFICANT CONDITIONS: Hypertensive Heart Disease	PART III IF FEMALE, WAS THERE A PREGNANCY IN THE PAST 3 MONTHS? Yes ☐ No ☐	AUTOPSY (yes or no): 25. No	CASE REFERRED TO MEDICAL EXAMINER: 26. No
(Probably) ACCIDENT, SUICIDE or HOMICIDE, or UNDETERMINED: 27a.	DATE OF INJURY: 27b.	HOUR OF INJURY: 27c. M	DESCRIBE HOW INJURY OCCURRED: 27d.
INJURY AT WORK: 27e.	PLACE OF INJURY: 27f.	LOCATION: 27g.	

A CERTIFIED COPY MUST CARRY THE EMBOSSED SEAL OF THE REGISTRAR OF VITAL STATISTICS.

I hereby certify that this is a true and correct copy of a certificate on file in the office of the Local Registrar of Vital Statistics of the Pinellas County Health Department, St. Petersburg, Florida.

May 30, 1985 [signature], Deputy Local Registrar

CERTIFICATE OF RIGHT OF ENTOMBMENT

CALVARY CEMETERY AND CHAPEL MAUSOLEUM

Know all Men By These Presents: That CALVARY CEMETERY, a cemetery member of Miserere Guild, Inc., the Grantor, a corporation not-for-profit, organized under the laws of the State of Florida, and under the jurisdiction of the Bishop of the Diocese of St. Petersburg, Florida, in consideration of the sum of **Three Hundred Seventy Five and 00/100 Dollars** ($ **375.00**), receipt whereof is hereby acknowledged, does hereby grant unto **THOMAS MANCUSO** **(Cremains)** his/her heirs, successors and assigns, the rights for entombment purposes only to Crypt(s) **Niche 4** Tier, **K** Location, **Corridor F, Complex I**, in Calvary Chapel Mausoleum, as designated on the plat of said mausoleum; subject to the rules and regulations now in existence or hereinafter promulgated by Miserere Guild, Inc. or by the Bishop of the Diocese of St. Petersburg — including but not limited to the following:

Permission must be obtained from the Grantor before taking any action concerning care or maintenance of the above described Right, or entombment therein.

No transfer or conveyance or assignment of any interest or rights acquired hereunder by the Purchaser, his/her heirs, successors, or assigns, shall be valid without the written consent of the Grantor and without the subsequent recordation of such transfer, conveyance, or assignment in the official records maintained in the Cemetery office.

The bronze memorial and entombment will be furnished without any further cost to the purchaser.

Perpetual care will be furnished, without any further cost to the Purchaser, from the income of the Endowed Care Fund.

At no time will flowers, wreaths or other decorations be permitted on the crypt front. Such decorations will be permitted only on benches provided by the Cemetery.

In the event Grantee fails to exercise the rights herein granted, within 99 years of date hereof, the same shall revert to the Grantor, and no right, title or interest shall thereafter exist in the Grantee or his/her heirs, successors or assigns.

In Witness Whereof, the said Miserere Guild, Inc. has caused this instrument to be executed by its duly authorized agent and its corporate seal affixed this **13th** day of **JUNE** 19**85**.

MISERERE GUILD, INC.

By G. F. Tschiderer

SEAL

51

Form 630 ... Department of Commerce and Labor IMMIGRATION SERVICE

SALOON, CABIN, AND STE...

LIST OR MA...

Required by the regulations of the Secretary of Commerce ...

S. S. TAORMINA

1	2		3	4	5	6
No. on List.	NAME IN FULL. Family Name.	Given Name.	Age. Yrs. Mos.	Sex.	Married or Single.	Calling or Occupation.
1	Scalia VL 192/937	Giorgio		M		
2	Palazzolo	Nicolo		M		
3	Tumbarello (grandmother)	Pietronilla				
4	Mancuso	Angela				
5	Mancuso	Giuseppe				
6	Mancuso	Ignazio				
7	Pulizzi	Francesco				
8	Lombardo	Giovanni				11-153113
9	[illegible]					
10	[illegible]					
11	Patti	Bernardo				
12	[illegible]					

my aunt Angie, uncle Joe, my father Ignatius (Thomas)

Subj: **(no subject)**
Date: 9/13/2005 10:45:52 AM Eastern Daylight Time
From: JSutton639
To: JSutton639

First Name:	*Angela*
Last Name:	*Mancuso*
Ethnicity:	*Italian South*
Last Place of Residence:	*..., Italy*
Date of Arrival:	*August 11, 1913*
Age at Arrival: *7y* Gender: *F*	Marital Status: *S*
Ship of Travel:	*Taormina*
Port of Departure:	*Palermo*
Manifest Line Number:	*0004*

VITO PATRINA TUMBARELLA/MANCUSO

THOMAS ANGELINA SARAH JOSEPH
YOLANDA IDA ALFRED

Alfred + Kay Tumbarelli/Moore

GETS BATTLE STAR

Pvt. Alfred Mancuso, 6723rd truck group, in its resupply mission, has been commended in a letter for the part he played, and is now entitled to a Battle Star.

Sarah Mancuso/Farina

Dolores Yolanda Joyce Henry Ida Bob Bobbie L. Joe

YULETIDE WEDDING IS SOLEMNIZED HERE

Miss Ida Mancuso is Bride of Henry Roache, of Doylestown

AT ST. ANN'S, SUNDAY

A Yuletide wedding in St. Ann's R. C. Church yesterday at three o'clock in the afternoon attracted a number of guests, when Miss Ida Mancuso, daughter of Mr. and Mrs. Vito Mancuso, of 2 Green avenue, became the bride of Mr. Henry Roache, Doylestown.

Mr. Mancuso escorted his daughter to the altar of the edifice, where the Rev. Fr. Peter Pinci performed the ceremony.

Members of the bridal party included: Miss Frances Caucci, Grant avenue, as bridesmaid; little Joyce Mancuso, Bristol Terrace, as flower girl; Mr. Joseph Caucci, Wood street, best man; and Fred Ricci, Trenton avenue, ring bearer.

The costume of the bride was white, her attendant wearing pink; and the flower girl yellow. The

Continued on Page Four

oridal gown was of satin, entrain;
he yoke being of net, and the
bodice trim being pearls. The
sleeves were long. The bride wore
upon her hair an orange blossom
wreath from which fell a net veil
over which were scattered small
satin bows. Her slippers were satin,
and she carried a bouquet of white
roses with a lavendar orchid in the
center.

Miss Caucci's pink gown was
fashioned of taffeta, it having
sweet-heart neck-line, with pearl
trim at the shoulders. Sleeves were
three-quarter length, and the skirt
had a short train. A cluster of
flowers on her hair matched the
gown, from this falling a pink
shoulder veil. Slippers were pink
as were also the roses in her arm
bouquet. The flower girl's costume
of yellow included a taffeta gown,
floor length, the skirt being ruffle
trimmed; the gown having sweet-
heart neckline and three-quarter
length sleeves. Her Juliet cap was
of taffeta, slippers were white, and

phillyBurbs.com

BUCKS COUNTY Courier Times

Home | Local News | News Archive | Local Sports | Sports Archive | Editorial
Columnists | Obituaries | Multimedia | Circulation | Feedback | Advertise

Sarah Farina (nee Mancuso)

Thursday, July 26, 2001

Sarah Farina (nee Mancuso), age 94, of Bristol, Pa., died on Tuesday, July 24, 2001, at the Temple Lower Bucks Hospital. Born in Italy, she was a resident of Bristol Boro for the past 89 years. She was a retired employee of Philco Corp. and Mancuso Bakery formerly in Bristol Boro. She is the sister of the late Angelina Bono, Alfred, Thomas and Joseph Mancuso. She is the widow of the late Samuel Farina. She is survived by her sisters, Yolanda Buzzatto of Orlando and Ida Roach of Doylestown; and several nieces and nephews. Relatives and friends are invited to call on Saturday 8:30-9:30 a.m. at the Galzerano Funeral Home, 430 Radcliffe Street in Bristol. Mass of Christian burial will be celebrated 10 a.m. at the St. Ann Church. Interment will follow in St. Mark Cemetery. There will be no evening calling hours.

Sarah Farina

Bristol Boro Resident

Sarah Farina (nee Mancuso), age 94, of Bristol, Pa., died on Tuesday, July 24, 2001, at the Temple Lower Bucks Hospital.

Born in Italy, she was a resident of Bristol Boro for the past 89 years. She was a retired employee of Philco Corp. and Mancuso Bakery formerly in Bristol Boro.

She is the sister of the late Angelina Bono, Alfred, Thomas and Joseph Mancuso. She is the widow of the late Samuel Farina. She is survived by her sisters, Yolanda Buzzatto of Orlando and Ida Roach of Doylestown; and several nieces and nephews.

Relatives and friends are invited to call on Saturday 8:30-9:30 a.m. at the Galzerano Funeral Home, 430 Radcliffe Street in Bristol. Mass of Christian burial will be celebrated 10 a.m. at the St. Ann Church. Interment will follow in St. Mark Cemetery. There will be no evening calling hours.

June 4, 2000

Dear Joyce:

Hapeing that youre summer is much better than here, It's been very HOT here plus the smoke from all the fires.

Hope your are feeling better — We are all doing fine

Enclose you will fine Two pictures of your Great Grandparents his name was Thomas & her name was Susanna I don't know if that's the Correct Spelling of Susanna I'm sure some put a Z in there somewhere. I had to go to Walgreen's to have the one of my Grandfather.

Have a nice summer & Hope to see you in Fl.

Love

Aunt Yolanda

6/'4

Joyce;
Finally got more information about my Grandparents my Grandmothers maiden name was Susanna La Fata, she married Ignazio (Thomas) Tumbarello they had 5 girls + 1 boy my uncle Martino, you probably remember him; my Grandfather worked for Marsala Wine Co. He was a paymaster.

Hoping all is well with you, I'm doing fine but it has been HOT & humid here.

Love
Aunt Yolanda

P.S. Thanks again for the enlarged photo of the family

Dear Joyce & Bob; sept.

Thank you for that beautiful letter you sure do a great job with that computer. My Aunt that lived on Seara St was Anna who had one daughter Theresa & son Tommy you probably remember them, there older than you. We are all doing well, but Summer was HOT, now we are looking forward to the cool mornings & cool evenings. Enclosed is a card

Page 2

I know your on the internet, I don't understand Computers or Internet, so see what you think of it. Hoping your Girls & their families are ~~good~~ doing Good.

Hope to hear from you when you get back in Fl.

Love
Aunt Yolanda

P.S. Finally got my new rugs & I love it.

Yolanda Buzzato

BUZZATO, YOLANDA, Funeral services for Mrs. Yolanda Buzzatto, age 87, of Orlando, who passed away Tuesday, September 13, 2005 will be held on Monday, September 19, 2005, 10AM, in the Woodlawn Funeral Home Chapel. Mrs. Buzzatto was born March 3, 1918 in Bristol, PA and is survived by her son, Joe Buzzatto of Orlando; sister, Ida Roach of Eoylestown, PA; her grandchildren, Alicia Gattenio of Elberta, AL, Brett Buzzatto of Saco, ME and Jodi Buzzatto of Deltona. Services are by WOODLAWN MEMORIAL PARK AND FUNERAL HOME. 407-293-1361.

Dignity Memorial

Published in the Orlando Sentinel on 9/17/2005.

Back

IGNAZIO THOMAS TUMMARELLO

SUSAN OR SUSANNA LA FATA / TUMBARELLA